GW01454996

The Hohenzollerns and the Nazis

The Hohenzollerns and the Nazis

A History of Collaboration

STEPHAN MALINOWSKI

Translated by Jefferson Chase

ALLEN LANE
an imprint of
PENGUIN BOOKS

ALLEN LANE

UK | USA | Canada | Ireland | Australia
India | New Zealand | South Africa

Allen Lane is part of the Penguin Random House group of companies
whose addresses can be found at global.penguinrandomhouse.com

Penguin Random House UK,
One Embassy Gardens, 8 Viaduct Gardens, London sw11 7bw

Penguin
Random House
UK

First published in German under the title *Die Hohenzollern und die Nazis* by Ullstein Buchverlage
2021
This translation published 2025
001

Copyright © Ullstein Buchverlage GmbH, 2021
Translation copyright © Jefferson Chase, 2025

The moral right of the author and of the translator has been asserted

Set in 12/14.75pt Dante MT Std
Typeset by Jouve (UK), Milton Keynes
Printed and bound in Great Britain by Clays Ltd, Elcograf S.p.A.

The authorized representative in the EEA is Penguin Random House Ireland,
Morrison Chambers, 32 Nassau Street, Dublin D02 YH68

A CIP catalogue record for this book is available from the British Library

ISBN: 978-0-241-59618-0

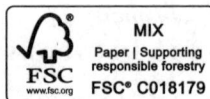

To Béatrice

Contents

List of Illustrations

Introduction

In the autumn of 1923, a member of the exiled German royal family set off in his sports car on a long journey. He would have to drive some 1,000 kilometres from the Dutch island of Wieringen to one of his family's ancestral homes, a Renaissance castle in the German province of Silesia. The day before he had started this trip, he had sent his father a letter full of confidence about the family's future prospects. On that very same day a political parvenu, while in hiding in the Alpine village of Uffing on the shores of the Staffelsee, composed his political testament. He even contemplated suicide. Two days later, he was arrested.

Before making his way back to his home country, Prince Wilhelm of Prussia, former crown prince of the German Empire, had posted the letter to his father, Kaiser Wilhelm II, who had for some five years also been living in Dutch exile. In the meantime, Adolf Hitler, the leader of an extreme right-wing splinter party, had gone down to defeat, together with his allies in the Bavarian capital, in a hail of gunfire from the Munich police. This was the end of an early, violent attempt to bring down the Weimar Republic. Both events, the return of the crown prince and the failed Munich putsch, made the front pages of the world's press.

There was no connection between either the events or the men in question. These two enemies of German democracy represented opposed poles of society and came from vastly different social backgrounds. One of the few things common to the Prussian former army group commander and the ex-private from Austria was that they both began agitating against the Weimar Republic at the same time. But their starting points couldn't have been more dissimilar. At this juncture in history, the significance of these two events remained unclear. It would have been difficult to imagine that the

I

future belonged to the Nazi movement while the German royal family would be left with little more than the past.

This book investigates how the social milieus of Prince Wilhelm of Prussia and Adolf Hitler converged and how various segments of the anti-democratic Right in Germany collaborated with one another. It will tell this story from the perspective of the Hohenzollerns, who before being deposed in November 1918 had been one of the most powerful families in Europe.[1] The focus will be on three generations: that of the Kaiser, Wilhelm II (1859–1941), that of his eldest son, Crown Prince Wilhelm (1882–1951), and that of the crown prince's six children, among whom his second son, Louis Ferdinand (1907–94), possessed the greatest historical significance. The centre of the analysis and the narrative of this group portrait and social study will be Crown Prince Wilhelm.

Post-1789 France is an example of how a nobility toppled by revolution can reinvent itself in 'de-aristocratized society', recasting and relocating itself between adaptation and counter-revolution.[2] After 1918, the same challenge was thrust upon the German aristocratic dynasties and their members, who had lost their centuries-old functions and roles almost overnight. Part of this story is the German nobility's reaction to the extraordinarily deep caesurae Germany went through in 1918, 1933, 1945 and 1990. Every one of these historical ruptures required an immense amount of adaptation and the creation of new figures to publicly represent the Hohenzollerns' self-image as a family. Often, they were accompanied by a new 'Head of the House', as the leading family member was known in aristocratic jargon.

As is the case throughout the history of the nobility, tropes and techniques, and not just bare facts, are what is most interesting. This book looks at specifically aristocratic forms of memory and representation. It is about estates, castles, hunts and memoirs but also paid family advisors and journalists, lawyers, historians, financial consultants, authors of evaluations and pamphlets, consultants, ghost-writers, spin doctors and public relations specialists. The gap between individuals and public personae is greater with aristocrats than with other social groups – and greatest of all for kings and heirs to the throne. Every biography that goes beyond the private sphere will inevitably place more importance on the figure than the person. Aristocratic personae were created by an effective publicity apparatus and the methods of modern propaganda – and even more by how they were seen and defined by the general public.

The nineteenth-century German poet and critic Heinrich Heine once remarked that aristocracy can only exist if people believe in it. This is only half true. The various instruments of power at the disposal of the nobility were as real as they were lasting, as many contemptuous adherents of democracy who prematurely dismissed the aristocracy would learn to their own, often physical, dismay. Even after 1918, millions of Germans retained the sort of faith that allows kings and noblemen to function as such. In theatre, kings are identifiable because of the deference and servility of the actors around them. No aristocracy can make do without representation, ornament and illusion. If aristocracy is indeed considered a kind of theatrical illusion, then the audience necessarily plays a crucial role. PR work and audience interpretation are crucial factors in whether an individual – be it an heir to the throne or a commoner styling himself as 'the Führer' – is considered a superhuman messiah or a laughable clown. That's another reason why, in addition to offering a portrait of three generations of the German royal family, this book concentrates on the history of communications between the Hohenzollerns and the general public. From its beginning to its end, the dynastic idea of Prussia carried intense, projected emotional energy. The Hohenzollerns' greatest capital was always the rapture they inspired in millions of Germans. That was what granted them special status, which was never fully exhausted.

Before the Wilhelmine Empire collapsed like a house of cards, the Hohenzollerns' power naturally went far beyond just the public imagination. In the midst of the First World War, the Cecilienhof Castle – really more of an estate – was opened in the Neuer Garten park in Potsdam. Symbolically, Crown Princess Cecilie had her youngest child baptized and moved into the new residence named after her alone. The ceremony took place on 9 November 1917, one year to the day before the Wilhelmine Empire would fall apart. The baptism 'was a private family affair . . . in keeping with the seriousness of the times', newspapers wrote,[3] and thus without the pomp and circumstance for which the Hohenzollerns were alternately admired and mocked around the world.

When construction began on the new residence of Crown Prince Wilhelm and Cecilie, the former Duchess of Mecklenburg, in 1914, it was seen as an intermediary residence for the heir to the throne, whose power and prestige were at their zenith, and his family. Amidst the ups and downs of the decisive year of 1917, many German navy men believed that Reich submarines were poised to bring down the British Empire and to defy the industrial might of the United States in the Atlantic Ocean. After all, Germany had already achieved military victory on the Eastern Front, and the occupation of the vast area known as 'Ober Ost' had German officers and planners dreaming of colonizing Eastern Europe.

At least nominally, Crown Prince Wilhelm commanded Germany's largest army group. And it was the mark of his significance that German newspapers were careful to assure readers that he had only briefly left the field to attend the Potsdam baptism. Part and parcel of the Hohenzollerns' image was the tradition of the Prussian princesses being photographed in military uniforms and the postcards of the prince's four young boys playing with a Gatling gun. But ironically, while the entire Hohenzollern family was at least symbolically at war, a new faux-English royal residence was being built for an heir to the throne who would become one of the most powerful men in the world – but only as long as Germany emerged victorious. This was the role and identity into which Wilhelm of Prussia had been born and for which he had been trained.

The central question of this book is: what was the relationship of the Hohenzollern dynasty to the Weimar Republic and to National Socialism? This question resurfaced in Germany five decades after the end of the Second World War for political and legal reasons. In the early 1990s, the Hohenzollern family filed compensation claims

for the Soviet expropriations after 1945. It was the start of a long process of legal discovery conducted, in part, in the public eye.
Historically, this dispute was about the question of whether the last
German crown prince had directly or indirectly supported National
Socialism. The dispute was the result of a peculiarity of the compensation regulations after German reunification. A 1994 law
regulating compensation claims excluded claims if the last owner of
the expropriated property had supported the Nazi dictatorship. The
total amount in dispute in the case of the Hohenzollerns has been
estimated to be in the hundreds of millions. Additionally, historically minded observers were, of course, keenly interested in the
question of how one of the formerly most powerful families of the
European high nobility had positioned itself in relation to National
Socialism.

The starting point of my own involvement with the former
crown prince's post-1918 activities was an expert evaluation I was
commissioned to write by the Ministry of Finance in Potsdam in
2014. For its part, the Hohenzollern family had engaged and financed
renowned historians as experts – including Christopher Clark,
Regius Professor of History at Cambridge University, one of the
leading historians of Germany worldwide, as well as Wolfram Pyta
and Rainer Orth, two excellent historians of the periods under discussion. The Hohenzollern family later also co-financed and
provided organizational support for an entire monograph by the
historian Lothar Machtan. It was launched at considerable expense
in the summer of 2021 at a gala featuring a musical band, the acting
German minister of finance and the acting 'Head of the House' at
Berlin's Kronprinzenpalais, a symbolic location in Berlin's historic
centre.

More than other historical debates, the dispute over the Hohenzollern claims played itself out between historical scholarship,
jurisprudence, politics and the mass media. By the summer of
2019, the debate had reached a popular audience, not primarily
through the work of historians, but rather through an investigative
story in the news magazine *Der Spiegel* and, even more, a satirical

segment by the TV comedian Jan Böhmermann. In a November 2019 programme, Böhmermann delivered an extremely cutting polemic against the family's claims to restitution. On his website, he published the four expert evaluations, which had previously been treated as confidential. This episode of Böhmermann's programme now has over 4 million views on YouTube.

By that point, the debate had attracted the attention of nearly all leading German media – newspapers, magazines, television, radio, blogs – as well as international outlets such as CNN, the *New York Times*, the *New York Review of Books*, *The Times*, *The Spectator* and *Le Figaro*. The regional state parliaments of the cities of Berlin and Brandenburg discussed the case, as did the Bundestag, which convened a commission of historical and legal experts. Meanwhile, Hohenzollern family lawyers sued newspapers, politicians and historians in more than eighty lawsuits.

The nature of German law means that the many court cases associated with the Hohenzollerns' restitution have to be focused on a lone individual, Crown Prince Wilhelm, forcing complex historical questions into an either/or, black-and-white straitjacket. This may appear right and necessary from a judicial perspective. But one task of historians is to try to relocate the individual figure in his proper societal setting. The questions surrounding the crown prince inevitably lead us back to his family and the conservative, anti-democratic segments of German society. There is no way to reasonably assess Crown Prince Wilhelm without placing him in the broader, historical context of post-1918 German counter-revolutionary movements.

The German revolution of 1918 may have done away with one of the most powerful dynasties in Europe, but it also made peace offers German aristocrats never accepted. Their refusal to do so is a key factor when historians consider whether the revolution could have more firmly and consistently established democratic principles in Germany. The figure of Wilhelm inevitably raises the issue of the German nobility, a dramatically under-researched topic, and immediately opens up a historical avenue rarely examined by leading scholars of the Weimar Republic. The history of the Hohenzollerns after 1918 is by no means *terra incognita*. There is a whole series of older[4] and more recent[5] studies on the German nobility after it was 'abolished' – at least in terms of political power. Nonetheless, and rather inexplicably, the Hohenzollerns and the aristocracy play next to no role at all in the standard histories of the Weimar Republic and the Third Reich.

One reason is that social historians tend to concentrate on group dynamics, whereas the nobility often seems to represent the very essence of stasis. Moreover, history generally tends to favour the victors, and the victors within the radical political Right of the Weimar Republic were clearly the Nazis. When compared to one of the unavoidable fixed points of twentieth-century European history, the darkness and destruction brought about by the Third Reich, the deposed royal family may seem little more than a footnote. Furthermore, after 1918, as in 1945, the aristocracy was indeed largely considered to have been abolished. For most proponents of democracy, which had seemingly emerged victorious, the Hohenzollerns and the rest of the German aristocracy remained an incomprehensible, indecipherable social clique, an 'exotic Indian tribe', as the pro-democracy man of letters and member of 'Young Germany' Heinrich Laube had put it back in 1830.[6] As a rule, adherents of democracy had little contact with this group and its ways of life, values and traditions. The result was that the public attitude towards the nobility in the 1920s was a mixture of contempt, incomprehension and resentment, with some occasional admiration thrown in for good measure. That persists today. But during the Weimar Republic and before the consolidation of the Nazi dictatorship in 1934, the Hohenzollerns remained an important factor in the survival of Germany's fragile democracy.

For a variety of reasons, many of them good, historians in the past few decades have renounced the traditional fixation on great individuals. The major political and cultural histories of the Weimar Republic, even those concerning the radical political Right, read the past in a way that is blind to the German nobility. In an astonishing parallel, just as post-1945 historians have lost track of the aristocracy and have seldom examined that group systematically, people in the Weimar Republic dramatically underestimated the resources of power of a nobility that had supposedly ceased to exist. Proponents of democracy tended to take parliaments and newspapers most seriously, whereas the aristocracy, at least internally, was thought to be more concerned with balls, horse races, casinos and hunting parties. Few Germans were able to perceive the influence of princes, country estates, clubs, pheasant shoots, salons and aristocratic networks 'not foreseen in the constitution'.[7] But that influence remained considerable until well after the Nazis' ascension to power in 1933.

The following six chapters will cover a century of interaction between the political leaders of the Hohenzollern dynasty and the general public, showing the former's roles in anti-democratic right-wing circles, the deals that they struck with the Nazi state and their attempts since 1945 to convince democratic, post-war Germany to buy into a self-serving, revised version of history.

I.

The Hohenzollerns in Exile: Outposts in
the Counter-Revolution (1918–23)

The Kaiser's 'Heroic Death'

What ultimately became known as the Allies' 'Hundred Days Offensive' of August–November 1918 culminated in the collapse of the German lines on the Western Front. The series of attacks that pushed German troops further and further back cost the lives of more than a million people on both sides. On the morning of 9 November 1918, as Germany's decisive military catastrophe was unfolding, a fateful meeting took place at German military headquarters in the Belgian town of Spa. Tersely and soberly, Field Marshal General Paul von Hindenburg told his king, emperor and supreme commander Wilhelm II that he could no longer guarantee his safety. Hindenburg didn't pull any punches. Revolution, he said, was spreading like wildfire from Kiel to Munich, and the Reich Chancellor and his emissaries were demanding that the Kaiser and the crown prince step down. There was no more chance of holding the German capital, Berlin, than there was of maintaining the Western Front, and rebellious German troops had seized control of the bridges across the River Rhine. When asked, thirty-nine German frontline commanders had said that, if Wilhelm II ordered it, they would beat an orderly retreat home with their men. But they would not mete out any counter-revolutionary violence against their fellow Germans.

Proudly and calmly, Wilhelm II dismissed both the idea of doing battle against the German people and concerns for his own security. In an address to his highest-ranking officers, he recalled one of his dinnertime speeches in which he had cited his ancestor Albrecht,

who had some five centuries before said: 'There is no more beautiful death than one surrounded by my enemies.' Without any
hesitation or further discussion, the Kaiser summoned four of his
six sons and a small cadre of officers – militaristic aristocrats from
Pomerania and Brandenburg – for a 'final ride'. A stretch of the
front with particularly heavy artillery fire was selected, and, without a word, the men, who had chosen to die, mounted their horses
and launched the final cavalry attack of the Wilhelmine Empire
with their emperor in the lead.

The military report of the incident read: 'The field marshal
moved uphill to gain an overview. Using his spyglass, he could see
the small group shrink as the men rode towards the horizon. Suddenly, as though a volcano had erupted, a horrific, massive hedge of
rock and earth shot up towards the heavens and descended again.
The riders could no longer be seen. Shocked, the field marshal
lowered his spyglass. His aged lips murmured: "The end of the
Hohenzollerns. Praise God, a worthy end."'

The events just described never happened. On the contrary, this
fictional vision of history appeared in the newspaper *Vorwärts*, the
central organ of the Social Democratic Party, as a sarcastic lampoon
flage of how the German monarchy actually collapsed. It was published on 9 November 1932, the fourteenth anniversary of the
Kaiser's flight to the Netherlands and fewer than three months
before the reins of power would be handed over to Adolf Hitler.[1] As
part of the ruse, the newspaper claimed that Hitler had ordered ten
million copies of the historical scene to be handed out in the schools
of what would shortly become the Third Reich. The bitter irony
was that the Kaiser's alleged desire for a hero's death – the failure of
which to materialize was the subject of millions of discussions, particularly within the German nobility and throughout conservative,
monarchist society – was just wishful thinking, divorced from reality. The truth was that the Kaiser and the crown prince had fled.

The lack of a forceful response to revolution in Germany and the
self-sacrifice the Hohenzollerns *hadn't* made immediately created a
need on the Right for vivid conservative fantasies which would

persist for decades. The royal behaviour *Vorwärts* ridiculed with its adroit satire was a deadly serious matter for conservatives. By 1932, the First World War lay fourteen years in the past, but the political Right was still obsessed with the heroic legacy the Hohenzollerns could have, but hadn't, left behind.

The heroic self-sacrifice *Vorwärts* caricatured could have happened in reality. At the very least theoretically, the Kaiser had four options in Spa on 9 November 1918: launching counter-revolutionary operations aimed at Berlin, 600 kilometres to the east; staying put and allowing himself to be captured and prosecuted by the Entente; initiating a targeted 'special offensive' on the front that would end in the spectacle of his death;[2] or fleeing to a neutral foreign country, for instance the Netherlands or Switzerland. These and other courses of action were indeed considered in response to revolution on the home front and calls for the Kaiser to abdicate. The idea of Wilhelm II pre-emptively renouncing the throne, for instance, was debated but discarded, and the suggestion that he could abdicate as German emperor but remain king of Prussia was deemed legally untenable.[3] It is uncertain whether the notion of the Kaiser riding out to meet his death was ever put to the man in question, but many of his underlings certainly discussed it.

Historical reconstructions and bitter debates among the officers and diplomats present about what actually happened on 9 November 1918 began to circulate immediately after the Kaiser's 'departure', as monarchist circles frequently termed it, to the Netherlands. Thanks to indiscretions on the part of eyewitnesses, accounts swiftly flooded the public sphere. In March and April 1919, the German press got hold of letters from the Kaiser to the crown prince and a retrospective written by General Count Friedrich von der Schulenburg, who vigorously advocated putting down the revolution by force.[4] These documents showed that the Kaiser had promised the general chief of staff of the Army Group German Crown Prince to stay 'with the troops' and not to abdicate the Prussian throne. The general's account, as passed on in the socialist press, read: 'I answered, 'If His Majesty would come to our troops at the front,

His Majesty would definitely be safe. Please promise me that His Majesty will stay with the troops come what may.' His Majesty took his leave with the words, 'I will stay with the army. I was allowed to kiss his beloved, strong hand, and I never saw him again.'[5]

Flight and Curse

Revisionist conservative narratives blamed – together with revolutionaries, southern German diplomats and 'weak-willed' civilians – Wilhelm Groener, the lone non-aristocratic member of the general staff, and Paul von Hindenburg for the Kaiser abandoning his troops. On 9 November, Wilhelm II himself sought to shift blame to Jews and freemasons and already foresaw a life as a 'pensioner' in a neutral foreign country as his most likely future. In his final wartime letter to his wife, he wrote about the possibility of 'falling here amidst those who remained true to the very end'.[6] But he didn't do any such thing. Ultimately, those who believed most in the supposed ideals of the monarchy – the nobility, the monarchists and, broadly speaking, the extreme Right – had to admit that the king had failed to anticipate the consequences of his actions and himself bore responsibility for following bad advice.

Crown Prince Wilhelm, who had taken part in the lengthy discussion in Spa and spoken with his father for even longer afterwards, quit the scene after several hours and returned, much to the surprise of various generals, to his own headquarters.[7] He had already been stripped of his command by the revolutionary government in Berlin, and his request to be allowed to lead his troops back to the German capital was denied. So, too, was his wish to return to his castle in Silesia as a 'private citizen'. The rationale given was that, if he did, the local farmers would 'beat him to death'.

Communications between Spa and Berlin made it clear that for domestic and international political reasons the social democrats had no intention of allowing the crown prince to return to Germany.[8] Moreover, the heir to the throne, too, had made promises to generals and others, one of whom wrote, 'He shook my hand and declared that he would stay with the army.' As early as 1917, he proclaimed that in the case of German defeat he would 'proceed to the head of his troops and seek death'.[9] But on 12 November 1918, two days after his father, he also hurried off the Netherlands.[10] Later on, in conversations with old and new radical right-wing elites, he would follow the Kaiser's lead in blaming 'limp-wristed' civilians, 'big-city rabble' and 'segments of Jewry' for Germany's military demise.[11]

Most of the nobility viewed the prince's flight no less critically than that of his father. It is nearly impossible to overestimate the significance that the two men's 'departure', without a fight, for a quiet life in the Netherlands had for the still-to-be-defined relationship between the political Right in Germany and the Hohenzollerns. The family's standing among broad swathes of the nobility suffered greatly from what was interpreted as a cowardly act of desertion, although the Hohenzollerns' prestige never completely dissipated. Still, although the bonds between the nobility and the royal family were by no means dissolved, the violation of traditional ideals profoundly changed attitudes among the lower aristocracy, officer corps and civil servants towards potential candidates for the throne.

The resulting power vacuum accelerated the rise of new images and figures of leadership. Long before the appearance of National Socialism, the vacuum was filled by ethnic chauvinists and the radical Right.[12] And the far Right wasn't alone in calling for Germany's figureheads to demonstrate strength and die a hero's death. The lawyer, officer, member of the conservative anti-Nazi resistance and post-1945 advocate for the Hohenzollern family Fabian von Schlabrendorff recalled his father, also a Prussian officer, privately demanding that all the Kaiser's sons should fall in battle. Only the crown prince should be allowed to survive since he was crucial to continuing the monarchy.[13]

Views like this were particularly common among aristocratic women. One week after the Kaiser fled, Princess Rosy zu Salm-Horstmar wrote:

It's really strange that there are so few true men in Germany! – The whole thing is terrible. But I don't believe that it was His Majesty's idea to flee. I think they must have captured him . . . I think it's much worse that his son followed in his tracks. In this regard, I must praise Prince Eitel! Personally speaking, it's not too bad about the other two. But the issue, the idea is different. It's as though humanity is in the grip of a disease that's twisting its spirit . . . Still, I must admit, the monarchic idea was an illusion and only worked with good monarchs. As soon as the fellow [on the throne] is useless, the cause is doomed. And it's now well and truly doomed.[14]

By the following February, she had subscribed to the popular notion that the bourgeois Wilhelm Groener, in particular, bore the blame for Wilhelm II's flight:

Groener seems to be primarily the one who convinced Hindenburg to send the Kaiser to Holland. The old fellow [General von Plessen] always advised the Kaiser to ride against either the enemy or on Berlin, even at the cost of his life. That was indeed the only possible path. But His Majesty was no doubt too weak for this! – In any case, the whole thing is horrible, and our enemies are getting more and more impertinent.[15]

Desertion and Internal Sacrifice

The historical record is full of attempts to come up with stories to compensate for what the nobility, in particular, viewed as this blemish on the House of Hohenzollern: the lack of a dramatic final battle during the demise of the monarchy. Again and again, observers speculated about internal struggles and the 'terrible tremors within the Kaiser's soul', essentially positing, in the absence of a short, dramatic final battle, a lifelong internal struggle within the monarch himself. From this perspective, Wilhelm II's flight to the Netherlands was seen not as an act of self-preservation or cowardice but rather as part of a never-ending, arduous journey and a massive act of self-denial for the benefit of the German people, which the Kaiser would carry around with him for the rest of his life. Apologists for the monarchy credited the crown prince, too, with taking a 'decision' that entailed 'selflessly serving' his people and his fatherland. In this reading, the prince absconded to the Netherlands not to save his own skin, but in a display of 'sacrificing his most personal wishes and his own happiness'.[16]

Monarchist publications would defend this notion for decades, and it was public knowledge the Kaiser amended his last will and testament in 1937 to read, for posterity: 'Out of love for my people, I made the greatest and heaviest sacrifice of which I was capable when I went abroad in November 1918, taking upon myself all the misinterpretations, scorn and mockery this step entailed.'[17] Accompanying the pseudo-religious themes of internal turmoil and self-sacrifice were countless reports of alleged danger the German royals faced in the Netherlands. The Kaiser, it was told over and over, faced the prospect of being kidnapped by commandos, assassinated, subjected to the constant surveillance of patrol boats or falling victim to a carefully planned communist attack. These dangers were either imaginary or grossly exaggerated – they never materialized.

In interviews, the Kaiser and the crown prince sought to encourage the belief in their boldness and courage. As early as February 1919, the crown prince submitted to 'informal' questions and put on a brave face – from the safety of his relatively secure haven – vis-à-vis the demands from the Entente that he be handed over. 'Je m'en fiche,' – 'It's all the same to me,' – he proclaimed, regurgitating the empty slogans of the previous November. 'They'll never take me alive.' The conservative German press praised such posturing as a bold 'challenge' to Germany's recent enemies.[18]

Before revolution erupted in Germany, Wilhelm II had ordered that the New Palace in Potsdam, to which the empress, four of their sons and their wives had retreated, be defended like a fortress. In a combative tirade, the Kaiser pronounced himself ready, in the interest of restoring order, to open fire on his own property, to march with a single loyal battalion on Berlin, to fight down to the final bullet, to answer his enemies with automatic weapons and to stand by his troops. He also pondered out loud whether he should commit suicide: 'I'm no coward and am not afraid of a bullet, but I don't want to be captured here . . . So, children, arm yourselves! I'm staying in the villa tonight. We cannot afford any more to be unarmed.'[19] On his subsequent flight he was protected by soldiers toting machine guns, and those who accompanied him in his motorcade carried rifles.[20]

It has been plausibly argued that demands for the Kaiser to give his life on the battlefield reflected modern rather than traditional role models. Heroic deaths or militarily staged suicides were by no means Hohenzollern traditions, no matter how often Germans stylized the alleged fearlessness of Friedrich II and the horseback duel and death by sabre in 1806 of Prince Louis Ferdinand of Prussia, after whom Crown Prince Wilhelm named his second son. Author Theodor Fontane had sung Louis Ferdinand's praises in a mid-nineteenth-century poem: 'In stature six feet tall / a god of war to regard / Admired by women beautiful / Beloved by brothers in arms / A blue-eyed, blond with swagger / And clutched in his youthful hand / Was Prussia's venerable dagger / Prince Louis Ferdinand.' When measured against the long tradition of much-ballyhooed Prussian culture and its putative modesty, readiness for sacrifice and heroism, however, the reality of November 1918 was very feeble indeed.

Demands that sacrifices be made and that the king should forfeit his own life were more in line with the modern figure of the charismatic leader, or Führer, than with the dynastic Hohenzollern kings. On this score, historians have correctly spoken of 'a neo-romantic and thus genuinely modern scenario'.[21] In his 1920 book *Storm of Steel*, right-wing intellectual Ernst Jünger rhapsodized about the 'princes of the trenches': battle-hardened, unbending warriors in comparison to whom the Kaiser and his sons appeared pathetic. The new breed of 'princes' could be noblemen, apothecaries' sons or manual labourers. Such stylized figures recur throughout the radical right-wing literature of the Weimar epoch, first and foremost Hitler's *Mein Kampf* in 1925. A highly decorated and frequently wounded soldier who fought in the trenches of the First World War, Jünger saw it as the prince's duty under certain circumstances to sacrifice himself: 'The prince has a responsibility to die in battle surrounded by the last of his own kind. The countless others who went to their deaths before him have a right to demand that.'[22]

The generations who were given their role models in the German educational system and military academies, where they were introduced to legends like the demise of King Leonidas and the 300 Spartans in the Thermopylae pass in 480 BC, found images of heroic deaths equally familiar and absurd.[23] The German version of the story of how Spartan warriors sacrificed themselves in battle against the Persians – 'Traveller, if you get to Sparta, announce there that you saw us lying here, as our law demanded' – was authored by no less than Friedrich Schiller, and after 1918 not only the aristocracy, but even more so the educated bourgeoisie, enthusiastically embraced the cult of the dead. Moreover, for decades, both the nobility and the educated upper classes had been pumped full of Richard Wagner's intoxicating scenarios of downfall and salvation in words and images.

Conversely, the modes of settling conflict invoked in this context were thoroughly archaic, not modern. In German interpretations of the country's defeat in November 1918, the updated, modern ideal of heroic death gained strength within the military families of the Prussian aristocracy and Wilhelm II's entourage from its connection with a specific cult of falling in battle.[24] Thus, the imperative that the Kaiser and his sons go down fighting is best understood as a hybrid of ancient and highly modern elements – a mixture that would later recur in National Socialism.

The fantasy of the king as a leader who would voluntarily go to his death among his men was ultimately the product of how Wilhelm II had stylized himself in the preceding decades. It's difficult to imagine similar expectations being projected upon Georges Clemenceau, Woodrow Wilson or Lloyd George. As soon as pretension and reality diverged, however, this bathetic image of military leadership came back to haunt the Kaiser and his sons – and the Hohenzollern family as a whole. After 1918, the anti-democratic movement made much of German soldiers' courage in dying at the front, a bravery the crown prince and his brothers had neither demonstrated nor possessed. To bridge the obvious gap, reactionaries required a host of anecdotes, suppositions and sub-narratives such as that of the crown prince's alleged refusal to disguise himself as a civilian or to remove his bear-skin cap with its death's head when he had himself driven into Dutch exile. Later, in conjunction with a planned attempt to escape back to Germany, the crown prince procured fake identity documentation with the name Johannes Hoogenstein, whose picture showed him wearing a presumably pasted-on moustache and a flat cap.[25] Another element of the motif of the noble, fearless Hohenzollerns consisted of stories of how the empress faced down a group of uncouth revolutionaries with dignity and courage in Villa Ingenheim in Potsdam.[26] For decades, narrative images of the Hohenzollerns' readiness to fight were disseminated and embellished into a determined struggle against a much-feared 'Bolshevik revolution' in Germany. In fact, the machine guns, hand grenades and battalions of guards that defended Potsdam Palais like a fortress conjured up a battle that had never in the event actually needed to be waged.

None of the Hohenzollerns or the other princes were ever threatened physically during the 1918 revolution. Even as people called on social democratic ministers to mow down rioters with machine guns and to attack apartment blocks in working-class neighbourhoods with artillery and warplanes, workers and soldiers' councils provided guards to protect the empress and crown princess. Nonetheless, the national and international media were deluged by hastily cooked-up fables, woven from the thinnest threads of facts, about the constant peril to the Kaiser and the crown prince from Sparticist Youth attacks, intricately plotted kidnappings and imminent revolutions.

In reality, the Hohenzollerns' transition to the Weimar Republic was as non-heroic as it was undramatic. The Kaiser's sons who had remained in Germany experienced the initial weeks following the overthrow of the monarchy away from home in the Pomeranian forests but nonetheless in the comfort of family estates and aristo-cratic networks. The crown princess returned with her six children to Cecilienhof guarded by security provided by a workers and sol-diers' council. The Kaiser's son Oskar wiled away his time at the country estate of his father-in-law, Count von Bassewitz, in Meck-lenburg. Oskar's brother August Wilhelm took up residence in a hunting lodge in Thuringia owned by Duke Carl Eduard of Saxe-Coburg and Gotha. Empress August Viktoria resided with her second-eldest son Eitel Friedrich in Villa Ingenheim.[27]

The empress didn't remain for long in Germany – she left for the Netherlands in late November in a special train escorted by social democratic guards. She wouldn't return to Potsdam until after her death in 1921. But the brief period in which August Viktoria remained in Potsdam, combined with the crown princess staying in Cecilien-hof, made the Hohenzollern women into symbols of strength and determination, the role vacated by the Kaiser and the crown prince. In Potsdam, the crown princess acquired a new stature, and not only among monarchists, as a combination of a loyally waiting Penelope, an iron-willed place-holder and an on-the-ground organ-izer of the battle against those Weimar Republic forces that wanted to seize the royal family's hereditary estates and cancel their entitle-ments. The figure of a princess steadfastly holding the line in difficult times summoned up the powerful mythology surrounding Queen Luise of Prussia during the Napoleonic Wars. Both were seen as shining examples of strength, hope and resurrection after a national catastrophe.[28]

Fear had initially led the German aristocracy to lie low, but soon there was no need for anxiety. One month after the Kaiser fled, a German princess wrote:

There we have it! At the start, things will be very bad for us, and some conditions like those in Russia will arrive in German cities.

Bolshevists – I mean. But after a time, they will be pushed aside by good troops. The republic will have its day, but it won't persist, 2–2½ months at most. Then a king will come again. Maybe not as he used to be, which was in fact quite bad, but a king who's like a king, like the old kings of Prussia. I already know what he'll look like. Things will be 'very bad,' as they say, for us, but it will strengthen us and we will grow old in happiness. No matter how everyone is weeping right now, and no matter dark things may look at the moment, I simply can't believe in Prussia's downfall, and I know it will rise again. There you have it! You see, I'm not worried at all about Prussia. I'm far more concerned with finding a reasonable tutor for the children.[29]

Despite the thoroughly comfortable conditions in which the revolution allowed the German royal family and other aristocrats to exist, they felt that they had undergone a uniquely precipitous fall, an unprecedented caesura and an unspeakable catastrophe. This subjective response deserves to be taken seriously, since, arguably, no part of German society ever fell from such great heights in so short a time as did the nobility in 1918. Nonetheless, only German aristocrats could interpret the revolution as an apocalypse. The first phase of their reaction was one of disbelief, fear of an imagined bloodbath along Russian lines, paralysis and speechlessness. Even twelve years after the fact, in 1930, the crown princess would write in her memoirs:

Thus came the most terrible blow we Germans have ever experienced in our two-thousand-year history. The revolution was at hand . . . There was a ceasefire and then, ultimately, the dictated peace treaty of Versailles. These events are so tragic that even today I can't bring myself to speak of them.[30]

These statements were manifestly untrue. In fact, from very early on, the crown princess and most of the Hohenzollerns rediscovered their tongues and their ability to organize themselves politically.

Contact with Counter-Revolutionaries

In December 1918, after an unexpectedly and remarkably non-violent first month of revolution, in which none of the deposed aristocrats suffered any physical violence whatever, Germany was sucked into cycles of brutal fighting between revolutionary and counter-revolutionary forces. By the first days of 1919, the signs of a potential civil war – a scenario that would dog the Weimar Republic until its end – were evident everywhere. Munich and Berlin became the two most prominent arenas of the conflict, which by mid-1919 had claimed 3,000 lives. Recent historians have described and analysed in detail the massive counter-revolutionary violence unleashed in December 1918 against a 'communist revolution' that was more imagined than actual.[31] The courts martial, the political assassinations and the deployment of artillery within the German capital and other events established new levels of tolerance for using violence that would mark an immense change in political culture in Germany.[32] Sharing responsibility for the explosion of brutality were the German military leadership, the Reichswehr, radical right-wing Freikorps militias and associations, segments of the social democratic movement and some other adherents of democracy.

Although they didn't assume leadership positions of any sort, members of the Hohenzollern dynasty joined counter-revolutionary organizations at an astonishingly early stage – a fact registered throughout Germany. On 11 December 1918, when the First Regimental Guards returned on foot to their Potsdam garrison, the troops were inspected by Prince Eitel Friedrich, and their commander Count Eulenburg delivered a monarchist speech.[33] Several days later, addressing the newly formed, ultra-right-wing German National People's Party (DNVP) in Berlin as the main speaker, Siegfried von Kardorff excoriated the revolution as 'the most terrible crime ever committed against the German people'.[34] The crown prince established initial contact with military leaders of the counter-revolutionary movement in the Netherlands before 1918 was even over. In articles by right-wing and anti-Semitic journalists in the US, the royal family commenced an overseas public relations campaign that also featured in the German media. Family ghost-writers fed the growing myth that Germany had been 'stabbed in the back' by leftist traitors.

The first revisionist monarchist pamphlets and brochures began to appear, obscuring the actual behaviour of the Kaiser and the crown prince in the final days of the war. In the summer of 1919, German national parties disavowed any responsibility for the First World War and Germany's defeat and demanded 'the restoration of the monarchy under the Hohenzollern sceptre'.[35] Around that, anti-democratic protest marches, often led by General Erich von Ludendorff, called for a return to the 'spirit of Potsdam', the seat of monarchist power. Such demonstrations were common in Berlin and Potsdam, particularly in the area around the latter city's Garrison Church, where the great German national symbol Friedrich the Great was buried.[36] In the central Berlin district of Mitte, the royal family's main administration – the so-called 'Ministry of the Royal House' as it was known until 1925 – resumed its work. In Bonn, the former royal family lawyer and constitutional expert Philipp Zorn, who would later re-enter the Hohenzollerns' service, composed the first of numerous briefs arguing that Entente demands for the ex-Kaiser and crown prince to be handed over were illegal.[37]

By that time, the Hohenzollerns had also already found legal experts to argue for distinctions between family and state property that would influence public German attitudes for over a century.[38] When the Weimar Constitution was ratified on 31 July 1919, the royal family had already started to redefine its role within the convoluted and organizationally still quite fluid anti-democratic camp in various forums. But, in the early days, their search for a new function and new allies took place outside Berlin. Two of the most important locations were in the Netherlands.

Leading Lights of Monarchism

During the 1923 fruit-picking season, Wilhelm II had himself driven in an open car through the municipality of Betuwe in the Dutch province of Gelderland. Whenever a pig came into view along his route, the 63-year-old is reputed to have doffed his hat and repeated three times: 'Good day, my dear little swine.'[39]

Viewed superficially, this anecdote might seem to suggest that the exiled former monarch had disengaged from the world he had lost in 1918 and was now just a peaceable nobleman who delighted in gazing upon the cherry blossoms and greeted the pigs amidst replendent Dutch fruit gardens. Upon closer inspection, however, this bizarre scene wasn't necessarily one of flowers and peace. Greeting pigs was a relic of a wartime superstition according to which the supreme commander could ensure victory in battles to come by issuing greetings every time he saw a pig behind German lines on enemy territory.[40] The story actually suggests that from the Kaiser's perspective the war still wasn't at all over in 1923. This was precisely the view adopted, perhaps out of necessity, by the politically relevant members of the Hohenzollern dynasty and the far Right during the Weimar Republic. That segment of society refused on principle to accept the outcome of the war and thought it was only a matter of time and organization before the conflict would be continued. Most members of this milieu still conceived of politics and Germany's future in military and martial terms. Meanwhile, the new rules of democracy remained equally alien to the Hohenzollerns, most of the nobility and a significant portion of the entire German population.

Two locations predominate in this chapter of Hohenzollern history: Doorn and Wieringen. Both offer insights into the two most important early political transformations the family was undergoing: the Kaiser's gradual drift into insignificance and the attempt to reinvent the crown prince as a leader who championed the opposition to the Weimar Republic. The Hohenzollerns' days in exile were simultaneously both a farce and a serious threat to the infant German democracy. In these two Dutch hotspots of German conservatism, the borders between reality and theatre, fact and rumour, flights of fancy and recurring themes and clowns and leaders were quite permeable. Correspondingly, there are two ways to interpret this mixture of the risible and the genuinely destructive: as a curiosity on the margins of the main history of the Weimar Republic or as a complex of contradictory impulses typical of the time, one which would recur in many twentieth-century dictatorships, including the Nazi movement and regime.

Theoretically, the monarchy, the higher nobility and the aristocracy had ceased to exist with the founding of the Weimar Republic. But it was naive to think that the aristocracy could be simply abolished by decree: the attempts to do so were toothless. In the reality of the Weimar Republic, German aristocrats retained their estates, castles, titles and most of their positions of authority, and it soon become clear that many were still a force to be reckoned with.

The story of the Hohenzollerns as part of the counter-revolution began almost immediately after the royal family arrived in Dutch exile and had multiple high points and more than one main protagonist. In the family logic, the 'head of the house' was considered the unchallenged leader, and the Kaiser's authority, based as it was on 'house rules', was binding not only on his sons, but on his grandchildren as well. This was explicitly described in the 1952 memoirs of Prince Louis Ferdinand of Prussia, the crown prince's second-oldest son and the 'head of the house' at the time, in which he tried to pass himself off as a supporter of democracy and an adversary of Prussian militaristic tradition and National Socialism. In Louis Ferdinand's retrospective telling, his grandfather in Doorn was the one who decided whether he as a young man would be allowed to travel the world, including the United States, write a dissertation, quit his jingoistic student fraternity, get married or fight a duel while enrolled at Bonn University.[41]

But after 1918 it was impossible to ignore the cracks that had opened in the family hierarchy. Although the Hohenzollerns remained firmly embedded in the anti-democratic camp, the authority of the 'head of the house' was now split between various centres of power. The German higher nobility and the historians who have chimed in to support the royal family's demands for the restitution of confiscated assets have perennially focused on the dynasty's oldest son, but a balanced historical analysis has to acknowledge a multitude of significant players. The Kaiser had seven surviving children and four siblings in the 1920s. All told, the crown prince and his six brothers and sisters had nineteen children, and their spouses also must be considered when taking stock of the three active adult generations of Hohenzollerns in the 1930s.

The Kaiser's children and their families continued to reside in various estates and villas in Potsdam, Silesia and elsewhere after 1918. Thus, any talk of the 'eradication' of the German nobility was as spurious concerning the Hohenzollerns as it was with any other aristocratic German family. Neither the individuals nor their codes, traditions, identity or political influence ceased to exist. Outside the authority of the democratic constitution, a parallel aristocratic world of antiquated titles, terminology, internal rules and rituals survived.

These three generations of Hohenzollerns played a role during both the Weimar Republic and the Third Reich. The Kaiser in Doorn, the crown prince in Potsdam and Silesia, the remaining princes in Potsdam and the Kaiser's second wife, who constantly shuttled between castles, salons, country estates and party headquarters throughout Germany, all remained people of consequence who were taken seriously at home and abroad, particularly in right-wing circles. Whether they were always visible to the public or not, the family continued to exercise important functions.

The defenders of the early Weimar Republic considered it sufficient to restrict what they regarded as the two potential aristocratic leaders of a counter-revolution to specific locations outside Germany – the Kaiser in Doorn and the crown prince on the remote Dutch island of Wieringen to the north – and to ban them from coming home. Female members of the royal family were granted greater freedom of movement. In late November 1918, the empress was allowed to return from the Netherlands to Germany. She was escorted by soldiers and travelled under the personal protection of a leading social democrat in a special train with three brand-new sleeping cars and two carriages full of luggage.[42] Other members of the Hohenzollerns were given full freedom of movement, as was the case for all members of former ruling dynasties deposed after the First World War. There was thus a constant stream of visits and communication between Doorn, Wieringen and Germany, which meant that the two Dutch towns became dual centres of German counter-revolutionary power between 1918 and 1923. They also unleashed different dynamics and have been documented by different levels of historical evidence. Whereas the crown prince's years in exile have had to be reconstructed like a puzzle from scattered sources, the Kaiser's exile in Doorn was unusually well documented. So this is the place to start.

Rumours and Counter-revolution: Doorn

In a moment of desperation in September 1919, the most loyal servant of the Kaiser in exile, Sigurd von Ilsemann, wrote in his diary: 'To sit for hours and hours as though nailed to one's chair and have to listen to the same old stories from the Kaiser is becoming intolerable.'[43] The author of these words was a highly decorated 33-year-old officer and lieutenant general's son who had accompanied Wilhelm II on his flight to the Netherlands and become his de facto right-hand man in Doorn. When he jotted down those lines, he had no way of knowing that his lamentable condition would last for another twenty-two years. As Ilsemann would note a decade later, 'Yes, it certainly isn't fun to chop wood, collect hay, pick flowers and water them for ten years in a row – God knows, it's sometimes barbarically difficult for me.'[44]

Again and again, the scholarly literature has portrayed the

ex-Kaiser as a duck-feeding, wood-carving curiosity.[45] But there is ample reason to look beyond the ducks, the forest, which was razed to the ground after two decades, and the Kaiser's hand-signed wood-work. Doorn was both a reflection and a major foreign outpost of the German far Right during the Weimar Republic.

In retrospect, the Dutch town appears like a dead-end road that diverged from the rest of the twentieth century or, as one observer described it, a 'brackish pool at the edge of lively current'.[46] But Doorn was anything but an insignificant backwater in the history of German hostility towards democracy. Like many aristocratic hubs, Doorn was part of the shadowy world of the counter-revolution, which adherents of democracy at the time weren't always able to adequately read and upon which historians up to the present day have rarely focused. The Kaiser, stranded like a castaway in the 'dismal landscape of the rain-soaked Dutch plains', was a symbol of the emasculation of the entire German nation. Doorn was like a never-ending puppet show depicting how a former world power shrank to miniature dimensions. As one contemporary wrote, 'The German eagle that once spread its wings and flew across the lands now sits in a tiny golden cage – he can't take flight because his chain is too short.'[47]

Early satirical caricatures depicted the Kaiser and crown prince as a pair of rats hiding in a Dutch barn and eating their way through wheels of cheese until they are discovered by three Hohenzollern-hunting enemies: a Dutchman with a cudgel, a socialist cat and an Entente bulldog. 'Get them!' the caption reads.[48] An American cartoon from the time renders the militaristic Prussian eagle as a helpless, plucked chicken tied up by international treaties. The caption reads 'Nothing left but the squawk.'[49] The combination of mockery with a residual underlying fear that the chicken could one day turn back into an eagle was typical of many caricatures of the day.

The isolated and psychologically broken Kaiser, for quite some time incapable of comprehending the world in which he now lived, may have seemed to have no major influence on right-wing organizations in Germany. But, upon closer examination, this view reflects our democratic biases one hundred years after the fact. Millions of people at the time saw the situation otherwise, and the monarchist camp certainly viewed Doorn and its exiled inhabitants in an entirely different light. Huis Doorn was, as many contemporaries pointed out, both a 'cloud cuckoo land' of German monarchism[50] and a fulcrum for the entire anti-democratic movement. Descriptions of the Kaiser greeting pigs and the impressive collection of curios he assembled during his Dutch exile only told one side of the story. Doorn was also a hub of the counter-revolution, a location where serious political work was done and a place from which the Weimar Republic would be attacked until its dying day. We have little cause to regard it with anything resembling nostalgia or romanticism.

In the form of a largely unedited diary, Ilsemann, who never departed from the Kaiser's side, left behind one of the most remarkable post-war sources of information on German monarchism. Ilsemann was married to the daughter of Count Godard van Aldenburg-Bentinck, in whose baroque, moated estate south-east of Utrecht, Kasteel Amerongen, the Kaiser spent the first one-and-a-half years of his exile, and he wrote his journals very much as a protocol for subsequent generations. When the invading Wehrmacht approached Doorn in 1940, he hid the documents in the walls of the estate, and fifteen years after he died his widow released them to the public. In 1967 and 1968, part of the diaries was published in two volumes by Harald von Königswald, a writer of pro-aristocratic works and a man with connections to the conservative resistance to Nazism.[51] Although Königswald made a number of editorial interventions to present the Kaiser more positively, there is no doubting the basic authenticity of Ilsemann's descriptions of events, constellations and statements – especially as they conform to his own biography and information from other sources, for instance the extensive diary kept by Wilhelm II's personal physician Alfred Haehner.[52]

Ilsemann, who took over the management of Huis Doorn in 1945 at the request of the crown prince, shot himself in the gatehouse of the estate in June 1952. His diaries attest to his keen powers of observation, sober judgements, great honesty and impressive if old-fashioned loyalty and fidelity to his 'lord'. These two volumes, accurately described as an 'involuntary cultural history',[53] are significant not so much for their reconstruction of Wilhelm II's hatreds and delusions as for their minute documentation of the aristocratic extreme Right, including eating and speaking habits, temper tantrums and personal animosities. With almost anthropological precision, Ilsemann reveals the codes and rules that governed this segment of society during the Weimar Republic.

Particularly noteworthy in the light of today's debates is the helpless rage with which conservative aristocrats reacted to the publication of the two volumes of Ilsemann's memoirs in 1967–8. If the author's son is to be believed, members of the royal family tried to suppress the second volume, which shed light on individual Hohenzollerns' relationship with National Socialism.[54] Numerous passages from Ilsemann's original manuscript in which the Kaiser raged against 'caste comrades' and common people were also stricken from the published volumes.[55] After its publication, criticism of the book took on bizarre dimensions. Some eagle-eyed critics wrote letters to newspapers disputing the idea that the Kaiser could have chopped down 13,000 trees a year. Calculations of this sort sought to undermine the credibility of the entire text[56] and led the sports section of the *Frankfurter Allgemeine Zeitung* newspaper to publish a debate about the Kaiser's performance with his saw.[57] Somewhat more interestingly, a former diplomat attacked Ilsemann and other advisors to the Kaiser for their 'servility',[58] while a conservative navy historian felt called upon to dismiss the value of the diaries as a whole.[59] The Kaiser's grandson Wilhelm Karl publicly stated that Wilhelm II had been the smartest and best educated person he had ever met, pillorying the diaries as a 'felony' and a 'violation of trust' that exposed private matters to an 'all-too-critical public'.[60]

In the end, Ilsemann's son remarked drily that the man 'sitting behind the walls in Doorn' had been exactly the person his father had described. '[This] was no enlightened old gentleman who had grown wise, acknowledged his own failings and saw new ways forward for his fatherland,' the son wrote. 'The letters to newspapers and the personal attacks against the diaries' editor of the preceding weeks show how powerful the hopes are in conservatives circles that the opposite was the case, hopes that live on – you would almost think – despite the authors' knowing better.'[61]

His Majesty's Perspective

The 678 pages of published Ilsemann diaries document Wilhelm II's at times farcical narcissism, a mixture of infantile fantasies of omnipotence and aggressive self-overestimation with an almost incomprehensible refusal to acknowledge reality. For the former Kaiser, the German people were 'utterly pathetic, a gang of scoundrels', who deserved what they got for 'hounding him out'.[62] Consumed by nebulous notions of widespread betrayal, the ex-monarch took every opportunity to speak, lecture, curse and write about almost every target under the sun, attacking his children, the German people, his advisors, the aristocracy, the tsars, the Italians, Austrian Emperor Karl I, his generals, Hindenburg, Groener, ungrateful German workers, cowardly German bourgeois, German civil servants, freemasons, conservatives, the British, his officers, pro-democracy liberals, Jesuits, Catholics, southern Germans and – increasingly and by way of shorthand for all other traitors – 'the Jews'. At table in 1921, he informed his fellow diners that

> the Jews have driven the 'German hare' back and forth between them . . . All they are interested in is established Jewish world dominance . . . If the tide turns in Germany, it will be the Jews' turn to suffer . . . They'll be forced to surrender everything – their accumulated wealth, their homes and everything they own.

Wilhelm II didn't stop there. 'Once and for all, they must be removed from their civil service positions,' he raged. 'They have to be brought down.'[63] Deeply religious and increasingly interested in theology, the former Kaiser became more and more susceptible to ethnically chauvinist interpretations of Christianity – a line of thought indebted to the racist theories of Houston Stewart Chamberlain among others. In 1923, Wilhelm arrived at the conviction that Jesus was 'a *Galilean* and thus *not a Semitic Jew*'.[64] Thanks to the mediation of the anti-Semitic, German-American journalist and publisher George Sylvester Viereck, the ex-Kaiser's theological 'insights' found an audience in the US, causing Wilhelm II to moan that it was impossible to get the 'truth' out in Germany because the entire press was in the hands of Jews and Jewish capital.[65] The ex-Kaiser manically edited and published 'historical tables' intended to show that he had been innocent of provoking the First World War. Ilsemann's diaries and other sources overflow with examples of Wilhelm calling for retributory blood to be shed, pathetic scoundrels punished, and his adversaries hanged or beheaded.[66] In future, he fantasized, no one but himself would have a say in anything. All the traitors, failures and advisors were to be done away with, and after his restoration he would have to wield 'the power of a shogun'.[67] The Kaiser's inflated self-image made itself felt even in those forums that, however significant they may have been for internal aristocratic communication, were far removed from the intellectual focus of the times. For example, in the hunting magazine *Deutscher Jägerbund*, a certain Count Finck von Finckenstein informed his readers how 'assiduously' Wilhelm was working to combat 'the lie of German culpability for the world war'.[68]

As abiding as the Kaiser's significance for the German Right might have been, it remains incomprehensible how he envisioned himself becoming a 'shogun'. The idea was as ridiculous as Prussian field marshal August von Mackensen, whose moustachioed, hypermasculine visage and characteristic gigantic hussars' busby made him one of the most photographed figures on the far Right in Weimar Germany, who wrote to the Kaiser in 1924 that 'Sharpened on my desk lies my sword / and all you have to do is give the word.' The laughable posturing of the field marshal, born to a bourgeois family and seventy-five years old, epitomized the fantasies of the Kaiser and his minions at this juncture.[69]

One of the best-known statements from Doorn, not made public until Hindenburg's death in the summer of 1934, sums up the world-view of this dotty, bitter former monarch throughout his exile. Upon hearing of his former military commander's passing, Wilhelm proclaimed: 'Blood must flow, lots of blood, above all from the nobility, from all who deserted me.'[70] This statement was suppressed at the request of the Hohenzollern family from the 1968 published edition of Ilsemann's diaries.[71] Other passages read like previews of the horrific abyss into which Germany would in due course descend. In August 1921, the Kaiser uncorked a bottle of champagne to celebrate news of the murder of former German finance minister Matthias Erzberger of the Centre Party. His reaction to the killing of the Jewish-German foreign minister Walther Rathenau the following year was similar.[72] In the summer of 1922, American newspapers asked why the Hohenzollerns had not officially denounced those who had assaulted the journalist Maximilian Harden, one of the Kaiser's fiercest critics. (In fact, there were suspicions, never proven, that the family had approved or even been involved in the murder.)[73] Wilhelm called Harden a 'loathsome, dirty Jewish fiend' and Rathenau a 'mean, deceiving, racial traitor'. In a similar context, the former Kaiser attacked the idea of 'world citizenship' and the Enlightenment of Goethe and Schiller as particularly corrupting.[74]

For several months before he was killed, the Jewish-born Harden, who had once been considered for the post of American ambassador, had spoken out against the crown prince, the Kaiser and the violence emanating from monarchist groups.[75] In early July 1922, Harden counted 317 victims of anti-democratic assassinations, writing that only intervention by the victorious Entente powers could stop the spread of massive monarchist brutality. One day later he was attacked in front of his villa in Berlin's leafy Grunewald neighbourhood by a 'hired gang' of radical right-wing thugs and beaten to within an inch of his life with metal bars. Harden never fully recovered from the attack and could no longer work as a journalist. 'You Germans will perish because of your solidarity with murderers,' he later said in court concerning the open and tacit support received by his attackers and those who had ordered the assault. Left-wing writer and editor Kurt Tucholsky would quote those words in the influential weekly *Die Weltbühne*.[76]

The situation was much the same with Erzberger, one of the German signatories of the ceasefire in Compiègne in November 1918. Long a target of far-right hatred, he had already survived one assassination attempt before he was murdered by the right-wing terrorist organization Consul. The champagne uncorked in Huis Doorn was part of a general drift towards brutality among parts of the German nobility.[77] Kurt Eisner, the Jewish-German socialist leader of the post-war revolution in Bavaria, had been shot twice in the back of the head in February 1919 in Munich by a young Bavarian count, who was subsequently celebrated as a hero by some aristocrats. Rumours spread that the Kaiser's youngest son, Joachim, had been involved in the assassination. Shortly before the murder, Joachim had been arrested in conjunction with an attempted putsch against the new, left-wing Bavarian government.[78] Wilhelm II also reacted with glee to the death of the German president, Friedrich Ebert. 'We'll drink some bubbly to that, eh, Ilsemann, right now while the paper is being read aloud!' he exclaimed. This was another passage censored from Ilsemann's diaries.[79]

The Kaiser was originally only supposed to reside at Kasteel Amerongen for three days, but his stay eventually turned into eighteen months. By the time the former monarch finally began looking for a suitable residence in Holland, fierce debates were already underway concerning the disappropriation of, and possible compensation to, the Hohenzollerns.[80] In the summer of 1919, the finance minister Albert Südekum, a member of the conservative wing of the social democrats, caused a stir with his proposal that the royal family should be given 10 million marks with which to acquire property. The notion met with considerable resistance from both the Right and the Left, as did a subsequent suggestion in 1920, which Südekum defended, that the Hohenzollerns should receive a blanket pay-off of 100 million marks. Both ideas were quickly abandoned.[81] Belying early fears about Bolshevik conditions in Germany, significant sums did regularly appear in the royal family's Dutch bank accounts. This significantly eased financial pressure on the Kaiser. By May 1921, the German government had transferred some 76 million marks to the Hohenzollerns.[82]

Nonetheless, the gap between the Kaiser's actual and putative wealth remained great and was obscured by assumptions and false information. Whereas Wilhelm II was considered even in the late Weimar Republic to be 'one of the richest Germans, if not *the* richest',[83] he himself continually complained about financial constraints and repeatedly considered selling off his valuable art collection. In 1929, his 'Berlin manager', as the *New York Times* reported, moaned about the vast expenses of maintaining the royal estates, the alleged losses generated by royal forests and the size of the extended royal family itself.[84]

In August 1919, Wilhelm II had enough money to acquire the property in which he would live out his life, purchasing Huis Doorn for 500,000 guilders. After carrying out extensive renovations costing a further 850,000 guilders, the Kaiser and his wife moved into their new home, located only a few kilometres from Kasteel Amerongen and some sixty kilometres from the Dutch–German border, in May 1920.[85] Huis Doorn was actually too small to accommodate the reported sixty-four freight train cars and thirty-six removals vans full of German royal belongings that arrived in the Netherlands.[86] But the advantages of the grounds, which had been redesigned in the late eighteenth century and included a moat, a large park and fifty-nine hectares of land, won over its new owners. The smoking room looked out on a pond and beds of irises, and for two decades the fallen Kaiser would receive navy officers, local generals, his children, grandchildren and relatives, race theorists, apocryphal ethnologists, anti-Semitic professors and writers, artists, historians, princes, admirers, delegations of aristocratic associations and, in 1931, Hermann Göring beneath a portrait of Friedrich the Great.

Nonetheless, Wilhelm didn't enjoy his early years of exile in Amerongen and Doorn. In his eyes, those years unfolded under the cloud of the terrible catastrophe of the German revolution. The Kaiser's radius in the Netherlands was restricted to one district of Utrecht province. The grounds of his estate were subject to constant surveillance, so that whenever he went out, he was trailed by a Dutch police vehicle. Even the airspace over Huis Doorn was closed.[87] From the Hohenzollerns' perspective, this was a time of real and perceived threat to their very existence. In 1920, his personal physician Haehner revealed that the former monarch always kept a loaded pistol on his bedside table.[88] Wilhelm lived in constant fear of being assassinated or, above all, of being handed to the victors in the First World War. In July 1919, the British prime minister David Lloyd George had repeatedly insisted in the House of Commons that the Kaiser and crown prince be extradited,[89] and segments of the Left in Germany supported the idea of the pair of royals having to answer to the Entente powers in court. For example, the pacifist Hellmut von Gerlach and the seventy-year-old theoretical patriarch of the Social Democratic Party Eduard Bernstein warned at a rally in 1920 of the dangers that the reactionary forces posed to the Weimar Republic and its 'new spirit'.[90]

For these reasons, Wilhelm and his advisors drew up a series of contingency plans for him to flee incognito by ship, car, ambulance or aeroplane to other parts of the Netherlands, the Black Forest, a monastery or a country estate in East Prussia.[91] The royal entourage was intensely worried that the former monarch could be paraded through the streets of Paris or London, beheaded or sent away to a prison in Algiers or St Helena or Peru. For a long time, the possibility of Wilhelm being extradited was real, as speculative plans were laid to have an American commando abduct the Kaiser and put him on trial in front of an international court. Protection from the Netherlands was Wilhelm's most effective defence.[92] Cartoons from the time show him cowering behind the voluminous skirts of a stereotypical Dutch woman who shelters him from the searching eyes of armed Entente officers.[93]

Such worries proved as unfounded as the fears that the German revolution would turn extreme, and Wilhelm II soon developed a rigid daily routine that included reading the newspaper, sawing tree trunks, prayer, lectures, receiving guests, long monologues, walks, dictation, correspondence and feeding the ducks. Ilsemann described the 'torment' of this unvarying sameness.[94] But routine could never relieve the permanent insecurity felt by the Kaiser and his entourage after their unprecedentedly precipitous fall. Rumours in the press about assassination plots in 1922 and 1932 highlighted the former monarch's tenuous position.[95] The Kaiser's inflated opinion of himself compensated for his vulnerability without doing anything to lessen it in reality.

One of the curiosities that best illustrates how Wilhelm gradually drifted off into a fantasy world was his passion for certain forms of archaeology and ethnology, particularly his enthusiasm for the teachings of the influential autodidact Leo Frobenius and his theory of cultural morphology. A 'working group' founded by the Kaiser himself combined top-class scientific research with shallow politicization and instrumentalization.[96] In October 1923, after a lecture by Frobenius, Wilhelm asked him to stay on in Doorn, enthusing:

> It's as though I've been redeemed! Finally, I know what future we Germans have and for which we are still called! All these years after the revolution, I racked my brains, but now I know: we will be the leaders of the Orient against the Occident! . . . We belong on the other side. Once we have taught Germany that the French and English aren't white people at all, but rather blacks, the French, for example, Hamites, they will go after these gangs.[97]

But even this statement, which combined the grotesque absurdity of earlier proclamations by Wilhelm and presaged his racist boasting to come, cannot be entirely dismissed as the rambling of an addled aristocrat. Back in Germany at the time, many intellectual elites were discussing similar ideas advanced by Oswald Spengler, and a bewildering number of 'barefoot prophets' from various ethnic-chauvinistic and racist movements had already begun to influence the political attitudes of millions of people.[98] The Kaiser's musings may have revealed his distance from reality, but they were typical of the self-deception of an entire caste, the intellectual fault lines of a shaken nation, and the radicalization, confusion and hatred growing not just in Huis Doorn but in an entire country.

In this respect, too, Huis Doorn was a mirror as well as just an oddity. The 'nightmare-like otherworldliness' of the place[99] and the copious evidence of how the Kaiser saw the world make it hard for observers today not to engage in psychological diagnosis. Reasonable arguments have been made that the countless remote diagnoses of the Kaiser as 'degenerated', insane, abnormal or lunatic often say more about those who made them than the object himself.[100] Nonetheless, while British historian John Röhl's view that Wilhelm suffered from paranoid delusions may overshoot the mark in the medical sense, [101] the closer one looks at the situation in Doorn, the harder it is to characterize the fallen leader's massive distance from reality, radical egotism and immense aggression in neutral terms.

The New 'Empress'

Doorn was also where the deepest rupture in the Kaiser's personal biography, one which would also have political implications, took place: his marriage to his second wife, Princess Hermine Reuss von Greiz. Nearly twenty-nine years his junior and a widow with five children, Hermine was five years younger than the Kaiser's eldest son. Empress Auguste Viktoria had died in 1921, and Hermine and Wilhelm married the following year. American newspapers reported that the Kaiser had married a 'lover of pomp and display', entirely dissimilar to level-headed Auguste Viktoria. 'Wilhelm has chosen second bride with temperament like his own,' wrote the *Evening Star* in Washington.[102] In later years, Hermine more than anyone else sought to steer Wilhelm towards National Socialism.

To legitimize his relationship with a much younger woman, embarked on so soon after the empress's death and much criticized among monarchists, the Kaiser put out a story in an interview that was, in the words of the periodical *Tage-Buch*, 'so awful you want to believe that the interview was invented or at least falsified'. In Wilhelm's telling, when Auguste Viktoria died, 'her maternal love . . . alone among women . . . flowing over the hospital gown of every wounded soldier', God had directed his attention to a letter written by a small boy, whom the Kaiser immediately recognized as a 'comrade'. He invited the child and his mother to Doorn, and in this fashion God led his new bride to him. 'I often felt that Romeo and Juliet didn't know the true meaning of love,' he pontificated. 'The "love that moves the sun and other stars" is the love between ripe men and women in whom knowledge has killed off romance.'

That was the tone in which the Kaiser had his ghost-writer Sylvester Viereck commune with his followers.[103] The 63-year-old Kaiser's unexpectedly quick remarriage elicited mockery among democrats and horror among monarchists. Like most members of Wilhelm's entourage, including all the royal children[104] and the crown princess,[105] Ilsemann opposed the marriage. The crown princess, who now found herself competing more or less openly with someone her own age, pointedly referred to the Kaiser's second wife as 'the new woman'.[106] The disruption of the Kaiser's relationship with the traditional nobility was registered as far away as the east coast of the US. The *New York Times* ran a story with the headline 'The Old Nobility Is Peeved', which contended that an aristocratic delegation, led by the influential landed nobleman Elard von Oldenburg-Januschau, was trying to persuade the exiled monarch to change his mind.[107]

Such efforts came to naught, but among the German nobility the Kaiser's second marriage was another permanent black mark against him after his flight to Holland. A substantial public relations offensive was launched to make Hermine palatable to conservative circles. Third-rate commissioned pamphlets written in the style of kitschy courtly romances praised her positive qualities and sought to elicit sympathy for the 'lonely' Kaiser. The pathetic level of texts with titles such as 'The Kaiser's Bride' only underscored what a thankless task it was to try to make the Kaiser's marriage to the young widow appear seemly.[108]

Hermine's ambitions for influence, power and a serious, public role quickly became the stuff of gossip and rumours in Germany and gave rise to an entire subcategory of jokes among pro-democracy segments of society. After their marriage, the 'Kaiser's bride', whose husband still used the signature 'Imperator Rex', tried to get the German consulate in Amsterdam and authorities in Berlin to change her passport to read 'Empress of Germany'.[109] In an English-language self-portrait of the 'imperial couple', produced in 1928 as a special PR measure for the British and American markets, she was referred to as 'empress in exile'.[110]

Around this time, in the satirical magazine *Simplicissimus*, the gifted caricaturist Olaf Gulbransson depicted the would-be empress trying to scale the outside wall of Kaiser Wilhelm's palace. Entitled 'The Climbing Hermine', the image showed the Kaiser's wife contorting her limbs and clawing at the 'historic corner window' in an attempt to hoist herself into Wilhelm II's former office, which was familiar to everyone in Berlin. Dangling from her left hand was Friedrich the Great's famous marshal's baton.[111] Playing on the fact that her marriage contract with Wilhelm spelled out where she was to reside, and the rooms had been equipped especially for her in the palace, sharp tongues around Germany mocked Hermine as the Kaiser's billeting officer.[112]

Despite the mockery, however, Hermine immediately established herself as a force within the microcosm of Doorn and within the royal family. This educated, ambitious and very energetic young woman became one of the most important emissaries of German monarchism both in the Netherlands and on her countless trips and visits abroad. Several rooms in Huis Doorn, most of them smaller guest bedrooms, were put at the disposal of the 'empress' and the five children she brought with her from her first marriage.[113]

From the moment Hermine arrived in the public eye until her death in 1947, the foreign press took a constant interest in her. Despite intense efforts to keep her wedding to Wilhelm in the autumn of 1922 private, the event was besieged by as many as 300 journalists seeking to get a look into the estate and the park.[114] The big American newspapers constantly reported on the Kaiser, Doorn and the royal family's estates, children and political activities. Papers in Albuquerque, New Mexico, ran photographs of the bride, while the New York press shared details about the colours of the wedding bouquets and ran pictures of hordes of reporters in front of Doorn's front gate and photographers balancing on the roofs of cars, and shots of the crown prince's arrival in an open car. Even the motorcade in which he left the island of Wieringen was deemed worthy of a pictorial feature. The *New York Times* reported that the Kaiser sold the rights to an exclusive picture of his wedding for $10,000.[115]

In a 1923 interview, the Kaiser described Doorn as a 'glass house' – both a panopticon where the Entente nations and the world press kept him under constant surveillance and a harmless place where he could maintain his external image of an apolitical patriarch going about his harmless hobbies and occasionally receiving his children and people wishing to speak with him. This was the way the Hohenzollerns would often be depicted,[116] and investigations of even the most minor changes in the royal circumstances became something of a journalistic sub-genre in the global press during the 1920s. In 1927, for instance, the *New York Times* found it fitting to interpret the installation of a new bathtub in Wilhelm's Berlin palace as evidence of an imminent royal restoration. That newspaper also followed stories about the ex-Kaiser losing weight and quarrelling with his wife as well as the fashion details of the overcoat worn by the crown prince to his father's seventieth birthday.[117] No sooner had the crown prince settled in Wieringen than reporters with hidden cameras began to track him, and the first stories about the 'celebrity prince' made their way across the Atlantic.[118] But the international media and paparazzi kept a constant eye on all members of the royal family wherever they went. The result was stories with headlines such as 'Honeymoon Walks Have Ceased and William Appears Much Older and Thinner' and 'First Exclusive Picture of Ex-Kaiser and His Bride!'[119]

A Parallel Universe

The miniature court societies assembled from old retinues and eighteenth-century furniture in Amerongen and Doorn were bizarre microcosms,[120] and it required an anthropological acumen to decode the rules, rituals and language of this monarchist parallel universe similar to that of Clifford Geertz's famous analysis of Balinese cockfighting. Both the cockfights and the imaginary aristocratic oases featured 'deep play', the performance of actions that external observers would have considered 'irrational'. But, for initiates in both cases, such rituals followed their own logic, whose meaning could only be understood within the system.[121]

This was true of even the most minor, ancillary customs in the anti-democratic outpost and mecca that was Doorn-Amerongen. A conflict in November 1919 shed light on the extent, contours and abstruseness of the attempts to carry on an *ancien régime* in exile. The empress's lady in waiting, Countess Mathilde Keller, nicknamed 'the hallelujah aunt' by mocking contemporaries,[122] insisted that, as a court marshal, the Kaiser-in-exile's host, Count Gontard, walk backwards before His Majesty with a gold-tipped staff whenever the ex-Kaiser entered the salon or the dining room. Keller rejected a compromise, suggested by the young Countess Bentinck, of using a bell to announce the arrival of the Kaiser instead – calling this an expression of 'socialist ideas'. A short time later, the older countess launched a campaign to prevent the tablecloths printed with the Prussian eagle from being used on inappropriate occasions.[123] Such minutiae might appear ridiculous. But they were part of the same battle over symbols, colours, standards, memorials and flags that was waged on the streets of 1920s Germany with fists, batons, daggers and firearms that continued throughout the history of the Weimar Republic.

Huis Doorn seemed to many observers to be frozen in time. It was a place where a fallen king could stand in front of gigantic military maps as his generals dozed off and retroactively won the battles of the First World War, where he could vanquish the republicans in the Spanish Civil War and where he could drive the occupying French army from German lands with the weapons allegedly concealed in the castles and manors of the Prussian nobility.[124] Or he could simply while away his evenings with endless monologues about his own infallibility and the shortcomings of others. Not coincidentally, Wilhelm II's entourage in Doorn consisted largely of old men, retired high-ranking officers who took turns 'performing their duty'.

Every day the Kaiser sat upon a saddle-shaped desk chair, cutting articles out of third-rate newspapers as though assembling a self-made collage to prop up his absurd view of the world. All the while he would 'drink his two glasses of port wine, one with water, and eat his seven or eight small sandwiches'. Cigarette in hand, he would ask his adjutant Ilsemann: 'So, my boy, what's new today?'[125] The majority of the entourage were more interested in shielding the Kaiser from reality than confronting him with it.

Wilhelm II never had any lasting contact with the language that expressed the political order of a new, radically different world. Ilsemann recorded in detail how stiffly members of Doorn society communicated. For example, in 1932, one of the Kaiser's stepsons withdrew from the Kaiser's presence with the words, 'Father, will you permit me to obediently take my leave?'[126] Two years later a grandson greeted him by saying: 'Grandpapa, I report for duty.'[127] Another eighteen-year-old grandson asked him in 1935: 'Dear Grandpapa, may I be allowed to express my most obedient congratulations on the occasion of your birthday?'[128] Wilhelm's children typically kissed his hand by way of a greeting.[129] His brother Heinrich referred to him in the presence of others as 'my most merciful lord'.[130] His son Oskar, a member of the right-wing paramilitary Stahlhelm (i.e. the Steel Helmet, League of Frontline Soldiers, Germany's largest conservative and anti-democratic veterans' organization), greeted his father with military stiffness,[131] and the greetings offered by his brother were so 'cold that Empress Viktoria Auguste began to weep'.[132]

In 1919, the Kaiser's 35-year-old son Prince Adalbert complained that he was still treated like a schoolboy.[133] Three years later, in his first volume of memoirs, the crown prince wrote about his father's 'hypercritical coldness', telling readers that of all the children only his much younger sister Viktoria Luise had been able to touch 'a warm place in the Kaiser's heart'.[134] Indeed family correspondence was also carried out in the harsh tones of Wilhelm's domination, in which his sons, even when high-ranking officers in their fifties, got dressed down like naughty children. In 1923, the Kaiser's second wife addressed him with the words, 'Would you allow me, exalted lord, to speak with [State Secretary] Kan for a moment in your presence?' Both in writing and orally, members of Wilhelm's retinue addressed him habitually with sobriquets such as 'exalted master'.

The continuing use of such formal language indicates a growing gap with reality that is better measured in anthropological observation than pro-democratic mockery. In 1934, Prince Friedrich zu Solms-Baruth began a letter to the Kaiser: 'Most serene emperor and king! Most merciful emperor, king and lord!' That piece of correspondence, written by a man who, ten years later, would be arrested in conjunction with the 20 July 1944 attempt on Hitler's life, ended with the words:

If it be not impertinent, my sister or I would propose reporting back to you soon. My mother has charged me with telling Your Majesty that she forever thinks of Doorn with gratitude and loyalty. I would like to bow down once more and present my most obedient thanks to Your Majesty for the gracious sympathy He has shown. I remain His Royal Majesty's most loyal servant, Friedrich Solms-Baruth.[135]

Historian Percy Ernst Schramm, one of Germany's most internationally respected medievalists at the time, who visited Doorn in
1930 with his wife, wrote with dismay about one of the Kaiser's
frigid, 'servile' adjutants:

> He was the pure embodiment of a 'court flunky'. He only moved
> when the Kaiser wanted something brought to him. In effect, he
> was the extended index finger of his lord, in front of whom he
> removed the monocle from his eye. The fact that the Kaiser puts up
> with such people is also characteristic.[136]

The tone that ran through the letters, postcards and tributes
addressed to the Kaiser was typified by a missive sent in September
1933 by Paul von Hindenburg, who, despite having fallen out of
favour with the royal family, was still, after all, the president of the
German Reich: 'Deeply moved, I bow down and present Your
Imperial and Royal Majesty with my most respectful gratitude for
His most gracious interest in my affairs.'[137]

As surreal as it may seem today, the Kaiser and the crown prince
spent a lot of time having photos taken of themselves that they then
sent, often autographed, to admirers. Grown men and women collected these images like icons.[138] The need to be visually represented
went hand in hand with the constant urge to issue pronouncements.
By May 1919, the crown prince had already been dubbed the 'most-
interviewed man in Europe' and the 'most-photographed of all
fallen luminaries'.[139] A bewildering array of photos, portraits and
likenesses of Crown Prince Wilhelm, mailed all over the world
together with letters and in postcard form, have thus been preserved
for posterity. The stream of images of various sorts that continued
until the prince's dying days can't help but remind observers today
of the innumerable selfies taken by twenty-first-century teen-
agers.[140] One obvious explanation would be a need for reassurance
that he existed in the political realm and continued to be publicly
perceived as an important figure.[141]

Among the Hohenzollerns' loyal followers, the act of preserving and responding to such images was a ritual way of proclaiming their undying loyalty. For example, in 1936, the cavalry captain and writer Adolf Victor von Koerber wrote to the crown prince: 'I would like to express my most obedient gratitude to Your Royal Majesty for the excellent picture of Yourself in a sports shirt that I was allowed to receive into my possession on 24 August.'[142] Three years later, Prince Max Egon zu Fürstenberg thanked the Kaiser for another image: 'The lovely picture Your Majesty bestowed upon me on my birthday hangs before me, and over and over my eyes rest upon the beautifully captured features of Your Majesty in inconvertible love.'[143]

The Kaiser frequently added eccentric comments to the countless variously shaped and sized photographs and busts of himself he presented to others. In 1927, he gave a former commander of an elite German military regiment, Hans von Tschirschky und Bögendorff, a photo of himself with the words, 'He who does not parry gets dismissed!' Ilsemann noted in his diary: 'Tschirschky is saddened because this inscription ruined the picture for him. He intends to cut it out, as he has no idea what the Kaiser's statement refers to.'[144]

Such incidents appear ridiculous today, and they also elicited scorn in the 1920s. Such laboriously maintained theatrical rituals were obviously and completely out of step with the times. A figure like Ilsemann, who challenged a man who insulted him to a duel in Huis Doorn's park[145] and who never wavered from the side of his lord despite his own better judgement, often seemed like a knight from a long bygone era: a north German Sancho Panza stoically accompanying his deranged master as he tilted against windmills in the Netherlands. Pro-democracy camp Germans were not the only ones who viewed the cabinet of oddities in Doorn with a mixture of scorn and pity. The contrast between past military glory and the aged Kaiser feeding ducks was also fuel for conversation among the nobility and the German Right. In public as well as privately, many conservatives cited four lines from Goethe's late poem 'Tame Invectives': 'Why is it that a single king / Is swept out as though with a broom? / Surely they'd still be standing / Tall, if it was a matter of more than one.'[146]

Arthur Moeller van den Bruck, one of the major prophets of the new Right in Germany, employed a variant on this motif in his 1923 bestseller *The Third Reich*. 'Royal majesty,' wrote van den Bruch 'had already disappeared from those who ascended to the throne, long before the loss of their crowns confirmed that they were no longer princes but eminently human beings.' It was down to this weakness alone that 'these representatives of royal majesty ended up as very common citizens, having emerged from the general tragedy without tragic greatness and departed the preserve of enigma for the most banal sort of private life'.[147]

Leading Lights and Military Colours

Nonetheless, Doorn was more than a museum of bizarre wax figures. It was there that a defence was mounted of a social milieu that decisively rejected the democratic German mainstream and that served as a beacon to all Germans seeking to restore a lost past. Doorn was a signalling station for the right wing and, directly or indirectly, its messages reached millions of people in Germany. Moreover, Doorn preserved and embodied the vivid splendour those millions of Germans remembered from the putative good old days.

An example of this language of symbols was the memorial ceremonies, documented for posterity in minute detail, in Doorn and Potsdam after Empress Augusta Viktoria's death in April 1921. In Doorn, a small circle of aristocrats and high nobility escorted the casket, which the Kaiser and the crown prince were not allowed to accompany to Germany, on the first leg of its journey to its final resting place. This scene was reminiscent of one of the most famous artefacts of Wilhelmine self-depiction: a photograph of the ceremonial issuance of watchwords on 1 January 1913 on the Schlossbrücke bridge in Berlin. It showed Wilhelm II and his six sons, with waving plumes attached to their pointed Pickelhaube helmets, in front of rows of military officers – a careful staged symbol of the majesty of the late Wilhelmine Empire. Eight years, a world war and a revolution later, the crown prince, his brothers, his brother-in-law and his father recreated this moment of splendour with the help of the other aristocratic mourners. In the dining hall of Huis Doorn, which had been transformed into a funeral parlour, 'four heavy silver candelabras' created a 'magical light'. At the start of the ceremony, Count Gontard, who bore the title 'court marshal', knocked with his sword against the oaken floor of the Dutch house. 'With firm steps' and, dressed respectively as a naval officer and a cuirassier, a hussar and a life hussar, the crown prince, two of his brothers and the Duke of Braunschweig descended the podium steps, 'all with sabres drawn, between them black-veiled ladies-in-waiting and courtiers, everything surrounded by wreaths and flowers – it was an arresting, truly Prussian image'.

The family would long retain its habit of attending weddings and funerals in military uniforms, even if the armies from which they originated had ceased to exist. Even the Hohenzollerns' house physician, otherwise a cool and critical observer of royal rituals, was very impressed by this spectacle, writing in his diary:

> The scene was splendid, when these four tall, well-built figures strode gravely and proudly into the room of mourning with their swords drawn. It was truly a source of joy and satisfaction to be able to show the Dutch in attendance, with their customary louche bearing and mostly small statures, this glorious image of Germany's former military greatness.

The Kaiser stepped forward, pale and dressed in the field grey of the First Infantry Guard Regiment. Kneeling down, the widower laid his head upon the casket and didn't move for several minutes of silent prayer. 'As though on command', the princes saluted the deceased empress by lowering their swords. Accompanied by the tolling of bells, the makeshift hearse – a military vehicle which the Kaiser had used to visit the front during the war and which had been painted black – rolled slowly over the gravel of the dark park of the estate. 'The way was illuminated by torches, and from the heavens the moon shed its bright light on this sad milestone in world history.'[148]

The casket was then taken by train to Berlin, now the capital of democratic Germany. Thousands of onlookers lined the rail tracks along the way, and hundreds of thousands followed the funeral procession to the park of Sanssouci Castle in Potsdam, where 6,000 officers formed a guard of honour at the neo-classical temple. Even a pro-democracy newspaper wrote, 'For a few short moments in Potsdam, the Wilhelmine era was revived into a ghostly, radiant existence,' although the paper also dismissed the spectacle as 'the parading of a corpse from an extinct era'.[149]

Months prior to the empress's death, the suffering of the 'mother of the nation' driven into exile had already been staged in a fashion that overtly referenced the popular myth of Queen Luise of Prussia, mother of Wilhelm I, who was seen as a martyr of the Napoleonic Wars and a symbol of German national renaissance.[150] Augusta Viktoria, whose youngest son had committed suicide in 1920, was also lionized as a woman who struggled through personal tragedy, the humiliation of her nation and the malice and hardship visited upon all of Germany under the yoke of foreign domination.

The plight of the Hohenzollerns in exile and the parallel physical suffering of the empress formed a narrative that was deeply and emotionally anchored on the German Right.[151] Even in transit from Doorn to Potsdam, the funeral party had been 'received with honours reminiscent of the bridal journey made by Marie Antoinette from the royal Hofburg in Vienna to Louis XVI in Versailles 150 years previously'.[152] In the first German city after the funeral train crossed the border, the local mayor presented the princely escorts with a laurel wreath. Upon the mourners' departure, they were also given a 'wreath into which a crown of thorns was woven as a symbol of the empress's suffering' and a hand-tied bouquet from the committee of the Women's Patriotic Association.[153]

The carefully staged ceremony in Potsdam, which superficially resurrected the Wilhelmine Empire for a day, was interpreted in various ways, depending on the observer's politics, but it was remembered, then and today, by people throughout the political spectrum. The German socialist press wrote of a 'Hohenzollern commotion the likes of which the post-war era had never seen before' and a 'monarchic review of the troops' – hardly an adequate interpretation given the military trappings of the event.[154] In the subsequent Prussian regional elections, left-wing parties criticized the Right for tugging at German heartstrings, and leading Social Democrats in the Reichstag objected to political parties instrumentalizing the funeral.

For people at the other end of the political spectrum, the veils, lowered swords, piles of red roses, bodyguard regiments, uniforms, funeral marches, flags, officers, clergy and princes projected dignity and strength and provided a visible demonstration that those qualities had not been lost to Germany but only concealed – and could thus be reactivated. The left wing of the socialist movement saw the spectacle as a 'belated Carnival parade', which is probably the impression most people today would get if they viewed the film footage of the event. *Weltbühne* pundit Hans Siemsen skewered the pompous spectacle with particularly incisive turns of phrase, one of which would be used over and over in the following twelve years to pillory monarchist rallies:

It is revolting to see older, adult men stuff themselves into such clownish jackets, hang pounds of medals from their chests and don the sort of helmets people no longer even wear in variety shows . . . They're not even officers any more. The uniforms they sport no longer exist. They retrieve them from their closets like people buying costumes from a second-hand shop, and they attend funerals as if they were masked balls. Just imagine if an everyday widower wore pink jerseys or a knight's armour to his wife's funeral.

Siemsen's text ended in a flurry of anger, however futile, at that significant part of the German population that didn't share his social democratic norms:

The Hohenzollerns and the Nazis

What kind of a people are we who applaud the men who have lied to us, sold us out and brought us ruination just because they misuse the burial of an old woman to stage a monarchist demonstration and a military masquerade? How tactless, cold-hearted, brutal and dumb.[155]

For impassioned democrats the pompous spectacle might have been farcical and overblown, but on the Right it was regarded as a dignified reinvocation of old traditions. The funeral procession behind the casket, borne on a carriage pulled by four black Trakehner horses, with the veiled crown princess and Prince Eitel Friedrich behind it, his sword drawn and in uniform like all the men, included at least seven of the princes from the regional states that made up Germany, representatives from practically all right-wing associations in Prussia and – in Hans von Seeckt – the head of the army command of the at least nominally democratic Reichswehr.

Although estimates vary as to how many people took part in total, there is no question that turnout was massive, with as many as a quarter of a million people making their way to Potsdam.[156] The ceremony turned into a powerful demonstration of monarchist power, but it didn't feature any concrete political demands. Rather, it mobilized emotions that undercut the Weimar Republic. This was one of the last great moments of Hohenzollern 'emotional politics', understood as a theatrically staged exchange in which the monarchy demonstrated its love for the people and received popular love and legitimation in return.[157] The funeral must clearly be seen as a significant indicator of the free-floating monarchist loyalties and emotions that could be harnessed in millions of Germans.[158] The dual events in the Netherlands and in Potsdam in April 1921 showed that Doorn, despite the wishful thinking of pro-democracy forces, was more than just a graveyard of decommissioned ideas and emotions. The empress's funeral demonstrated how little those forces understood the emotional household of Germany's anti-democratic Right.

Huis Doorn was a symbolic centre of the old world, and from

there disruptive signals were broadcast out into the Weimar Republic. The Kaiser, who would never again leave the Netherlands, remained a key figure until his death in June 1941. Together with his second wife, and sons and advisors who came and went from the estate, he was a leader who could not completely be ignored by the anti-democratic Right. Wherever principles of legitimacy were taken seriously, and particularly among older monarchists, the Kaiser remained a focus of attention. And within the Hohenzollern family, Wilhelm II's often brusquely issued commands to his sons and the clan as a whole were still considered just as binding as a superior's military orders.

The Crown Prince on the Isle of Wieringen

The Hohenzollerns also had a second counter-revolutionary outpost with its own accents: a brick house on the desolate island of Wieringen, about 150 kilometres or a half day's journey from Huis Doorn. Here the crown prince lived in exile until November 1923. It was more the antithesis to than a poor man's version of Huis Doorn and utterly unlike Cecilienhof, the estate built especially for him, in which his wife still resided, making her the highest Hohenzollern representative on German soil. It was said of Cecilie's post-war lifestyle in Potsdam that she existed 'unrepentantly according to her whim', altering nothing of 'the overall contours of her life of luxury'. As one contemporary observed, 'there are still the same number of ladies-in-waiting, court functionaries, maids and servants as before the revolution'.[159] That was anything but true of the crown prince. After fleeing Germany, Wilhelm arrived on the island of Wieringen on 22 November 1918. Press photographers captured him disembarking from the small ferry, and the images were published the world over. 'On his way to oblivion' was the caption in a Chicago newspaper.[160]

There, Crown Prince Wilhelm moved into an austere, decidedly unglamourous, two-floor parsonage, where he began to fashion a political identity of his own. Pictures of the island taken by non-journalists show it to be rainy, barren place of simple houses standing in mud.[161] Mockingly compared by caricaturists to Napoleon in his final place of exile, Saint Helena, the crown prince existed behind a wooden fence in this dull rural landscape. Today a landfill connects Wieringen to the Dutch mainland, but until 1924 it was a roughly 10-kilometre-long island in the Zuider Zee populated by dairy farmers and fishermen. A 1919 caricature in postcard format juxtaposed two images. One showed the prince in 1914 with a drawn sabre and a death's head cap, leading German troops to the front. It was captioned: 'We battle [German: *Wir ringen*] to the end; we battle to the death.' The other image depicted him in 1919 wearing his uniform with ridiculous large wooden shoes and staring at an hourglass in the light of a petroleum lamp. The caption there: 'Wieringen to the end, Wieringen to the death.'[162] Like his father, Wilhelm was banned from returning to Germany, but he was able to reach Wilhelm II's estate in exile in a few hours by ferry and car. The crown prince maintained many of his political contacts with Germany via an older officer named Louis Müldner von Mülnheim, one of his closest and most influential advisors. A cadre of officers, civil servants, photographers, journalists and writers performed what today would be called the prince's PR work, creating the basis during his years of exile for the narratives and images that would later be employed politically.

Like the Kaiser, the crown prince feared for a long time that he would be assassinated or extradited to the Entente nations. In 1919 and 1920, he offered to sacrifice himself on behalf of the other individuals wanted by the victors, writing to King George V: 'If the allied and associated governments require a sacrifice, let them take me instead of the 900 Germans whose only fault was that they served their fatherland in war.' Previously the Kaiser's brother and other princes had offered themselves up in open letters 'Take us in his stead. Or along with him!'[163] But these suggestions were cleverly calculated but ultimately empty displays of nobility and courage.

The crown prince's public gesture elicited no response and

worsened his conflicts with his father.[164] Wilhelm's fall from grace was just as steep as the Kaiser's, but the depths to which he fell were far lower – at least in terms of material conditions. In the winter 1918–19, he took refuge in a 'worrisomely primitive house' whose rooms could hardly be heated, living a life of waiting, reading, writing, conversing with followers, mostly from the military, and taking walks through the cold, 'impenetrable fog'. In the autumn of 1919, the *New York Times* ran a profile of the crown prince, contending that he was so impoverished he had been forced to sell his fur coats in Amsterdam.[165] The American press, which can be said, without exaggeration, to have developed a decades-long obsession with the Hohenzollerns, was full of detailed 'home portraits' with headlines such as 'The Crownless Crown Prince and His Island'.[166]

Gradually, Wilhelm succeeded in setting up a household that included a chef and a maid from Cecilienhof as well as motorized transport. In 1920, American newspapers reported that the crown prince's 100-horsepower Benz was one of the fastest cars in the world. If he so desired, Wilhelm could reach even the faraway Spanish border in no time, within two days at most.[167] Two former officers who lived at least some of the time in the two-storey house served the crown prince as adjutants, private secretaries, servants and social companions who helped him with his 'work'.

After the initial waves of rubberneckers, photographers and journalists had subsided, the prince was visited by members of wealthy families from Amsterdam and elsewhere, who occasionally sailed to Wieringen in their yachts. Wilhelm borrowed money from his mother, and the wife of an Amsterdam jeweller furnished his house for him. The Kaiser's personal physician reported in 1921 that the island's famous guest was very popular among the natives and was well looked after.[168] Wilhelm regularly called at Doorn and received increasing numbers of visitors, once in a while his wife and children. Still, when one thinks of the halls of mirrors in the royal castles in Potsdam and other examples of pre-1914 Prussian pomp, it's hard to imagine the crown prince sitting at a wooden table in the parlour of his brick house over a glass of beer with the former general chief of staff Count Friedrich von der Schulenburg, future army general chief of staff Ludwig Beck, Dresdner Bank director Eugen Gutmann, Field Marshal General Hans von Plessen, Count Heinrich zu Dohna, Prince zu Solms-Baruch and the Duke of Braunschweig.[169]

But that was undoubtedly what his reality was really like. Wilhelm learned 'tolerable' Dutch, speaking with the fishermen and farmers in their homes every day, and wrote letters in an endless series of variations on military staccato concerning the same basic topic: 'I'm suffering from this nameless filth in Germany. I lack anything genuine to do. I miss my family, my house, the soil of March Brandenburg, my thoroughbreds and my old friends.'[170] In February 1919, after only a few months in exile, he wrote to an officer with whom he was cordial: 'I live here in part like a fisherman or farmer, read, write a lot, play music, draw and work in the village smithy. You can't let yourself be dragged down.' He signed off the letter with the words 'Your old commander', adding in parentheses, 'How is the expansion of the rear positions?'[171]

Throughout his exile, the crown prince was able to keep in contact with old and new German military elites. With outmoded arrogance, he wrote to Ludwig Beck in 1921 of the newly reconstituted Polish state: 'Poland is nothing but a bad joke of world history that will disappear again when the time is right.' Along with maintaining such friendships, Wilhelm also made connections to influential German right-wing militia leaders. Among the visitors to Wieringen was the former navy officer Hermann Ehrhardt, one of the best-known and most charismatic figures in the paramilitary Freikorps, who led the national German counter-revolutionary movement and would later make a name for himself as a planner of political assassinations.[172]

The brusque tone for which the crown prince was known throughout Germany continued in his correspondence in exile, as did the simplistic mindset that thought complex political issues could be solved by sufficient demonstrations of force. In 1921, for instance, he wrote that all it would take to resolve all Germany's border conflicts with Poland was to 'bring together all Germany's regular military and volunteer associations and give the Poles a proper thrashing'.[173]

The crown prince shared the opinion with military elites and most of the German right-wing camp that the world war wasn't truly over and would be continued by a new leader in a new form. This idea was less the wishful thinking of a prince in exile than a *sine qua non* for Wilhelm to earn his place on the recoalescing German Right. In a major 1919 interview with the *New York Times*, the crown prince declared that there would be another large-scale war within a decade. The *New York Tribune* quoted this statement, noting sarcastically that its author had to know what he was talking about since starting wars, after all, was one of his specialities.[174] The spectacle of a fallen crown prince in wooden clogs vowing from his little island house that renewed world war was inevitable once again combined ridiculousness with a harbinger of darkness to come. Even in clogs, the seemingly laughable crown prince remained part of the forces that were about to redefine the political Right in Germany.

The Resentment of the Socially Demoted

In the early phase of the German counter-revolution, various ideologically and organizationally fluid circles overlapped. There were no hard-and-fast distinctions between monarchist intransigence, paramilitary cults of violence, racist esoterica, global anti-Semitic conspiracy theories, terrorists, assassins and would-be putschists. The fluidity within the political Right as a whole made it easier for the Hohenzollerns to make connections to significant new figures and their ideas.

A decade before the Nazi movement established itself as the leading right-wing force in Germany, unprecedented bridges that would become a reality in 1933 were already under construction. One notable example of the openness of early German counter-revolutionaries to new forms of collaboration was the unlikely biography of the spy and global adventurer Ignaz Trebitsch-Lincoln,[175] whose 'secret' and 'mysterious' connections to the crown prince's cadre of advisors was controversial enough in 1919 to attract intense interest abroad.[176] A series of more or less sensationalist reports portrayed Trebitsch-Lincoln as a mediator in early plans for a putsch. One plot envisioned the Kaiser being declared mentally incompetent and Hindenburg elected German president, whereupon he would step down so that that Crown Prince Wilhelm could be crowned.[177] Like much that emerged from the early counter-revolutionary movement, such ideas may have sounded like penny-novel fantasies, but there was some astonishing substance at their core.[178]

Upon his release from a British prison, where he had served three years for fraud, the former British member of parliament and con artist Trebitsch-Lincoln meandered, hungry and penniless, through the streets of post-revolutionary Berlin. There, in a grotesque political match-up, despite being born a Hungarian Jew, he won the trust of the racist writer Reinhold Wulle, one of the leading lights of the radical right-wing press. Trebitsch-Lincoln, who was known in Germany for his scathing anti-British texts, impressed the anti-Semite Wulle with his claim to have connections with no fewer than 320 American publications. Wulle introduced Trebitsch-Lincoln to one of the top figures of the anti-democratic movement, the Ludendorff intimate and former artillery officer Max Bauer.[179]

Bauer and Trebitsch-Lincoln both regarded Crown Prince Wilhelm as a legitimate candidate for the throne, which made it necessary to bypass the Kaiser.[180] Trebitsch-Lincoln was able to get various American newspapers to report rumours that the Kaiser had lost his mind, wandering through Amerongen Castle screaming, incapable of recognizing his surroundings.[181] Trebitsch-Lincoln failed in his attempt to meet Wilhelm II at the castle, but he was received on Wieringen by the crown prince's adjutants, whom he informed about his ideas for restoring the monarchy. The advisor in question had little time for his insistence that the prince would have to assert himself like Caesar and Jesus.[182] Nonetheless,

Trebitsch-Lincoln continued to enjoy Bauer's trust, retained contact with leading monarchist insurgents and even played a not unimportant role in the Kapp Putsch.

In 1919, the crown prince had articulated his wish to create an instrument of 'massive propaganda' that would constantly remind people everywhere of what he saw as the Social Democratic movement's culpability in Germany's defeat. The former colonel Bauer was among the most powerful of the German putschists when he swore his unqualified loyalty to Wilhelm in early 1920. The time wasn't ripe for the heir to the throne, Bauer conceded, but his propaganda was starting to work. Bauer gave the prince a plan drawn up by Trebitsch-Lincoln, saying how they shared 'professional interests' with the former spy.[183] The scenarios envisioned in that document, in keeping with its peripatetic author, freely mixed fantasy and reality. Long before the Kapp Putsch, fantastic visions of the restoration of the German monarchy ghosted around the global press. Some reports claimed that the crown prince had secretly returned to Germany a while ago and was already at work steering the counter-revolution, which would involve two million men, from his Silesian estates. Fantasies of the Kaiser's son assembling a million-strong army 'like Caesar in Gaul' and leading it against the Weimar Republic would recur in later radical right-wing pamphlets.[184]

As things turned out, once the Kapp Putsh had failed, it didn't take long for both the Kaiser and crown prince to distance themselves rhetorically from the attempted coup d'état, although it had initially put the Hohenzollerns 'in a very happy mood'.[185] This was hardly surprising. One of the two men's primary concerns was not to lose the protection of the Dutch government. The crown prince's position was worrisome enough to British and Dutch authorities that they temporarily prohibited him from leaving Wieringen and deployed a torpedo boat to monitor his activities.[186]

The extensive travels of Trebitsch-Lincoln, who was manic-depressive,[187] took him to many places, but he never personally met the crown prince. A windbag and wanderer between worlds, he would heap public scorn ten years later upon the 'stupidity' of putschist circles who could not even agree on a pretender to the German throne.[188] This three-chambered burlesque of princes, putschists and confidence men was no secret to Germans at the time. In 1928, the star director of German avant-garde theatre Erwin Piscator used the figure of a highly strung spy to depict a 'society of scoundrels'. Played by Curt Bois, the Trebitsch-Lincoln character was paired with Ludendorff in an 'international farce of cheats and criminals', written by Leo Lania and scored by Kurt Weill, which mixed post-war German reality and grotesque exaggeration.[189]

At first glance, the encounter between one of the leaders of the militarized far Right in Germany and an imaginative Jewish conman who was trying to win the crown prince's support for a putsch may seem like the stuff of fiction. But, as with other historical episodes, this was more than a mere oddity. In her seminal analysis of totalitarian movements, Hannah Arendt describes a constellation that has existed since the late nineteenth century and whose basic contours were also visible in Weimar Germany: the cooperation between members of a fundamentally threatened or simply fearful elite with picaresque adventurers, would-be visionaries and self-proclaimed dragon slayers from well outside respectable bourgeois society. As Arendt tells it, elites may begin to openly admire people from gangster and criminal milieus in situations of economic and political upheaval. The result is new subcultures that bring together people from all walks of life who feel socially demoted.

First published in 1951, Arendt's analysis examined the examples of the militaristic far Right in 1890s France, the brutally racist African colonists around 1900 and the rise of fascist movements after 1918. Arendt described these new constellations of people with the word 'mob'. But they didn't consist solely of the lower classes. On the contrary, they were like a caricature of society in its entirety: alliances of people who had been pushed down the social ladder, the angry and the avaricious, individuals from all classes who had been rendered superfluous and who were now reconstituting themselves in a new type of group.

Alliances arising at key historical junctures between the high nobility, the military, armed militias and disreputable mediators and agents often remained quite unstable and ended up amounting to nothing. So did many of their principal figures. In the years that followed, Trebitsch-Lincoln's German patron Wulle vacillated between collaboration with and opposition to the Nazi regime and was arrested in 1940. He survived the Sachsenhausen concentration camp, where he was held under special conditions that included permission to receive cigars sent by the crown prince.[190] Following his career as a putschist and a global counter-revolutionary advisor, Bauer died in Shanghai in 1929 while working for Chiang Kai-shek.[191] Trebitsch-Lincoln himself, who by that point was ordained as a Buddhist monk, met his end in 1943 as an agent of the Japanese secret service, also in Shanghai. This picturesque, enigmatic middleman and trickster, whose biography defied alignment with any usual twentieth-century political categories, seems to have absconded to China all the way back in 1921.

The partial opening-up of elite segments of society and their partnerships with figures with whom they would have by no means consorted before the war were both a novelty and a model for the future – one which is frequently present at the beginnings of twentieth-century dictatorships. While Trebitsch-Lincoln was shuttling between Berlin, Doorn, Wieringen and other parts of the world, a painter of postcards from Austria in post-revolutionary Munich was discovering his talents as a radical right-wing orator and his appeal as a guest, whip and holster on full display, in the homes of wealthy patrons.[192] When seen in the context of Hitler's early contacts to leading political, military and social circles in Munich, Trebitsch-Lincoln's presence on Wieringen seems much less implausible and bizarre. It was an expression of the anti-democratic Right's willingness to experiment and of the new social alliances that soon played a central role in the rise of Nazi movement.

The realities of the crown prince's first five years after the First World War have been buried under 100 years of romanticization. While Wilhelm undoubtedly led a stark life of relative privation early on, he soon existed in fairly comfortable circumstances and was able to move around. Overall, this half decade remains something of a blank spot in the crown prince's biography. Politically, these years allowed the prince to keep his distance from the violent turmoil of the early Weimar Republic. That was precisely the strategy advocated by Wilhelm's advisors operating on various estates and in Berlin and Wieringen. As one of them wrote, 'My policy for him is: keep your mouth shut, don't be drawn on any issues, don't engage in politics, build a new life seriously and assiduously, don't reveal any vulnerabilities in your personal life – and wait for your time to arrive.'[193] It was a sign of things to come that the crown prince's return to Germany in November 1923 coincided with the failed putsch by Hitler and Ludendorff. The crown prince required a period of exile for him to accrue the legend and nimbus of a matured and hardened prodigal son. In terms of how their respective images developed, it is hardly absurd to compare Wilhelm with Hitler following his release from Landsberg prison after serving his time for his role in the Beer Hall Putsch.

Crown Prince Contra Kaiser

The differences in the images of the Kaiser and the crown prince quickly became greater and greater. Compared to the ageing former monarch amidst his stunted twenty-four- to fifty-person court,[194] the trim, athletic prince zipping across his island and the mainland on his motorcycle, accompanied only by a few loyal 'adjutants', was as crass a contrast as Huis Doorn was to the simple parsonage on Wieringen. Photos of the younger Wilhelm on his motorbike were published as far away as New Jersey.[195] Even in early 1919, this father–son relationship was portrayed as one of alienation and division, in which the Kaiser, stuck in the past, was confronted with a highly dynamic heir who allegedly favoured not a putsch, but a popular monarchy with parliamentary support. This notion itself was a product of propaganda launched on behalf of the crown prince.[196]

The carefully staged images of the crown prince in exile built on publicity work and a reputation established before 1914. Even then, Wilhelm's ghost-writers and advisors were already trying to conceal his well-publicized affairs and tendency towards frivolity and brazenness behind a façade of his alleged qualities as a modern leader. Thanks to some national reported public appearances, the crown prince had already positioned himself politically as the preferred option and ally of the radical right-wing and anti-Semitic opposition to the Kaiser. In the summer of 1914, after he had levelled insults at German chancellor Theobald von Bethmann-Hollweg and just before the left-wing publication *Vorwärts* labelled him a warmonger,[197] a self-sponsored pamphlet argued the case for the crown prince and his leadership style in a way that presaged his later attempts at PR. At the time, the radical Right was searching for an alternative to Kaiser Wilhelm, who was seen as too 'liberal'. After the war and the Kaiser's abdication, images of the crown prince prepared in 1914 could be used more freely in an increasingly open political arena. Or, to state matters the other way around, Crown Prince Wilhelm had already constructed a persona as the type of man lionized by the Right after 1918, four years earlier.

In the months preceding the outbreak of the First World War, writer Paul Liman, who had already made a name for himself as a *claqueur* of Bismarck, published a book that sought to identify and distil leadership qualities from the crown prince's happy-go-lucky life of operettas, hunting trips and gambling. Playing upon the clichéd aristocratic and neo-conservative disdain for formal education,[198] Liman argued that the prince's sporting, macho, easy-going manner was proof that he had the right stuff to be a modern political leader. 'Only a philistine can demand that a prince constantly attend lectures or deny him recuperation that comes from intellectual relaxation,' Liman gushed.

A bit of clever tomfoolery never ruined anyone's taste or character . . .
A prince, too, should learn how to laugh, how to laugh himself back

to health . . . and not just always search like Iphigenie for the land of Greeks in his soul or share in Tasso's desperation.

Liman delighted in recounting the prince's achievements in hunting, gaming and sport, together with his physical attributes.

And indeed, in appearance and habits, the crown prince was the antithesis of not just his father, but also his brother Eitel Friedrich, with his 'terrible plumpness as a result of his horrid obesity' and 'wife of colossal girth'. Compared with many a monocle-wearing, beer-bellied right-wing political leaders, for example the media mogul Alfred Hugenberg, Wilhelm was a paragon of modern masculinity. His trim young body, trained twice a week with a boxing coach, commanded respect even among his critics and was seen as a sign of the serious effort being put into becoming a leadership figure.[199] The constant emphasis on the crown prince's physique was another way of distinguishing him from Wilhelm II, with his congenitally withered arm, which he tried to keep concealed all his life. But no matter what camera tricks were employed, as a horseman, swordsman, dancer and hunter (to run through the central disciplines of the German aristocracy), the father was condemned to be dramatically overshadowed by his son.

Liman drew a connection between the healthy body and the political farsightedness of the future leader:

> Just as Crown Prince Wilhelm surveys the hunt and its pleasures from a higher vantage point, rather than as a sport to combat boredom, a running theme can be seen in his overall attitude toward athletics. He doesn't hesitate in the face of the boar's teeth or the wild predators of the jungle. He rides the most excitable horses, courageously scales all obstacles and is a skilled swimmer, fencer and gymnast, with hardly any peer among Germany's aristocratic youth. Trimmer than trim, taut, his clear eyes homing in on his opponent's weaknesses, he can hold his own in battles from the tennis court to the fencing arena. Why can we find wrong in that?

On the contrary, Liman concluded, Wilhelm was to be admired for 'leaving behind the listlessness and excess of his early life in order to offer his young body, healthy and strong, to the national community'.[200] All in all, Liman's homage presented readers with the ideal image of a modern leader as man of the people, conspicuously different from Wilhelm II. In many respects, the book was reminiscent of the pre-war far-right-wing screed *If I Were the Kaiser*, written by the ultra-nationalist Heinrich Class.[201]

In 1922, the influential journalist Maximilian Harden, the bête noire of the Kaiser, published a similar portrait of the monarch's son. In Harden's portrayal, the crown prince was a loner, a keen-eyed hunter stalking deer from Scotland to India, his belt cinched tight to emphasize his svelte waistline, every inch the sportsman even in uniform, his cap cocked at a dashing angle and with a gait closer to a stroll than a march. Modest, courageous in the face of danger, admired by his men and existing in exile in 'small, humble, barely heatable quarters', Wilhelm seemed to be pursuing in everything he did the goal of distancing himself from his father and the latter's clunky, vacuous pomp. The Kaiser had no choice, wrote Harden, but to put up with the 'existence of a crown prince and rival who had for too long remained an apprentice and a cavalry lieutenant'.[202]

This was an astonishingly sympathetic portrait of the crown prince from one of the most sarcastic journalists in Europe, but Harden wasn't the only influential voice to depict Wilhelm in a glowing light. Around the same time, soon-to-be-chancellor Gustav Stresemann praised the prince's constant 'running and riding around . . . boxing and swimming' as a 'revolt of nature against the enforced monotony of military service, just as his whole being was a revolt against the symbolic aspect of the royal calling, as excessively embodied in his eyes by his father, the Kaiser'. Stresemann continued:

The gaze of his imperial father became as stiff as that of a statue, when, for instance, he showed himself and the empress to his regiment in Potsdam, field marshal's baton in hand. His son's eyes sparkled with lust for life, and his cap was worn just as slanted and his uniform just as irregularly as the film version of Friedrich the Great.[203]

The merging of Prussian tradition and modern cinematic illusion was a positive quality, not a black mark. From the very beginning, American star reporters also did their best to create the image of the crown prince as a congenial, approachable and vivacious heir to the throne.[204]

A Modernized Kaiser

From early on, the crown prince conceived of himself as a modern, contemporary aristocratic leader and considered his father to be a relic of the past. It was easy for Wilhelm to stylize and distance himself as someone different from the hermit-like Kaiser with his military maps, duck ponds and woodcutting. In 1920, in conversation with his personal physician Alfred Haehner, he was already referring to his 'old, ossified Papa', who was 'terribly divorced from the world'. Wilhelm II would have been perfectly at home in the world of Louis XIV, the crown prince scoffed. The Kaiser's attitudes were 'completely outmoded'. The people knew nothing of him, and he knew nothing of the people, past whom he had always sped in his car in Berlin, taking nothing on board. By contrast, the crown prince saw himself as a militarily trained populist leader who did his own shopping, was able to joke with shop girls and soldiers and rode his motorcycle through the streets of Utrecht, where he was universally recognized and greeted.[205]

Several months before these statements, as already discussed, he had irritated his father by offering to take the latter's place and allow himself to be extradited to the victorious Entente powers.[206] Through gritted teeth, Ilsemann noted how well informed the crown prince was compared to his father 'about the state of the world and especially Germany'.[207] From the outset, the contrast between the crown prince's connection to everyday reality and the Kaiser's dream world was glaringly obvious. Supported by his own circle of officers and right-wing authors for advisors, the crown prince published two volumes of ghost-written memoirs in 1922 and 1925,[208] although his own contribution to them was minimal – a fact known even outside Germany.[209]

The crown prince's propaganda was particularly crass, combining false demonstrations of humility with commissioned, hagiographic biographies. For example, in the summer of 1919, the *Tägliche Rundschau* newspaper printed an open letter from the heir to the throne to the intelligence officer Kurt Anker, who had published a book entitled *Crown Prince Wilhelm*. 'You have done this without my knowledge, and that was right of you, since if you had asked me beforehand, I would have said: save yourself any further effort – the world is unteachable right now,' Wilhelm wrote. 'I trust that with time the accusations against me would collapse on their own. It runs against my nature to rush too quickly to demand justice.'[210]

Nevertheless, the response to the crown prince's first volume of memoirs in 1922 already demonstrated how difficult it would be to turn him into a post-revolutionary hero and leader. French literary journals took a profound, keen and mocking interested in this 'portrait of the man he would like to have been'.[211] Even for his experienced PR team, it was no easy task to explain Wilhelm's role before and after the start of the First World War, his dubious military performance during the conflict and his flight to the Netherlands. Nor were his publicists able to extinguish the eyewitness accounts and stream of anecdotes about the easy life Wilhelm had led behind the frontlines. They were a constant wildfire threatening to burn the crown prince's reputation to the ground.

Wilhelm's preferred ghost-writer was an Austrian war correspondent and opponent of anti-Semitism, Karl Rosner. Rosner was a good choice for creating a new image of the crown prince as a clear-eyed observer who had seen the military disaster coming all the way back in 1914,[212] had sought to ward off the worst and was now looking to build a broad consensus in the social mainstream. But compromises made on behalf of the ideal of national unity and the new moderate tone raised the hackles of the racist Right, who responded by spreading rumours that Rosner was secretly Jewish. Members of the anti-Semitic pan-Germanic League, who had courted Wilhelm as their preferred leader before the war, now attacked him as a Jew-lover. The main Nazi newspaper, the *Völkischer Beobachter*, mocked the 'Jew crown prince', writing, 'How you've gone to the dogs, you Hohenzollerns!'[213]

The radical right-wing German opposition, which had already trained its sights on the Kaiser, now presented itself as both the heir and the vanguard of racist anti-monarchism: heir because the images it used had been around since the Wilhelmine Empire and vanguard because it was absorbed and radicalized by a part of the Nazi movement. Picking up on an idea advanced by the 1912 anti-Semitic tome *Semi-Gotha*, much feared by the German nobility because it purported to document the 'Jewification' of the aristocracy, racist circles began debating around 1920 whether the Kaiser himself might be a 'Jewish half-breed'.[214]

On the other hand, a French review of Rosner's book *The King* dismissed it as one of the most laughable works ever written about the war. That statement was debatable, but its essence hit the mark.[215] Moreover, the crown prince's ghost-written memoirs had to compete with the recollections of the Kaiser, put into words by a Pan-Germanic writer named Eugen Zimmermann. They ran through editions of around 300,000 copies, and the global rights brought in significant money.[216] A Dutch newspaper reported in 1922 that the American edition had earned 800,000 marks. The article was accompanied by a caricature of the Kaiser crying gold ducats like tears into a large jug as he jotted down his memoirs.

In the years that followed, the Kaiser constantly sought to have his mediators directly intervene to control what was published about him. For instance, he had Zimmermann complain to the Berlin publisher Ullstein about the supposed manipulations of truth in its books critical of the monarchy. One such work was the thoroughly negative memoir of former German chancellor Bernhard von Bülow, whom Zimmermann accused the publisher of providing with office supplies and 'a mademoiselle to do the typing'. Hans Ullstein dismissed Zimmermann's objections with the succinct remark that Ullstein was, after all, an 'anti-monarchist publishing house'. The former Kaiser also sought to warn foreign writers about the pernicious influence of Ullstein and its 'Jewish publications'.[217] The Kaiser's own writings were buttressed by apologist works he himself commissioned, provided information for, edited and censored. Among this genre were the volumes written by Austrian historian Karl Friedrich Nowak, who attended the Kaiser's lectures, the contents of which he dictated in the evening to a Princess Kropotkin for typing, without making any effort to confront what he had heard with the empirical imperative of always questioning the source.[218]

Many of the Hohenzollerns tried, often with some success, to influence German and international opinion via the American press. Interviews, pictorials, pre-arranged news reports and stories were constantly being placed in leading American media outlets, where they also reached the British, French and German press. Such efforts did not always bring about the desired results. In the 1920s, for example, Sigmund Freud drily commented about the most recent interview by one of Wilhelm II's most important American press agents: 'By the way, you know that my respect for the Kaiser was always quite meagre, and you can add that my regard for the ex-Kaiser hasn't grown.'[219] But, on the whole, the monarchist camp got roughly the same amount of influence out of its propaganda efforts on Western media as the effort it invested in them. The attempts to put the Hohenzollerns' views on the world stage via the American media were doubtlessly one of the most effective ideas the spin doctors working for the royal family had. And it would continue to be a focus for decades.

While the marketing of autobiographical Hohenzollern material could be politically influential and economically lucrative, it could also do damage in the wrong context – a recurring issue over the years. Some examples of this long tradition of trying to politically instrumentalize history were the attempts after the Second World War by the Hohenzollerns' 'PR department' to suppress the publication of the crown prince's and princess's rather hastily written memoirs and plans to make the princess's life into a film and to find a biographer capable of massaging Wilhelm II's difficult biography and to improve the family's nationally and internationally battered reputation.[220]

The 1920s German public knew the Hohenzollerns' ghost-writers by name, and there was no shortage of scorn among reviewers concerning the quality of their work and the Kaiser as 'the world's best-paid author'.[221] The Kaiser's memoirs appeared at roughly the same time as three other books from the crown prince's smaller but more productive propaganda staff, whose authors did their best to depict Wilhelm *fils* in a positive light for the masses and with regard for the democratic reality of Weimar Germany.[222] That required completely ignoring the crown prince's character and past deeds, portraying him as a keen strategist, a brave soldier, a salt-of-the-earth defender of the common people, a statesman and a leader for the future. The serial publication of such propagandistic works would continue after Crown Prince Wilhelm returned to Germany.[223]

The prince's increasing alienation from his father was manifest in the fact that Kaiser knew nothing of his son's books before they were published and was angered by them, remarking that no one wanted to read an obituary written by his own offspring.[224] Commentators outside the royal family also saw the crown prince's writings as a 'vivisection of his father, tactless and with the only possible aim of promoting himself as the better Kaiser'.[225] British diplomats charged with assessing the probability of a monarchist putsch already spoke in late 1919 of a genuine animosity between royal father and son.[226] Wilhelm II's anger at his son's perceived manoeuvring to topple him from the throne was reinforced by his second wife, who characterized the crown prince as 'cowardly, dirty, stupid, conniving' and 'unmasculine'.[227]

Wilhelm II's conflicts with all his sons extended down to the level of style and dress. They are interesting not just as an example of the ridiculous dimensions of the enmity but as a typical fault line in the Hohenzollern family. The Kaiser accused his son August of 'dandy-isms', writing:

> He changes his clothes four times a day, always with new outfits making an appearance. Evenings, instead of his uniform, he wears a tuxedo with diamond-and-ruby buttons on the vest, shirt and cuf-flinks. He even dons a woman's bracelet. The crown prince isn't much different. I don't know from whom these fellows got that.[228]

Even during the war, the 'young man', as Wilhelm II often referred to the crown prince, had 'flitted about in affected get-ups of the sort no other officer in my army wore'. After the war, the ex-Kaiser carped, 'Instead of reading my memoirs, which I have placed at his disposal, he races around all day on his motorcycle and in his car.'[229]

Circles close to the Kaiser repeatedly described the cold-hearted brusqueness with which he treated his sons,[230] and those private tensions would later influence the political lines of conflict within the family. They emerged clear as day in the crown prince's half-hearted, never completely realized attempts to make political decisions independently of his father.

The Laughing Man

From early on as heir to the throne, officer and public figure, the crown prince cultivated a style that was – to use a term popular among Prussian military aristocrats – 'dashing'. Among the countless anecdotes about Wilhelm, one story stands out above the rest. In October 1913, a young lieutenant in German-occupied Alsace announced he would give 10 marks reward to every one of his recruits who cut down a French civilian with his blade. This prompted a conflict between civilian and military authorities that ended in a constitutional crisis known as the 'Saverne Affair'.[231] At the height of the controversy, the then thirty-year-old crown prince sent a telegram whose contents soon became famous. Before long, hundreds of thousands of postcards were printed, depicting Wilhelm on horseback, his sabre drawn, proclaiming, 'Always with a firm grip.' By the fall of 1914, a theatre on Berlin's Nollendorfplatz square was staging 'a patriotic musical production' with that phrase as a title.[232]

The image of Wilhelm as a man of skull-and-crossbones caps, cavalry attacks and unflinching brutality would feed into the drastic caricatures of wartime French propaganda. The title of the anti-German war novel by Louis Dumur, *The Butcher of Verdun*, was clearly intended to conjure up a Crown Prince Wilhelm as the butcher of Verdun.[233] Constantly cited by both friend and foe, this four-word sobriquet would stick to the prince until his dying day. Before the SS co-opted the death's head symbol, the white skull above crossbones on the tall fur caps of the hussar bodyguard regiments embodied the supposed fearless courage of the light cavalry. The fact that at no point in his life had Wilhelm shown any such bravery may explain why there was a perceived need for the story of him daringly insisting on wearing his skull-and-crossbones cap while crossing the border when he fled to the Netherlands on 12 November 1918.

Compensating for Wilhelm's decidedly unheroic life, at least superficially, were the imposing uniforms that lent him an aura of bravado. The style was very much in demand in the post-1918 political and aesthetic competition for attention. His alleged derring-do dovetailed with his casualness, typified in his habit of wearing his officer's cap cocked at an angle. This soon gave rise to a nickname, *L'homme qui rit* (The Laughing Man), as the French described him during the war.[234] The sobriquet may have seemed congenial. In fact, the phrase was taken from a well-known 1869 Victor Hugo novel, in which the main character, whose face has been surgical disfigured on the orders of the king, is condemned to exist forever wearing an artificial smile in a world that is nothing to laugh about.[235]

One of the crown prince's major supporters, Stresemann, also found his constant smiling seriously problematic: 'It gave the impression of a person of frivolous blood, who had no inkling of the gravity of the world and his own duty and who was only interested in appearances.'[236] In retrospect, this combination of certain military derring-do with the occasional pose of a man of the people doesn't seem devoid of promise. In fact, a decade later, corresponding attempts were made to stylize Wilhelm into a military leader who had also exhibited his 'lust for life' on the battlefield, who had truly tried to reach out to the warriors of the frontlines and who had motivated them to fight on with his dashing humour and constant smile. This was compatible with the image of a leader who also got up at the crack of dawn to take care of 'man and horse'.[237]

For his part, Wilhelm of Prussia would maintain his early image as a modern, dashing, uncomplicated swashbuckler throughout his life. His five years of exile on a barren, treeless island[238] accorded him little opportunity to develop his dashing reputation, but he did have plenty of time and space to ponder what the outlines of a modern leader should look like. Within the political constellation of the Weimar Republic, it did no harm to the prince's image to be seen as someone present in various contexts, albeit as a dilletante, without being defined and deformed by a single role. For all the scorn heaped upon the Hohenzollerns, the possibility that Wilhelm or one of his sons could play a leading political role was held up both as a hope and a fear depending on people's own politics. But, in both cases, that possibility was taken seriously.

Stylized images of the hero being formed by deeply instructive years of actual or imaginary privation was one of the basic tropes of twentieth-century ideas of modern leadership. In contrast to the Kaiser, bemoaning the state of the world amidst his caricature of a court, the crown prince could claim after he returned to Germany that he had been prepared for a higher calling by his purported years of Robinson Crusoe-like isolation.

If his years in war and exile are taken together and considered as one chapter, the prince lived apart from his family for some nine years before they were reunited in November 1923. In both the elaborate depictions of his propaganda staff and apparently in his own

memory, this time was elevated into a period of noble enlightenment in keeping with both the Prussian aristocracy's cult of austerity
and the military ideals of leadership popular in the day.[239] Contemporary depictions tended to show the prince as habitually depressed
and disgruntled, whereas later accounts cast him as a leader forged
by years of hardship, who had matured into a figure worthy of a
king thanks to a process of ascetic self-discovery and who was now
well equipped for a homecoming of Odyssean dimensions.[240] In her
1930 memoirs, the crown princess sought to conjure up the idea of
her husband's persistence as something he owed 'exclusively to the
youthful, hardened body and the philosophy of life' he had acquired
in exile.[241]

A 1926 book, one of many attempts to reshape and reinvent the
prince, described his transformation from a youthful, bold warrior
to a mature political leader with a common touch. The author of
this work, Georg Freiherr von Eppstein, a monarchist writer from a
Jewish family and an ordnance officer in the First World War who
would perish in the Theresienstadt ghetto in 1942, filled his work
with bathetic images of seagulls, ocean storms, cold and loneliness:
400 pages of the sort of kitsch present everywhere that literary
ambition, monarchist loyalty and military culture overlapped in the
1920s. 'Hissing, shaking and rolling, a small steamship bore me
across the stormy Zuider See to the crown prince's island of Wieringen,' the author wrote. 'The deck was crowded with hard-working
men returning home, among them Jan Luyt, a well-known blacksmith.' Contemporary readers were quite familiar with the unusual
combination of crown prince and blacksmith. 'In Wieringen, the
smith so strong / And the blows of his hammer became song,' the
text continued in cod verse, before moving on to describe an
encounter with the prince's closest companion, his adjutant Major
Müldner von Mülnheim. He is described as manfully weathering
the cold and damp 'upright and straight as always, the loyal companion of his master, standing beside him as unshakably in exile as
he once did among the enemy'.[242]

The satirical magazine *Simplicissimus* used the kitschy image of the prince in a smithy to encourage the heir to the throne in exile to remember the words of his grandfather: 'Learn to suffer without advertising it!' *Vorwärts* quipped that it was now clear where the crown prince got the money he deposited in crooked banks – he had earned it as a blacksmith.[243] The sharp tongues at this left-wing newspaper also devoted a number of mocking poems to the crown prince, reviving the image of him as a blacksmith the week before he unexpectedly returned to Germany:

> Disgusted so much of
> What a prince hates to see
> Lives Friedrich Wilhelm of Prussia
> In a Dutch isle in the sea.
> As a smith manfully hammering away
> And telling reporters what was on his mind
> He spent the biggest part of his day
> While sobbing his eyes out at night . . .
> Friedrich Wilhelm intervenes
> With his powerful blacksmith's hands
> To fulfil the German destiny
> Everything will be simply grand.[244]

Among the prince's most prominent supporters and visitors to Wieringen was Gustav Stresemann, then the chairman of the nationalist, free-market, pro-democracy German People's Party (DVP). He would publicly come out in favour of the prince's cause and later, as German chancellor, would be instrumental in Wilhelm being allowed to return to Germany, despite criticism at home and abroad.[245]

When admitted to the humble rooms of the parsonage and coming face to face with the heir, Crown Wilhelm's hagiographer Eppstein could hardly suppress a sob: 'He cut the same lean and mean cavalryman's figure as ever, but a grey sheen hangs over his blond hair. Congenial, unpretentious and open in his attitude and his questions.' In Eppstein's eyes, the supposed inner transformation undergone by the prince, to whose achievements as a wartime military commander Eppstein devoted so many words, had left its physical mark on the would-be king and leader: 'Time, suffering, the deaths of his comrades young and old and his heavy, bitter thoughts in the distant loneliness of exile have chiselled deep furrows in his noble Hohenzollern visage.'[246]

As of 1918, all members of Germany's former ruling dynasties – and especially the princes of Prussia and above all the crown prince – were forced to redefine their roles. In the summer of 1920, when Wilhelm's youngest brother, Joachim, shot himself in a palace in Potsdam, the liberal *Vossische Zeitung* newspaper wrote in its obituary that the man had 'been undone by being a prince'.[247] That was reference to the expectations and presumptions attached to the title and such a massively significant family name, neither of which had any clear place any more in the Weimar Republic. In the political vacuum of his foggy island, the crown prince had more time and space than his siblings to adapt his persona and image to this radically different reality.

Female Visitations

There is no doubt that monarchist propaganda dramatically overstated the barren asceticism of Wilhelm's years in exile. By contrast, in their private correspondence, friends, fellow officers and advisors fretted that the heir to the throne's mercurial, libidinous nature could be neither controlled nor concealed. Writer Kurt Anker – one of the prince's closest advisors before converting to the cause of democracy and falling from grace in monarchist circles[248] – warned Wilhelm in 1920 to be on his guard, even if it was still possible 'now and then to secretly pick some flowers and nosh on their berries'.[249] For his part, the prince dismissed the countless entreaties by his advisors to devote himself more seriously to intellectual pursuits and his political restoration.[250] In early 1922, there was a debate in front of a regional court in Frankfurt an der Oder and in the daily press about the truth of allegations that during the war the crown prince had 'kept a harem' in his headquarters, made a 'harlot' of an 'innocent girl' and arranged for her parents to be forcibly displaced.[251]

Rumours and reports about the crown prince's extramarital affairs abounded before, during and after the war, forming a veritable literary genre of their own that competed with the stylized images of Wilhelm as an amateur blacksmith and contented contemplator of life. Newspapers ran stories about a young 'Amsterdam lady' who had moved to the fishing island to become a milliner and who received regular visits from Wilhelm. Allegedly outraged by the immoral scenes unfolding in the 'milliner's' house, islanders were said to have protested vocally outside and chucked stones at the unequal and illicit couple. A story in a Washington newspaper entitled 'Mob Prince for Visiting Modiste. Young Hohenzollern Flees from Crowd' (sic) claimed that the police had to be summoned to restore order on the tiny island.[252] Lending credence to such narratives was a letter from the mayor of Wieringen to the Dutch government official responsible for the Kaiser's and the crown prince's exile. It stated that Müldner von Mülnheim had apologized for the 'sad incident' and the abuse of Dutch hospitality. Other sources also attest to Wilhelm carrying on similar sorts of affairs.[253]

Relevant in this regard was a defamation-of-character lawsuit filed in Nancy in 1921 by a young Frenchwoman who felt herself depicted as one of the crown prince's many lovers in the novel *The Butcher of Verdun*. Author Louis Dumur denied basing his character on the woman, and her case was dismissed, but the trial attracted considerable press attention in both France and Germany.[254] The public discussion of the crown prince's sexual adventures during his time as army group commander behind the front lines was part and parcel of the literature of scandal that flourished after 1918. One particularly notable example was the dramatic description of the situation behind the Western Front by the soldier Heinrich Wandt, whose efforts attracted the attention of military and judicial authorities and earned him not only a stretch in prison but also

a more-than-200,000-copy bestseller. In 1923, Wandt had been forcibly removed from French-administered Düsseldorf and taken to
Potsdam, prompting talk of a 'German Dreyfus affair'.[255] John
Heartfield, the famous Weimar Germany graphic artist, created a
cover for Wandt's book, retained through all subsequent editions,
that featured a military officer clutching a glass of champagne and
a prostitute.[256] Wandt, who was sentenced to six years' in prison by
a national court in 1923, dedicated his book to the frontline soldiers
'forced to endure Allied barrages and chemical weapons in filth
and blood so that the "victorious" persevering warriors could continue to stuff their faces, whore around and fence stolen goods as
long and as comfortably as possible at a safe distance from the
bullets'.[257]

Co-opting and recasting the myth that German troops had been
betrayed by leftists on the home front, Wandt's socialist and pacifist
narrative excoriated 'those who today cry out for vengeance' as the
ones who 'ground down the morale of the fighting troops with
their shameless debauchery and were the true backstabbers of the
German front'. Combining facts, rumours and exaggerations, the
author served up a coarse mélange of violence and pornography,
providing copious details of aristocratic officers, many referred to
by name, who had sought 'access to the garishly lit shagging houses
in which they squandered their money, indulged their urges and
danced obscene dances at night with the harlots'.[258]

In keeping with the images constantly being used against the
crown prince were Wandt's descriptions of backline aristocratic
officers 'who had naked harlots on their laps in the most elaborately
decorated expensive bordellos behind the stock exchange around
the main market square'.[259] Wandt offered his readers a section specially devoted to the 'amorous pleasures of the crown prince', who
was introduced as 'the most active representative of the much
ballyhooed Hohenzollern sense of family'. Charleville, the location
of German military headquarters, was presented as a place full of
hungry French street urchins begging from German troops with
the words: 'Hey, soldier, give me a piece of bread, and I'll show you

where your crown prince goes to f***.'[260] This trope, which would wind its way through the post-war provincial American press like a snake,[261] continued to feature in left-wing polemics. Even at the high point of the crown prince's political influence in 1932, the social-democratic press scoffed that the 'conquests' made at his military headquarters in Charleville 'had definitely *not been achieved over French males*'.[262]

And during Wilhelm's years in exile the story never changed. The embarrassingly precise medical notes of his personal physician bore witness to his affair with the young Dutch Baroness Lili van Heemstra.[263] And other sources mention a lengthy relationship with a young German woman that allegedly produced a child and contended that the crown prince later visited his illegitimate offspring in Munich.[264] A 1919 postcard caricature showed a gleeful crown prince in wooden clogs with two young women, one stereotypically Dutch, one stereotypically French, sitting on his lap. The headline read: 'I may be lonesome, but I'm not alone.'[265] A variation of this joke mockingly depicted Wilhelm on his island in his spurs and hussar's uniform while young women waved to him from the mainland.[266]

As in all scandals, it's difficult to distinguish fact from fiction, but there's no doubt that the crown prince gravely violated the ethical codes of his own caste. Colonel Max Bauer, one of the most energetic members of the army high command during the war, once received a worried report that Wilhelm was 'engaging in physical relations with French women'. He was even purported to have commissioned an oil painting of one particularly attractive mistress and appeared in public with her. Rumours to this effect spread like 'wildfire' through the trenches and threatened to undermine the Hohenzollern family's reputation as a whole.[267] The surest indication that there was considerable truth to the constant, damaging rumours can be found in the recently published diaries of Colonel Walter Nicolai, the head of military secret service.[268] In the inhibited language customarily used by Prussian officers when talking of private matters, Nicolai refers to the 'tender bonds' and 'amorous adventures' that took place on the Western front. The diarist wrote in the plural, leaving no doubt that the general staff was aware of what was going on. He even alludes to an affair with a Jewish woman at the start of the war.

It seems impossible that the situation could have remained concealed from the upper echelons of the aristocracy and military and political elites. And it is hard not to be astonished today by the spectacle of the head of German military espionage, the general chief of staff and a circle of ranking officers fretting in the army's main headquarters on the Western front about the crown prince of Prussia and Germany's regular tête-à-têtes with his French lover in a villa at safe remove from the fighting. The crown prince's critics were concerned both that the woman might inadvertently pass on confidential information, or even be a foreign agent, and that the stories increasingly seeping through to frontline soldiers would be embellished, as rumours are wont to be, and wash back, out of control, to Germany.

For a time, a press officer close to the prince was considered as a potential mediator, but it then emerged that he, too, was having an affair with a Frenchwoman. Nonetheless, despite all the nervous discussion among the general staff officers, even the most upstanding of them were far too toadying to directly raise the issue with the commander of the largest German army group. The officers were so exasperated that they considered informing the Kaiser of his son's transgressions, believing that only paternal censure would have any effect on Wilhelm. Instead, with Germany occupying parts of France, the prince's military entourage sent the young woman – whose name was Gabrielle Beurier and who was deemed 'not to conform in any respect to even the most modest demands of good taste' – to Lille, where she was quartered in a detached house and watched over by military police. Breaking his word, the crown prince continued to visit her there until she was sent to Brussels, where Wilhelm threatened to 'put a bullet in his head' if anything happened to his lover. Amidst this uncomfortable situation, and with Germany's military collapse looming, he summoned up the bravura to declare in mid-September

1918: 'If our cause goes down in failure, I will fall anyway with my last battalion.'[269] Two months later, he would, of course, revise that position.

The astonishing and sometimes grotesque aspects of military life behind the front illustrated what would be a significant general development. The private was becoming the political. The more that was revealed about the private life of the crown prince and his family, the more difficult it became to control, especially given the gap between pretence and reality in Wilhelm's major transgressions against the moral codes conservatives claimed to uphold. The prince's behaviour during a war in which millions were sent to their deaths, some under his command, was like an acid bath for his reputation. Despite the constant lying, Wilhelm's propaganda staff, charged with creating the image of him as a shining leader, were increasingly at a loss as to how to counter questions about not only the prince's military and political abilities, but also his personal integrity. In this media no-man's land, transgressions gave birth to scandals, more or less distorted versions of which were passed back and forth. Yet they never made Wilhelm untenable as a public figure.

The lurid details of soldierly life far from the front did not just entertain the public, they also revealed the considerable propaganda work undertaken to salvage the crown prince's reputation and presaged later attempts to invent a figure that never existed in reality. It was just a taste of the crass lies that the crown prince's staff would use to deny what they knew to be true and create a whitewashed public persona. The main issues concerning the prince's character were well established by the end of the First World War, and would-be kingmakers would spend the next two decades trying to smother them. They included doubts about Wilhelm's political judgement, leadership abilities, actions late in the war, closeness to everyday people and capacity to live up to standards of honour and morality he himself propagated.

The extramarital trysts he organized in occupied villas far from the fighting were the symbolic pinnacles of the heir to the throne's generally less than warrior-like record. Just like Wilhelm's brother Oskar, who spent the war behind a desk after suffering a nervous breakdown in 1914, the Kaiser, his heir and the other princes were perfectly content to remain in observation posts far from the horrible realities of mass slaughter they themselves helped bring about. Later recollections by frontline soldiers drastically contradicted the official accounts coming from regimental commanders. People began to question, for instance, whether Oskar of Prussia, who had allegedly suffered 'heart palpitations' in the vicinity of the front, had ever lived up to the ideals of the Prussian military's first family. 'Where is the military heroism?' the socialist newspaper *Vorwärts* was still asking in 1932.[270]

Conversely, the Hohenzollerns began early on trying to imagine a past in which they had stood side by side with the frontline soldiers. The armistice was not even four weeks old when Crown Prince Wilhelm discovered his love of peace and remembered his camaraderie with his men, telling the Associated Press 'My soldiers, whom I loved and with whom I lived continuously, and who, I may say so, loved me, fought with the utmost courage to the end, even when the odds were impossible to withstand.' Notably, even in such self-stylizing autobiographical statements, it was 'his' men, and not Wilhelm himself, who had demonstrated immense courage.[271] And indeed a rapidly growing number of accounts after 1918 depicted the crown prince as a fellow who had been witnessed in many places during the war, but never anywhere near the front. It was not only the socialist press but also members of the traditional ruling elites who recalled the past in this way.[272]

As they did when questioning Wilhelm's military achievements, proponents of German democracy compared the prince's private 'shortcomings' with the ideals propagated by the Hohenzollerns. This was an effective strategy politically, even if the critic in question didn't actually share those ideals. By 1926, for instance, Reichstag deputy Fritz Sänger declared in the German parliament: 'I think we can safely say that never has a dynasty gone down as dishonourably and ignobly as the Hohenzollerns.'[273]

Battle of Images

By contrast, during the war, American reporters of German extraction generated positive images of the Hohenzollerns, which were then disseminated as pro-German propaganda. In them, Wilhelm was the epitome of a popular military leader who graciously acknowledged the great courage of his French adversaries and whose leadership and strategic talent made him a role model for all young German officers.[274] Moreover, despite the many rumours about and the reality of the crown prince's life behind the front, Cecilie was highly regarded as a symbol of conservative womanhood. The crown princess often posed for postcards in a white dress, surrounded by her children in sailor suits, among wounded German soldiers. After the war, even in the American press,[275] attempts were constantly being made – not without some success – to protect Wilhelm's reputation from being damaged by the scandalous aspects of his private life. Monarchist propaganda used the princess and her children's rare visits to Wieringen to present a façade of intact family life. One image from August 1920 depicts the crown prince, dressed in Scottish tweed and a white turtleneck, with his hands resting on the shoulders of his youngest sons. Off to the side, his smiling wife and two of his other children stare into the camera.[276]

These staged images promoted the idea of Cecilie, travelling with her children to visit her husband in his ascetic life in exile, as a loyal, loving wife and a role model. Such trips were, however, hardly an exercise in asceticism. In the fall of 1919, the crown princess travelled from Potsdam to the Netherlands in a special railway salon car placed at her disposal.[277] Prearranged photos snapped by photographers from major newspapers documented the crown princess and her younger sons' time at Wieringen, and there was a group portrait of the happily reunited family. Motifs included the family's arrival at the dock, the young sons in sailor suits beside their harmoniously smiling parents, laughing island residents, the crown prince sitting on his new motorcycle, and the crown princess clinging to his side and smiling for photographers as they journeyed on to Amerongen.[278]

Pro-Crown Prince Wilhelm propaganda vacillated between denying and whitewashing his amorous adventures. Great energy was expended to counter the 'stories' relating to his alleged behaviour behind the frontlines in the war. Meanwhile, the 'weaknesses' of a man 'very able to distinguish between the pretty and the ugly' were also reinterpreted as signs of the prince's misogynistically stylized 'bold' masculinity.[279] The pinnacle of the campaign to depict Wilhelm as an upstanding fellow in his private life was an anonymously authored 1923 book titled *The German Crown Prince and the Women in His Life*,[280] which was announced in advance in the American press.[281] Over the surprising length of 200 pages, it sought to refute, undermine and reinterpret the most common rumours about Wilhelm's activities. One possible author was Wilhelm's advisor and former intelligence officer Kurt Anker, who was probably paid to put a positive gloss on what he knew about the prince's private life.[282]

Contemporaries were appalled that such a book could even exist, and early reviewers focused on the question of who had commissioned it. By the mid-1920s at the latest, the public began to ridicule the 'imbecilic legend' of the Hohenzollerns' 'exemplary' virtuousness.[283] Readers today might find this book, along with much of the output of the royal family's propaganda staff, alternately fascinating and cringeworthy. Remarkably primitive in both language and argument, works of this sort made the crown prince look foolish and only added fuel to the fire of those who mocked him. In the case of *The German Crown Prince*, the list of the 'women in his life' was dumbfoundingly long: from the 'wonderfully beautiful nineteen-year-old French cigarette salesgirl . . . who possessed all the charms of her race' and later denied under oath engaging in any improper 'intercourse' to the various daughters of good repute described as 'unusually captivating in appearance'. Yet, despite it all, the crown prince was depicted as steadfastly resisting even the most powerful temptations of the prettiest women of the day, who, seductively dressed, tried physically to entrap him. With his 'great appreciation of grace and beauty', Wilhelm was often 'enflamed in the manner of a troubadour' but always remained 'the complete, congenial gentleman'. In one episode, he rescued a black cat belonging to an older French lady decked out in a 'white, tropical outfit'. On another occasion he is described as intervening in 'gentlemanly fashion' when another Frenchwoman wanted to stay at the side of her lover, a German officer. 'The girl must not be abandoned!' he commands. 'This is a case where respectability and chivalry must be shown!'

In this context, the author asks: 'Was it such an accursed crime, if one or another officer or soldier from the army group staff diligently worked his twelve to sixteen hours and then – since the opportunity presented itself and the heart began to speak – wiled away a free hour with Yvonne, Marcelle or Josephine? My God, who got hurt?' After alluding to a woman for whom the crown prince was allegedly prepared to commit suicide, the author writes of 'unusually strong affinities', adding: 'She was a creature that would have made an impression on any man with healthy sensibilities – all the more so as her physical charms were combined with intellectual qualities.'[284]

The final pages of *The German Crown Prince* refer readers to Schopenhauer, reminding them that the pleasure of luxury in all its forms can lead to the abyss – the implication being that Wilhelm had long taken this advice to heart. The upshot after 200 pages is that 'The heir to this empire has made his way on his own through humid darkness with extreme self-discipline and mature masculinity.'[285] Ultimately, however, there were simply too many windmills to be tilted at to portray the crown prince as a caring family father in line with conservative moral ideas, and subsequent propaganda gave up on the idea or emphasized other sorts of flattering images of the heir to throne. In the end, the loosened moral codes of the Weimar Republic as a whole made Wilhelm's private transgression seem less scandalous.

Ultimately, all attempts to make a public scandal of the crown prince's private life failed. In the long run, Wilhelm was able to massage his media image, and the heir to the throne's many relationships with young, beautiful, glamorous women caused little lasting offence. On the contrary, many people saw them as evidence of positive attributes of a virile modern leader and evidence of Wilhelm's connection to ordinary people. As was the case with countless other twentieth- and twenty-first-century leaders, the private life of the Kaiser's son was successfully associated with the ideal of a 'bold,' 'natural' character and common images of masculinity. Wilhelm's 'amorous adventures' helped transform the crown prince from a relic of yesterday into the leader of tomorrow. After 1945, even pro-Hohenzollern servants of the royal family would relate anecdotes about the 'coarse humour of the Hohenzollerns' and the men's nights in Cecilienhof and their copious amounts of sandwiches, beer, liquor and cigarettes, presided over by the crown prince with his propensity for lewd remarks and dirty jokes told in Berlin street dialect.[286]

Once ideas of leadership had transitioned from the straight-laced Wilhelmine Empire to the freewheeling Weimar Republic, the crown prince's dubious reputation was no longer an insurmountable obstacle. The general administrator of the Hohenzollerns' affairs after the Great War, Count Hardenberg, may have been wary about allowing his daughters to get too close to Wilhelm, in all senses of the word.[287] But it didn't deter him from serving as the crown prince's primary underling and fixer.

Conservatives and upholders of traditional morality in the Weimar Republic of course viewed the situation differently. The crown prince's extramarital adventures were the stuff of conversation among the officer class, in the press and in anti-monarchist pamphlets. In the officer corps, Wilhelm's predilection for pretty women made him look weak and lacking in self-control. A common joke went that if there were three connecting bedrooms, with the prince in the first, the crown in the third and several beautiful women in the second, the monarchy would be never be restored because Wilhelm would never make it from room one to room three.[288] This was typical of the lascivious jokes told, occasionally even in Wilhelm's presence, in smoking salons and officers' messes, and among diplomats and at private evenings frequented by military elites.[289] Meanwhile, the crown prince's lifestyle, known and caricatured throughout Germany, was completely at odds with his wife's equally visible patronage of the strictly conservative Luise Association, which railed against modern 'dissipation' and preached 'moral stringency'.[290] Already hard to maintain during Wilhelm's exile, the façade of a functional marriage between Wilhelm and Cecilie became even more difficult to prop up when he returned to Germany. All the hypocritical admiration for the 'feisty' heir to the throne notwithstanding, left-wing satirists and caricaturists had a field day with the image of the Kaiser as a randy old man living together with a woman the same age as his children and a crown prince cavalierly disregarding sexual constraints.

Men and women reacted differently to the prince's inability to control his sex drive. What was the stuff of mocking male banter, but still only banter, among military officers was no laughing matter for many leading aristocratic ladies, as one 1925 letter critical of Crown Princess Cecilie shows:

> A woman who has so little moral sensibility and wishes to restore to the German people a Kaiser capable of doing the things the crown prince has done as a married man does not belong at the head of such an association! Even if some episodes have been exaggerated, a large number of them have actually transpired. I can understand if she forgives the man because she truly loves him. But I cannot comprehend why she would want such a man to be Kaiser and a role model for her entire people. I fear that the crown princess only wants this because she wishes to become empress.[291]

Pro-democratic moral judgements about the princely couple were naturally more critical than those of conservatives. In 1929, Wilhelm's fellow aristocrat and man-in-the-know Baron Kurt von Reibnitz endorsed the republican view that, since returning to Germany, 'the crown prince has relapsed into his pathological fondness for amusement, only worse'.[292] And the prominent pro-democracy chronicler of the times Count Harry Kessler made no bones about his contempt for Wilhelm the following year:

> Despite his grey hair, he is still at heart the young prince who as a hussar longed for a refreshing, high-spirited war only to wave from his window in Stenay, dressed in his pyjamas and with French whores in tow, at the mutilated regiments returning from Verdun. In him, the genetic debility of the Hohenzollerns has taken on nearly monumental proportions.[293]

In his famous metaphor of the 'king's two bodies', the scholar of medieval history Ernst Kantorowicz advanced the notion that royal monarchs have a physical existence that is both mortal and immortal. The constant buzz around the crown prince's private life during the Weimar Republic made it clear that even his sexual activities were now accepted as a legitimate topic of public discussion. Yet the more Wilhelm's biological body became the subject of salacious popular discussion, the more the figure of the king, conceived as eternal, began to be moulded by general popular longings for a new kind of leader.

Neither in 1920 nor in 1930 was Wilhelm ever as ridiculous as his democratic adversaries would have liked to think. Without doubt, he was a mediocre person, but his public persona reflected the strengths and weakness of the other leadership figures at the time. In this regard, too, the contrast with his father was stark. Visual representations of Wilhelm II were those of an elegant, gracefully ageing gentlemen in the public eye whose dark suits suited him just as well as his full, grey beard. The ex-Kaiser was frequently depicted with a silk handkerchief, a cane carved of exquisite wood, cravat, white shirt collars and spotlessly polished leather shoes and spats, sitting on a white bench in the park of his Dutch estate, a dog at his side, elbows locked with his wife or with one arm around one of his grandchildren. And the images of him strolling around and working away with gigantic saws to cut wood were more the stuff of private snapshots and home movies.[294] Wilhelm II thus had nothing of the populist Führer so longed for in the discourses that arose during the 1920s. Tellingly, in 1930, one right-wing publisher who advised the former Kaiser about his public image asked for an image for an illustrated magazine that showed him 'engaging in an activity', for example reading, but requested that he 'leave out the monocle'.[295]

Conclusion: The Reinvention of the Crown Prince

In their aesthetics and breadth, visual depictions of the crown prince were altogether different from those of the 'resting' ex-Kaiser. Whereas the latter's persona was possibly intended to echo the nationalist legend of Friedrich Barbarossa sleeping inside Kyffhäuser mountain, representations of the former were designed to embody disruption, dynamism, change and readiness for a new era – with a dash of humour, impudence and transgression. The images were all about the possibilities for and limits upon creating a modern, 1920s leadership figure. During his years of exile, representations of Wilhelm as a soldier, commander and army group leader were augmented by pictures of him sitting on a bench talking to the widow of a Dutch farmer, smiling modestly at the fence surrounding his humble domicile, dressed in a Scandinavian sweater and knickerbockers with a bicycle while visiting his father's stately residence,[296] standing next to a lorry in a long, black leather overcoat, black gloves, a black cap and driver's sunglasses, or posing in the entrance to a village blacksmith's workshop, muscles flexed as he held a hammer and a horseshoe. In similar fashion, pictures of the crown prince next to a simply dressed older woman made their way across the Atlantic and gave rise to the headline in a Canadian newspaper: 'Once Arrogant German Crown Prince Enjoys Chat with Dutch Housewife'.[297]

It's not hard to see such images as an attempt to create modern concepts of the aristocracy or – to be more precise – the difficult task

87

of updating aristocratic ideals for the modern world. This went as far back as the popular nineteenth-century comic opera *Zar und Zimmermann*, which premiered in 1837 and depicted Tsar Peter I travelling incognito in the northern Netherlands and being taught the art of shipbuilding. The symbolically loaded scenario of an aristocrat of the people, the king-in-exile secretly and invisibly preparing for his return during the Weimar Republic may not have been completely new, but it was a perfect fit for the political situation of the day. The pictures of the smiling prince in his wool sweater riding his bike weren't random snapshots. They were conscious, carefully staged images made by professional photographers.

The poses the crown prince struck for pictures taken during exile are conspicuously non-military. The images sought to depict Wilhelm as a likeable, harmless civilian and facilitate his return to Germany. Work on the narrative of the prince as a man who had been quick to recognize both the chance of a German victory and, later on, Germany's coming defeat,[298] and who now put his faith in Woodrow Wilson and wished only to return home as an ordinary citizen, indeed a 'labourer', was already underway before the war had even come to an end.[299] In the immediate wake of the post-war revolution in Germany, Wilhelm's brother Eitel had also declared that he didn't want to be anything more than a simple citizen.[300]

In the English edition of the prince's 1922 memoirs, the photographic illustrations offered a much clearer look at how he hoped to reinvent himself than the bloated, unreadable prose of his ghostwriter. The images show Wilhelm hunting elephant in India, fighting in the trenches, consulting with general staff officers in his field headquarters, measuring distances on a military map under the expert eye of his chief of staff, Count von Schulenberg, and travelling amidst a convoy of wounded soldiers near St Quentin. In the second part of the book, readers were treated to the sight of the crown prince next to an old Dutch widow, and once again in the workshop of his 'friend', the village blacksmith, and his son, wielding a large hammer in his royal hand. The two final images juxtaposed the impressive New Palace in Potsdam and the simple pastorage on Wieringen.[301] The message was not how far down Wilhelm had slipped in the world, but rather how he had joined the ranks of everyday people.

Another source of images was postcards showing the heir to the throne, for example sitting in a starched white shirt on a cliff, contemplating the vastness of the sea, with three ships on the horizon – every inch the future ruler patiently waiting for his moment to arrive. Countless other pictures portrayed the crown prince more as a stableman than a nobleman, the epitome of a 'brash', 'athletic', modern masculinity. This was the opposite of how he was seen in *Simplicissimus* caricatures, left-wing op-ed pieces and the private correspondence of acquaintances who doubted his leadership qualities. In words, positive and negative, as well as in the surviving photos, Wilhelm appears as a figure with various facets and roles, a chameleon of scintillating changeability, similar to a number of the twentieth century's most successful leaders. Historian Heinz Reif's characterization of the aristocracy as a 'master of visibility' seems particularly appropriate here. Amidst the rather drab self-depiction of the Weimar Republic and its political representatives, the crown prince and his assemblage of props seemed vivid and vibrant. A variety of images were generated in the 1920s to complement the soldierly one of Wilhelm in his uniform, hussar's cap, sword belt and leather boots. There was Wilhelm the hunter, shooting a twelve-point stag; Wilhelm the athletic sportscar driver in three-piece tweed; Wilhelm the excellently dressed, elegantly trim gentlemen in a dark suit or casual attire for a day at the races; Wilhelm the smiling philosopher with his handkerchiefs, greyhound and tight-fitting, slim-waisted jackets; Wilhelm the youthful tennis player on the most expensive courts in Berlin's upper-crust Grunewald district; Wilhelm the chain-smoking clubgoer, horseman, equestrian and enthusiastic attendee of car and bicycle races, theatrical plays, comic operas, movies and boxing matches; Wilhelm the excellent swimmer; Wilhelm the skier and bobsledder in St Moritz; and Wilhelm the sophisticated conversationalist and maker of bawdy remarks in Berlin street language.

Before and after his years of exile, until 1933, a never-ending flood of kaleidoscopic images depicted the heir to the throne as an estate owner and hunter in Silesia, an officer in Potsdam, a civilian strolling along the shores of the picturesque Mondsee lake in Austria and a self-assured man of high society adept at moving confidently among Europe's military and political elites. Few political leaders during the 1920s could compete with this sort of symbolic visual variety.

One of Wilhelm's options in 1918 would have been to withdraw completely from the public eye. He could have boarded a ship to Argentina, relocated to a Swiss villa or lived as a private *grand seigneur* in a castle in Silesia. But few Hohenzollerns decided to take this route, and there is little evidence that Wilhelm ever seriously considered it. Even throughout his quiet years in island exile, he never ceased conceiving and redefining himself as the Prince of Prussia, the heir to the throne and a political leader. And, among serious monarchists, there was no bypassing the Kaiser's eldest son. Jean-Paul Sartre wrote in a 1940 diary entry:

> The Crown Prince has a reserved, accomplished future as soon as he appears in the world. His being is a 'being-to-reign', just as man's being is a 'being-to-die'. As soon as he's conscious of himself, he finds before him that future in which to reign is his most essential and most individual possibility. And if there are even Crown Princes who refuse to reign, they still make their decisions in the face of their essential destiny. They cannot evade their 'being-to-reign': they cannot cause themselves not to have been Crown Princes, in their innermost natures; they cannot cause being-to-reign not to be a quasi-existential characteristic for them.[302]

The leading light of French existentialism, pondering the would-be German Kaiser, three months before the Wehrmacht attacked France, formulated an idea that can help us today understand the figure of the heir to the throne and his political significance. Earlier, in one of the most important novels of the Weimar period, *The Man Without Qualities*, Robert Musil wrote:

> By the time they have reached the middle of their life's journey few people remember how they have managed to arrive at themselves, at their amusements, their point of view, their wife, character, occupation and successes, but they cannot help feeling that not much is likely to change any more. It might even be asserted that they have been cheated, for one can nowhere discover any sufficient reason for everything's having come about as it has. It might just as well have turned out differently. The events of people's lives have, after all, only to the least degree originated in them, having generally depended on all sorts of circumstances such as the moods, the life or death of quite different people, and have, as it were, only at the given point of time come hurrying towards them.

Most people, Musil continues, are like a fly who initially only gets stuck by a single hair to the sticky paper that holds and gradually envelops them 'until they lie buried under a thick coating that has only the remotest resemblance to their original shape'.[303] It is precisely on this score that a crown prince differs from other people. No crown prince comes to his role in life by accident. It makes very little sense to separate his character, his strengths and weaknesses, from the calling he himself and millions of observers presume he possesses. It is conceivable that such people can escape this role, but, as Sartre points, kings simply are 'another human species'.[304]

One of the most famous sentences in Hitler's *Mein Kampf* is his (untruthful) account of how he learned of the German revolution as a wounded soldier in a military hospital and reached a resolution while crying into his pillow: 'It was then I decided to become a politician.'[305] Hitler became a modern Führer and Germany's dictator thanks to political and social circumstances, personal decisions and his own qualities. The crown prince – even though he was a fallen heir to the throne and not, as Sartre wrote, a king – didn't even have to make a decision to abide by his 'being-in-order-to-rule'. He was born to it.

Nonetheless, the creation of the crown prince as a figure, like that of the Führer, had less to do with the man himself than with what others ascribed to him – all the more so because he played a leading role in a tragedy, then was part of a farce. Generally speaking, as both Sartre and Musil knew, it's hard for aristocrats to completely invent a new biography and image, and for an aristocrat as important as a crown prince it's more or less beyond the realm of possibility. This is a useful way of understanding the reinvention of the crown prince in exile and his later reception in both Germany and the foreign media. It is a way of comprehending the gap between a figure who appears utterly empty in so many respects and the considerable significance accorded to him by outsiders. Millions of monarchist Germans couldn't simply ignore the Kaiser and the heir to the throne. Even the insistence back then and today among democrats upon referring to Wilhelm as the 'ex-crown prince' was an acknowledgement of the special qualities they wanted to dissolve and assimilate – an enterprise that never fully succeeded.

Wieringen remained a romanticized episode in Wilhelm's life, put forward to connect the swashbuckling figure from the Wilhelmine Empire with the values that prevailed afterwards. Meanwhile, Huis Doorn remained a site of anti-democratic broadsides and internal right-wing, political intrigue until Kaiser Wilhelm II died in the summer of 1941. But the most effective guerilla warfare the Hohenzollerns waged against the Weimar Republic from beginning to end was organized primarily within Germany itself.

2.

Guerrillas: The Hohenzollerns Versus the Weimar Republic (1923–31)

Followed by four horsemen in chainmail bearing lances and shields with the black, white and red of Imperial Germany, Crown Prince Wilhelm of Prussia rides across a wooden drawbridge over a deep chasm. Calmly and firmly, he holds the reins of his white stallion in his left hand, as he and his companions pass through a wooden gate with a sign reading 'Republic'. Trailing behind them, off to one side, is a corpulent fellow in morning dress: German chancellor and later foreign minister Gustav Stresemann. The title of the 1924 cartoon depicting this scene was 'Stresemann, the Bridge Builder'. It stylized Wilhelm's return to Germany as a scene from Fritz Lang and Thea von Harbou's spectacular film 'The Nibelungs', in which Siegfried enters the Burgundian Empire. The image and the text combined various temporal levels. The Stresemann quote used here as a caption – 'We don't want an intentional contrast between the old and the new Germany. Our task consists of building a bridge between past and present' – would have reminded historically informed readers of Napoleon.[1] The drawbridge 'Knight Wilhelm' crosses has been especially lowered for him. But the most arresting detail in this illustration, which was published in *Vorwärts*, was that his tunic is covered in swastikas.

Four months later, in early 1925, the paper ran another cartoon. This one depicted the crown prince in the Busch Circus in Breslau (today: Wrocław). Surrounded by cheering spectators, Wilhelm in his hussar's uniform stands poised before a wall to be jumped over with a hobby horse attached to his waist. On the other side of the wall, the spurs-wearing circus director – representing the aristocratic leader of the Silesian Regional Association – bows deeply in a swastika-covered impresario's frockcoat. He even wears swastika cufflinks.[2] Left-wing caricaturists drew connections between the planned restoration of the monarchy and the Nazis surprisingly early on. The 'emperor's birthday edition' of a pro-democracy humour magazine around this time depicted Wilhelm II riding a gigantic elephant that is stomping across porcelain and leaving a trail of destruction in its wake. The beast's head, atop which a herald sits blowing into an outsized horn, is adorned with a huge swastika.[3] The democratic Left in Germany clearly saw the crown prince's return to the country as a threat to the Weimar Republic and a harbinger of a new alliance between monarchists and the still amorphous forces of the radical Right.

The crown prince didn't return to his native land in November 1923 on a horse or an elephant. He arrived by sports car, accompanied by a second vehicle containing a handful of loyal vassals. Nonetheless, the cartoons were a basically accurate depiction of Stresemann's role in Wilhelm's return and foreshadowed the political cooperation that would develop between these two men in the years to come. The revolution in Germany, the flight of the monarchy's highest pair of representatives, the rival royalist headquarters of Doorn and Wieringen and the undefined role of the other members of the royal family had destabilized the strict hierarchical and fixed symbolic system of the Hohenzollern family that existed before 1918. The question of what would become of the family's assets, major properties and immense wealth had still not been answered when Wilhelm came back to Germany, and the family was being forced to rethink its public communication and parry democratic attacks. It was entirely unclear at the point of the crown prince's homecoming whether the Hohenzollerns would come to some sort of arrangement with Weimar democracy and its principles or would seek to undermine them in the longer term. Wilhelm had a host of political options in the period from 1924 to 1931, and his future role remained undefined. A number of interpretive battles and preliminary decisions led Wilhelm to position himself as he did in the decisive years of 1932 and 1933. But his stance didn't emerge from nowhere. It had a substantial prehistory.

Gustav Stresemann, Bridge-builder

The return of the German heir to the throne was, on the surface, simply an individual relocating from one place to another, but it was also a national and international political event of the highest order. Even the stops Wilhelm made on his roughly 1,000-kilometre-long journey illustrated how well the old aristocratic networks still functioned in democratic Germany. Wilhelm spent three nights at the estates of prominent aristocratic critics of democracy before arriving on the fourth day, after nine years of absence, five of which had been in exile, at Oels (Oleśnica) Castle near Breslau. Monarchist propaganda later depicted the homecoming as a latter-day version of Odysseus returning to Penelope in Ithaca. Before Wilhelm even reached Silesia, despite the commotion at the time surrounding Hitler and Ludendorff's attempted Beer Hall Putsch in Munich, the story was front-page news for the French press. Meanwhile, British newspapers ran headlines about the return of the 'war criminal', and diplomats exchanged agitated dispatches concerning the event.[4] Most French daily newspapers treated Wilhelm's homecoming as a threat to peace, and excitable French readers followed every detail of the trip until the prince arrived back in Silesia.

Even after 11 November 1923, the French press devoted more attention to Wilhelm than to analyses of Hitler and Ludendorff's uprising in Munich. French observers immediately distrusted Stresemann's contention that the crown prince was only a private citizen and by no means the worst of Germans, seeing his homecoming as a sign of a new anti-democratic current in the German mainstream. Even conservative French newspapers ran headlines such as 'A New Danger – the Crown Prince'.[5] France's cabinet was very concerned that anti-democratic attacks on the infant Weimar Republic would be stepped up, while the British government took a more relaxed attitude. British foreign secretary George Curzon dismissed Wilhelm as a pathetic figure and Stresemann's facilitating role in his return to Germany as a foolish foreign-policy provocation, remarking that the German chancellor had to be an even bigger ass than the crown prince. But by the time the British and French had coordinated their opposition to Wilhelm's planned return, he had already crossed the Dutch–German border.[6]

The crown prince arrived back in a country in the 'uproar of turmoil', a republic undermined by attempted putsches, hyperinflation and the French military occupation of the industrial Ruhr Valley.[7] His return established another centre of counter-revolution alongside Doorn – only this time on German soil and with Wilhelm as a now mobile leader. Although a financial settlement with the Weimar Republic government was still three years off, the heir to the throne and 'private citizen' had a selection of estates and city palaces and huge material wealth at his disposal. Depending on their political outlooks, Germans viewed Wilhelm's return with concern, hope and indifference. In the pro-democratic camp, a basic tone of mockery gradually gave way to worries that 'reactionary' currents were gaining strength. It was unclear why the Weimar Republic, with its shaky foundations, had in the first place not only allowed, but financed the return of the second leading anti-democratic figurehead after the Kaiser himself. That question was hotly debated during the 1920s.

Both in cartoons and political reality in 1923, Stresemann was the principal architect of the bridges that allowed Wilhelm's return. A short-term chancellor who would later serve for years as Germany's foreign minister and share the 1926 Nobel Peace Prize with the French socialist foreign minister Aristide Briand, Stresemann is remembered as one of the leading advocates of German democracy. His death in October 1929, which came almost simultaneously with the Wall Street Crash, is considered a major caesura in the history of the Weimar Republic. The son of a Berlin tavern owner, innkeeper and beer merchant, Stresemann wasn't born with aristocratic connections. He wrote a doctorate on the bottled beer business, served as a representative in the Association of German Industry and ascended to the top of the pro-democratic, patriotic-nationalist German People's Party (DVP) by advocating imperialist positions.[8] Until the final days of the world war, he had supported aggressive policies of annexation, but as the chairman of the DVP he had transformed himself into a mediator, leading a broad-based 'grand coalition', including the social democrats, that elected him chancellor during the crisis year of 1923.[9]

A lifelong monarchist, he had visited the crown prince in 1921 in Wieringen and authored an influential defence of the crown prince, entitled 'Fathers and Sons', the following February. This short text repeated established motifs of the royal publicity apparatus, chiefly that the enlightened crown prince, matured by his years in exile, should – like Friedrich the Great – be judged not by the sins of youth but by the qualities of adulthood. The prince's time was the future, not the past. Stresemann had many good things to say about the Hohenzollern monarchy, particularly, with an eye to appeasing left-wing democrats in the cabinet, its social welfare policies. Such policies, he argued, set Germany positively apart from France, where socialist ministers had ordered troops to open fire on striking workers. Stresemann heaped praise, as fawning as any publisher's blurb, on Wilhelm's not-yet-published first book:

> On his distant, isolated island in the Zuider Zee, the crown prince has, I'm told, written down his recollections, which are to be made publicly available in the foreseeable future. They will yield a very different picture of the nature and views of the crown prince than people have previously had . . . People will have to take this book seriously because it was written by a man of intellect and experience who had more opportunity to record his impressions than most of our contemporaries.[10]

Stresemann presented the prince as a political realist, influenced by classical writers such as Lessing and Goethe, who had warned about what the future could hold immediately after the 1914 Battle of the Marne and who actively demonstrated his concern in 1917 for the 'older family fathers' among his troops. This wasn't very accurate. Wilhelm had enthusiastically supported pan-Germanic positions even before 1914 and had pilloried 'those who shirk their duty' throughout the war in harsh, unforgiving terms.[11] But, by the time Stresemann penned his warm words, there were contrary narratives vying to dominate public opinion. Stresemann's text more or less explicitly envisioned the crown prince's eventual return to Germany – which the author himself would then help arrange as German chancellor eighteen months later.[12]

Indeed, Stresemann was the key political figure in the detailed long-term planning of how to get Wilhelm back home. He was the one who saw to it that the prince was issued a passport, and brought the SPD ministers in the cabinet and the influential Prussian Social Democrats Otto Braun and Carl Severing on board with the idea. For his part, Wilhelm was careful to always refer to himself as a private citizen and a family father in conversation and in his correspondence. He also forwent his title of crown prince. When seeking support from adherents of democracy, he pointedly signed off with the words 'Your most devoted Wilhelm'.[13]

But Wilhelm wasn't always this submissive. While in the Netherlands, with help from his wife in Silesia, the crown prince had spent years commissioning lawyers to prepare briefings and file lawsuits to get the royal estate in Oels declared Hohenzollern private property.[14] Using arguments that some legal specialists – then as now – regarded as flimsy, evaluators and the regional court reached conclusions that set the Hohenzollerns on a long-term 'path to victory' concerning the family's holdings. German law, administrative practice and jurisprudence, which was the purview of judges and civil servants who had mostly been appointed during the Wilhelmine Empire and who were guided by the pre-democratic legal system and a mentality that privileged private property over constitutional finer points, enabled Hohenzollern lawsuits to pressure the leaders of the fledgling Weimar Republic. The former's lawyers felt confident enough to advise their opponents, with astonishing presumption, not to appeal, arguing that the appellate court in Breslau was favourably predisposed to the royal family and would surely follow the recommendations of the Hohenzollern-commissioned evaluators.[15] In fact, it was often difficult to tell who legitimately owned what. An American report from 1924, for instance, also conflated art works acquired by the Prussian crown on the market in 1821 with those that had been looted and taken to Berlin during the war.[16] Conversely, the wide-ranging claims advanced by Hohenzollern legal teams sometimes made even grotesque demands seem plausible. It was reported in Washington that the Kaiser had claimed two works by Jan van Eyck that had actually been stolen by German troops when they plundered Ghent Cathedral. The works had since been returned to that city, but the Kaiser still insisted they were his private property. It was a uniquely unusual and presumptuous demand, noted the *Washington Post*, while adding that, bafflingly, the Kaiser had come out the winner every time he had gone to court.[17] French newspapers also passed on rumours that the crown prince had 'borrowed' priceless vases from a Berlin museum and was now refusing to return them.[18]

Stresemann's argument that Wilhelm's presence in Germany was perfectly compatible with democracy wasn't the only significant element in his courting of mainstream democrats and the subsequent attacks on the Weimar Republic by the far Right. It was also highly important that the support of Stresemann, whose wife was from an assimilated Jewish family that owned department stores, implicitly distanced Wilhelm from anti-Semitism. 'He felt himself equally free of that mentality which sees in every person of Jewish blood an individual to be fought against,' the rather misguided chancellor proclaimed.[19]

But the most important resistance that had be overcome to such a symbolic figure returning to Germany came from abroad – and particularly France. Even the press in faraway French colonies railed against the 'most shameless affront thus far to the Allies'.[20] But Stresemann did his best to generate support for Wilhelm's cause among Germany's enemies in the war. *The Times* in London passed on Stresemann's assurance that the prince had 'no intention of allowing himself to become mixed up in the intrigues of this or that national or militarist clique'. The paper also recapitulated

Stresemann's arguments that Wilhelm had no connections whatever to the far Right in Germany, that his sympathies lay with the
constitutionally elected government and that any republic unable to
tolerate the presence of a crown prince on its soil was no true republic at all.[21]

In soliciting the support of the German bourgeoisie, Stresemann
came up with the rather far-fetched image of Wilhelm as a figure
deeply rooted in high German culture, trotting out names such as
Schiller, Lessing, Goethe and Friedrich the Great as alleged intellectual peers. In the loneliness of exile, the story went, Wilhelm had
become a thinker and a scholar, rounding out his personality by
studying the liberal bourgeois literary canon. Stresemann's praise
for the intellectual achievements of the heir to the throne was so far
removed from Wilhelm's widely known, true nature that his pane-
gyric attracted immediate scorn.[22] In a letter to Wilhelm in October
1923, the chancellor stressed how long he had been advocating for
the crown prince's return and reported that the governing cabinet
had 'taken under advice your declaration that you will refrain from
political interference'. The letter was signed 'Most devotedly in genuine esteem for His Eternal Imperial Majesty, Stresemann'.[23] There
was a broad network of support for Wilhelm's return in 1923, but
Stresemann was clearly the leader in making the necessary political
arrangements.

Controversy abounded from the very beginning of Stresemann's
lobbying on behalf of Wilhelm – and it remains a side topic in
today's historical debates about how to view the German chancellor and foreign minister.[24] Throughout the Weimar Republic,
Stresemann would be seen as the man who had brought the crown
prince back to Germany and given him unlimited, state-financed
opportunities to engage in anti-democratic agitation. For a decade,
observers vigorously debated what promises had been issued to the
prince and precisely how he had formulated his pledge, as a 'private
citizen', not to get involved in politics. The issue of Wilhelm's 'word
of honour', as will be discussed further, was more than just a detail.
At stake was the prince's trustworthiness and the potential threat he

represented. There were disagreements on all sides. But it is beyond doubt that the crown prince promised the democratic supporters of his homecoming that he would refrain from politics. Equally without doubt, some of those democrats took him at his word and saw his return as a gesture of conciliation towards the monarchist camp. Tellingly, the issue would flare up in 1922 and then again in spring of 1932, the second time in conjunction with Wilhelm's public support for Hitler.[25]

The It Boy: Public Attention as a Resource

Like all leading European aristocratic families, the Hohenzollerns were well versed in creating, maintaining and adapting personae to advance their aims. There was a decades-long, indeed centuries-long, tradition of artfully creating gaps between image and reality. Staffs of advisors spewed out words, created images and commissioned historians and other authors.[26] Early on, a multipolar apparatus coalesced between Doorn, Wieringen and various Hohenzollern outposts in Germany. Among those who contributed to the crown prince's post-1918 reinvention was a team of writers, lawyers, historians and PR advisors who constantly massaged his image. Another component was the immense attention the figure of Wilhelm generated at home and aboard.

Edward Bernays, a nephew of Sigmund Freund and one of the fathers of the modern concept of PR in the United States, taught that the battle for attention was one of the most important political struggles of the 1920s.[27] And it was generally true that the crown prince and his staff of advisors impressively mastered that art, maintaining it over the years without any real achievements to Wilhelm's name.

The decade between the conclusion of the First World War and the end of the 1920s, when Wilhelm would unambiguously position himself within the right-wing radical segment of society, can be characterized as a grey period, in which the crown prince as a figure lacked contour and wasn't always easy to pin down. Interest in the heir to the German throne continued unabated during this time. To adapt the contemporary concept of the 'It Girl', which originated in 1920s Hollywood, Wilhelm could be described as something of an 'It Boy' – a figure whose fame rested on the sheer fact that he was famous. The main difference from the It Girls was that the attention around him had a clear source. The unique position of being a crown prince created a figure that would have major significance so long as the monarchy was conceived as an alternative to democracy. Moreover, Wilhelm was a figure whose radiance would persist for as long as he recalled the purportedly better times, glory and power of a fallen empire amidst the psychological ruins of the early Weimar Republic.

This was the function of the crown prince for millions of Germans. The entire Hohenzollern family remained the subject of headlines in everything from the political and cultural sections of respected newspapers on down to the lowliest tabloids and pamphlets. The countless reports about the family's minutiae and banalities indicate the level of public interest elicited and the emotional charge it still carried. In Hans Christian Andersen's 'The Emperor's New Clothes', it's a child who ultimately points out that the monarch is in fact naked. There were analogous clarifications about Wilhelm, but what today would be called a 'culture of presence' helped the German aristocracy and the crown prince maintain their social influence.[28] Presence in this context can be understood as a quality connected to physical and symbolic attributes that are more or less opposed to understanding, explanation and analysis. Viewed rationally, the crown prince's new clothes were non-existent, but his presence – the traditions and strengths he represented – remained nonetheless attractive to millions of German observers.

At the high point of the Terror in 1793, the anti-Enlightenment French counter-revolutionary Joseph de Maistre compared his two bêtes noires to a child who breaks his favourite toy to see how the mysterious internal mechanism works.[29] This idea, from de

Maistre's *Lettres d'un Royaliste*, still held sway among 1920s German monarchists. The desire and capacity to overlook the naked truth about the Hohenzollerns was a fundamental requirement for monarchism during the Weimar Republic.

Such attitudes were encouraged by the possibilities and mechanisms of modern media and publicity. Although not yet known as such, advertising men, the blossoming sector of public relations specialists and the masters of political propaganda in the 1920s knew how the 'economy of attention' worked.[30] In the battle to captivate the popular mind, Wilhelm achieved some remarkable successes, constantly remaining an object of projection not just for those tabloid reporters with little better to do than pass on what fabulous outfits various princes and princesses wore and what splendid locations they visited, but among serious political journalists as well. Astonishing attention was given to where and when the crown prince appeared in public. Such news was also reported abroad in stories from Vienna's 'The German Crown Prince Visits His Parents' to Baltimore's 'Former Crown Prince Ends Visit to Ex-Kaiser'.[31] One paper in the Austrian Capital even found it fit to run the headline 'Crown Prince Not in Vienna'.[32]

Even in 1932, the crown prince was famous enough abroad that a French newspaper led with a story entitled 'The Ex-Crown Prince and Chancellor von Papen Attend a Film Screening in Berlin'.[33] In 1934, another French paper informed its readers 'Correction: Former Crown Prince Did Not Stay in Provence'.[34] Few public figures at the time were so famous that reports were filed about places they *didn't* visit. The same holds true today. Only British royalty can make headlines with the news that the Queen was *not* planning to watch an upcoming TV programme.[35] It's beyond question that the crown prince behaved as he did in the knowledge that the eyes of millions were upon him.

In the campaign preparing people for Wilhelm's return to Germany, one set of carefully controlled publications stand out. The first was an open letter by the crown prince presenting German and international audiences with a hitherto unknown Wilhelm who was perfectly compatible with and reconciled to democracy. Meticulously prepared and dated 15 October 1921, it was addressed to Philipp Zorn, a septagenarian professor emeritus of governmental law and former crown functionary with whom Wilhelm had studied during a brief course in law and who was now made out to be the prince's teacher and mentor. In this missive, probably composed by ghost-writers and approved by Stresemann, the prince talked of his 'self-chosen exile', his rejection of all attempted putsches and his acceptance that Germany's form of state had been settled. The letter, which proved a massive publicity coup, depicted the prince as a man who, 'after long years of loneliness', now felt 'a yearning for [his] wife and children and a family life independent of any further demands, as any thinking person will be able to understand'.[36] As its tone also made clear, the letter was primarily aimed at the liberal, pro-democratic segment of the bourgeoisie, and it did indeed draw positive reactions from the 'liberal' camp.[37] The roughly simultaneous photo series, discussed in the previous chapter, of the prince as a cyclist, thinker and congenial conversationalist with 'ordinary' older ladies, served as the visual component of this broadly targeted charm offensive.

The Racist Nationalist Campaign

One of the most interesting aspects in the debate unleashed by the crown prince's return came from the far Right, which was split along lines that would also preoccupy the Hohenzollerns in the following years. Count Ernst von Reventlow, one of the sharpest and most confrontational writers in the pan-Germanic movement and for years one of the staunchest detractors of the royal family, openly questioned whether it was desirable for the crown prince to come back to Germany at all. In a series of articles, the final one published after Wilhelm's convoy of sports cars had already crossed the German border, the count portrayed the heir to the throne as a weakling and a failure who was trying to re-enter the country on the back of the liberal 'Jewish half-breed' Stresemann and propaganda from the 'Jewish press'.

The accusation that the Kaiser, the crown prince and the entire high nobility were insufficiently anti-Semitic would continue until well into the Third Reich. Wilhelm's open letter had combined self-praise and ex-post-facto claims to have known what was coming with an attempt to cosy up to the advocates of democracy he believe could enable his return. The crown prince claimed that, as early as 1914, with the failure of the Schlieffen Plan, he had considered it impossible for Germany to win the war, and that by 1917 he argued for a negotiated peace. In Reventlow's eyes, such statements made the prince an example of the sort of lukewarm 'half-heartedness' that had in fact robbed Germany of victory.

The approval the crown prince's letter elicited from a segment of democratic German society, actually a notable success, was interpreted as a sign of his proximity to 'Jews and their friends', with Reventlow warning: 'Behind Stresemann's pseudo-monarchism is Jewry.' It was embarrassing, the count continued, to have to read that a Prussian crown prince wanted to withdraw to his 'royal fiefdom' in Oels in the Silesian provinces.[38] Reventlow, many years Wilhelm's senior, also attacked with almost parental severity the latter's tactical false pledge that he would live his life back in Germany as a private citizen, father of his family and estate owner: 'There's no helping him who betrays himself. Whoever is too soft to be something other than a private citizen is disqualified. But the monarchist idea in Germany will not be smothered alongside him.'[39]

Himself a member of a renowned aristocratic family from the northern German region of Holstein, Reventlow offered a telling example of the two-sided monarchist perception of the emperor's body. The 'weakling' who existed in reality, Reventlow argued, could be understood as an unfortunate link in a chain that would be followed by stronger leaders. One weak man at the helm was no reason to dispose of an entire system. There was no reason to destroy a painting because the nail supposed to keep it hanging on the wall proved insufficient to the task. The 'failure of one wearer of the crown,' Reventlow insisted, didn't 'discredit the monarchist principle'.[40] The tone and content of such attacks became harsher with every missive Reventlow penned. To his mind, an heir to the throne who had settled for hollow compromises with the Weimar Republic, bowing down verbally before it, and a would-be king who proclaimed that he was only interested in his own private happiness had discredited himself as a future leader. For Reventlow, Wilhelm was nothing more than an egotistical and opportunist loser and lickspittle.

Like many racist nationalists, Reventlow superficially cleaved to guiding conservative concepts, but his critique of actual members of the former ruling family twisted the meaning of the words 'aristocracy' and 'monarchy' to the point of opaqueness. Little remained of the traditional significance of the monarchy, its institutions and personifications in the count's attacks.[41] It was only logical that, several years later, Reventlow renounced monarchism and joined the Nazi movement.

Reventlow's anti-Hohenzollern offensive was typical of other conflicts between the royal family and the new racist far Right. One example was the feud in 1926 and 1927 between Prince Oskar of Prussia and Hermann Ehrhardt, a wartime torpedo boat captain, organizer of political assassinations and probably the most charismatic leader of the paramilitary Freikorps movement. In 1919, Ehrhardt had conspired to liberate the Kaiser from Dutch exile in a surprise raid, but he later became an increasingly vocal critic of the Hohenzollerns' fighting spirit and the Kaiser's hesitancy. The break between the royal family and one of the main Freikorps idols caused considerable fretting in military and officers' associations and serious concern within the Kaiser's entourage.[42] The difference between the ponderous, old-fashioned style of Princes Oskar and Eitel and the crisp masculinity of a war hero like Ehrhardt was all too obvious and to an extent mirrored the rift between the old and new Right in Germany.

This basic constellation would persist, although increasingly characterized by the attempt to bridge the gaps. From exile, the crown prince responded in proxy to Reventlow's attacks through an ally who had stayed with him during his early days in the pastorage in Wieringen and one of the leading writers on his propaganda staff.[43] Baron Ehrenfried Günther von Hünefeld was a kind of aristocratic jack of all trades, a monocle-sporting son of an officer,[44] a diplomat, a writer and a pilot whose spectacular flights over the North Atlantic and in East Asia would earn him international fame and would show up the Weimar Republic with his monarchist feats of derring-do.[45] Hünefeld's defence of Wilhelm against Reventlow's attacks was notable for the almost servile respect with which he treated the 'most honourable count'. These rather impotent responses once more stressed the crown prince's purported salt-of-the-earth, selfless qualities, repeatedly citing Reventlow's admission that everyone who truly got to know Wilhelm inevitably 'loved' him.[46] Wilhelm's propaganda apparatus invoked this idea constantly, and it never completely disappeared even in mocking portraits of the heir to the throne. In 1926, a Dutch aristocrat published a book under the pseudonym of 'Baron Ermine', in which he depicted the life and loves of a barely fictionalized crown prince on the island of 'Wiereland' in the form of a 400-page adventure novel. Although the figure of the fictional prince occasioned much concern and anger among the advisors of the real-life Crown Prince Wilhelm because of the protagonist's many indiscretions, in tone and style he was sympathetically depicted as a bon vivant with a fondness for earthly pleasures: 'No matter how fast his car went, his old companion, melancholy, always got in the vehicle and drove along with him . . . Only a little bit of loyalty remained in his heart, fleeting, like the scent of a beautiful flower.'[47]

What was astonishing about the campaign preparing for the crown prince's return was the distance between the lines the principals tried to straddle. They extended from the Social Democratic ministers in Stresemann's cabinet to the radical right-wing, racist camp, whose as yet unformed potential, best embodied around 1922 by Reventlow, was no secret to Wilhelm's advisors. The astonishing gymnastics Hünefeld put himself through trying to court the

aggressive detractors of the monarchy attest to the great significance the crown prince and his lobbyists attached to far-right,
anti-Semitic groups. The fantasies and plots to topple the Weimar
Republic by force would go down in flames in the succession of
attempted putsches from Kapp to Hitler. These failures revealed,
among other things, the rifts within the German Right. From that
point on, it was essential to the crown prince to call for unity across
the right-wing spectrum and offer to help bridge any gaps. This
gambit was already evident in 1922, although the message was
occluded by verbal concessions to the Weimar Republic, whose
gates were only to be opened so that it could be attacked from
within. Two years further on, it became impossible to deny that
Wilhelm had become a figure only rallying the Right.

That figure needed to be overhauled in the autumn of 1923 if
Wilhelm were to be allowed to return to Germany. This was the
political equivalent of squaring a circle. Worries among the democratic wielders of power had to be assuaged, no cause was to be
given to the radical Left to mobilize its revolutionary cohorts and
the Allied authorities were to be denied any pretext for intervention. At the same time the monarchists could not be disappointed,
and the conservative and military segments of society needed
reason to believe that, some day in the future, the Weimar Republic
would be destroyed. In light of Wilhelm's nearly hopeless starting
point, his transformation from a largely despised refugee in 1918 to
a possible king in 1932 was nothing short of a triumph.

Pro-Democracy Cassandras

The debates about Wilhelm's return to Germany came in a phase
of grave political upheavals and amidst a wave of radical right-wing
violence. Three occurrences stand out among the many political
assaults and assassinations. In January 1920, the centrist Matthias
Erzberger, who had signed the armistice ending the First World
War in Compiègne in 1918, was shot and lightly wounded in an

attempted assassination in Berlin. He survived that attack but was killed seventeen months later, in August 2021, by two assassins who shot him twice in the back of the head while he was lying on the ground. On 4 June 1922, the social democrat Philipp Scheidemann, who had proclaimed the Weimar Republic in 1918, was the victim of an acid attack, which he only survived thanks to chance. Three weeks later, German foreign minister and industrial tycoon Walther Rathenau, hated by many as a Jewish politician whose sole goal, his enemies believed, was to fulfil the demands of Germany's former adversaries, became the most prominent bourgeois figure to be assassinated. He was murdered in broad daylight in his open-topped car in the genteel Berlin neighbourhood of Grunewald.

The killers in these and other cases were members of Freikorps circles, in which military, racist, radical right-wing and monarchist variants of hatred for the Weimar Republic intermingled.[48] For a time, the series of murders strengthened pro-democracy forces' willingness to defend themselves and elicited visible and audible outrage from the political centre. After the killing of Rathenau, the centrist politician and German chancellor Joseph Wirtz explicitly pointed out the connection between homicidal paramilitary organizations and the radical Right in the Reichstag. In June 1922, in words soon to become well known throughout Germany, he would take conservative deputies to task: 'There stands the enemy, who has dribbled his poison into the wounds of a people. There stands the enemy – and there can be no doubt. The enemy stands on the right.'[49]

One of the reactions to the wave of political assassinations was the first version of the Law to Protect the Republic.[50] When the draft legislation was debated, social democrats wanted to direct the law 'against people and associations whose goals include endangering democratic governments, killing their representatives and using violence against republican forms of state'. The Hohenzollerns and crown prince were repeatedly named during these debates. SPD deputy Toni Pfülf criticized 'the members of the families that once ruled the land who have shown no gratitude for the fact that after

November 1918 not a single hair on their heads was harmed'. Pfülf demanded that the central institutions of power be protected from the influence of former princes. Communist Wilhelm Koenen went a couple of steps further, calling for the aristocrats to be 'smoked out' of Germany so that no symbols glorifying monarchism would take root in the soil of the Weimar Republic. Shouted interjections such as 'The crown prince and his harem' and 'His face looks like it's been slapped' led to scenes of tumult in the German parliament. By contrast, a legal expert for the right-wing DVP, Wilhelm Kahl, saw the return of the crown prince as an expression of a 'natural human right' whose abrogation would be 'a cruelty of an unheard-of sort'. Stresemann hedged his bets, calling the murdered foreign minister Rathenau a statesman who had never generally rejected a monarchist form of state. Acting as though not directly involved, Stresemann mentioned in passing that he had heard tell that the prince had filed a petition to be allowed to return home.[51]

Considerable reservations about Wilhelm's return persisted, and long-term arrangements were required to overcome them. The very day the crown prince set out from Wieringen on his way home, the German government discussed concerns that as soon as the prodigal son returned to Silesia, he would be 'covered by the mantle' of the political Right.[52] The pro-democracy *Frankfurter Zeitung* newspaper announced that, while others had for now taken over the active conspiring on Wilhelm's behalf, he would soon be at the centre of attempts to undermine the Republic. The returning prince was considered a 'source of danger' from which a 'perspicacious government of good character needed to protect itself'.[53] The pretence of Wilhelm's 'private' return was not to last long. In April 1924, the prince was already being lionized at a military event in Silesia, one which *Vorwärts* mocked as 'Hohenzollern fiddling' while declaring 'Stresemann's protected fellow is allowing himself to be worshipped.'[54] Meanwhile worries were growing in western Germany as to how French occupiers would react.[55] Democratic observers already reported that the crown prince had negotiated with the leader of the ultranationalist DNVP, Count Westarp, about who would stand as the lead candidate in the next national election.[56] Concern that visible political activity by the Hohenzollerns might provoke Entente and particularly French repression were in evidence across the journalistic spectrum, and the option of punitive action was openly discussed by the French media.[57]

Let us spring forward ten years now to a debate in the spring of 1932 that looked back on the arrangements for the crown prince's return in 1922 and 1923. After Wilhelm again intervened in a key political issue with a public statement, a wave of newspaper articles recalled the promises he had made back in 1923. One argument advanced by supporters of the heir to the throne was that the assurances he had given a decade earlier had expired with Stresemann's death in 1929 – a bewildering line of reasoning since his promised non-interference concerned the state and not an individual statesman. Others claimed that Wilhelm had never made any such promise. When that idea was discredited, a third argument contended that the crown prince had meant something else. That, too, prompted a furious quarrel. On the one side, Wilhelm's camp, once again coordinated by his adjutant Müldner von Mülnheim, proposed that the heir to the throne had referred to 'interference' but not political 'participation' as such.[58] Pro-democracy critics countered that, if this was so, then either Stresemann or the prince was a liar.[59] The manager of Stresemann's estate was questioned, and the Social Democrat Wilhelm Sollmann, who had served as interior minister in Stresemann's cabinet in 1923, interceded in the debate, describing the assurances the SPD had been given and expressing the opinion that Stresemann, in his 'romantic pride', had believed he and the crown prince had reached a 'gentleman's agreement'. But extensive debates continued over what precisely had been promised and fixed in oral and written form.[60] Neither for the first time nor for the last in the history of the Hohenzollerns their public image, a respected historian was commissioned to draw up an evaluation.

The historian in question was Friedrich Thimme, the head of the Reichstag library and the editor of the most important edition of documents concerning the First World War. He was an excellent choice from a Hohenzollern PR perspective. Thimme's abilities in handling historical source material were beyond reproach, and he was known as a liberal democrat and an independent mind, who had maintained his distance from the radical Right and criticized the Kaiser's 1923 memoirs.[61] At the same time, on numerous occasions, he had tried to promote a positive view of the heir to the throne and the Hohenzollern dynasty. All the way back in 1920, Thimme had characterized the crown prince in the *Prussian Yearbooks* journal as an 'empirical . . . simple and humble personality' who was 'well-rooted with his feet on the ground' and who rejected all pomp – in positive contrast to the romanticism of his father.[62]

Thimme had also visited the crown prince in the Netherlands in the summer of 1922 and had published several complementary pieces about him immediately after returning to Germany the following year, emphasizing Wilhelm's 'work ethic and devotion to duty' and the 'historical, political and social studies' he had undertaken while in exile. At a point when the liberal bourgeoisie was being asked to accept the prince's new role, Thimme followed Stresemann in proclaiming that Wilhelm's return poised 'no domestic danger' whatsoever and 'on the contrary was a boon for Germany'.[63]

Nine years later, in the spring of 1932, with the believability of the internationally scrutinized crown prince eliciting massive scepticism, Thimme again offered his services, dismissing the idea of Wilhelm having given his word of honour to Stresemann as a 'legend'.[64] The conservative press treated the historian as its star witness, citing Wilhelm's 1923 correspondence, in which he had emphasized his desire to be reunited with his family. 'Familial relations' and his children's education, Thimme argued, had demanded that Wilhelm be allowed to return to Germany, where he intended to devote himself to 'managing his agricultural properties'. Without a hint of irony, the crown prince's publicity staff's strategy tried to portray him as a simple private citizen and farmer who just wanted to live with his family.[65] At the same time, French observers scoffed that breaking his word was not a problem for a crown prince who was cheered on by 20,000 spectators in Berlin's Sportpalast arena.[66] The French press was generally concerned about Wilhelm's increasingly aggressive visibility.[67]

Ultimately the 1932 debate about what Wilhelm had and had not promised in 1923 highlighted Stresemann's influence, the creativity of the crown prince's staff and the deep rifts about how much honour there was in Wilhelm's 'word of honour'. Parts of the German press continued for some time to compare the heir to the throne's behaviour to the blatant, politically motivated lies told by Göring, Strasser and Hitler.[68] In the newspaper *Tage-Buch*, Stresemann's arranging of Wilhelm's return was deemed a 'swindle', and Stresemann himself, who agreed with the crown prince about 'the entire menu of revisionist demands', as a manifestation of the Weimar Republic's innate weakness.[69] New York newspapers called him a 'Napoleonic modernist' who had created a rickety coalition with feudal lords and other enemies of the nation.[70] *Vorwärts* suggested – then as now plausibly – that the 'intimate connection' between Stresemann and the crown prince deserved to be considered a special chapter in the history of the German bourgeoisie. Later generations of historians, the newspaper argued, would view Stresemann's immense 'will to climb the social ladder' in precisely this light.[71]

Among the many bourgeois observers left scratching their heads at Stresemann's patronage of the prince was his son Wolfgang Stresemann, a lawyer and orchestra conductor.[72] The events of both 1923 and 1932 reveal a lot about the aims and techniques of the publicity advisors trying to create a suitably modern image of the Hohenzollern dynasty. They also offer insights into the motives and misconceptions of that segment of the bourgeoisie which continued to invest trust, hope and loyalty in the family, the heir to the throne and the concept of Prussia. After all, it was only thanks to patronage from bourgeois circles and the projections of millions of ordinary Germans that Wilhelm could accrue the significance he did as a public figure. This was as true in 1923 as it was in 1932. The admission into the Weimar Republic of perhaps the most important symbol of the anti-democratic aristocracy, arranged in the face of considerable resistance, wasn't a major shift in German society, which was grappling with much graver issues in 1923. But no political camp considered it a triviality, either. Over the years, Wilhelm's presence in Germany lent an undeniable stature to the initially amorphous mélange of anti-democratic groups, and that influence would continue until at least 1934.

Masses of Assets

Overnight, upon his return to Germany, the crown prince exponentially expanded his radius for physical movement and for political action. But to fight against the Weimar Republic, the Hohenzollerns also depended on their material wealth. This was at the heart of the struggle during the 1920s over the family's assets.

The 1918 revolution in Germany had toppled the monarchy and raised the question of what should become of royal holdings. In the case of the Kaiser, who had been Germany's wealthiest individual before 1914 and remained one of its richest men,[73] this was a political and symbolic as well as a financial issue. It would take eight years for the tug-of-war over the Hohenzollerns' assets to be legally resolved, and in several aspects the debate of 1921 persists today, more than a century later. The eight years between the seizure of royal assets in November 1918 and the eventual legal settlement in October 1926 were full of hard-fought negotiations, including a 'settlement commission', numerous legal trials, battles between appraisers, parliamentary debates and heated political campaigns. This issue was a permanent fixture of German society in that time. In the six months preceding the agreement ultimately concluded between the former ruling dynasty and the state of Prussia, left-wing parties staged a popular referendum on whether the assets of the entire German aristocracy should be confiscated with no compensation at all. That referendum failed in June 1926, and the first attempt at a legal settlement followed several weeks later.

The compromise was signed on 6 October 1926 and ratified by the Prussian parliament shortly thereafter. The revolution hadn't gone after hereditary aristocratic assets in revolutionary fashion, treating them instead as an issue to be resolved legally and not politically. The early decision to address the question according to the presumed legal continuity between Wilhelmine Germany and the Weimar Republic ultimately produced a half-hearted result from a democratic-republican perspective. In the end, the 1918 revolution merely staked a claim to the Hohenzollerns' royal and private assets without actually confiscating them.

Sixty-four lorries full of the Kaiser's belongings and millions in private capital were released in 1919 and 1920, and, as early as March 1919, there were already discussions about lifting their formal expropriation.[74] The revolutionary energy necessary for a political solution – state expropriation in return for lump-sum compensation – quickly waned and was restricted legally by guarantees concerning royal assets in paragraph 153 of the Constitution of the Weimar Republic, which took effect in the summer of 1919. Social democrat attempts to compromise with bourgeois parties meant that the issue of royal wealth was placed into something of a permanent waking coma. Once thrust into the legal arena, the matter proved so complicated that negotiations could have stretched out for a century or more.

The crux of the debate was where private and state aristocratic assets began and ended. The regulations concerning such assets that had been drawn up during the eighteenth and nineteenth centuries were difficult enough already, but after the 1918 German revolution they became so complex that they still have not been completely resolved to this day. On the issue of domains alone, which crystallized in the late nineteenth century, the leading expert on the topic has written:

All these masses of assets with their extended, attached capital funds . . . together represent a scarcely transparent agglomeration of wealth, concerning which it was only sure that the state could continue to stake a claim to them, that the Hohenzollerns were obviously multimillionaires and that not everything had transpired legally.[75]

Professional evaluators – in this case four renowned legal scholars and law professors commissioned in early 1919 – had a huge influence on defining what would be considered private property. The expertise of these specialists, all of whom were warmly disposed towards the Kaiser and some of whom were part of the liberal camp,[76] would greatly impact years of decisions by courts, commissions, ministers and governments. The preliminary rulings made between 1919 and 1924 were the products of these evaluators, who 'wielded an academic power and majesty untouchable on their terrain' – as long as everyone involved shared their basic political convictions.[77] Today's constitutional scholars have very different fundamental views, in particular on issues concerning the wealth of the crown and the legal status of the so-called *Kronfideikommissrente*, an annual sum paid to the crown for the state use of royal assets. Contemporary scholar Heinz Holzhauer writes: 'A house of cards constructed by card cheats could not have been ricketier than the construction with which [the evaluators] sought to show that the *Kronfideikommissrente* was a legitimate part of Wilhelm II's private assets.'[78]

The views expounded in the evaluations proved very effective in the main court cases and in the public conflicts at the time. The same was true of the extensive publicity work, which covered everything from the Reichstag and the conservative German press to letters to the editors of American newspapers written by Hohenzollern lawyers complaining about what they claimed was inaccurate reporting.[79]

The royal family's adversaries continually tried to highlight the Hohenzollerns' enormous wealth. For instance, in 1922, the communist parliamentary deputy Theodor Neubauer – the son of an agricultural estate inspector, a reserve lieutenant and a historian with a doctorate – came up with some dizzying and not always accurate numbers: 484,406 hectares of land, 300 million marks in private wealth, 500 million marks in art and an overall wealth of 2.6 billion marks. In contrast to this astronomical data, the annual military pensions paid by the Weimar Republic were amounts imaginable to everyday Germans: 10,074 marks to the former division commander Prince Eitel Friedrich, 7,554 for Prince Oskar as a former colonel, 17,127 to the Kaiser's brother Prince Heinrich, an ex-grand admiral, and 3,030 marks for the former major Prince Joachim. (By way of comparison, the monthly wage of a unionized German worker in 1920 was around 130 marks.) Social democrats repeatedly raised the issue of the massive amounts of state money going to the high nobility. In 1922, they gleefully publicized the fact that Prince Oskar had complained about not receiving his wages as a brigade commander in the final three months of 1918.[80] 'Up with the princes!' was the sarcastic title of a December 1924 article about the former Duke of Meiningen, who successfully sued for compensation of 8.25 million gold marks and a monthly pension of 4,125 gold marks in a Leipzig court.[81]

So long as the sums involved were generally comprehensible, conservatives had difficulty rebutting the critics. In 1926, for example, the legal expert Friedrich Everling – the leader of the monarchist 'League of the Upstanding', editor of a publication called the *Conservative Monthly* and a later member of the Nazi Party – spoke at a Reichstag debate about the pensions enjoyed by the Kaiser's sons. The princes, Everling argued, had only applied for the pensions during the 1923 economic crisis 'when they weren't doing well', adding that anyone acquainted with Prince Oskar knew that he heated his own stoves and went without a personal servant. The parliamentary record notes 'laughter' at this point in the debate.[82] In a June 1928 interview with the *Daily News*, Prince August Wilhelm denied joining the 'German Workers' Party' while insisting that he enjoyed being around workers very much. As August Wilhelm told it, he was so poor that he could no longer afford taxis and had to take the bus, as a result of which he had also determined how congenial the bus conductors were and how much he liked being among the working classes.

The Failed Disappropriation

Behind the façade of such self-depictions, Hohenzollern lawyers worked right from the start, and successfully, to regain confiscated royal family assets. Until this avenue was legally closed off in February 1926, lawyers for members of the high nobility were remarkably adept at suing for the return of the latter's property in civil damage compensation trials. Their lines of argument included such odd manoeuvres as the Kaiser demanding the restitution of his personal colonial assets in German Southwest Africa,[83] which by then was under South African mandate, after colonial German troops had waged a genocidal war there in 1904. Demands for the restoration of two farms in what is today Namibia, which would eventually be reacquired with capital from spouses marrying into the family, applied at least theoretically also to confiscated Hohenzollern assets in reconstituted, post-World-War Poland.[84]

The individual legal triumphs leading aristocrats were able to achieve against state authorities attracted particularly keen interest. Along with a 1924 victory for Prince Friedrich Leopold there was a national court verdict of 18 June 1925 that restored the aristocratic estates seized by a left-wing government in 1919 to the former ruling family of the duchy of Saxe-Coburg and Gotha. The beneficiary of this verdict was, as the 'head of the family', Duke Carl Eduard of Saxe-Coburg and Gotha, who had already made a name for himself as an enemy of the Weimar Republic and a patron of the far Right. Shortly thereafter, he would become one of the most influential aristocratic supporters of the Nazi movement.[85]

In November 1925, amid a growing number of successful aristocratic civil suits against the state, the communist KPD proposed novel legislation allowing for the seizure of the entire wealth of royal families and their members without any compensation whatsoever. The subsequent petition for a public referendum marked the beginning of what an American newspaper called one of the most astonishing experiments in decades within a functioning democracy.[86] This leftist political and propagandist trial balloon would have reallocated major amounts of land to farmers and small leaseholders, transformed aristocratic estates into spas and orphanages, established new museums and redistributed wealth to wounded veterans, the unemployed, widows and those hardest hit by hyperinflation. For tactical reasons and under pressure from their constituency, the social democrats supported the initiative, after initially raising serious concerns about it. Together the SPD and the KPD put forward the petition in January 1926. Nine months of intense propaganda battles followed, but the debate was far less about the legal details of aristocratic wealth, which few people understood to begin with, than about the origins and persistence of extreme social inequality. The conflict was between equality and private property, which were viewed as absolutely incompatible.

The plan for a referendum initiated by Germany's two main working-class parties and conducted in the first half of March 1926 was astonishingly successful: 35.5 per cent of voters supported the proposal – more than the percentage of the electorate that usually voted for the parties themselves. There were, however, regional differences. Support was strong in Berlin, Leipzig and Hamburg and weak in Bavaria and eastern Germany. The petition got more than three times the proportion of votes needed to meet the quorum for a referendum. Conservatives were thunderstruck at the petition so easily clearing this hurdle and immediately mobilized their forces. A 'Working Committee to Combat the Petition' united nearly all of the major right-wing political parties, the Stahlhelm militia, right-wing associations of all sorts, agricultural and industrial, both major churches, Germany's largest aristocratic league (the DAG) and the wealthy interest groups of the former princes. Backed by huge sums of money, the conservative counter-campaign included reports placed in leading media to speakers who addressed Germans of all walks of life, right down to farmers in the most remote villages in East Prussia.

The Hohenzollerns and their representatives in the German capital played an active role in the organization of this counter-campaign.

The 'general administration' reported back extensively to the ex-Kaiser about plans to systematically influence various segments of the press, the use of picture agencies and the hiring of constitutional scholar Carl Schmitt to deliver an evaluation to the parliament's judiciary committee. The Hohenzollerns' staff in Berlin were deeply involved in the formation of an 'Association for a Legal Settlement of the State with the Prussian Royal House', consisting of seven renowned university professors acting in the interests of the family and producing further expert evaluations. The staff also actively communicated with the anti-democratic Scherl publishing house, officers' associations, right-wing political parties, the churches and the Agricultural League. They dispatched spies to leftist political events, mass-printed fliers and encouraged leading aristocrats in Silesia and Westphalia to put pressure on regional bishops, who in turn wielded influence over deputies from the Catholic Centre Party.[87] In the summer of 1926, Wilhelm II contended that in 1919 he had 'acquiesced' to negotiations in the spirit of generosity but that, owing to public incitement, all sense of proportion had subsequently been lost. The defence of aristocratic interests, he continued, should not primarily be a 'material' one: it needed to be elevated to the 'heights of a great idea'. To leave no doubt, the ex-Kaiser proclaimed: 'This idea is the battle for the inviolability of private property.' He, the former monarch, had no choice but to lead this struggle for the entire German people, even if most of those people weren't yet capable of comprehending its complete import.[88]

The discussion surrounding an unqualified defence of private property also prompted a fundamental decision on the right-wing extreme of the political spectrum. At its February 1926 conference in Bamberg, the Nazi Party, whose leftist wing initially sympathized with the idea of confiscating aristocratic wealth, vigorously pledged its fealty to the principal of private ownership. It subsequently launched a garish, very vocal propaganda campaign proposing to confiscate the assets not of the aristocracy, but of the 'eastern Jews', who had migrated to Germany after 1914.[89] German President Paul von Hindenburg, aided by right-wing legal experts, succeeded in establishing the controversial idea that any blanket disappropriation would require an amendment to the constitution. That meant that any proposed legislation would need an absolute rather than a qualified majority to become law.[90] The referendum was defeated on 20 June 1926, after garnering only 14.5 million instead of the required 20 million votes.

One cartoon in the pro-republican campaign for the referendum featured two images of the same aristocratic estate under the headline 'What Should Become of This?' The first image showed a bald king wearing an enormous crown faced by deeply bowing lackeys. On the margin, officers in jack boots, teeth bared, brandish their sabres at fleeing civilians. In the second image, showing the estate transformed into an orphanage, seven happy children dance in a circle.[91]

Similarly, in the run-up to the June 1926 referendum, German cinemas showed a political film entitled *Not a Penny for the Princes*. It juxtaposed images of magnificent castles with grim scenes of Berlin workers living in squalid courtyard hovels. The unemployed, the film informed viewers, received 27 pfennigs of assistance per day, while the Kaiser's daily pension was 1,650 marks. This drew an objection from right-wing lawyers to the highest office for monitoring film content in Berlin.[92] They argued that the daily sum of 1,650 marks went not to the Kaiser alone but to the 'members of the former imperial house'. The film, they contended, was thus intentionally misleading. Those arguments fell on deaf ears, and the film was approved to be shown, with the social democratic press promoting it as a 'fine piece of propaganda in the fight against the larceny of the princes'.[93] Left-wing journalist Kurt Heinig, one of the most active advocates of the disappropriation initiative, published a 'primer' detailing the assets and capital wealth of the higher German aristocracy. The dizzying sums listed were a vivid representation of just how much wealth was at stake.[94]

The conservative counter-campaign branded the initiative a fundamental attack on private property per se and excoriated it as a 'cowardly act of theft against the property of defenceless princes'.

Speakers told audiences in many rural villages that ordinary people's homes, farms and livestock would be confiscated next. As soon as the 'holy principle' of private property was violated, they argued, there would be nothing preventing the state from seizing factories, carpenters' workshops, department stores and small retailers, allotment gardens, banks and the savings accounts of everyday workers, shop owners and farmers.[95] Anticipating later levels of debate, parallels were drawn between the massive wealth of leading aristocratic families and what farmers had acquired with their own two hands. A conspicuous undertone ran throughout the pro-aristocratic campaign whose credo could be expressed as: 'The corrosive Jewish spirit of Bolshevism knows no bounds.'[96] Or, as Baron Karl von Plettenberg, former commander general of the guard corps and general adjutant to Wilhelm II put it, the 'Jews and comrades of Jews' who made up the political elite of the Weimar Republic have 'consciously worked towards the destruction of all we used to consider great and holy.'[97]

Prince Eitel Friedrich told the press that nothing would fan the flames of communism or more greatly threaten German prosperity than a seizure of the royal family's assets.[98] The conservative counter-offensive always focused on the inviolability of the bourgeois order based on private property. Obscured by the passions engendered in the debate was the fact that aristocratic wealth was usually not the deserved reward for personal labour in line with the bourgeois work ethic but rather the result of legally enshrined hereditary privilege, which less to do with the rules governing bourgeois ownership and the bourgeois work ethic than with the legalities of civil law.

Estimates made for the settlement ultimately adopted in 1926 started from the premise that the Hohenzollerns would be compensated for around three-fifths of the overall value of the family assets. The pro-democracy *Weltbühne* boiled down the complex deal into the following: instead of a lump sum of 10 to 30 million marks, which Prussian state premier Otto Braun and others had suggested,[99] the Hohenzollerns would receive 250,000 acres of land, around a dozen estates, including the Old Palace and the Dutch Palace on Unter den Linden boulevard in Berlin, two dozen villas and large utility buildings, removal vans full of valuables, three-quarters of the 'Hausfideikommiss-Kapitalienfonds' (the inherited wealth of the Hohenzollern dynasty passed down the generations), one half of the 'Kronfideikomiss-Kapitalienfonds' (the fund used to maintain the royal household during the monarchy), all of its jewellery as well as 15 million marks from Prussian taxpayers – and this at a time when Prussia was having to borrow to service its debts. The total cost of this expression of public appreciation, according to estimates made by the Hohenzollerns themselves before the First World War, would have been at least '125 million gold marks,' excluding a long list of further amenities.

Two side aspects would continue to play a role in later decades. One was the idea that 'the free state of Prussia' would place

> Cecilienhof in the New Garden near Potsdam at the disposal of the former crown prince and his wife as well as their children and grandchildren for a residence as long as they live since these well-born personages were unlikely to be able to make do with Oels and the dozen estates remaining to them.

The other was the aforementioned 'blemish' that 'according to the agreements the House of Hohenzollern was entitled to name its own court archivist for the royal archive in the Charlottenburg district to record a clean version of its history' and that His Majesty's general representative would be allowed a voice on the supervisory board. With that, observers prophesied in 1926, the royal family, financed by alimony from the Weimar Republic, would continue to shape the historical depiction of the House of Hohenzollern. That would indeed be the case for many years. Around the same time, Wilhelm II's general administration reported that the house archive would only be available for use with permission from his general representative. This would 'ensure that nothing can be published, viewed or otherwise used without the express consent of Your

Majesty's representative'. The report was part of a longer briefing about the broad, direct attempts to influence German media and popular opinion to serve Hohenzollern interests.[100]

The *Weltbühne* piece wasn't sparing in its contempt for the result of the negotiations. In reaching this compromise, the paper wrote, the free state of Prussia was behaving 'like its beloved king's quartermaster', accommodating 'Wilhelm II's wish to have the estate and park in Homburg vor der Höhe as a residence for himself and his wife for the rest of their lives. The author added: 'There's no more cordial way to call upon Wilhelm II to return.' Cuttingly, the article concluded with the statement that the Prussian government was 'afraid of giving taxpayers and the homeless even the most general information of what the Hohenzollerns were in fact likely to get from the deal.'

Richard Lewinsohn, who was responsible for the *Weltbühne's* business section for a decade, came up with his own set of metaphors for the social democrats' propensity for swallowing whatever was forced down their throat. 'We know that like all lower forms of life, the Left in Germany has excellent digestive organs and chokes down whatever the right puts in front of it,' he wrote. 'But the Hohenzollern compensation agreement might just make them sick to their stomachs.'[101] In September 1926, the *Weltbühne* announced that it would no longer report on the crown prince's extramarital affairs, arguing that 'following him to bed is just the equivalent of subserviently recognizing a non-existent significance'. It was far more worrisome that

> completely blind social democrats had supported his return to Germany, creating a sort of monarchist hub that did an excellent job on the issue of compensation for leading aristocrats. His eternal litany 'I will only live in Germany as a humble private citizen and never involve myself in politics' was the pinnacle of all the Hohenzollerns' [empty] promises.[102]

People on the left of the political spectrum saw the situation much the same way and were correspondingly outraged. In October 1926, the decisive vote on the proposed legislation stalled in the Prussian regional parliament. Communists vocally opposed the draft compromise, and the SPD faction withheld its vote, not wanting to provoke the anger of the party's base. Four months after the failure of the popular referendum, the mood was so heated that the decisive vote could only be held after incendiary debates during the third reading of the proposed resolution or, as it was described, a 'four-hour voting battle'. Members of the communist faction briefly succeeded in turning the plenary hall into a literal battleground after some yelling and physical altercations. Files were tossed, vicious insults and blows traded, and court bailiffs grabbed elected deputies and ejected them from the hall. Three people were injured, and while an angry crowd demonstrated against the compromises made to the 'Hohenzollern thieves' in front of the building, chairs were being thrown inside it.[103] The protestors repeatedly left sacks full of money rendered worthless by hyperinflation in front of the Berlin Palace for Wilhelm II to see, and there were street brawls and exchanges of gunfire over the issue. British newspapers reported the parliamentary president being doused in ink and a general increase in 'Anti-Hohenzollernism in the widest sense'.[104]

Thus, in the autumn of 1926, almost eight years of negotiations, lawsuits and debates yielded an 'unreadable mess of dates, paragraphs and court verdicts' that concealed the immense concessions made by the state. In *Weltbühne*, Carl von Ossietsky ridiculed the 'middlemen' who were not only willing to pay the Hohenzollerns in the interest of compromise but, wherever they deemed necessary, were even ready to trade blows in parliament with communist deputies on the aristocracy's behalf.[105] Leftists never tired of stressing in speeches, brochures, campaign communications and the social democratic press that the entire matter should have been settled politically, not legally. But, every time organs like *Vorwärts* summoned the rhetorical fortitude to denounce what was going on, they contradicted years of SPD policy.[106] Even Ernst Heilmann, who led the right wing of the SPD in the Prussian state parliament, warned that 'it's dangerous for the Republic to put such a huge mass of wealth in the hands of its natural enemies.' But ultimately Heilmann, a lawyer, tried to convince fellow party members outraged by the concessions that the Prussian state had little chance in front of the courts and that only the German national government could confiscate aristocratic holdings.[107]

The communist press in France mocked the social democrats, satirically envisioning the prodigal Kaiser confirming party leaders in their government posts and awarding them medals.[108] In general foreign journalists didn't hold back from ridicule, reporting on issues in detail down to the level of quarrels concerning the crown princess's silverware.[109] Above all in France, Jacobin energies and anti-aristocratic and anti-German hostility discharged itself in broadsides against the Hohenzollern family and its purported plight. Alongside objective reports about the course of the negotiations came attacks upon a 'family of vultures and thieves'.[110] Many of the barbs were aimed at the malleability of the SPD leadership. It was noted with a certain Schadenfreude that the most gifted SPD ministers had succeeded in banning ranking police officials from wearing monocles, which were considered reactionary symbols,[111] while, on more important matters such as the crown prince's return to Germany and the deal concerning royal assets, pro-democracy advocates hadn't shown any comparable energy – a fact that left party functionaries in many places in the country struggling to explain themselves.

Like the entire social democratic movement in the 1920s, the leaders of the SPD were caught between radical left-wing demands and centrist calls for conciliation and compromise with parties from the bourgeois middle. The result was a combination of revolutionary-sounding sloganeering in public and constant willingness at the negotiating tables for eight long years to seek deals between the German state and the royal family.[112] The truth was that the state had hardly exhausted its legal options. Although it categorically rejected revolutionary solutions, the stance of SPD leadership as the years of legal wrangling dragged on was otherwise contradictory, half-hearted and inconsistent.[113]

The hesitancy of the pro-democratic camp may appear surprising in retrospect, but it did have its reasons. After the onset of revolution, SPD leaders and Germany as a whole had more pressing worries than the coffers of the exiled Kaiser. The Hohenzollerns profited from being relatively low on the list of priorities as the future of the Weimar Republic was being laid out. Government inconsistency was the product less of a lack of backbone and more of a realistic evaluation of the strength of its opponents, particularly in view of the conservative dominance of the German judicial system. Moreover, the same mechanisms at work in other political areas blocked radical impulses where the potential seizure of royal assets were concerned. The actions of Russian revolutionaries, in particular the symbolically charged execution of the Romanovs, together with both the real and, even more, imagined threat of Bolshevism spreading into Germany, frightened many social democrats into insisting on compromise with the bourgeois centre.[114] The debate about the potential seizure of royal assets was thus shot through with what historian Hans Mommsen called an 'almost neurotic fear of communist anarchy'.[115] Such anxieties were the basis upon which German aristocrats, above all the Hohenzollerns, could deploy their remaining power to conclude new arrangements. None of the advocates of democracy celebrated the eventual compromise as a triumph. Conversely, the Hohenzollerns' dissatisfaction with what had been attained was great enough that Friedrich von Berg, the chairman of the larger German aristocratic association, was dismissed from his post in late 1926.[116]

'Smuggler Princes'

The eight years of wrangling over royal assets was only one of many conflicts surrounding private wealth in general in Germany and one of many cultural strands concerning how the country should deal with its extreme social inequality. Members of the Hohenzollerns were repeatedly thrust into the public eye in a series of scandals and incidents the pro-democracy camp sought to exploit. The questions Germans began asking with increasing volume as of 1918 were directed not just at where the royal family had got its wealth but how its assets were moved around. Suspected illicit transfers of capital were all the more controversial because leaders of the Hohenzollern clan lived abroad.

One particular burden on Weimar Germany was the perception of it being the product of a national defeat and a 'republic of crooks'. In a society in which fighting and dying side-by-side in the trenches were a prominent measure of collective identity, alleged 'wartime profiteers' on both the Right and the Left were seen as dastardly villains. In 1922 and 1923, Germans from all social classes endured one of the most radical devaluations of currency ever seen in modern history. Things got so bad that one-billion-mark coins were minted, and the issuance of a 500-billion-mark banknote convinced many people that nothing was secure any more and that the world had been turned upside-down. The ravages of hyperinflation hit those who saved money immeasurably harder than those who owned property or land.[117] Against this backdrop, there were constant conflicts over whether some Germans were concealing assets and evading taxes by transferring huge sums of money abroad. The political Right blamed not just the consequences of the war, but the Weimar Republic itself for this perceived injustice. The villainous stereotype of the cowardly, crooked embezzler was often used to defame Jewish financiers and merchants, some of whom had risen meteorically up the social ladder amidst the economic chaos of post-1918 Germany.

The media, legal and parliamentary debates about whether the Hohenzollerns were concealing immense amounts of money and assets abroad really got going around 1921. Newspapers in New York and Washington ran headlines reading 'Hohenzollerns Involved in Big Smuggling Plot' and 'Royal Germans Smuggle Millions'.[118] At the centre of the controversy were the activities of privy councillor and banker Josef Grusser, whose private bank had helped the wealthy, including some well-known aristocrats, to move money abroad illegally. The Hohenzollerns particularly relied on access to liquid capital in the period between the confiscation of royal and private property in November 1918 and the settlement reached in October 1926 – no one more so than Crown Prince Wilhelm, who remained partly dependent on his father's largesse and indeed almost ran out of money in his early days in Wieringen.[119] Grusser, who more than once personally drove suitcases full of his clients' jewels and other valuables in a luxury car from Germany to Amsterdam,[120] was arrested in 1925, but not before his relationship with the Hohenzollerns had attracted public controversy.

There was no shortage of suppositions and discussions concerning irregularities connected with several royal family members, particularly the crown princess. It was widely known that, at the start of his Dutch exile, Crown Prince Wilhelm had borrowed a large sum in guilders from Grusser. The crown princess maintained an account with Grusser's bank via which, according to the family itself, an 'entirely above-board sale of jewellery had been carried out'. In the spring of 1921, a court fined the Kaiser's second-oldest son, Prince Eitel Friedrich, 5,000 marks for having a covert bank account. Called to testified before a Berlin regional court, Prince Eitel – who in the absence of Wilhelm II and the crown prince was serving as the 'deputy head of the family' – had tried to excuse his transgression by saying he was a soldier, not a businessman, and that he had only tried to put aside 'a little bit of money for emergencies' for his wife. The account was registered under the code name 'Prince of Eitel'.

The size of this 'little bit of money' – 337,000 marks deposited at an Amsterdam bank – made many ordinary Germans prick up their ears. The court case attracted international attention and produced a few curiosities. For example, there was a disagreement at the court as to whether Eitel should be referred to as 'His Royal Highness', 'the prince' or simply 'the defendant'. For his part, Eitel always appeared before the judge in military dress and wearing an Iron

Cross.[121] The socialist and communist press had a field day comparing the sums at stake in the case with the financial realities of their readerships, continuing to do so even after the verdict had been rendered. In late 1922, for instance, leftist newspapers reported on an immensely valuable tiara the Kaiser had brought to Doorn as a gift for his wife:

> Who can blather on about the 'misery of the Hohenzollerns' at a time when war widows and cripples, pensioners and invalids, in the hundreds of thousands go to the dogs . . . People able to scoop a tiara worth hundreds of millions from their fully packed jewellery boxes should at least have enough shame in days like these not to talk about their own 'misery'.[122]

The contrast between the opulent settlement received by the Hohenzollerns and the reality of those crippled in the war remained a running theme, and the notion formulated on the Left that the Kaiser's sons were siphoning off lucrative officer's pensions from the 'coffers of the Republic' caused additional outrage.[123] At this juncture and later, this debate was more about political than legal and financial issues: the question of how German social inequality had arisen, why it persisted and whether it was legitimate.

In November 1920, the Reichstag debated the issue of royal assets being transferred abroad. Three excellently prepared legal experts, who, as became immediately apparent, were getting instruction from the Hohenzollerns' staff, spoke on behalf of the royal family: professor emeritus Adelbert Düringer, a former president of the leading German association for 'Law and Business'; former superior administrative court councillor Count Kuno von Westarp, who was the chairman of the conservative-nationalist party DNVP; and the renowned prosecutor Wilhelm Kahl, a deputy for the centrist DVP, whose remarks Stresemann seconded at various points in the discussion. Kahl criticized the 'hounding of the Hohenzollerns' by the Left and recommended mildness in the face of 'the manifold unhappiness and the force of fate that has come down upon this house'.

Nonetheless, there was no glossing over the royal family's connections to the dubious practices of the 'niche banker' Grusser and no plausible answers to the question posed by the SPD's Philipp Scheidemann as to why the bank accounts in question had not been opened at an established financial institution rather than at a 'money-laundering bank'.[124]

It's hard to imagine a greater gap than that between the two conflicting interpretations of the situation. Social democrats accused the Hohenzollerns, including the crown princess, of illegally spiriting assets worth around sixty million marks out of Germany. Conservatives insisted that the disgraced banker had only visited the princess on one occasion 'in order to deliver a letter from the unhappy crown prince'.[125] There's was no bridging these two views. On behalf of the DNVP leadership, Westarp asked deputies to consider who was more credible: the renowned legal expert and professor Karl or a socialist journalist, an unreliable 'youngster' who published 'lies and incitement' in *Vorwärts*. Concerning the undeniable fact that items of great value had indeed been taken outside Germany, the count engaged in rhetorical excursions that crossed the boundary into kitsch:

> Please ask any German woman, regardless of class, whose husband lived abroad penniless and threatened by extradition to the enemy, whether she would hesitate to use the jewellery at her disposal to ensure her husband could keep himself alive. I believe that there can be no doubt what she would answer. No German woman would shy away in the face of formal regulations that might stand in the way. Instead, she would do what she considered her duty according to her heart, her own needs and her relationship to her husband.[126]

On the other hand, the debate was also accompanied by false rumours that the crown princess had succeeded in 'smuggling some twenty million marks of her enormous wealth into Switzerland'.[127]

In a pamphlet, pro-democracy parliamentarians mocked the legal experts as 'Hohenzollern lawyers' who had 'sold out their

professional reputations, dispensed with any shred of judicial thinking and recklessly made themselves into custodians of the deeply
compromised Hohenzollerns and their dirty business'.[128] This line
of attack was led by Rudolf Breitscheid, at the time a member of
the Independent Social Democratic Party (USPD):

Let us assume that the House of Hohenzollern truly could point to
all of the great deeds in the past the gentlemen on the Right credit
it with. What in the world would convince us not to go after these
acts of theft and money laundering if there had been a break in the
present with such a noble past? How dare you speak to us of historical piety? I don't want to delve into the history of the House of
Hohenzollern here. I don't want to delve here into how it acquired
its wealth. I don't want to delve into how the German people has
had to suffer under the Hohenzollerns. Let me just say this . . . the
past achievement of your Hohenzollerns doesn't outweigh the fact,
if it is true, that these Hohenzollerns are behaving like the worst
sort of profiteers who got rich during the war and are now taking
their wealth out of the country to the detriment of the German
people and the German republic . . . It has recently become fash-
ionable among the gentlemen on the Right to put forward the
Hohenzollerns in exile as the poorest and most pitiable people . . .
Alas, ladies and gentlemen, as far as I'm informed, the head of the
House of Hohenzollern currently still possesses a palace while
there are many people here in Berlin who don't even have a room
of their own . . . You can't tell me that the former crown prince of
the German Empire lacks the basic necessities over there in Holland. And if that's true, well, he's a healthy young man, so he should
get a job . . . Despite this, we are prepared to support him . . . But
our standpoint is that the House of Hohenzollern is itself greatly
responsible for this moral calamity . . . They say that personal valets
have no heroes. We now want to show the entire people what these
emperors look like in their new clothes.[129]

The international press immediately jumped on the Reichstag

debates. The *New York Times* ran a story entitled 'Smuggling Princes Hit in Reichstag', putting the sum out of which the Hohenzollerns had cheated the state at 250 million marks.[130] An even more extensive and dramatic story in the *Boston Daily Globe* bore the headline 'Kaiser's Family Charged with Stealing'.[131] Regarding the royal family's assets, the paper devoted a whole page to a question asked with astonishing rarity: 'How the Kaisers [sic] Got It'. The accompanying article traced the details of how the Hohenzollerns acquired their controversial wealth all the way back to the Middle Ages, citing an analysis recently presented to the legal committee of the Prussian parliament by two social democrats: Ernst Heilmann, a legal expert and one of the party's best orators, and Arnold Freymuth, the senate president of the Prussian Superior Court of Justice. Accustomed as lawyers of Jewish background to facing massive hostility, the authors of the report mustered a series of legal, historical and political arguments for seizing the majority of Hohenzollern assets.[132] A brochure presumably put together for the subsequent German election offered a kind of dumbed-down version of their analysis. It was ambiguously titled 'What the Hohenzollerns Have Earned'.[133]

In late 1920, Heilmann also defended a resolution in the Prussian parliament to strip royal assets, claiming to 'represent the interests of the people against the Hohenzollerns'. He calculated for his fellow deputies that the Kaiser received 33 million marks in annual income and planned annual payments under the status quo of 48 million marks to the Hohenzollern family. In sharp language, he questioned what if anything among the disputed family assets could truly be considered private property.[134] The social democratic women's magazine *Die Gleichheit* ran a long analytic article on the topic entitled 'Thieves' while *Vorwärts* published a sarcastic ballad that had the Hohenzollerns' 'personal and court smuggler' packing the 'princely treasure chest' into his car and driving off with it.[135]

At the same time, with the so-called Südekum Settlement of 1920, in which social democratic finance minister Albert Südekum had offered broad concessions to Hohenzollern negotiator Count von Schulenburg, the SPD had itself created a thorny legal situation for the years that followed.[136] Südekum was often caricatured as a labour leader 'with the usual three diamonds on his fingers'. And the fact that in 1920 he lived at least part-time as a tenant in the idyllic Dacrow estate on the River Havel in Potsdam, a property confiscated from the Hohenzollerns, didn't add to the credibility of the SPD's negotiator.[137] There was no denying that the party itself was also responsible for the state's conciliatory stance towards the royal family,[138] and the SPD was constantly open to attacks from the communist KPD, which called for a 'revolutionary tribunal' and accused social democrats of helping to 'sanctify private property'.[139]

Starting with present-day financial irregularities, 'What the Hohenzollerns Have Earned' and the report upon which it was based traced the royal family's wealth back hundreds of years and raised general questions about where it came from and how it had increased. If its authors were to be believed, the overall wealth of the Hohenzollerns was unimaginable – in part because lawyers and negotiators for the family had done their best to conceal its true size.[140] The report covered everything from medieval legal concepts to wars and land seizures to the later acquisition of property in Berlin and annexations after the 1866 Austro-Prussian War. It recalled sceptical questions asked abroad, particularly in France, as to how a government capable of doling out 100 million marks to the Hohenzollerns could be so strapped for cash that it couldn't afford reparations payments. At the time, this was an argument taken very seriously indeed.[141]

Cunningly, the report also harkened back to Prussia's self-enrichment at the expense of Hanover and the Electorate of Hesse in 1866, citing Bismarck, who justified harsh Prussian treatment of its adversaries by saying that the English had not paid support to the Scots after defeating them because the Scots could have then raised an army against England.[142] Referring to the monarch of Hanover, the Iron Chancellor had snapped, 'We owe King Georg nothing.' The 1920 report and pamphlet echoed those words: 'We owe

Wilhelm nothing.'[143] Following Bismarck, the leitmotif of the entire pamphlet warned against the Weimar Republic bankrolling its future enemies. Summing up the parliamentary debates, a triumphant, full-page report in a USPD newspaper proclaimed: 'A Black Day for Monarchists'.[144] But the pro-democratic self-confidence that flickered here didn't last. Like Breitscheid, those who identified a serious danger in concessions to the Republic's enemies wouldn't survive the demise of that state for long. Freymuth and his wife committed suicide in Paris in 1933 after fleeing the Nazi regimes. Heilmann, who had refused to seek exile, was arrested in 1933 in Berlin and murdered in 1940 in Buchenwald.

Ne'er-Do-Wells and Drones

As long as it was conducted in the realm of mathematics and financial law, the battle over the Hohenzollerns' assets remained an abstract one. Probably for this reason, the royal family's republican critics sought to translate their arguments into personal terms. The image of the smuggler aristocrat was supplemented by the figure of the extravagant, noble ne'er-do-well who contributed nothing to the welfare of the community. A series of authors borrowed images from the Enlightenment, Jacobinism and historical social democratic anti-monarchism to create a new enemy: the work-shy, dissipated, decadent aristocratic profligate forever whinging about his purported financial misery. 'What the Hohenzollerns Have Earned' more or less denied the Hohenzollerns had earned anything at all during their family history: 'Idiots, wastrels, sex obsessives and partial and complete lunatics, of the sort the Hohenzollerns have given us en masse, should in future no longer be present at the head of the state.'[145]

Some foreign newspapers continued to use the vitriolic contempt of wartime propaganda. In December 1918, a portrait of the Hohenzollerns published in a Kansas paper wrote of Wilhelm and his horde of handsome, birdbrained sons. With cutting sarcasm, and little understanding of the lives of European aristocracy, the author mocked princes for spending the war far from the frontlines and being completely useless as civilians. In this interpretation, the family was nothing but a clan of decadent, cowardly shirkers.[146] Even as far away as Alaska, in 1919 the Kaiser and his sons were characterized as 'unemployed' – a term somewhat ignorant of the standards and self-image of the European aristocracy without, however, being entirely inaccurate.[147] The motif of 'useless', parasitic aristocrats remained a prominent element of left-wing, pre-Weimar Republic publicity before being co-opted by the radical Right in its campaigns against 'useless mouths to feed'.

One increasingly prominent element in the pro-democratic repertoire was questioning the royal family's service during the war. The flight to the Netherlands of the Kaiser as commander-in-chief and of the crown prince as the supreme commander of the largest army group was a constant line of attack which monarchist propaganda could do little to counter and which appealed to almost all political camps. In addition, advocates of democracy increasingly began to analyse whether other prominent individual Hohenzollerns had endured the battles, perils and horrors of the front as they so often claimed. A crown prince, clad all in white, playing tennis far from the front was a hard sell in post-war Germany, but attacks featuring that image were legion.[148]

In stark contrast to the accounts of their achievements and sacrifices in battle that filled the 'heroic memorial pamphlets' published by aristocratic families after 1918, the Hohenzollerns became increasingly branded as 'one of those rare German families who didn't lose any members during the war'.[149] The Kaiser and his sons had run around in 'gleaming officers' uniforms', but none of them had suffered 'so much as a scratch'. This view persisted for decades and often occurred in conjunction with references to the 'fat wallets' of this 'family of heroes'. As one critic put it, 'the only battle this family ended victoriously was the battle for the princely compensation'.[150] In 1914, Prince August Wilhelm had broken some bones in a car accident behind the front. The left-wing press described those injuries as the result of a 'drunken joyride with some ladies' – and it was true that they were not the product of anything related to the fighting.[151]

Whatever people's opinion about the military capabilities of the princes, there was no disputing the fact that Hohenzollerns had spent the war not in the trenches wearing gas masks but in high-command positions on requisitioned aristocratic estates. The Left utterly rejected the idea that the Kaiser had been denied the opportunity to die in battle with his men in 1918. Wilhelm II's flight reflected nothing other than cowardice, newspaper readers as far away as Atlanta could read.[152] And critics recalled that the crown prince had been conspicuously cast as a swashbuckling cavalry officer and once rhapsodized about the sweetness of dying on horseback in battle. 'But the crown prince didn't die,' the social democratic press pointed out succinctly in 1932, adding that in four years Wilhelm had had ample opportunities to die a hero's death on the battlefield. Instead, in 1917, as the last German strongholds before Verdun were falling in 'homicidal slaughter', he had ordered by telegram from a Berlin jeweller '25 gold ladies' wristwatches with illuminated faces . . . for 25 beautiful ladies' who lived near his main quarters in Charleville.[153]

Citing both the bourgeois and the working-class ideal of labour, opponents increasingly dismissed the royal family's competence and contributions to a modern, meritocratic society. The family no longer had the job of representing a monarchist state, and, in a republic emphasizing the values of hard work, achievement and performance, traditional forms of aristocratic self-legitimation inevitably faced a profound crisis. The German princes had never been hardened in the proverbial storm of steel, nor were they compatible with the ideal of the 'worker' who would reorder the modern world.[154] Amidst constant references to princes' absence from the frontlines and lack of any activity that could be understood as labour, the aristocracy was dismissed as a collection of drones – a metaphor from the insect world that was hard to combat.[155] For instance, in 1929, an aristocrat who had broken with his class wrote of the crown prince and his brothers:

It's strange that the Kaiser's five sons are ashamed of living like drones. When the war came to an end, all of them were young enough to learn and practise a trade. They could have taken other German princes from former ruling families as role models.[156]

In pro-democracy eyes, the post-1918 Hohenzollern family combined the lack of any social contribution with immense demands for state support. A 1931 issue of *Vorwärts* wrote that, twenty-nine years previously, August Bebel had already asked what the crown prince actually had to show for himself. Now he was older and grey-haired – but he still hadn't achieved a thing.[157]

As the crown prince was allowed to return to Germany, foreign correspondents wrote of Eitel Friedrich trying his hand as a 'gardener', August Wilhelm setting up his folding chair next to 'Don't Walk on the Grass' signs in Potsdam's parks and painting cheerful landscapes in oil, and Oskar strolling through the streets of the garrison city 'entirely openly as a man who had nothing to do and little money to spend'. Sporadic princely apprenticeships in bourgeois careers such as banking went nowhere fast.[158] It wasn't until the generation of the Kaiser's grandchildren that they began to change, at least symbolically. When the crown prince's second-oldest son got a doctorate in economics and stuck his toe into the working world during his long periods abroad, the *Manchester Guardian* ran the headline 'A Hohenzollern Goes into Banking'.[159]

Nevertheless, journalists and other observers from proletarian and middle-class backgrounds largely remained in the dark as to what, in the absence of governmental and representative functions, the members of the former ruling family actually did with their time. It was obvious that the norms of work and leisure life didn't apply to the royals. But ordinary people had only vague ideas, rarely going beyond guesswork, accusation and caricature, about how the Hohenzollerns occupied themselves.

One eloquent illustration of how the Hohenzollerns and their spokesmen viewed the bourgeois triad of performance, achievement and wealth was a 1929 attempt to downplay the Kaiser's assets to roughly a third of the figures in public circulation. The key, Hohenzollern management argued, was not what any individual possessed, but rather the fact that the wealth in question had to be divided between sixteen households with forty-nine members. None of these forty-nine people probably ever considered working for their money. Aristocratic circles considered the idea of getting a job and paying one's way as absurd as the demand to be provided for from annual stipends, and existing wealth was assumed to be self-evident.[160] Foreign observers recorded the debates about royal wealth with interest and scorn, yielding a corpus of lasting images. In 1932, a radical right-wing French newspaper ran a caricature depicting the crown prince reclining on the back seat of a luxury limousine. The lovely young lady at his side asks: 'Say, Your Majesty, will you have to renounce your stipend as a prince if you become Kaiser?'[161]

The Hohenzollerns' attempt to evade the bourgeois and proletarian work ethic and to insist on the rectitude of their inherited, non-earned wealth didn't always proceed without friction. In early June 1926, the crown prince's staff and a 'Committee for the Battle Against a Popular Referendum' approached Walter von Molo, one of the Weimar Republic's most successful writers, a friend of Stresemann and the author of widely respected books about Schiller and Friedrich the Great, who seemed a likely candidate to sign a petition against the confiscation of royal assets. But the attempt to recruit Molo – particularly because his name was presumptuously added to the petition without his permission – was a publicity dud. In a full-page rebuttal in a pro-democracy newspaper, the bestselling author denounced being drafted into the royal propaganda ranks against his will and ironically distanced himself from the overtures and promises that he could become a crown prince advisor. He ended his missive with the words:

I'm not a member of any caste or clique. I only love hardworking people regardless of whether they call themselves bourgeois, noble or proletarian! . . . Work alone creates and maintains humanity.

Only working people give us a future. I despise all others from the deepest depths of my soul.[162]

At the same time as it was becoming increasingly difficult to justify the aristocratic lifestyle, the ideal and image of the aristocrat bon vivant who existed outside this world of rewards for labour still found support even in the Weimar Republic and inspired defiant rhetorical responses.[163] The idea that ordinary people had to try to become something while the nobility enjoyed the happy lot of being *born* something was recast in the 1920s.[164] Defenders of the monarchy and the ruling aristocracy always at least partly distanced themselves from the ideal of hard work: 'In a monarchy, the human being who is stands above the human being who achieves. Therein resides the superiority and the ethical substance of the form of state.'[165] As nebulous as talk of 'the human being who is' or, to paraphrase novelist Robert Musil,[166] human existence not fragmented by the demands and challenges of modern life may have been, many 1920s non-aristocrats, especially among the bourgeoisie, still believed in it. That notwithstanding, opponents of the aristocracy continued to search for exemplary personifications of the high-born wastrel and found a number of candidates in the House of Hohenzollern, which came to represent the 'nobility', the military and the upper classes in general.

Two figures particularly stood out as work-shy 'spendthrifts'. Empress Victoria Augusta's brother-in-law Friedrich Leopold of Prussia, who was fifty-three years old in late 1918, was a fabulously wealthy son from one of the ancillary Hohenzollern bloodlines and a former general in the Prussian army who had raised the red flag at his hunting lodge near Klein-Glienicke at the onset of the German revolution.[167] In his youth, he had been considered the 'wealthiest unmarried prince in Europe' and a 'dandy from head to toe', whose meteoric rise through the ranks in the Prussian army prior to 1914 had been admired as far away as America.[168] His identically named son, who was twenty-three at the end of the First World War, had been exempt from frontline service and had spent 1914 to 1918 painting and collecting art in various palaces and castles from Lugano to Glienicke to his family's west Prussian estates. He lived relatively openly with his homosexual partner. The pomp-and-circumstance and martial trappings of the main branch of the family remained foreign to the younger Friedrich Leopold, with his fondness for mink coats and cashmere.[169] In many respects, he was the opposite of his two brothers, one of whom had fallen at the front in 1917 while the other, a nationally renowned equestrian, would die ten years later – together with his horse – after a fall.[170]

Advocates of democracy were never particularly fond of either the father or the son. Putting even the eccentric dandyism of Oscar Wilde and Marcel Proust to shame, this pair of bon vivants were perceived as being incompatible both with the ideals and demands of republicans and with the lifestyle of the rest of their extended clan. The hostility persisted even after Friedrich Leopold *père* resigned from the Hohenzollern family association and joined the left-wing German Democratic Party (DDP). It was even said that he refused to swear the oath of loyalty the Kaiser's brother had demanded of all family members.[171] After the raising of the red flag, legend had it, Friedrich Leopold's estate had been 'stormed' by a lieutenant loyal to the Kaiser who had restored order by hoisting the red, white and black imperial German standard in its place – a bit of provincial farce that amused the international press. The prince soon left Potsdam for Italy and Switzerland, but he remained a potent symbol in Potsdam and Germany as a whole, and the scorn heaped upon his alleged thirty-seven pairs of black, patent-leather shoes and boots and his skin-tight riding britches, in which he was unable to sit or bend down, went on for decades. The Hohenzollern family repeatedly tried to have both father and son placed under conservatorship, and the republicans sought to extend a legal action originally taken by Wilhelm II as the 'head of the house' against his cousin. That attempt was dismissed in 1921.[172]

Pro-democracy advocates criticized the two men's sale of irreplaceable works of art and the liquidation of property republicans considered state property. The prince repeatedly sought to sell parts of the renowned park grounds on the River Havel as land for construction. He also had plans drawn up to build a hotel.[173] Social democrats in both the regional parliament and the Reichstag fretted over the whereabouts of a flute that had once belonged to Friedrich the Great, which together with art of immense value was in the prince's possession. Between 1921 and 1924, Friedrich Leopold sued to retain control over his estate in Fatow-Krojanke, which at almost 22,000 hectares was almost a miniature state in itself and had been valued before the war at 25.7 million marks. In addition, the German finance minister transferred 1.7 million marks in gold francs to Switzerland to cover the debts father and son had racked up there. Other lawsuits filed by Friedrich Leopold *père* concerned capital investments, the Palace of the Order of Saint John in central Berlin, authority over the district of Düppel-Dreilinden and his estates in Klein-Glienicke.

In June 1924, his lawyers, employing legal 'sleight of hand' in various forms, won a significant victory before the national Reich Court.[174] The case set a major precedent for later lawsuits filed by the main branch of the Hohenzollern family and for the larger conflict over legal definitions of what assets of former ruling royal houses could be considered private property. Immediately after the verdict in question, pro-democratic voices objected that, because of the judge in charge of the case, all legal argumentation was 'hopeless' and that the only thing left was to 'suffer without complaint'. Republican objections established themselves in the public consciousness but had no legal traction. As one critic sarcastically asked his readers, 'Did no one ever teach you that the burgrave of Nuremberg bought the Mark Brandenburg in 1415 with money from his own purse and that, strictly speaking, you are all tenants who can be happy that Wilhelm doesn't demand the rent?'[175]

At the same time as scandals were being created about individual members of the Hohenzollern clan, the public was also given more precise public depictions of other figures, events and places. The Berlin court's verdict finding Eitel Friedrich guilty of illegally transferring money, the debate about how to view the vast sums of royal wealth, the image of spendthrift, physically and psychologically bloated princes and the constant, emotionally heated journalistic reports ultimately gave rise to bitter verbal sparring and tumultuous scenes in the Reichstag.[176]

Democratic critics of the royal family focused on dissecting not only individuals but symbolic locations and pastimes. The casino in Campione, a picturesque Italian exclave on the shores of Lake Lugano in the Swiss canton of Ticino, which opened in 1917, became the epitome of post-feudal decadence. If contemporary accounts are accurate, the casino, which had been a nest of spies in the final year of the war, served as a kind of Magic Mountain for Europe's deposed princes, who spent entire nights at the gambling tables winning and, more frequently, losing fortunes. Among them was Prince Friedrich Leopold as well as the youngest of the Kaiser's sons, Joachim, who was often accompanied there by his older brother Eitel Friedrich. The Hohenzollerns even purchased villas in the town of Castagnola on the banks of the lake.[177] News of the royal family's swanky life-style in Ticino travelled far and wide. A newspaper in Minnesota, for instance, reported that Crown Prince Friedrich had urged Italy's King Victor Emmanuel III to shut the casino where his cousin and youngest brother were losing vast sums of money. Indeed, the gambling house would in fact shut its doors in the summer of 1919.[178] Attempts within the Hohenzollern family to plug leaks by having members put under 'conservatorship' are evidence of the increasing difficulty it had in keeping the clan's wealth in the hands of the 'head of the house' under the new conditions.

But scandalizing accounts of embezzlement, crass inequality and obscene wastefulness didn't benefit the republican camp in the long term. On the contrary, talk of deceit, corruption and wartime profiteering turned into a powerful instrument of the political Right. At the same time as a settlement was being reached with the Hohenzollerns, right-wing propagandists were able to turn the narrative of corrupt, decadent princes on its head thanks to the 1924–5 'Barmat scandal'. One of the most spectacular stories of corruption in the Weimar era, it centred on Ukrainian-born Jew Julius Barmat, whose crooked investment company cost the Prussian state several million marks and implicated a number of social democrats. The far Right seized on the affair to connect the ideas of wartime profiteering, fat cats, illicit financial deals and corruption with Jews, democracy and the Weimar Republic.[179] The basic constellation of 'Jewish interlopers' cheating the German public would be reprised in the similar 'Sklarek scandal' later in the decade. In the war of images and slogans, improprieties like these helped distract from financial irregularities within the conservative camp. The figure of the Jewish crook became – as an illustrated book with an introduction by the brother of right-wing philosopher Ernst Jünger put it – the 'face of democracy'. In 1926, amidst the great propaganda battle over whether the Hohenzollerns should be stripped of their wealth, Nazis drove trucks around German cities with giant billboards reading: 'Disappropriate the princes' assets – Barmat needs money!'[180]

Potsdam Guerillas

As long as the Kaiser and the crown prince remained in exile, the Kaiser's sons Eitel Friedrich, Oskar and August Wilhelm took on representative functions, and Potsdam, where they and the crown prince's sons resided in their estates and villas, was one of the most important symbolic and organizational bases of reactionaries. From the earliest days of the Weimar Republic, monarchists and democrats battled to determine the symbolic significance of places. Military cadets lining up in rows for inspection by General Ludendorff and Prince Eitel Friedrich attracted keen attention abroad and started violent altercations in many places in Germany.[181] Potsdam and in particular the Garrison Church became one of the most important locations for right-wing marches and events following 1918. Here, a bewildering variety of small and large organizations and associations found somewhere to deploy their multitude of forms and colours. Again and again, male and female members took on central roles in such mass events.[182]

The symbolic battle for Potsdam was waged across three generations. The crown prince's two eldest sons, Wilhelm and Louis Ferdinand, attended the city's military academy in the 1920s. The two brothers, who as small children had already ridden with elite cavalry troops and had grown up around their grandfather, the Kaiser, continued to enjoy a special status in 1920s Potsdam. One aristocratic classmate, who described the awestruck deference with which the Prussian princes were treated, recalled teachers simply ignoring the results of the German revolution. He described one school building: 'In the auditorium three gigantic paintings depicting the royal couple and eagles flying around Hohenzollern Castle – no one would have thought of taking them down after 1918.'[183] In an early version of his 1952 memoirs, in which he would try to pass himself off as a democratic, easy-going, cosmopolitan aristocrat, the crown prince's son Louis Ferdinand described his older brother and himself becoming leaders at school, in their class and in Potsdam in general. It was, to borrow a sports term, a home match. In concordance with other sources, Louis Ferdinand, who gleefully styled himself as a 'rebel prince', wrote of his monarchist teachers, hard work, broad interests, sporting achievements and his experience together with his brother making their mark on a Potsdam that was anything but democratic.[184]

The republican camp was occasionally successful at challenging right-wing anti-Weimar symbolism, but it failed to establish predominance. One instructive example of the tug-of-war between republican and monarchist symbolism was the visit paid in October 1924 by the French-German literature scholar Victor Basch to a conference on world peace.[185] A freemason, supporter of Dreyfus, member of pacifist French organizations and an advocate of French–German reconciliation,[186] Basch was invited by the League of Human Rights to hold a talk in the Potsdam Concert House. But conference organizers had overestimated conservatives' willingness to tolerate a speaker who was not only a Frenchman, an intellectual and a pacifist, but a Jew born in Budapest. Indeed, bringing a person who embodied everything the Right loathed to Potsdam was the equivalent of hoisting the Prussian eagle in Alpine Bavaria. Pro-democracy organizers were no doubt well aware of this and sought to exploit Basch's visit for its symbolic political value. The Stahlhelm militia marched throughout the city in protest, the conference was forced to change venues and required massive protection from police and pro-Weimar Republic Reichsbanner units, whom the right-wing radicals mocked as 'cardboard helmets'. Reports of the confrontation were shot through with hostile right-wing stereotypes of a republic rendered defenceless by 'lame' civilians and undisciplined, slack democrats who allowed themselves to be photographed in bathing suits, exposing Potsdam to ridicule.[187] For his part, Basch tried to build a bridge in his speech between 1920s Weimar Germany and an idealized Germany around 1800, passing over the imperial Wilhelmine era. Germany, Basch argued, would blossom into a centre of European culture. Following Basch at the speaker's podium was Ferdinand Buisson, an 83-year-old French pedagogue, educational politician and Parisian pacifist, who would be honoured with the Nobel Peace Prize in 1927 together with German pacifist Ludwig Quidde.

Conservative newspapers railed against the 'Baschists', moaning that intolerable insults had been publicly hurled in 'the city of the great Friedrich'. The Stahlhelm pledged their readiness to a man to prevent the 'marvellous Monsieur Brasch under any circumstances' from taking the stage. In the Prussian parliament, the conservative-nationalist DNVP formally enquired whether Basch had made a joke calling monarchists 'Potsdam idiots'. The Reichsbanner militiamen were defamed as the 'traditional troop of deserters and mutineers' and the 'bodyguards of the French', and left-wing activities in Potsdam's hotbed of monarchists were decried as something close to sacrilege, with one conservative declaring: 'Potsdam is holy ground! A soldiers' city!'[188]

The social democrats had specifically chosen the garrison as a symbol of the cultured 'spirit of Weimar', taking the offensive against the militarist-monarchist 'spirit of Potsdam.'[189] This pacifist, social-democratic attempt to stage a pro-democracy 'Potsdam Day' would persist in local memory. In March 1933, when the Nazis organ-ized their own Potsdam Day, Basch's appearance was recalled as a moment of national shame, endured by the city populace with manly fortitude.[190] In fact, the pacifist event was a fleeting, atypical moment. During the German occupation of France many years later, the then eighty-year-old Basch would be arrested together with his wife in Lyon by French militias and both were murdered by the head of the city's Gestapo.

In 1924, *Vorwärts* had written, 'The youths of the Stahlhelm and the German racists of Potsdam believed they could defend their ter-ritorial dictatorship in the city, if nowhere else.' The paper went on to skewer 'the terrible reign of brainlessness' and – referring to the alliance between the Stahlhelm and the racists – 'black, white and red swastika terror'. Such choices of words reflected the sort of street politics that would be increasingly dominated by the Right in the years to come.[191] Within the conflict, the Kaiser's sons, residing in Potsdam, were significant political beacons.

Historians have used the term 'street politics' to analyse various forms of conflict in Wilhelmine Germany, primarily taking place between parts of the labour movement and the authorities.[192] With a pinch of irony, it could also be turned on its head to describe the guerilla warfare waged by the Right and the Hohenzollerns against the Weimar Republic from its inception to its final days. The gueril-las in this metaphor were members of an indigenous population (the populace of an imaginary empire led by the Kaiser) waging a small-scale war against external occupiers (democrats, socialists and Jews), during which they exploited familiarity with the terrain and operated a multitude of bases. In 1921, the *New York Times* indeed described monarchist counter-revolutionaries in Germany and their paramilitary organizations as 'guerrilla chieftains'.[193] This was a rea-sonable characterization of the militaristic segments of the German Right. Chairman Mao famously remarked that guerilla fighters had to move through their environment like fish in water.[194] In Potsdam and elsewhere, anti-democratic groups, with whom the Hohenzo-llerns were deeply interwoven, could count on that level of support among a segment of the populace and the military, police and court apparatuses.

The metaphor of guerilla warfare is also appropriate given the militarist aggression at right-wing events, which not infrequently ended in physical violence. The 'street politics' of anti-democratic groupings was always aimed at establishing symbolic dominance over streets, public squares, buildings and days of memorial. Everyone involved understood that laying down markers was a way of staking a claim to rule – this is the only way of comprehending the bloody determination with which symbols and emblems were fought over in the Weimar Republic.[195] Anti-democratic groups combined organized presence, physical confrontation and paramilitary violence with a set of symbols every bit as vivid and complex as those of the political Left. Even before 1914 it had been hard to fully comprehend the dynamics of the street politics and the 'men who felt most German'.[196] Now there was nothing civil about the 'civil war' pro-democrats accused the Stahlhelm of fomenting.[197] The basic tenets of militias of street brawlers who purported to be defending Germany were to never forget the previous war, continue behaving in war-like fashion and prepare for the war to come.

A complementary component was the Right's loudly proclaimed contempt for the 'system', which recurred through the discourse of the Hohenzollerns, right-wing associations and nationalist intellectuals. 'The day on which the parliamentary state collapses in our grasp, we will proclaim a national dictatorship and it will be our highest holiday,' wrote Ernst Jünger in 1925 with typical subtlety.[198] More and more, the Right saw hatred for political enemies as an emotion to be encouraged.[199] In the 1928 'Finsterwalde Declaration of Hate', endorsed by Prince Oskar, Stahlhelm leader Elhard von Morozowicz summarized the right-wing credo:

> We hate the edifice of the state as it blocks our efforts to liberate both our enslaved fatherland and the German people from the lie of war guilt and for winning the necessary space to live in the East that will make the German people free again.[200]

Pictures and reports of members of the House of Hohenzollern prominently appearing at anti-democratic events can be found for every year, indeed every season. Here, too, reality, perception and hearsay intermingled. During the unsuccessful Kapp Putsch of 1920, for instance, Eitel Friedrich, once accused of betraying his father back in Germany, was mooted as a potential successor to the throne.[201] Not infrequently, critics supposed rather than demonstrated Hohenzollern involvement in counter-revolutionary activities. Foreign observers saw Prince Oskar's anti-democratic speeches and symbolic appearance beside Hindenburg at monarchist funerals – as well as the crown princess's sale of a painting by Dutch master Meindert Hobbema worth 300,000 marks and considered by the SPD to be state property – as an indication that the royal family was preparing to step up its battle against the Weimar Republic.[202]

The reconfiguration of individual groups on the political Right gradually changed their styles, codes and concepts of honour. Dividing lines between the behaviour of the imperial armed forces and the open brutality of the radical right wing in the Weimar Republic blurred. The shifts proceeded slowly, over two decades, and took place in a grey area of countless tiny intersections. For example, in 1926, when Prince Oskar wrote a friendly note and sent a pack of cigarettes to an imprisoned would-be assassin who had planned to murder Stresemann, he crossed a line that was immediately publicly identified and discussed. A pro-Weimar satirical magazine published a cartoon featuring an exquisite carved wooden box full of equally exquisitely rolled cigarettes and a photographic portrait of Prince Oskar. With sarcastic reference to demands that the royal prince should be reminded of his duty to defend the republic, the caption read: 'We oppose this measure most decisively. You can't demand the world of those whose loyalties lie abroad.' The situation was similar with a provocative visit paid by August Wilhelm to a prisoner accused of murdering a member of the Reichsbanner.[203] The pro-democracy camp knew nothing in the 1920s of the champagne uncorked in Doorn when Rathenau and

Erzberger were assassinated, but the royal family's increasingly frequent participation in growing anti-republican activism was followed in minute detail. Merely nostalgic reminiscences about allegedly better times gone by were as infrequent in Doorn as they were among the politically active Hohenzollerns in Potsdam and Berlin.

The brutalization of political culture manifested itself in changes to symbols and language. People talked about violence differently, and political violence had a different public status, with conservative elites, including the Hohenzollerns, increasingly not only accepting, but openly embracing it. [204] The royal family's basic mode of behaviour became militaristic and confrontational. In 1920, the surgeon and writer Carl Ludwig Schleich landed a bestseller with his memoirs, entitled *Sun-Kissed Past*,[205] and there was definitely a market for idyllic portrayals of better, peaceful days gone by. But the Hohenzollerns contributed nothing to this trend. Royal family members weren't interested in the contemplative search for an idealized past but in the violent conquest of a better future. The idea of dreamy nostalgia, of a melancholy rededication to better days gone by, theoretically fitted in well with the conservative tradition, but it was entirely unsuitable to the aggressive posturing of the House of Hohenzollern.[206]

Prussian authorities suspected Prince Eitel Friedrich of being aware of or even somehow involved in vigilante far-right murders of figures considered traitors, including the assassination of Rathenau, but those suspicions never hardened into concrete accusations.[207] The lines between Freikorps paramilitaries, radical right-wing secret societies and organizations in the Potsdam military milieu were indistinct. In 1927, at a time when one of the Kaiser's sons was being named in court as a possible planner of a political assassination, Eitel Friedrich, Oskar and August Wilhelm were provocatively marching through Berlin alongside Carl Eduard von Saxe-Coburg and Gotha, already a member of the Nazi Party, 'in the first instance as Stahlhelm men without any official rank'. Meanwhile the 'Prussian flag' was flown at the Old Palace on Unter den Linden, the Berlin residence of the 'empress' Hermine.[208] Some years later, the former King of Saxony, the crown prince and princess and their eldest son participated at a Stahlhelm rally in Breslau, mockingly nicknamed the 'parade of the princely fawners'.[209]

The constant movements of the so-called empress Hermine, who used parts of the Old Palace and the Dutch Palace both as a private dwelling and a 'residence', were interpreted as speculative indicators of whether Wilhelm II was getting ready to return to Germany.[210] While Berlin and Potsdam remained the centres of the monarchist anti-democracy movement, the conflicts igniting there also spread to countless other parts of the country. These weren't always merely symbolic.[211] In May 1924, a purported 200,000 men took part in a nationalist rally in the city of Halle that marked the re-erection of a statue of Field Marshal Helmuth von Moltke that had been torn down by communists. The marchers came from various segments of society but contained a heavily racist, ultra-nationalist component. A motley mix of Stahlhelm and Wehrwolf paramilitary groups, veterans' associations, shooting guilds, vocal clubs, fraternities and the like paraded for hours in front of far-right general Erich Ludendorff, while speakers called for a 'new empire' and the unification of 'all Germans living in Central Europe'. Ludendorff and Prince Oskar 'inspected' the 'troops'. Events of this nature occupied whole cities. One eyewitness described how 'straight as ramrods and enthusiastic, the men pass by – battalions, regiments, divisions, whole armies'.[212] Swastika flags waved next to Stahlhelm symbols, and one of the stars of the show was Prince Oskar. When marchers ran into a communist counter-demonstration, the result was hours of street fighting using batons, knives and handguns, leaving people dead and seriously injured. Newspapers reported that one police officer and ten 'communists' had been killed. Prince Oskar's role in this 'putschist march' became the subject of heated debate in the Prussian parliament.[213]

Around the same time, the crown prince caused a stir by visiting the Dutch Embassy in Berlin. A potential diplomatic row was avoided when the visit was declared 'private', but Britain's *Observer* newspaper saw this as a new tactic in which Wilhelm would appear as a private citizen and let others do the political work behind the scenes. It was an accurate bit of analysis. The crown prince's new role was in part an extension of his activity as an army group leader, during which his leadership was largely symbolic, while others did the military work. It was also a continuation of his period of exile, when his publicity staff wrote his books and texts while he sought to emerge from his father's shadow, posing for photographers and serving as the subject of symbolic images.[214]

The general perception of German supporters of democracy and foreign journalists was correct. The Hohenzollerns were increasingly present and active in the anti-democratic movement, lending it their symbolic weight. Nervous republicans registered not only the constant, ritualistic right-wing marches, but also the political character of supposedly private encounters and the various displays of public sympathy for the Kaiser's sons in places such as Potsdam. Officially, it was a private occasion when former imperial army generals, the crown prince and his other brothers gathered in August Wilhelm's villa to celebrate Wilhelm II's birthday, but the hundreds of supporters who assembled outside to cheer clearly made it a political event.[215] Individual figures, including the crown princess, were perceived as exercising particular influence. In 1924, foreign observers considered her the most popular person in Germany, while portraying the crown prince as a calm, calculating 'Machiavelli', reserving his 'sword' for the most opportune moment.[216]

Pro-democracy advocates couldn't understand the mass popularity of members of the House of Hohenzollern, and their bewilderment was reflected in their accounts of the situation. They were dumbfounded that socialist scorn heaped upon the royal family did nothing to decrease support for the clan among broad segments of the populace. In 1926, the crown prince caused a stir when he attended an indoor cycling race in Berlin's Sportpalast arena. A Swiss newspaper described the 'infernal spectacle' as the mood among some of the spectators soured and turned against the unusual onlooker. A cardboard sign was dangled on a string from the upper rows, reading: 'Not a pfennig for the princes. All the money for the racers!' The crown prince manfully put an end to this provocation by grabbing the sign and tearing it to pieces. When the arena announcer stated that the 'well-known sports supporter from Oels' had pledged a 500-mark prize for the race winner, tumult broke out, and the police had to intervene. It's impossible to precisely reconstruct the sequence of events in the Sportpalast.[217] But the appearance of a German crown prince at a sporting event that was part of Berlin working-class culture was clearly something remarkable, as was the strong emotional reaction his presence elicited.

Supporters of the Weimar Republic were particularly concerned about obeisance and all other forms of positive reaction towards the crown prince. The year prior to the tumult in the Sportpalast, the crown prince made a considerably more successful appearance in a friendlier environment, the aforementioned Silesian Regional Association in a Breslau circus, where the heir to the throne was greeted with standing ovations. Association chairman Baron Prätorius von Richthofen had nothing good to say in his speech about the Weimar Republic and German democracy, and social democrats demanded an 'investigation' after it was reported that a civil servant, who owed his loyalty to the democratically elected government, had kissed Wilhelm's hand.[218] It was noted that the crown prince had, at that moment, 'emerged' from his political non-involvement.[219] It was five days later that *Vorwärts* published the aforementioned cartoon depicting the crown prince as a circus show rider performing for adoring audiences in front of an impresario whose jacket was covered with swastikas.[220]

Not long after this successful test appearance near Wilhelm's Silesian estate, French sources reported him showing up at a horse race in Berlin, accompanied by a retinue of German princes. Officers in eighteenth-century uniforms rode in formation for him, and some 5,000 spectators serenaded him with the German national anthem.[221] Two weeks later, following the death of the German president Friedrich Ebert, a French newspaper speculated on whether the crown prince could possibly succeed him. That article closed by recalling the millions of dead in the First World War and predicted the emergence of a German revanchism, led by Wilhelm, that would cost significantly more lives.[222] Around this time, the crown prince remarked privately to confidants that he didn't see himself as either a private citizen or a farmer and that he knew little about agriculture: 'In terms of my nature and inclinations, I'm primarily a soldier and a political leader.'[223]

The constant flag waving, regimental days, military memorial ceremonies and parades were a thorn in the side of many democrats. Prohibitions, cordons and attempts to symbolically 'protect' military barracks from Hohenzollern wreath-laying had very limited success.[224] The arcane rituals of knighthood under the Order of St John in the presence of the Hohenzollerns, extremely difficult for laypeople to understand, led to angry polemics against the 'small-minded followers of authority who would rather be hounded from one war to the next than give up their reverence of princes and the lickspittles who slink in front of the gates of aristocratic castles, ecstatic whenever they catch sight of a couple of general's bars'.[225] Outrage, scorn and bewilderment were all evident in an account of a ritual during which Prince Oskar appeared, on behalf of his father, before a huge imperial German flag in the guards' club on Sophien-strasse in Berlin. It quoted Oskar as saying: 'In the name of my father, His Majesty Wilhelm II, I am charged with presenting the silver *Fahnennagel* [a small metal military decoration].'[226]

This arcane ritual in the 'theatre of the monarchy'[227] obviously had great emotional value, as did the so-called battle of the flags, the intensely bitter debate about the Weimar Republic's public representation domestically and internationally.[228] The political duel between the democratic black, red and gold and the conservative, monarchist black, white and red persisted throughout the Republic and even brought down a government in 1926. In Potsdam, where the DNVP-led local authorities often blocked democratic organizations from using public spaces, support for monarchist symbols, including the imperial flag in public buildings and a picture of the

Kaisers in academies and school, was especially hardcore.[229] Military and conservatives circles maintained their own individual set of symbols despite all attempts to establish democratic alternatives. The struggle between these two symbolic worlds would rage on until ultimately both sides were overwhelmed and broken by Nazi symbolism.

The guerilla struggle waged by the Right against the Weimar Republic had political, symbolic and terrorist components, and it utilized forms of political communication not foreseen by Germany's democratic constitution. In salons, clubs and private estates, at horse races and on hunting expeditions, conservatives had little trouble creating forums advocates of democracy could neither understand nor access. By the mid-1920s, it was established practice for anti-democracy elites to come together in their own circles outside the institutions of the Republic.[230] Indeed, associations, state administrations, the courts, government ministries and above all the military were determined to tread upon those very institutions. The military leadership was as central to the 1918 revolution, the 1920 Kapp Putsch and the plans for a coup d'état in 1932 as it would prove to be in planning and fighting the later Nazi wars of conquest.

In 1926, as the settlement was being reached with the Hohenzollerns, one moment crystallized republican concerns about the growing monarchist charisma in the military. It was sparked by some fairly ordinary Reichswehr manoeuvres in Münsingen, south of Stuttgart. Taking part was twenty-year-old Prince Wilhelm of Prussia, the crown prince's eldest son, whom some monarchists considered a candidate for the throne. In keeping with family tradition, Wilhelm had joined the First Guard Infantry Regiment on his tenth birthday in 1926 and had been given the rank of lieutenant. The young man – an athlete, a law student and a member of the Stahlhelm's youth organization – took part in an exercise with the elite Infantry Regiment 9 in Potsdam, which had inherited the traditions of the Guard Regiment and was nicknamed 'Count 9' because of its large number of aristocratic members. The combination of the 'heir to the throne' and this elite regiment carried enormous symbolic weight among military enthusiasts, and reports of the prince's role in the manoeuvre spread swiftly through the entire German press. Initially, denials were issued, but the facts in this case were more than obvious.

At the start, journalists mistakenly reported the 'temporary engagement of the [crown prince's] eldest son in the Reichswehr'.[231] Once this error had been corrected, critics scoffed that the 'temporary Hohenzollern volunteer' would hardly have signed up for the normal twelve years of service.[232] That left the army leadership having to answer embarrassing questions about its recruitment practices, which violated agreed limits on Germany's remilitarization and which were closely monitored abroad.[233] Angry social democrats complained that monarchist traditions were being covertly continued and laws concerning a democratic army violated. They also objected that the left-wing Reichswehr minister, who had not been informed about the prince taking part in the manoeuvre, was being made into a mere 'harlequin'.[234] The affair might seem like a triviality or something from a comic opera, social democrats warned, but the Republic could not accept 'the officers corps and troops being men indoctrinated in right-wing circles and with a mentality bred in officers' clubs and common soldiers' boozers that was diametrically opposed to that of democratically minded segments of societies'.[235] One of the most renowned generals of the old German army would later remark about the imperial officers corps: 'The officers were as a matter of course trained morally, and we didn't tolerate democrats or Marxists in our ranks.'[236] This was basically the same attitude that had applied in 1926.

Rhetorical broadsides from other members of the House of Hohenzollern poured more oil on the fire. By the time of the Kapp Putsch, Germans had to ask where Reichswehr leaders stood on the Weimar Republic and how much influence monarchist undercurrents had on the military leadership. At a monarchist rally in Nuremberg, Prince Oskar had proclaimed: 'I bring you the greetings of our family's younger recruits who hope they can serve in a resurrected German army.'[237] Journalists at *Vorwärts* began to comb the military rolls in search of officers with the title 'prince' in their names. They found what they were looking for in Saxony[238] and interpreted the affair surrounding Prince Wilhelm as a test of strength between the Republic and 'militarism'.[239]

Who was responsible for the scandal? It soon emerged that the DDP Reichswehr Minister Otto Gessler – a southern German lawyer with no military experience – was pretty much the only one who had not been informed about what was going on.[240] That spoke volumes about the relations of power between political authorities and the military leadership. As a political consequence of the affair, the monocle-wearing head of the army command, General Hans von Seeckt, was forced to submit his resignation, which Hindenburg reluctantly accepted. Conservatives suspected a plot by the Entente's supervising military authorities, while left-wing democrats believed they had uncovered the start of a monarchist putsch. The affair illustrated three things about the Hohenzollerns: their increasing assertiveness, their connection with the Reichswehr leadership and the immense commotion even a young Hohenzollern prince could generate by publicly appearing in uniform.

In the *Berliner Tageblatt* newspaper, Theodor Wolff, one of Germany's leading left-wing democratic journalists, drew attention to a long-standing French regulation that barred the heir to the throne and his children from entering the country and prohibited the other French princes from assuming positions in the army, the parliament and the civil service. Wolff contrasted that with the situation in Germany not just within the Reichswehr but also in positions of leadership throughout the Weimar Republic: 'Never before has there been a state in which hostile pretenders to the throne, who hope for the fall of that state, have been accepted into the ranks of the army.'[241] Carl von Ossietsky used similar words in *Weltbühne*, writing that a comparable affront 'would have been unthinkable even in the darkest days of the French republic'. He added: 'There is no republic in the world where the pretender to monarchic legitimacy is allowed to do an internship in the army . . . alternately in civilian dress and in uniform – in part even in the uniform of the old armed forces.'²⁴² Observers also noted the special ambitions of the crown princess, to which she devoted considerable energy, exploiting personal connections, to bring her eldest son into close proximity with the Reichswehr.²⁴³

At least some of the foreign press interpreted Seeckt's dismissal and the negative reaction to the prince's symbolic participation in the military manoeuvre as a sign that the Weimar Republic was establishing itself.²⁴⁴ In London, the *Economist* wrote of the 'Hohenzollern nuisance'.²⁴⁵ In the tone it took and the result it achieved, the Republic acted with an astonishing stringency considering its shakiness in the years to come. Even moderate voices described the decisive stance of republicans as 'the first time the new regime has provided a welcome display of self-confidence and energy'.²⁴⁶

The Hohenzollerns' overall image in the 1920s suffered from insurmountable shortcomings. With its members scattered across various places, the family had no recognizable geographical centre. The performance of the Kaiser and his sons at the front had been meagre, hardly measuring up to the most important post-war trope of the far Right: the trench-tested warrior. Nor did the public wrangling over assets, which lawyers argued were private property, lend much glory to the family. Portraits of princes doing gardening and painting landscapes were ill-suited to increasing the Hohenzollerns' prestige or combating the oft-used drone metaphor. The situation was exacerbated by the family's inability to prevent members' private lives from being dissected by an anti-aristocratic or merely voyeuristic public.

Crumbling Façades

Individual scandals and crass violations of the rules and standards of the world gone by heightened internal Hohenzollern family tensions. Among them was the short-lived 1927 marriage of the Kaiser's sister Viktoria to the Russian taxi-dancer and swindler Alexander

Zoubkov, thirty-five years her junior, who not only ruined the princess's reputation but relieved her of much of her substantial fortune.[247] The resulting scorn continued even after the princess's death in 1929. The *Irish Times* reported on the passing of the bankrupt 'Frau Zoubkov', and English newspapers mocked the 'Zubkov sale' in Bonn, at which portraits of the crown prince were flogged off at laughable prices.[248]

The family's economic losses and fragmentation shattered old customs and forced members to search for new ones. Making matters worse was a previously unthinkable series of divorces – three alone among the crown prince's brothers – and laboriously maintained façades that could never completely conceal the failed marriages like the one between the crown prince and Cecilie. The veneer protecting royal self-depictions quickly peeled off under the constant scuttlebutt, press hostility, divorce trials, petitions to declare family members mentally unfit and countless rumours bandied about in far-off America.[249] Together with the intense rivalries within the family itself, all this made the potential heirs to the throne seem, to the outside world, flighty and morally ambiguous.

The mass media reported fairly discretely about the suicide of the Kaiser's youngest son, Joachim, whose wife allegedly cheated on him with another swindler, but the press still passed on the fact that his parents in Doorn had refused to grant their blessing for a divorce, after which the prince shot himself in one of his brother's Potsdam villas.[250] International reporters blamed the suicide on his impending marital separation, his congenitally weak nerves, his purported 'paranoid' personality, his fear of losing everything because of decisions beyond his control and all manner of speculative causes. What were well-documented were his serious psychological problems, his broken marriage and his toxic relationship with his father.[251] Joachim, who was twenty-nine when he killed himself, left behind a young son, prompting a highly public, years-long custody battle between the mother, Princess Marie Auguste von Anhalt, and representatives of the Hohenzollern family.

The Kaiser's second-eldest son, Eitel Friedrich, divorced in 1926, but the alleged infidelity and 'inappropriate' behaviour of his wife, Sophie Charlotte von Oldenburg, had attracted negative publicity and prompted legal action all the way back to 1919.[252] In 1922, Eitel Friedrich sued at least four German newspapers for reporting on her purported affairs, with the disputed details including such banalities as whether the princess had kissed a certain Baron Plettenberg or merely spoken with him on the telephone.[253] This litigiousness did little good one way or the other since the reported details of his and his wife's private lives had already been disseminated by the New York press. Love letters were read out loud in German courtrooms, while papers in New York gleefully told the story of the princess's 'unrestrained passion' and the 'remarkable Hohenzollern family scandal'.[254]

Four years later, the marriage was finally terminated. The reasons cited by the court were neglect and emotional cruelty – a real sensation, as one Baltimore newspaper remarked.[255] After the divorce, the princess married a younger ex-cavalry officer-turned-police-officer and became active in politics. In 1930, she was one of the first high-level German aristocrats to formally join the Nazi Party. Eitel Friedrich continued to live in the oversized Villa Ingenheim on Lake Templin in Potsdam. During the divorce proceedings, the prince accused his wife, a renowned beauty from one of the wealthiest and most well-respected northern German aristocratic families, of aspiring to be a 'movie star'. In response, the princess called her husband a 'degenerate'. Seats in the court gallery were given exclusively to family members, as the New York press reported in 1926.[256] When the prince resigned from his position as grand master of the Order of St John in the wake of his divorce, the social democratic press compared the scandal to a bit of theatre 'from the early Middle Ages'.[257]

The divorce of Eitel Friedrich's probably homosexual young brother August Wilhelm in 1920 also attracted damaging publicity. A Hohenzollern family physician testified that the wife, Princess Alexandra zu Schleswig-Holstein-Sonderburg-Glücksburg, suffered from 'nymphomania'; and her affairs with 'underlings' caused unusually hurtful scandals. The court presiding over the divorce deemed her solely responsible for the failed marriage, and custody of their seven-year-old son was awarded to August Wilhelm.[258] The princess then married a former navy officer below her station and led an unconventional life as an artist, for many years in the United States.[259]

There were also wild reports from 1919 onwards, apparently stitched together from various rumours, that the crown princess was also mulling over a divorce. They had a certain credibility because of Wilhelm's notorious lifestyle, even though they had no basis in fact. Readers as far away from Europe as San Francisco were treated to warmed-over gossip that the crown prince abused his wife and that Cecilie had fled to Switzerland to seek refuge with her Russian mother, whose life was full of an impressive set of scandals all her own. The crown princess had been stopped at the Swiss border, the story went, and sent back to Berlin.[260] Rumour also had it that the only thing preventing a divorce was the express wish of Empress Viktoria Augusta, an idea that persisted for years. The ever-observant personal physician of the Kaiser and the empress, by contrast, considered the crown princess 'too clever' for a divorce.[261] Mixing factual details about a marriage that was mere façade, rumours and the stuff of penny dreadfuls, the *Washington Post* devoted a whole page to a portrait of the crown princess as a woman humiliated and physically abused by her husband, who had been prevented from fleeing and dreamed of living in the US. A large drawing depicted Cecilie cowering on the floor in fear of the raised fist of her uniformed husband.[262] Reports of this sort would combine salaciousness and voyeurism with elements from a real struggle for power as long as the family was not completely demystified and was held up for judgement according to its own proclaimed standards.

The blurring of reality and perception, facts and rumours, gave all depictions of this fractured ruling dynasty in a democratic country an unreal, theatrical quality. In the period in question, a former paramilitary and an impoverished young ethnic German from what is now Latvia, Harry Domela, caused a national stir by passing himself off as the young Prince Wilhelm. After becoming homeless and working selling cigarettes in the 1920s, Domela learned how to imitate aristocratic mannerisms and invented a title for himself. His physical resemblance to Wilhelm gave rise to rumours that he was actually the Kaiser's grandson, leading him to be invited to aristocratic soirees and stays at luxury hotels. He was arrested in 1927 and immediately composed a bestselling memoir translated into English as *A Sham Prince: The Life and Adventures of Harry Domela as Written by Himself in Prison at Cologne, January to June 1927.*[263]

Domela became a darling of the left-wing media. His story illustrated how trapped the Weimar Republic remained in the mores of the Wilhelmine era with all its servility, obsession with status, illusions, lies and deceits.[264] The lines drawn between the values the royal family ostensibly embodied and pure theatre, indeed farce, were increasingly dissolving. But the Hohenzollerns weren't the only ones at fault. In Jean-Paul Sartre's theatrical Dumas adaptation *Kean*, the title protagonist, an actor, personifies the blurring of what a person is and what the public wants to see in him. In one scene, Kean tells the audience: 'Behold the man. Look at him. Why don't you applaud? Isn't it strange. You only care for illusion . . . Listen – I am going to tell you something. I am not alive – I only pretend. Ladies and gentlemen – your humble servant.'[265]

Kean's 'confession' is relevant to nearly all the scenarios in which the 'aristocracy' communicated with observers. Kings don't exist without an audience. By 1930, this truism applied not only to the figure of the 'crown prince', which only existed as such thanks to the collaboration of millions of onlookers, critics and claqueurs. It also described the mechanism by which a painter of postcards was transformed into the 'Führer'.

From today's perspective, it is irrelevant to what extent the individual scandals, with their merging of reality, interpretation and supposition, were invented. What is significant is the astonishing intensity with which the political and personal details of the Hohenzollerns were followed even in places far from Germany – and how much and how quickly the scandalization of royal family members' private lives, which had been successfully prevented prior to 1918, corroded the Hohenzollerns' image. The many transgressions against conservative morality and the fragmentation of the family were both real and impossible to ignore.

As a result, it was increasingly difficult for the Hohenzollerns to plausibly depict themselves as an intact family unit embodying continuity of values and pointing the way towards a better future based on those venerable traditions. No longer were they able to personify the idea that the world of yesterday could be the world of tomorrow. A ruling dynasty disintegrating to the extent that the Hohenzollerns were might have been capable of attracting attention and bundling negative energy directed against the current 'system'. But it could no longer claim to represent the conservative values of the pre-war high aristocracy. Even conservatives had to admit that, under the circumstance, the Hohenzollerns could in no sense continue to embody change, morality, honour and order.

Many observers credited the monarchies in Scandinavia, the Netherlands and Britain with unifying citizens of their nations across party lines, but the prospect for anything like that in Germany was impossibly remote. The House of Hohenzollern was completely unsuitable for bringing together people across class and party divides – or symbolizing the long-existing idea of 'popular community' propagated by the Nazis and others. On the contrary, Germany's royals were active protagonists in a symbolic and de facto civil war. By the mid-1920s, the family was already less of a potential national unifier than one of the factions trying to bring down the Weimar Republic.

To an extent, the dissolution of traditional codes and standards of behaviour liberated Hohenzollerns as individuals, who enjoyed increasing opportunities to join new groups and redefine themselves with their own sets of political values. In the reconfigured German Right, and the Nazi movement that would soon come to dominate it, extramarital affairs, divorces, dirty financial deals and anti-government agitation were no longer insurmountable obstacles. It may have been becoming increasingly impossible to positively depict the ruling family as a whole. But that was not the case with leader figures who could be portrayed as combining the old and new worlds.

The Path to the Right

The public role played by the Hohenzollerns in and against the Weimar Republic was a complex one, but two unambiguous, political conclusions can be drawn. Both male and female family members actively opened themselves to the radical right-wing camp. And not one family member underwent a transformation that led him or her to actively support Weimar democracy. Several minor members of the Hohenzollern clan retreated into unconventional private lives. For instance, Prince Joachim Albrecht, a wounded veteran of the First World War, took up poetry and music. After getting involved in a fistfight with French officers in Berlin's Adlon Hotel in 1920, making him the first Hohenzollern to be convicted of an offence in a court of law,[266] he lived out his days until his death in 1939 as a private citizen and composer. He married a commoner, travelled to the US and developed an interest in jazz. In 1932, French journalists chatted amiably with him in a Berlin cabaret theatre.[267]

But, as a rule, the core members of the Kaiser's family never completely disappeared from the public eye, just as none were ever reconciled to the Weimar Republic. The only exception among Wilhelm II's children, his middle son, Prince Adalbert, a navy officer, eschewed the public eye. Together with his wife, Princess Adalheid von Sachsen-Meiningen, he withdrew, first to the spa town of Bad Homburg, then in 1928 to a villa on Lake Geneva in Switzerland, where he died in 1948.[268] Various photos showed him wearing Bavarian mountain garb with Alpine lakes in the background. A 1921 profile depicted him as a wealthy man who enjoyed a comfortable life after stepping back from politics. But he was an exception. The other, publicly active members of the main family – the Kaiser and his wife in

Doorn as well as the other Hohenzollerns spread between Berlin, Potsdam and Silesia – were drawn ever further to the political Right.

For the crown prince, the years 1924 to 1929 were a time of searching, and his appearance at right-wing events still seemed restrained. His staff of advisors believed that his new role had to be prepared quietly over time. Until the 1926 settlement between the Hohenzollerns and the Prussian state, Wilhelm had trouble financing his lifestyle. Despite the generous yearly allowances the crown prince received from the family coffers and significant government subsidies, his adjutant worried that he would have to give up either Oels or Cecilienhof.

Nonetheless, the prince's financial constraints shouldn't be overestimated. Around 1925, Wilhelm lived his life between racetracks and polo fields, the tennis courts and villas of Berlin's wealthy Grunewald district, and hunting trips in Silesia. His days were filled with horse breeding, receptions with his dogs and Silesia country aristocrats in the smokers' salon at Oels, dinners with Stresemann, Schulenburg and Hindenburg in Cecilienhof, restaurants, theatres and clubs on Berlin's Kurfürstendamm, annual chamois hunts in the Salzkammergut, visits to Lucerne and Locarno and trips to Doorn and East Prussia, where he once approvingly remarked: 'You notice next to nothing of the Republic here.' He also described a reception committee of veterans associations and patriotic clubs arranged for him in an East Prussian estate by the landed aristocrat Elard von Oldenburg-Januschau, a living legend and the epitome of a Prussian reactionary. Together with his sons, the crown prince 'inspected the ranks of the veterans'. His description of this ceremony rang true; his assertion that he felt 'strong distaste' taking part in it, less so.[269]

The tour of East Prussia the crown prince undertook with his wife and his sons Wilhelm and Louis Ferdinand in 1925 was passed off as a private trip. In fact, it was an extended, minutely organized publicity jaunt, during which he solidified contacts with right-wing organizations. The French press, together with its German counterpart, reported in great detail on Wilhelm's appearances and the cries of 'Come back!' that they unleashed.[270]

One observer noted around this time that the crown prince led 'the life of a wealthy and elegant private gentleman'.[271] While hardly untrue, this remark overlooked Wilhelm's constant and increasingly visible political activities and his close contact with German political and military elites. It was hardly possible for a crown prince to live solely as a private citizen within the counter-revolutionary circles of a fragile republic. Among the military men with whom Wilhelm met were later German chancellor Kurt von Schleicher, the head of the army's personnel office, and philosopher of world power Joachim von Stülpnagel, Schulenburg, up-and-coming Reichswehr general Ludwig Beck and Lieutenant Colonel Baron Friedrich Wilhelm von Willisen, who oversaw Germany's illicit rebuilding of its air force and was one of the leading military officers in the German Gentlemen's Club (Deutscher Herrenklub), an association of industrialists, bankers, large property owners and high-ranking ministry officials. In the political arena, Wilhelm's connections spanned the right wing of the Centre Party, the DVP, the DNVP, far-right Freikorps officers and Hermann Göring.

All of this was hardly part of the life of just an 'elegant private gentleman'. Nonetheless, the strategy of the crown prince's advisors to avoid or keep low-key any political activity persisted, at least in rudimentary form, until the end of the 1920s.[272] In spring 1928, Wilhelm's top advisors counselled him against formal membership of the Stahlhelm as counter-productive, arguing that the façade of non-partisanship as a potential heir to the throne was far more valuable. He was advised not to inspect troops at parades alone, but rather 'as part of a circle of the most elevated guests of honour'. Conversely, it was unthinkable that the crown prince would march in the ranks of ordinary Stahlhelm fighters. A pretender to the throne couldn't 'wear a windbreaker and parade past national leaders'[273] – although Wilhelm's brothers had done precisely that at 125,000-man-strong Stahlhelm marches in Potsdam and Berlin.[274]

It wasn't easy to balance the roles of heir to the throne and military man, as was evident in the salutations Stahlhelm leaders used when corresponding with Wilhelm. He was greeted with 'My most honoured, dear Prince' while letters ended 'With comradely regards and best soldierly wishes for your health, I remain Your Royal Majesty's loyal . . . '[275] As late as 1931 the Kaiser himself intervened to prevent the family's greater involvement with the Stahlhelm, which would have involved founding a unit bearing the crown prince's name, but the heir to the throne continued to be frenetically celebrated at Stahlhelm rallies.[276] In one of his reports concerning a particularly aggressive event, the British ambassador to Germany emphasized the prominent presence of the crown prince and princess.[277] By the end of the 1920s, it had become impossible to overlook two things: the royal search for forums where they could put in openly visible political appearances and the drift further and further to the right. That closed the gaps between the Hohenzollerns and the Stahlhelm, the extreme wing of the DNVP and organizations that took their models from fascism.

The 1928 discussions about whether it was unseemly for the crown prince to don a military windbreaker made no bones about his great enthusiasm for fascism. This made him more willing to publicly identify with martial attitudes and behaviours. In 1929, he and his son Wilhelm planned to drive to fascist Italy with the German National Automobile Club.[278] The former Kaiser and the crown prince had discussed conceivable future models for the monarchy in Doorn all the way back in the summer of 1922. Some ten years later, the son tried to explain to his father, who was becoming increasingly divorced from reality, 'that if any monarchy at all was to come it would have to be constructed differently from previously'. The crown prince added: 'Something along Italian lines. That means that the cares and burdens of today's age can no longer rest on a single pair of shoulders but will have to distributed across several.'

There is copious evidence of Crown Prince Wilhelm's early fixation on the idea of a 'popular Kaiserdom', broadly anchored in the masses, with which the heir to the throne unsettled old guard monarchists.[279] Ever fickle, the Kaiser's first reaction was to reject this model – although not because he was outraged by fascism but because he opposed all ideas that challenged his own absolute right to rule. He berated his son as an immature youth but soon thereafter sent one of his right-hand men to Rome to court Mussolini. That emissary had even less success bringing the two sides together than the crown prince.[280]

Directly after political power in Italy was handed over to Mussolini, the Kaiser had remarked: 'The most recent events in Italy without question represent a turning point. I think that fascism will spread to Germany and that the monarchy will be restored.'[281] The Kaiser's enthusiasm for the Italian fascist by no means faded, with Wilhelm II once writing of Mussolini: 'He has achieved admirable things, and people will imitate him the world over.'[282]

In 1928, the crown prince made another of his trips to Italy, after which he waxed lyrical to his father about Mussolini. Wilhelm was especially taken with the fascist practice of shaving the heads of communist leaders and painting the Italian flag in oil on their skulls.[283] In Italy, the political enemy, the prince reported, had been 'eradicated, torn up by the roots'. Wilhelm explicitly stressed the 'brilliant brutality' employed by the fascist regime. In keeping with the basic tone of his correspondence and the main current of his political ideas, he praised the 'ruthless energy' with which all of Italy had been turned on its head.[284]

By violently suppressing and fracturing the political Left, Italian fascism achieved what the crown prince dreamed of in more than two decades of his correspondence. In 1928, Wilhelm indicated that Stahlhelm leader Wilhelm Seldte was his preferred dictator – before that there had been others, and others would follow, before a wider consensus emerged around Hitler. What remained constant from the very start was the crown prince's obsession with political models centred around a dictator, characterized by militarism, fascism and violence, which was expressed in the idea that 'ultimately only a dictator can pull the cart out of the mud'.[285]

Mussolini received the crown prince on multiple occasions, and various direct contacts were maintained in both Berlin and Rome with the other political elite. Wilhelm's sons also got to know the world of fascist Rome. In his 1952 memoirs, Louis Ferdinand would casually recall the audience his father arranged for him and his brother with the dictator in 1933. With the market value for fascist contacts having fallen dramatically nearly twenty years after the fact, Louis Ferdinand presented his encounter with Mussolini, whom his father 'met every time he was in Rome', as a droll anecdote. This recollection was full of the snobbery and ex-post-facto denials of proximity to fascism characteristic of most post-1945 aristocratic memoirs.[286] In Louis Ferdinand's telling, the young German princes weren't intimidated at all by Mussolini the dictator, who allegedly reminded them of an everyday Italian village restaurant owner, albeit one with thoroughly passable French. Louis Ferdinand responded in Italian, which he claimed to have learned from 'fanatically' anti-fascist fishermen in Rapallo. This depiction of events was very similar to the prince's accounts of Hitler, of whom he allegedly heard for the first time in 1930 from his 'landlord' and who reminded him of a 'Viennese porter'.[287]

Louis Ferdinand's Italian anecdote illustrates the effort of three Hohenzollern generations to court Mussolini's favour.[288] The crown prince's admiration for the dictator was so great that he kept a signed portrait of the dictator on his personal desk at Cecilienhof[289] and was a member of the pro-fascist 'Society for the Study of Fascism',[290] in which Duke Carl Eduard von Saxe-Coburg and Gotha, Waldemar Pabst and radical right-wing leaders set the tone, wove networks and debated the ideas of leading anti-democratic intellectuals. Recent apologetic accounts of the society notwithstanding, membership in it alone was a sign of support for fascism and its goals, and the name of the crown prince was always printed first on the enrolment list.

Apologists may downplay this sort of engagement as not truly 'active',[291] but a crown prince could hardly have been expected to assume a bureaucratic office such as treasurer or custodian. Symbolic memberships were indeed typical of 'active' support from leading aristocrats,[292] and they were understood as such by the upper classes in Germany. This impression was reinforced by the fact that the crown prince's brother advocated the Italian model very visibly, for instance, by fulsomely lauding Mussolini in Rome in a November 1931 speech.[293]

It was also Prince August Wilhelm who established the earliest and most direct connection between the Hohenzollern family circle, the Nazi movement and the Nazi Party. Like his brothers, the Kaiser's fourth-oldest son – whose military career as an officer was as unsuccessful as his marriage and whose ghost-written PhD dissertation in political science was as unimpressive as his dilettantish landscape paintings – initially sought to attach himself to the Stahlhelm. August Wilhelm's journey to the political Right had its stops and starts. Although by 1924, the Wagner Festspiele in Bayreuth, despite being imperial black, white and red, had already come under the influence of Nazism,[294] one year later, August Wilhelm knowingly let himself be photographed with the 'Jewish Wotan' Friedrich Schorr, one of the superstar bass-baritones of the time. This was perhaps done to protect the singer against the storms of racist criticism he faced.[295] It was also an exception. As a rule, the Wagner family and Houston Stewart Chamberlain[296] were conduits connecting parts of the bourgeois elite, European aristocrats and the ambitious new radical Right.[297] And it was in this company that August Wilhelm and other Hohenzollerns became acquainted with the style, tone, ideas and leaders of the Nazi movement. The crown prince established early relations with Göring, and August Wilhelm's initial contacts around 1926 pointed towards a political career with the Nazis, culminating in his joining the party and the SA in 1930. That created a national and international stir, since the Nazi movement was beginning to emerge as the most dynamic force on the German Right. Connections with the German royal family gave a powerful legitimization to Nazism and right-wing radicalism generally during the final years of the Weimar Republic.

In the German national elections in September 1930, the National Socialists made a huge leap, increasing their share of the vote from 2.8 to 18.3 per cent and claiming 107 seats in the Reichstag. This electoral success was bolstered by the political activities of the crown princess, the ever-industrious would-be empress Hermine, the Kaiser in Doorn, and the imperial budgetary and financial administration and crown prince's advisors in Berlin. Every one of these agents worked intensely and continuously to undermine the Weimar Republic. Engagement in various right-wing organizations was seen as key to restoring the monarchy. The left-wing newspaper *Vorwärts* wrote:

> Hitler has his Auwi [August Wilhelm], and the Stahlhelm its Fritzwi [Friedrich Wilhelm]. The gentlemen of the House of Hohenzollern are seeking to cover all bases by allying themselves with everyone they expect to make a move against the Republic. Because they're such a large family, they're capable of forming Hohenzollern cells all over the place. They believe a new day is dawning.[298]

And in Göring the royal family had an early, stable connection with the Nazi leadership. In 1926, the crown prince personally congratulated Göring on his election to the Reichstag as a Nazi Party deputy, joking about the latter's 'physical strength' – much to the delight of Göring's aristocratic wife, who also regaled her mother with stories of the Nazis' beer-hall brawls with 'highly criminal' communists. Such contact offered enormous potential for expansion.[299]

Conclusion: The Counter-Revolution and the Nazi Movement

Karl Marx once sarcastically remarked that the various monarchs in nineteenth-century German-speaking Europe reacted to every half-revolution with a full counter-revolution. That was also true of post-1918 Germany, where the deposed House of Hohenzollern remained a central ideological and symbolic focus and the counter-revolution had several hubs, including some in Prussia directly connected with the royal family. One way of writing the history of the counter-revolutionary milieu is to focus on its hotspots, the places in which ideas, networks, publications and associations were organized and which were seen as beacons. In the case of the Weimar Republic, these places have largely fallen into obscurity, overshadowed by the sites central to National Socialism: arenas like the Feldherrnhalle and the Sportpalast or the Nazi Party Rally Grounds in Nuremberg.[300]

For the Hohenzollerns themselves, Doorn was the important centre abroad together with various major domestic ones. The leading political members of the family are all associated with specific places; the Kaiser with Doorn, his sons with their villas in Potsdam, the crown prince and his wife with Cecilienhof and Oels, and 'Empress' Hermine with Doorn, the Kaiser Wilhelm Palace in Berlin and her various other palaces.

These locations alone make it obvious that leading German aristocrats didn't adapt to fit the bourgeois-democratic reality after 1918, but rather continued in many respects to live their lives in what were essentially aristocratic enclaves within the Weimar Republic. This was true above all in the place that would become probably the most important modern symbol of the royal family: Cecilienhof. Conceived as a residence for the crown prince in Potsdam's New Garden park, it was built for a future that never materialized. Planning started in 1905, basic construction commenced in 1913, and the palace was completed the same year as the Russian Revolution. Set amidst lakes and the generous expanses of the park, it was the last palace the Hohenzollerns ever had built.

When Crown Princess Cecilie of Prussia moved into the mock Tudor building in August 1917, she was a highly cultivated, beautiful woman of thirty-one who was nine months pregnant with her sixth child. The palace was officially inaugurated on 9 November 1917, one year to the day before the proclamation of the German republic and the Kaiser's flight to the Netherlands. The United States had just joined the First World War, and breakthroughs achieved by British tanks in western Europe foreshadowed Germany's coming defeat. Far away from the fighting, the crown princess enjoyed the services of two valets, five servants, eight lady's maids, two chefs, five assistant chefs, three chauffeurs, eighteen chambermaids, a stoker and a telephone operator.[301] As the war raged on, the crown princess enjoyed the views from the gigantic main hall of Jungfernsee lake and the Brandenburg forest, played the piano, hosted society events and, surrounded by nurses clad in white, posed as the perfect housewife taking care of soldiers wounded at the front. From the estate, Cecilie would actively and publicly promote conservative ideals of womanhood and her charitable activities throughout the 1920s, maintaining and expanding them as though in competition with the Kaiser's second wife.

When the crown princess took possession of the palace-cum-estate, its 175 rooms, forty chimneys and twenty-eight telephone lines already seemed like something from a bygone era. In the middle of a world war, the ruling German dynasty had built a palace in the style of a Renaissance English country estate, a 'pastiche of various, heterogenous ideas' that afforded the princely couple nineteen, and their five children thirteen, rooms when they moved in (a sixth child was born later). All palace residents enjoyed the latest technological conveniences.[302] American observers considered the palace, even before it was finished, a clear break with tradition and a modern mélange.[303] Elements conceived by architect Paul Schultze-Naumburg before 1914 as a homage to the Hohenzollerns' aristocratic relatives in England now stuck out like a sore thumb. 'I cannot conceal how sad I am that the "German" crown prince forced you to create such a costume structure and that you allowed yourself to be forced to build an English estate while we are locked with the English in a life-or-death struggle,' architect Theodor Fischer wrote to his colleague Schultze-Naumburg. 'May the vengeance of destiny not strike you too hard.'[304] In fact, destiny's revenge would turn out to be mild. Both Schultze-Naumburg and the interior architect Paul Ludwig Troost would become two of the most influential National Socialist architects and members of the Nazi leadership's inner circle in the 1930s.

The crown princess – the former Duchess of Mecklenburg and sister of the queen of Denmark, who was very popular with the German populace – initially moved into the building with her retinue but without her husband. Since 1914, the politically active Cecilie had eagerly assumed the role of representing the crown prince while he was away at the front. The palace was briefly seized by the government in 1918 but the following year the Weimar Republic granted the Hohenzollerns the right to reside there for three generations. It has never attracted much attention. But if we consider the situation not as usual in retrospect, looking back from Nazism, but forwards from the perspective of the Hohenzollerns and the rest of the German aristocracy in 1918, the estate was hugely significant. With its palaces, Garrison Church, veterans' memorial ceremonies, elite military regiments, dense conservative traditions and symbols, militaristic associations, jackbooted officers, right-wing women's societies, four resident sons of the Kaiser and a populace that gave the ultra-nationalist DNVP more than 50 per cent of the vote in 1924, Potsdam was one of the right-wing strong-holds in Germany.[305] And within it, Cecilienhof was a more than just symbolic hub.

There is good reason to focus on the city when considering how the alliance between National Socialist and conservatives developed. As one of the crown prince's grandsons later wrote, the heir to the throne used Potsdam 'to invite prominent personalities to gentlemen's dinners'. The guest lists included not only the German chancellor Heinrich Brüning but also 'boisterous circles of artists, journalists and famous sportsmen'.[306] There was a clear political direction at Cecilienhof, and centrist politicians such as Brüning were hardly the rule. Congregations in the estate's gentlemen's and smoking rooms were blunt, Prussian-style military-dominated affairs.

The city of Potsdam and its flourishing scene of aristocratic and bourgeois anti-democratic elites has been called a 'laboratory for radical right-wing political experiments'.[307] Cecilienhof served as a home, meeting point and base for extremists in Potsdam and Berlin and at rural events in Brandenburg. The palace was equipped with the most modern means of transport. The crown prince had two BMWs, a Mercedes and a DKW at his disposal, the crown princess drove a Maybach and a Mercedes, and even Wilhelm's adjutant Louis Müldner von Mülnheim had a Mercedes of his own.[308] Alongside Doorn and Cecilienhof, the third significant place for the Hohenzollerns' relationship with the political Right lay 400 kilometres southeast of Potsdam. Oels Castle in Silesia became the crown prince's official 'rural residence' in the 1920s, the 'country' in the typically amphibious, town-and-country existence led by wealthy aristocrats. This massive building, built in the Middle Ages, had been redesigned a number of times to make it one of the largest Renaissance palaces in Europe. It first came into the Hohenzollerns' possession in the late nineteenth century, and the royal family's lawyers succeeded in making it part of the 1926 compensation settlement.

The fiefdom of Oels encompassed fifteen manors and some 10,000 hectares of forest, and it was the preferred centre of life for the crown princess in her de facto separation from her husband. Wilhelm for his part was drawn more to Cecilienhof, Potsdam and Berlin, using Oels primarily in hunting season. All in all, the crown prince and princess spent approximately half the year in Cecilienhof, and the other half in Oels and travelling, usually separately.[309] The crown princess had no fewer than nine rooms of her own at Oels, while her four sons and two daughters occupied an entire wing of the building. Located 30 kilometres north-east of Breslau, the palace with its thirteenth-century walls was the antithesis of Cecilienhof and Berlin. Oels represented pre-modernity, country life, the rural aristocracy, vast property, powerful landowners' associations and hunting parties. Wilhelm set up a Trakehner stud farm to demonstrate the horsemanship that was part and parcel of being a member of the nobility. His rooms in the palace were full of hunting trophies from the region and from India, while a bearskin rug lay in front of the fireplace in the great hall. It was here that Wilhelm's six children spent formative parts of their youth.[310]

Other rural and urban Hohenzollern hubs included the City Palace in central Berlin near the government district, the Reichswehr Ministry, the major embassies and the most prominent political clubs and salons. The crown prince and princess had used the palace as their winter Berlin residence until losing it during the German revolution – a painful moment for the royal family. Atypically, the Weimar Republic kept possession of the palace, the birthplace of the final German Kaiser, using it as a rare example of the end of the old order. In the first year of democracy, it was remade into the National Gallery, and the art historian Ludwig Justi quickly staged there the world's first exhibition of contemporary twentieth-century modernist works of art, including French Impressionists, members of the Berlin Secession and the German expressionist group Die Brücke.

That loss was compensated for by another important Hohenzollern base in central Berlin, the Kaiser Wilhelm Palace (also known as the Old Palace) on Unter den Linden, which the Hohenzollerns were allowed to keep under the compensation agreement and which was one of the most splendid of the city palaces. 'Empress' Hermine resided on the first floor during her Berlin visits. Meanwhile, to the right of that building, General Wilhelm von Dommes, the Hohenzollerns' head political advisor and general agent, and his staff performed their duties in the Dutch Palace, which had previously belonged to the first king of the Netherlands. The crown prince even maintained a pied-à-terre there, in the very centre of the Weimar Republic's capital.

The compensation agreement allowed the royal family to retain a series of further palaces, estates and other properties. Throughout the Weimer Republic, all seven of the Kaiser's children owned and resided in palaces and villas, mostly in Potsdam. Every time they moved within Germany – for holidays, stopovers or visits to a political or cultural event – they could call upon a dense, nationwide, functional network of castles, residences, estates and city palaces in which their 'class comrades' maintained an almost invisible world of their own, well off the pro-democratic radar.

The network of aristocratic locations branched out as far as noble bloodlines did. To name just one example, Hermine and her sons from her first marriage, all of whom were early participants in the

Nazi movement,[311] owned properties such as the early baroque Saabor Castle in Lower Silesia and (between 1927 and 1933) the breathtaking Burgk Castle on a mountain plateau in Vogtland. For at least sixteen weeks every year, Hermine travelled around to manage her property and to do political work while her three sons commuted between their universities in Bonn and Berlin and Saabor and Doorn.[312] Other hubs were the right-wing political salons in Berlin, particular the one hosted by Viktoria von Dirksen in her villa in Berlin's central Tiergarten district,[313] the network of 'national clubs', the annual dinner at the German Gentlemen's Club (Deutscher Herrenklub)[314] and the villas and luxury flats in Berlin, Potsdam and other German locations. Their significance persisted until the National Socialists created their own version of 'polite society' after 1933 – and even then the role of the higher nobility went beyond that of mere decoration.[315]

It is not easy to get to grips with the function of the various counter-revolutionary centres and hotspots. Among the places at the crown prince's disposal, Cecilienhof and the Hohenzollerns' palace in Berlin were the military and political centres of power in Potsdam and the capital respectively, while Oels Castle in Silesia was a bastion of the reduced but still significant influence of the rural aristocracy and large landowners. Sometimes these locations, above all Cecilienhof/Oels and the ex-Kaiser's residence in Doorn, also competed as centres of power.[316]

The fragmentation of the Hohenzollern clan and of their power during the revolution was mirrored in the separation of locations, administrations, budgets and staffs of advisors. This was a family in which the father constantly sought to humiliate his sons, his relatives, the aristocracy as a whole and his subjects, accusing them of treachery, and in which the sons typically only began challenging the patriarch's authority when they had passed the age of fifty. Such problematic father–son relationships had featured in successive generations of the Hohenzollerns over the preceding centuries. It was difficult for commoners to decipher the complex puzzle of various sons from various generations who were touted as possible heirs to

the throne, a widow-'empress' who was wildly jealous of her similarly aged stepdaughter, and princes who married below their station
and were commensurately shunned by aristocratic society.[317]

And what of Doorn, whose significance we examined in detail in
the previous chapter? There, the former Kaiser continued to draw
up battle plans while seated atop a saddle at his desk. In the summer
of 1934, to take one late example, Wilhelm used newspaper articles
to draw up a global, strategic plan that had a German-led Europe
allying itself with Japan to lead the fight against Bolshevism, 'subjugate' the Soviet Union and triumphantly proclaim a new world
order in the Kremlin. That June, he personally presented this pipe
dream at a meeting in Arnheim am Rhein to the 23-year-old son of
Winston Churchill, telling him to pass it along to Britain's governing cabinet. 'They won't believe their eyes,' Wilhelm promised.[318]
From our perspective, there seems, at least at first glance, no option
but to classify Wilhelm's combination of childish rage and aggressive self-overestimation as a form of delusion, of interest mainly as
a curiosity. But, as was the case with the crown prince, millions of
contemporary Germans took the ex-Kaiser seriously. And, of
course, in 1940 a military alliance with Japan *was* signed, and the
Soviet Union *was* invaded a few days after his death.

For monarchists around 1930, Doorn and its main resident were
far more than mere curiosities. Thus, the Kaiser's Dutch home in
exile was both a never-never-land *and* a continually important
coordination and information centre for the political Right. During
this time, the ever hyper-dramatic Wilhelm II complained:

> No one helps me any more, the outcast, fated, denigrated, slandered
> scapegoat who has outlived his time . . . I've reflected that when
> you've passed the age of seventy and have only been cursed, criti-
> cized, complained about and deceived, you don't expect anything
> more from life. It was simply too much. I don't ask anything any
> more of life.[319]

But in his less depressive moments, the former Kaiser did in fact expect quite a bit of life, starting with mastery of Europe. And the enemies of democracy had no choice but to pay attention to him as a figure.

Moreover, Wilhelm II's sons, daughters, advisors and political helpers managed to connect him, despite his being self-restricted to his estate and park, with the extreme Right in the Weimar Republic. Hermine Reuss was the main intermediary. At her own estates, the Wagner festival in Bayreuth or the Nazi Party rallies in Nuremberg, she made contact with a host with right-wing radicals. As early as 1926, Hermine met Hitler, whose opposition to the seizure of aristocratic assets had been noted with approval among the upper nobility. Along with Prince August Wilhelm, Hermine was the element in the Hohenzollern family who most deeply aligned herself with National Socialism and supported the movement with the greatest energy. In 1924, the Kaiser's brother Heinrich had still dismissed followers of Nazism as 'Hitler socialists'; but the Hohenzollerns' traditional pronounced contempt for the 'rabble' in the ultra-right, racist movement, parts of which were openly hostile to the aristocracy, waned over the years.[320] While the crown prince declined to actively participate in Nazism during the mid-1920s because of its putative 'proletarian' core,[321] his stepmother was establishing contact with the movement with the help of Bayreuth and a number of 'class comrades' and political salons. The ex-Kaiser's staff of advisors in Doorn were split between condemning and approving of Hermine's efforts, which reached their symbolic height when Hermann Göring visited the estate for exploratory talks in January 1931 and May 1932.

There is no doubt that she constantly tried to win over her husband for the Nazi movement as the only political force that would be able to arrange his return to the throne. The independent attitudes, energy and political activism of the princess and her sons from her first marriage, who joined the Nazis early on, shouldn't be underestimated. They had considerable influence on the former Kaiser's political views in Doorn. But, as we know today, the notion that Wilhelm was a helpless victim of the malign influence of his wife has little basis in fact, much as the ex-Kaiser's associates and Hohenzollern family historians might have wanted to believe in it.[322]

Also, to an extent without the help of his family, Wilhelm remained in contact with the far Right via powerful intermediaries in the foreign and particularly the American press. One such intermediary was George Sylvester Viereck, a Munich-born German-American and pro-German agitator who sang the praises of both the Hohenzollerns and the Nazis. A photo that turned up in New York in 1928 showed a group of men taking tea in front of some neatly stacked piles of wood in the park at Doorn: Wilhelm, Sigurd von Ilsemann, General Wilhelm von Dommes, a Dutch guard named Van Houten and Viereck. The image of this meeting between military men and the journalist was an effective piece of political propaganda. Years later, Goebbels would still make use of the writings of Viereck, who never tired of paying homage to the former Kaiser.[323] Viereck was described as 'the best paid and most important American propagandist for the German cause' during the 1930s. He saw Nazi anti-Semitism as a 'negligible by-product of a movement that eminently deserved support because it was desperately struggling for world peace'.[324]

Views like this could already be heard in the garden in Doorn in 1928. The year before that, the socialist lawyer and journalist Fritz Solmitz wrote an impressively precise portrait of the German Right, in which the Kaiser had 'lost all currency'. Sober businesspeople, Solmitz added, now treated the 'state' as a guiding principle and had long since 'discarded' the 'completely devalued stock' they had previously put in the monarchy. Viereck in America responded by sneering, 'This nonsense isn't worth the paper it's written on.' Solmitz, who would be murdered in 1933 in the Fuhlsbüttel concentration camp, underestimated how much the Kaiser's currency would rise in value in the years leading up to 1933.[325]

A few years after Solmitz dismissed Wilhelm as irrelevant, a socialist newspaper expressed pity for the ex-monarch as a 'person who's lost himself in the pose of the Kaiser'. Unlike Bismarck, who after his dismissal retired to his estate with his black jacket, floppy hat and long pipe, Wilhelm II 'never got beyond being a spectral part in a play-acted version of a past that lay behind him and could never be recovered'. Unable to acknowledge and atone for his own failings, he remained trapped in an absurd bit of aristocratic theatre: 'The curse of megalomania and the insanity that came with the military limped like a ghost behind him and pushed him down into his armchair as a vivid expression of the grotesque. That's just the way he is.' This description of the daily farce in Doorn was typical of pro-democracy analysis in both its precision and in its underestimation of the forces at work there. At the time when this portrait of Wilhelm's 'spectral' exile appeared in the summer of 1931,[326] Göring had already visited the ex-Kaiser, and the 'currency' of the Hohenzollerns was back on the rise.

The former Kaiser had no coherent political outlook on or stance towards the Nazi movement. Wilhelm II's only constants were his ridiculous egocentrism and hyper-dramatic emotional ups and downs. He continually drifted off into fantasy worlds of conspiracy theories, imaginary wars, general rage, strong-sounding but empty phrases, racism, anti-Semitism and the conviction that he himself was the solution to all of Germany's and Europe's political problems. In a 1927 letter, he opined: 'The press, Jews and mosquitoes are a plague from which humanity must free itself. I believe the best would be gas?'[327] This remark was hardly a harbinger of the genocide to come, but it did document the morass of crass hatred and anti-Semitic fantasy in which the ex-Kaiser was sometimes submerged.

General von Dommes, one of the men closest to Wilhelm II, regularly attended Nazi events in Potsdam in 1930, often in the company of Prince August Wilhelm. The presence of individuals from former court society as well as of former officers who lived in Potsdam, was conspicuous enough to attract political surveillance.[328] The crown princess at the time had contact with Göring and Ritter von Epp at the residence of her brother-in-law August Wilhelm.[329] The prince later claimed that he was first introduced to Hitler by his brother, Crown Prince Wilhelm, and that Göring, a frequent guest at Cecilienhof, had brought the two together.[330]

The Hohenzollerns showed a clear political preference for the future when they associated themselves with the Stahlhelm para-militaries and the Nazi movement and when they supported the anti-democratic, right-wing extremist Harzburg Front in October 1931. Observers across the political spectrum noted the huge increase in activity of Hohenzollern princes in the Stahlhelm, and some both inside and outside the clan predicted that the family would reclaim power via the office of Reich president.[331] It was still pos-sible in the early 1930s to conceive of monarchy and Nazi dictatorship as opposites. But clearer-eyed observers saw the two as collabora-tors. A satirical monthly magazine in Vienna published a cartoon in March 1933 entitled 'The Steps Up to the Hohenzollern Throne'. It depicted Wilhelm sitting in his throne atop four steps bearing the words: 'Junkers/barons', the 'Evangelical Church', 'militarism' and 'National Socialism'. The final step consisted of a giant swastika.[332] The illustration was one expression of the common illusion at the time that the Nazi movement could be instrumentalized to restore the monarchy.

3.

Almost a King

The Hohenzollerns in 1932

In late March 1932, Prince Wilhelm of Prussia, the former crown prince and possible heir to the throne, was laid up with lumbago. Nonetheless, despite being bedridden, he received a cabal of monarchist hotheads and self-appointed kingmakers at Oels, where, over the course of hours, they presented a spectacular plan. During the meeting, also attended by the crown princess, at the bedside of a would-be monarch in a Renaissance castle in Silesia, the German presidency and a return to the throne did indeed seem within reach. The plot, conceived as a surprise coup, ended on 1 April, when the crown prince endorsed Adolf Hitler in a run-off election for the presidency. It was a harbinger of things to come – although several newspapers that reported on it felt the need to assure their readers that it wasn't an April Fool's joke.

The whole episode, which featured officers and publicists hastily shuttling by car, train and plane between Oels, Berlin and Munich, indeed had something of the comic opera about it. Nonetheless, there were two very serious sides to this incident for the history of both the house of Hohenzollern and the anti-democratic movement in Germany. Firstly, Prince Wilhelm's endorsement aligned him once and for all with right-wing extremism – a position he would never formally renounce, even after 1945. Secondly, the prospect of a Wilhelm–Hitler alliance lent the crown prince a renewed political influence that would peak in the following months.

Opposition or Collaboration

This chapter will examine the elevation of the crown prince to a figure seen domestically and internationally as a leader capable of channelling the anti-democratic movement towards either dictatorship or monarchy. The period between March 1932 and Hitler's appointment as German chancellor on 30 January 1933 gave a negative answer to the question of whether any forces on the political Right would be able to oppose the Nazi movement. It also decided the issue of how the crown prince, who at least theoretically could have headed a conservative alternative, would position himself. Politically and symbolically, Prince Wilhelm and his family had two options: opposition or collaboration. The notion that a Hohenzollern king could have presented a monarchist option to Nazi dictatorship persists to this day and has been part of the conservative narrative about the end of the Weimar Republic since the 1930s. On what was it based? And to what extent did the crown prince himself encourage the belief in such an alternative?

The writer Reinhold Schneider, an enthusiast of the Hohenzollerns and Prussian monarchism, recalled a conversation with Wilhelm after 1945:

> The crown prince gestured toward the chairs and told me that years ago Hitler, Göring, Goebbels and Röhm had sat there. Hitler had said to him: 'My goal is the restoration of the empire under a Hohenzollern.' The crown prince was convinced that Hitler only abandoned his original plan to restore the monarchy in May 1933.[1]

This story reflects two elements central to the crown prince's thinking and behaviour. On the one hand, we find Wilhelm fantasizing about the restoration of the monarchy under his leadership and issuing an open invitation to the Nazi leaders to explore their common ground. On the other, we see him assuming ex post facto the role of victim who was lied to by the prominent Nazis sitting in their armchairs in Cecilienhof's Great Hall. The House of Hohenzollern, it was implied, had been betrayed.[2] But, conversely, we should also ask why Hitler, Göring, Goebbels and Röhm came to be sitting in those armchairs in the first place and what the subject of their discussions was. The scene encapsulates Wilhelm's failed attempt to marshal his personal and symbolic resources and advance his aims by concluding an alliance with National Socialism.

How did the political and symbolic communication between the Hohenzollerns and the Nazi movement develop over the course of 1932, a year in which the restoration of the monarchy, however implausible, accrued a chimeric influence? All the ideas debated within the House of Hohenzollern of how to restore the throne involved Nazi cooperation. It is crucial to keep that fact in mind while examining the grey areas, nuances and conflicts within the monarchist camp. In the eyes of Hohenzollern supporters, the crown prince came closer to re-establishing the throne in 1932 than his father had in all the preceding years. For a time, it seemed that Prince Wilhelm and his various representatives could in fact walk a very fine line. On one side was the inconsequential joke of an heir to the throne some of his pro-democracy opponents regarded him to be. On the other was the modern, populist leader his supporters dreamed the crown prince could become, especially during 1932.

It is probably true, as Prince Friedrich Wilhelm would write many years later, 'that the rapidly increasing popularity of the crown prince reached its high point' in 1932.[3] But at no point were the personal qualities and political abilities of Wilhelm as an individual the crux of the matter. Both supporters and detractors fretted about the political direction in which the immense symbolic capital of the concepts 'German crown prince' and 'Prussia' – capital that was by no means Wilhelm's to utilize as he saw fit – would flow. Even before 1914, the prestige of these concepts had become the object of emotional public battles, and after 1918 it consisted almost entirely of what could be salvaged in media debates and public perceptions.

Reich President Crown Prince Wilhelm

The most conspicuous attempt to politically exploit the charisma attached to Wilhelm as Prussian and German crown prince came in an appeal in the monarchist newspaper *Fridericus* on 20 March 1932. In an editorial taking up the entire front page, its anti-Semitic and far-right publisher, Carl Friedrich Holtz, had offered a vision of 'Our Reich President Crown Prince Wilhelm'. Holtz was not at all interested in erecting a bulwark against National Socialism, as the article made clear: 'This is the only way to achieve a change of system. Under the crown prince's Reich presidency, enough room for action would remain for Hitler. Give your motor all the petrol it can take, and everything will still turn out fine in the end.'[4]

The presidency was the Weimar Republic's highest office. In the intervals between the main and run-off elections of 1932, with the Right undecided about which candidate it should unite behind, the crown prince was won over to the idea of himself standing for the office, as a representative of the National Socialists and nearly the entire traditional conservative camp. For that to happen, however, both Hindenburg and Hitler would have had to withdraw their candidacies. Wilhelm had mulled over running for the presidency since 1928. The Stahlhelm began discussing the possibility of his candidacy as of 1930, and the Nazi movement had been part of the equation since 1931.[5]

With actions like his very prominent participation in the Stahlhelm's 'Day of the Frontline Soldier' in Breslau in May 1931, Wilhelm positioned himself ever more clearly among the ranks of possible leaders of the anti-democratic Right. This was also true, if less powerfully, for his brothers. Both the left-wing and the right-wing press ran reports about the four Hohenzollern princes marching together at far-right rallies to ever greater applause and public acclaim.[6] In Doorn in January 1931, Wilhelm gave a speech at his father's birthday celebrations in which he characterized 'le roi de Prusse' as his ultimate goal. The 'national movement', he said, was making progress and 'he and his brothers were fighting, too, at the vanguard, each so to speak with his own combat strips and within his own limits'.[7] Wilhelm would never revise his official line concerning the desirability of an alliance between traditional conservatives and National Socialists. As one biographer would remark, the Stahlhelm had been his 'home base' during 1930 and 1931.[8] As of January 1932, considerably before the Nazis' stunning electoral gains in elections that year, attempts to curry favour with the Nazi leadership emerged from the general affiliation with the far Right.

In his 1955 memoirs, Hitler's former chief press officer Otto Dietrich claimed that, even before the first stage of the presidential election, Wilhelm had told Hitler he would be willing to stand against Hindenburg if that's what the Nazi leadership desired. Dietrich didn't give a date for this offer, but, if genuine, it must have been made in early March 1932.[9] In the first stage of that vote, Wilhelm sent out mixed signals. At the same time as he and his brothers were appearing as a group in black velvet suits at Stahlhelm events, Wilhelm also turned up at Nazi rallies, where his brother August Wilhelm raged against Hindenburg.[10] The foreign press again immediately registered the Hohenzollerns' 'greatly increased activity' on the stages of the radical Right.[11]

Documented attempts were made between 14 March and 1 April 1932 to negotiate a plan for Hitler and Prince Wilhelm to jointly take power. Working under extreme time pressure, advisors of the crown prince shuttled between Doorn, Bochum, Berlin and Oels, trying to get Hitler to support Wilhelm standing for the office of Reich president. The Nazi leadership's interest in this astonishing scheme probably stemmed from the conviction that Wilhelm would be easier to get rid of than Hindenburg and that a candidacy by the former would create problems for the latter.[12] Along with the highest office of state in the Weimar Republic, unofficial internal discussions also featured the idea of a Reich 'administrator', a figure who would prepare for the return of Kaiser Wilhelm II or the coronation of the crown prince or even the latter's eldest son. The ideal scenario, according to this thinking, was that Hindenburg would

withdraw his own candidacy, leaving Prince Wilhelm to face competition from the Left. Once elected Reich president, Wilhelm
would then name Hitler as 'his' chancellor.

In a hasty burst of improvised activity, three officers – Günther
von Einem, Eberhard von Selasen-Selasinsky and Joachim von
Ostau – succeeded in initially winning over not only Wilhelm and
the crown princess but also Hitler, Göring, Goebbels, Frick and
Strasser to the idea. The plans culminated in the scene at Oels
described at the beginning of this chapter, in which the laid-up
prince received emissaries while lying in his 'very lovely bed', smoking in his 'wonderfully beautiful and majestic castle'.[13] Joachim von
Ostau was particularly important here. A barely thirty-year-old son
of an estate owner, Ostau had joined the Nazi Party the year before.
He ran various theatres and managed Nazi propaganda in northern
Westphalia until the autumn of 1932, when he fell out of favour
within the Nazi movement because of his monarchism.[14]

The crown princess, who took part in at least some of the talks,
vigorously supported the attempt to win over the bedridden crown
prince for a direct, public alliance with Hitler. She was also charged
with securing the Kaiser's support in telephone conversations with
Doorn. But those efforts came to naught because of one of Wilhelm's assistants, Baron Ulrich von Sell, a critic of the Nazi
movement to whom we will return later.[15] Thereafter, it was decided
to personally deliver all correspondence by courier. The crown
prince communicated his decision in two letters – addressed to
'Dear Mr Hitler' and 'Dear Papa' – that were sent by train to Doorn
and plane to Munich. Colonel Selasen-Selasinsky frenetically criss-
crossed the Weimar Republic between Silesia and the Netherlands.[16]
Hitler and his closest circles agreed to the plan on the condition that
Hindenburg wouldn't run. The crown prince would have to put
himself forward as a consensus candidate for the entire political
Right against the communist Ernst Thälmann. The outcome of
such a run-off election would have been easy to predict. Prince Wilhelm later said that he had told Hitler: 'The best thing is if I'm
nominated for the presidential election, and then you'll become my

chancellor.'[17] The idea of the crown prince as a marginalized and a cartoon figure of the sort mocked by his pro-democratic detractors was clearly belied by the fact that Schleicher, Hitler, Goebbels and other Nazi leaders took him very seriously in 1932, seeing him as a political trump card of the highest order.

The plan to have the crown prince stand for election ultimately failed because of inadequate time to prepare and because of Wilhelm II's refusal to sanction it. Selasen-Selasinsky was given a very cool reception by the ex-Kaiser's wife, who treated him brusquely and refused him an audience with the former monarch. As the crown prince told it, Wilhelm II 'ordered' him to give up the plan, and he followed his father's wishes, much to the dismay of his advisors, who wanted him to emulate the legendary Prussian General Ludwig Yorck von Wartenburg in 1812 and disregard royal instructions.[18] In December 1933, the Kaiser would cite monarchist writer Reinhold Schneider's dictum that a Prussian king could not be a father and a Prussian heir to the throne could not be a son.[19] Crown Prince Wilhelm was a fifty-year-old man who still felt required to ask his father how he should dress and whether he was allowed to become president of the German Reich. For his part, Wilhelm II found the mere idea of being elected to the highest office of the Weimar Republic and swearing an oath of office to a democratic constitution completely out of the question.

In the mind of the Kaiser, self-centred as always, the episode again proved his politically inexperienced sons' lack of ability, and once more, in supercilious missives, he tried to defend the traditional monopoly of the head of the family in making decisions. In a 'decree of the highest order', he stated: 'As an unshakable basis, the Hohenzollern monarchy has legitimacy. That fundamentally distinguishes it from the dynasty of a usurper . . . Every other path is impossible and leads to ruination.' Another sharply worded statement made it clear that his sons Wilhelm and Eitel Friedrich were not to exceed their authority and were also required without exception to abide by the decisions of the family head even during his 'current residence abroad'.[20] At the same time, Wilhelm also addressed the crown prince in letters as 'my dear boy'. In a letter in which he once more treated his oldest son like a fool, he raged against the 'undigested thoughts in an addled skull' that could only be classed as 'absolute nonsense'. By refusing to sanction his political plans, the ex-Kaiser told the prince, he had spared him a 'major humiliation'. Wilhelm II concluded his paternal letter by writing: 'I consider it thoroughly necessarily that you seek as always peace and rest in the south or at a spa.' Around the same time, he wrote to Prince Oskar that he had luckily been able to avert a 'stupid juvenile prank by politically clueless greenhorns who tried to misuse poor W'.[21]

Proximity

Although the improvised plans for a formal political alliance ultimately failed, they did bring the crown prince close to National Socialism in a lasting way. Immediately after the demise of his plans and the ire of his father, Prince Wilhelm wrote to his advisor Selasen-Selasinsky saying that he had now seen with his own eyes in Doorn that 'certain facts' could not be overcome. Nonetheless, Wilhelm identified a 'positive outcome', writing: 'My relationship with the Nazi Party leadership . . . has undergone a decisive bolstering to which the speech I will make this Sunday will surely also contribute. This is an area for future activity. Deferred does not mean ruled out.'[22] That same day, Wilhelm expressed his gratitude in similar words to his other emissary, Günther von Einem, the son of the former German war minister: 'The final chapter has yet to be written, and it is certainly of significance for the future that relations between me and the leadership of the Nazi Party have definitely been reinforced by the past few days of talks.'[23]

The idea that the crown prince was standing 'at the ready' to 'intervene and assist as Reich administrator and then as King Wilhelm III', with the backing of the Reichswehr and the 'moderate elements' of National Socialism remained in currency. Even Kaiser

Wilhelm II's former ghost writer did his part to promote the notion in his reports from Berlin.[24]

Details of the failed alliance quickly became public knowledge in Germany and made their way into the American press within a couple of days.[25] Knowledge of the talks between the crown prince's and the Nazi camps nourished month-long rumours in the domestic and international press that Hindenburg was going to step down as president and that Wilhelm II would be appointed Reich administrator.[26] The German word for administrator, *Verweser*, is nearly identical to the German verb for 'to decay', *verwesen*, inspiring the magazine *Der Wahre Jakob* to run a cartoon depicting Wilhelm dressed in a hussar's uniform with a spade in his hand standing in front of a ditch in which the German Reich lay malodorously rotting. The caption of the cartoon proposed that the crown prince had found 'a thoroughly fortuitous formulation for the nature of his intentions'.[27] 'Hitler promises the ex-Kaiser the throne,' it was proclaimed three weeks after the crown prince had endorsed Hitler in the presidential election, and the left-wing press passed along fictitious reports that Kaiser Wilhelm had donated a quarter of a million marks to Hitler's campaign and pledged to make him a prince.[28] Even several weeks later the *Welt am Abend* newspaper was still asking: 'Will the ex-crown prince become Reich administrator?' Pro-democracy newspapers seriously discussed the rumour that the crown prince was headed to London on a foreign policy mission to improve the chances for a restoration of the Hohenzollern monarchy.[29] In the summer of 1932, a cover story of the Catholic magazine *Der gerade Weg*, published by Centre Party supporter and opponent of the Nazis Fritz Gerlich, was entitled '1,000 Princes and a Metalworker: On the Natural History of the National Socialist German "Workers Party"'. Heading a list of 'Heavy Labourers as Members or Friends' was the crown prince followed by August Wilhelm.[30]

The former state secretary Hans Schäffer, a confidant of the ex-chancellor Heinrich Brüning, was convinced that summer that the Reichswehr minister Kurt von Schleicher planned to install Prince Wilhelm in political office. The crown prince had a 'hands-on role' in the plans, Schäffer contended, and some of the crucial meetings were taking place at Cecilienhof.[31]

Reports on various options for a likely restoration of the Hohenzollern monarchy spread all the way down to the provincial press in France, and the alleged plan for a regency was discussed in astonishing detail, often on front pages.[32] French journalists in the autumn of 1932 believed that the Papen government was considering how best to publicly declare the resurrection of the monarchy while others predicted that the restoration would happen in stages from Hindenburg to Schleicher to Hitler to the monarchy itself.[33]

The international press in English, including the major dailies in London, New York, Dublin, Boston, Toronto, Austin, Texas and Shanghai, continually reported during the Papen administration that the monarchy was making a comeback and that concrete talks had taken place between the government, the army, the Stahlhelm paramilitaries, the crown prince and Doorn. Readers in New York were told that 20,000 people had turned out to frenetically cheer the Kaiser's five sons in the Sportpalast arena.[34] Belgian writer Georges Simenon, the inventor of famous detective Maigret, passed on news that the Kaiser's wife had taken tea with Hitler in Berlin's Kaiserhof Hotel – which the foreign prince interpreted as confirmation that the monarchy would be returning.[35] French correspondents wrote of seeing the crown prince received and accompanied by an official escort of Nazis in Berlin.[36]

It barely took twenty-four hours for the world press to spread the news of public appearances, statements and speeches made by individual Hohenzollern family members. When, for instance, Prince August Wilhelm boasted in the Spandau district of Berlin that his father would soon reclaim the throne and that 'Prussia's iron fist' would smash Germany's foes, the prince's words immediately became the stuff of extensive discussion in London and Washington.[37] In the summer of 1932, some media reports even gave specific dates on which the monarchist coup could be expected.[38] Mussolini, too, was convinced in November 1932 that Germany would return to being a monarchy within the following two years.[39]

A subject of constant debate was the role and stance of the inscrutable Nazi Party. The idea that the Kaiser was indebted to party financiers and that Hitler was among those leading the restoration efforts recurred in the most unlikely places, for instance a June 1932 story in the *Minneapolis Star* entitled 'Hitler Playing Leading Role in Monarchy Plan'. Supposed clandestine meetings between the Kaiser and the Crown Prince in Zandvoort, Netherlands, were such a badly kept secret that they were reported on in Texas.[40] As bogus as many of these reports may have been, they still documented the heightened foreign interest in the Hohenzollerns and their activities, alleged or actual.

The most outlandish rumours did in fact overlap considerably with the actual and vastly more intense activities of the tangled networks of various monarchist associations, whose actions were often based on ideas divorced from reality. Plans and consideration often grew into scenarios straight out of novels. One example was a rumour concerning the navy officer Baron Alexander von Senarclens-Grancy. Grancy, a Nazi supporter from venerable Swiss nobility and an adjutant and advisor of the Kaiser in exile, was said to have drawn up a plan in the summer of 1932 to send a navy commando to free Wilhelm II from his Dutch exile, to bring him via the North Sea to Wilhelmshaven in Germany and to escort him there onto land so that he could proclaim his return as Germany's sovereign.[41]

The notion of close ties between National Socialism and the Hohenzollerns was omnipresent in the latter half of 1932. Depending on the variant, either the Hohenzollerns would usher Hitler into power or, conversely, the Nazi movement would prove a vanguard of the restored monarchy. In November 1932, *Simplicissimus* ran a four-panel cartoon entitled 'The New Tale of the Frog Prince'. The first panel shows a fat, ugly frog with a swastika armband that lives in a 'brown swamp'. The caption read: 'He has nothing but a big mouth and isn't much to look at or listen to.' In the second panel, Franz von Papen and Kurt von Schleicher persuade the virgin Germania to take the frog as her husband. In the third panel the young woman follows their instructions and kisses the frog in a conjugal bed decorated with the Prussian eagle. And the fourth panel, the frog has been transformed into a smiling Prince Wilhelm of Prussia who, decked out in a crown, jack boots and a uniform, holds Germania in his arms.[42]

In October 1932, the German government denied a report in *Vorwärts* about imminent talks between the crown prince, Papen, Schleicher and Hindenburg, calling it 'a product of pure fantasy'.[43] Such speculations were nothing new. Years before, the 'left wing' of the Nazi Party had trumpeted that 'the former crown prince is about to join Hitler's party'.[44] In April 1932, the American Germany correspondent Edgar Ansel Mowrer, who would win the 1933 Pulitzer Prize for his reporting on the rise of National Socialism, wrote of heavily monarchist tendencies in the Nazi Party and believed the Nazi movement was 'also being supported from Doorn and encouraged by the princes'.[45] The Social Democratic press in Austria criticized what it called a 'secret plan' hatched between the Kaiser and Hitler and contended that the Hohenzollerns had placed a portion of their 'enormous wealth' at the Nazis' disposal in order to reclaim the throne with the help of the movement.

Both the pro-democracy and the communist press repeatedly claimed that Hohenzollern family members and other nobility had made large donations to the Nazi Party.[46] At the same time, the *Weltbühne* proposed that Hitler aimed to establish a hereditary monarchy and reported in great detail, albeit without evidence, that the Hohenzollerns had arranged for 220,000 reichsmarks to be paid to the Nazi-affiliated Franz Eher publishing house and had supported the 'Hitler movement' to the tune of a half-million marks. That support was allegedly augmented by donations from the Duke of Saxony-Coburg-Gotha, the Grand Duke of Mecklenburg and the Duke of Braunschweig.

Fritz Gerlich also claimed to have been told by a courier that 'enormous sums of money' were flowing from Doorn into the Nazi Party.[47] Hitler, the story went, wanted to get rid of the 'revolutionary elements' in the movement. The most likely candidate to inherit the throne was the crown prince's eldest son.[48] The 'swastika Kaiser', as the left-wing press repeatedly referred to Wilhelm II, supported the Nazi movement from Doorn both financially and by deploying his sons.[49] The newspapers offered no proof of their assertions. *Vorwärts* referred to the mediation of the Berlin salon hosted by Hitler admirer Viktoria von Dirksen, who had allegedly introduced the Nazi leader to the crown princess and arranged financial support for the SA.[50] The American secret service more or less plausibly traced connections to the Kaiser's wife, Hermine, who was thought to funnel some of her independently inherited wealth to the Nazi Party.[51]

The Crown Prince as 'Campaign Worker'

The 1932 presidential election revealed how close the Hohenzollerns and the Nazis had become. During the campaign, Prince Wilhelm allowed himself to be photographed in civilian garb and an overcoat next to campaign workers wearing sandwich boards advertising the Nazi Party. The foreign press published this image with a caption declaring that the former crown prince was going to vote for Hitler.[52] If French papers were to be believed, the photograph was taken on 13 March, which would have meant that prince Wilhelm had already declared his support for the Nazi leader during the first phase of the election.[53] Hitler visited Cecilienhof on a number of occasions, and the crown princess warmed to the idea of an alliance with National Socialism. 'The crown prince', as his biographer and contemporary Paul Herre would write in 1954, 'was now part of the National Socialist camp in all its forms.'

Wilhelm continued to decline to join the Nazi Party. But Herre would write, correctly:

> In public he was considered a follower of Hitler . . . He had no scruples about taking part in Nazi events or receiving party leaders at his home. The crown princess, too, was in Hitler's camp and sought to win over General Schleicher, who still rebuffed him. Ultimately with complete success.[54]

Conversely, Goebbels's diaries suggest that Wilhelm was right to believe he had increased his own status within the circle of Nazi leaders around Hitler. In June 1932, Hitler was still mulling over a 'reformed monarchy' as a viable form of state and held the crown prince in high regard.[55] The international press also recognized Wilhelm's conspicuous presence at gigantic Stahlhelm rallies like the one in September 1932 that saw 190,000 armed men converge on Berlin's Tempelhofer Feld parade ground in Berlin. Starting at five in the morning, endless columns marched for five hours in front of up to a million spectators, creating 'the most brilliant military display since the days of Ex-Kaiser Wilhelm.' The prince watched the proceedings from a seat of honour, while two of his brothers marched within the ranks.[56]

The presence of some twenty former princes, Chancellor Papen, Reichswehr Minister Schleicher, the crown prince, his brothers and their remaining wives at such a huge, anti-democratic rally was not viewed without concern in France. French correspondents cited the 120,000 pairs of sausages, the 30,000 litres of milk and an indeterminate quantity of beer consumed by the troops 'goose-stepping' past the former heir to the throne.[57] Reports came into Paris of a seven-hour march in the presence of the Reich chancellor, 'the entire aristocracy and all of the generals of the Wilhelmine Empire'. The first table at the subsequent gala dinner at the Kaiserhof Hotel, at which Stahlhelm leader Theodor Duesterberg was seated between Prince Oskar and Prince Eitel Friedrich, made the front page of the French daily *Paris-Soir*.[58] The communist press in France wrote of the deployment of 'the army of the fascists and industrialists'.[59] With good reason, after the events in Berlin-Grunewald and the public appearances of the Bavarian crown princes the following day, one French newspaper remarked that 'the German princes are showing their true faces'.[60] The Stahlhelm's day of celebration was captured in a propaganda film. When it premiered in October 1932 in a Berlin cinema, Chancellor Papen and Prince Wilhelm turned out to watch. Paris newspapers ran photographs of the crown prince grinning for the cameras in the chancellor's box.[61]

But the incident that most highlighted the Hohenzollern's relationship with the Nazi movement for both the domestic and international press was Wilhelm's electoral endorsement of Hitler on 3 April 1932. A few days after the collapse of his plans for getting himself elected president with Nazi help, the crown prince decided to back Hitler in the run-off vote. A press statement, written in his typically terse military tone, announced: 'The withholding of a vote in the run-off of the Reich presidential election is incompatible with the idea of the Harzburger Front. Because I consider a national front unconditionally necessary, I will be voting for Hitler in the run-off.'[62] This endorsement explicitly enlisted the aura and authority of Prussia for Hitler and against Hindenburg, contradicting the position of the Stahlhelm.[63] It was signed, in an attempt to ape the bourgeois customs of the Weimar Republic, 'Wilhelm, Crown Prince.'

The endorsement, composed in the Silesian provinces of Oels, was published by all the major news agencies, resulting in headlines including 'The Right Man for Hitler' (Berlin), 'Je voterai pour Hitler!' (Paris), 'Hitler Wins Vote of Ex-Kaiser's Heir for "Nazis"' (New York), 'No Gentleman' (Edinburgh), 'Hitler's Crown Prince' (New Zealand) and 'Ex-Crown Prince Creates a Sensation' (Shanghai). The news of Wilhelm endorsing Hitler spread like wildfire and was deemed a sensation worthy of front-page headlines not only in the German[64] and German-language press[65] but also in many non-German papers abroad.[66] In Bombay, the *Times of India* wrote of the 'prince's manifesto'. Within twenty-four hours, it was all people in Germany could talk about and was known around the world. A widely read Viennese newspaper ran a cartoon featuring Hitler in a page's hat and an SA uniform bowing before Kaiser Wilhelm II, who was shown holding an axe lying on a block of wood in one hand while presenting the Nazi leader with a thick wad of reichsmarks with the other. Meanwhile, a grinning Crown Prince Wilhelm, adorned with a gigantic hussar's cap, gives the politician a note reading 'Vote for Hitler', which the latter greedily grabs.[67] Echoing this idea, an exclamation-mark-heavy headline on the middle of the front page of the *Chicago Daily Tribune* read: 'Elect Hitler! Crown Prince Tells Germany!'[68]

Prince Wilhelm's endorsement was probably the most public act of Hohenzollern support for the Nazi movement prior to Hitler attaining power in January 1933. Nonetheless, pro-Prussian historians after 1945 only noted, drily, that the endorsement had 'attracted widespread attention'.[69] Crown Prince Wilhelm's charitably inclined biographer Klaus W. Jonas merely remarked that the endorsement had 'stirred up a lot of dust'.[70] Herre, who knew the crown prince personally and was writing less as a historian than as a historical eyewitness, recalled the endorsement dropping like a 'bombshell' on public opinion: 'It was a step that didn't seem necessary in any way and that caused the greatest commotion on all sides. General von Schleicher, who had hoped to utilize the heir to the throne to defeat Hitler, was beside himself.'[71] The daily press vigorously discussed 'the crown prince's advertising for Hitler' and warmed up old rumours about the exiled Kaiser's and the high nobility's alleged financial support of the Nazi Party.[72] The title of a story in *Welt am Montag* read: 'The Crown Prince as Election Worker: A Secret Agreement with the House of Hohenzollern'.[73] Reports of Wilhelm's surprise endorsement also made their way onto the front pages of newspapers in France's overseas colonies.[74]

To appreciate how far the crown prince had moved away politically from the mainstream conservative camp by 1932, we need only look at the intellectually inclined magazine *Der Ring* of the German Gentlemen's Club and the debates within the German Aristocratic Society (DAG). The need to choose between Hindenburg and Hitler compelled everyone active on the political Right to stake out a position.[75] Individual commentators diagnosed the crown prince's endorsement as 'self-destructive' and rightly predicted: 'Monarchism has now been completely swept aside. In a tragic misapprehension of the political developments, this representative of the dynasty has abdicated his duty and calling.'[76]

An Endorsement Without Effect?

With good reason, recent research has treated Wilhelm's endorsement of Hitler in early April 1932 as one of the key documents of Hohenzollern history. Yet this statement of political affiliation was one in a long series of steps taken by various parts of the Hohenzollern political apparatus to cosy up to Nazism. In the preceding weeks, at the same time as the hastily improvised attempt to form an anti-democratic duo of Hitler and Wilhelm, the crown prince had called upon several of the most powerful right-wing representatives in Germany to support the Nazi leader. On 23 March, Wilhelm sent letters to Franz Seldte and Alfred Hugenberg, criticizing their potential abstention in the run-off election and demanding that they publicly back Hitler.[77] He was following the lead of the Kaiser's head advisor Magnus von Levetzow, who had written to radical right-wing elites such as Heinrich Class and Göring, announcing his opposition to Hindenburg as an ostensible friend of the Weimar system and giving his support for Hitler. The rear admiral was convinced that Hitler, 'once granted power, would call upon the finest forces of the nation and its best men to work with him'. Alongside far-right general and Freikorps leader Count Rüdiger von der Goltz and Duke Carl Eduard von Sachsen-Coburg und Gotha, one of the most energetic patrons of the Nazi movement in the high nobility, Levetzow had pledged his loyalty to a form of political agitation that was aimed particularly at military circles and often featured in the Nazis' *Völkischer Beobachter* newspaper.[78]

After the fact, the crown prince himself also portrayed his endorsement as a major expression of support for the Nazi movement. In June 1934, Wilhelm bragged to the British newspaper mogul Lord Rothermere that he had 'secured' two million votes from traditional conservatives for Hitler in the 1932 presidential run-off election. In clumsy English, the crown prince said he had supported Nazism since the time 'when Adolf Hitler, whose genius had understood to hammer into the broad masses of the workers the faith in a new nationalist socialist Germany, began his ascent'. He added:

> Thus I also joined Adolf Hitler, already at a time, when wide circles of the Stahlhelm and particularly of the German Nationalists refused to recognize him . . . May I remind you of our last conversation at Cecilienhof and of the things I had to say then in favour of Hitler? May I summarize it once more shortly: I had tried repeatedly to include already Chancellor Brüning to retire voluntarily, and to recommend Hitler as his successor to the Field Marshal. I continued these attempts under the Chancellorship of General von Schleicher. At the Presidential elections I stated publicly that I would vote for Adolf Hitler and against the Field Marshal. I believe to have thus secured for Adolf Hitler about two million votes from my Stahlhelm comrades and from the German Nationalists. I also intervened personally to obtain the cancellation of the interdiction against the Nationalist Socialist formations.

Wilhelm wound up by stating that it had been a happy day for Germany when Hitler was finally appointed Reich chancellor: 'All I can say is that on that day indescribable jubilation went through the whole German nation.' Hitler's own position was being increasingly jeopardized by radical elements, Wilhelm claimed, blaming Goebbels in particular. The best way for Hitler to consolidate his own status was by uniting his regime with the monarchy. The exact circumstances under which that merger was to happen would be just a 'a question of staging'.[79]

Contemporary observers rated the effect of the crown prince's endorsement very highly,[80] but both they and contemporary historians have questioned Wilhelm's boast that he had delivered Hitler two million votes.[81] There's no quantifying the effect of the endorsement. That said, it would be absurd to think that the support of the Kaiser's eldest son and heir to the throne would have had no effect whatsoever on the right-wing camp, and there is no denying that the endorsement prompted intense discussions both in Germany and abroad. Here again was a leading representative of the House of Hohenzollern helping Hitler to seem like an acceptable political ally. In his second dissertation of 1981, Prince Friedrich Wilhelm of Prussia – Crown Prince Wilhelm's grandson and a historian whose first dissertation was rejected ex post facto for plagiarism – speculated that the crown prince's endorsement perhaps reflected the Kaiser's wishes at the time.[82]

Support for the SA and the SS

The historian Prince Friedrich Wilhelm was much more direct in his evaluation of another endorsement. On 13 April 1932, the crown prince and princess had spent four hours with Hitler in Göring's apartment, where they reiterated the heir to the throne's interest in a restoration of the monarchy with the help of the Nazi movement.[83] He also tried in vain to reach the generals Schleicher and Wilhelm Groener by telephone to secure their support for the idea.[84] The following day, Wilhelm wrote a letter to Groener, who was Germany's Reichswehr and interior minister. In it, he vigorously opposed one of the most effective measures the Weimar Republic ever took against the Nazi movement: the ban on the SA and the SS that had been issued the day before. The contents of that letter would become public knowledge some months later.[85]

The ban on the SA and the SS was very controversial among the German officer corps and on the political Right in general. In May 1932, Groener's career would come to an end after he gave a particularly weak speech in the Reichstag defending the ban. It made the lieutenant general and quartermaster general of the Army Supreme Command seem like a feeble old man past his time. Groener's position had already been undermined by his second marriage to a woman thirty years his junior, who gave birth to a child only a few months after their wedding. Playing on the fact that the child had obviously been conceived out of wedlock, Groener's son was nick-named 'Nurmi' after a champion Finnish middle- and long-distance runner. The son of a paymaster from Württemberg, Groener was never fully accepted by the inner circle of the leading Prussian military fans anyway, and he had attracted their direct ire for his role in the Kaiser's flight to the Netherlands. His fellow generals considered him a 'politician, only too ready to compromise'. His opposition to the SA and the SS was the last straw. In the end, all the attacks from the old military guard simply wore him down.[86]

Opposition to the ban on the SA and the SS, which the crown prince criticized as a 'grave mistake', also helped bring down the Brüning government.[87] Wilhelm wrote to Groener, 'It is incomprehensible to me how you in particular, as the Reichswehr minister, could help to break up the wonderful human materiel that has been put together in the SA and SS and is enjoying valuable training there.' Young people were being given a 'preliminary education in the sport of self-defence', the crown prince asserted, and would stand at the ready in case of border conflicts and as a reservoir for a future army. It had been his desire 'right from the very start', Wilhelm explained, to create a 'relationship of trust' between the Reichswehr Ministry and the Nazi Party.[88]

A short time later, the crown prince wrote to Hindenburg recommending that he take a hard line against the left-wing press, put down the 'obstructionists' in southern Germany, ban the KPD, lay 'a number of communists at some point out on the pavement in eastern Germany' and generally 'not to be gentle' in any of these endeavours.[89] His grandson, the historian Friedrich Wilhelm, would write forty years later: 'Without question the crown prince did his part to make the Nazi Party acceptable to right-wing circles.'[90] It speaks volumes that Germany's Reichswehr and interior minister, Groener, thought it necessary to send a four-page answer to an heir to the throne who had no official governmental function. In that letter, the general reached very different conclusions to those of the crown prince about the quality of the 'human materiel' united in the SA and the SS and the 'blood injected into them'.[91]

When Wilhelm's letter was reproduced in the press, it unleashed outraged debate in German-language newspapers. In a report on what it called the prince's attempt to unite Stahlhelm, the SA and the SS, Vienna's working-class *Arbeiter-Zeitung* played on the phrase 'human materiel', writing that Wilhelm was promoting the 'wonderful homicidal materiel' in the Nazi Party's main organizations.[92] The pro-democracy camp celebrated the ban on the SA as a major success. The pacifist journalist Carl von Ossietzky, then serving time in prison for publishing an article about Germany secretly building up an air force, wrote about the 'brutal culture of marauders', illegal caches of weapons on country estates and the flood throughout the country of SA men, who hadn't learned any skills other than 'standing at attention and bashing heads'. Rather prematurely, Ossietzky concluded that the ban on the SA was a decisive step towards demystifying the Nazi movement and ensuring the triumph of the Weimar Republic.[93]

Three weeks after writing this notorious letter, Crown Prince Wilhelm celebrated his fiftieth birthday. The illustrated magazine *Sport im Bild* devoted a half-page portrait showing him posing casually in bright tweed and riding trousers.[94] A London illustrated magazine devoted a whole page to the occasion.[95] Among those invited to the celebrations were military elites from the imperial armed forces, leaders of the Reichswehr and representatives of the most important right-wing groups. Late in the evening, Göring – in civilian dress – appeared and withdrew with the crown prince and princess for an intimate chat in the Great Hall at Cecilienhof.[96] In the central district of Berlin-Mitte, monarchists had rented Berlin's largest dancehall, the Konzerthaus Clou, for a party decked out in imperial red, white and black that was reported on by the Chicago press.[97]

Among the various members of the Hohenzollern clan who viewed a restoration of the monarch with Nazi help as a viable option were the Kaiser, his wife Hermine, the crown prince and crown princess, the crown prince's eldest son (another royal who was probably personally acquainted with Hitler and Göring)[98] and

Prince August Wilhelm and his son Alexander. In 1931 and 1932, Hitler and other Nazi leaders were frequent visitors to August Wilhelm's residence, the Villa Liegnitz in Potsdam, located on the edge of the royal Sanssouci Park some 3 kilometres removed from Cecilienhof. Eighteen-year-old Prince Alexander, who formally joined the Nazi Party in 1931, worked on behalf of the Nazi leadership in his father's home and at right-wing salons and mass Nazi events. In his memoirs, Hitler's press officer Otto Dietrich recalled that Hitler, before abandoning monarchism once and for all in 1933, considered the well-liked Alexander a possible future 'Kaiser' – although no one within the Hohenzollern family shared that view.[99]

Limits of Convergence

By endorsing Hitler, the former crown prince had positioned himself against Hindenburg, and all the most important conflicts on the Right revolved around how conservatives should approach National Socialism. The broad spectrum of options stretched from membership of the Nazi Party and the SA, close alliances and tactical cooperation to attempts to 'contain' the Nazis and Hitler, attempts to 'contain' the Nazis without Hitler, sceptical distance and open hostility. In 1932 corresponding lines of conflict ran through the ultranationalist DNVP party, the Stahlhelm, the monarchist associations, the Reich Agrarian League, Germany's many aristocratic advocacy groups and the Reichswehr. Ultimately, the two largest right-wing militias of the Weimar Republic, the Stahlhelm and the SA, would have more in common than not, and in January 1933, the Stahlhelm would be represented in Hitler's first governing cabinet. The behaviour of the crown prince, a former army group commander and a poster boy for the Stahlhelm, was very influential in reconciling the two factions on the political Right.

Nonetheless, the two main right-wing German political currents butted heads in the months before and even after Hitler assumed power. The Stahlhelm and the SA differed dramatically in style, age structure and politics. Parts of the SA dismissed the Stahlhelm as a league of ossified, backward-looking reactionaries while some Stahlhelm leaders rejected the Nazi Party as a fundamentally 'socialist' party, whose platform, at least in April 1932, resembled that of the SPD. The implication was that only a strong DNVP and a bolstering of other traditional right-wing parties would bring about the desired alliance between conservatives and National Socialists.[100] During the autumn of 1932 and the Papen government, Nazi propaganda stepped up its attacks on the aristocrat-dominated 'cabinet of barons' and the old elites. Conversely, from the Stahlhelm leadership on down to its local chapters, traditional nationalists objected to the SA's rough manners and pseudo-socialist demands. A cartoon published in the Stahlhelm press in October 1932 depicted three aristocratic SA leaders – Count Bernd von Wedel, Count Wolf-Heinrich von Helldorf and Prince August Wilhelm – with swastika armbands in the Kaiserhof Hotel in Berlin: Through an open window they can hear anti-aristocratic chants coming from the street. In response to the question, 'What kind of savage proletarian din are the communists kicking up down there?', the Berlin SA Leader Count Helldorff answers, 'You've got it wrong – those are our party comrades.'[101]

Often mocked as a 'party for the upper crust', DNVP conservatives and Stahlhelm members turned the tables by drawing attention to aristocrats and 'upper crust' in the Nazi Party.[102] During election campaigns, Nazi newspapers never ceased attacking the 'barons', the Gentlemen's Club and the circles around Papen. In response, conservative newspapers went after Goebbels as a 'male Rosa Luxemburg . . . unattractive in physical form and Jewish of appearance'. Conservatives didn't fail to take note whenever Goebbels sneered that the Kaiser had failed to live up to the duty simple soldiers had been able to fulfil, 'namely to stand by your people in need'.[103] For many traditional right-wingers, the Nazi propagandist was a rabble-rouser and liar with no control over his emotions. Referring to the early Goebbels endorsement of socialist-sounding slogans, they accused him of proclaiming 'Hail Moscow' not so very long ago. By contrast, conservatives pointed out, the Stahlhelm had opposed Bolshevism before the Nazi movement even existed.[104]

There is ample evidence in places like rural Brandenburg of a split between DNVP-loyal aristocratic estate owners and increasingly Nazi-leaning farmers.[105] Such conflicts came to a head in countless towns and cities. Throughout Germany, there were 'planned acts of terror' carried out by SA units on DNVP and Stahlhelm events. The conservative press reported on SA commandos setting off fireworks, firing gas pistols and releasing mice as well as brawls at event venues and the use of batons, knives and even firearms. In one instance, SA men forced their way into a Stahlhelm event in Düsseldorf and drowned out attendees attempts to sing the German national anthem, the 'Deutschlandlied', with a version of the Nazis' own Horst Wessel Song. DNVP newspapers branded this SA action as an expression of the group's 'subhuman' nature.[106]

In October 1932, the DNVP booked a traditional labour movement venue, the 'beer palace' Neue Welt in the working-class district of Neukölln, for a rally, underscoring the Stahlhelm's desire to make their presence unmistakably felt in left-wing areas. Nazis took up positions throughout the arena before the event began, and their coordinated disruptions caused a riot in which truncheons were swung, beer glasses thrown and people seriously wounded. SA units, who had arrived at the venue with their own regimental doctor, chanted 'Heil Hitler – and to hell with [DNVP chairman] Hugenburg.' The DNVP press accused them of using 'Bolshevik methods'.[107]

The aggression between Nazis and traditional conservative nationalists were more than just theatrical rituals, leading to calls on both sides for the resentments and animosities to be resolved. Well-respected and highly visible mediators were needed. Few, if any, leaders from the aristocratic-military camp were as suitable for this purpose as the crown prince, and Wilhelm duly called upon his Stahlhelm comrades to join with the SA and the SS. His argument that the organizations should unite Germany's youth as those who would embody Germany's capacity to defend itself militarily was hotly debated in the German-speaking press.[108]

In a long letter to Hitler in September 1932, Wilhelm reiterated his call for an alliance between the DNVP and the Nazi Party, particularly between the Stahlhelm, the SA and the SS. 'Dear Mr Hitler,' the crown prince wrote. 'Do not let the many people who welcome and support your movement from the depths of their hearts waver and become confused . . . Please put personal feeling to one side and lead this marvellous national movement into fruitful labour.' Not only the German papers, but also the *Times* in London reported on Wilhelm's call for unity between the Stahlhelm and the SA.[109]

The appeal for right-wing solidarity was consistent with the idea of 'taming' National Socialism advanced by Schleicher, Papen and other conservatives. Hitler's superficially polite but arrogant answers, which reiterated his demands to become Germany's new leader, left no doubt that this plan was destined to fail. Hitler portrayed himself as a man from the bottom of the social ladder who preferred to work 'thirteen to fourteen hours a day . . . bloodying his hands' with common labourers than to accept a promotion from above. The time of the old elites was past, the Nazi leader none too subtly suggested. The future belonged to the movement he and he alone had built.

The crown prince sent a copy of this correspondence, in addition to some information about his latest hunting achievements, to his father in Doorn. A short time later, in September 1932, the Kaiser's sarcastic commentary fell into first Göring's, then Hitler's hands. Any relationship the crown prince might have imagined he had built with the Nazi leadership was badly damaged.[110] As the director of the Ullstein publishing house, Hans Schäffer – a Jewish lawyer and financial expert and keen observers of his times – subsequently surmised, 'something very heavy must be weighing upon the house of Hohenzollens, otherwise it would not be coming apart as it is'.[111] Despite his constant proclamations of alliances and loyalties, at least between March 1932 and early 1934, the crown prince 'pinned all his hopes on Hitler and National Socialism', and the contours of the new monarchy he envisioned, aside from his own central role in it, remained vague.[112] The same was true for the Kaiser's leading political advisors in Doorn and Berlin and at least partly this applied as well to Kurt von Schleicher and the Reich chancellor, Franz von Papen, Schleicher himself had helped install. Conversely, Hitler seems to have been worried about being trumped by the crown prince if it came to a direct confrontation.[113] The Nazi leader had a healthy respect for Wilhelm's prestige and charisma at this point and alternately feared and courted him.[114]

Yet, although there were plenty of potential conflicts between the crown prince and the Nazi movement, and the Hohenzollerns' relationship to the various groups and potentates in charge of the Nazi party remained constantly unstable, the failure of the envisioned alliance to materialize in late March 1932 was regarded as a missed opportunity, probably never to come again.[115] Following in the tradition of Nazi Party attacks on the German nobility, the regional party leader of the Ostmark, Wilhelm Kube, took the crown prince and his ambitious wife to task in late 1932. A trained journalist with experience in organizing campaigns on the racist Right, Kube depicted Wilhelm as unfit for any and all positions of leadership in the coming Third Reich.[116] Even months after his opening salvo, he still railed against 'those intoxicated with beer and business' who 'confused the resurgence of the nation with a royal birthday ball'. Hitler alone, and 'no one else in Germany', Kube exclaimed, had 'crushed the skull' of the 'beast of Marxism'.[117]

Kube was a parliamentary group leader in the Prussian regional parliament, a self-proclaimed 'socialist and nationalist' critic of Hindenburg as a coward who had placed his 'sword' at the disposal of the social democratic revolution in 1918. He depicted Wilhelm, by contrast, as a laughable fool drawing up pie-in-the-sky plans with Papen in Cecilienhof and the 'extraordinarily ambitious crown princess' as a power-hungry woman with a 'scheming nature' thanks to the 'southwestern blood' in her veins. The crown prince's eldest son, Kube claimed, had disparaged Hitler, while the crown prince himself, like his own father, had an 'embarrassing soft spot' for Jews.[118]

As far back as 1921, right-wing publishers had offered to commission a book documenting the crown prince's staunchly anti-Jewish stance, but angry anti-Semites never tired of accusing Wilhelm of making common cause with 'fat-cat Orientals' and Stresemann, portraying the latter as part of a Jewish conspiracy.[119] The well-to-do Berlin district of Grunewald became a dog-whistle term, reminding people that the crown prince consorted with members of the Jewish bourgeoisie.

Two days before assuming power in Germany, Hitler 'absolutely excoriated the feudal lords of 1918', a group Goebbels dismissed as 'cry babies'. Before that, in *Mein Kampf*, the Nazi leader had also skewered the alleged decadence of the hereditary German nobility and the behaviour of the princes in 1918.[120] The racist camp had been honing its attacks on the aristocracy and the royal family ever since the Wilhelmine Empire, and parts of the Nazi movement had adopted and sharpened these arguments. This hostility had been a constant throughout the Weimar Republic. Several years prior to Kube's attacks, the aristocrat Louis Müldner von Mülnheim challenged a racist publisher to a duel, after the latter accused him of having Jewish ancestry.[121]

There were waves of anti-monarchist tendencies in the Nazi movement cresting in early 1934, when public warnings were issued that the Nazis would 'crush any aristocratic underminers [of the new political order] just as we did the Marxists and communists'.[122] The authors of that statement were Reich Administrator Wilhelm Friedrich Loeper and Kube. For the latter it was an astonishing about-face. As recently as June 1932, Kube had come out in support of the Hohenzollern monarchy and against a confiscation of aristocratic property in the Prussian regional parliament.[123] But in the minds of the racist Right, there was no contradiction between these two positions. They were used at different times and in different situations. As part of the general attempt to portray the Nazi Party as an organization of common people, the ideology advanced by

Goebbels, Kube and 'Reich Farmers Leader' Richard Walther Darré could be tactically modified for use in both the agricultural community and the working classes.

In the latter half of 1932, speculation was rife about a restoration of the monarchy. The emergency decrees issued by the Papen and Schleicher governments and the dismissal of the democratically elected government in Prussia in July 1932 had largely pulled the rug out from under the feet of defenders of democracy, and the Stahlhelm openly marched with 150,000 men through Berlin. In this situation, and with the Nazi movement losing both its unique aura and its larger number of votes in the November national election, Nazi propaganda dramatically turned up the volume of its anti-capitalist components. But this was a good example of Nazism's ability to adapt, chameleon-like, to its environment, and it modulated between rejection of and cooperation with the monarchist, conservative camp. There was never a permanent rupture with conservative functionaries and elites. Still, the conflicts remained both real and visible. The most vocal and hardest-edged attacks were seldom directly launched against the crown prince or the Hohenzollerns. Instead, a significant minority of Nazi followers were generally critical of or even hostile towards the aristocracy. The most conspicuous fault line between old nobility and the New Right was one the Nazis had inherited from the ethnic chauvinism of the Wilhelmine Empire. A portion of the self-appointed representatives of the ethnically conceived German *Volk* in the late nineteenth and early twentieth centuries considered themselves to be the new aristocrats and rejected the existing nobility as decadent, incompetent and 'Jewified'. A 1912 paperback genealogy called the *Semi-Gotha* went so far as to list all the factual and purported relations between aristocratic and Jewish families, piling considerable pressure on many princely dynasties, including that of the Hohenzollerns. Along with Kube, Darré and at times Goebbels were the most anti-aristocratic of the Nazi leadership.

The German literature specialist Hans F. K. Günther, also known as an 'anthropologist' and nicknamed the 'pope of race', had called for the creation of a new German aristocracy all the way back in 1924, creating concern and unease within the hereditary nobility.[124] Two years later, he argued in a book called *Aristocracy and Race* against the idea of equality of noble birth, proposing that non-Nordic aristocrats should be stripped of their status and contended that any 'Nordic' farmgirl was genetically far superior to any non-Nordic princess.[125] In 1927, a physician wrote of Wilhelm II that the laws governing equality of birth among the nobility had led to a 'prevalence of genetic deficiencies and near-degeneration'. For that reason, the author argued, the historic aristocracy was largely useless as a leadership caste. The new 'German aristocracy' – equipped with 'blond hair, narrow skulls, blue eyes, good intellects . . . self-assured and distanced manners, and pleasing gaits' – would have to be created according to the rules of modern eugenics.[126]

Darré radicalized these ideas in his 1930 anti-aristocratic screed *New Aristocracy of Blood and Soil*.[127] In an oft-cited passage, he proposed that the historic nobility no longer had enough 'good blood' in its veins to 'measure up to a farm boy from a northern race'. For that reason, the aristocracy was unsuitable to lead the coming Reich.[128] Traditional nationalist newspapers often had difficulty countering the aggressive attacks of the Nazi agricultural leader, including his accusations that prior to 1914 the former had brought Marxists into Germany and allowed 'broad streams of Jewish blood to flow into German aristocratic families'.[129] With a nod towards Cicero, one DNVP newspaper asked on its title page, 'How much longer, Darré?' This may have resonated with graduates of humanistic academies, but it was hardly sufficient to discredit the Nazi press with the masses. Nor were traditional conservative attempts to turn the tables and uncover the Jewish ancestry of Nazi leaders. The name of the DNVP newspaper was the bland *The Party* while the Nazis had *The Attack (Der Angriff)*.[130]

The crown prince faced the same dilemmas as other aristocrats, who simultaneously wanted to influence, contain, repel and co-opt the aggressive style of the Nazi movement. This amounted to a political aporia. When Prince Wilhelm had returned to Germany in

1923, there was no way for him to appease both disgruntled traditionalists and radical anti-Semites, and that situation hadn't changed by 1932.

The concept of a new aristocracy propagated as of 1930 by the Argentine-born merchant's son, frontline officer and doctor of agricultural sciences Darré was among the most direct challenges to the traditional nobility to come from the Nazi Party.[131] It attacked the aristocracy as a whole and with it the Hohenzollerns on two central points, ideological and economic: ideological insofar as it used racism and eugenics as a weapon against the nobility both high and low, and economic since Darré's promotion of relatively small agricultural units was a declaration of war on the *latifundia* of the traditional large German aristocratic estates. Large-scale aristocratic landowners often called the Nazi movement 'Bolshevik' – and there was vigorous aristocratic opposition within the Brüning and Schleicher governments to National Socialist ideas for settlement programmes. Meanwhile, Germany's most important agrarian interest group, the Reich Agricultural League, agitated on behalf of Hitler.[132]

The 'socialist' tendencies of the Nazi Party caused the wild mood swings of the ex-Kaiser to reach a low in the autumn of 1932. In a letter, which ended on a note of melancholy nostalgia, to one of his advisors, he wrote that Hitler was increasingly showing his true nature as a socialist and that he, Wilhelm II, no longer expected anything from the Nazi leader. As always, the ex-Kaiser depicted himself as the sole solution: 'The swastika flag is simply too red . . . The monarch and supreme wartime commander is the only one who can perhaps bring Hitler to reason. There's a lot of rain here, but it's warm. Today's Sunday. How nice it used to be. Your Wilhelm!'[133]

A general anti-aristocracy undercurrent, occasionally extending to the Hohenzollerns, was an undeniable aspect of the movement, but it never predominated as either ideology or practice. Kube, an excessively corrupt figure even by Nazi standards, was relieved of his posts in 1936 before being reactivated as an organizer of violence and genocide in Germany's war in eastern Europe. The influence of Darré – whose wife was herself an aristocrat – also waned until the start of the Second World War. Hitler, Goebbels, Himmler and Göring all concluded numerous arrangements with the aristocracy and supported compromises concerning traditional aristocratic property.[134] The uneasy relationship between the house of Hohenzollern and the Nazi movement can best be seen as an extension of the openly anti-aristocratic strain in earlier right-wing racism.

The statements issued by Hitler and Nazi leaders always remained vague enough to leave room for monarchist ideas, and conversely the emotional connection monarchists felt towards the crown remained powerful enough to maintain illusions about alleged monarchist aspirations within the Nazi movement. For example, in June 1931 a monarchist lawyer and officer in the reserves recorded his subjective impression of Hitler stopping August Wilhelm to greet him during a parade in the city of Chemnitz: 'His greeting was not that of a leader of a movement to one of the movement's followers, however, prominent. It was a greeting of someone with military training towards a prince.'[135] Indeed, some conservatives continued to believe well into 1934 that Nazism was 'actually' a monarchist movement. But there was scant evidence for that belief.

Hitler and Schleicher: Imaginary Options

Among his many connections to anti-democracy military and political elites, Crown Prince Wilhelm's relationship with Kurt von Schleicher played a particularly important role in the latter half of 1932. The former general was one of the most powerful conspirators among the many bourgeois and aristocratic elites who sought to bring down the Weimar Republic by instrumentalizing the mass popularity of the Nazi Party. Schleicher was the leading political mind within the military, the minister of the Reichswehr, the architect of the Papen government and, for two months, the final German chancellor before Hitler, and Wilhelm engaged in an on-again, off-again political collaboration with him.

Schleicher and his circle of anti-democratic advisors – top military officers, leading lawyers and journalists – tried out a number of ways in the second half of 1932 to institute a state of emergency and create an authoritarian regime. They included variations with and without Hitler. With the idea of installing a temporary Reich administrator and vague conceptions of restoring the monarchy remaining in currency, the crown prince accrued an increasing importance within the anti-democratic camp. The attempts to form an alliance with Hitler in March and Wilhelm's endorsement of him the following month led to further discussions and negotiations about potential cooperation, engendering both fears and hopes among the populace at large. The phase lasted for around five months between the 'Prussian blow' on 20 July 1932, in which powerful elites led by Chancellor Franz von Papen dismissed the elected Social Democratic regional government of Prussia, and January 1933, when Papen agreed that Hitler would be named chancellor.

Schleicher knew the crown prince from their youth in the prestigious military academy in Plön in northern Germany,[136] and the two were close enough for Schleicher, in a 1920 letter, to address Wilhelm as 'My Dear Crown Chap'. Given the customarily fraternal tone of the military and the aristocracy, it's difficult to say whether the pair were friends or had a relationship of mutual convenience. What is certain is that, by the end of 1932, the crown prince would give in to political pressure and drop the idea of a government of Schleicher without Hitler for one of Hitler without Schleicher. Schleicher would later be murdered in the 1934 Nazi purge known as the Night of the Long Knives. Major General Ferdinand von Bredow, who would be assassinated shortly thereafter, noted in November 1933 and January 1934 that, where Schleicher was concerned, the crown prince and the House of Hohenzollern had 'a skeleton in their closet'.[137]

What Schleicher, Bredow and the crown prince shared was not a fundamental enmity towards National Socialism, but rather a staunch rejection of the Weimar Republic and a desire to destroy democracy by uniting the political Right. That included the

Die Söhne des Kronprinzen am Maschinengewehr.

Eigenhändige Aufnahme Ihrer Kaiserlichen Hoheit der Frau Kronprinzessin in Zoppot.

The four sons of the Crown Prince and Crown Princess pretending to man a machine-gun during the First World War.

Die Kronprinzessin und Prinzessin Viktoria Luise in Uniform.

Phot. G. Berger, Potsdam.

Wilhelm's daughter Viktoria Luise and Crown Princess Cecilie in commander's uniforms.

3. Wilhelm with his entourage chopping wood in Huis Doorn's park.

Doorn.　　　　Huize Doorn.　　　　Verblijfpaats Wilhelm II.

4. Huis Doorn.

Kronprinz in Wieringen

5. Ex-Crown Prince Wilhelm in 1920 in Jan Luijt's smithy on the then island of Wieringen.

Kronprinzessin Cecilie
und die Prinzen Wilhelm, Louis Ferdinand u. Hubertus
inmitten von verwundeten Kriegern.

6. Crown Princess Cecilie with her three eldest sons during a visit to the military hospital in the seaside resort of Zoppot (now Sopot in Poland), 1915.

7. The ex-Crown Prince in a modish suit next to a motorcar, July 1931.

8. 'Stresemann the Bridge-Builder': The ex-Crown Prince enters the German Republic as a knight wearing a robe decorated with swastikas. The cartoon parodies a poster for Fritz Lang's film *Die Nibelungen*. Reich Chancellor Gustav Stresemann was instrumental in enabling the ex-Crown Prince's return from exile in November 1923.

9. The ex-Crown Prince and ex-Crown Princess in front of Oels Castle in Silesia (now Oleśni‹ in Poland), after his sensational return from his Wieringen exile (1923).

10. Emperor Wilhelm II with the Crown Prince's sons Wilhelm and Louis Ferdinand, around 1910.

1. The Cecilienhof Palace, Potsdam, 1918.

)ie Stiege zum Hohenzollern-Thron

12. An Austrian cartoon from 1933 showing the steps Wilhelm needs to climb to get back his throne: first the Prussian nobility, then the Evangelical Church, then militarism, then National Socialism.

13. The ex-Crown Prince with pro-Hitler-campaigners during the second round of the 1932 presidential election.

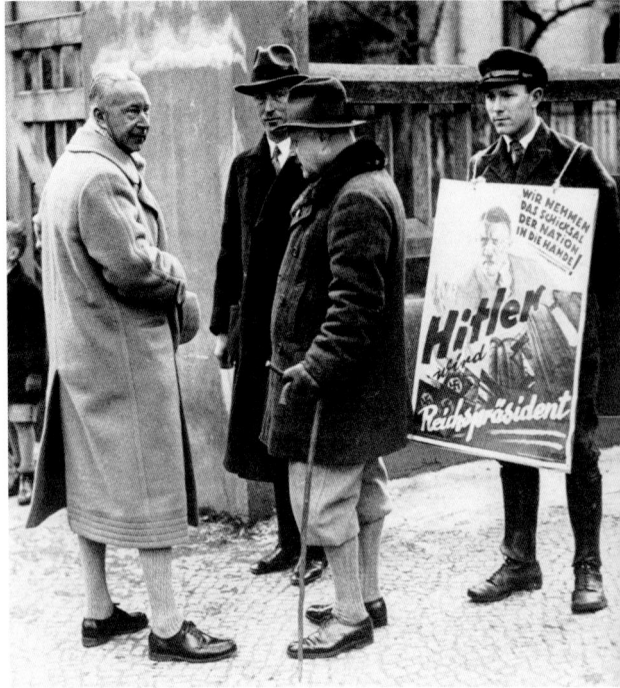

14. The ex-Crown Prince performatively shaking hands with Hermann Göring in front of the Berlin Cathedral, 5 February 1933.

'reasonable' segments of the Nazi movement. Wilhelm often moved amorphously and unpredictably within the anti-democratic right wing in Germany, but, as his contemporaries recognized, there were two constants. Every move he made was directed against democracy and at bringing himself to power and, if possible, to a not-further-specified throne. He also shared his 'friend' Schleicher's officious tone, exaggerated self-regard, contempt for Nazi arrivistes and enthusiasm for everything military.

Like Schleicher, Wilhelm was capable of modulating between multiple right-wing options, including Italian-style fascism, utterly vague notions of monarchist restoration, a government run by emergency decrees and a military dictatorship, and potential allies, which spanned the Reichswehr, the DNVP, the agrarian associations, the Stahlhelm, the SA, Schleicher, Göring, SA leader Ernst Röhm, his father, the ex-Kaiser, and Adolf Hitler. The consequences for Schleicher when he could no longer keep these many balls in the air were fatal. By contrast, to stay with the metaphor, with Wilhelm, the balls merely stayed on the ground. The crown prince had already begun to turn his back on his 'friend' Schleicher even before Hitler was named chancellor. Ten days before Schleicher's murder, Wilhelm wrote in a letter to the British newspaper mogul Lord Rothermere that, although Schleicher had the best of intentions, he didn't possess sufficient will and energy for genuine action, which was why he, Wilhelm, together with many of his comrades in the Stahlhelm, had joined forces with Hitler.[138]

Recent historians have contended that Crown Prince Wilhelm reached the height of his political influence amidst the crisis of state in November 1932, becoming a key figure in conservative plans that excluded Hitler.[139] But the historical record doesn't support this view, and there is good reason to doubt that Wilhelm was very actively involved in allegedly anti-Hitler circles around Schleicher in the latter half of that month. On 19 November 1932, the crown prince announced he was travelling for two weeks to the picturesque Salzkammergut for the express purpose of 'escaping the political turmoil'. The fact that he took a holiday in the Austrian mountains near Mondsee Lake until early December clearly belies the idea that he was engaged in a tireless political battle against Hitler's chancellorship.[140]

The crown prince has often been depicted as being a major source of ideas and having excellent connections to a purported group of right-wing 'Hitler detractors'. But the documented flow of information and the results of the schemes in which Wilhelm took part paint a different picture. They portray the prince as a blowhard whose transparently tactical vacillations between the Reichswehr, the Stahlhelm and diverse factions of the first and second guard of National Socialism significantly damaged a potential united conservative position.

The entire upper aristocracy maintained a habitual distance from Hitler and concerns about socialist strains in the Nazi movement while showing a willingness to cooperate with both. Nine days before Hitler's appointment as chancellor, Otto II, Prince of Salm-Horstmar wrote to the ex-Kaiser in Doorn from his estate in Varlar in western Germany. In his letter, the prince – a leader of the Pan-Germanic League and a supporter of the Harzburg Front – complained about Schleicher's 'shiftiness' and voiced hopes that Papen would regain the chancellorship. To bring that about, the latter would have to get Hitler to join the governing cabinet 'so that the fraternal fight within the anti-Marxist camp finally comes to an end'. The results, the prince predicted, would be the disempowerment of parliament, a revision of voting rights and a reintroduction of the monarchy.[141] This was the core idea and illusion with which Crown Prince Wilhelm and most of his set operated at the time.

In this period, the extent of the crown prince's 'friendships' with Nazi leaders was becoming a problem. There was no way to keep open various anti-democratic options together with their respective leaders without friction, and Wilhelm was flexible enough to drop one or the other, depending on which political camp he was interacting with. In December 1932, for reasons of political expedience, he was forced to defend himself against accusations that he had allied himself with Ernst Röhm. The more

Röhm's homosexuality became a topic for internal discussion, the more assiduously Wilhelm stressed his distance from the SA leader.[142] The Nazi press was vigorously attacking Schleicher by this time. Rumours were spread that the Kaiser had prohibited all members of the royal family from joining the Nazi Party and that Prince August Wilhelm had already forsaken Germany for Italy, but these were lies apparently emanating from anti-aristocratic circles, which were also discredited in the Nazi press.[143]

In contrast to the view propounded by the embittered general Groener,[144] at no point did the crown prince and princess merely repeat whatever Schleicher whispered in their ears. Within the unstable camp of the Right in Germany, the crown prince vacillated between various positions and options represented by Schleicher, Bredow, Hitler opponent General Carl-Heinrich Rudolf Wilhelm von Stülpnagel, the landed gentry of the Reich Agricultural League, Hitler and Göring and various influential 'aristocratic comrades'. Wilhelm's private correspondence contains evidence of vague support for Schleicher as well as equally vague hopes that Hitler would liberate himself from the 'radical elements around Goebbels'. There are also repeated assertions that the crown prince had worked hard to create an alliance 'between the Stahlhelm and the SS and the SA'.[145] In early December, he stressed that Schleicher, despite the danger that he would prematurely be ground down like Papen before him, 'still represented the most valuable bridge to this great, valuable but also very difficult popular movement'.[146]

National Socialists Against Hitler?

This was a time in which a high-ranking Bavarian SA leader, Franz von Hörauf, still considered it possible that Hitler and his party rival Gregor Strasser would reach an agreement in which the latter would become 'leader on matters of substance'. Hörauf recommended that Wilhelm play his cards close to his chest. Following the turmoil of a leadership battle, a 'longing' for a pole of calm to rally round – i.e. the German crown – would become ever stronger.[147] This was the idea, put forward two weeks before Hitler became chancellor, that the crown prince took with him into the first months of the Third Reich. There is no evidence whatever, though, of any dedicated opposition to Hitler by Wilhelm, only of a rapid succession of arrangements that all envisioned an alliance with National Socialism. Circles close to the crown prince confirmed that he was pleased by the Nazis' loss of support in the German national election of November 1932. One of his strategies was to hope that the rise of the Nazi Party and its influence within the anti-democratic camp could be weakened, then controlled. Two days after the November vote, Müldner von Mülnheim also expressed his satisfaction at the decrease in Nazi support.[148] The monarchist camp very much saw the Nazi movement as a containable junior partner and not as the most powerful force in a new conservative alliance. The notion of using Strasser to rein in Hitler as the leader of the 'reasonable' Nazis – although the notion was built on thin, indeed rapidly melting ice – typified monarchist efforts to reach an arrangement with Nazism, not to oppose it. In December 1932, Hörauf questioned 'whether Hitler will come to reason'. The answer he gave was: 'Only under Strasser's leadership will the cooperation desired by His Imperial Majesty between the Nazi Party and the rest of the nationalist forces be possible.'[149]

In late 1932, there was considerable consternation among the crown prince's staff at Goebbels' cutting and 'impudent' attacks upon the Schleicher government. Nazi newspapers were branded 'communistic', and in their private correspondence monarchists fantasized about jailing the soon-to-be German propaganda minister for life.[150] Throughout 1932, traditional conservatives clung to the illusion that Hitler was a 'reasonable' man negatively influenced by 'radical' elements in the Nazi party leadership.[151] Historian Ian Kershaw later masterfully characterized this line of thinking as 'If only the Führer knew' reasoning.[152] Papen, Schleicher and the other architects of the Nazi-led government would all demonstrably fall victim to this false reading of Hitler and his henchmen.

It is highly questionable – in the context of both the importance of Strasser and his allies in the rise of the Nazi movement and of the arcs of those, including Crown Prince Wilhelm, who so quickly and clearly distanced themselves from the forty-year-old diabetic after he had lost the battle for control over the party – whether the Strasser circles and the comparatively 'good' elements of the Nazi Party deserve to be described as Hitler adversaries.[153] In any case, Wilhelm's and Schleicher's main objective of cooperating with Strasser was not to split or destroy the Nazi party but to gain influence over a segment of the party in hopes of steering it to their own ends.

It seems both disingenuous and implausible to look for 'opponents' of Nazism among the circles of the party's second most powerful figure (Gregor Strasser), an SA leader and later commandant of the city of Łódź (Franz von Hörauf), an SS officer and later camp physician at Auschwitz, deeply admired by Hörauf (Baron Franz von Bodmann), a man who would later become one of the most powerful SS leaders (Kurt Daluege), a brutal organizer of various political assassinations (Paul Schulz), a later Reich finance minister and one of the architects of the disappropriation of German Jews (Walter Funk), the Gauleiter (regional leader) of East Prussia and latterly Reich Commissar for Ukraine and one of the most powerful figures in German-occupied eastern Europe (Erich Koch), the later Reich interior minister, who would go on to cover up Röhm's murder (Wilhelm Frick), the head of the Gestapo in Frankfurt and later an SS Obergruppenführer (Karl Kaufmann), or the Gauleiter of Westphalia and a state secretary in the Minister for the Occupied Eastern territories during a genocidal war (Alfred Meyer). Nonetheless, within the movement, these people were indeed considered part of the 'reasonable' Nazi camp, which at least for a time was more or less closely associated with Strasser.[154] The epithet 'reasonable' frequently referred to Nazis with good connections to industry. Strasser, for instance, took up the post of director at a subsidiary of the Schering company after he withdrew from politics.[155]

There are good reasons to regard Schleicher's alleged plan to split the Nazi Party as nothing more than a myth, albeit one that persisted after 1945 for political reasons. Schleicher's attempts at taming the Nazi movement between 1930 and January 1933 may have been a scheme, in a variety of directions and invariably unsuccessful, to use its potential so that traditional conservative elites could destroy the Weimar Republic.[156] But that hardly means that a broad conservative front almost succeeded in coalescing in opposition to Hitler, and the fact that the idea has been so often repeated doesn't make it any more true.[157]

Schleicher's concepts sounded much like the macho slogans of Crown Prince Wilhelm, if on a higher and more nuanced intellectual and political level. Wilhelm's temporary support for Schleicher's plan reflected both men's hostility towards the Weimar Republic and personal arrogance, which helped to doom both of their ambitions to failure. Schleicher and the crown prince didn't represent a last-minute alternative to Hitler. On the contrary, they stood for the final destruction of any conservative alternative to Hitler.

On the Night of the Long Knives, the Nazi dictatorship, led by a head of government who hurried from place to place with pistol drawn, began violently dispatching its own former allies in the fashion of a criminal underground. But the roles played by Ernst Röhm, Gregor Strasser, Edmund Heines, Kurt von Schleicher, Edgar Julius Jung or Crown Prince Wilhelm in creating that Nazi dictatorship were not annulled by the fact that they were all either murdered or marginalized from political life.

A Monarchist Alternative?

Although some historians are still attracted by the idea that there could have been a conservative alternative to Hitler emanating from the circles around Schleicher and supported by the crown prince, the only arguments for it consist of mere counterfactual speculation.[158] Such notions do no justice to all the political groups that actually did oppose Nazism in historical fact rather than just in ex-post-facto thought games. They also downplay the importance of traditional conservatives' collaborations with Nazis, which today appear so unseemly, creating illusory connections between the former and the anti-Nazi resistance. Moreover, speculative reasoning can neither be proven or disproven empirically. If things had been different, so the thinking runs, everything might have turned out differently. As we will see, this is the same logic the German royal family retrospectively employed to present itself as a putative alternative to the Nazi dictatorship.

The myth of a monarchist alternative is invariably connected to Schleicher, whose actions remain untransparent, powerful circles within the military and industry, and various conservative pressure groups. So it's worth taking a closer look at them. 'Are the Hohenzollerns Coming Back?' British press mogul Lord Rothermere answered this question in a June 1932 edition of London's *Daily Mail* in the affirmative. There was no more frequent prediction at the time in Europe than that Germany's royal family would return to their throne within the next eighteen months.[159] Whether in Germany or abroad, a Hohenzollern restoration was considered a very real possibility in the latter half of 1932.

It's hard to say how many people at the time favoured or feared this option. What is certain is that it was the subject of lively discussions at all levels on both the Right and the Left, in Germany and abroad, and among ex-patriots, aristocrats, military officers, the working classes, professors, communist newspapers, liberal journalists, cartoonists, constitutional law experts, intellectuals, government ministers, German chancellors and the Hohenzollern family itself.[160]

Even the day the chancellorship was transferred to Hitler, 30 January 1933, some belated rumour-mongers were still repeating the fantasy that the crown prince would become Reich administrator, with Hitler under him, and that the monarchy would be restored.[161] A cartoon in a left-wing Viennese daily depicted Hitler as the 'liveryman of the reactionary right', wielding his whip as a group of SA 'horses' pulled the coach of state. The passengers of this

Hitler-driven vehicle included a stereotypical capitalist carrying a humongous sack of money, the Kaiser in his helmet and the crown prince in his hussar's uniform. A segment of German press also interpreted Hitler's appointment as chancellor as a preliminary stage of possible monarchist restoration.[162]

Neither the Right nor the Left lacked imagination when it came to fantasies about the potential power of monarchism. But how much of an actual force was it in the Weimar Republic? To answer this question, it's useful to define who and what were meant by the word.[163] What existing political positions, organizations and personnel were available to the cause of restoration? There are serious gaps between the post-1945 tales of alleged monarchist resistance to Hitler and the historical record. History as a discipline can hardly be expected to explain away the discrepancy between the immense messianic expectations invested in the German monarchy, on the one hand, and its actual weakness, on the other. Nonetheless, this is precisely the gap that can and must be discussed.

At various points during the Weimar Republic, vague notions of a Hohenzollern restoration appeared like the lesser of two evils compared to a Nazi dictatorship. Barely any of the post-war interpretations of history neglect to quote two Winston Churchill statements from 1945 and 1946. 'This war would never have come unless, under American and modernising pressure, we had driven the Habsburgs out of Austria and the Hohenzollerns out of Germany,'[164] opined the British prime minister. 'By making these vacuums we gave the opening for the Hitlerite monster to crawl out of its *sewer* on to the vacant thrones.' He later added: 'If the Allies at the peace table at Versailles had allowed a Hohenzollern, a Wittelsbach and a Habsburg to return to their thrones, there would have been no Hitler. A democratic basis of society might have been preserved by a crowned Weimar in contact with the victorious Allies.'[165]

Churchill's blithe assertions are part of a line of conservative thinking about German history that still persists today. Another major component of this logic came from the memoirs, first published in 1970, of the former German chancellor Heinrich Brüning, who posthumously claimed that he had planned to restore the Hohenzollern monarchy. The idea was to create a conservative military dictatorship supported by the Reichswehr and the 'moderate' segments of Nazism, which would have paved the way for a restored monarchy. This, Brüning proposed, was the final and only alternative in late 1932 that could have 'prevented Hitler'.[166]

Like all attempts to promote the idea of a monarchist alternative centred upon the Hohenzollerns in 1932–3, this has no more basis in fact than recent homages to the British and Scandinavian royal families, 1920s dime-store novels and clichés of friendly Dutch princesses waving from bicycles. As charming as the beaming faces of Swedish princes and as compelling as the heroes in Peter Jackson's *Lord of the Rings* might be, they have no more to do with the reality of German monarchism in 1932 than Sir Lancelot does with Crown Prince Wilhelm. The historical reality of the waning Weimar Republic was entirely different.[167]

There are various reasons why image didn't match up with real life. The first is that all monarchist counter-revolutions need to agree on a pretender to the throne. Unlike republicans, who are not bound by dynastic lineages, monarchists can't choose their own leaders. Conversely, every functional monarchy must be able to withstand a series of weak or poor kings.

Where there are doubts as to the reputation or popularity of an heir to the throne, two tropes of rehabilitation have been part of European nobility since the days of Antiquity. One is that of the prince who matures into a worthy king after enduring hardships. The other – which runs from Homer to the Brothers Grimm and plays a role in the great European counter-movements to the French Revolution – is the king who returns from exile after a period of wandering, privation and battles to restore his former glory.[168] Supporters applied these images both to the Kaiser and to his eldest son. Weimar monarchists were perfectly capable of distinguishing between personalities and ideas. And criticism of the king and hopes for a (new) king weren't mutually exclusive. In his famous study *The King's Two Bodies*, Ernst Kantorowitz writes that political mysticism loses its power and significance when it is divorced from its origins.[169] Over time, the German monarchy suffered this fate. Nonetheless, to stay with Kantorowitz, the office of the king retained its dual embodiment throughout the Weimar Republic. It was still possible for German monarchism to overlook the short-comings of the two candidates for the throne. They were still seen to embody immortal ideals and principles and could be understood as placeholders for a future king who would physically return and rule over a yet-to-be-created kingdom.

For this reason alone, despite his meagre personal achievements, the crown prince could not simply be passed over. As long as a political system contains counter-revolutionary forces that dream of a reconstituted monarchy and the 'return of the king',[170] a crown prince will retain great importance, even if he is considered a complete incompetent. From King Arthur[171] to Tolkien's Aragorn, centuries of people have been fascinated with the figure of the returning, initially unrecognized, king who changes everything. Unfortunately it is the original archetype from which the twentieth-century figure of the secular leader, or Führer, emerged.

Post-1918 Germany was the perfect breeding ground for such a sacral figure in a modern guise. It was a country of shattered illusions and the European centre of hyper-emotional political dreams, which bubbled up throughout the Weimar Republic. It is worth recalling the poet Heinrich Heine's sarcastic remark that the devil, aristocrats and Jesuits could only exist if people believed in them.[172] That *bon mot* neatly sums up the power of political imaginations in post-1918 Germany, where, strictly speaking, there was no such thing as an aristocracy or a crown prince.

Centuries of aristocracy, monarchy, kingdom and divine right had not only been based on institutional power. They had also depended on projection, on imagined qualities and wishful thinking, something neither the nobility nor the monarchy could do without. That was very much the case in post-1918 Germany with its prominent cult of leaders and leadership. Without such projection, there is no way of explaining Hitler's mercurial rise or his subsequent aura.[173] Both precedent and general historical mechanisms made it unlikely that the heir to the throne of a just-toppled monarchy who was active in a lasting and significant reactionary political environment could ever be a completely marginal figure.

Obviously, the structural weaknesses of German monarchism were bound up with the weakness of the crown prince. And a great many people at the time did indeed draw that connection. Examples of scorn being heaped upon Wilhelm could be found practically on every corner of the Weimar Republic. The cutting tone of these sentiments was reflected in dismissive words formulated by former French ambassador to Germany André François-Poncet, who was close to the circles around Schleicher. In François-Poncet's post-war memoirs, he had little good to say about Wilhelm:

> He was a completely inconsequential figure, a bon vivant without any serious interests or talent. At a time of great historic decisions and the most drastic caesura, he was a wan, pale figure who never attracted a circle of men of importance, neither in the Wilhelmine Empire nor in the Weimar Republic nor under Hitler. When history renders judgement upon him, it can only be: 'He stepped upon the scale and was found to be too lightweight.'[174]

François-Poncet without doubt had an excellent sense of the relations of power and key figures in the Weimar Republic, and Wilhelm himself provides few arguments against the French diplomat's judgement. If the significance of the crown prince and the monarchy as an imaginary option nonetheless deserve to be treated seriously, it's not because of the qualities of the individuals in question, but rather down to the importance of human imagination, symbolism and the monarchy's emotion legacy. By the nineteenth century at the latest, the power of German monarchs and would-be kings was derived more from the aura of the figure than from the actual individuals concerned.

Monarchy Without a Monarch

To appreciate the specific position of monarchism in post-1918 Germany, we need to keep sight of two seemingly, but only seemingly, contradictory elements: the great emotional energy that connected millions of people with the splendour and glory of the Wilhelmine Empire and the fallen Hohenzollern dynasty, and the political feebleness of the various monarchist movements. Arguing for a restoration on the basis of comparisons with other countries' royal families, counterfactual speculation and high literature meant fundamentally ignoring the political realities of the Weimar Republic.

Around 1932, the chances for a restoration of the Hohenzollerns were decided not in Britain or Hollywood, but in East Prussia, Silesia, Berlin and Potsdam. If pigs had wings, the saying goes, they would fly. Following the same logic, if there had been a powerful monarchist movement in post-1918 Germany and a royal dynasty that had pushed for the British model, Germany would have been like Britain. Likewise, had the Hohenzollerns unanimously opposed Nazism, or if Wilhelm II, his second wife and his sons had been different people, post-1918 German history might have taken a different course. And something similar applied to old and new fantasies about the possible return of a German king under a constitutional monarchy. Thus, we need to leave the realm of the hypothetical and focus on the actual conditions in 1932, including, not least, the personnel available.

Monarchies are bound to the principle of succession – kings, princesses and crown princes can't be chosen on the basis of merit – so by necessity the Hohenzollerns were the centre of all speculations about a monarchist alternative to Nazi dictatorship. A restoration is unworkable when the monarchy in question doesn't agree on one pretender to the throne. And, with the Hohenzollerns, no fewer than nine potential candidates from three different generations were considered. A royal family in such a state could only encourage the rise of a dictatorship, not present an alternative to it.

Tellingly, in December 1935, the Social Democratic Party in exile (SOPADE) received a report from inside Nazi Germany of a staff officer summarizing discussions within the military leadership in which the monarchy was said to have a 'personnel issue'. Unlike Italy, Germany didn't have any one person suitable for embodying an aristocratic reaction to the status quo.[175] The problem revealed by the clandestine social democratic network remained the same whether it was July 1944 or 1918. The main internal reason why the monarchist idea did not represent a genuine alternative to Nazism was the personal weakness of the leading royal family members.

The problem started in Doorn. It was difficult for German monarchism to simply ignore the Kaiser, who continued to live in Dutch exile, and his very active political apparatus in Germany. We have already seen how the former monarch had gradually drifted into hatred and self-pity, but in terms of the rules of monarchism, this unfortunate slide didn't change his top rank in the designated line of succession. On the contrary, to use the language of high nobility, he remained the 'head of the house' with an unbroken, constant claim to the throne. But we need only look at the statements from the ex-Kaiser's closest circles, collected in Ilsemann's diaries, to see that Wilhelm himself was one of the greatest liabilities of post-1918 German monarchism.

As early as October 1919, during his first visit to Doorn, the crown prince was appalled at the illusions under which his father laboured while still nurturing hopes for a political future.[176] In 1920, the ex-Kaiser's brother-in-law, Prince Friedrich-Karl of Hessen, was convinced that Wilhelm would never be able to recapture the throne.[177] When Ilsemann travelled to Germany in late 1920, he didn't encounter a 'single person' among the aristocracy and the political right-wing parties who believed that the Kaiser would someday regain his former position. Ludendorff and Crown Prince Rupprecht of Bavaria also discounted Wilhelm as a viable candidate for a restoration.[178] Nobles from the Wilhelmine generation such as Count Detlef von Moltke were no more sanguine about the ex-Kaiser's prospects,[179] and the sharp-tongued Crown Princess

Cecilie, getting straight to the point, dismissed the whole idea of his returning to Germany either as a monarch or a private citizen. No one had time for Wilhelm any more, she scoffed. He was 'all played out'.[180]

In April 1923, Ilsemann jotted down the sad impressions he had received during a ten-week trip through Germany in which he had met with representatives of the old elites in various parts of the country. The picture he came away with was very dark:

> My overall impression of the mood concerning the Kaiser back in his homeland is catastrophic. His marriage and his publications have made my lord a dead man in many circles. Whereas on my previous trips to Germany, lots of people asked after their former Kaiser, this time almost no one said a word about him. Those who did usually made bitter accusations or even voiced contempt.

Meanwhile the ex-Kaiser's most loyal servant saw the mood towards the crown prince as somewhat more favourable:

> Those who are still willing to even consider a monarchy think of the crown prince, his son or his son under the regency of his mother. The crown princess is extraordinarily admired and respected. Everyone is full of praise for her. In general, the idea of a monarchy seems to be gaining support.[181]

Count Friedrich von der Schulenburg, the crown prince's former general chief of staff, also commented around this time that the Kaiser was 'over and done with', among other things because of his second marriage. His views on Wilhelm's son varied, but Schulenburg did rate the crown prince's prospects as somewhat better, remarking that the crown princess was 'the only man in the family' – a vicious put-down in the context of Prussia's militaristic aristocracy.[182] There were even rumours among leading officers about the tireless activism of Count Westarp, one of the most determined monarchists of the Weimar period,[183] who was attempting to bring the Kaiser's oldest grandson to the throne. The *New York Times*, too, identified Prince Wilhelm as the candidate best suited to retaking power.[184]

Foreign observers were also left without a clear idea of who the focus of the monarchist camp was after the German Revolution of 1918. Late that year, the British ambassador to the Netherlands sent London an evaluation of German monarchist plans in which he identified the possible pretenders as 'either the ex-Emperor at Amerongen and the ex-Crown Prince at Wieringen, or for the purpose of placing on the German throne a son of the ex-Crown Prince or some Prince who is not a Hohenzollern'.[185] The fragmented extreme, racist right wing, too, considered the issue of succession 'complete chaos'.[186] Both Count von Fürstenberg, one of the Kaiser's few personal friends, and Alfred Niemann, whom observers considered one of Wilhelm's main propagandists, considered it impossible for him to reclaim the throne. In 1923, before concluding a visit to Doorn, the crown prince stated that people now only laughed at 'Papa'.[187]

In the summer of 1927, the crown prince, crown princess, Prince Friedrich Eitel and other family members vented their dismay at how divorced from reality Wilhelm had become, obsessed with his return to the throne and drawing up plans on giant military maps to win the First World War after the event. 'How is it possible', the crown princess asked an adjutant she had taken to one side, 'that this fundamentally clever fellow constantly comes out with such fantasies and contradicts them with his own person?'[188]

With tears in his eyes, the Kaiser's admiring younger brother Heinrich described the endless series of tirades of his domineering sibling as 'pathological'.[189] Several of his most loyal attendants considered it a 'crime' to encourage Wilhelm's hopes of restoration, and one of the most clear-headed advisors in Doorn, Baron Ullrich von Sell, began to doubt that his presence there made any sense. To Sell's mind, if anyone had a chance at the throne, it was the crown prince. Sell spoke of the 'crazy eyes' of the Kaiser, who had become 'his wife's puppet', had lost direction among empty, superficial rituals like the bestowing of titles and who was always posing for photos and film footage.[190]

Princes Oskar and Adalbert, two of the crown prince's brothers who felt very close to their father, held emotional discussions about why no one in the family was telling him the 'truth', but within the Hohenzollern's communicative labyrinths, neither found a way to do that himself.[191] In 1931, eighteen-year-old Prince Alexander of Prussia, who like his father August Wilhelm was in the process of joining the Nazi Party, opined that it was best for his grandfather not to know what his grandchildren really thought about his prospects for a return to Germany.[192] With a fateful marriage of his own in the offing, Prince Wilhelm, the crown prince's oldest son, also said he was horrified by how divorced from reality his grandfather's ideas were becoming.[193] In March 1932, the Kaiser's only daughter, the Duchess of Braunschweig, and her older brother Oskar, an active Stahlhelm member, proclaimed that 'Papa is pinning all his hopes on Hitler' and predicted that he would be terribly disappointed. 'No one is shouting for him to come back.'[194]

The self-images of both the Kaiser and the crown prince had little to do with the sober, analytical assessments royal advisors dared only whisper. Until his dying day, Wilhelm II regarded himself as the only possible solution to all the major political issues faced by Germany, indeed all of Europe. There is evidence that his minions continued to try to help him back to power at least until 1934, even though that amounted to little more than pandering to the fantasies created by old men and continually embellished by the Kaiser's second wife. Wilhelm's actual political prospects entirely depended on a still older man, Paul von Hindenburg, the conservative general who served as German president, the highest political office in the Weimar Republic, from 1925 to 1934. At least in theory, Hindenburg insisted on a strictly legitimist, Doorn-oriented, political line that, while not actively demanding the ex-Kaiser's return, effectively blocked any other monarchist options. Even in his political last will and testament, Hindenburg clung to this rigid position.[195]

In the subsequent generation, much like his father, Crown Prince

Wilhelm saw himself as the only suitable candidate for the throne, and in his case, too, his ambitions were vigorously supported by his wife. A 1925 trip to East Prussia convinced him that powerful currents of monarchism remained, and this inspired an exaggerated sense of self-importance that would persist until at least the summer of 1934.[196]

The ambitions of Hermine and Cecilie, both ever industrious, were important in their own right. In October 1932, the daily German press was full of opinions about why the Kaiser had no chance to return to power while the prospects of the crown prince, if allied with the Nazi movement, were eminently realistic. The chatter focused on the planned revision of electoral laws, the liquidation of the Weimar Republic and the path back to a monarchy via the crown prince as a Reich administrator, which the Papen government was bandying about under the slogan 'The New State'.[197] These speculations made their way as far as the readers of daily newspapers in Toronto and Shanghai.

Leading social democrats also took this scenario seriously. During a speech in Berlin, Rudolf Breitscheid warned about the crown prince's growing influence, and the idea of a 'monarchy without a monarch' was debated across much of the German capital.[198] What had been a mere phantasm six months earlier, English readers in Shanghai were told, was now the most discussed political option in Germany.[199] The crown prince purposely remained nebulous about his actual plans. His answer when a reporter for the *Daily Herald* asked him if he aspired to become a monarch was: 'I will serve my country until I die.' This inspired the liberal press to nickname him 'The Sphinx of Oels'.[200]

Fathers and Sons

As mentioned before, the field of potential candidates for the throne during the Weimar Republic went considerably beyond the former Kaiser and his eldest son. The power structures that had once been clearly focused on the Kaiser as the 'lord of the centre'[201] had become a borderless puzzle in which individuals from three generations were mooted as potential successors and attracted support from diverse factions within the monarchist camp.[202] Kaiser Wilhelm II positioned himself against his sons and grandsons on individual issues and matters of principle, the crown princess rejected the Kaiser's second wife, and the latter struck out at a number of advisors from venerable aristocratic families, who in turn plotted against one another within a constantly shifting system of divergent loyalties, political outlooks and personal vanities.

Serious conflicts recurred as various Hohenzollerns made attempts to court the Nazis that were coordinated either badly or not at all. For example, in September 1932, after connections had already been established between several royal family members and Nazism, the crown princess celebrated her forty-sixth birthday in Cecilienhof, and among the invited guests was the former fighter pilot and political ally of the crown prince Hermann Göring. The talk turned to a letter from Wilhelm II to his son in which the ex-Kaiser had mocked Hitler and National Socialism.[203] In one version of events, the crown prince fetched the letter himself and presented it to Göring during the celebrations, whereupon relations between Doorn and the Nazi leadership cooled markedly. The would-be empress Hermine, it was reported, immediately suspected the crown princess of engineering the stunt to knock the Kaiser out of running for the imaginary restored throne once and for all.[204]

There is ample evidence of the Kaiser and the crown prince competing for Hitler's favour in 1931,[205] with Doorn and Cecilienhof operating as rival monarchist political centres – at least where potential alliances with Nazism were concerned. Nonetheless, in his clearer-headed moments, the former Kaiser seem to have realized that the idea of a restoration with the help of the Nazis was a chimera. The most obvious manifestation of Wilhelm II's disappointment in the Nazi movement was the dismissal in December 1932 of Baron Magnus von Levetzow, whose main task had been to build connections between Doorn and Hitler's movement. Still, even Levetzow's firing did not bring about a definitive break between the two sides. On the contrary, Wilhelm II behaved in the same ambiguous fashion he would in the years that followed, constantly complaining about attacks on him in the Nazi press and venting his disappointment at Göring's allegedly broken promises while his advisory staff scrupulously kept doors to the Nazi Party open. Thus, as late as January 1933, Wilhelm II still told Levetzow that he naturally still recognized 'the value of the nationalist ideas of National Socialism'.[206] Another royal advisor with particularly good connections to the Nazis, Leopold von Kleist, was also dismissed in late 1932 in addition to Levetzow. But as Baron Ulrich von Sell, one of the ex-Kaiser's advisors more critical of the Nazis, stressed, neither of those personnel moves signalled a general rejection of Nazism. Sell himself considered the Nazi movement 'the protector of our national desires' and emphasized the need for unity within the nationalist Right. Four years later, the royal advisor was still trying to dispel the notion that Wilhelm II had come out against Nazism in 1933.[207]

As we have seen, much of the ill will towards the Kaiser and the crown prince within the Prussian nobility and on the German Right stemmed from them fleeing the battlefield in 1918. In his correspondence with Prince von Salm in 1919, Count Arnim, the grand seigneur of Brandenburg and the final president of the Prussian House of Lords, compared the crown prince to a 'deserter' and deemed his private life 'impossible'.[208] The entirety of Schulenburg's correspondence speaks much the same language, vacillating between hopes that the prince would change his ways and become a useful figure and depressive despair at how much Wilhelm's personal shortcomings were shaking the monarchy to the core. A 'weakling' and 'milksop' was how Schulenburg termed his former commander in 1920.[209] Like most of his family, this decommissioned general and manic writer of letters, notes and memoirs joined the Nazi movement after 1930.

Advocates of democracy also engaged in lively discussion about the difficulties faced by a monarchy that couldn't even agree on who should be monarch. Shortly after the crown prince's return to German soil in November 1923, the social democratic newspaper *Vorwärts* wrote: 'The return of the crown prince once again underscored the fact that the monarchists would be at their most desperate if they actually had to name a pretender to the throne.'[210]

Joachim von Stülpnagel, an influential officer within the Reichswehr Ministry, confessed similar misgivings to an adjutant of the crown prince 1924: 'The question of monarchy or republic depends on his own person. If he fails, the Hohenzollern dream is over.'[211] Also in 1924, Lieutenant General August von Cramon, aide-de-camp to the Kaiser, sighed that he didn't know upon whom monarchist propaganda should focus: 'The father has no chance, his eldest son makes too many damaging mistakes, and his son is still too young.'[212]

The antagonisms within the Hohenzollern family in general remained as bitter as the rivalries were among the potential aspirants to the throne. The running conflict between Wilhelm II and his sons was the most important, among other things because it reflected the gap separating the Wilhelmine generation in the Netherlands from the younger one in Germany. During family quarrels, Wilhelm II constantly treated his sons, all in their fifties and sixties, like unruly schoolboys. The pattern of behaviour is particular evident in the correspondence following the crown prince's unhappy attempt to ally himself with Hitler to seize the office of German president. It was 'high time that I come back,' the ex-Kaiser wrote in late April 1932,

> or do my gentlemen sons think that one of you is capable of taking over this task, you who have been exclusively trained for your specific tasks? You may know a bit about tactics, but you can only rule Germany if you have been schooled for years and collected experiences, as I have. Should any of you dare to undertake any such thing as the crown prince just did, I as the head of the family will simply disown you . . . After everything I have endured psychologically in these past long years, I know how to clean out the sort of pigsty you have at home! You won't believe your eyes. There's a reason I've

spent time here studying the methods of Lenin and Mussolini for so long and in such detail.[213]

Wilhelm II also dismissed the crown prince as a liar and a 'frondeur' (political rebel) directly acting against his own father.[214]

The idea of 'betrayal' was a constant of how the ex-Kaiser saw the world, his own family explicitly included. Outraged over the co-option of the word 'Führer' by the Nazis for Hitler, the former emperor, reduced to feeding the ducks in his pond in Doorn, insisted that only he could be the true leader since that was a mission bestowed by God upon his family centuries ago. He began a 1930 speech by quoting a passage from the Gospel of John, which he claimed applied to both Jesus and himself: 'I am the vine; you are the branches. If a man remains in me and I in him, he will bear much fruit; apart from me you can do nothing.'[215]

Two Queens

In a fireside chat at Cecilienhof in 1934, the crown prince said that the royal family would be sad, but also relieved, if his father were 'called to meet his Maker'. He, the crown prince, could have seized power during Wilhelm II's moments of weakness all the way back in 1908, he claimed, and, if he had, world history would have taken a different course. He had now learned to bide his time, but his wife could hardly wait any longer for a restoration.[216] Three years before that, in 1931, the prince admitted to feeling 'jealousy' that 'his Göring' had visited Doorn.[217]

The constant carrousel of possible candidates for the throne surprised even members of the inner royal circle. In March 1928, for example, Ilsemann was stunned to discover that the crown princess harboured very specific hopes not only that her eldest son would have a political career in the future but also that her husband could soon become first the commander-in-chief of the German armed forces, then a 'regent'.[218] Cecilie's objection 'We parents are still here!' in response to discussions of her son as potential heir to the throne[219] was frequently echoed in Doorn, where the Kaiser's wife kept an aggressively distrustful eye on the activities of her stepchildren. The attendant officers at the Dutch estate referred to Hermine and Cecilie as 'Kriemhild and Brundhild', and the foreign press also reported for years about a 'battle between two queens in the style of the *Nibelungenlied*, which will have a fateful political conclusion'.[220] Ilsemann depicted Cecilie constantly referring to Hermine as 'the new woman', while Hermine never ceased trying to turn the Kaiser against his sons.[221] The accounts of the women, written in the main by men in tones of misogynistic scorn, portrayed them as power-hungry harridans. Nonetheless there is considerable hard evidence of the rivalry, ambition, energy and activity of these two nearly identically aged women.

Much to the dismay of contemporaries, particular in the right-wing camp, the crown princess was an agent in her own right, with a personal agenda, in the scramble for power. Across the political spectrum, Cecilie was described as a systematic, tactically adept schemer. In October 1932, the pacifist journalist Hellmut von Gerlach wrote an article on monarchist hopes for a period after Hindenburg. When he mentioned Cecilie's speeches at a Stahlhelm rally in Magdeburg, he characterized her as the true driving force behind this political current. General Wilhelm Groener took much the same view.[222]

Cecilie was very popular among broad segments of the German people and, like her husband, she created her public identity from a wide variety of roles and symbols. She was alternately the pretty-as-a-picture young duchess from a castle in Schwerin, the daughter of a Russian *grande dame*, an elegant, upper-class fashion icon and a mother of the nation who, like Penelope in the *Odyssey*, had run Germany's first family during her husband's exile, maintaining its wealth and prestige, raising six children and confidently interacting with the country's elites on every stage of culture, diplomacy, politics and power.

She was also a leading figure in the largest conservative women's association as well as in the National Ladies' Automobile Club, chaired by Princess Olga von der Lippe. The club, in which aristo-cratic and upper-bourgeois ladies raced around in expensive sports cars, embodied a very specific sort of modern womanhood.[223] It lost its autonomy at the end of 1932, moving to the extreme political right under the stewardship of its new chairman, Duke Carl Eduard von Sachsen-Coburg und Gotha. But before that the club was an arena for what the noblest of noblewomen described as 'national motor driving' and used to create a hybrid modern and conservative image.[224] In short, Cecilie was a female leader who felt equally at home in castles and estates, at aristocratic balls and charity events, on hunting expeditions and at Stahlhelm rallies, and could converse comfortably with young nurses, ranking Reichswehr officers, ambassadors and world famous musicians such as Wilhelm Furt-wängler and Herbert von Karajan.

No Hohenzollernist

A strong, independent princess at the side of a crown prince often dismissed as a ne'er-do-well did nothing to simplify the question of who monarchists wanted to be crowned the next king. There simply was no consensus at the time about which candidate was best suited for a restoration. In his much-debated memoirs, Brüning claimed to have supported Prince Louis Ferdinand, a 27-year-old with no polit-ical experience at all. In June 1933, Crown Prince Wilhelm's eldest son, Prince Wilhelm of Prussia, who ranked above Louis Ferdinand in the traditional line of succession, disqualified himself with his 'unseemly' marriage to Dorothea von Salviati and voluntarily renounced any claims to the throne. With that break, the ex-Kaiser considered naming Wilhelm's youngest brother, Friedrich, or his middle brother, Hubertus, royal successor.[225] By this point, Wilhelm II had spent a decade unleashing tirades against the 'clique' of mon-archists in Potsdam, whom he called 'dogs' and 'a thoroughly repulsive, dangerous gang', and living in fear of his own supporters abandoning him for the crown prince.[226]

The situation wasn't any clearer within the DNVP. In 1929, when a German admiral called upon party chairman and media mogul Alfred Hugenberg to take a more monarchist stance and asked who the official pretender to the throne was, he received no answer.[227] In late 1932, an intimate of Crown Prince Wilhelm summed up the sizeable gap between the monarchist clichés spouted by the right wing and political reality by calling Hugenberg a 'Bismarckist but no Hohenzollernist'.[228] Invoking Bismarck could mean many different things to different people on the Right during the Weimar Republic, but loyalty to the House of Hohenzollern was not among them.[229]

As if that weren't enough, monarchists within the Nazi movement, as Goebbels noted, never excluded either August Wilhelm or his son Alexander, both card-carrying fascists, from the conversation about who should occupy the throne.[230] Meanwhile, monarchists from the circles around Papen and the office of the vice-chancellor were said to favour Crown Prince Wilhelm's youngest son, Friedrich – an option also supported by some of the English nobility.[231] Near the end of the Third Reich, the right-wing fringe of the conservative opposition to Hitler seems to have also discussed the idea of an 'elite monarchy' that would have elevated 'not the first, but the best pretender of the ruling house to the throne'.[232]

There may have been many domestic and international factors working against a restoration of the German monarchy, but it is important to remember that one of the main reasons it never materialized was that the House of Hohenzollern also divided the monarchist camp. Options that would have seen members of the royal families of Bavaria, Mecklenburg and Saxony take over the imperial throne were mooted.[233] As early as the 1920s, the legal abdication of the Kaiser and the crown prince, the oath of loyalty all six of Wilhelm II's sons swore to him and the considerable ambitions maintained by various royal wives were seen as insurmountable obstacles.[234] In April 1932, Schulenburg remarked that, while the monarchist idea was making something of a comeback, it was bound to fail due to the 'lack of a single candidate after the downfall of the House of Hohenzollern'. At that point, the Kaiser's fifth son, Prince Oskar, a Stahlhelm member held in high regard by conservatives, was being discussed as a potential monarch, and such speculations made it all the way to Paris and Hong Kong.[235] The prince had been the subject of an influential 1930 essay of the extreme right monarchist writer Junius Alter. In it, the author lobbied for an alliance of all right-wing associations, including the Nazis, and invoked the image, adapted from early iteration of jingoistic nationalism, of a future Kaiser slumbering in the Kyffhäuser mountain like the mythical Friedrich Barbarossa. In one chapter, in which Alter handed out grades like a schoolmaster to all the Hohenzollern princes, or 'Stahlhelm princes', as he called them, in terms of their suitability for leadership, he dismissed Crown Prince Wilhelm in two sentences. Instead, Alter focused on the soldierly and 'simply' structured Prince Oskar, although his qualities would, over the course of the essay, be deemed inferior to Hitler's.[236] Meanwhile, Hugenberg was promoting Oskar via his media empire. The Harzburger Front also proposed the prince, who remained active in the Stahlhelm, as a unity candidate to oppose Hindenburg in the 1932 election.[237] In conversation with the British ambassador to Italy in November 1932, Mussolini called Oskar the natural candidate for the throne.[238] The pro-democracy aristocrat Baron Kurt von Reibnitz, who analysed the conservative inability to decide on a candidate for the throne with great glee, ended a 1929 portrait of the Kaiser with the words:

Wilhelm II might as well have had himself driven to [the East Prussian towns of] Cadinen or Roiminten after he abdicated. Not a hair on his head would have been harmed. He would only have to have kept his peace and lived as a solitary widower. But the crown prince, when he was rightly relieved of command of his army, should have ridden back home as an officer with some regiment or another. As a socially minded estate owner and modern agriculturalist, he would have found enough to do in Oels. His brothers, too, should have done some gainful labour. There is no place in Germany for drones.[239]

Strikingly, these mocking, malicious lines came from the pen of a member of the old Silesian aristocracy who had broken with his social milieu and joined the social democratic movement.

Yet, notwithstanding the cutting criticism from observers and the scorn of the caricaturists, the real obstacles were internal conflicts within the Hohenzollern family itself and the disruption of the fundamental principle of legitimacy upon which monarchies are based. That principle of legitimacy – the political aorta of any monarchy[240] – had been shattered in 1918, and there was no way to repair it by nominating a replacement to the highest royal office. The anti-Semitic journalist Count Ernst von Reventlow hit the mark when he scoffed in 1926 that a monarchy could not simply be put back on its feet like a toppled stool.[241] A similar image was used in a long, sarcastic article by the Pulitzer Prize-winner Frederick T. Birchall in the *New York Times* in the autumn of 1932. He caricatured the monarchs of Europe in general as listening to marching band music in upper-class spas while waiting to be returned to power. Among them the Hohenzollerns were depicted as particularly prone to wishful thinking, hoping against hope that the throne would, sooner or later, be retrieved from a museum and its wobbly legs patched up and reinforced.[242]

The images of a restored monarchy and the return of the king continued to appeal to some Germans, and Crown Prince Wilhelm profited most from them. But it remained unclear what sort of monarchy was being envisioned or how the broken components of the Wilhelmine Empire could ever be put back together. The lack of a consensus pretender was thus only one of the insurmountable obstacles faced by post-1918 monarchism.

The Impossible Restoration

The restoration of the German monarchy was an improbability and ultimately an impossibility due to factors both internal and external to the Hohenzollern family. Moreover, from contemporary observers to the present day, the picture of what sort of renewed monarchy was even envisioned has remained remarkably vague. No matter what political camp, what source or what decade they have come from, the assertions made on this score have been extraordinarily diffuse.

Writing from his Paris exile in the summer of 1935, Count Harry Kessler summarized a long conversation he had had with the former German chancellor Heinrich Brüning about the latter's purported efforts to prevent Hitler's rise to power by restoring the monarchy. The plan had been scuppered by his dismissal in May 1932, Brüning claimed. Kessler wrote: 'I assume that his policy was simply to restore the monarchy in whatever form and regardless of who the monarch was. But you can't make an omelette if you have no eggs.'[243] Kessler, a keen observer of the highest levels of German politics for decades, was echoing a sentiment that had been formulated ten years previously at the other, right-wing racist end of the spectrum by Reventlow, who cited Bismarck saying: 'To make roast hare, you need a hare, and for a monarchy you need a king.'[244] Even the best-informed contemporaries couldn't keep track of who had promised to whom what sort of monarchy with which monarch.[245] And later historians greeted the Catholic nationalist Brüning's putative plans for a restoration, which he only announced to the world in his posthumously published memoirs in 1970, with healthy scepticism.[246] The most recent research has cast lasting doubt upon them as well.[247]

Even if men like Brüning did in fact seriously consider a Hohenzollern restoration to ward off Nazism, none of the necessary conditions were present. According to a recent, very convincing biography of one of the leading monarchists of the Weimar Republic, Count Kuno von Westarp remarked that his contact with the crown prince had strengthened his conviction that 'the monarchy as an idea in urgent need of preservation desperately needs to be protected from its current personnel'. There is ample evidence of numerous attempts within the advisory staffs of both the Kaiser and the crown prince to 'protect the monarchy against itself'.[248] And when asked by the American deputy chief prosecutor at the Nuremberg trials in 1947 who was envisioned as a restored king in the case of a collaboration, Crown Prince Wilhelm couldn't even answer the question.[249]

In addition to the lack of a consensus pretender to the throne, the many reasons for the political weakness of Prussian monarchism are easy to identify.[250] For starters, the Kaiser and his son had been discredited in the minds of many Germans as deserters. A malicious caricature published in the British magazine *Punch* showed Wilhelm II cowering on the ground behind the skirts of a Dutch woman in fear of French and British authorities.[251] This view was echoed even within families of the old Prussian aristocracy and the high German nobility. In 1929, the Duke of Mecklenburg, who was also the royal consort of the Dutch princess, told one of the Kaiser's adjutants that Wilhelm II should have followed the counsel of his advisors and remained with his men instead of fleeing to the Netherlands.[252] The irreparable damage done by the flight of father and son was the subject of innumerable heated discussions, particularly among the Prussian and northern German nobility and the officer corps.[253]

Moreover, the various regional monarchies never succeeded in agreeing on a structure for the restoration of the German national princes. In addition to the Hohenzollerns, various other disempowered princes continued to make demands after 1918. In 1932, princes from various offices – for example Duke Adolf Friedrich zu Mecklenburg, the older brother of the Dutch royal consort – were considered as potential Reich administrators. That October, State Secretary Erwin Planck remarked to the director general of the Ullstein publishing house, 'You have no idea how many pretenders there are from various dynasties.' He meant pretenders to both the German throne and the position of Reich administrator.[254]

Instead of a coherent plan for establishing a monarchy, as Brüning's posthumous memoirs implied had existed, sources from the time provide evidence only of aimless drifting between various strands of wishful thinking. Precisely those circles that most passionately advocated a 'national bloc' or 'national front' considered it impossible to restore the old multitude of German princes. In September 1933, the head of Hitler's Reich Chancellery, Hans Heinrich Lammers, asked an emissary of the Kaiser: 'Surely you don't want to make Schwarzburg-Sondershausen a fully fledged regional state again?'[255] Whether it was treated as the butt of scornful jokes or as a serious constitutional problem, the question of whether the countless tiny duchies in Germany should be reactivated was another dilemma legitimists could never resolve.[256]

Despite the lip service President Hindenburg paid to monarchism, he never backed it and refused to support any of the Kaiser's sons.[257] And, in terms of their ability to mobilize support, the political organizations of Prussian monarchism remained empty vessels with little actual power. In June 1932, the correspondent of the *New York Times* calculated for his readers that roughly 25.5 million voters out of an electorate of 44 million were deeply opposed to a restoration. That newspaper also published an analysis by the journalist and university lecturer Ernst Jäckh about the structural impossibility of a monarchist comeback.[258] Throughout the Weimar Republic, the weakness of the small, politically insignificant monarchist organizations sapped the vast, free-floating energies of monarchism in general and many Germans' emotional attachment to the Kaiser, the Wilhelmine Empire and their symbols. Hellmut von Gerlach was correct when he scoffed in 1932 that monarchism was without exception 'a phenomenon at the bottom of the pyramid in the animal kingdom'.[259]

While shadowy monarchist networks did play an important role in the reconstitution of the German Right and were strong enough to stoke desires for a strong leader, they remained too weak to bind such desires or produce any candidates of their own.[260] Another failing was monarchism's decreasing appeal to younger generations. Everywhere in Germany, monarchist organizations lost younger members, who joined more modern, radical alternatives. All German aristocratic organizations worried about this loss of support.[261]

It has been perennially suggested, from Brüning's memoirs to the recent speculation about possible monarchist alternatives to Nazism, that the British monarchy could have served as a model. The Scandinavian and Dutch royal families and the Second Empire in France under Napoleon III have also been held up as promising potential alternatives to the Third Reich. But such comparisons are implausible and even absurd. Particularly bizarre are the flights of fancy into French history, including supposed parallels with Napoleon III's 1852 coup, which paved the way for him to go from elected head of state to quasi-emperor. As Napoleon's nephew, Napoleon III was the product of the French Revolution, a factor with no equivalent in Germany. Crown Prince Wilhelm possessed no comparably broad wellspring of popular support. And the nephew of a famous uncle launching coups d'état was completely at odds with the fundamental principle of legitimism and the German counter-revolutionary movement as it actually existed in 1932.

Comparisons with other northern European monarchies and the British tradition of compatibility between monarchy and democracy are likewise misplaced.[262] Around 1933, there was no designated heir to the Hohenzollern throne able to fill the role of the Dutch Stadhouder (governor) or the British 'king in Parliament'. As the philosopher Ludwig Marcuse said about the Hohenzollerns after the start of the Second World War, 'the comparison with a parliamentary majority like the British one is mere verbiage from those who cherry pick through history.'[263] The idea that Heinrich Brüning aspired to a parliamentary democracy along British lines is hardly credible and deserves to be dismissed as one of the legends with which the ex-chancellor sought to rewrite his political biography while in American exile.[264]

In any case, it was never envisioned that the Crown Prince could take power along the lines of British parliamentary monarchy. If there was a model, it was that of the monarch–dictator combination that had ruled Italy since 1922. The Kaiser's and particularly the crown prince's amply documented enthusiasm for Italian fascism, expressed in their multiple trips to Rome and their membership of something called the Society for the Study of Fascism, was based on its perceived ability to combine a mass movement, charismatic leadership and monarchist symbolism. 'The most recent events in Italy no doubt mark a turning point,' opined the Kaiser only a few weeks after Mussolini's theatrical March on Rome in 1922. 'I believe that fascism will spread to Germany and that it will restore the monarchy.'[265] In 1926, Wilhelm II promoted fascism as a way of concentrating the strength of the political Right: 'Finally a bloc is beginning to coalesce, upon which, God willing, the "red international flood" incited by "world Jewry" will break. Germany must do its part by forming a common front against omnipresent Juda under the leadership of the German Kaiser!'[266] The crown prince kept a photo of Mussolini on his desk in Potsdam, and his brother August Wilhelm represented the Nazi Party in Rome at rituals in which the party expressed its admiration for Italian fascism. In 1932, the Italian model of having both a king and a *duce* was discussed as a solution that could unite Hitler, Schleicher and the crown prince.[267] By June 1933, the disillusioned Kaiser may have declared: 'Germany shouldn't have an English or Italian monarchy. I alone am the monarch who decides everything. I will never agree to externally imposed conditions.'[268] But his sons and grandsons continued to pursue pie-in-the-sky plans based on various theoretical possibilities for alliances with the extreme right-wing forces of the day.

The Mountain King

The word 'Prussia' and the title 'crown prince' still possessed immense appeal, however difficult to quantify, for those millions of Germans who continued to feel emotionally attached to the pre-1914 monarchy and its representatives. People at the time stressed this fact, and historians have amply confirmed it. Indeed, such loyalty resonated in the term 'republicans by reason', which late converts to democracy such as historian Friedrich Meinecke and the author Thomas Mann used to describe themselves, implying that, in their hearts, they still felt a fondness for the monarchy.[269]

European history is full of examples of kings in exile and pretenders in waiting taking on, almost automatically, a heightened significance. Figures of this sort were common to nearly all reactionary conservative movements since the French Revolution. That event created not only a new social order but a new counter-revolutionary tradition. The result was countless pretenders to numerous thrones, many of whom could be dismissed personally as 'empty vessels' but whose political significance was beyond dispute.[270] One thinks, for instance, of the final Scottish pretender to the throne, Charles Edward Stuart, better known as Bonnie Prince Charlie. The perceived splendour of monarchs and kings, who were elevated above the everyday earthly world, had always derived its power more from the imagination than from reality. For this reason, Crown Prince Wilhelm needs to be evaluated equally as a real person and an imaginary figure. Germany had never lacked myths about leaders to come, and the venerable and compelling trope of the king in waiting remained very powerful after 1918.

Probably the most prominent of these myths were the many variations of the legend that Emperor Friedrich II from the medieval Staufer dynasty, also known as Friedrich Barbarossa, was slumbering in Kyffhäuser Mountain, waiting for his moment to return. The monarch was pictured sleeping on an ivory throne, with his long red beard growing down through and around it. Every hundred years, according to the myth, he would awaken and send out a dwarf to check whether ravens were still circling the mountain. Only when a mighty eagle drove them away would Barbarossa and his followers come back to life, leave their mountain and found an empire of peace and majesty. This myth was co-opted and adapted to the times by early nineteenth-century German nationalists and Romantics.[271] For example, in 1817, the poet and Orientalist Friedrich Rückert composed the lines:

> He never died in any way
> He lives on there as we speak
> In his castle he hid away

Sitting down for a mighty long sleep.
He took with him, so we learn,
The Empire's great majesty
But with it he will one day return
As soon as he is ready.[272]

With the founding of the Wilhelmine Empire in 1871, if not before, the Hohenzollerns laid claim to this legend for themselves. Directly above a statue of the reawakened Barbarossa, a more than 80-metre-high Kyffhäuser monument was built in Thuringia depicting Kaiser Wilhelm I as unifier of the German nation. In 1900, the so-called Kyffhäuser Association became the umbrella organization of all German veterans' groups. It had more than two-and-a-half million members and continued to exist during the Weimar Republic, changing its name to the German Warriors Association Kyffhäuser. Various Hohenzollern princesses paid visits to its Potsdam headquarters, lending their glamour to the group.[273] Thus, the Kyffhäuser legend was just as much a part of Weimar culture as jazz bars, the women's movement, Josephine Baker, Bauhaus and social democracy.

As every myth must, if it is to survive for any duration, the Kyffhäuser story was reinterpreted countless times. After 1918, the political right assigned the role of the unholy circling ravens to socialists, democrats and Jews. Who would play the role of the awakened king was left open, reflecting the indeterminacy of right-wing hopes for salvation in general during the 1920s, but there was no shortage of militarist, ethnically chauvinist iterations of Barbarossa emerging from the mountain with his sword drawn during the Weimar decade.

To appreciate the power of such myths of restoration, we can't just calculate the number of members of monarchist organizations, tot up how many cabinet members or Reichswehr officers held pro-Kaiser speeches or count the statues at the headquarters of the DNVP, the German Gentlemen's Club, the country's aristocratic associations or the Stahlhelm. The persistent power of monarchical longing that cropped up here and there throughout the Weimar Republic needs to be conceived as something fluid influencing the emotions and political attitudes of millions of people. This power expressed itself less in the form of organizations than as an unstable configuration of various social strata and circles. They included weekend warriors who spent their Sundays in military enthusiasts' clubs recreating famous battles with tin soldiers; officers and militia fighters who marched in the boots and uniforms of no longer existing armies through November rains under the Wilhelmine red, white and black flag with no actual clear goal in mind; and segments of the academic and intellectual elites who transformed the idea of the 'new aristocracy' and modern leadership into the two guiding concepts of the new Right in Germany.[274]

After 1918, the concept of the aristocracy and the figure of the king were politically and intellectually up for grabs. The leading conservative minds in the Weimar Republic defended both, but with an eye towards reconfiguring rather than preserving them in the form they had had before the World War. The more unclear it became who could be considered for the throne and forge a new aristocracy to topple democracy, the more the concepts of king, leader and nobility took on new meanings. What united the tin-soldier strategists, marchers in the rain and the crème de la crème of the intellectual Right was their hatred of the Weimar Republic and fervent longing for a better Reich to come. As the Kaiser's political envoy communicated to Hitler in August 1932, Wilhelm II derived the strength to work for the Nazi movement 'from my burning hatred, unsurpassed by anyone in Germany, my sacred hatred of the contemptible November Republic, conceived in filth and humiliation and illegitimately born amidst treason and betrayal'.[275]

The redefinition of kingship made itself seen in everything from racist hate pamphlets to the rarefied theorizing of right-wing intellectuals. Particularly important for the uppermost strata of conservative thinking was the circle around the poet Stefan George and the almost inexhaustible arsenal of coded messages it introduced into 1920s discourse. One particularly telling example is a

1927 study, quite well known at the time, of the thirteenth-century Staufer Emperor Friedrich II by the medievalist Ernst Kantorowicz.[276] As it was read at the time, this study conjured up the mythical power of an ideal leader figure as a way of paying homage to the conservative 'hidden Germany'.[277] Kantorowicz's work inspired readers to search for new leaders of the sort probably not envisioned by its author. Hitler was said to have read it twice, and Göring gave Mussolini a signed copy of it.[278]

Kantorowicz came from a bourgeois Jewish family and had fought at Verdun and as a member of the paramilitary Freikorps against left-wing revolutionaries in Munich. He emigrated from Germany in 1933, becoming a professor at Berkeley and establishing a global reputation. He later distanced himself from his early works and criticized the seductive power the intellectual Right had exerted in the Weimar Republic. In the US, he used to refuse to sign copies of his book on Friedrich with the remark that the author of that work was long dead.[279] In the winter of 1943–4, he held a series of lectures to teach young American officers the basics of German history and give them insights into what had made Hitler possible. During those lectures, the former George disciple deemed Germany's tendency to believe in political prophecies the main evil in the country's history.

Kantorowicz's concerns about the connection between myth and politics overlapped with ideas put forward by some of his fellow German emigrés at the time: political scientist Eric Voegelin's concept of 'political religions', for instance, or Hannah Arendt's analysis of totalitarianism.[280] Kantorowicz – knowing all too well that the answer to the 'George question' was part of the answer to the 'Hitler question' – frankly admitted that he had also previously politicized myths and mythologized politics.[281] The desire for a saviour was a dangerous longing, which he himself had stoked two decades previously:

The wave of political prophesying . . . rose again, higher than ever, when the war was lost in 1918. There was not a single schoolboy

who wasn't aware of the unkept promises and who didn't long every
day for salvation, just as people during the Middle Ages expected the
Final Judgement to arrive at any moment.[282]

Kantorowicz had begun his 1927 book, which stylized the Staufer
emperor into a 'wonder of the world', by citing Virgil's famous
prophesy from the Fourth Eclogue that a saviour would be born.
He concluded it with a cryptic variation of the Kyffhäuser legend in
which not the Kaiser, but the German people itself was sleeping
inside the mountain. Today, Kantorowicz and his interpretation of
these symbols are a topic for academic specialists. But in the 1920s
they were familiar to every German secondary school student. Even
more important were the countless connections between the high
and low ends of the intellectual spectrum, in which general expectations were conditioned by historically laden images of sleeping
kings, golden ages and leaders of empires to come. What was true
for the remnants of conservatism was also true for the ramblings on
the new Right about empires and leaders who would arise from
nowhere. Such nattering was powerful enough to summon up
slumbering energies but too weak to bind them politically. The
Hohenzollerns would ultimately lose, once and for all, their privilege to determine who would lead Germany. But, before that, all
the chatter about a new aristocracy and new types of leadership
would undermine the Weimar Republic and offer the royal family a
distant glimpse of actually retaking power.

Many rungs below the George Circle on the intellectual ladder,
Hermine von Reuss, the Kaiser's second wife, revived the Kyffhäuser motif in a 1927 book written for an English-language audience:
'Huis Doorn confines Wilhelm II like the mountain prison walls the
red-bearded Kaiser. But, unlike Barbarossa, Wilhelm II never sleeps.
Impatiently he scans to see if the fateful ravens are still circling over
Germany.' The renegade aristocrat Reibnitz cited this passage in his
cutting 1929 portrait of the ex-Kaiser and his wife, writing that 'The
pose is turning into a farce, and ridiculousness is deadly', and that
the 'Empress' had 'driven the final nail in the Hohenzollern's

coffin'.[283] But this rare advocate of democracy from the old aristocracy was premature in his assessment. The monarchist narrative in Weimar Germany was hardly dead. On the contrary, it derived vitality from the venerable, if newly iterated, Kaiser-king-leader trope as well as from the fact that most Germans still didn't comprehend how the various German ruling families could have disappeared from the political stage so suddenly and unexpectedly in 1918.

Expectations for a Führer

Recent historians have used the apt metaphor of 'vagabond monarchism'[284] to describe two basic phenomena: on the one hand the weakness and transience of post-1918 monarchist currents, which, with the exception of Bavaria, never came together into a coherent, politically effective movement, and on the other the flexibility of monarchist desires, whose intensity never diminished even as they moved further and further away from the original dynasties that had ruled up to 1918.[285] For most Germans, the unexpected abolition of the Kaiser and the German kings and princes was a side-effect of the greatest military catastrophe in German history. The collapse of a familiar world left behind a vacuum that was not only political, but also symbolic and emotional.

The widespread longing for and expectations of a new leader, or *Führer*, was without doubt one of the most potent elements in the political chemistry of the Weimar Republic. On the political Right in particular, there were always messianic, religious components to the hope for a saviour who would overcome democracy and rescue the German people from its purported misery.[286] Lively debates were held within the Hohenzollern family about widely divergent variants of the expectations for a Führer and the sense of having a historical mission. In early 1933, the crown prince wrote to his sister Princess Viktoria Luise that ten years previously he had spoken with the apocalyptic cultural historian Oswald Spengler about a leader to come who would be neither a prince nor a general. In Hitler,

Wilhelm added, the figure he and Spengler had predicted had now appeared.[287]

Widespread German desires for an iron-fisted leader were significant for the Hohenzollerns in two respects. Segments of the monarchist camp interpreted this social phenomenon through the lens of the Kyffhäuser legend, interpolating a popular longing for a return of the royal family, in the person of either the ex-Kaiser himself or one of his heirs. With a mixture of anger, disappointment and growing hopelessness, Schulenburg spoke in April 1928 of the Hohenzollerns' duty to 'provide us with a pretender, and then may Heaven give us the man who can wield power in our interests when the moment is ripe'.[288] The subsequent transformation of legitimist pipe dreams into a far more modern hope for a Führer is very evident in the correspondence between this advisor and the crown prince. Even before Schulenburg and most of his family joined the Nazi Party, his hopes for a strongman leader were powerful, if vague. 'Only a titan', he wrote in his letters over many years, 'can master these things, a titan we don't have on either the Right or the Left.' In late 1929, Schulenburg dreamed of a leader who 'would arise from masses' and 'jerk the steering wheel to the Right'. Using images that bore comparison to Fritz Lang's *Metropolis* as well as the speeches of Mussolini and Gregor Strasser, the crown prince's former military tutor invoked the idea of a *homo novus* who would 'build bridges of reconciliation between the ruling caste and the working classes'. In this idealistic vision, the air for a 'monarchy' was growing increasingly thin.[289]

On the other hand, the longing for a non-aristocratic Führer had even spread to the House of Hohenzollern itself, as the royal family pondered the prospect of one of its members assuming a largely symbolic office alongside Adolf Hitler. As far back as 1924, the crown prince had concluded that 'ultimately only a dictator can drag the wagon [of state] out of the muck'.[290] That same year, Wilhelm's brother Prince Oskar beseeched God to help their fatherland by 'giving it just one man who strikes out brutally to the right and to the left and to the right again to get everyone in the same camp'.[291]

As we have seen, the crown prince and his brother were probably thinking about Mussolini, but their thoughts would soon turn to his fascist contemporary in Germany.

Conclusion: The Crown Prince as a Signal

In 1932, the cause of establishing a conservative monarchy as a counter-movement to Nazism had no consensus choice for king and no followers of any note. Various anti-democratic models – monarchy, military dictatorship and fascist state – overlapped and seemed to change from week to week. A monarchist solution or a military dictatorship without the Nazis was never seriously suggested, nor would it have been possible. The debate was solely about how to bring together the various right-wing groups. This is precisely where Crown Prince Wilhelm came in. The heir to the throne was an important mediator between the Reichswehr, the Stahlhelm, the SA, the SS, the Nazi Party, the DNVP, the Gentlemen's Club, veteran's associations, traditional organizations and other conservative groupings. That was due to his unique symbolic influence.

The liberal democrat Friedrich Naumann had described Kaiser Wilhelm II in 1909 as a 'signal individual'. Given the uniform focus on the Kaiser within the apparatus of rule and large segments of the public sphere in Wilhelmine Germany, metaphors of this sort – a signal, the lord of the centre, a beacon – seem quite accurate. One early essay on modern propaganda deemed Wilhelm II as symbolically important for the Wilhelmine Empire as Mohammed was for Islam or the issue of equal distribution of wealth was for the social democratic movement or a registered trademark was for an entrepreneur. Referring to the congruence of power, faith and symbolism at play, journalist and critic Maximilian Harden dubbed the Kaiser the 'Dalai Lama in uniform'.[292] Even during Wilhelm II's reign, there was no way to generate charisma and visibility without mass media, and long before 1914 the Kaiser had lost control over this process. Nonetheless, Wilhelm II remained a figure of paramount importance for both critics and admirers. After 1918, German monarchism was fragmented and dispersed and no longer had any such focal point.

To an even greater extent than his father, whose position was at least institutionally anchored, the crown prince had no choice but to be a media figure, a figure of the imagination created above all by publicists and the mass media. In his role as a potential heir to the throne capable of representing a new mixture of Hohenzollern legacy and the spirit of a new age, Crown Prince Wilhelm was far more effective than his aged, exiled father, lost in a world of personal fantasy. The public roles of the crown prince and princess were without compare within the Hohenzollern family.

Much later in history, Prince Wilhelm Friedrich of Prussia would write that his grandfather, the crown prince, was 'an important symbolic figure for all conservatives in the Reich'.[293] That is an apt description of his main function. At no point did the crown prince ever become the lord of the centre, a Prussian Dalai Lama or an undisputed focal point. But he did send signals that were difficult to overlook. For the traditional German Right, he embodied the fusion of all anti-democratic forces. He was far better suited to this role than the ponderous Hindenburg, who didn't speak the language of the modern era and who as president of the Weimar Republic could never entirely rid himself of the stigma of having gone over to the enemy, however partially. Hindenburg had advised the Kaiser to make his 'departure' to the Netherlands, or at least had not prevented it. He had sworn to defend the Weimar Constitution, signed laws aimed at protecting the republic, tolerated political coalitions that included social democrats and allowed the black-red-and-gold flag of democratic Germany to be flown atop the Reich Presidential Palace. In agreeing to lead a democratic republic, the field marshal general discredited himself in the eyes of many people on the right, including the Hohenzollerns. In contrast, the crown prince's anti-democratic credentials were beyond reproach.

Special times, the Kaiser told his grandson Louis Ferdinand in early 1923, called for special measures. For that reason, he said, he had allowed his sons August Wilhelm and Oskar to join the Stahlhelm and the SA, two organizations of great 'energy' he seemed to think were two divisions of one movement.[294] Despite all the differences between the traditional conservative and National Socialist anti-democratic agitation, Wilhelm II recognized the importance of uniting the political Right. And, both in the Kaiser's imagination and in reality, that role fell to the crown prince.

Within the right-wing camp, with all its various leaders, tribes and clans, Crown Prince Wilhelm was an important mediator both factually and symbolically. Today's business consultants would call him an enabler and facilitator between the Nazi movement and conservative groups.[295] The crown prince was uniquely suited to the role of resolving conflicts within the extreme right and the anti-democratic camp and helping the two develop full synergy within the group as a whole. By the end of 1932, this role was well established, and in the next chapter we will examine how it was expanded and reached its zenith.

4.

Collapsing Constraints:
The Hohenzollerns in 1933

In December 1945, writer Erich Kästner related how the Crown Prince Wilhelm – by then a 63-year-old – had moved to the southern German town of Hechingen with a very young woman he described as 'pretty as a picture'. There is a black-and-white photo from this period that, with the help of a number of auction houses, has been preserved today. It shows a young actress kneeling on the floor before the bare walls of an apartment at the foot of Hohenzollern Castle, looking up at the grey-haired crown prince reclining on a chaise-longue. The young woman has her arms wrapped around a German shepherd sitting next to Wilhelm. In an interview with the Swiss weekly *Weltwoche*, the crown prince openly discussed his new romance and his past, touching on Adolf Hitler, who had 'visited' Potsdam and always treated him very 'respectfully'. Back then, Wilhelm added, he had considered the German dictator an 'agent of Providence'.[1]

In September 1946, two weeks before judgement was rendered against the major German war criminals in Nuremberg and the full extent of Nazi atrocities was revealed to the public, the crown prince also answered journalists' questions, granting an interview to the French Resistance newspaper *France Soir* from a villa at the foot of the now French-occupied royal castle. When a reporter from South Africa asked what Hitler's gravest mistake had been, Wilhelm, strikingly, answered: not reaching agreement with France to proceed jointly to subjugate Britain after Germany's early victories in Western Europe. *France Soir* concluded that the German pretender and former army group leader was a 'man who hasn't understood anything'.[2]

Two years later, Wilhelm's brother August Wilhelm testified in front of a court about his activities during the Third Reich. August Wilhelm, now incarcerated by American troops, had been present during the torture of prisoners at an ad hoc SA prison in 1933 and had inspected the Dachau concentration camp. 'Those were good facilities,' he told the court. 'Better than what we have here in the internment camps.'[3]

These vignettes illustrate what would seem to be the astonishing inability to learn from the past among those Hohenzollern family members who had actively supported Nazism. The historical record suggests that they were largely incapable of acknowledging their own mistakes or engaging in self-criticism. Both the Kaiser and the crown prince laboured under a mix of foolishness and massive self-overestimation. And those basic characteristics were one reason why, as of 1933, the crown prince and other Hohenzollerns gladly served the young Nazi regime.

Post-1945 Narrative Threads

In a 1954 memoir entitled *Veiled Day*, writer Reinhold Schneider, who had personal connections with the Hohenzollerns and later became close to the Christian, conservative resistance against Hitler, wrote the following about his conversations with Wilhelm: 'It struck me that the crown prince had a guilty conscience about having ingratiated himself with the Nazis. He suffered a lot from having done the unforgivable when he donned those 'strange trousers', the brown ones, at the parade on Tempelhofer Feld and marched past the *maître d'* [SA Gruppenführer Karl] Ernst'.[4] During the 1970s, one of Wilhelm's former servants remembered a moment in Cecilienhof when the crown prince, incensed at being dressed down by a common National Socialist Motor Corps leader, burned his SA uniform, including hat and overcoat, in an oven.[5] With the snobbery typical of the high nobility, the Kaiser made fun of the SA uniform and once opined that it made his son 'look like a security guard'.[6] No doubt, the notoriously vain crown prince, who devoted a lot of times to his 'outfits' (as we today would put it) and who complained about the 'appalling' official dress of the republican Reichswehr,[7] would have preferred many other military tunics to the garb of the SA – and not just on fashion grounds. The assertion that the heir to the German throne somehow accidently ended up wearing the swastika uniform or that the swastika meant nothing to him persists in some quarters even today.[8] As late as 1962, Wilhelm's sympathetic biographer Klaus Jonas captioned a picture of him in a SA Motor Corps uniform with the claim: 'He always regretted the 1933 picture in that uniform.'[9]

The stories the former royal family repeatedly told and had others tell about itself after 1945 are full of alleged misunderstandings, mistakes, gestures that were actually meant very differently and, over and over, deceptions to which guileless royals had fallen prey. A main thread of the tale the family has been weaving since the end of the Second World War is that its members tried but failed to tame Hitler and the Nazis.[10] This is not entirely untrue. Like most of the elite aristocratic and bourgeois functionaries who allied themselves with the Nazi movement, the Hohenzollerns did imagine they could rein in, steer or somehow co-opt the potential of Nazism. One of the most frequently used metaphors among the upper classes was that of the constraining guardrails they supposedly placed upon Hitler and his henchmen. This chapter will examine how such 'constraints' began to collapse almost immediately and how, from the perspective of the Hohenzollern family, the roles of horse and rider were quickly reversed.

Twenty-five years after Klaus Jonas's biography of Crown Prince Wilhelm, written in the US, the historian Friedrich Wilhelm of Prussia boiled his own description of his grandfather down to three pages of his 1985 dissertation. As an 'automotive enthusiast', the crown prince only joined the SA Motor Corps in order to avoid being forced to join the Nazi Party, Friedrich Wilhelm claimed, and he had suffered 'greatly' at having to wear their 'funny trousers'. The 'danger of Nazis disappropriating the royal family' had been severe, and the Stahlhelm uniform with the obligatory swastika had offered 'refuge' from the far worse uniform of the SA. In this interpretation of history, the crown prince was someone pressured and threatened into choosing a 'compromise'. Stahlhelm events, Friedrich Wilhelm insisted, had 'no connection whatsoever' with Nazism, and the crown prince felt a conscious desire to support the conservative militia against the Nazis. Starting in 1933, Wilhelm had 'in reality involuntarily got caught up in numerous political activities surrounding Hitler'. It was just as impossible for the crown prince as for any other German citizen to refuse 'to politically participate in any form at all'. This extremely compact depiction of Crown Prince Wilhelm is astonishing, as is the extent to which its basic ideas have been developed over the last decade or so.[11] Some historians only seem to mention instances of close contact between Wilhelm and Nazism in order to downplay their significance. The uniforms, symbols and rituals of National Socialism were ridiculous, Hohenzollern apologists have argued, but it was often impossible for the prince to avoid them.

'Strange Things Happen in Germany' – Two Coffins in Berlin

The reality of 1933 was very different from the tales that were told after the Second World War. Royal family members didn't take part in Nazi marches or pose in swastika armbands by accident, nor did they need to be coerced into doing so. Their behaviour was neither a clever disguise nor a regrettable mistake. Crown Prince Wilhelm's endorsement of Hitler in the 1932 election, connecting the House of Hohenzollern with Nazism, was a conscious political decision. It's no exaggeration to say that both the crown prince and his brother August Wilhelm put themselves on parade for the new regime throughout 1933.

In a sense, after the inauguration of the Hitler cabinet, the starting point for these rituals was 5 February 1933. It was on that day that the Nazi regime, only a few days old, staged a massive ceremony for two men who had been shot to death on the night of 30 January 1933: the sergeant constable Josef Zauritz and the SA leader Hans Maikowski, who had made a name for himself as the head of the ultra-brutal Mördersturm 33 (Murder Storm 33, as the unit had been nicknamed in reference to its particularly brutal attacks) in the Charlottenburg district of Berlin.[12] In February 1933, some 4,000 SA men, backed up by police units, had already held a Nazi-style wake in the neighbourhood. Presaging what was to come under the new dictatorship, the buildings in this working-class area were illuminated with klieg lights, and men with machine guns were deployed on the streets. Presiding over the ceremony were the SA leaders Count Wolf-Heinrich von Helldorff and Prince August Wilhelm of Prussia.[13]

This two-day official state commemoration on 5 and 6 February was devoted equally to the representative of traditional government power and the trigger-happy Berlin SA leader, anticipating what would follow, in expanded form, six weeks later with the 'Day of Potsdam'. The funeral of two martyrs allegedly killed by communists elided the gap between the police officer and the SA man in the minds of many in attendance at Berlin Cathedral, as Hitler 'took a seat together with the crown prince in rows directly in front of the altar reserved for family members'. The press particularly emphasized the presence of the crown prince.[14] Photos from the ceremony showed two silver-plated coffins lying next to one another, one bedecked with an imperial red, white and black standard, the other with a swastika flag. Eight police and eight SA men, all in uniform, stood guard over the coffins. To the left of the photos were swastika flags, and in front of the coffins were some two dozen wreaths, some also decorated with swastikas, and SA men and police standing in the centre aisle of the cathedral.[15]

Photos of the funeral procession show masses of people on Berlin streets wet with February rain – and staged images of harmony between police units and formations of SA men performing the Hitler salute. Hundreds of wreath bearers, police, Stahlhelm members and SA and SS units lined up in rows or trailed behind the two coffins.[16] Some half a million people were estimated to have witnessed the procession between Berlin Cathedral and the Invalidenfriedhof cemetery some 2 kilometres away. But only the 24-year-old SA leader, who had been born in Berlin, was buried there. Zauritz's remains went sent on to his native Silesia for interment.

The funeral was broadcast live on the radio and captured in a one-hour propaganda film entitled *Germany Awaken*. It showed the crown prince both in Berlin Cathedral and then six weeks later at the Day of Potsdam. There Prince Wilhelm stood together with Hindenburg and Field Marshal August von Mackensen in a symbolically charged moment of greeting and later directly beside Macksensen as they jointly inspected the troops parading to the customary blaring marching music. In 1942, the aged Nazi Party member Mackensen claimed that the Day of Potsdam was the first time he had ever personally met Hitler.[17]

Photos shot from various perspectives show the crown prince conversing with Göring atop the steps of Berlin Cathedral during the funeral,[18] and the doleful radio reporter didn't neglect to comment upon Crown Prince Wilhelm's arrival. Pro-democratic newspapers, which had not yet been forced to toe the Nazi Party line, noted with astonishment how much Goebbels's new 'brown broadcaster' had focused on the presumptive heir to the throne.[19] In his diary entry about the impressive mass spectacle, Goebbels himself recounted driving through the 'endless human walls' of what he claimed had been 600,000 people. The funeral brought Goebbels face to face for the first time ever with Wilhelm, who was subsequently described as 'throwing himself' at the propaganda minister both in person and in letters.[20] The fact that the crown prince had 'laid a wreath upon both coffins' was front-page news even in the provincial press. It was also noted that, during the service, the heir to the throne had sat in the front row next to the families of both 'martyrs'.[21]

Crown Prince Wilhelm didn't attend the burial ceremony, where the deceased SA leader was celebrated as a young 'warrior' who had 'fallen in the battle against animalistic human beasts'.[22] But his appearance at the funeral service was reported around the world, including in a detailed, page-long account in the *New York Times* entitled 'Strange Things Happen in Germany'. Wilhelm was depicted as the most prominent figure at the ceremony, sitting in symbolic harmony next to the uniformed Hitler at the very front of the cathedral. No Stahlhelm or Nazi rally any more, opined the author of the report, could be considered complete without the crown prince and his brothers.[23]

A live radio recording of the ceremony also focused on the SA leader Maikowski. In a tone that turned hysterical towards the end, the broadcast emphasized the merging of old and new, a crown prince who stood with SA men on the steps of the cathedral and a new Germany without class and caste differences.[24] The funeral mingled Christian burial traditions with elements of an act of state and the death cult so prominent within the SA.[25]

One of the big American dailies, the *Chicago Tribune*, which predicted a likely return of the Kaiser to Germany,[26] also reported extensively on the funeral and the 'closeness' between Hitler and the former crown prince. The banner headline read 'Ex-Kaiser's Son Joins Hitler at Nazi Funeral'. The counter-revolutionary stance of a fallen royal family still allowed to be active in its home country was without historical parallels, asserted the paper, adding that Wilhelm was 'literally acting like Hitler's manservant'.[27] The French press ran headlines such as 'Ex-Crown Prince in the Middle of Massive Funeral Procession', accompanied by photos of Wilhelm and Göring's handshake.[28]

One of the earliest and most influential analyses of Nazi dictatorship was *The Dual State*, first published in the US in 1941 and written by lawyer and political scientist Ernst Fraenkel. It described the formation of a dual apparatus of rule.[29] One part – the state of norms – remained connected to continuing laws and traditional institutions, while the other – the state of measures – intervened situationally, as needs demanded and often in contravention of the state of norms. Five days after power was handed over to the Nazis, the dual structure Fraenkel described was nowhere near established. But the convergence of regular and irregular power – of police and army, on the one hand, and SA and SS, on the other – apparent at the funeral revealed the contours of the polycratic organizational monster of the Nazi state in its embryonic form.[30] This new kind of ritual, in which Germany's crown prince paid tribute to death, blood and violence, was the highest form of symbolic consecration the conservative camp could bestow on the new duality of old and new state power.

The political and symbolic distance Wilhelm had travelled by this point was truly enormous. The pretender to the German imperial throne, the man made a Prussian army lieutenant at the age of ten, the officer in Prussia's elite regiments and the commander of an army group in the First World War was paying tribute, before the eyes of the nation in Berlin Cathedral, to the unity of the police and the SA and publicly honouring a convicted street brawler and murderer.[31] It remains unclear whether, two weeks previously and thus before the Nazis were handed power, Wilhelm had also laid a wreath in honour of the cultishly worshipped SA leader Horst Wessel.[32] Several newspapers had reported him performing such a symbolically freighted gesture, although it seems difficult to reconstruct whether they were confusing Wilhelm with August Wilhelm.[33] In any case, the pro-democracy camp considered the two brothers equally close to the Nazi movement. Nonetheless, one recent, very detailed account of the February funeral contends that the crown prince only wanted to pay his respects to Zauritz, that he had no way of knowing about the serious crimes of the SA leader and that, for reasons of piety and social 'constraints', had 'no choice other' than to engage in a gesture that necessarily looked as though he were honouring the brownshirt Maikowski.[34]

Theoretically it was possible, if extremely unlikely, that the crown prince knew nothing about the doings of the SA, which had been marauding through German streets for more than a decade and which in the early days of the Hitler dictatorship alone detained, mistreated and abducted more than 10,000 social democrats and commenced a reign of terror in makeshift, 'wild' concentration camps.[35] But there is no doubt that the funeral – the largest propaganda event of the regime, which was still only a few days old – was inspired by the same basic idea as the Day of Potsdam six weeks later. The event in Berlin Cathedral powerfully displayed the purported harmony between the regular powers of state and the troops of the Nazi dictatorship by despotic decree.

In his 1932 book *Hitler's Way*, the pro-democracy opponent of Nazism and later president of West Germany Theodor Heuss described the role the Hohenzollerns played within the Nazi movement in business terms. Heuss, a trained economist from an affluent south-western German family who had written his dissertation on vine dressing in Heilbronn, employed a metaphor reminiscent of the merchant caste described in Thomas Mann's famous novel *Buddenbrooks*. The Hohenzollern princes, Heuss wrote, were not part of the capital stock of National Socialism, but they were listed in its advertising books.[36] This was a telling metaphor, especially at a time when Nazism still required 'advertising' to win over conservative elites. To remain with this image, the crown prince and princess, together with other family members, were among the Nazis' most important endorsement figures for potential traditional right-wing customers. One of the fundamental rules of consumer psychology is to keep advertising messages simple and to repeat them as often as possible in highly visible locations. The politically active Hohenzollerns did precisely this on numerous occasions, often attracting international attention in the process.

Masquerade: Two Coffins in Potsdam

The *Gesamtkunstwerk* that became known as the Day of Potsdam, an act of state on 21 March 1933, is particularly prominent. It was one of the most important acts of self-presentation of the yet-to-be-consolidated Nazi regime, which was still trying to convince doubters and sceptics among Germany's conservative elites.[37] The stability of the Nazi government depended on support from conservatives, many of whom strongly objected to the revolutionary undercurrents in Hitler's movement.

Immediately after a fire destroyed the interior of the Reichstag on 27 February 1933, plans were drawn up to have the German parliament convene elsewhere. Although Hitler himself suggested Potsdam City Palace, the decision was made on 2 March, three days before fresh national elections on 5 March, in favour of Potsdam's Garrison Church – or, as General Wilhelm von Dommes called it 'a holy site . . . for every Prussian [and] the resting place of two great Prussian kings'. But in the national elections, despite the terrorization of voters, the Nazis attracted only 44 per cent of the vote, clearly missing an absolute majority. At this point, the German government was a Nazi–conservative coalition that could act only on the basis of emergency decrees sanctioned by Germany's president, Hindenburg. He and the elite functionaries close to him were the primary audience targeted by the state act in Potsdam and Berlin on 21 March.

That event was a frenzied piece of theatre, witnessed by hundreds of thousands of people, a staged coming-together of Nazis and traditional conservatives that falsely suggested a continuation of Prussian traditions.[38] Although the Day of Potsdam focused on Hindenburg, the Reichswehr, Germany's military associations and its churches, the presence of the crown prince, three of his brothers, the crown princess and other family members provided a highly visible personification of the reconciliation of old and new. As was the case during the ceremonies that transferred power to the Nazis in January, the emphasis was less on the Nazi movement per se than on the creation and representation of conservative–Nazi alliances.

The regime was several months away from being able to compel the various apparatuses of state power to toe Nazi lines. Thus, this symbolic event, which encompassed both living and dead members of Germany's former ruling dynasty, carried great significance. 'No attempt at claiming political authorization in the Third Reich', historian Martin Sabrow has written, 'was more successful than the state act of 21 March 1933, which was exalted into a "Day of Potsdam".[39] The Garrison Church in the centre of that city was where Friedrich II and Friedrich Wilhelm I lay buried and had been a mecca for Prussian conservatives and right wingers in the 1920s, a place where the 'spirit of Potsdam' could be summoned in opposition to the 'spirit of Weimar'. The act of state was broadcast live on the radio and filmed with twenty cameras mounted in the church. Children were given the day off school, and an unspecified number of public events took place in Potsdam and nearby Berlin. The act of state itself was the most elaborate spectacle yet staged by the new regime.

At least superficially, the choice of Potsdam and the Garrison Church was a nod to the old Prussian elites and their military traditions. The Hohenzollerns played no role in the parliamentary voting taking place in the ersatz Reichstag, as the official explanation had it.[40] Their task was to embody the cooperation between old and new, Prussian tradition and National Socialism.

Senior advisors of Kaiser Wilhelm had asked the crown prince not to attend the event, and, if Ilsemann can be believed, he had promised not to.[41] If so, it was another broken pledge. Decked out in his hussar's uniform, Crown Prince Wilhelm was quite visible in the background of the adroitly staged main ceremony in the Garrison Church. Surviving photographs taken inside the building reveal a setting so arranged as to direct the gazes of most of the spectators in the overcrowded church onto Hindenburg and Hitler. Goebbels and his staff had tinkered with the seating arrangement 'until the wee hours of the morning' in order to 'leave an indelible imprint on the memories of the generations alive at the time'.[42] The symbolic solution they found was to have a standing Hitler speak to the seated Hindenburg, behind whom the crown prince sat, perpendicular to the line of sight of the spectators but nonetheless prominent, at floor level in a former 'empress's loge'.[43]

As a result, when Hitler was speaking, Germany's new chancellor, President Hindenburg and the 'imperial family' were lined up from the audience's vantage point.[44] This inspired one reporter to write: 'The former empress's loge was particularly opulent. It was in this loge that the former crown prince took his seat.'[45] The empress's seat and three further ones were left symbolically empty and adorned with wreaths. The significance was obvious – and not just to monarchists and those generations familiar with the Kyffhäuser legend of the emperor slumbering in his mountain and waiting to return. The spot for the German king remained unoccupied.[46]

In his speech, Hitler rejected the idea that Kaiser Wilhelm bore any responsibility for the First World War. The correspondent for French newspaper *Le Petit Journal* interpreted this as a hand extended to the Hohenzollerns and wrote that Hitler had looked over at the crown prince as he spoke these words. 'The only thing missing for a complete resurrection of the past', added the correspondent, 'was the man waiting in his estate in Doorn.'[47]

The Hohenzollerns' symbolic contribution to the event was bolstered by the presence of three of Crown Prince Wilhelm's bothers, together with their sons. Some observers also claimed to have spotted the crown princess. Photos of the other princes also appeared in the French press.[48] The highpoint of the ritualistic event in the Garrison Church occurred when President Hindenburg, dressed in his field marshal's uniform, descended the steps to the crypt alone to pay his respects to the Prussian kings lying at rest. At the beginning and the end of the act of state, Hindenburg raised his field marshal's staff in acknowledgement of the royal family.[49] That gesture could be interpreted either as a tribute to the absent Kaiser or as a tribute to the present heir to the throne, but either way it underscored the importance of Crown Prince Wilhelm. The reactionary conservative *Kreuzzeitung* newspaper reported the following day:

At precisely twelve noon, the Reich President made his entrance, and the organ music swelled, while those in attendance fell silent. With his raised field marshal's staff, the aged military commander greeted the son of the House of Hohenzollern, which he had faithfully served for so many long years.[50]

At no point was the crown prince the main attraction, but the attention he commanded was noted by numerous domestic and international observers. The French ambassador to Germany André François-Poncet, for instance, wrote of the crown prince personally reviewing the marches of the SA, the SS, the Reichswehr and the Stahlhelm.[51] The foreign press also extensively described the activity of Crown Prince Wilhelm and his brothers in the Stahlhelm. Pictorial reports published in London in 1930 documented the Hohenzollerns surrounded by 125,000 Stahlhelm men in Koblenz. The explanation for their presence, even back in 1930, was that the ideals of the Stahlhelm were largely the same, albeit with a monarchist inflection, as those of Nazism.[52]

That was also the perception in March 1933, and the press again picked out the crown prince as a figure of note. One regional Cologne newspaper even thought it worth relaying one of Wilhelm's gestures: 'The crown prince greeted the Reich president to cries of "Heil!" from the crowd.'[53] The Bavarian colonel and later Wehrmacht field marshal general Baron Maximilian von Weichs recalled in his memoirs:

> Among the most conspicuous figures, the German crown prince in his hussar's uniform, a very popular costume in Potsdam, was seated on the VIP stand. That gave us the impression that the Hohenzollerns were seeking to connect themselves in a certain sense with the new regime, which was still presenting itself as a coalition government of right-wing nationalist parties.[54]

A photograph that first resurfaced in the 2014 debate about whether the Hohenzollerns were entitled to compensation from the Federal Republic of Germany shows Hitler and a fur-hat-wearing Crown Prince Wilhelm grinning at one another. It has become the most frequently used image to represent the Hohenzollerns' connections with Nazism. Other photos, also printed as postcards, depict Wilhelm deep in conversation with Hitler to his right and Göring to his left.[55] Another picture exists of the crown prince next to Hindenburg and Mackensen.[56]

It has rightly been pointed out that this staged spectacle could additionally be read as depicting not just the putative unity of the Right but also the continued existence of traditional conservativism parallel to fascism.[57] Overall, however, it's difficult to see the coming together of Stahlhelm and the SA, crown prince and Göring, imperial standards and swastika flags, Hindenburg and Hitler as anything but as an advertisement for the sort of right-wing unity the regime still lacked.[58] The power of these images came not least from their openness to various interpretations. The keen-eyed conservative Berlin correspondent for the French newspaper *Le Matin* recognized that the ceremony derived its force precisely from 'not having specified the meaning of this symbolic pilgrimage' to Potsdam. The extreme right-wing journalist Philippe Barrès, who mentioned the crown prince multiple times in his report, saw in the event a harbinger of a potential, if not imminent, restoration.[59]

Several years previously, Gustav Stresemann had mocked the increasingly visible, jack-booted Hohenzollerns at extreme right-wing rallies as the 'promotional princes'.[60] Stresemann's choice of words may well have expressed a modicum of regret at his own role in releasing the monarchist genie from its bottle. In any case, the phrase was very appropriate to the appearance of the entire Hohenzollern clan at the Day of Potsdam since all Hohenzollern family members present were essentially doing publicity work for the new Nazi regime. Even if there were more black-white-and-red than swastika flags on display and Hitler, clad in top hat and tails, seemed to shrink in stature beside Hindenburg, the event can hardly be considered a victory for the traditional Right in the battle for symbolic pre-eminence.[61] It was no accident that the swastika flag designed by Hitler in 1919 reused the imperial colours.[62] That emblem anticipated exactly the convergence the Nazis were trying to promote in Potsdam. The morning ceremony in Potsdam was an exercise in visual and acoustic mimicry, which came to an end a few hours later and 30 kilometres to the east of Potsdam.

That afternoon, when the first working session of the German parliament commenced at the Kroll Opera House near the Branden-burg Gate in Berlin, SA and SS men stood in a guard of honour, arms raised, at the building's entrance. To enter the makeshift par-liament, deputies had to walk through rows of fascists performing the Hitler salute and thereby demonstrating the power of Nazism.[63] By this point, eighty-one communist and twenty-six social demo-cratic deputies had fled or been taken into 'protective custody' and tortured.[64] Starting in January 1933, 81 per cent of KPD deputies, 59 per cent of SPD deputies and 9 per cent of deputies from all other parties (above all the Centre Party and the DDP) were either killed, imprisoned in camps or driven into exile.[65] As early as April 1933, socialist newspapers reported that SS head Heinrich Himmler had ordered the construction of a concentration camp at Dachau for '5,000 Communists and pro-democracy Reichsbanner activists'.[66] Pro-democracy and socialist deputies later recounted feeling threat-ened in front of the Kroll Opera House on 21 March 1933. By contrast, photos from that day show a relaxed-looking crown prince, all smiles, shaking hands with Nazis in the guard of honour. Hitler appeared at the building in his SA uniform and took a seat among the Nazi deputies. SA and SS men watched over the entrances and exits, and Göring, in his role as president of the Reichstag, made a speech in front of a gigantic swastika that had replaced the red-black-and-gold democratic German eagle in the concert hall. In addition, the name of the Platz der Republic (Republic Square) had been restored to Königsplatz (King's Square).[67]

The foreign press noted Crown Prince Wilhelm's clear visibility in the diplomatic loge of the new provisional parliament building, where he passed his time conversing with the French ambassador to Germany[68] and from where he waved to his brother August Wil-helm, who was seated among the Nazi deputies between the leaders of the SA and the SS.[69] The opulent special editions of German illustrated magazines also featured images of the crown prince in his loge.[70]

On the front pages of the major French newspapers,

correspondents described the crown prince's beaming face and gestures of approval. Nor did they fail to fail to notice his ostentatious applause at various points in Göring's speech.[71] Articles and pictures also documented the Kaiser's eldest son being 'greeted ceremoniously and reverently by the members of the government cabinet and the Reichstag in front of the building'. The uniformed, jack-booted Nazi deputies marched in two columns into the building like – to paraphrase two commentators sympathetic to the Hohenzollerns – paramilitaries occupying a street or village.[72]

At the opening of another Reichstag session on 17 May, the crown prince, wearing his military uniform, entered the building through an honour guard of SS men giving raised-arm salutes. At the end of the session, the members of the Nazi parliamentary group, also decked out in uniforms and again with raised arms, sang the first verse of the 'Horst Wessel Song', the anthem about a fallen Nazi 'martyr'. The decisive act of self-emasculation of the German parliament and the de facto start of the Nazi dictatorship, however, had already taken place on 23 March, less than forty-eight hours after the Day of Potsdam. The vote for the 'Law for Alleviating the Misery of the People and Reich', better known as the Enabling Act, handed Hitler emergency dictatorial powers. Only the remaining social democrats had opposed it.

Interpretations of a Staged Performance

The 'sophisticated smoke and mirrors act'[73] in Potsdam didn't aim to represent a new, unified Nazi state, from which one could distance oneself by wearing an imperial death's head hussar's uniform.[74] The spectacle was intended to suggest complete cooperation between old and new, monarchist-conservative and Nazi Germany. The atmosphere in Potsdam was by no means dominated by Nazi slogans such as 'Clear the Street – the SA Is Marching'. Instead, the emphasis was on discipline and unity, with joint marches and torch-lit parades featuring the SS and the SA, the Reichswehr, the police

and the Stahlhelm, cheered on by frenetic onlookers. Security officers had difficulty keeping the rubberneckers behind the barriers
erected in many spots.[75] It was no accident that Nazi newspapers
ran pictures of Friedrich the Great on their front pages that day.

The skilfully engineered images of symbiosis between old and
new in countless locations in Germany that day were designed to
represent an alliance that allegedly summoned the collective
strength of tradition and updated it for the future. In the Garrison
Church, organizers succeeded in filling the south gallery to the left
of the royal crypt with uniformed, decorated veterans who had
served in the wars from 1864 to 1871 that had unified Germany as a
nation.[76] The following day, the Junker conservative deputy Friedrich von Winterfeld gave a speech in the Prussian parliament
celebrating the defeat of Marxism and expressing his hope that the
monarchy would be restored. Nazi deputy Wilhelm Kube stood
up and pointedly shook his hand after the speech.[77] Symbolically, the
aged veterans in the Garrison Church implied traditionalists' support
for nineteen-year-olds in the SA, the SS and the Reichswehr. A large
sign was hung from the metal struts of the Glienicker bridge over
the River Havel between Berlin and Potsdam. It informed those
travelling towards the latter: 'We welcome the New Germany.'[78]

To stage this alliance, representatives of *both* sides were needed.
The four Hohenzollerns in attendance, and particularly the crown
prince, were the principal representatives of traditional conservatism. The Nazi *Völkischer Beobachter* newspaper promoted stylized
images of the 'grey and brown armies marching shoulder to shoulder' in a report on an interview given by Crown Prince Wilhelm in
August Wilhelm's residence, Villa Liegnitz. Wilhelm's son, the
twenty-year-old SA man Prince Alexander of Prussia, opened the
estate gates to admit journalists who waited in silence for his father.
'Now all is still,' the report's author wrote. 'Memories spread over
the venerable painted cupboards of Villa Liegnitz. Eyes traverse the
walls. Prussian history comes to life. Images from a grand past
speak unambiguously . . . The door opens. "Heil Hitler!" '[79]

The figure of the crown prince in his death's head hussar uniform was an important component in both the staging and the interpretation of the spectacle in Potsdam. It was also symbolically significant that Hindenburg – a major protagonist and object of projections at this act of state – appeared not in civilian dress, but in his Prussian field marshal general's uniform. It was precisely the combination of old and new uniforms and military decorations that created the illusion of continuity the Nazis wanted. Units of police, SA, SS, Stahlhelm and the Reichswehr, including groups from elite Prussian regiments, marched together side by side.

The mix of Hohenzollerns in attendance reflected the idea of the convergence of various traditions: the crown prince as a death's head hussar, August Wilhelm as a high-ranking SA leader, and Oskar and Eitel Friedrich in field grey at the head of Stahlhelm units.[80] That was exactly the constellation that had arranged for Hitler to be handed power. The crown princess, as the patroness of Germany's largest conservative women's association, also appeared, as did various other princesses and princes, many of them members of the SA or Stahlhelm, who were recognized and admired by the crowds. In addition, 'other members of the former royal dynasties' were spotted as well.[81]

To jump ahead in time for a moment, it's instructive to compare the Day of Potsdam with the funeral of Wilhelm II eight years later. Prior to the ex-Kaiser's death in June 1941, he and his staff had resisted the idea of the Nazi regime exploiting his passing for propaganda purposes. The former emperor refused to be buried in a non-monarchic Germany or be given a state funeral amidst a sea of swastika flags. Significantly, as Wilhelm II lay dying, only weeks before Germany's attack on the Soviet Union, Hitler still thought it worthwhile to enlist the symbolic power of the Hohenzollerns for the regime. But in 1941 he failed to do so – or perhaps more accurately, Doorn engineered a symbolic compromise by inviting representatives of the Third Reich to stand watch alongside Hohenzollern family members and figures from the old guard.[82] By contrast, in 1933 the Hohenzollerns made no recognizable attempt, either in Potsdam or Berlin, to resist being obviously co-opted.

On the contrary, the traditional conservative press was positively enraptured by the Hohenzollerns' role in the Day of Potsdam. The *Kreuzzeitung* described what it saw as onlookers' boundless enthusiasm when Princes Oskar and Eitel Friedrich marched in the Nazi ranks.[83] That was significant because in prior years aristocrats had particular difficulty stomaching this sort of symbolic integration and subjugation. Organizations such as the Stahlhelm, the SA and the SS demanded that members from the landed aristocracy subsume themselves in the collective and, if called upon, march through the streets not only beside but sometimes behind their estate managers. This repeatedly gave rise to arguments with aristocrats either quitting or being expelled from those organizations.[84]

The 'Stahlhelm Princes', as Oskar and Friedrich Eitel were nicknamed, publicly performed the required gestures of subsummation. As one populist segment of the Nazi movement, taken over from the ethnic-chauvinist tradition of the nineteenth century, never tired of demanding, 'We want leaders, not lords.' This perspective rejected the term 'conservative' as 'another name for liberalism with some wrinkles ironed out'. At its core, the Nazi concept of leadership implied a turn away from all established forms of hereditary 'lordship' and saw this sort of revolution as solely possible within the Nazi movement.[85] In the minds of many at the time, if the aristocracy was to march, it could only be within the ranks of the entire German people.

These symbolic experiments of the Day of Potsdam were intended to bolster the notion of popular ethnic community (*Volksgemeinschaft*), which had not yet been completely co-opted by the Nazi movement. One example of this was the electoral alliance Battle Front Black, White and Red, founded in February 1933, which included the Stahlhelm, the DNVP and the Agrarian Association.[86] Although a weak parliamentary force, this group shared a major donation from industry with the Nazi Party, one which had significant influence on the general election of 5 March 1933 and the forging of a two-thirds majority for the Enabling Act.

Creating a conservative backdrop, whose most conspicuous

component was the presence of members of the royal family, was one way the Nazis tried to get elite functionaries in the Reichswehr and civil service, the aristocracy and the upper classes to cooperate with them. Without such collaboration, the Third Reich neither could have been created, nor would it have been able to function. The presence of the Hohenzollern princes at acts of state underscored a message crucial to the consolidation of Nazi rule: the Nazi movement was no longer revolutionary but would, instead, band together in new forms with the forces of the old empire. This message was aimed at the entirety of the non-Nazi Right. The aristocracy was one major influence on that segment of society, encouraging people to build bridges between old and new elites.[87] No group was better suited to represent the new coalitions than the nobility and, within the nobility, the princes of Prussia. On 12 March 1933, inspired by and echoing historic examples, Hitler made a reassuring radio speech directed at the elites of the *ancien régime*. Its wording was remarkably like that used by Napoleon to solicit support from pre-revolutionary elites after his 1799 coup d'état.[88] Anticipating the core message of the Day of Potsdam, Hitler suggested that his movement's fourteen-year 'struggle' had 'now reached its conclusion, visually and symbolically'.

Even after 1945, Crown Prince Wilhelm still emphasized how deeply Hitler's speech in the Garrison Church had moved him – and how deeply he had believed in the restoration of the monarchy. In 1934, he had proclaimed that Hitler's words had been 'more profound and moving' than anything he had 'previously heard from a German statesman'.[89] Despite a few superficial flaws, the spectacle in Potsdam enormously influenced the traditional conservative camp. Even the pointed absence of Hitler and Goebbels, both born Catholics, from the Catholic service did little to disrupt the consolidation of the new conservative–Nazi solidarity. Hitler and Goebbels had boycotted the religious services to express their displeasure at Catholic bishops' criticism of Nazism, preferring instead to lay wreaths at the graves of their 'murdered SA comrades' in Berlin's Luisenstädtischer Friedhof, which was located in a working-class district.[90] For their part, the ethnic-chauvinists and racists of the extreme Right were very pleased at this remarkably blatant anticlerical gesture.[91]

Gestures of this type helped to mollify that part of the Nazi movement which constantly talked about revolution and resisted the idea of bowing down before conservative symbols in a staged, patent-leather-shoe atmosphere.[92] It was the role of Vice Chancellor Franz von Papen, first and foremost, to provide symbolic balance. While Hitler was paying his respects to his Nazi comrades in Berlin, the Catholic estate owner with excellent connections to Rome assumed the role of ersatz 'Führer' at the service in Potsdam. Much like the Hohenzollerns, Papen – a former diplomat – had the task of embodying the Janus face of Nazism, bringing together conservative tradition and the activism of brutal streetfighters under one tent and symbolically granting the latter the legitimacy of the established elites.

The Nazis continued to play with conservative symbols even in the loftiest locations in the German capital and in countless weekly cinema newsreels, on the radio and on posters and stamps. On 21 March 1933, the Nazi leadership had a 4-metre-high portrait of Wilhelm II hung back on the wall in Berlin's Rathaus.[93] The traditional conservative press was only too happy to participate in the illusion of Nazi monarchism following the Day of Potsdam. The headline of the *Kreuzzeitung* the day after the ceremony was 'Hitler Honours Hindenburg'.[94] Not neglecting to mention the Hohenzollern princes, the monarchist press sang the praises of this 'awakening Germany' and depicted the act of state as a decisive step towards a royal restoration.[95]

The *Kreuzzeitung*, the leading reactionary conservative newspaper, anticipated a restoration to come while admitting that there would be no going back to the old Reich. Instead, the paper expected an 'ethnic German state the likes of which we've never had before'.[96] There were countless other acoustic and visual elements of this melding of old and new. The bells of the Garrison Church became the new interval signal on German radio, and the Reich postal service printed commemorative postcards, still in circulation today, that featured portraits of Friedrich the Great, Bismarck, Hindenburg and Hitler in a row. 'What the king conquered, the prince formed, and the field marshal defended, the soldier rescued and unified' was the postcard's slogan.[97] The Day of Potsdam ended with a fireworks display, a 'gleaming spectacle of fire', which was later repeated at the Kieler Woche sailing regatta. Shining in the sky as night fell were the heads of Friedrich, Hindenburg and Hitler – far above those of the people in the crowd.[98]

Potsdam Is Everywhere

Potsdam was the most spectacular and important in a series of events including Hohenzollerns that demonstrated the alliance of old and new in Germany. In May 1933, for example, a memorial ceremony featuring 100 warplanes and 70,000 Hitler Youth was held in Düsseldorf to mark the tenth anniversary of the death of the 'martyr' Leo Schlageter, who had been executed by French occupation forces. As reported in the local press, the Kaiser and the crown prince sent huge wreaths that were laid and watched over by SS men.[99] Two months later the crown prince and the imperial field marshal Mackensen were central figures at the 'Day of Weapons' of the German cavalry, a gigantic military fair and parade staged as a mass summer festival, open to the public at large, in the Rheinstadion arena. It completely dominated the city for several days.[100] Whereas previous versions of the event were a mix of military tradition and folklore, the July 1933 one mutated into a 'marriage of the symbols of the old guard and the new strength' like the one Hitler had praised in the Garrison Church.[101]

The crown prince was everywhere to be seen on the main stages in Düsseldorf. On one occasion, 1,000 SA men, carrying torches, accompanied by flares and singing the 'Horst Wessel Song', marched in two rows and formed an oval into which twenty old regiment standards were brought. 'You couldn't have staged it any more clearly,' wrote one observer. 'The old army was surrounded by the new brownshirts, and former imperial soldiers were absorbed into the ranks of the Nazi Party soldiers'.[102] The crown prince also had one of his attachés tell the press that he had placed two bouquets of roses on Schlageter's grave, accompanied by an SS man, after the ceremony – and that he was moved and impressed by the unity the SA and the SS had demonstrated.[103]

This sort of behaviour was the exact opposite of 'inner emigration'. In *Eichmann in Jerusalem*, Hannah Arendt once observed: 'The only possible way to live in the Third Reich and not act as a Nazi was not to appear at all: "Withdrawal from significant participation in public life" was indeed the only criterion by which one might have measured individual guilt.'[104] Crown Prince Wilhelm could have refused to appear in public. But Wilhelm and the other 'princes of promotion' chose to be constantly, politically and unambiguously present.

From his Dutch exile, Wilhelm II followed his sons' political doings in minute detail, commenting upon them and issuing 'commands' in response. Although he generally supported the princes' participation in the Stahlhelm and the DNVP,[105] he tried to prohibit them from taking part in the Day of Potsdam. But, in contrast to his potential candidacy for the Reich presidency, the crown prince this time ignored his father's instructions.[106] Far away in the Netherlands, the ex-Kaiser mocked the 'Friedrich circus', which could only serve to make the Republic respectable. He could only have meant the Hitler regime. Since even the Stahlhelm had failed, Wilhelm II added, it was high time for him to personally intervene. But then, assuming the line the entire Hohenzollern family was following, he went on to say: 'I cannot do this without the Nazis; we need to use the Nazi upsurge.' A few days later, when Ilsemann reported to his lord on Hitler's speech to the Reichstag, in which he had said that a restoration was out of the question for the time being, the news hit the former Kaiser like a 'bullet to the chest'. Staring ahead blankly, stress lines etched across his face, like a condemned man hearing his verdict read out, Wilhelm II was only capable of uttering a single word: 'So!'[107]

In October 1931, Hitler had pointedly refused to greet the Stahlhelm units parading at the 'Harzburg Front' in traditional military
fashion. At that point no one would have called the German Right
unified. A year and a half later, the Day of Potsdam made a major
step towards bringing the two sides together. The crown prince, his
wife, his brothers and the rest of his family moved about in the pul-
sating milieu of right-wing extremism like the proverbial fish in
water. Moving between various leaders and organizations, none of
the Hohenzollerns occupied the top ranks of power or was among
the main architects of the alliance between the Nazis and Germany's traditional conservatives. Nonetheless, various royals, first and
foremost the crown prince, served as major mediators, accelerators
and symbolic representatives of that alliance.

Journalist Hans Georg von Studnitz, who had attended school
with the crown prince's sons in Potsdam and later became a member
of the Gentlemen's Club, the Nazi Party and the Nazi Security Service, wrote in his memoirs that the German revolution of 1918 had
never seriously rattled 'Prussia's Potsdam heart'. That heart had
'only stopped beating', he added, 'when the Day of Potsdam with
its encounter between Hindenburg, Hitler and the crown prince
ushered in the end of Prussian history'.[108] The message Studnitz
wanted to send with this philo-Prussian statement was, of course,
that what came next couldn't possibly have had anything to do with
Prussia itself. Staudnitz's post-war conservative interpretation of
the past anticipated later assertions that the Hohenzollerns in Potsdam, the heart of their own family history, had been exploited,
misused and even 'prostituted'. Crown Prince Wilhelm's son Louis
Ferdinand came up with that final image, which is still used in some
quarters today.[109]

The truth was that the House of Hohenzollern thought it had to
participate in the biggest propaganda event of the nascent Third
Reich. Six months before the Day of Potsdam, the pacifist writer
Hellmut von Gerlach had come up with an apt description of the
political and symbolic division of labour within the family and the
Hohenzollerns' contribution as a whole:

The Hohenzollern princes have divided up different roles. Some do their work in the Stahlhelm, others in the Nazi Party, with the crown prince serving as the liaison officer between the two ostensible separate fronts. He's active in the Stahlhelm and assists Hitler, whose candidacy for the presidency he endorsed in the run-off election.[110]

Without doubt, the crown prince posing for photos in Potsdam and his brothers marching alongside Nazis lent all the force possessed by their name, tradition and charisma to the new regime.

In keeping with the function of a liaison officer, the crown prince alternated between Stahlhelm and Nazi greetings, whatever was most opportune. He signed off an April 1933 letter to Goebbels, for instance, with the complicated formula, 'With heartfelt greetings, Heil Hitler and Hail to You in Battle, Most Respectfully, Wilhelm'.[111] The conglomeration of black-white-and-red and swastika flags at right-wing events also signalled the crown prince's preferred alliance.[112] All of these gestures blurred the lines once and for all between the formerly separate traditional conservative and fascist camps – a convergence the crown prince was all for. The core agenda of the heir to the German throne combined, on the one hand, insistence on the value of old Prussian symbols and traditions with a reinterpretation of Prussian history, on the other, to meet the needs of the Third Reich. This was the background of Crown Prince Wilhelm's continual calls for 'undying Prussian-ness' to be amalgamated with the spirit of the new age.[113]

The Ladies' Event – Cecilie's 'Day of Potsdam'

Other Hohenzollern family members also fuelled the process of amalgamation. Of particular note is the intense political activity of the crown princess, especially her engagement in Germany's largest conservative women's organization. Cecilie garnered a lot of publicity at an event for women three weeks after the Day of Potsdam that reinvoked the alliance symbolically forged at that ceremony.

As the 'first lady' of Germany, the crown princess served as patroness to the Queen Luise Association, an anti-democratic women's group and the first women's organization to exclude 'Jewesses and members of foreign races'.[114] The association was considered a female version of the Stahlhelm, with which it was closely connected in terms of both ideology and organization. Cecilie and Wilhelm often appeared together at group events, with the former giving a speech while her husband inspected parades of uniformed, saluting Stahlhelm troops.[115] In addition to raising money for charity, the Queen Luise Association politically indoctrinated its members, who numbered 200,000 in 1933. At mass events, the Luises, as they were known, were all attired in white-collared cornflower-blue dresses. The dress code was the female equivalent of the Stahlhelm uniform. As of 1931, Cecilie had also posed in this garb, although she never neglected to signal her distinction optically by adding pearl necklaces, silks and luxuriant furs.[116]

The crown princess regularly appeared at the association's annual celebrations. In the autumn of 1932, with Wilhelm at her side, she held the keynote speech before an audience of 5,000.[117] Cecilie and the group's other leaders shared the crown prince's political affinities and went on organized tours of Italy to learn more about the fascist social model they so greatly admired. They were even received by Mussolini personally.[118] Nationally, the association's leader supported the dissemination of conservative, ethnic chauvinist and racist, and anti-Semitic views among women from all walks of life. Its Silesian leader Maria Theresia von Buddenbrock, for instance, once faced police investigation after defaming Jews as bacteria, filthy rabble and boils on society in a 1929 public speech.[119]

When a group of SA men in the Silesian town of Potempa bestially stomped a Polish worker to death in front of his mother, an act that shocked people throughout Germany, the Queen Luise Association was among the conservative political organizations to lobby for the killers to be spared capital punishment.[120] Like Crown Prince Wilhelm, Buddenbrock also endorsed Hitler in the 1932

German run-off election.[121] The association immediately welcomed the Hitler government after the Nazis were handed power on 30 January 1933 – its leadership had included active female Nazi supporters for some time already.[122]

There is no doubt that Cecilie supported Nazism at this time. The most visible manifestation came when she spoke at a 14 May 1933 Nazi anniversary celebration staged at Potsdam's Stadion am Luftschiffhafen arena, Berlin's Sportpalast and the Kroll Opera House. Attendance was estimated at between 20,000 and 45,000. In her speech, the crown princess proclaimed, 'For the first time, a women's organization has succeeded in filling the great circle of the Stadion am Potsdamer Luftschiffhafen.'[123] In Berlin's Sportpalast, the speakers were escorted to the podium by cornflower-blue-wearing Luises and a Stahlhelm and an SS member. Photographers and a propaganda film documented the event.[124] The photos show the arena draped in swastikas and uniformed women standing in astonishingly perfect formations in the style of totalitarian mass events.[125] The aesthetic here was much closer to the symbolic universe of fascism than the pseudo-conservative masquerade in the Garrison Church.

Encircled and escorted by Stahlhelm troops, the rows of women in blue uniforms with white collars formed more than just an antithesis of the clichéd liberated, lascivious, scantily clad *new woman*, who danced her nights away in Berlin clubs – the image that has dominated the collective imagination from the nightmares of conservatives during the 1920s to the kitschy Weimar nostalgia of the present day. For participants and spectators, the arrangement of space, colour and lines of human bodies was a new visual experience, one similar to culture theorist Klaus Theweleit's description of how soldiers imagined servile femininity in his seminal book *Male Fantasies*.[126] Along with the crown princess, Countess Ina Marie von Bassewitz-Levetzow, the wife of the Stahlhelm leader Prince Oskar, also took part in the ceremony. In keeping with tradition for prince's wives, conservatives tended to refer to her as 'Princess Oskar'.

Details of the event were passed on by newspapers far away from the German capital.[127] The local Cologne press reported on the 'threefold Heil' with which it concluded.[128] The speeches about the 'boldness of the female leaders' and the 'hopes for final victory', other journalists commented, reflected the search for a combination of old and new formulae. The same was true of the event's success in wedding Germanic elements to the association's typical idealization of women as homemakers. 'Years of most courageous struggle' lay ahead, gushed the press – struggle in which women would be the 'guardian of the people's most precious assets'. The provincial newspaper *Teltower Kreisblatt* proclaimed:

> Never will a people flourish and prosper, if its women do not preserve their dignity and most loyally fulfil their God-given tasks. In the old Germanic sense, a woman and mother is the priestess of the sacred home hearth, a loyal helper of her husband, a faithfully caring mother to her children, whom she raised with a firm, loving hand to become strong, joyful people.[129]

The association's deputy leader, Baronness Charlotte von Hadeln, whose husbands and sons were active in the Nazi Party, the SA and the SS, solemnly declared that the organization stood firmly behind Adolf Hitler. As the symbolic main speaker at the event, despite being said to have grave private concerns about aspects of Nazism, the very composed crown princess signalled her support for solidarity and cooperation. As part of a 'broad front', Cecilie announced from the podium of the massive hall to more than 20,000 listeners, 'national women' had come together. Adolf Hitler, she added, was due 'heartfelt gratitude' for protecting German women so that they were now 'able to fulfil their patriotic duties without constraint'.[130]

French newspapers also reported 'the ex-crown princess delivering an encomium to Hitler', correctly stating that Cecilie was Hitler's most important female propagandist at the juncture.[131] In the end, though, the Queen Luise Association's attempts to cosy up to the Nazis were in vain. Like the vast majority of traditional conservative organizations, the association could never free itself of suspicions of attracting malcontents and reactionaries, and it was absorbed into the National Socialist Women's League in 1934.

Beyond Potsdam

Throughout 1933, the crown prince's political activity seemed hyper-active and harried. The sheer number of levels upon which he acted, simultaneously or successively, was conspicuous: in his family, among comrades and friends, at public events, in uniform, in civilian clothing, at Nazi marches, in private conversations with Hitler and Göring, as a writer of letters, as a stylish raconteur at political salons, as a frequently posing figure in weekly newsreels and photos and in circles of high-ranking Wehrmacht officers or Silesian landed aristocrats. It was with a member of that final group that Wilhelm sought an arrangement in a June 1933 letter, written from Oels, to the leader of the Stahlhelm in Silesia. In it, the crown prince expressed his pleasure at the 'common front of unity between the national forces in National Socialism and the Stahlhelm'. Because of his family connections, among other things, the Silesian Stahlhelm leader Count Sylvius von Pückler, who would later become an SA Oberführer and then a Wehrmacht officer, made an ideal correspondence partner for the crown prince. Pückler's older brother, Count Carl Friedrich von Pückler-Burghauss, the husband of the princess of Sachsen-Altenburg and later an SS general and convicted war criminal, was then the head of the Silesian SA.

These two brothers were members of venerated Silesian nobility and part of the region's landed elite, so they could help the crown prince communicate his message that the entire political Right needed to come together. Excerpts of his letter were printed six months later in the *Kreuzzeitung*. They clearly expressed Wilhelm's hope that the Stahlhelm would remain a separate organization while calling upon the traditional conservative camp to support the Nazi regime.[132] In the first half of 1933, ex-Kaiser Wilhelm II also said on numerous occasions that he welcomed an alliance of the Reichswehr, the Stahlhelm, the SA and the SS.[133]

These were two of many voices advocating that the Stahlhelm, the SA and the SS be united into a single fighting force. In the autmn of 1932, the crown prince had allowed his Nazi friend Joachim von Ostau to publish an open letter from him calling for the organizations to be merged. Repeatedly, Crown Prince Wilhelm emphasized the military potential of the German youth concentrated in these associations.[134] In May 1933, the crown prince appeared in Wittenberg with Stahlhelm leader Franz Seldte, who had joined the Nazi Party and who declared that his organization would stand 'as one' behind Hitler.[135] It was no great secret what the future held in store. Even socialist newspapers at the time correctly predicted that the Stahlhelm would be disbanded and amalgamated into the Nazi power apparatus.[136]

In September 1933, several months after the crown prince's letter to Pückler, he made another high-profile appearance at the Stahlhelm's Reich Leaders Conference in Hanover. The event, held on the city's Maschwiesen exercise grounds, was a gigantic rally with parades, banners and marching bands, during which well-drilled combinations of Stahlhelm, SA, SS and Reichswehr soldiers displayed their new-found unity. Photos show the uniformed crown prince wearing a swastika armband and marching in the front row alongside SA leader Ernst Röhm and Himmler.[137]

The foreign press again noted the presence of fascist symbols and ran a close-up photo of the crown prince next to Röhm captioned: 'A Hohenzollern Wears the Nazi Emblem'. French newspapers commented that since the Nazis had come to power there had been no recognizable difference between the Stahlhelm and the SA and that the joint march in Hanover had been a demonstration that the two groups were one.[138] Hundreds of thousands of people had followed this propaganda event, at which Wilhelm had called the Stahlhelm one of the 'most valuable and solid supporting pillars of the Nazi house of state'. During the parade of troops and the 'great Führer appeal', the prince had stood next to Heinrich Himmler on the grandstand, and during Hitler's speech he raised his arm in salute beside Papen. Some 60,000 Stahlhelm men and 6,000 Stahlhelm banners, journalists wrote, had been 'registered' for the event.

The event was captured for posterity in a propaganda film entitled *Swastika on a Steel Helmet*, made by the influential director-producer Hubert Schonger. It featured the crown prince giving autographs and standing next to Hitler, Himmler and Röhm. The film, produced using state-of-the-art technology, took its title from the SA version of a traditional paramilitary song: 'Comrade give me your hand / Let us stand together true / Others may fight against us / But our spirit will never be subdued. / Swastikas on steel helmets / A blood-red band connecting the same. / And Storm Division Hitler / Will be our brand-new name'. Close-up shots in the film showed the crown prince in the grandstand seated next to Seldte, Röhm and Himmler.[139]

In October, one month after the gigantic rally in Hanover, the crown prince appeared at a similarly staged event, a Stahlhelm chapter meeting in the Silesian capital, Breslau, only 30 kilometres from Oels. Photos suggest that he was a central figure, standing on the grandstand between two huge swastika banners, with his hand clutching a third such flag. Other images show him at a parade of some 80,000 people publicly marching beside Röhm, with whom he led the masses through the city.[140] Such photos were also printed in foreign newspapers.[141]

In the run-up to the national election of November 1933, in which the Right presented a unified electoral list and at which Germany's withdrawal from the League of Nations was to be ratified, the crown prince wrote an appeal entitled 'November Days' published in at least three different newspapers. Appearing on 9 November, fourteen years after the German Revolution and a decade after Hitler's failed Beer Hall Putsch in Munich, the article praised the Nazi leader as a keen-eyed, radiant 'torchbearer', who, after a 'ten-year struggle, waged with incomparable strength of conviction and willingness for sacrifice', had earned the right to lead the German people. Wilhelm added that following Hitler was a 'duty, matter of honour and an obligatory expression of gratitude for everyone . . . with a German heart beating in his breast'.[142]

While one of the studies later commissioned by the Hohenzollern family may have downplayed the significance of the crown prince's support for the merging of the SA and the Stahlhelm,[143] people at the time viewed the merger of the two as a decisive caesura. This was also and especially true within the Hohenzollern family itself. The amalgamation of the two groups caused conflicts over everything down to the smallest details concerning uniforms, flags and insignias. A perfect example was the quarrel between the crown prince and the Kaiser in late November 1933 about whether the former should be allowed to wear a swastika armband together with his trademark hussar's uniform.[144] Wilhelm II seems to have tried to prohibit his son from combining the conspicuous uniform of the elite imperial regiment with the insignia of the Nazi movement – an optical gesture which would have transferred the power of the death-head as a Wilhelmine symbol to the SS. It was a sign of the politically charged fusion of Prussian tradition and Nazism that the crown prince was constantly advocating.

Here again, it would be wrong to call Crown Prince Wilhelm a 'Nazi', but he was one of many aristocrats who mixed his symbols and gestures. As early as 1932, Prince Adolf zu Bentheim-Tecklenburg, the 'aristocratic marshal' and the leader of the largest association of German nobility, which at the time was leaning towards Nazism, had already begun signing his letters with both the traditional military and Nazi greetings, 'Front Heil' and 'Sieg Heil'.[145] Never one to turn down donning a swastika armband with his field greys, the crown prince also sought to visually embody this fusion at all levels and in a language comprehensible to millions of Germans. In December 1933, a left-wing Austrian newspaper captioned a photo of Wilhelm in a Stahlhelm uniform with a swastika armband with the words 'An illustrious Nazi', writing 'Finally the German crown prince has arrived where he has belonged for quite some time . . . The swastika was what Wilhelm was lacking more than anything else.'[146] The detailed language of symbols melded the patina of the old with the dynamism of the new, including such minutiae as the slow metamorphosis of the caps, death's heads and crossbones the crown prince sported in public. At first glance, Wilhelm's 1933 headgear appeared to be the traditional hussars peaked cap. But upon closer inspection, the rather blockish death's head of the hussars gradually shrank to the size of the death's head emblem on SS uniforms, and death's heads begin to appear on the crown prince's collar tabs. Meanwhile his appearances alongside SA and SS men grew increasingly jovial and 'comradely'. At several of his 1933 appearances he 'even deviated from the norm by wearing death's heads on the collar of his hussar's uniform, suggesting a similarity with the SS uniform'.[147]

It's entirely possible that the symbol- and fashion-conscious heir to the throne ordered his tailor to customize his outfits. In a social setting in which fine differences of this sort were keenly noted, such changes carried considerable communicative force and would have been read as an expression of the crown prince's increasing conformity with the new holders of power and their rules. A satirical cartoon from Austria depicted Wilhelm in his hussar's uniform next to a Carnival harlequin, who says to him: 'In hard times like these, even I have little success, but you . . . are in another league entirely.'[148] A year later, a Belgian cartoonist drew Wilhelm wearing the knickerbockers of Nazi uniforms under the sobriquet 'The Clown Prince'.[149]

Recent commentators have made astonishing claims about the heir to the throne being allegedly 'bound by duty' to pose for images wearing swastika armbands.[150] The truth is that Wilhelm was under no compulsion whatsoever to be a member of a right-wing extremist, military organization that would fuse with the SA or to appear in uniform wearing a swastika at countless events throughout Germany. No institution could have required the heir to the German throne or his children to use political symbolism benefitting the far Right. It has also been put forward in all seriousness in recent debates that the crown prince was unaware of his own symbolic significance, that he merely enjoyed the 'cosy feeling of belonging

to a familiar club' in the Stahlhelm and that he had no way of understanding why he should have quit the SA.[151] Those who want to
interpret history in this way are free to do so. It may be true that, in
1933, just like most of the German populace, the majority of the
German high nobility didn't spend their lives marching under swastikas next to Röhm and Himmler across Germany's parade grounds.
But the idea that the crown prince acted under duress or in igno-
rance is empirically untenable.

Symbols of Nazi authority were even used in private spaces in
Cecilienhof. A series of photographs, introduced as evidence in
court in the late 1940s but only recently rediscovered, feature the
crown prince and his children posing in their home for foreign
photojournalists in April 1934.[152] The short introduction remarked
that the crown prince was 'cautious' about Nazism, suggesting he
didn't fully identify with it. The carefully staged images aimed at an
audience from various countries told a different story. They depict
Wilhelm in an athletic pose, wearing a wristwatch and a white shirt,
in front of a crooked oil portrait of his father and working out as a
lithe 52-year-old with a punching ball in front of his smiling children
Cecilie, Friedrich and Hubertus. Hubertus and Friedrich appear in
various uniforms with swastika armbands in front of the mock
Tudor façade of the estate, Wilhelm sitting with them on the sofa.
The scenes were photographed from below. Viewers see three
Hohenzollern princes, six black jackboots and crossed legs in SA
uniforms and three swastika armbands in the central visual axis.
The subjects of these photos all changed costumes numerous times
during the shoot.

Other photographic series showed the lord of Cecilienhof at his
desk with his cherished picture of Mussolini. A book seems to just
happen to be lying open in the middle of the image – Göring's
Revival of a Nation – while the crown prince strikes a pose as if he
were working at his desk. The visual high point of the series featured Wilhelm ruminating in front of a mirror. Shot from behind
and to one side, this portrait captures the crown prince both in profile and, in his reflection, frontally. The props in this photo were a

white porcelain container, Wilhelm's brown SA motor brigade uniform, a leather belt on which his left thumb is casually hooked, a rather random Iron Cross dangling before his midriff and a prominent, protruding swastika that commands the viewer's gaze.[153]

This meticulously staged set of images was first published in a popular illustrated weekly in Britain and appeared in slightly different form in the Netherlands and Denmark. In other words, Wilhelm arranged for a coordinated, pan-European portrayal of himself and his family under the sign of the swastika. The fact that such images were taken in the crown prince's living room and the Cecilienhof Park invalidates the notion once and for all that he was somehow 'forced' to pose with Nazi symbols. The headline in the *Illustrated London News*, in which the crown prince opted to depict himself in this way, was 'The Ex-Crown Prince Wears the Nazi Swastika: The Ex-Kaiser's Heir and Two of His Sons as Storm Troopers'.[154] The crooked oil portrait of Kaiser Wilhelm II suggested that he was part of the past in contrast to the two generations of young, future-oriented princes ready and willing to play active roles in the Nazi regime as leaders in the modern fascist sense.

By this point, Berlin stationery shops were already well stocked with postcards featuring the prince in a brown shirt and a swastika.[155] And as the crown prince and his family endorsed the Third Reich in word and image, the British press was running extensive, remarkably prescient analyses of how a regime supported by the eastern German aristocracy was continually ratcheting up pressure on Jews and how political fugitives, male and female, were being 'shot while trying to flee' in all corners of the country. It's no accident that the first American anti-Nazi film was made at this time.[156] There was no shortage of foreign headlines that read 'The Former Crown Prince in Nazi Uniform' above a picture of him posing casually, in fascist garb, in front of automobiles.[157]

Whether it was to compete with or to supplement this photographic series, the *Illustrated London News* published a home portrait of Wilhelm II in Doorn that December. Along with images of a dinner, the estate grounds, the ex-Kaiser's beloved ducks and

Collapsing Constraints: The Hohenzollerns in 1933

Hermine with her daughters doing their homework, it showed the former monarch ostensibly engaged in political work and remarked upon the crown prince's collaboration with the Nazis in several asides.[158]

Kings and crown princes are ultimately actors playing roles. This has been a fact of life, at least since the French Revolution, in republics with counter-revolutionary movements promoting restoration as an alternative to democracy. For that reason alone, the most pernicious effects of Hohenzollerns undermining the Weimar Republic may have been at the symbolic level. The adult male and female members of the House of Hohenzollern were entirely aware of their social status, the aura of their name and their influence within the conservative camp. Moreover, all members of the clan who sought the limelight were surrounded by advisors who carefully worked to shape their masters' images. Hohenzollerns didn't make public appearances by chance. There was no way those appearances would remain unnoticed or could unintentionally come to mean something other than what was actually intended.

Yet alongside the symbolism very assiduously maintained by the former German royal family between 1930 and 1934, the House of Hohenzollern was also concretely active in the various networks of the political Right. As important as high-profile public appearances may have been, the aspect of Hohenzollern activity that remained invisible to the general populace – the conversations and correspondence, which can only be partially reconstructed today – was also significant. On 14 March 1933, for instance, the crown prince wrote from the so-called Dutch Palace (Niederländisches Palais) in Berlin to his close acquaintance Eberhard von Selasen-Selasinsky, promising to lobby Papen on his behalf for a government post. 'We can be not only proud but filled with joy at the positively wonderful development of things in the past few weeks,' Wilhelm proclaimed:

For me it's especially satisfying that I have now finally attained the goal to which I've devoted myself with all my heart and which many

291

people who thought themselves cleverer than I were unable and refused to understand. We must all now see to it that this wonderful national front is further strengthened and supported and not destroyed. Regardless where they come from, all attempts at corrosion must be prevented by all means imaginable.[159]

In his response two days later, Selasen-Selasinsky – who, as we have seen, was a key figure in attempting to arrange a deal with Hitler in March 1932 – stressed how happy he was, how much he himself had done to help the rise of the Nazis and how vigorously he had striven to bring about an alliance with Nazism: 'I have worked in exactly the same sense of Your Royal Majesty and always [advocated] the unity of all nationalist forces.' He expressed his optimism in the cavalry metaphors typical of the aristocracy: 'I'm convinced that we'll ride again in the foreseeable future . . . We always got as far as the Brandenburg Gate, and now the march will go from there to the Palace!'[160]

Two days after receiving this response, the crown prince sent very clearly worded letters to the head administrators of his estates in Oels and Primkenau:

To get rid of any doubts as to my attitude toward the current domestic political situation, I announce to you the following. I most warmly welcome the coming together of all nationalist forces in a united front of the black-white-and-red front and the National Socialist movement and take great personal satisfaction in seeing the goal I have pursued for years with all my heart finally being reached. Unfortunately, there are still would-be patriotically minded people who take a wait-and-see and even mistrustful attitude toward this act of solidarity. I have no choice but to condemn this sort of lukewarm nationalist thinking in the sharpest possible manner. There is nothing to wait and see about here! Every single national-minded German must act, without regard to individual personal interest, so that this wonderful national front is supported, preserved and strengthened. I expect from all my civil servants, employees and workers that they correctly understand the great times in which we have been placed and actively and completely devote themselves to the idea of the nation, just as I do. I would like this attitude of mine to be made generally known and for it to be noted that I neither can nor will tolerate any other behaviour.[161]

The Rejuvenation of the Thoroughbreds

Around the same time as the German royal family's appearances in Potsdam in the spring of 1933, which entailed new forms of self-representation, there was another episode in which private life, inheritance laws, generational conflicts and debates about modern leadership overlapped. That June, the crown prince's eldest son, the almost 27-year-old Prince Wilhelm, married Dorothea von Salviati, a woman below his station, against the will of his family. Since 1931, the family had sought to scupper the relationship, which had started during the prince's university years in Bonn – Kaiser Wilhelm II remarked in this regard that making half-breeds out of thorough-breds was intolerable. There was even thought of sending the rebellious prince abroad in order to avoid competition between multiple rival heirs to the throne. 'It's bad enough that the all-corroding Jewish spirit of the age has also not passed by our house, as the lamentable marital decisions of several of your father's brothers demonstrate,' Wilhelm II wrote to his grandson. 'For that reason, those of the lineage *called to the throne* need to take regard of their *duties* all the more strictly.'[162] Hohenzollern princes who married below their station would find their annual financial perquisites cut to a minimum, the ex-Kaiser threatened. Wilhelm II's right-hand man Dommes cautioned the young Prince Wilhelm that, if he went ahead with his plans to wed Salviati, it would deal a 'mortal blow' to the idea of the German kingdom. And much to Ilsemann's dismay, instead of keeping the affair private, the ex-Kaiser had his 'court marshal', Count von Schwerin, issue Prince Wilhelm a written rebuke.[163]

Salviati was a member of the lower nobility and of Italian origin whose title only went back to 1830.[164] Even worse by the standards of the Prussian nobility, her mother was the daughter of a Hamburg merchant family. By marrying such a person, Prince Wilhelm, third in line to the throne, was breaking the unwritten 'house rules', calling the line of succession into question and causing unrest within the Hohenzollern clan. When it became clear in April 1933 that young Wilhelm had indeed married his fiancée, tensions between the ex-Kaiser and the crown prince worsened. Whereas the former adhered strictly to the principal of equal birth from the *ancien régime*, meaning a prince would have to marry a princess of the same rank, the latter had a far more liberal, modern outlook. A fundamental debate about the House of Hohenzollern's identity could no longer be avoided. As late as 1940, the family's financial and assets administrators still drew up lists of which young princesses from various lineages of high nobility were suitable for marriage according to the third section of the Gotha, the guide to aristocratic genealogy.[165] Other lists of potential female marriage candidates contained critical notes in the margins. For instance, concerns about the 'dubious' reputation of candidates' mothers was enough to get them removed from consideration.[166]

Documents from the family archive reveal that after 1933 the concept of equal birth quickly became more flexible, as the drastically reduced number of 'equally noble' princesses forced a hasty rethink. In heated discussions between family members, financial administrators and the family council, concerns were expressed, in cautiously general language, that incest could lead to the Hohenzollerns' decline. But the statutes that were agreed emphasized the importance of 'German and related blood' and imposed the radically anti-Semitic rules of the German Aristocratic Society, which barred individuals whose 'bloodlines' contained marriages with Jewish spouses after 1750.[167] Prince Oskar insisted that assiduousness as a housewife was a necessary criterion for the future, which not every daughter of the high nobility possessed. Moreover, since many members of the high nobility could no longer afford to keep their spouses in massive estates and castles, but rather had to get along as married couples in more usual dwellings, potential partners had to be on the same wavelength emotionally. Instead of causing 'degeneration', Oskar argued, an opening of the circles in which Hohenzollerns were permitted to marry could help the family produce sound progeny who stood by their responsibilities and were capable of serving as modern leaders.[168]

In 1941, the crown prince made the most radical statement by some distance by asking whether 'the daughter of a Westphalian farmer', provided that she was 'Aryan', wasn't a more suitable marriage partner than a degenerate noblewoman.[169] This question, posed shortly before the death of his father, raised the possibility of a revolutionary change in the prevailing standards within the high nobility. Wilhelm's question invoked a radical break with tradition and represented a potential bridge with, and indeed an echo of, demands made for decades by racist populists, right-wing intellectuals and the anti-aristocratic current of Nazism. The crown prince made it clear to his fellow Hohenzollerns that relaxing marriage strictures would also be good PR, saying 'The abandonment of our strict rule of equal birth would make a good impression on the public at large.'[170] Crown Prince Wilhelm's suggestion appears remarkable when compared with what came later. Even after 1945, Hohenzollern rules concerning 'equal birth' remained in place and still haven't been scrapped today, at least for the 'head of the house'.

In any case, back in 1933, the open violation of these rules shocked the ex-Kaiser and deepened the rifts within the royal family.[171] In the middle of the conflict, the crown prince travelled to the 'Coppa Mussolini' equestrian tournament in Rome, a journey the foreign press deemed worthy of pictorial features.[172] In the Italian capital, he and his sons Louis Ferdinand and Hubertus met with the Italian dictator and the country's royal couple.[173] Wilhelm II ordered him to immediately return to Germany, but the crown prince ignored his father, leaving the ex-Kaiser to fume in angry diatribes and letters. Never had the patriarch of the House of Hohenzollerns been forced to read such a letter from a son, Wilhelm II raged. In shrill tirades, the emperor in exile railed to his retinue against the *'fronde'* of the two younger generations – the 'big-headed impudence', arrogance, vanity and 'dishonourable conspiring' of his son, the crown prince.

The relative calm with which Crown Prince Wilhelm reacted to his own son's act of rebellion reflected his own quite flexible moral standards and his significantly more modern understanding of leadership. By contrast, his father in Doorn immediately invoked mechanisms of punishment and sanction whose language and methods came from times long gone. It probably seemed grotesque to the crown prince that the ex-Kaiser's 'instructions to the princes in uniform' came in the form of orders-in-council. But Wilhelm II insisted on preserving precisely this tradition, once instructing his financial administrator Baron von Sell: 'You and Dommes are to draw up a *cabinets ordre du roi à l'héritier* that he is required to take *ad notem* and his brothers have a duty to acknowledge. Let me make no bones about this! We need absolute clarity. A Prussian-Hohenzollern line! Anyone who doesn't obey is out!'[174] The crown prince was told to depart from Italy for Germany immediately, go to the house of his son's bride in Bonn and 'vigorously intervene with these women'. This conflict was another example of why there could be no place in the brand-new Third Reich, which was still taking shape, for the ex-Kaiser. And it showed that the generations of Hohenzollerns after Wilhelm II enjoyed a far greater freedom of action than they traditionally would have.

Tiger Hunter and Construction Worker: The Battle of Images

Every form of public solidarity with the so-called common people and every populist gesture on the part of the royal family risked being read differently in the public sphere. Left-wing newspapers around 1932 depicted the heir to the throne Wilhelm as a frivolous 'fascist prince' tossing a few coppers out of his window in the Dutch Palace because it amused him to see jobless people on the street below scramble after the money. Some papers even published photographs of such scenes, but it's impossible to confirm or deny today whether they were authentic.[175]

This anarchistic gesture suggests that there were limits to how much the crown prince could simulate closeness to the German people. It would have been unthinkable for a modern, twentieth-century leader like Hitler to rain pennies down upon a crowd from a castle. Crown Prince Wilhelm either could not or refused to close the central performative gap between the allegedly hard-working Führer, who shared the destiny and the uniforms of his comrades, marching alongside them and eating the same humble meals, and the luxury-loving lord casually tossing alms from his royal residence. Wilhelm could not speak to workers at the Krupp factory in the industrial city of Essen, as Hitler did,[176] or join the ranks of 'his SA' as a former army message-runner. Those abilities were based on genuine affinities, a kind of street credibility completely beyond the reach of members of the high nobility.

Contemporaries constantly made jokes about this gap. For instance, in September 1932, a Viennese monthly magazine imagined the prince being addressed on Berlin's luxury Kurfürstendamm by one of his many female tennis partners, who says, 'Now that you've given your heart to a party for workers, you'll probably have to start doing some work.' Wilhelm looks down at his manicured fingernails and responds. 'I beg your pardon, noble lady. No one said my sympathies extended *that* far.'[177] Expressions of scorn of this sort were typical not just of the organized political Left, but of the entire German working classes. Conversely, many observers, not just on the Right and internationally as well as in Germany, emphasized the athleticism, visibility, popularity and ambitions of the crown prince, who continually frequented the highest political circles.[178]

If we consider the crown prince as a potential leader, which was how a segment of the German population certainly saw him, we can't fail to be struck by the contrast between his persona and the image Hitler had spent years meticulously creating. Hitler was seen as an ascetic, a bachelor, a non-smoker, a teetotaller and a vegetarian who neither sang, danced nor engaged in sports, a workaholic who slept little and worked weekends, and a former frontline soldier who lived close to his men in great simplicity, who was wedded only to the Nazi movement and Germany and who had clawed his way up from nowhere. This was the exact antithesis of the crown prince's biography and image. Wilhelm was a prince born to the uppermost echelon of society, the lover of scores of spectacularly beautiful women, a man of hunting trips, soirées, light opera, clubs, cocktails, dinners, theatres, galas and tennis courts, a child of privilege living on a Potsdam estate and racing around Potsdam and Berlin in a powerful sports car like the son of a nouveau riche industrialist, a daddy's boy and an aristocratic jerk who tossed cigarettes to soldiers from his bright red car while keeping safely behind the frontlines and threw pennies down to the unemployed from his palace. The affection some people who met him sometimes felt seems to have come not despite, but precisely because of these flaws.[179] Meanwhile, aristocrats who may have found the crown prince's lifestyle contemptible saw no way of doing without him as a figure. He necessarily remained the focus of all legitimists who regarded him as a link in a chain, an intermediary and the personification of ideals of which he could not be stripped.

In the competition of these two figures of leadership, Hitler, of course, triumphed in the end. The appeal of the grave, cold-hearted, shouting, fanatical, joyless leader far exceeded that of the trim, elegant, cosmopolitan, constantly smiling bon vivant, tiger hunter, army group commander and equestrian. Ultimately Hitler, and not Wilhelm, was the better screen upon which Germans could project their hopes for the future.

People at the time in the Weimar Republic also saw what may today appear like the contrast between an energetically bellowing gorilla and a playfully snobbish but elegant aristocrat as a contest between two different types of leadership. The crown prince was no worse a speaker than Hindenburg or Hugenburg, whose oratorical abilities bordered on non-existence, but anyone who views the scant, sound-film footage of Wilhelm will recognize his limits as a public performer. For instance, in one three-minute interview he gave in English for Fox Movietime News in Salzburg in 1932, the casually dressed crown prince shakes hands with the journalist with the pinky and ring finger of his right hand, while his other two fingers hold a burning cigarette. In ponderous phrases, possibly read from cue cards held aloft, he informs his interlocuter that Germany 'will always in the end come out on top'. He hopes, he adds, to visit the US very soon, saying, 'I take the opportunity of sending my heartiest greetings, to all Americans.'[180] It is easier to understand today how and why this sort of figure would come out second best in a competition of two radically different political styles.

Prince Wilhelm's lustre – the enormous energy that coalesces when millions of outsiders project their desires onto a single individual – derived from the name Hohenzollern and Germans' attachments to it, not from the personality of the man himself. With Hitler, the case was the precisely the opposite. It is a mechanism that has been described by observers and scholars from various disciplines for around a century. Historian Wolfgang Schivelbusch once asked:

> How could Hitler with his fits of rage ever been taken seriously? There are many accounts of how this non-descript product of the masses would first stand silently in his beer halls before sucking in energy from the arena as though by some hydraulic process. He needed masses of people in order to see himself among them. At the same time, he absorbed the masses into himself.[181]

In 1934, the crown prince himself called Hitler an 'incomparable teacher of energy', whose 'magnetism' he greatly admired.[182]

It is precisely this dialectic give-and-take between sender and receiver that the crown prince could never channel. Wilhelm's appearance and the stiff choreography of the Stahlhelm made it obvious why traditional conservatives could never summon up the sort of power Hitler did. One key to the Nazis' success was their hostile takeover of central socialist gestures. In a famous essay from 1935, cultural critic Walter Benjamin remarked that fascism gave the masses a form of expression while denying them their rights.[183] In this vein, it must be said that the crown prince and his conservative supporters promised the masses neither their rights nor a form of expression. But that didn't lessen Wilhelm's influence over the conservative German elites, who had never been favourably disposed to the rights of the 'masses' anyway.

Foreign Promotion

Along with being visible on big stages, which he sought out like an ambitious actor, the crown prince supported the new regime by writing a series of letters to leading personalities in Germany, Britain and the US. For instance, in late March 1933, the crown prince addressed an open letter to the German-American anti-Semite and Nazi propagandist George Sylvester Viereck, one of Nazi Germany's most effective PR men in the United States.[184] In it, Wilhelm defended the German government against what he claimed was completely baseless, foreign 'horror propaganda'.[185] The crown prince's public use of a phrase so common in Nazi propaganda was no accident. It was part and parcel of his high-profile activities promoting the regime at home and abroad. Thanks to Viereck's impressive connections, Wilhelm's statements often found their way into the foreign press and had an unlikely reach, landing, for instance, on the desk of Sigmund Freud.[186]

On 11 April 1933, the crown prince sent a letter, signed with 'Heil Hitler', to Goebbels. It contained a copy of a piece of correspondence he had sent to his lifelong friend the American opera singer and actress Geraldine Farrar.[187] In it, he tried to elicit the support of this superstar, equally famous in the US and Germany, for the Nazi regime, writing that 'socialists, deserters, cowards, war profiteers and sadly also a large portion of Jews' had stabbed the German armed forces in the back in 1918. Jews had pushed Christians out of

the civil service elite, he claimed, while socialists had secretly controlled the country and were essentially responsible for its economic
failings. The Nazi 'popular movement', directed by its 'brilliant
leader Adolf Hitler' now needed sufficient time for 'certain clean-up
operations'. In the final analysis, Germany was leading the fight
against communism 'for the entire world' and would shortly return
to 'complete calm', Wilhelm assured Farrar.[188] 'Toady!' and 'nausea-
inducing!' wrote Goebbels in his diary about the sycophantic letters
he received from the crown prince.[189] Goebbels – who tended to
side with the anti-aristocratic faction of the Nazi movement but
also maintained an adjutant from the high nobility and perennially
tried to integrate compatible members of the old aristocracy into
the new high society of the Third Reich – considered Wilhelm a
clever 'trickster'.[190] He often voiced his personal disdain for the heir
to the throne in his diaries, although that didn't prevent him from
regarding and treating Wilhelm as a player of primary importance
in the run-up to the Nazis gaining power and trying to consolidate
their dictatorship.

In late March 1933, the crown prince received Goebbels at Cecilienhof. Photos from the following summer that show Wilhelm laughing
and conversing with the propaganda minister and his wife, Magda, in
the Baltic Sea resorts of Heiligendamm and Kühlungsborn suggest
that the two men must have been on the same wavelength in certain
situations. The crown princess also received Magda Goebbels multiple times during this period, and the French press took note of the
crown prince applauding Hitler's attacks on US President Franklin
D. Roosevelt.[191] Ultimately, Goebbels viewed the crown prince in
the same way as Lenin did what he allegedly called his 'useful idiots'.
The propaganda minister's diary entries on Wilhelm are a treasure
trove of instances of personal antipathy cynically combined with a
willingness to explore political cooperation.[192]

In March 1933, the crown prince's personal initiative was part of a
concentrated propaganda campaign, also involving the Stahlhelm,
that defended the state's attacks on Jewish-owned assets in Germany and culminated in an anti-Semitic petition being sent to

Roosevelt.[193] As part of their reporting on this event, the large national newspapers ran Wilhelm's public declaration on their front pages. Echoing the words of Hitler, the crown prince told American readers that 'no one in Germany is made to suffer any hardships because of his religion'. Side articles reported on the initial successes of this German 'counter-propaganda'. Chicago's *Herald Tribune*, for instance, professed to reveal 'the truth' in Germany.[194] Citing the *Daily Telegraph* and *The Times*, the *Kreuzzeitung* wrote in April 1933 of the 'ebbing agitation' in England as a direct result of German 'counter-propaganda'.[195]

To understand the import and timing of such sentiments it is worthwhile taking a closer look at what the crown prince termed 'clean-up operations'. Wilhelm meant three things with this phrase: the destruction of the democratic state apparatus, the first wave of boycotts and acts of terror against German Jews, visible to the entire world,[196] and the establishment of ad hoc or 'wild' concentration camps.[197]

The crown prince's endorsement of anti-Semitic repression was remarkable because Wilhelm personally wasn't very anti-Semitic, particularly compared with the Nazi movement as whole, usually formulating denigrating remarks to allow exceptions for the Jewish-German upper classes. Nonetheless, the 'clean-up operations' of which he spoke included massive acts of terrorization first and foremost by the SA, which even the Nazi leadership could hardly control, against actual and imagined opponents of the regime.[198] Throughout Germany in the latter half of March 1933, there were countless, systematic instances of symbolic and physical violence against Jewish-owned department stores, shops and hotels and those who frequented them, as well as personally against Jewish lawyers, doctors, judges, merchants and teachers. This terror campaign culminated in the so-called 'Jew Boycott' of 1 April 1933, a state-orchestrated measure against Jewish economic life that masqueraded as an expression of popular outrage.[199]

Outside Germany, particularly in Britain, the US and Palestine, Jewish organizations protested against the increasing violence and called for various boycotts of German goods. The Jewish scholar of Romance languages Victor Klemperer noted on 27 March 1933 in his later world-famous notebooks:

> The government is in hot water. Atrocity propaganda' from abroad because of its Jewish campaign. It is constantly issuing official denials, there are no pogroms, and has Jewish associations issue refutations. But then it openly threatens to proceed against the German Jews – if the mischief making by 'World Jewry' doesn't stop.[200]

Hannah Arendt, too, would recall in a legendary television interview how she documented everyday anti-Semitic acts in Germany for a Zionist organization in March 1933, an activity for which she spent a week in prison.[201] Only two weeks after the Day of Potsdam, the social democratic press in Austria published a photo of the newly opened concentration camp in Dachau. Another image showed a contentedly laughing, corpulent Prince Eitel Friedrich with the caption: 'They sense their time is at hand. Prince Eitel Friedrich enjoys himself with his kind in the Clou concert hall about the new age in Germany.'[202]

The crown prince's appeal came at the same time as official government propaganda claiming to be 'self-defence against horror propaganda'. An 'action committee' of the Nazi Party proclaimed that 'no German should buy from a Jew', even as assurances were given that foreigners would be exempt from this dictum. The official state line was that the anti-Semitic measures were a 'disciplined defence measure directed exclusively at German Jews'. The *Kreuzzeitung* devoted its entire front page to a story entitled 'The Great Struggle Against Lies of Horror: Nationalist Movement and Reich Government Hand in Hand'. Once again, the Stahlhelm pledged its loyalty to the regime. Goebbels was quoted as saying it was tempting to offer a reward to anyone who could name a single Jew 'who had died during the national revolution'.[203] In fact, by this time Rudolf Benario, Ernst Goldmann, Arthur Kahn and Erwin Kahn, whom some historians consider the first people murdered by the regime, were already being detained. They would be killed in Dachau some two weeks after Goebbels' statement.[204]

While Nazi propagandists called for 'enlightenment' to be brought to businesses, among workers and 'down to the smallest farming village,[205] the crown prince made similar proclamations abroad. On 25 March 1933, Goebbels wrote of Wilhelm's assistance: 'Horror propaganda. The crown prince is greatly helping me with an open letter to Viereck in New York, which I wrote for him and which will be cabled to America tonight.'[206] This missive attracted considerable attention in the German and international press and was printed in the *Völkischer Beobachter*.[207] Meanwhile, the crown prince's friend Göring told foreign reporters on 25 March 1933: 'There is not a single person in Germany whose fingernails were ripped out or whose ear lobe was pulled off, and no one has lost his eyesight.' As Göring was saying these words, some 100,000 political prisoners were being held in concentration camps – a number that would double by the end of the year.[208] And French correspondents in Berlin reported that foreign journalists who spread 'false' information about Germany would 'now face imprisonment'.[209]

While the crown prince was calling for the international community to show understanding for Germany's 'clean-up operations', SA units were torturing regime opponents in Berlin and Brandenburg basements in every fashion imaginable and unimaginable. And Wilhelm was promoting the lie that the new regime didn't use violence, according to the credible testimony of one torture victim, despite his brother August Wilhelm being present as a spectator and cheerleader at sessions where people were tormented. In a former Social Democratic Party building in the Berlin's Charlottenburg district, socialists who had been tortured were allegedly paraded like trophies past August Wilhelm and the Berlin-Brandenburg SA leader Karl Ernst.[210] In a detailed account in a German exiles' newspaper in 1937, Stefan Szende, a member of the left-wing, socialist resistance to the Nazis, described being mistreated in a basement full of brutally abused victims with August Wilhelm in attendance.[211]

Nonetheless, on 23 March 1933, the *Berliner Lokal-Anzeiger* news-paper asserted: 'In not a single case have Jews been molested by uniformed National Socialists . . . On the contrast, SA men have defended Jews most energetically against any such humiliations.'[212] By this time, the real situation in Germany was so apparent that even foreign diplomats described it in cables to their foreign minis-ters.[213] Contradicting the crown prince's perspective as an ally of Hitler, Göring and Röhm, Klemperer wrote on the Day of Potsdam of the 'most frightful pogrom threats . . . together with gruesome medieval reviling of the Jews'. A day later he added: 'In a pharmacy toothpaste with a swastika. – A mood of such fear as must have existed in France under the Jacobins. No one fears for their lives *yet* – but for bread and freedom.'[214]

As we have seen, a few days after his appearance at the Day of Potsdam, the crown prince put his exalted position and his extensive foreign contacts at the disposal of the propaganda minister of the yet-to-be-consolidated Nazi state.[215] Wilhelm's open letter was reported on everywhere from the provincial press in southern Brandenburg to the major German broadsheets to the newspapers of record around the globe.[216]

The crown prince continued his series of letters promoting the new regime with a four-page missive the following June to Lord Lothian. In it, Wilhelm tried to convince the British public of the appeal and advantages of the 'new Germany'. The letter celebrated 'our popular chancellor Adolf Hitler', whose perspicacity, strong leadership and 'brilliance' had made him into a leader 'for whom all our hearts beat in loyal devotion'. The crown prince went into detail about the situation of Jews in Germany, writing of 'a small circle of established Jews . . . who are just as fine citizens and just as nation-alistically minded as other upstanding Germans – I personally know some such men'. But he added that after the First World War, as was not easy for the British to recognize, Germany had been completely 'flooded' by 'eastern Jews' (i.e. Jews from eastern Europe) who had come to dominate many parts of social life. For that reason, it was necessary to 'ruthlessly fight Jewry'. The Stahlhelm, the DNVP, right-wing associations and the Nazi movement, Wilhelm proposed, had worked together to 'root out communism', and reports about atrocities in Germany were nothing but wartime propaganda – although a 'ruthless' struggle was being waged against Jewish 'corruptors of the people', in which certain 'severe practices' were regrettably unavoidable.[217]

This surge of written defences of the Nazis' anti-Semitic measures obliterated the more differentiated positions the crown prince had taken during the early Weimar Republic and the scepticism he had formerly, at least in private, maintained towards radical anti-Semitic views.[218] Before Hitler was elevated to power, Wilhelm kept his distance from radical, racist anti-Semitism despite being susceptible to traditional anti-Jewish stereotypes. He rejected being labelled an 'anti-Semite', saying that his enemies were above all the 'eastern Jews'. At the same time, he demanded that bourgeois Jewish Germans decide 'whether they wanted to be viewed as patriotic Germans or foreigners flirting with internationalism, against whom every upstanding German had a right to fight'. In 1931, he told an Austrian magazine, to which he gave an extended interview while on holiday, about a 'humorous statement of a Jewish lady in Berlin', a 'female friend' whom he had once driven around at high speeds in his car. She remarked that an accident at such speeds could lead to the sorts of compound fractures that would put him in the royal crypt and her in Berlin's Jewish Cemetery.[219] In 1932, he insisted in interviews with foreign newspapers that he had nothing against 'assimilated' and 'nationalistically minded' Jews. At the same time, however, he insisted that Germany would have to expel, by force, if necessary, all Jews who had immigrated to the country after 1918.[220]

The crown prince continued to be attacked by radical anti-Semites, and there is no evidence of him participating in the most brutal forms of racist discourse and practice. But that doesn't mean that when we look at the Third Reich's policies of repression and genocide we should emphasize, as some have chosen to do recently, the allegedly 'moderate' or 'reactive' anti-Semitism of the crown prince or the ex-Kaiser.[221] It's useful here to recall Ian Kershaw's oft-cited statement: 'The road to Auschwitz was built by hate, but paved with indifference.'[222] More recently that notion has been revised to read: 'The road to Auschwitz was built by hate, but it wasn't paved with indifference. It was paved with collaboration.'[223]

No one in their right mind would regard the waves of unfiltered anti-Semitic hatred coming from the ex-Kaiser in Doorn as 'moderate' – they were only that in comparison to Himmler, Streicher, Heydrich and their ilk. And there's little reason to cite as evidence in Crown Prince Wilhelm's favour his acquaintance with upper-class Jewish individuals and 'many young women of the Jewish faith'.[224] Anti-Semitic attitudes and selfishly motivated relationships with individual Jews are by no means mutually exclusive. The historical record shows that the crown prince was a morally flexible opportunist and not a racist fanatic. That was most likely the reason why he publicly supported the Nazi regime's anti-Semitic policies and for his particular hostility towards 'eastern Jews' – and precisely the sort of indifference and collaboration just cited that were preconditions of genocide.[225]

The nuance evident in the crown prince's mild-tempered 1931 holiday interview later disappeared from his public statements. On 5 July 1933, after multiple requests, Wilhelm was received personally by Hitler in the Reich Chancellery. All indications are that the crown prince coveted this privileged reception as a way of improving his reputation and counteracting the various rumours and accusations floating around about him.[226] One month later, on 4 August, Wilhelm again exceeded himself in his efforts as an international propagandist for the Nazi regime. In an article in the British *Evening Standard*, he turned his attention back to what he dismissed as the false picture of the new Germany abroad. As reported back home by the *Vossische Zeitung*, the crown prince praised the Nazi leadership's 'sense of moral responsibility', which had enabled the first-ever 'revolution without bloodshed'. Foreign reports about the worrisome situation in Germany were dismissed as merely empty agitation. On the contrary, Hitler and Hindenburg had 'achieved something for which the entire German people . . . forever owes them a debt of gratitude'. The time wasn't far away when all of Europe and the whole 'world of culture' would thank Hitler for saving 'civilization' from Bolshevism.[227] The reality was, of course, very different. To cite only one figure: in the weeks between the Reichstag fire on the night of 27–8 February and 25 March 1933, almost 250 people were killed in 'political confrontations' in the Berlin police precinct alone. That was roughly five months before the crown prince's article, by which time Nazi terror tactics had markedly increased in severity.[228]

Also in August 1933, the crown prince authored a full-page article in a New York newspaper that attracted considerable attention back home in Germany. The piece featured a large illustration of Wilhelm on horseback, holding a shield in his left hand and a swastika banner in his right, and his saddle also draped with the Nazi symbol. The article was entitled 'Why Is the World Against Us?' Never had a revolution proceeded so bloodlessly and been morally legitimated by such 'fairness' as that of January 1933, the crown prince assured his readers. The cultivated world would soon see, he added, that Hitler would protect not just Germany but the entire fabric of civilization against Bolshevism.[229] It was no great secret which parts of the cultivated world Wilhelm meant. His brother, the SA leader August Wilhelm, was a visual arts enthusiast, himself an oil painter and the president of the German Society for Art. Perhaps in the interest of division of labour or perhaps in competition with the crown prince, August Wilhelm conspicuously stepped up the vitriol of his anti-Semitic agitation and sought to cosy up to the Nazi leadership by increasing his SA activity in 1933.[230]

Fifteen years earlier, during the German revolution of 1918, August Wilhelm had taken refuge in the villa of Jewish banker Eduard Arnhold on Wannsee Lake in Berlin – a service for which he thanked Arnhold in a privately printed laudation. For this reason among others, many members of the art world were particularly taken aback by the prince's anti-Semitic fury.[231] But once he joined the Nazi Party, August Wilhelm completely renounced his previous liberalism, which had, for instance, led him to defend a Jewish opera singer playing Wotan at the 1925 Wagner Festival in Bayreuth.[232] As early as 1930, Heinrich Arnhold, the banker's brother, sent the prince a sharply worded letter criticizing his ingratitude.[233] It is worth noting that Crown Prince Wilhelm published his whitewash of Nazi Germany in the *Evening Standard* three months after the public book burnings on Berlin's Opernplatz on 10 May 1933. The destruction of the art world envisaged by the crown prince and his younger brother was already underway, but by the Nazis, not by Jews.

Facilitator for the Political Right

Acts of political symbolism were followed by major adjustments on the conservative political front and within the military. Stahlhelm members – among them Wilhelm, Oskar and Eitel Friedrich together with various sons of theirs – were issued a final call to deliver hand-signed oaths of complete allegiance to Hitler or face expulsion from the organization. Despite members from three generations of Hohenzollerns vigorously objecting to family members kowtowing to the regime, royal 'resistance' to the Nazi regime never went beyond private complaints and concerns that assets might be confiscated. All the Hohenzollerns concerned provided the required statements. Foreign media, from flagship publications down to local newspapers, ran articles featuring images of a smiling Wilhelm in his Nazi Motor Corps uniform with swastika armband and headlines such as 'Ex-Crown Prince Joins Nazis' and 'L'ex-kronprinz adhère au parti hitlérien'.[234]

Ilsemann kept a record of Wilhelm II's dismay and irritation at all the photos in the German and international press showing the crown prince 'with the Nazis'. It pained the ex-Kaiser in exile to see traditionally military emblems being progressively overwritten with symbols of the new German authorities. Yet, as always, the former monarch's attitude towards the new symbols was also unclear and incoherent. At one point, he was glad to hear that the Koehler publishing house wanted to publish his text on the origins of the swastika, only to learn from lawyers that the Nazi symbol was a registered trademark and could not be used for copyright reasons without permission on the cover. He was also willing to allow the Majolika factory he owned in the East Prussian town of Cadinen to produce busts of the Führer with the inscription 'Heil Hitler!' 'That's great,' he remarked. 'Let them make as many Hitler busts as they can. Business will be good.'[235]

Around roughly the same time, during animated discussions while visiting Doorn, the crown prince urged his father to 'fight for Hitler's soul so that the good in him comes out on top and he can triumph over the radicals together with his friends on the Right'. The crown prince was against any strategy of distancing the royal family from German fascism, insisting that 'the crown can only be won back with Hitler's help and the only alternative is to reach a clever pact with the Nazis'. The Kaiser's demand for absolute restraint, Crown Prince Wilhelm added, was 'wrong-headed'. Hermine and various advisors also weighed in on the arguments over whether a Hohenzollern crown prince 'should be allowed to wear a swastika on his hussar's uniform'.[236]

Against this backdrop, the crown prince's membership in the Nazi Motor Corps was an optimal compromise. It avoided a visual transformation of the heir to the throne into a party comrade while allowing him to be connected to Nazi organizations. According to Ilsemann, the younger Wilhelm argued that in this way he could serve his fatherland in case of a general mobilization.[237] But it is questionable whether many people believed that his decision to join a Nazi organization and publicly appear in SA uniform were solely expressions of his enthusiasm for 'motor sports' and 'the comfort of a tightly knit club' or that the incorporation of the Stahlhelm into the SA merely entailed a superficial change of label.[238] In any case, royal family members wearing fascist uniforms and swastika armbands remained a continual source of strife within the House of Hohenzollern.[239]

International observers didn't fail to register and publicly discuss the decisions of individual royal family members to sport swastikas, and such images were reproduced well outside Germany. In addition to the photo in newspapers around the world of the crown prince reclining on a sofa in Cecilienhof together with his sons Hubertus and Friedrich in SA Motor Corps uniforms with swastikas, the foreign press also reported on Wilhelm appearing in that same uniform at a large rally on Tempelhofer Feld in March 1934 and at a swastika-decorated event in the ballrooms of the Berlin Zoo one year later.[240] In July, he attended the Day of Weapons of the German Cavalry in Düsseldorf's Rheinstadion arena, sitting in the grandstand under an enormous swastika with a tiny death's head on his collar patch.[241] That September he was photographed at celebrations of the Langemarck myth in Nuremberg surrounded by gigantic, torch-lit Nazi flags and schoolchildren, cigarette in hand and swastika on his arm, very much at the centre of the masses' attention.[242]

Caricatures also thematized the royal association with Nazism. The July 1933 edition of the Austrian monthly *Leuchtrakete* ran a cartoon entitled 'Race of the Hohenzollerns for the Nazis' Favour' and subtitled 'Crown Prince Wilhelm Joins the Nazi Motor Corps'. It depicted Wilhelm driving a gleaming convertible, his arms raised in a Nazi salute, past a grandstand full of swastikas where Hitler, Röhm and Goebbels stand. The bonnet of the car is decorated with a little swastika flag and bears the inscription 'Crown Prince Wilhelm'. Running breathlessly behind the vehicle in an SA uniform, with a fist raised, is August Wilhelm, who complains: 'Stop him. It's not fair for him to drive ahead in his car. I've been in the Nazi Party longer than he has!'[243]

No one – either in the public at large or the Hohenzollern family – interpreted using swastikas, joining a Nazi organization or continually demonstrating support for the new regime and its symbols as a 'change of labels' or a desire to be 'part of a club', as later apologists were sometimes wont to do. In 1934, Ilsemann deemed the incorporation of the Stahlhelm into the SA one of the severest blows of the monarchy's time in exile and wrote of the ex-Kaiser: 'His family is divided. Some of its members have already gone over to the Nazis, this anti-monarchist party, as His Majesty sees them, and the rest will probably also follow suit.'[244]

The Eternal Parade: The Codes of Military Clans

The idea that membership of the Stahlhelm was merely an expression of harmless 'fraternity' and 'belonging to a club' is as absurd as the notion that the crown prince's support for the SA never went beyond 'small favours' like picking up the tab for an evening's worth of beer or a motor brigade's tanks of petrol.[245] The various factual and symbolic connections the crown prince sought to establish with the military and the paramilitary segment of society speak volumes. It is hard to overestimate their significance for the regular army, militia organizations and veterans' groups, all of which felt deep emotional attachment to the lost war and harboured passionate desires for revenge.

Nowadays, the Weimar Republic is primarily imagined as a society of modernism, theatre, nightclubs, jazz and Bauhaus architecture. But it was also one that never succeeded in getting over the First World War, where metaphors of struggle, triumph, battle, offensives and war were constantly used across the political spectrum. Ideas such as members' 'desire to be part of a club' do little to help us understand the societal substrate and spirit of Weimar Germany's veterans' associations and paramilitary organizations. Even in peacetime, the trivial and not-so-trivial mutual experience bound together former warriors and those who considered themselves as such within a matrix of military codes, according to which German politics and society could be interpreted. At the core of the identity of the Prussian military clans was a cultish worship of war and battle. In 1880, with a nod towards Kant, Count Helmuth von Moltke had proposed:

Lasting peace is a dream, not even a sweet one, and war is a link in the chain of the divine world order. It allows the noblest of human virtues – courage and renunciation, duty and willingness to sacrifice – to arise as men risk their lives. Without war, the world would be decay into a materialist swamp.[246]

The general guidelines issued by the supreme general staff to Prussian officers in 1902 questioned international legal attempts to limit the scope of war. Those guidelines openly scoffed at the 'humanitarian views that more often than not degenerate into sentimentality and mushy emotionalism'.[247]

Some two decades and one lost world war later, the crown prince and the influential would-be putschist Colonel Max Bauer agreed that the most pressing task of the day was to strengthen Germany's armed forces – and that undisciplined civilians bore the blame for the country's defeat. The terms 'spineless' and 'spinelessness' were abbreviations for an early and still private version of what would become the 'stab-in-the-back legend', the right-wing myth that Germany's troops had been betrayed by the leftist home front.[248] Throughout the Weimar Republic, even comparatively sophisticated right-wing intellectuals hewed to the same military formulae that informed the thinking of the Reichswehr leadership. None of the politically active Hohenzollerns succeeded in breaking with this mindset before 1945. Even though they had shown no heroism on the battlefield, military life remained the environment and the army the institution within which the royal family understood society and politics.

The aristocratic warriors who had commanded German troops during the past war and were planning for the next one as something unavoidable and necessary oriented their lives around countless sorts of military pursuits. The result was grown men between the ages of thirty and sixty pushing tiny figures and artillery around on long tables in the Tin Soldiers Club, Reichswehr officers, excitable, knapsack-toting schoolboys, wide-eyed girls in pigtails and crowds of other enthusiastic onlookers admiring heavy-artillery guns at autumnal military exercises, and soldiers who carried out make-believe manoeuvres using tanks made of cardboard.[249] The upper strata of the Prussian military milieu in which the Kaiser's sons were socialized remained a world of simple, stable codes that provided support and orientation. And although the fraternity within the Stahlhelm and the traditional military organizations may have been different from the brutal, brawling style of typical SA units, there were various ideological and political connections between the two.

It was astonishing how homogeneous this military milieu remained in a society in which, despite the official German army being limited to 100,000 men and 4,000 officers, an illegal, unofficial Reichswehr arose. Millions of men engaged in war games in forests, on rural estates and in private clubs, using tin soldiers, military maps and model railroads, continually celebrating themselves. From imperial Germany to the Weimar Republic to the Third Reich, stable linguistic and symbolic codes and unvarying rituals cultivated a form of military masculinity and a specific notion of the fatherland. Men were willing to march through the streets in uniforms and jackboots through both pouring rain and 'Hohenzollern weather', as sunny days were known in this milieu. There were marching bands, chest-thumping speeches and cries of 'Hurrah!' and 'Hail to the Front!' There were officers without an army and uniformed soldiers without wages, a general longing for order, structure and hierarchy, a specific form of comradeship and friendship, and nights of drinking beer and singing battle songs.

Support for incessant marches and parades of the sort the Hohenzollerns provided was not a given in the aristocracy or the high nobility. In some aristocratic circles, particularly outside Prussia in Catholic Bavaria and other parts of southern Germany, members objected to the self-celebratory militarism in which three generations of the royal family publicly partook. The journalist Baron Erwein von Aretin, an advisor to the crown prince of Bavaria and one of the most brilliant minds within the Bavarian nobility, repeatedly spoke up on behalf of the old Bavarian aristocracy to reject the perennial and continuing Prussian obsession with everything 'parade-ish'.[250] Aretin feared that the familiar rituals would lead only

to a 'permanent army and navy commemoration event full of rat-
tling sabres and crashing waves that doesn't advance Germany a
single step and is condemned to forever occupy the realm of
fantasy'.[251]

Prince Wilhelm, the crown prince's eldest son, had attracted
negative attention in this regard all the way back in 1928 at a celebration for the Bavarian crown prince in Munich's Löwenbräukeller.
Bavarian monarchists found the Stahlhelm style of the young
Hohenzollern offputting, and one witness described his behaviour
as 'posing of the sort I understood neither from the prince nor the
party and that was certainly utterly miscalculated for the Munich
mentality'.[252] One year previously, Crown Prince Rupprecht of
Bavaria had himself remarked: 'The idea of leadership [in the Stahl-
helm] reminds me vividly of the belief in the coming of the messiah
among latter-day Jews who have now been waiting in vain 1,900
years for their saviour to arrive.'[253]

Even then, Aretin considered the Stahlhelm speeches a 'lame'
copy of Hitler.[254] By late 1930, the baron was even more direct:

> Whenever I see the Prussian princes' enthusiasm for National Social-
> ism, I always think of the eldest son of the Duke of Orléans, the
> Duke of Chartres, who always acted as a steward for the Jacobins –
> the Nazis of 1790 – until he found his father beheaded and himself
> imprisoned in the Chateau d'If, as soon as the Jacobins came to
> power. Mercantile houses had more to do with making him King
> Louis Philippe. How frenetically the Jacobins celebrated Louis XVI,
> when he donned the Phrygian cap, the swastika of 1790. I do indeed
> trust the political attitudes of Hitler, Epp, etc . . . But in the case of
> true social upheaval, which I regard as unlikely since we have no
> talent for major revolutions, such men will scatter like chaff in the
> wind, leaving behind a fanaticized proletariat who will execute their
> generals when they suffer defeat and terrorize everyone of property
> under the justification that they are 'comrades of the Jews'.[255]

There was no Hohenzollern equivalent of the Bavarian scepticism that excessive militarism would lead to Jacobinism and destroy the substance of the monarchy from within. Leading members of the royal family around 1933 certainly did not share Prince Louis Ferdinand of Prussia's antipathy, expressed in a lengthy 1987 television interview in which he claimed that he never liked Nazism because the militarism, constant marches and never-ending parades rubbed him up the wrong way.[256] While only a minority of the German nobility may have actively been involved in military culture and eager to put their willingness to fight on constant display, none of the other European royal families were anywhere near as directly and conspicuously aggressive as the Hohenzollerns.

The militarist culture of the Stahlhelm was related to, if not identical with, the belligerent National Socialist idea of German ethnic community and the fraternal ideal of the SA. Thus, the constant, always reported participation of the crown prince and the 'Stahlhelm princes' in Nazi culture possessed undeniable significance. The 190,000 Stahlhelm paramilitaries who marched through Berlin in September 1932, for instance, made for an impressive spectacle, and the presence of the Crown Prince Wilhelm and his brothers, which was also noted in the international press, augmented its importance.[257] Countless private Prussian military and aristocratic archives attest to the continuing significance of marches and parades – sometimes, rituals and codes gain rather than lose significance when the world that gave rise to them disappears. That was very much the case with the lonely war games played by the ex-Kaiser in the Netherlands on his maps and the fawning letters his sons sent him from Germany to document the immortality of the aristocratic, military caste and its values. The correspondence is full of military motifs being used to express passion, security, identity and even love. Within German reactionary conservativism, many of the strongest and deepest emotions were linked to values, rituals and dreams that are difficult for observers today to understand as the past, as British novelist L. P. Hartley once put it, is a foreign country.[258]

To understand the codes that continued to inform aristocratic, military culture across political discontinuities, it's worth taking an anthropological look at the particularities of language and symbols. The immense passion able to inspire paramilitaries and weekend warriors of various sorts to march across muddy fields may completely baffle observers today, but that doesn't diminish its obvious power in the past. The Prussian Guards' interception of the French retreat at Battle of Gravelotte in 1870 or the march of the XVII Army Corps under August von Mackensen against the right Russian flank in 1916 were no less electrifying for the militarist-nostalgic segment of German society than Le Corbusier's *Plan Voisin* was for city planners in the Weimar Republic or the Marxist idea of global revolution was for the German Communist Party. Sources repeatedly relate grown men bursting into tears, overcome by emotion, when military units representing past glory marched by or aristocratic estate owners gave bellicose speeches. Uniforms, medals, banners and marching formations were able to summon these most intense of emotions.[259] The feelings attached to everything military, to specific ideas of order and greatness and to traditional designations of rank deserve to be taken seriously. To appreciate the intensity of the emotions carried by rituals, signs and codes, we must remember how much the military influenced the early education of German aristocrats. Small children not yet able to write were taught how to ride tall in the saddle and hold the reins alongside their fathers. Photographs from the period show them as tiny white dots within formations of black-clad hussars.

Battles, regiment names and army commanders as well as anecdotes, minor material details and places of remembrance were anchors of aristocratic identity. The entire high nobility may not have been this way, but the three to four generations of Hohenzollerns who cleaved to military traditions certainly were. War and the military remained their most important point of reference. Military rituals offered support, tradition and an ever-available bridge between Doorn and Berlin and across generations – even though the family no longer had any an actual army at its command. In 1930, Prince Oskar still reported how he, representing his father, the

Kaiser, had brought together the former officers of the Royal Grenadiers, collected tributes to the ex-monarch and ensured the continuity of Prussian military tradition.

The reading material consumed by the Hohenzollerns also remained centred around the military. In that same report, Prince Oskar also recommended to his father three volume of war memoirs: Joseph Douillet's *Moscou sans voiles* (Moscow Unmasked), Baron Hans Hennig Grote's *Die Höhle von Beauregard* (The Cave of Beauregard) and Josef Magnus Wehner's *Die Sieben vor Verdun* (Seven Before Verdun).[260] Even during the Third Reich, Wilhelm II's sons would send him purposeless reports of military details intended to reassure the patriarch about his past and present importance. For example, in 1937, Oskar wrote from Vienna, where he had been sent by his father's 'highest command' to attend the funeral of a member of the high aristocracy, about a conversation with the king of Spain: 'He was still very well informed and asked about gorget patches, grenadiers' eagle helmets, Gibraltar armbands, leather port-épées in the infantry regiments. We met until about 11.30 p.m.'[261]

In 1934, Prince Eitel Friedrich wrote about the march of elite Prussian regiments in Berlin, thanking his father for his 'most gracious telegram' and reporting: 'One's heart leaped again when one saw these tall, strapping people with their disciplined military posture, to which no passage of time could make them unaccustomed.' Eitel Friedrich used the same familiar terse wordings and images. The pastor 'held a brief, full-blooded sermon about vigilance, determination in faith, manliness and strength'. The company, led by Count Schwerin, made a very 'strapping' impression, although 'Naturally, the day was won by the guards, who were most strongly represented and marched by like a single wooden board – Count Finkelstein had the liberty of leading the fusiliers by in a light-footed fusiliers' march.' (The former Kaiser underlined the words 'light-footed fusiliers' march' in his son's letter.) In Berlin's Lustgarten park, 'pea soup and sausage' had been served, which inspired Eitel Friedrich, the least intellectually gifted of Wilhelm II's sons, to attempt a joke: 'It's said that the grenadiers ate up all the fusiliers' sausages.' He followed that up with accounts of the lively activity at the 'small calibre shooting booths', a large amount of beer and the 'awarding of prizes in the [palace restaurant] Alter Fritz until the wee hours of the morning'. He signed his letter 'Your loving and obedient son, Fritz'.[262]

Whether in the Wilhelmine Empire, the Weimar Republic or the Nazi dictatorship, military codes connected members of the traditional conservative minority and enabled them to fantasize about how they might prevail even in the hostile environment that was democracy. Although the aristocratic, military clans, the guards regiments and the leading noble families differed markedly in style from the Nazis, the SA and the SS, military codes were one of the main things they had in common. For aristocrats, the Nazis' hypermasculinity, cult of leadership, hatred of democracy and love of marches, war and battle made them into kindred spirits, if not brothers. Nonetheless, the shift from the codes and concepts of honour of the imperial armed forces to those of the far more brutal extreme Right in the Weimar Republic were significant, and the transition required two decades and a grey area of countless tiny overlaps.

Right Versus Right: The Limits of Collaboration

The reconfiguration of Germany from a republic into an almost hermetically sealed dictatorship proceeded astonishingly quickly, albeit not overnight. In its early years, the Nazi faced not only democratic and left-wing opponents but conservative critics and right-wing competitors. Theoretically, at least, the segment of society the crown prince represented was capable of containing the Nazis and could have become a rival camp. The Reichswehr officer corps, the Stahlhelm with approximately half a million members, the DNVP and the agrarian association of the major aristocratic estate owners were the most likely rallying points for a conservative alternative to Hitler. In the first few months of the Nazis in power, organizations that called themselves conservative sought ways to preserve their independence and prevent amalgamation. In particular, the Stahlhelm, with its high-profile royal members, was a potential focus for conservative forces and one of the few right-wing organizations capable of rivalling the SA and the Nazi movement.

This does not mean that Stahlhelm was in any sense a 'resistance organization', as the Hohenzollerns' financial manager and other defenders of the crown prince and his brothers sought to claim following the Second World War, when the Dutch government retook possession of Huis Doorn. This idea recurs in a number of prominent post-war conservative legends and was part of Hohenzollern efforts to preserve family assets in 1947 – and it still attracts supporters today despite its patent absurdity.[263] On the other hand, there were real and, at least for a time, great differences between the Stahlhelm and the SA, and without question, in their detailed descriptions of the former, the crown prince's defenders were justified in distinguishing between the two groups. We need to locate the conflicts on the German Right within the larger history of political violence and compare the Stahlhelm with the actual direction in which the Nazi movement was headed.[264] The disagreements between the two most important paramilitary organizations of the anti-democratic Right went beyond the mere rivalry that saw the Stahlhelm eventually dissolved. They included an entire universe of serious discord, starting with the Stahlhelm leadership's disgruntlement with the SA, up to those leaders' ultimate arrest and murder.[265]

In late March 1933, conflict arose between the Stahlhelm and the Nazis in the city of Braunschweig, and the local Nazi authorities had the SA and the SS take more than 1,400 people into custody. Local Stahlhelm leader Werner Schrade, who would later be executed as a member of the conservative resistance to Hitler in 1944, wrote to the organization's deputy national leader Theodor Duesterberg: 'My biggest worry that we will soon be crushed and overrun by the Nazi Party . . . If the Stahlhelm falters now, our bright future will be in serious jeopardy.'[266] The following month, in

April 1933, DNVP Chairman Alfred Hugenberg sent a twenty-five-page letter to Hitler and the acting German interior minister Wilhelm Frick protesting against the abuse and brutality his party's members had suffered at the hands of the SA and the SS.[267]

Around Germany, the SA, in particular, targeted members of traditional conservative organizations,[268] and rivalries with the Stahlhelm flared up in countless places in the twelve months following the spring of 1933. A handful of Stahlhelm leaders were taken to concentration camps, something noted even in the foreign press.[269] In June 1933, Hohenzollern financial advisor Arthur Berg described a disconsolate mood within the Stahlhelm as some of its officers were taken into 'protective custody' by the SA. This was a matter the Hohenzollerns took quite 'personally'. Nonetheless, Berg advised Crown Prince Wilhelm to continue to support the merger of the Stahlhelm and the SA and counselled him about which propaganda events he should visit in the future.[270] During the final discussions about whether the Stahlhelm should be dissolved, Hitler complained about the 'undermining work' being done by 'individual princes such as Eitel Friedrich'.[271] Thus, at the time, the Stahlhelm still represented a forum for lines of conservative opposition, which would stretch until the failed attempt on Hitler's life in 1944.[272]

The faultlines were evident in the most important traditional conservative party, the DNVP, as well as in the major aristocratic associations, in the aristocracy as a social group and in the rifts in individual families. 'The German nobility is in a pickle', wrote one sarcastic commentator in the autumn of 1932, 'because it doesn't know where it should go or to whom it belongs. To Hugenberg, Duesterberg and the Stahlhelm or to Prince Auwi, Adolf Hitler and the Nazi hordes.' The author went on to cite two contrary petitions by aristocrats on the issue of whether the nobility should further cosy up to the Nazi movement or not.[273] Nazis and traditional German nationalists were smashing one another's skulls in with chair legs and beer mugs, it was reported. That raised the question of internal quarrels within the House of Hohenzollern, whose members were, after all, divided into two camps.[274] As we have seen, the conflict reached its zenith in the autumn of 1932, and it would take some two years to finally smooth it over or, in some cases, smother it. As long as the relationship between the Nazis and traditional conservatives remained ambivalent, prominent representatives of the high nobility and, first and foremost, the Hohenzollerns, had enormous influence on whether conflicts were heightened or levelled.

Like practically all organizations of the political Right, the Stahlhelm was divided between supporters of an open alliance with the Nazis and those who wanted to maintain political and structural independence. For more than a decade, the Stahlhelm had been one of the most important anti-democratic fighting corps in the Weimar Republic and a bastion of anti-democratic propaganda and indoctrination. Given the group's close collaboration with the Nazi movement, it would be ridiculous to interpret membership in the Stahlhelm or wearing Stahlhelm regalia as an act of distance from Nazism.[275] Although there were conservative groupings like the Confessing Church that did genuinely oppose the Nazis, the Stahlhelm in 1933 wasn't one of them. It had more in common than not with Hitler's movement.[276]

The extensive cooperation between the two right-wing groups was reflected in the fact that the Stahlhelm leader Franz Seldte was made part of Hitler's governing cabinet when he assumed power on 30 January 1933. Late that April, Seldte joined the Nazi Party and declared that he and the Stahlhelm would subordinate themselves 'as a unified military unit to the Führer', and, in June, Seldte prohibited Stahlhelm members from joining any political party other than the NSDAP.[277] In a gradual process of self-liquidation, age group by age group, Stahlhelm men were incorporated into the SA Reserves I and II.[278] Due to takeovers of other organizations and new memberships, the SA's membership between 1933 and 1934 swelled from approximately 430,000 to, at least formally, some four million.[279] The Stahlhelm nominally continued to exist until November 1935, when it was officially disbanded.

To 'contain' Nazism as the architects of the new Hitler-led coalition government envisioned in January 1933 would have required a conservative counterweight and diverse centres of power, including Germany's industrial and finance leaders, who had little contact with the Hohenzollerns and the rest of the German nobility. There were various forces aligned with the political Right that could have prevented or at least 'tamed' the Nazi movement's complete seizure of power: the Reichswehr, the Stahlhelm, the DNVP and the agrarian, monarchist and aristocratic associations. All these groups had vocal anti-Nazi opponents and critics within their ranks. One of the most important effects of the crown prince's activities was to stifle those voices.

Several recent historians have focused on the crown prince's relationship with his 'friend' Kurt von Schleicher, treating Wilhelm as a key figure in a putative alternative to Hitler. Interpretations of this sort see the crown prince as an active detractor of Nazism and one of the earliest embodiments of the anti-Hitler resistance in Germany. But the historical record from the first few weeks of the Third Reich and the year 1933 prove the opposite. There is no doubt that both Kaiser and crown prince were enthusiastic about the formation of the Hitler cabinet.[280] The day the new government was inaugurated, the crown prince told Ilsemann how happy he was that the sort of nationalist government he had been striving towards for a year had now been created in Germany.[281] Wilhelm and Hitler also exchanged cordial telegrams.[282] Prince Louis Ferdinand spent 30 January 1933 at the wedding of a Prussian princess at which, symbolically, both a Stahlhelm and an SA band played.[283]

In the weeks and months that followed, the crown prince stepped up his efforts to promote the Nazis in his family, circle of friends, the officer corps, aristocratic circles, large estate owners and the Stahlhelm. He wrote open letters to influence American and British opinion and made public appearances that reached millions of people in Germany and abroad. The attempts made by individual historians from 1947 to the present day to reinterpret such actions seem baffling given the unambiguousness of the evidence.[284]

One of the most famous statements in the creation of the Nazi dictatorship is attributed to Franz von Papen, the man most responsible for handing Hitler power, during the first weeks of the regime. 'He's working for us,' Papen told one conservative sceptic concerned about the alliance with Hitler. To another he said: 'What's your problem? I'm the one with Hindenburg's trust. In two months, we'll have pushed Hitler so far into a corner he'll squeak.'[285]

There's no way of confirming the authenticity of such statements, but the two metaphors they contain have been passed down for decades because they so perfectly capture the mixture of arrogance, self-overestimation and misunderstanding from which traditional conservatives like Papen suffered. More than fifty years ago, Volker R. Berghahn concluded his ground-breaking study of the Stahlhelm with a sentence about all the would-be conservative 'containers' of Hitler, including the crown prince and the other royal members: 'They called for a dictatorship and got one – only to find they had fallen victim to their own political illiteracy and intellectual limitations.'[286]

Conclusion: Promoters of the Third Reich

As we know, the birth of the Nazi dictatorship in January 1933 was *not* down to electoral results. In the national election of November 1932, the Nazi Party lost large numbers of votes, tallying only 33.1 per cent. Hitler was not elected chancellor. He attained that post thanks to a long series of backroom discussions and deals after traditional conservatives abandoned the strict lines drawn between themselves and the National Socialists. People at the time used to joke, with reference to the omnipresence of Hindenburg's son Oskar at his side, that the Weimar Constitution didn't foresee the Office of the Son of the Reich President. The joke was a reminder of the power some individuals possessed to take major decisions outside republican institutions and contrary to the rules of democracy.

This is the context in which we must understand the crown prince's activities in connecting the Nazis and the traditional conservative camps. To achieve that bond, two things were needed: 1) communication and the building of networks in gentlemen's studies, clubs, officers' messes and at country estates, which were beyond democratic scrutiny and followed the rules of conspiracies and arcane rituals; and 2) the acceptance of the Nazi movement as a viable ally by aristocratic and bourgeois elite functionaries. The latter, especially, was anything but a given. Considerable hurdles had to be cleared to win over sceptics like Count Friedrich von der Schulenburg, the crown prince's advisor, critic and former army group general chief of staff. But by April 1933 this eminently talented general himself gushed: 'Hitler's success in the Reichstag has been astonishing. It was delightful to see how he battered the social democrats right from the outset. In any case, whoever got old Hindenburg to make Hitler chancellor will go down in history.'[287]

On 6 March 1933, having just returned from a trip to St Moritz, the crown prince wrote to his friend Colonel Ferdinand von Bredow using brutal language to express some familiar ideas. Schleicher should never have been allowed to assume the chancellorship, Wilhelm argued. After Papen's resignation in early December the only solution would have been Hitler as chancellor in an alliance with Schleicher. Here the crown prince summarized his plea for conservatives to work together with the Nazis, which would lead to the 'Day of Potsdam' two weeks later. One passage of the letter read:

> The main thing now is to support the cohesion of this government in every respect and smack anyone in the gob who tries to introduce unrest and mistrust into this cohesion. In a variety of ways in the most recent days and with the necessary ruthlessness, I have taken care of this 'smacking [our enemies] in the gob'. Wishing you all the best and hoping that you will continue to employ your strengths for the national cause, I remain, in old friendship, your Wilhelm.[288]

This piece of correspondence, written to one of Schleicher's closest associates, is utterly at odds with any notion of the crown prince as a covert agent for the conservative resistance to Hitler *avant la lettre*. Without doubt, at least in theory, for a few months, Schleicher was the strongest advocate of subsuming the Nazis into the crown prince's agenda. At the same time, Schleicher's lasting attempts to use Gregor Strasser to co-opt parts of the Nazi movement for a coalition under his own control are also undisputed historical fact, as is their swift and utter failure. From the crown prince's perspective, Schleicher was simply one option among many. What's more, Schleicher's murder by the Nazis did nothing to prevent Wilhelm from engaging in domestic and international publicity work for Hitler, Nazism and the regime. Every 'upstanding German' had always hated the Weimar Republic 'from the depths of his soul', the crown prince told the British press magnate Lord Rothermere in June 1934.[289] In late 1934, he addressed Hitler as 'my Führer' in a letter he concluded with the words: 'In hopes of having the pleasure to see you again in the new year, I remain, with heartfelt greetings, your loyal Wilhelm.'[290]

This second letter was written well after the killing of Röhm, Schleicher and others in the Night of the Long Knives, which many people knew Hitler had personally authorized. In August 1934, six weeks after Schleicher's murder, the crown prince granted a front-page interview to the right-wing Paris daily *Le Petit Journal*. In that interview, which seems to have been the first time he had talked to the French press since 1914 and which was reprinted in translation in newspapers from other countries, including Switzerland's *Basler Nachrichten*, he proposed that France, England and Germany needed to stand together against the Slavic and Asian peril. Wilhelm added:

> Foreign countries cannot appreciate the enormous debt of gratitude the German people owes to Adolf Hitler. He's an incomparable 'teacher of energy'. There was nothing we needed more. Through the power of his magnetic personality, he has diverted the German nation's historical development in a different direction. Nothing the future may bring will change that.[291]

Such statements competed with the crown prince's betrayal of his former allies in favour of kowtowing to the new regime. But, unbeknownst to him, Wilhelm's descent into political meaninglessness had already begun.

5.

Abysses: The Hohenzollerns in the Third Reich (1934–45)

An oral anecdote from the winter of 1940 records the moment when the ex-Kaiser was forced to recognize his own definitive descent into insignificance. The Wehrmacht had been occupying the Netherlands for months, and, while walking in the forest near Doorn, Wilhelm II happened upon a young German soldier guarding a depot. The former Kaiser gregariously inquired where the young man was from, only to find to his dismay that the man didn't recognize him. When asked, the soldier was unable to name either the 'lord of the land' in his home region of Thuringia or any other German prince. Nor did he know anything about the Kaiser, who had left Germany twenty-two years earlier and now resided in the Netherlands. The ex-monarch returned home 'pale' and distraught from this encounter and never went walking in that part of the woods again.[1] 'Here come my soldiers,' the Kaiser had exclaimed in May 1940, when the first Wehrmacht units arrived in Doorn. But the encounter at the depot several months later showed definitively that these were not the Kaiser's troops. The following year, three days after Nazi Germany's invasion of the Soviet Union, an obituary for Wilhelm II in the weekly newspaper *Das Reich* would cite precisely this anecdote.[2] With a few modifications, similar stories could have been told about the entire House of Hohenzollern to illustrate its members' increasing irrelevance.

The ex-Kaiser lived for only six months after the episode at the depot. Following a last burst of enthusiasm at the Luftwaffe's successful landing on Crete, he died on 4 June 1941 in Huis Doorn, which at that point was cordoned off from the outside world by German soldiers.[3] He had refused on multiple occasions to return to Germany and had instructed in December 1933 that no wreaths or swastika flags be laid on his grave.[4] He also ruled out being buried in Germany as long as the monarchy hadn't been restored To this day, his remains lie interred in a mausoleum specially constructed for them in Doorn.

Decoupling

In the first phase of consolidating power, the Nazi regime dismantled the Weimar Republic and its institutions and focused its terror tactics on leftist and pro-democracy organizations and leaders. Within months, the Nazis successively destroyed the organizational basis of the Europe's strongest labour movement as well as all the institutions that had supported and defended Weimar democracy.[5] In the second phase of consolidation, which was characterized more by violence than by political emasculation, Germany's new Nazi masters increasingly shed their conservative partners and allies and other self-proclaimed representatives of traditional conservativism. The resignation of the figure intended to be the 'strong man' within the Hitler cabinet, DNVP leader Alfred Hugenberg, who later called supporting Hitler the 'greatest stupidity of my life', typified the folly of trying to simultaneously exploit and contain the dynamism of the Nazi movement.[6] With only few exceptions, for instance, the German Aristocratic Society, which maintained its autonomy and status as the largest group of its kind in Germany, monarchist and traditional conservative associations and their leaders were amalgamated into the Nazi state and stripped of their influence.

Over the course of a single year, the 'useful idiots' from the final days of the Weimar Republic became politically useless baggage, an irritating remnant the Nazis first shrugged off with increasing frankness, then discarded entirely like a spent battery. The present chapter will look at how the Nazi dictatorship decoupled itself from the conservative midwives that had assisted at the birth of the Hitler government. As part of this divorce, the regime marginalized Germany's former ruling dynasties, in particular the Hohenzollerns, although without ever substantially attacking their existence.

The arrangements with the Nazi regime reached by the Hohenzollerns and other prominent aristocratic families were born of opportunism, adaptability, self-effacement and acceptance of the new national order. There was no place in the long term in the Nazi ideal of 'popular ethnic community' (*Volksgemeinschaft*) for the German nobility and, in particular, Germany's former ruling dynasties. There was thus no avoiding conflict between the traditional identity of the high nobility and the Nazi ideal of the Führer who bridged class divides.[7] Transforming princes and dynastic rulers into 'ethnic comrades' was an extremely difficult endeavour, both symbolically and factually. Thus far, historians have only traced the careers of a select few members of the high nobility in the Third Reich, for example, Prince Josias zu Waldeck und Pyrmont and Duke Carl Eduard von Sachsen-Coburg und Gotha, both of whom supported the regime early on and radically.[8] Nonetheless, together with the roughly 250 members of the Nazi Party from former ruling dynasties, they showed that it wasn't impossible for people of the highest birth to transform themselves into 'racial comrades' and even to take on positions of responsibility in the Nazi state.[9]

As a rule, though, German princes rarely offered more than recruitment aid and symbolic support for the Nazi Party – services of immense importance up to 1933 but increasingly of irrelevance as of 1934 and afterwards. The career of Prince August Wilhelm had brought him, at least symbolically, into close contact with the inner circle of Nazi elites. Yet in the summer of 1934 his constant efforts to become a fully accepted member of this circle were rebuffed in humiliating fashion, and he was shunted off to the side.[10] Still, even personal defeats of this sort didn't mean complete exclusion from public life. August Wilhelm still retained enough influence in 1943 to get a sailor sent to a concentration camp for critical remarks made about the regime to his barber.[11]

After 1933, all Hohenzollerns had a variety of options, including to withdraw into a private sphere of luxury. Some members did in fact choose to while away their days between Berlin, Potsdam, Silesia, Austria and Switzerland, travelling the world and enjoying the company of Germany's upper crust. In 1940, August Wilhelm could draw on a yearly allowance of 48,000 Reichsmarks, roughly double what a government minister earned, and lived rent free in the Villa Liegnitz in Potsdam.[12] And he was only in the middle of the pack in terms of the estimate financial leeway enjoyed by members of the royal family.

Of course, the desire to retain assets and opportunistically satisfy material desires didn't mean that there were no ideological and political commonalities between the aristocracy and the regime. On the contrary, lust to get revenge and teach Marxists, republicans and Jews a lesson remained powerful motivators for the Hohenzollerns, as did their wish to somehow compensate for their disappointment at Germany's defeat in the First World War. Thus, despite various tensions and conflicts, arrangements based on common enemies and ideological common ground continued unbroken until 1945.

Two main Hohenzollern concerns were protecting the family's status and wealth and negotiating a path through private and political life. With the demise of the Weimar Republic, the clan immediately lost a great deal of visibility with the matching demise of the democratic press that had always taken an intense, sometimes obsessive interest in the royal family. The Nazi press spilled little ink about the high nobility and the Hohenzollerns, depriving them of something the Weimar Republic had not only allowed but provided in abundance: attention and the corresponding aura of being something special. As discussed earlier with reference to the theatre, a king can only exist as such as long as others bow and scrape before him. Nazism took away the Hohenzollerns' extras and their audience.

The monarchist wager on Nazism was obviously a very bad bet. Having had their hopes raised by the Day of Potsdam, numerous representatives of Wilhelm II personally broached the possibility of restoring the Kaiser to the throne with Hitler between May 1933 and April 1934. But the Kaiser's perception of reality contrasted starkly with the Nazis' quick devolution of what little monarchist power remained. Plagued by increasing moments when he realized what was actually going on, the Kaiser ghosted around the halls of Doorn in front of the empty façades of a world gone by. Three days before Hitler assumed power, Wilhelm II celebrated his birthday together with guests including the former kings of Saxony and Württemberg. It was like a re-enactment of the *ancien régime*. One reason the ex-Kaiser and his eldest son were so enthusiastic about the Hitler cabinet was their mistaken belief that it would put the royal restoration back on the agenda.[13] Three weeks later, Hermine reported from Berlin that several police units had been put at her disposal and that she was already negotiating with Vice-Chancellor Papen. But the celebration was premature. In July 1934, the ex-Kaiser was already complaining that German schools were teaching pupils too much about the republics of Ancient Greece and Rome and not enough about ancient German history and the divine right of kings. He ordered his adjutants to draw up 'historical tables' to be used in instruction. And, several days after Hindenburg's death the following August, an agitated Wilhelm II demanded that the German army swear an oath of loyalty to himself and not Hitler.[14]

That same month, after conversations with his 'lord', General Friedrich von Unruh remarked: 'The world wouldn't believe that anyone with such unmodern views still exists today. He interprets everything, even the most important political questions, through his own personal lens, and there's no one left he can lean on.' Even Wilhelm's sole remaining friend, the fabulously wealthy, eighty-year-old southern German *grand seigneur* Prince Max Egon zu Fürstenberg, had gone over the Nazis, joining the SA and delivering propaganda speeches in front of thousands of people.

By contrast, the ex-Kaiser hoped that the old guard, a handful of men aged sixty to eighty, would prop up his power.[15] As we've seen, a decade previously, August von Mackensen had told him that his sword lay ready on his desk and that the Kaiser need only whistle for him to take it up. But even back then the field marshal general – the son of a bourgeois family who had become the most important personification of the Wilhelmine Empire after the ex-Kaiser himself – was already seventy-five years old. His sharpened sword was mere metaphor.[16]

In 1933 and 1934, Hitler clearly answered the question of restoring the monarchy in the resounding negative. On at least four occasions, leading monarchists raised the issue at the highest levels of the new regime. But they might as well have tried to bite off a chunk of granite. The Prince of Bentheim-Tecklenburg-Rheda's proactive displays of obedience managed to get the German Aristocratic Association, the largest organization of the German nobility, exempted from the February 1934 ban on monarchist groups. That, however, was as far as Reich Chancellor Hitler was willing to accommodate the aristocrats.

In the spring of 1933, Hitler received the Wilhelm II loyalist Friedrich von Berg and made some vague noises about the monarchy of the future, which could be established after a victorious war. But, at a second meeting that October, Hitler was already noticeably more hostile to the idea. The officer's arguments that the Führer needed the Hohenzollerns to head off 'atomistic battles' and secure his 'works' for the long term left Hitler utterly cold. The same was true for Berg's statements 'that the entire younger generation of the House [of Hohenzollern] has joined the ranks of the movement' and that the crown prince would have liked to have served as a mediator for Hitler during his talks in Rome with Mussolini. Hitler 'passionately' rejected Berg's monarchist agenda, telling him that the priority was to put down communism and 'Jewry'. While he had nothing against the Hohenzollerns, Hitler added, the crown prince as a person and the monarchy as an institution weren't 'steely enough' for this task. In February 1934, Hitler finally gave the monarchist emissary a completely cold shoulder. In a supercilious tone, the Nazi leader said he no longer wished to be disturbed in his 'reconstruction work' by the German princes. To achieve his goals of 'rooting out the criminals of the November Revolution' and re-establishing the Reichswehr, Hitler continued, he would need twelve to fifteen years.[17]

Although the petitions made by these monarchist geriatrics already displayed an astonishing distance from reality, they were very much outdone by the missive from another prominent aristocrat. Former Lieutenant General August von Cramon, who once privately boasted that he was willing to be sent a concentration camp for his beliefs,[18] composed a bewildering memo in October 1933, in which he suggested that Wilhelm II be restored his powers as emperor and king as a gift for his seventy-fifth birthday the following January. Cramon, himself seventy-three years old, claimed that the wisdom and dignity of age had been added to ex-Kaiser's 'hereditary wisdom of lineage'. He added that the logical extension of the 'Führer idea' was 'the eternal leadership of the hereditary monarchy' and that Hitler himself would help bring about the restoration: 'Adolf Hitler is, as far as we know, himself a monarchist.'[19] Men like Cramon also reflexively clung to the crown prince. Without a family or dynasty of his own, the logic ran, Hitler was by necessity a transitional figure paving the way for a future king. Such utterly implausible wishful thinking was typical of the dwindling numbers of post-1918 monarchist aristocrats.[20]

Wilhelm II's private correspondence reveals that as early as the summer of 1933 he was aware of the end of the rule of law in Germany and the growing power of the Gestapo, which he saw as a 'Cheka' (secret police) 'modelled after Moscow'.[21] The ex-Kaiser's main point of dissatisfaction with the new regime was the fact that the Nazis made no attempts to reverse his own disempowerment. A September 1933 letter, written in English, to one of his sisters illustrates the extent to which he lived in a world that had ceased to exist back in 1918:

> I am glad you were able to lodge and feel comfy in my 'Hotel' – with our Schloss and *Papa's* Palace on one side and next door to *Grand-papa*!!! What an ignominious situation to be deprived of all rights acquired by birth and tradition!!! ... It is horrible to have our

feelings trampled on like that! No tradition any more! Brutality! Willy.[22]

Several months after Cramon's memorandum, on 27 January 1934, the old and the new German Right collided heavily in Berlin on the ex-Kaiser's birthday. The conflict was a caesura after which it was no longer possible to overlook the Nazi regime's hostility towards monarchist symbols, rituals and organizations. Whereas in faraway Doorn 'princely personages' came together 'in their old colourful uniforms' and 'ladies' fabulous jewellery was on display to admire',[23] the main celebration in the opulent marbled reception hall of the Berlin Zoo was stormed by marauding SA troops. This incursion was announced in advance. Various Nazi leaders, including the deputy Berlin Gauleiter (regional leader), Arthur Görlitzer, and the head of the political police, Rudolf Diels, had explicitly warned 'reactionaries' against organizing celebrations or raising money to mark the ex-Kaiser's birthday. Monarchist machinations, they threatened, would be treated the same as communist agitation.[24]

In early 1934, the 26-year-old southern German aristocrat and SA leader Count Hans von Reischach published a verbose, widely read treatise supporting that organization's anti-aristocratic and anti-monarchist credo. The authorities, he argued, had thus far been far too circumspect in dealing with those old elites who were seriously impeding the creation of the new state. In a front-page article in a Silesian Nazi newspaper, he also opined: 'We have fought together side by side with the German worker and the German farmer against the November state, while broad swathes of the aristocracy took pleasure in the tedious company of "their own kind".' It was too late for such people to expect to be incorporated into the new regime, Reischach insisted. In the Nazi state, there would no longer be staircases with signs reading 'access for lords only'. Henceforth, people would only be measured by performance and diligence. It was unacceptable that some people of days gone by 'seek to avoid the re-formation' and remained 'insoluble foreign elements in the melting pot of the German revolution'. To raise the issue of a 'throne' and a restoration was a 'crime against the nation'.[25]

The report filed by the seventy-year-old retired major general Count Rüdiger von der Goltz, the chairman of the aristocratic Reich Association of German Officers and a card-carrying Nazi since the previous May,[26] about the events during the monarchist celebration in Berlin was shot through with the older generation's horror at the new. Goltz's outraged description of what happened following his birthday speech for 'our former commander-in chief' was full of dramatic language:

> Two hours after the speech, a horde, partly dressed in civilian cloth-ing and partly disguised as brownshirts, occupied the space like Bolsheviks, mistreating officers and their wives, destroying furni-ture, firing deafening gas pistols and fireworks that ruined the ladies' gowns . . . I said to those in attendance, Adolf Hitler would never approve of what we've just endured. Do not let that disrupt your loyalty to him.[27]

The ageing aristocrats at the celebration were far more horrified at violence being turned against themselves than at the Nazi Party's policies or true goals. Nonetheless, this and other events in early 1934 permanently buried the idea that Nazism would be a vehicle to return Wilhelm II to the throne. According to an account by the Jewish society writer Bella Fromm, a 'horde' of SA men also forced their way into another aristocratic ball in January, pushing several elderly gentlemen to the floor, kicking around officers' helmets like footballs and threatening ladies with revolvers.[28] The old-fashioned protest of a geriatric retired lieutenant general and the aggressive response of a young Nazi, in Fromm's retelling, illustrated how little the old monarchist guard understood the new fascist style and the tenor of the times.

Younger aristocrats, who were engaged with the new reality and served as SA, Wehrmacht or SS officers, discarded the language of the past and banished the idea of the restoration into the realm of political fantasy. 'All Germans reverently bow their heads before the memory of the Wilhelmine Empire,' wrote SA leader Achim von Arnim in mid-1933, 'but as long as our Führer is constructing the New Germany, the monarchist question is on ice.'[29] Monarchism had lost most of its appeal to and contact with the younger generations and could no longer help construct a dividing line between conservative political outlooks and Nazism. In February 1934, the former general and Hohenzollern financial administrator Wilhelm von Dommes complained to Hitler after Reich Food Minister Walter Darré had told a crowd that the Kaiser could be glad he hadn't been beheaded for his failed policies towards farmers. But that letter had no effect – it was just as impotent as Dommes's expression of regret that he was unable to challenge Darré to a duel.[30]

On the contrary, an extensive series of anti-monarchist articles and speeches began fomenting hatred for 'reactionaries' of various stripes, and among the explicit targets were the crown prince and his Silesian estates. This hostility towards the monarchy and nobility did not go unnoticed at home or abroad.[31] American newspapers correctly concluded that the Nazis now felt sure enough of themselves to launch a 'battle against the reaction' and monarchism despite the considerable support for the movement among the nobility and the military. Rallies in Frankfurt at which a Nazi student leader berated the Kaiser as a deserter whom the younger generation would never follow also attracted considerable attention.[32] The German Labour Front also staged an event at which it was proclaimed that reactionaries would be 'pulverized', and the organization's official newspaper demanded that monarchists 'return to the comfort of their mouseholes', since Nazis had 'no desire to make themselves the laughing stock of the world because of antics performed under the imperial crown'.[33] The anti-aristocratic attacks during this period were vitriolic enough for Major General Count Conrad Finck zu Finckenstein and other advisors to counsel Hermine not to travel to Berlin for fear the SA would arrest her for her widely known monarchist views.[34]

In a speech to the Reichstag on 30 January 1934, the Nazis' first anniversary in power and three days after the disruption of the Wilhelm II birthday celebrations, Hitler threw his weight behind the attacks upon putative conservative 'reactionaryism'. Göring introduced Hitler by underlining the importance of the occasion: 'As long as there is German history, 30 January will not only be a milestone. It will remain the turning point in the destiny of our German people.' Hitler directed the focus back to Germany's future form of state, promising, 'What once was will never come back.' He then became more explicit, saying that 'past dynastic interests' could not be recognized 'under any circumstances'. There was no space for the German princes to return to power. The Nazi policy of unity would be also enforced against any 'feeble successors and heirs to the politics of the past' who believed they could stand up to the new era. Hitler stressed the profundity of the 'historical revolution' that had unfolded over the previous year and dismissed any chance of restoring the monarchy, declaring, 'The question of the definitive form of state of the German Reich is now completely beyond discussion.' He also utterly rejected the principle of monarchic legitimacy: 'He who occupies Germany's ultimate pinnacle is called by the German people and is obliged solely to the people.'[35]

The Nazis' decoupling from traditional conservatives went well beyond rhetorical jibes. They directly followed up Hitler's Reichstag speech with a campaign against monarchist organizations. Göring protested vigorously to Interior Minister Frick against every instance of monarchist propaganda, which he considered an attack on the state, particularly when it targeted young people. Göring demanded that monarchist groups be banned and dissolved:

> The new state has not been created in fierce battle against the Left only so that new profiteers from the other side can put their own interests first. Everyone who encroaches on Adolf Hitler's Reich and state must be combatted to the utmost . . . The new state knows no quarrels over the form of government. Monarchy and republic are both alien to us. Both have failed.[36]

Observers in Doorn reported that, after being given a report on the speech, 'our poor lord has been suffering unspeakably'. The ex-Kaiser spoke of a 'declaration of war against the House of Hohenzollern', exclaiming, 'The enemy is on the Right.' A bit later, he received the news that the National Association of German Officers had been prohibited from using the word 'leader' to refer to anyone but Hitler. Whereas two months before Hitler's speech, Wilhelm II had listened to the crown prince advising him 'to make a pact with the Nazis and be clever about getting them on board', the Kaiser now ordered his sons, at least in the short term, to 'maintain absolute distance' from Hitler's movement.[37] The historical record reveals that the royal family was beset at the time by a mixture of anger, helplessness and worry. It is also full of evidence of various levels of opportunism and adaptation, fine adjustments concerning terminology, symbols, speeches, swastikas, uniforms, parades, greetings and the like.

What the crown prince meant by reaching a 'clever' pact with the Nazis entailed private talks at the highest level with Nazi leaders, but those conversations always came to naught. The royal family was influential enough to help the Nazis to power but not influential enough to push them in any given direction once they'd gained it. In August 1934, Goebbels noted in his diary: 'Conversation crown prince. Question of monarchy. They all believe in a restoration. I made no bones. Would be our greatest stupidity. We are arrivistes and must stay that way.'[38] Long before that, whether apocryphally or not, the French press reported Hitler telling the crown princess at an ambassador's reception: 'As long as I live, [a restoration] won't happen.'[39]

Amidst and beyond the acrimony of 1934, there was a considerable grey area of compromise and adaptation. For example, although Colonel General Karl von Einem, the commander of the German Third Army and former chairman of the monarchist League of the Upstanding, wrote to Mackensen in 1934 criticizing the 'action of the little man Hitler and other would-be greats against the pro-Kaiser movement', he couldn't help but admit that 'many people loyal to the Kaiser are now loyal to Hitler', especially among the German officer class.[40] Einem was one of the most influential monarchists in Germany. In March 1932, his son had been one of the mediators who had tried to broker a deal between Hitler and the crown prince, and Einem himself had publicly welcomed the handover of power to Hitler the following year.[41] He sent the Nazi leader a telegram of congratulations at the same time Hermine was assuring the ultra-monarchist August von Cramon, 'The Kaiser absolutely recognizes the scope and seriousness of your movement and is very impressed by your most recent speeches'.[42]

Applauding Murder: The Night of the Long Knives

30 June 1934 represents a major milestone in the Nazi regime's decoupling from those conservative groups, including the royal family, that had accompanied its rise to power. The murder spree colloquially known as the Night of the Long Knives, in which an armed Hitler himself went around by car after dark directing a nationwide killer commando, may not have set a completely new standard for brutality.[43] But this complex operation, ostensibly launched to ward off a 'Röhm putsch', stuck out in a number of respects from the regime's previous acts of terrorizing opponents. For starters, the eradication of the SA leadership under Röhm fulfilled a demand made by representatives of practically all of Germany's elite state functionaries. There was a broad consensus from Hindenburg and Reichswehr Minister Werner von Blomberg to a majority of the Reichswehr leadership, heads of industry, aristocratic large estate owners, university professors, conservative journalists and a group in the vice chancellor's office that the hugely powerful SA had to be reined in. The proletarian and, in some regions, small farmer make-up of the SA,[44] Röhm's demands for more authority, the challenge the group posed to the Reichswehr and the calls for a 'second revolution' that were making themselves heard in all corners of the Third Reich led to a great many people approving the decision to achieve that end via a series of murders.

The beginning was the famous Marburg Speech, delivered by Vice Chancellor Papen on 17 June 1934, written by the close Papen advisor Edgar Julius Jung and considered to this day to be the final public address to criticize the Nazi regime's bid for absolute power.[45] In it, the vice chancellor drew upon views common among anti-democratic, right-wing intellectuals to warn, 'with sensational sharpness', against 'permanent revolution' and 'eternal rebellion from below'.[46] The tone and thrust of the speech reflected the concerns felt by the upper classes since the Nazi Party platform of 1920 about the 'Jacobin' elements of Nazism. Papen cautioned against 'all the talk about a second wave to complete the revolution'. His words attracted considerable support, including from the crown prince, who seems to have sent him a letter expressing his agreement.[47] This was no great surprise. For a brief moment, the elites who collaborated with the Nazis while deceiving themselves that they were reining in Hitler must have believed their ideas of 'taming' and 'limiting' the fascist leader were working.

Yet, if the liquidation of the SA leadership fulfilled a long-standing demand of conservative elites, Hitler also targeted right-wing individuals who still possessed symbolic or actual power, including Gregor Strasser, Hitler's imagined and potential rival from late 1932, and Jung, who in addition to being Papen's speech writer was one of the most influential anti-democratic authors of the Weimar Republic. Schleicher was gunned down together with his wife in broad daylight in a luxurious Berlin suburb, and Colonel Ferdinand von Bredow belonged to Crown Prince Wilhelm's circle of military friends. The murder spree was designed to send the message to conservative elites that they could be the next targets of Nazi terror – sudden, extra-legal arrests, detention in concentration camps and executions in basements, forests and barracks court-yards. The killings can also be seen as an experiment, a test of what the power elites would tolerate and what sort of open terror most Germans would accept. The answer the regime got was, from its perspective, an affirmative go-ahead. The Reichswehr leadership's support for the operation, the gestures of submission from the completely intimidated SA leader Prince August Wilhelm of Prussia, the fawning interview the crown prince granted to the Swiss press about Hitler's 'magnetic power' and an essay entitled 'The Führer Is Protecting Law and Order' by Schleicher's former constitutional legal advisor Carl Schmitt – a text that remains deservedly notorious to this day – were just four conspicuous examples of conservative kowtowing.[48]

Two weeks after the murders, Hitler declared in the Reichstag that throughout history 'mutinous divisions' had been 'brought into line' not by regular courts, but through 'decimation'. He had acted in precisely this sense, he told his listeners:

> I issued the order to shoot the main culprits in this betrayal, and I furthermore ordered that the boils resulting from well-poisoning at home and our poisoning abroad be lanced down to the raw flesh . . . Let everyone know now for all time that, should he raise his hand against the state, his fate will be certain death.[49]

The upper classes reacted to these extraordinary words with a varied mixture of horror and relief. Many members of the high nobility and other upper social echelons displayed an astonishing nonchalance towards the Nazis' methods. Princess Olga zu Lippe, for instance, wrote in a letter:

> What would interest me is who will accompany Hitler at official occasions, since Hitler will now definitely not be able to get by without a lady . . . And how Hitler will master all this work – the party, the Reich chancellorship and the Reich presidency – while still keeping control over his own people. After the Röhm Putsch, that's more important than ever. Important problems! May he be blessed with the ability to achieve his goal.[50]

In Doorn, the Kaiser's dismay at open 'gangsterdom' and conditions 'like Chicago' was drowned out by Hermine's aggressive support for what had been done. Even the crass taboo of killing

Schleicher's wife Elisabeth, the daughter of a Prussian cavalry general, did nothing to dampen Hermine's enthusiasm for Hitler's 'clampdown'. The Kaiser's wife, who only one month before the murders had proclaimed that her husband's aims were completely identical to the Führer's,[51] added that German officers should have acted the same way when revolution broke out in 1918.[52]

The Hohenzollern inner circle was put on high alert, however, when the Nazis arrested the crown prince's adjutant Louis Müldner von Mülnheim and began pressuring his ghostwriter Karl Rosner and Müldner's associate Walter Nicolai. Eitel Friedrich was also interviewed by the police. None of those interrogated or detained were physically harmed, and Dommes negotiated Müldner's release after about three weeks.[53] But the upper classes worried for quite some time that they could be lumped together with 'communists, social democrats, old-school German nationalists and other members of their caste' by Röhm's successor Viktor Lutze.[54]

This episode made the Hohenzollerns realize that, although they had escaped this time, the threat was indeed getting closer to home. Hundreds of articles in the foreign press speculated about what role the royal family had played in events and what the fate of the crown prince would be. For a time, confused reports documented a general belief that the Hohenzollerns and the crown prince had taken a stand against the Nazi regimes and that the royal family would be completely broken up. The former crown prince was said to be in protective custody or in exile in Denmark. He was allegedly spotted in southern France, mistaken for a waiter and banished to the Netherlands along with his brother. But by 2 July 1934 even the provincial American press had correctly recognized that, while Schleicher had been killed, Papen was still a free man and the entire House of Hohenzollern had been 'immune' to the violence. The Kaiser's sons officially declared in a variety of outlets that they were unharmed.[55] The foreign media's explicit and implicit expectations that the Hohenzollerns would engage in opposition to Hitler proved to be erroneous.

Arrangements

Even before they were spared the extreme violence meted out upon conservative rivals of the Nazis during the Röhm murders, all three politically active generations of Hohenzollerns had begun to develop strategies for adapting, compromising and reaching arrangements. In 1933, Hitler received Louis Ferdinand in the Reich Chancellor's Office for an hour of talks.[56] It is difficult to know exactly why the Nazi leader would have wanted to speak with a 26-year-old who had no political function, but it seems certain that they discussed the United States and the Ford Motor Company. Hitler and the planners of Germany's imminent rearmament appear to have put great stock in Louis Ferdinand, a doctor of economics who possessed longstanding contacts in the US and a name considered glamorous by the American upper classes. (Conversely, his American contacts saw him as someone with the best of connections to German state elites.) In 1929, equipped with the blessing of the ex-Kaiser and a letter of recommendation to Henry Ford, the then 22-year-old had set off for a long trip to the US and Argentina. During an apprenticeship at Ford, he had got to know all aspects of modern industrialism there, from the conveyor belt to management to the corporate boardroom. This trim, elegant, handsome and by all accounts thoroughly charming young man returned from his extended trip with direct contacts that included Germanophile American journalists, Henry Ford himself and more than one later US president.

In July 1934, Louis Ferdinand returned to Dearborn, Michigan, as one of the negotiators between Ford, the German state and representatives of a planned Volkswagen factory. The talks, carried out at the highest levels, revolved around an ultimately unsuccessful project to build a complete new Ford factory on the banks of Germany's River Elbe.[57] As part of his attempts to convince Ford to make a significant business investment in Germany, the young consultant also negotiated with Wilhelm Keppler, one of the most fanatical

German industrialist supporters of Nazism.[58] German-American commercial circles appreciated Louis Ferdinand's value as a go-between, with one contemporary asserting, 'He has, of course, free access to everybody and everywhere and might be very useful.'[59] In January 1935, he tried to elicit support from Henry Ford's son for Germany and the Nazi regime. The restrictive measures of the Nazi authorities had been unpleasant, he argued, but necessary to keep the communists in check. Germany would no longer make any more territorial demands, the prince added, and the socialist tendencies within the Nazi movement had been beaten back.[60]

As an automotive representative with connections to the arms industry, the House of Hohenzollern and the Nazi regime, the abilities of the 'royal salesman', as the American press nicknamed him, were already very impressive.[61] Given the ambivalent and flexible perceptions of the US in the Third Reich and among Nazi elites, as well as the Hohenzollerns' great popularity among Americans, the prince was a credible intermediary.[62] Meanwhile, the general German fascination with American industrial production and Fordism opened further doors for Louis Ferdinand at home.[63] Lastly, his personal acquaintance with Hitler's former advisor Ernst Hanfstaengl, who had studied at Harvard and sheltered the Nazi leader after his failed putsch in 1923, was likewise a useful connection.

Central to the close relations maintained by three generation of Hohenzollerns – the ex-Kaiser, the former crown prince and Louis Ferdinand – with illiberal, Germanophile, anti-Semitic American elites were the circles around Henry Ford. In 1938, Louis Ferdinand and his wife were received in the White House by President Roosevelt's son. The prince's image was that of a cosmopolitan who nonetheless was in touch with 'the common people'. Just as his father, Crown Prince Wilhelm, had posed in exile for press photos with the blacksmith and inquisitive villagers in Wieringen, Louis Ferdinand presented himself, adorned in a suit and tie, shaking hands with an American 'pal' working on the assembly line at the Ford factory, to which the young prince had now 'returned'.[64]

After his time with Ford, Louis Ferdinand had worked for

Lufthansa, the company that had since 1926 been most involved with the illegal re-establishment of the German air force prohibited under the Treaty of Versailles. The firm was closely connected with Göring's Aviation Ministry.[65] The American press saw the prince as a kind of trump card Hitler deployed now and again on international missions, for instance to Britain, where Louis Ferdinand flew in a self-piloted plane and where he was described in the press as 'Hitler's Royal Right-Hand Man'.[66]

Around this time, Crown Prince Wilhelm received American pilot and hero Charles Lindbergh – who later spearheaded anti-Semitic, Nazi-friendly publicity campaigns as the figurehead of the American First Committee – at Cecilienhof.[67] Wilhelm also held an internationally closely followed meeting with ace German pilot Ernst Udet, one of the leading planners of German aerial rearmament.[68]

No member of the royal family became part of what we today might call the 'military-industrial complex'.[69] At the same time, it would be inappropriate to completely dismiss the poorly researched intersections between the political, military and business interests of the Hohenzollerns as insignificant 'adventures' or expressions merely of their interest in 'sports' and fast cars, as if the family had depoliticized itself, in one fell swoop, after 1933.

The 1936 Olympics were another occasion when the German high nobility and the Nazi regime cooperated extensively. Both the Winter Games in Garmisch-Partenkirchen and the Summer Games in Berlin offered the Nazis the chance to present the outside world with their biggest charade to date. The recently published diaries of the British conservative Henry 'Chips' Channon give a taste of the common ground between the anti-Semitic and anti-democratic segments of the British and German high society. Taking afternoon tea in Cecilienhof, Channon got to meet the crown princess and some of her sons. At wild parties until the wee hours of the morning at the villa of the German ambassador to Britain Joachim von Ribbentrop, he celebrated the New Germany with the 'fantastic Goring', with the two men discussing the possibility of a royal restoration some day. Men like Channon represented a channel of communication between Nazi Germany and Prime Minister Neville Chamberlain and British appeasement circles.

Among the functions of the newly reconfigured high society of the Third Reich was to further secure the support of elite state functionaries and generally improve Germany's reputation abroad. Members of German dynasties and select families from the lower nobility played a conspicuous role in this regard, as, of course, did the Hohenzollerns.[70] All of this led to Channon, in reality a Chicago-born parvenu, writing in the summer of 1936: 'England could learn many a lesson from Nazi Germany. I cannot understand the English dislike and suspicion of the Nazi regime. Personally I believe, and it rends my heart to say so, that England is in the retrograde.'[71]

Louis Ferdinand's arrangements with the Nazi regime ran parallel to those of his father, the crown prince, who also sought out opportunities to demonstrate his cooperativeness and recommend himself as a builder of bridges between old and new. In early 1934, discussions about Wilhelm as a potential future leader had by no means come to a complete halt, as was evident in a book by an officer and friend of the crown prince, Carl Lange. Originally published in different form in 1921 and widely discussed before its re-release, [72] this work was the latest in a series of publications emanating from the crown prince's PR staff that purported to show the 'true face' of the heir to the throne.[73]

The revised version put out in 1934 left out multiple passages included in the original twelve chapters. The chapter 'Love of Animals', for instance, was nowhere to be found, and the tome now concluded with a chapter entitled 'The Present Day'.[74] On the whole, the book 'underscored Wilhelm's important ambassadorial role for the new state, which he has fulfilled thanks to his personality and his global status as the former heir to the throne of the German Empire'. Lange emphasized the crown prince's contribution to defending the Nazi regime against the foreign, and in particular the American, press as well as his loyalty to Adolf Hitler and, more broadly, his 'commitment to the present day'. Because of the author's long and close 'acquaintance with the former crown prince', this book was touted as 'a valuable source for how the man wished his words and doings to be understood and evaluated'.[75]

Meanwhile, Wilhelm continued making high-profile domestic and international appearances wearing a swastika armband as a sign of his affirmation of the new era. Particular attention was attracted by a pictorial report in the *Kreuzzeitung* showing the swastika-sporting crown prince with his casually posing son Louis Ferdinand during a 'winter excursion' of the National Socialist Motor Vehicle Corps. The caption read, 'German products are superior in all classes'.[76]

The cooperative signals Wilhelm sent didn't change the attitudes of the regime towards the Hohenzollerns in the slightest. In an internal May 1935 memo, Hitler's deputy, Rudolf Hess, instructed party leaders and speakers not to talk about the monarchy. Instead of concerning themselves with superfluous issues like the form of state, they should instead study the Führer's views as expressed in *Mein Kampf*. The battle was not about whether Germany was better off as a republic or a monarchy, 'but whether there will be a German people for the next thousand years'.[77]

In May 1938, Louis Ferdinand married Grand Duchess Kira Kirillovna of Russia. The opulent wedding ceremonies, celebrated at the start of the month, first in Cecilienhof, then Doorn, brought together segments of the European high nobility, and the crown prince personally informed Hitler about the marriage. (It is unclear whether the Nazi leader was an invited guest.)[78] During the gala dinner, those family members who had married below their station were seated at a side table in a demonstration of the continued power of internal 'house rules'.

Louis Ferdinand's marriage to the cosmopolitan daughter of Russia's Grand Duke Kyrill Vladimirovich established a direct connection to those Romanovs who had survived Bolshevik assassination attempts and gone into exile following the murder of the tsar's family. Born in Paris in 1909, Kira Kirillovna had fled from Russia via Finland and the German city of Coburg back to France. Most White

Russians considered her father a pretender to the Russian throne. As of 1924, the grand duke took to referring to himself as 'emperor-in-exile' and divided his days between a *maison de maître* in Brittany, palaces in Nice and the Edinburgh Palace in Coburg.[79] After Kyrill Vladimirovich's death in October 1938, Kira's brother Vladimir Kirillovich became the 'head' of the House of Romanov.

In 1938, rumours swirled in the French press that, thanks to German assistance, Kira's brother might help bring together anti-communist forces in Ukraine. This was immediately denied.[80] In fact, during the Second World War, Louis Ferdinand's Russian brother-in-law lived partly as an estate owner in Occupied France, where in June 1941, days after the German attack on the Soviet Union, he issued an anti-Bolshevik call to arms and supported the German military campaign as an antidote to the Communist Internationale.

At this point, American journalists let their imaginations run two steps ahead, speculating that in the case of a swift victory to the east Hitler's plan was to erect a Slavic kingdom with Louis Ferdinand on the throne. A newspaper in Maryland, for instance, served up its readers this idea accompanied with a photo of Louis Ferdinand and Kira captioned 'Russian Throne?' Reports from the British Foreign Office and lengthy press summaries also document the currency of this notion. The media would promote the idea of a connection between the White Russian camp and an active political role for Louis Ferdinand 'in the East' for quite some time.

The press spent considerable energy in the summer of 1941 discussing relations between the Hohenzollerns and circles of anti-Bolshevik Russians in exile.[81] Kira's brother Vladimir spent the Second World War in a castle in the town of Amorbach in Lower Franconia. If only symbolically, the connections between the Houses of Hohenzollern and Romanov created an anti-Bolshevik German-Russian superpower with maximum hostility towards the Soviet Union. Kira's family probably also legitimized the longstanding connections between anti-revolutionary Russian exiles and the German Right in Munich and Berlin.[82] In 1942, *The New York Times* characterized Louis Ferdinand as a passionate supporter of the [German] war on Russia. And to encourage him to issue more anti-Bolshevik statements, the Gestapo appears to have arrested advisors of Kira's brother in Brittany during this time.[83]

In her reports to the Office of Strategic Services (OSS), the intelligence division of the American War Department, the former Berlin correspondent Sigrid Schultz characterized Louis Ferdinand as the monarchists' strongest figurehead and a charismatic personality the Nazi regime was exploiting abroad. His wife, Kira, too, had been reportedly considered for a time as a contact for anti-Bolshevik groups inside and outside Russia. After her activity as a spy was over, Schultz also opined that Louis Ferdinand and the monarchist movement had enough potential in late 1942 to serve as a potential counter-pole to the Nazi regime, one which might even be acceptable to the Soviets.[84] By contrast, she called the Kaiser's daughter Viktoria Luise, who was married to the Duke of Braunschweig, a 'fanatical National Socialist', whose estate in the Alpine Austrian town of Gmunden had been a 'breeding ground for Nazi agents' before Austria was amalgamated into the Third Reich in 1938. Schultz, who was able to file her reports until 1941, drew attention to the Hohenzollerns' numerous foreign contacts, particularly in Britain, and the continual social and amateur diplomatic services various female and male members performed on behalf of the Nazi regime. She also regarded two of Viktoria Luise's sons as having close relationships with Nazism and the SS.

There weren't many married couples in the Third Reich who represented lines of contact to both the heart of US centres of power and leading White Russian exiles. But, in addition to Kira's symbolic connections to anti-communist Russia and Louis Ferdinand's factual ones to large-scale American industry, the crown prince's son Friedrich was connected with England, where he was interned in 1940 and later married the daughter of a British earl. The crown prince's daughter Cecilie also made numerous contacts during diverse stays in London, for example, with Prudence Jellicoe, a granddaughter of the commander-in-chief of the Grand Fleet during the First World War.[85] Meanwhile, Hermine sought to elicit the support of a British general and attaché who kept in close touch with the ex-Kaiser. On one occasion she wrote:

> May England in this critical moment for Germany put all trust in our great 'Führer Adolf Hitler' [and] help him and Germany for the best, peace and quiet of Europe . . . I heard by radio the Führer's wonderful speeches – which cannot be translated as they are utterly German – but one must know him and hear his tremendous feeling – we say: 'innere Bewegung' to understand.[86]

The Hohenzollerns played a marginal role in the signing of the Munich Agreement in late September 1938 – the final and greatest of British and French concessions to Nazi expansionism – in two ways: an exchange of letters between Prime Minister Chamberlain and the former crown prince, and the loose contacts between the latter's eldest son, Wilhelm, and circles of officers who dismissed Nazi foreign policy as dilettantish. But the German high nobility's foreign contacts were by no means evidence of any personal anti-Nazism. When Crown Prince Wilhelm wrote to Chamberlain in 1938, his intention wasn't to preserve peace but to improve German prospects for victory in the war to come.[87] His initiative was based on the social, cultural and ideological common ground shared by the German high nobility and the appeasement-oriented segment of the British upper classes, with their strong, mutual anti-communist tendencies.[88] In the run-up to both of the world wars, German planners considered keeping Britain out of the conflict key to eventual victory.

Crown Prince Wilhelm did not suddenly become a pacifist in the autumn of 1938. He was an amateur diplomat, of whom the Nazi regime repeatedly availed itself, together with other members of the German high nobility. A major component in this collaboration was the fear of all varieties of communism that ran through the British, German and European aristocracy. On this basis, and thanks to the complex interrelatedness of noble families throughout

Europe, aristocratic channels provided a communications conduit away from the public eye.[89] But such channels did not result in opposition to the Nazi regime in 1938 any more than aristocrats' connections with sceptical military men like the army general chief of staff Ludwig Beck did.

It takes considerable imagination to interpret the 'September conspiracy' – in which some elite state functionaries allegedly plotted to stop the poorly advised Hitler from drifting into war – as principled opposition to Nazism.[90] Crown Prince Wilhelm was in fact on good terms with Beck, but at that point the latter was not the leader of the anti-Hitler opposition he first became in 1944.[91] The two men's cordial relations arose from their discussions about the issue of German rearmament in the early 1920s, the hypothetical plans for the next war and their common enthusiasm in 1933 for the formation of the Hitler government.[92] Obviously, the Hohenzollerns would feel closer to anti-democratic military elites than to Nazi Party leaders, but that's no indication of any proximity to the anti-Hitler opposition.

In any case, the 'September conspiracy' itself never progressed beyond the realm of the hypothetical, and none of the Hohenzollerns ever played a leading role in it. There's no supporting evidence for the legend that that the 'conspiracy' included forming a commando to assassinate Hitler, of which the crown prince's eldest son Wilhelm was often thought to be part.[93] The fact that the main figure and herald of this alleged plot was supposed to be Friedrich Wilhelm Heinz, a military officer who was one of the main leaders of extreme right-wing murder and terror organizations in the Weimar Republic, may explain why today's Hohenzollern apologists have opted not to further investigate or highlight this myth.

Five years earlier, while in the United States at the start of the Nazi-led government, Louis Ferdinand had impressed upon reporters the enormous support Hitler had among the German populace. Hitler was improving economic conditions and constantly working towards greater fairness internationally, the prince said. After his brother's marriage below his station, Louis Ferdinand had replaced

Prince Wilhelm as his generation's pretender to the throne. Now he tried to sell the American public the idea that Hitler was a 'true conservative' trying to unite the German nation. The symbolism of a Prussian prince promoting Hitler as a national unifier reprised a main leitmotif of the Day of Potsdam.[94]

Along with the many proclamations of his father, Louis Ferdinand's statements to this effect help polish the new regime's image abroad. They also signalled the Hohenzollerns' willingness to cooperate with the Nazi leadership. The Kaiser's wife in 1934 at least interpreted Louis Ferdinand's stay in the United States and the contacts he made there as a kind of publicity campaign for the Third Reich.[95]

In a television interview in 1987, Louis Ferdinand himself claimed that he had hardly followed Hitler's rise to power or German politics in general because he had been in the US during their decisive phase. In his autobiography from the 1950s, he recalled regularly meeting during the first months of 1933 with Nazi diplomats such as Hanfstaengl and Ribbentrop, although he purported to have resisted their attempts to recruit him for the Nazi cause since it violated the values installed within him by his grandfather, the Kaiser.[96]

In that television interview, the prince seemed to have forgotten several details from fifty years back in and around 1933. On the Day of Potsdam, Louis Ferdinand had written from Doorn to a Nazi-supporting banker and influential anti-Semite, Ernest Liebold, who was one of Henry Ford's closest advisors. In his letter, the prince explained in four pages of clunky English why he voted for the Nazi Party in the German national elections of 5 March 1933. An immense wave running through the 'new Germany', he said, had swept him along, and the alternative to Nazism was: 'Bolshevism. Chaos and death for all propertied people.' For that reason, the new regime, which had brought 'perfect order' to Germany, deserved support. Foreign creditors especially should now offer Hitler their assistance, Louis Ferdinand wrote. A peaceful German revolution was underway, and those who objected to the severity of the Nazis should consider how severely they had been persecuted by their opponents throughout the years. Much of the criticism from abroad was unfair. The DNVP was too old-fashioned, leading Louis Ferdinand to proclaim 'that the Nazis have my full sympathy'. At the end of his letter, the prince pointed out his close relations with the German ambassador in Washington and offered to serve as a mediator between the US and the Nazi regime.[97] Louis Ferdinand was not forced in any way to write a letter of this sort, a clear example of the prince doing publicity work for the Nazi regime. By the time his English and German autobiographies appeared in the 1950s, this former Hitler voter and mediator for the Nazi regime had transformed himself into a member of the German resistance.

Servility and Security

The vacillating attitudes of the ex-Kaiser towards Nazism in theory and practice didn't fundamentally change after 1934. From William II's supercilious comments in 1929 to his death in 1941, the only constant was the tactical consideration of whether collaborating with the Nazis would help restore him to the throne. His rhetoric and symbolic activities swung back and forth depending whether the signals sent by the Nazi regime were compatible with his fantasies of ruling Germany again. After 1934, the negative statements from Doorn concerning Hitler and the Nazi state increased. But it's impossible read any 'opposition' to the regime in them. There's little more to be gleaned from his volatile pronouncements than William II's bitterness at the demise of his own illusions, his enthusiasm for a war of aggression and the extreme egotism of his fragile psyche, whose origins John Röhl laid bare in his monumental Wilhelm II biography.[98] Yet, even as he sank into insignificance, the ex-Kaiser remained willing to cooperate with the regime.

On many occasions, Wilhelm II's private criticism of Nazism was cancelled out by other statements, especially in public. Two months after Germany defeated its Western European neighbours in the Second World War, the ex-Kaiser recalibrated his attitude towards

Britain according to a bizarre mixture of Protestant, chiliastic, anti-Semitic and paranoid elements centred around the bête noire of 'Juda'. In a letter to a countess friend in August 1940, he wrote:

> Then God sent us the war he had Juda, the Antichrist, start with the help of his slaves in England, as Juda intended to set up a great international Jewish world empire with the assistance of the British. At that point, God intervened and gave the German people victory. Juda's plans were smashed, and it was swept from the European continent!

Wilhelm's interpretation of Germany's defeat in 1918 remained the same but was expressed in far more drastic language. The First World War had been 'ignited by Juda with Satan's encouragement'. The ex-Kaiser imagined himself as a would-be benefactor betrayed, above all, by Jews. 'I invited Jews to my table and supported and helped Jewish professors. And their answer was mockery, contempt, world war, betrayal, Versailles and revolution!'[99] As early as 1919, the ex-Kaiser had developed an enthusiasm for the vulgar anti-Semitism of the sort found in the works of racist author Artur Dinter,[100] and animosity towards Jews is one of the few red threads running through Wilhelm's errant speeches in exile.

Back in Germany, the crown prince made fewer and fewer public appearances, and they were reported on more frequently by the foreign, especially French, not the Nazi-dominated German press. International journalists continued to take interest whenever and wherever Wilhelm did turn up: at a Hitler reception in 1935, that same year, again with Hitler, at the parades to celebrate the introduction of compulsory military service, and in 1936, in conjunction with the Olympic Summer Games, at a major state reception in Berlin's state opera house to honour Göring.[101] The French also continued to cite the crown prince's prediction that Europe would soon feel grateful to Hitler.[102] In 1937, a French newspaper wrote about Wilhelm's abiding popularity by describing how he and Cecilie had received a standing ovation, lasting minutes, when they appeared at a Berlin opera house. According to this account, at least, even the orchestra and the conductor applauded. In Germany, Goebbels prohibited all reports on this incident.[103]

As previously discussed, on one occasion the crown prince was allegedly so upset with the regime that he had wanted to burn his SA uniform,[104] and the former heir to the throne's displeasure at situations in which he had to allow himself to be bossed around by small-time Nazi leaders was a recurring motif in the international press. Not without a healthy dose of schadenfreude, American journalists passed on anecdotes of men of modest origins in SA uniforms reproaching the former army group commander for his relaxed posture during roll call and for having his picture taken with his hands in his pockets. American newspapers also accurately reported on Nazi grandees whose reputations were bolstered by royal princes helping them on with their overcoats. When Crown Prince Wilhelm joined the NSKK, one US paper commented that the crown prince had now become a 'truck driver'.[105] Likewise when August Wilhelm was spotted on Berlin's Unter den Linden collecting money for the Nazi charity Winter Assistance, foreign journalists dubbed him the 'beggar prince'.[106]

In the end, the tension between the crown prince's presumptuous manner and the new rules of the Third Reich led to a break. In May 1936, Wilhelm took it upon himself to send a telegram of congratulations to Mussolini, my 'much-admired Italian friend, the Duce', after he had conquered Ethiopia. (In this late colonialist war of aggression, the modernized Italian air force had used a considerable amount of poison gas – 400,000 to 700,000 Ethiopians, mostly civilians, died in the fighting – drawing sharp censure from the League of Nations.)[107] The Italian press jumped on the story. But Wilhelm's enthusiasm for Mussolini and presumption concerning what was an official matter of state didn't sit well with the SS newspaper *Das schwarze Korps*, which lambasted the 'pretender to the throne' – the article itself placed that title in inverted commas – for 'interfering' in German foreign policy.[108] This animosity didn't escape the notice of the foreign press. Despite passing on erroneous rumours that the crown prince was now being kept under close Nazi surveillance, one French paper correctly analysed the underlying conflict. The anti-Semitic magazine *L'Intransigeant* also wrote that the gulf between the crown prince and the Nazi regime had widened.[109] In the end Wilhelm resigned from the National Socialist Motor Corps[110] and would never again belong to a Nazi organization.[111]

As the major events of the Third Reich unfolded, members of the House of Hohenzollern constantly reconfigured their relationship with the Nazi regime, although public appearances and statements were invariably made with the family's material interests in mind. A particularly vivid example came after the Night of Broken Glass pogrom on 9/10 November 1938 and the days that followed, when hundreds of Jews were murdered, some 30,000 sent to concentration camps, and more than 1,400 synagogues and Jewish meeting places destroyed.[112] Credible internal documents from Doorn attest to the ex-Kaiser's brief outrage at the homicidal campaign against Jews and other victims and the destruction of Jewish institutions. Wilhelm was even reported to have called the perpetrators 'gangsters'. In a letter to Britain's Queen Mary, the Queen Mother, he blamed what had happened in Germany on 'Bolshevism'.[113] Within his family, he was more critical than ever before about the methods of the Hitler state and his son August Wilhelm's obsession with the Nazi movement. But there were no familial consequences, and Wilhelm II said nothing publicly during this apparently brief phase of outrage. Verbally, his attitude may have bordered for a moment on the sort of deep, malicious satisfaction displayed by his wife after the Night of the Long Knives four years earlier. But his private comments never went beyond the traditional upper-class conservative disdain for 'rowdy anti-Semitism' – a fleeting sentiment that as a rule was never expressed beyond the private sphere. Nonetheless, scholars continued to write for decades of the ex-Kaiser proclaiming that the pogrom made him 'ashamed to be a German'. This assertion still appears in the most recent pro-monarchy depictions of the past,[114] although it is mere legend based on a fake interview which the ex-Kaiser himself later disavowed, and which was quite possibly produced with the help of the British secret service to help discredit him with the Nazis.[115]

The situation with Wilhelm II's private correspondence was much the same,[116] and any expectations that the ex-Kaiser might take a public stand against the violence were clearly misguided. All of Wilhelm II's known public statements concerning the Nazi regime's anti-Semitic policies were ones of approval, not condemnation. Tellingly, on 10 November 1938, the ex-Kaiser's daily, telegraph-style notes mixed the news of anti-Semitic rampages with a record of the weather: 'Kemal Pascha †. Jew pogroms in Berlin and Germany. Synagogues burned. Overcast, still, wind from the SSE. Night + 3° thick fog. Heavy dew.'[117]

Two weeks after the pogrom, the male Hohenzollerns convened in Doorn. The purpose of this meeting was not to try to coordinate a unified family policy – the time for that was long past – to say nothing of an anti-Nazi one.[118] In fact the crown prince headed off an initiative by his father to prohibit August Wilhelm from continuing to promote the Nazis, and the latter remained the family member most active in Nazism. There were good material as well as political reasons for the royal clan to continue its established opportunistic cooperation with the Hitler regime. Democratic legal reforms had done away with the entailments that traditionally anchored aristocratic ownership of their vast assets, sending the nervous high nobility scurrying in search of alternatives ways of protecting their wealth and privileges. But it wouldn't be until early 1939 that the Nazi regime enforced the dissolution of entailments, so there was an incentive for the Hohenzollerns to stay on the Nazis' good side. To understand why we need to look more closely at laws governing aristocratic property.

Hereditary aristocratic land rights had technically been abolished during the Weimar republic, but the actual implementation had largely been put off and hadn't been resolved by 1933. The landed aristocracy in general and the former ruling dynasties especially worried right from the start about what the Nazi regime might do.

The Hohenzollerns, like all large-scale landowners, particularly fretted that the state could divide up or even confiscate their family assets and wealth. It was thus one of their highest priorities to reach new legal arrangements with the regime that would avoid such divisions and keep their property in the hands of a single heir. Under some circumstances, the institution of 'hereditary farms', or *Erb-höfe*, could be used to replace the older one of 'fee entails', or *Fideikommisse*, which had been legally eradicated after 1918. *Erbhöfe* were meant to guarantee long-lasting ownership within one family since they could not be divided, sold or mortgaged.[119] Many of the formerly ruling houses tried to secure exceptions to the legal limit of 125 hectares, which required them to demonstrate 'Aryan descent' and 'farming ability' (*Bauernfähigkeit*), by exploiting contacts with the Nazi leadership and demonstrating loyalty to National Socialist views.

Members of families, even those who had been 'disinherited' or whose property had been divided up under Weimar legal reforms, could now hope to recover what had been lost. The head of the family could offer younger siblings smaller packages, if approved by a judge, from what used to be 'household assets' as compensation. Another option was to obtain exceptional permission for an entailed estate to help younger siblings establish their own lines of ownership. The registration of assets as an entailed estate was subject to the whims of the Nazi state apparatus and informed by economic and ideological criteria. As part of its Four-Year Plan to achieve self-reliance and preparations for the Second World War, the Nazi regime insisted upon high-performance agricultural estates for the coming 'battle of food production'.[120] But if it toed the Nazi party line and curried favour with the right officials, the landed aristocracy could avail itself of arrangements, family-intern 'house laws', contracts and exceptions to avoid inheritance regulations, sidestep taxes and preserve aristocratic ideas of concentrating property in a single hand. Thus, many of these families had immense, concrete material incentives to follow the wishes of the Nazi regime.

The interests of the eldest sons (*Oberhäupter*) and their younger siblings and children often diverged,[121] but in general the search for a secure replacement for property guarantees, without which the nobility itself was difficult to imagine, remained one of the most important issues for the landed aristocracy. Not surprisingly, individual aristocratic attitudes towards the Nazi state depended on whether the people in question believed that the state would offer acceptable solutions or not. There was hope for new Nazi regulations alongside constant fears that the Nazi state would legally confiscate aristocratic assets in a way that the ex-Kaiser repeatedly termed 'Bolshevist'.[122] All the way back in September 1933, General von Dommes indirectly had his concerns about compulsory handover of land raised with Hitler.[123] Even foreign newspapers reported about the Hohenzollerns' fears of being stripped of their wealth.[124] In February 1934, Ilsemann recorded the Kaiser saying, 'If the Nazis take away my wealth, I'll sell the valuable paintings I have here and live out my days on the proceeds.'[125] Brothers of the crown prince declared that they would be 'kicked out of the country' and expropriated if they didn't bend to the regime's demands. In later interviews with newspapers in communist East Germany, the crown prince's valet said his former master had been permanently terrified of being stripped of his wealth.[126] German exiles in Paris noted a 1937 article in the Nazi press that criticized the Hohenzollerns for 'not wanting to give up any land' – an accusation that had also been reported internationally three years earlier.[127] National Socialism had helped the German princes escape planned disappropriation back in 1926, the thinking ran, and it was now time for them to show their gratitude by voluntarily forfeiting some of their property.[128]

In the summer of 1938, Baron von Sell, one of the anti-Nazi detractors among the ex-Kaiser's advisors, was detained and pressured by SA men at the German–Dutch border, so that Sell thought it possible he could be arrested at any time. The actual arrest of the monarchist journalist Reinhold Wulle also caused considerable consternation in Doorn.[129] Waves of actions targeting German aristocrats and princes recurred throughout the Nazi dictatorship, and parts of the movement talked constantly of confiscating land from the nobility for settlements. Conversely, in 1938, Hitler himself again publicly condemned the sporadic outburst from the anti-aristocratic factions within the Nazi leadership, explicitly describing renewed conflict with the dynastic German houses as undesirable.[130] Amidst the general enthusiasm of the ex-Kaiser and his wife for Germany's military victories in 1940, Göring tried in his capacity as 'Reich Master Hunter and Forester and High Commissioner for Nature Conservation' to convince Wilhelm II to sell his hunting estate Rominten in East Prussia. The sale of that property was concluded after the ex-Kaiser's death and brought in 700,000 Reichsmarks.[131]

Nonetheless, at the latest by 1938, it became clear that aristocrats, as long as they demonstrated a willingness to work with the regime, would not be among the dispossessed, but rather among the dispossessors and profiteers. The Nazi regime's policy remained that of controlling, not confiscating, private property, unless it was owned by Jews.[132] The Hohenzollerns invested heavily in acquiring formerly Jewish-owned companies that had been broken up and reconfigured with various levels of compulsion and violence. Although the topic has never been researched in detail, there were several cases in which members of the aristocracy helped themselves to parts of department store chains and Silesian cement plants. Everything from investments in the arms industry to the massive westward transfers of capital near the end of the Second World War show that the crown princes' financial administration, now going by the name 'general administration', successfully advanced aristocratic interests and knew how to profit from rearmament, conquest and wartime pillaging – as well as defeat and retreat.[133]

Depending on the political winds, the nobility transferred large amounts of capital back and forth inside and outside Germany, particularly using financial institutions in the Netherlands and Switzerland as conduits. In December 1940, for example, after Germany's great 'armed triumphs', Dommes advised Wilhelm II to increase his investments in German stocks. According to calculations by economic experts early on in East Germany, the balances achieved by the Hohenzollerns' financial managers more than doubled, from 18 to 37 million Reichsmarks, between 1933 and 1942. The family administration took account of both the military victories of 1940 and Germany's impending defeat in 1944. Hohenzollern tax documents from 1942 indicate raw assets of more than 84 million Reichsmarks, half of which were invested in stocks.[134]

In addition, economic opportunities were available in the Wehrmacht officer corps and in conjunction with the 'space' that was 'won' in the east, and some aristocratic families directly tried to profit from German military offensives in eastern Europe. Starting in 1939, members of the high and low, rich and poor nobility enquired of the SS leadership whether it would be possible to acquire estates in the territory Germany conquered. The settlements of occupied areas showed that the 'people without space', as the Nazis were fond of calling the Germans, now had lots of space but not enough people to fill it. Proposals to resettle industrial workers in the east proved so unpopular that 'Aryan' foreigners were also considered as potential settlers.[135] By contrast, some German aristocrats, especially those whose estates had been lost or who had come under economic pressure, saw such ideas as a unique chance to provide their families with property for generations by exploiting territory earmarked for settlement.

Enquiries made to Himmler and high-level SS officers document the intense interest various groups of aristocrats had in acquiring large plots of the 'eastern land'. Aristocratic applications formulated very specific desires. Enquiries directed during the war by Grand Duke Nikolaus of Oldenburg or Heinrich von Bismarck's wife directly to Himmler or to the responsible government officers revealed a keen interest in the endless possibilities of space that was to be conquered, planned, and settled 'out East'. Duke Nikolaus wrote:

Since I have 6 sons, I would like to acquire further property for the younger ones. I would be very grateful if you would briefly inform me whether there will be the basic possibility for me to purchase larger plots in the east after the end of the war . . . With friendly greetings and Heil Hitler . . .

He received a positive response.[136] The house of Schaumburg-Lippe, for instance, provided the male line of the family with land in eastern Europe or 'Aryanized' properties in German cities.[137] As of 1941, the Schaumburg-Lippes' vast properties were administered by the same leading agricultural manager as the Hohenzollerns' real estate, and both families employed many of the same lawyers and notaries. Essentially, all property confiscated from Jews was up for grabs.[138] The family had no compunction in 1940 about giving Prince Friedrich-Christian zu Schaumburg-Lippe, a younger son and adjutant of Joseph Goebbels, 'in lieu of cash property in the newly acquired eastern territory' as an inheritance.[139] Later examples included the services performed by SS leader Prince Josias zu Waldeck und Pyrmont for another Schaumburg-Lippe prince, a relative-in-law, who was interested in acquiring cheap land in the east, and the purchase of 'Aryanized' property in Berlin, including parts of the Hackesche Höfe complex of courtyards in a prime location in the centre of the city.[140]

When the Nazi state formally abolished historical entailments in early 1939, many families in the high nobility compensated younger members from their former 'household assets', although as a rule the amounts were well below what the beneficiaries would have received under common law governing inheritances. When further assets were acquired as compensation, as long as they were registered as entailed estates, they were subject to laws governing that legal form. That gave younger family members an incentive to behave obediently towards the regime. Moreover, in return for acquiring property, the nobility was required to subjugate themselves fairly comprehensively to ideological and practical guidelines from the Nazi regime. An example from July 1938 illustrates how arrangements over aristocratic estates were reached. The main counsel for the House of Hohenzollern wrote to Nazi state secretary Hans Heinrich Lammers, requesting approval for the purchase of 500 to 1,000 hectares of land for the crown prince's eldest son, Wilhelm, at a price of between one-and-a-half and two million Reichsmarks. Because of inheritance renunciations and contractual agreements, the crown prince was to become the sole heir of the family fortune, so the idea was to procure a new estate that would belong to his oldest son. And to protect it against state confiscation, the royal family requested that the property be declared an entailed estate, or *Erbhof*.[141] Lammers passed on the request to Reich Farmers Leader Walther Darré, who had no objections, after which Göring and Hitler both personally approved the purchase. The Nazi calls for settlements, which now and again included talk of confiscating land, can be seen as part of an atmosphere of vague threat. But aristocratic concerns about being disappropriated never led to any resistance, only to additional forms of opportunistic collaboration.

One month earlier, in June 1939, the crown prince wrote directly to his friend Göring. The letter revealed the general pressure under which aristocratic large landowners could come as a result of the settlement programmes run by a part of the Reichsnährstand (State Food Society), the Nazi government body set up to regulate food production. Employing a variety of arguments, Wilhelm asked for permission to preserve parts of his holdings in Silesia as a single property unit. Like other princes who had applied for entailment estates,[142] Wilhelm stressed the sacrifices he had already made in the form of handing over land for settlement by farmers.

This was part of a wider concessions system. Large-scale landowners from the high nobility who had been deemed 'capable of farming' and whose holdings had been recognized as an entailment estate often ceded a small portion of their territory to small farmers. But not all the arguments advanced by the crown prince for his

1939 request were equally persuasive. His nostalgic reference to the happy childhood his mother had enjoyed on these Silesian estates was probably unconvincing, as was his mention of the beauty of the flora and fauna and the enjoyment of guests from the world of industry on periodic hunting trips. More in line with the Nazi leadership's expectations were the assertions of the production capabilities of undivided, large-scale agricultural lands amidst preparations for war. That argument was likely to have been more responsible for keeping Darré's staff's settlement plans stored away in their desk drawers.[143]

Some historians have treated the settlement plans, which had many vocal advocates, as an indicator of the latent threat to which the Hohenzollerns were subject.[144] This may indeed have been one major aspect of the situation, but the fact that no Hohenzollern properties were ever confiscated and that the family's wealth did not grow smaller but rather significantly increased between 1933 and 1943 surely overshadow any hypothetical concerns. And, as far as we know, negotiations over specific tracts of land were focused on solutions members of the high nobility particularly loyal to Nazism had already reached with the regime.[145] Where wealth was concerned, those solutions massively favoured the 'heads of families', who were declared free, unencumbered owners after the dissolution of entailments, while their younger siblings were disadvantaged. The arrangement the Hohenzollerns' lawyers pushed through in November 1918 made the crown prince the sole owner of the family wealth a few days before the dissolution of entailments, and Wilhelm had to soothe the apparently considerable dismay of his younger brothers, who felt unfairly deprived.[146]

There was a long history of special conditions for aristocratic large landholders stretching back to the latter days of the Weimar Republic. Within the framework of what was known as the 'Eastern Aid' (*Osthilfe*), both the Hohenzollerns and the family of the ex-Kaiser's wife had profited from significant tax-free lines of credit.[147] The often dubious practice of handing out massive sums of financial aid to aristocratic large landowners, including the Hindenburgs, had led in 1932 and 1933 to the final major political scandal of the Weimar Republic.[148] Through the years, both contemporaries and some historians have argued that the need to hush up the controversy was an important motivation for naming Hitler Reich chancellor.[149] In January 1933, Count Harry Kessler wrote of a 'mixture of corruption, backroom dealings and nepotism reminiscent of the worst era of the absolutist monarchy'.[150] The day before Hitler's appointment, Theodor Wolff, one of the Weimar Republic's great pro-democracy journalists, spoke of the 'hungry ravens' circling ever closer to 'the old tower'. In Wolff's analysis, this was a case of the 'large East Prussian agricultural barons and their liaison officers, the high nobility and the upper ranks of the military' preparing the Hitler cabinet to advance their own material interests.[151] The scandal and the beginning of the Third Reich in January 1933 once again recalls the long series of arrangements that inspired individual Hohenzollerns to hope not only for a return to power, but also for material benefits under fascism. The Junker east of the Elbe also had a vested interest in ending the public outrage that had resulted from the 'Eastern assistance' scandal. But more important to them were the potential ways in which they could profit from Nazi policies of rearmament and militaristic-colonial conquest of land in the east. In this regard, the ex-Kaiser, his wife and several of his sons were among the huge parade of people, from all walks of life, who benefited or hoped to benefit from Nazi campaigns of pillage. But rather than speak generally, as historian Götz Aly does, about a Nazi dictatorship based on providing for Germans loyal to the regime,[152] it seems more useful to differentiate between various situations and interests. The materialistic calculations of large-scale aristocratic estate owners fundamentally diverged from those of miners, shop owners, saleswomen or university professors. Along with their long-term interest in a restoration of the throne, the Hohenzollerns shared the specific desires of the landed nobility as a whole.

While the Hohenzollerns were busy reaching arrangements to

secure their wealth, they were being pushed further away from the centres of actual political power. In his speech to the Reichstag in January 1939, Hitler dug unusually deeply into the arsenal of anti-aristocratic metaphors, contrasting the Nazi power of the new as an antipode to everything historically ossified and useless. It is impossible not to interpret one passage from the Nazi leader's address as a dig at the Hohenzollerns and the inheritance laws: 'I have no sympathy for the attempts by soon-to-be-extinct social classes to shield themselves from real life and thus preserve their existence by hiding behind a hedgerow of desiccated class laws that have nothing to do with reality. As long as this is just about them securing a peaceful cemetery to die in, I have no objections. But if they want to put up barriers to the progression of life, the storm of youth blowing forward will sweep away this ancient undergrowth before they know it.'[153]

Unused Counter-Charisma

Many historians have tried to associate the Hohenzollerns with the thinking of traditional German conservatives, including the military circles that actively resisted Hitler. But when Germany provoked the Second World War in September 1939, the male members of the royal family offered no opposition at all to that act of aggression. Instead, they were content to occupy lower positions of leadership in the Wehrmacht and were among those who most loudly applauded the Nazi's early military triumphs. All the way back in October 1934, the crown prince's son Hubertus had joined the military, and when Germany launched its aerial attack on Poland, Louis Ferdinand was a member of the Luftwaffe.[154] This was noted in the international press. *The New York Times* listed eight actively fighting Hohenzollern princes in September 1939, but the list was incomplete. In fact, 'all able-bodied Hohenzollern princes' had been drafted, and at the onset of hostilities thirteen family members were 'directly serving at the front'.[155] One newspaper report, in which Prince Oskar declared his family's loyalty to the regime after Georg Elser's attempted assassination of Hitler, named twenty-two Hohenzollerns at the front.[156]

Six weeks after the attack on Poland, the crown prince's eldest son, Wilhelm, reported that things were calm at the front with 'plenty of milk, eggs, butter and poultry'. The campaign had been 'instructive', he added, writing to an old friend with considerable experience of battle: 'Here in Poland, there is fighting again, but of a completely different sort than we learned.' Considering the extreme brutality of Germany's war in Poland,[157] it would have been interesting to learn more about the differences contained in this missive. A bit earlier on, Prince Wilhelm revealed: 'We are already mentally preparing ourselves for the west, where fundamentally different methods of fighting will have to be used.'[158]

Ironically, Wilhelm – the most military-minded of all the crown prince's sons – wouldn't survive the first two weeks of fighting in the west. On 23 May 1940, three days before Germany opened its major offensive, the 33-year-old was badly wounded in the Battle of Valenciennes just behind the Belgian border. The heroization of the prince that commenced immediately after his death included vivid, stylized descriptions of his end, evoking the fighting spirit, leadership, selflessness and sacrifice that were allegedly typical of Prussian military clans.[159] 'Tempestuously' First Lieutenant Wilhelm, the radiant idol of his company, led the charge, taking bullets to the lungs and stomach. But while lying wounded in the line of fire he maintained an overview and continued to give commands to his men, rescuing German victory and saving the lives of many comrades, before succumbing to his injuries the following day in a field hospital.[160]

Wilhelm's cousin Oskar, the son of the crown prince's brother of the same name, had already fallen while leading a company in Poland in mid-September 1939. But it was the death of Prince Wilhelm that would open a further gap between the Hohenzollerns and the Nazi regime.

The military funeral for the popular prince, who had caused a

nationwide stir in 1926 merely by appearing at Reichswehr manoeuvres, turned into the sort of event that didn't sit well with the Nazi
regime, and it continues to this day to be interpreted as evidence of
the royal family's opposition to Hitler.[161] On 29 May 1940, some
50,000 people turned out to form a guard of honour between Potsdam's Church of Peace and the Antique Temple in Sanssouci Park.[162]
As had also been the case with the 1921 funeral of the former
empress Augusta Victoria, the massive turnout could hardly be
interpreted as anything other than a public display of connection
with the royal family. But the funeral-goers didn't necessarily see
monarchy as a preferred alternative to the existing regime. Their
engagement was prompted by a charismatic officer who had fought
on the frontlines against Poland and France and whose 'hero's
death' came about as part of Germany's successful conquest of
Europe: France had been defeated, and the British military exped-
ition was surrounded near Dunkirk. The masses who turned out in
Potsdam most likely also wanted to mourn the first 50,000 young
Germans who had lost their lives in the Wehrmacht.

Thus, there was just as little reason to interpret the event as a
symbolic stand taken by conservativism against the Nazi regime as
there had been with the Day of Potsdam seven years previously.
Even the appearance of military grandees such as the omnipresent
Mackensen, wearing their old medals and imperial hussars' uniforms with fur caps and short tiger-skin coats, needs to be seen for
what it was. In 1935, Mackensen himself had accepted as an endow-
ment from Hitler his 1,250-hectare Brüssow estate and, a bit later, a
one-off payment of 350,000 Reichmarks. By 1940, one of his sons
was a decorated Wehrmacht lieutenant general, and another would
become an SS Gruppenführer.[163] 'As long as God grants me life, I
will remain loyal and grateful to Adolf Hitler, the leader and rescuer
of my German fatherland,' the 93-year-old field marshal would proclaim in late 1942. 'He is the German man I have looked for in my
fatherland since 1919.'[164]

Nonetheless, the Nazi leadership felt that a potential rival power
had shown its face in Potsdam. Hitler's reflexive aversion to anyone

who might in any sense be considered a successor and the great energy he invested in suppressing any forms of emotional or political affinity beyond the regime's control made further distance between the monarchy and the dictatorship inevitable. The Nazi regime had long desired clearer borders between the military leadership and the Hohenzollerns. For this reason, the crown prince's son had been denied a post as an active Wehrmacht officer, and Crown Prince Wilhelm's brother Oskar, who had been a regimental commander at the start of the war, was nominally promoted to major general and transferred to the reserves. Following the funeral for Prince Wilhelm, the regime issued the 'prince decree', which prohibited members of the former ruling family from being deployed in battle. The decree was enhanced in May 1943 when all members of the former 'ruling houses' were technically excluded from the Wehrmacht, although a few exceptions to the rule were allowed.

For Prince Hubertus and several other princes, this meant that the regulations concerning whether they could serve in the Wehrmacht varied up until 1944, although one grandson and the stepsons of the Kaiser were stationed on the Eastern Front in 1942.[165] The crown prince tried on multiple occasions, without success, to get family members back into the fighting forces. He also sought to secure permission for relatives from the House of Hessen to continue in combat roles – with a similar lack of success.[166] Such decrees saved a whole male generation of German princes, including some Hohenzollerns, from dying in battle. Conservatives by no means unanimously rejected these restrictions. A letter received by Princess Marie zu Ysenburg from her sister read:

We have also heard that there have been great losses among the high nobility. Your assumption concerning why the princes have been held back from the army seems plausible, but I hope there was a more humane reason. After all, we need the highest and most elevated classes in our people.[167]

After he was also discharged from the Wehrmacht, the crown

prince's son Hubertus lived as an 'agrarian' in the Wildenbruch estate in western Pomerania. Following the end of the war, he would emigrate to southwest Africa, where – together with his younger brother, who had married into money and reacquired former colonial lands – he would devote himself to raising Karakul sheep. He died in Windhoek in 1950.

The crown prince's youngest son, Friedrich, before and after 1945 the family's main connection with Britain, never fought in battle. The young man, who had studied at Cambridge and worked under a pseudonym for a London bank, was interned as a hostile foreigner while on a hunting trip to Scotland when the war started. Rumours that he had enlisted in the British armed forces quickly proved unfounded. As a British POW, partly in Canada, he dreamed of warm gloves and a farmer's life, and in one of his letters he asked for a copy of Erasmus of Rotterdam's *In Praise of Folly*.[168] His father, the crown prince, knew nothing of his whereabouts. In January 1941, Wilhelm wrote to his friend Geraldine Farrar: 'I wonder when we will see each other again? I do hope that this war may end soon, it is very sad that white people kill each other. From my son Fritzi I have no news.'[169]

The Hohenzollerns' exclusion from the Wehrmacht can be seen as part of a series of major and minor blows to what remained of the royal family's influence. A letter was written by none other than the general chief of staff and confidant to the crown prince, Count Friedrich von der Schulenburg, himself a former general from the old Brandenburg aristocracy, to a high-ranking military officer in March 1938. In it, Schulenburg, who joined the Nazi Party in 1930 and later became first a high-ranking SA leader on Röhm's staff, then an SS general, complained about the German princes being present at military rituals. These sentiments not only showed how significant the presence of Hohenzollerns in the officer corps was still considered, they were also a huge about-face. Although his feelings and opinions fluctuated over the years, the always cool-headed and keenly analytical Schulenburg had once placed great hopes in the crown prince as a potential leader and, as recently as 1929, he had also defended Wilhelm II against his many detractors.[170] But by 1938, SS General Schulenburg, a bearer of the Pour-le-Mérite, had given up any nostalgic monarchist hopes and also rejected any sort of military dictatorship. On the contrary, he claimed that the entire world envied Germany for the 'divine gift' of the Führer:

> Name me one general or admiral capable of replacing Hitler, who is backed by at least ninety per cent of the people. The unity of the German nation created for the first time in our history by Hitler can only be achieved by an extraordinary genius of his sort and cannot be transferred.

Therefore, Schulenburg demanded, princes and other members of dynastic families who were not committed Nazi Party members had to be excluded from rituals, manoeuvres, ceremonies and command posts. He also explicitly called for the crown prince and his brothers to be kept away from all military events. Otherwise, Schulenburg reasoned in another letter, there was a risk of officers being attracted to them, creating symbolic rival centres of power. Young aristocratic officers, in particular, might face a confusion of loyalties.[171]

What Schulenburg described was exactly the scenario the crown prince and his brothers could have tried to bring about shortly before and after the transferral of political authority to Hitler – had they been willing. Five years before the count's letter, during the transition of powers, the Hohenzollerns had in fact deployed their charisma – but for and not against the Nazi regime. Half a decade later, the same men who had formerly been coveted allies had become potentially disruptive figures the Nazis needed to isolate once and for all.

Although they had been marginalized by the regime, it took the Hohenzollerns years to realize that their dwindling chances for a share of power had now completely crumbled. The loss of their remaining symbolic capital proceeded far more swiftly than members of the royal family could comprehend. In December 1938, four years on from Dommes' unsuccessful attempt to challenge Darré to a duel, Wehrmacht commanding officers prohibited their men from celebrating the ex-Kaiser's eightieth birthday in any form, including speeches, toasts and congratulatory postcards. In the case of someone raising a glass to Wilhelm II in the officers' mess, those present were ordered to immediately leave the room and report the incident to their superiors.[172]

The period of the Nazis tactically taking care not to offend monarchist sensibilities was over. Whether former elite state functionaries were simply pushed aside or integrated into the new dictatorial apparatus depended on their ages and politics. In 1938, the Wilhelm II loyalist Dommes was over seventy and thus at the end of his career anyway. By contrast, General Wilhelm Keitel was only fifty-five when he issued the above-cited orders as the top commander of the Wehrmacht. The interval between Dommes dreaming of defending his lord and master's honour in a duel and Keitel's coolly issued command marked the collapse of the monarchist cloud cuckoo land, although not the end of the relationship between the Hohenzollerns and Nazism.

As they had during the Weimar Republic, the Hohenzollerns continued to send signals – a mixture of private criticism and public declarations of loyalty – from East Prussia, Potsdam and Doorn. The family was relatively enthusiastic about the military victories Germany achieved up until the summer of 1940, as it had been about the formation of the Hitler cabinet seven years prior. Notably, before these summer victories, the ex-Kaiser's wife in Doorn had enquired about the possibility of her husband returning to Germany to live a 'simple, withdrawn life' on a Hohenzollern estate in East Prussia, in case the war reached the Netherlands. Hitler answered in the affirmative.

With the opening of Germany's western offensive and its attack on the Netherlands in May 1940, Britain made an offer to take in Wilhelm II as well. Backed by George V, Churchill and his advisors considered using private channels to offer the ex-Kaiser the chance of resettling in England, promising he would be treated with 'consideration and dignity'. The plan was in fact communicated as a possibility. But Viscount Halifax, himself one of the leading British proponents of appeasement, found the idea absurd, characterizing Wilhelm II as an 'expansionist' and a Nazi sympathizer who was waiting for the throats of Germany's neighbours to be slit. 'I cannot for the life of me see why the old architect of evil should be allowed to come here,' Halifax objected.[173]

It's hard to know what to make of these rival offers other than as a competition between Nazi Germany and Britain. Wilhelm II living in exile in London would have been a powerful symbol, as would an ex-Kaiser supporting the Nazi regime from East Prussia. In June 1923, Wilhelm had presented Churchill's 23-year-old son with his already mentioned global strategy at a meeting in Arnheim am Rhein. It had envisioned Europe being led by a Germany that would ally itself with Japan, march to do battle with Bolshevism, 'subjugate' the Soviet Union and triumphantly celebrate the creation of a new world order at the Kremlin.[174]

But in May 1940, Wilhelm declined both offers to flee the war, telling the British he would rather shoot himself than go to England and let himself be photographed with Churchill.[175] His decision not to return to Germany evinces an uncharacteristic late moment of realism. To be king in waiting was at least to be a symbolically important figure with an aura of his own. Living out his days as an old man in Bad Homburg or transforming himself into party comrade Wilhelm II was tantamount to complete capitulation to Nazism and its political symbolism. This realization was probably something that stayed with the ex-Kaiser for the rest of his days.

Although his decision to remain in the Netherlands did carry a bit of symbolic significance, the former monarch did nothing to distance himself from the Nazi regime in May and June 1940. On the contrary, when a Wehrmacht unit showed up on the doorstep of Huis Doorn, the ex-Kaiser seemed as though he had been dipped in a fountain of youth. His personal physician described the scene in detail:

His Majesty stood, with his Iron Cross First Class pinned to his chest, beaming among the soldiers. He looked thirty years younger, happier and livelier than we had ever known him . . . He then invited everyone for breakfast with some fine coffee. A long table was set for the soldiers . . . Later a first lieutenant of the army fighting in the area arrived and delivered a very nice letter from the Führer, who offered the Kaiser the protection of the German Wehrmacht and asked whether there was anything he desired. In case he wanted to move elsewhere, he could choose the location. The Kaiser decided to remain in Doorn . . . Soldiers carrying hand grenades pressed forward . . . up to the private chamber of the Kaiser and wouldn't leave until the emperor and empress had shaken their hands. All of them wanted autographed pictures.

The ex-Kaiser had tears in his eyes and ordered 'champagne to be brought' for the evening. 'It's impossible to describe everything revitalizing.'[176] Hermine noted the 'great joy' the rejuvenated former Kaiser felt every time he saw another German soldier. The crown prince deemed Germany's triumphs 'beyond our wildest expectations', and Cecilie wrote from Potsdam to Doorn about 'how grateful and proud we can feel towards the army and the leadership'.[177] In lengthy eulogies, Hermine gushed over 'the genius of the Führer' and the 'glorious' times at hand and had swastika flags raised above her holdings in expectation of 'the final battle against the English'.[178] In June 1940, she told a friend: 'The Führer could not have done this any better or more beautifully.'[179]

The Nazi regime received regular telegrams of support from Doorn, Berlin and Oels, although after 1945, amidst Hohenzollern attempts to regain these properties, the family disputed that its members had written these messages. But we are not talking about an individual wayward telegram, rather a veritable flood of indisputably servile communication and correspondence. The assertive tone of the ex-Kaiser's 1932 letters to Hitler had disappeared completely from the missives he sent in 1933 directly to the Führer or the

Reich Chancellery. They were a mixture of supplication, subjugation and opportunism. It was the beginning of a ritual royal kowtowing to the Nazi leader at the end of every year and on Hitler's birthday.

Lammers as the head of the Chancellery answered such fawning messages from the royal family soberly, coolly and reservedly, and decisions were made carefully about which responses were to be sent to the crown prince or signed personally by Hitler. The crown prince addressed Hitler alternately as 'Mr Reich Chancellor' and 'My Führer' and usually wished the dictator 'God's blessings' and 'the strength to complete your work'. It was common for Wilhelm to express 'feelings of admiration', and his signoffs varied from the commonplace 'with friendly greetings' to 'I remain with particular respect' and even 'Sieg heil!'

On the twentieth day after Germany attacked Poland, the crown prince contacted his 'Führer' with a 'warm heart', telling him that every soldier's pulse was now beating faster and proclaiming how proud he was of the achievements of the Wehrmacht Hitler had created. In that message, the prince repeated his request that he and his sons be allowed to serve in the military, a wish that he had also communicated via the supreme commander of the army, Walther von Brauchitsch.[180] In June 1940, in what was probably his most obsequious telegram, the crown prince praised Hitler's 'genius leadership', which had secured victory in the west, invoked the 'final settling of accounts with perfidious Albion' and extended his hand 'as an old soldier and German full of admiration'. This telegram, which was signed with 'Sieg heil', was sent four weeks after the death of his son Wilhelm.[181] The ex-Kaiser's congratulatory telegrams to Hitler also told of him greeting Germany's victory in Poland with a 'warm heart' and stressed that nine Hohenzollern princes were serving at the front. The former monarch also called Germany's triumph over France 'God-ordained', expressing his personal gratitude to Hitler and his hope for 'peace'.[182]

The linguistic gymnastics performed in the responses authored by the former monarchist Lammers, who by 1940 held the rank of an SS Obergruppenführer, had an equivalent in the other direction. Neither side seemed to be on solid ground in terms of etiquette. Submission, sycophancy and uncertainty about how to translate old hierarchies into a form compatible with the 'ethnic community of the German people' took a toll on the German language itself. Formulas of greeting became a confusing mix of the old and the new. For example, in a letter of April 1939, Cecilie wrote to Göring with birthday congratulations she asked the recipient to pass on personally to the Führer. Hitler's petty bourgeois personal assistant responded that it 'was an honour' to acknowledge receipt of the flowers the crown princess had sent. His message ended, 'With a Heil Hitler I have the honour of being Your Imperial Majesty's most reverentially submissive [Willy Meerwald]'.[183]

It's tempting to see the flood of telegrams as rituals of submission intended to shore up what remained of the Hohenzollerns' former position, but that doesn't mean their authors didn't sometimes genuinely feel that way. In June 1941, two days after his father's death and shortly before Germany invaded the Soviet Union, the crown prince sent a telegram to Göring, telling him: '[My father] died in the conviction that the fierce battle for Germany's honour, rights and freedom by the Wehrmacht under its brilliant leadership will bring a final German victory. Please express my gratitude to your dear wife as well. Your Wilhelm.'[184]

Don't Put Up Any Resistance: The Hohenzollerns and 20 July

The failed assassination attempt on Hitler of 20 July 1944, which would later play such a fundamental role in creating the national narrative of the Federal Republic of Germany, marked the final break between the Hohenzollerns and the Nazi regime. Even at the time it was seen as the point at which the conflict between the Nazi dictatorship and the 'conservative resistance' became impossible to ignore. There are two important aspects here. The first is that the assassination attempt was led by military and state functionaries from the old elite, including a conspicuous number of aristocrats, whose determination and courage was most prominently personified by the charismatic Colonel Count Claus Schenk von Stauffenberg. The second is the notion that 20 July was the work not just of a tiny clique but represented practically all segments and groups of the populace, although it was launched by ranking, often aristocratic, officers, diplomats and statesmen. Just as some historians see a military dictatorship under Schleicher as the sole alternative to a Hitler government, others regard the Wehrmacht officers and civil servants, who were often integral components of the dictatorial Nazi apparatus, as the only realistic chance to destroy the regime from within. In this view, during both the beginning and the end of the Third Reich, the anti-democratic, non-Nazi Right was necessarily the core of any realistic resistance. For obvious reasons, this interpretation of history remains immensely significant for conservative politics in Germany today.

Hitler himself spoke immediately after the assassination attempt of 'one of the vons' trying to take his life, saying that before long the crown prince would be revealed as having been behind it.[185] Three weeks after the failed assassination, the *Völkischer Beobachter* ran a lengthy article full of anti-aristocratic resentment about how the 'final hour of the reaction was now at hand'.[186] The author raged against the 'clique of conspirators' that had consisted of 'degenerate bearers of noble names' or, as the Reich Nazi Party director Robert Ley put it, 'blue-blooded swine'. This is one of the standard phrases cited by historians when they want to emphasize how obvious the gulf became between the criminal Nazi leadership and the aristocratic elites who were prominent members of the anti-Hitler opposition.[187]

As impressive as quotes like this may appear, many of those who were part of the coup attempt, aristocratic or not, had supported the Nazi state in 1933, and most of the conspirators had occupied leadership positions within the Nazi machinery of dictatorship and violence and had served the cause of the Nazi regime doing far more damage on its behalf between 1933 and the first years of the war than they were able to do to it in the summer of 1944. Moreover, the vast majority of Germans with the word 'von' before their last names had no desire to see Hitler dead. On the contrary, after the assassination attempt, the chairman of the German Aristocrats Society made a speech assuring the regime of the nobility's loyalty and claimed that the conspirators were pariahs from the aristocracy just as they were from the populace at large. Even after the attempt on Hitler's life, there was no definitive break between the nobility and the Nazi state. That August, Count Albrecht von der Schulenburg, whose brother Fritz-Dietlof was a former Nazi and later had become one of the leading planners of the assassination plot, wrote to Himmler, pointing out in detail the heroic actions of his other brothers, who had fallen on various battlefields. Concerning Fritz-Dietlof, 'a person who used to be my brother', Schulenburg emphasized 'the shame a scoundrel has brought upon us and the legacy of his father and his dead brothers during the most infernal act in German history'. Himmler's response was very cordial, stressing the honourable memory of the Schulenburg family and its patriarch. He even invited Albrecht, who had fallen sick, to recover from his illness in the SS sanatorium in Karlsbad (today: Karlovy Vary).[188]

As soon became clear, the crown prince had nothing at all to do with the planning or execution of the would-be coup. It is thus astonishing how generations of Hohenzollerns have succeeded in suggesting that their ancestors somehow 'had connections' with the anti-Nazi resistance – a myth based on nothing more than a handful of conversations and the personal acquaintances of members of the royal family with individuals genuinely connected with the attempted assassination. This myth still attracts believers today. For example, in July 2019, a Hohenzollern lawyer expressed regret that 'unfortunately in the public debate it's often forgotten that the family also had contact with the resistance'. The lawyer also falsely claimed that the resistance had 'chosen Crown Prince William as the head of state' of a post-Hitler Germany.[189] Several years before those statements, the current 'head of the house', Prince Georg Friedrich of Prussia, made similar assertions in an interview, proposing that Louis Ferdinand and the crown prince 'maintained close contact with the resistance right from the start with the clear aim of restoring the monarchy in Germany'. In the summer of 2021, Georg Friedrich repeated the claim that his grandfather Crown Prince Wilhelm had taken part in the resistance, risking the lives of his family and himself.[190] As of this writing, no empirical evidence for these tenuous assertions has ever been presented.[191]

The preferred Hohenzollern version of the past sees Louis Ferdinand's alleged participation in the resistance movement as the final chapter in, and the last word on, the family's relationship with Nazism, while questioning 'whether it might not have been the assassination attempt itself that caused Hitler to go uncontrollably amok'.[192] The notion is as fanciful as the cavalier assertions about the 'family's role in the resistance' proclaimed on several major public occasions.[193] Tellingly, Hohenzollern apologists over the past decade have never seriously tried to establish the idea or build their arguments around it – with good reason. No proof has been found for such a connection beyond isolated conversations, known since the 1950s, between Louis Ferdinand and genuine members of the resistance, which have been handed down mainly through his and his friends' own accounts. But there is no indication that the Hohenzollerns, and especially Crown Prince Wilhelm, ever played any active role in the anti-Nazi movement.

Even the most imaginative storytellers from the circles of the military resistance to Hitler never mentioned the crown prince and his family.[194] The prominent 1946 account of the German lawyer, former reserve officer and resistance member Fabian von Schlabrendorff, one of the major historical sources concerning conservative anti-Nazism, contains no mention of the Hohenzollerns doing anything to further the assassination attempt or being envisioned as supplying a future head of state.[195] Nor do any of the most recent analyses of resistance networks,[196] evaluations commissioned by the family itself, the German Resistance Memorial Centre in Berlin[197] or the latest works of history.[198] A form of resistance so covert that no trace of it could be uncovered by expert researchers over seven decades would require a radical redefinition of what historians can consider resistance in the first place. There is no simple way to describe the shifting terrain of collaboration, submission, imagined threat and real pressure upon which the royal family operated as of 1934. There were limits to the common ground between the Hohenzollerns and the regime and its rules, as was the case with the other princely families and the low nobility. Nonetheless, to a greater extent than with other aristocratic lineages, the traditions and values attached to the name of 'Prussia' could have been a source of opposition to the regime's hunger for absolute power. While this situation generated constant tension between the regime and the royal family, on no occasion did it result in any acts of resistance.

Klaus W. Jonas's 1961 biography *Crown Prince Wilhelm*, which was praised by such formerly powerful anti-democratic figures as Papen and DNVP grandee Baron Magnus von Braun,[199] established what remains one of the most important narratives about the ex heir to the throne. In it, Jonas claimed that in 1944 the 'enmity' of the Gestapo turned against the House of Hohenzollern, with the secret police's 'hatred' increasing against the crown prince in particular.[200] Historians, however, are all too familiar with the methods used by the Gestapo against opponents of the Nazi regime and others who incurred their ire.[201] As a rule, the secret police didn't keep individuals under observation without taking action against them. The conversation Louis Ferdinand had after the assassination attempt with two Gestapo officers in the salon of his East Prussian estate, under the watchful eyes of an oil portrait of Kaiser Wilhelm in his field marshal's uniform, bore no comparison with the threats of violence and persecution the secret police used when interrogating those thought to be potential enemies. On the contrary, more than once the prince described how he had drunk wine and smoked cigars with the pair of Gestapo officers, from modest social backgrounds, who chatted with his wife about the weather, addressed him as their 'Royal Majesty' and left his estate, hours later, 'in high spirits'.[202]

The Hohenzollerns remained entirely untouched by the waves

of arrests after the assassination attempt, known as both 'Aktion Gitter' and 'Aktion Gewitter', which saw some 5,000 people land in prisons or concentration camps.[203] Louis Ferdinand later stressed his gratitude to his friends among the conspirators that they had not revealed his name, even under torture, and had saved his life with their 'loyalty until death'.[204] In 1965, the Jewish-Dutch businessman, collector and Holocaust survivor Maurice Frankenhuis, who had lived through Theresienstadt, interviewed Louis Ferdinand in New York. Frankenhuis knew an astonishing amount about the political arrangements the House of Hohenzollern had concluded with the Nazis and repeatedly asked the prince why it had not been possible to gun Hitler down from close range. No one had been able to get a weapon anywhere near Hitler, the prince always answered. So how come Stauffenberg had succeeded in bringing a bomb in a briefcase to a meeting with the Führer, Frankenhuis wanted to know. Ask Fabian von Schlabrendorff was Louis Ferdinand's answer.[205]

There is evidence that the right-wing, anti-Semitic fringe of the resistance led by the lawyers Johannes Popitz and Carl Goerdeler did consult about the future form of the German state and considered establishing a monarchy and contacting Louis Ferdinand. It is also a matter of historical record that the prince had several conservations with individual members of the conservative resistance. Popitz and Goerdeler occupied high offices within the Nazi state, and Popitz was a supporter of Carl Schmitt's anti-democratic ideas.[206] The diplomat Ulrich von Hassell, who was seen as a potential new German foreign minister by both the 1920 Kapp Putsch and the Stauffenberg conspiracy, was also among the minority of older conspirators still prepared to think in monarchist terms. But the speculations of individual plotters in 1942 about a possible restoration were just as vague as they had been a decade before in the waning days of the Weimar Republic. And, by the time the assassination attempt was made in July 1944, the nebulous notions of a Hohenzollern leading the new Germany had long been discarded.

The fact that Louis Ferdinand had talked on various occasions to members of the resistance who approached him was the result his friendship with the lawyer Otto John.[207] The two men knew one another from their mutual time with Lufthansa, where Louis Ferdinand had worked after his discharge from the Luftwaffe as a kind of *maître de plaisir* and go-between with foreign contacts. John, who managed to avoid arrest after the failed assassination, later became the scandal-plagued first president of the Office for the Protection of the Constitution in democratic West Germany. His memoirs are one of the main sources cited to back up the notion of Louis Ferdinand's 'resistance' during the Third Reich.[208]

Other connections require further analysis. For instance, after the Second World War, Louis Ferdinand stressed his contacts with Field Marshal General Georg von Küchler, who had been stripped of his command the previous January after disagreements with Hitler and whom the prince had visited on 20 July 1944, as the assassination plot was being carried out. But Louis Ferdinand neglected to mention that Küchler had taken a particularly hard line in the 'final resolution of the ethnic battle' in Poland in 1940, had supported the 1941 order that all Soviet commissars were to be executed after the start of Operation Barbarossa, had commanded the shock troops who had murdered the seriously ill in Nazi-occupied Europe and had been sentenced to twenty years' imprisonment for war crimes at the Nuremberg Trials in April 1949. In the edited 1968 version of Louis Ferdinand's memoirs, the general was only described as 'a Prussian officer of the best old type'.[209] In this and other cases, there is more to the story of the Hohenzollerns' relationships with ranking Wehrmacht officers than just their purported or actual attitudes on the afternoon of 20 July 1944.

There are simple explanations for the few 'connections' the Hohenzollerns did have to the core of the conspiracy. Planned coup d'états always entail the question of who should replace the deposed leader, and it was logical that, as part of the attempts on the part of the conservative resistance to identify a successor who could match the Führer's charisma, the right wing of the resistance and those members from the crown prince's generation would consider various Hohenzollern princes. As had been the case in the 1920s, when a restoration was completely off the agenda, several candidates of various ages were mooted in the most general way, without any hint of a consensus. The search for a pretender was no easier towards the end of the Second World War than it had been in 1932. Once again, in violation of all principles of legitimism, monarchists compared individuals of various lineages and generations as though they were items in a supermarket. But by the 1940s, the selection on offer was considerably reduced, and there was significant antipathy towards the crown prince, particular among younger officers. While Stauffenberg, his brothers and most of the youthful officers in the anti-Hitler Kreisau Circle were without doubt aristocratic elitists, they had little romantic attachment to Hohenzollern kings.[210] So it came to be that a minority of the older conspirators with monarchist tendencies focused on Louis Ferdinand as the member of the royal family who could hypothetically serve as a figurehead for the coup. His non-military manner, excellent connections with the US and close contacts with Henry Ford and Roosevelt – as well as his younger brother's connections with Britain and the generally positive English and American perception of him, spoke in favour of the 36-year-old Junker in 1944.[211] But any contacts between 1941 and 1943 were no more than gently exploratory conversations. The attitudes of the youngest and most active part of the resistance towards the Hohenzollerns ran from antipathy to extreme, fundamental antipathy.[212] By the time of the assassination attempt itself, none of the conspirators seriously considered involving the royal family in any way.

It is no great surprise that for a time older conspirators, long-standing opponents of democracy who retained their monarchist sensibilities, were open to the idea of calling upon the Hohenzollerns.[213] After all, a long European tradition existed of monarchs-in-waiting representing potential opposition camps to existing regimes, and the toppling of Mussolini in the summer of 1943 provided an obvious model for mobilizing a monarchy against a dictatorship. One member of the conservative resistance even drafted an impressive-sounding post-coup proclamation of a Hohenzollern prince as king. But this document was neither written nor endorsed by any Hohenzollern family member.[214] A part of the resistance may have initially courted the favour of the Hohenzollerns and pondered various possibilities, but conversely no Hohenzollern ever approached the resistance or offered any options. It was standard practice for generations for the royal family to maintain close relations with the officer corps, whose ranks included men, bourgeois and especially aristocratic, who played more or less leading roles in the coup plans. But this was an expression of the Hohenzollerns' closeness to the army, not to the conspiracy. The friendship between the crown prince and the military leader of the would-be coup, Ludwig Beck, went much further back than 1944, stemming from their mutual interest in undermining the Weimar Republic. By the time of the assassination plot, the two men were no longer in contact, and Beck rejected the idea of the Crown Prince Wilhelm playing any sort of leading political role.

When examined closely, little remains of the crown prince and the other Hohenzollerns' 'connections' with the resistance other than the fact that the royal family was considered, then rejected, for a symbolic, representative role at an early certain stage in the planning of the would-be coup. As had been the case with the vague speculations for a restoration in 1932, overpowering structural factors doomed all notions of enlisting the Hohenzollerns' help against Hitler twelve years later. And, just as in 1932, one of those factors was the inability of even the monarchist segment of the anti-Hitler opposition to agree on a suitable royal alternative. The type and content of the conversations[215] carefully initiated by some members of the resistance give an impression, as one historian put it, of 'how deeply many "decent" and "respectable" conservatives were implicated in the Nazi debacle from the start'.[216]

The most precise analysis of the contacts between the royal family and the opposition remains the 1954 book by the respected conservative historian Gerhard Ritter, himself a friend of Goerdeler with a variety of connections to the resistance.[217] Drawing on both original source material and personal knowledge, Ritter wrote about, among other things, two conversations held in the house of resistance theologian Dietrich Bonhoeffer about potential roles for the Hohenzollerns in the opposition to Hitler.[218] In these talks, Louis Ferdinand held open the prospect of participating in the resistance as a 'private citizen' but rejected all of the major symbolic roles put forward. What's more, the prince said that he would have to ask his father, Crown Prince Wilhelm, for his blessing before engaging in any activity. Ritter wrote: 'There was no doubt among anyone who knew the crown prince what his attitude would be. He immediately rejected the idea. And warned his son urgently and successfully against any further contact with such conspiracies. With that, the prince's political role was terminated for ever.'[219] The crown prince, who was by then the 'head of the house', not only avoided, but actively obstructed any family members who could have had any genuinely conceivable connection to the opposition. For thirty years, Louis Ferdinand repeated the contents of his father's warning, which within the internal codes of Hohenzollern family discourse amounted to a prohibition on any oppositional activity, and the prince's account has been confirmed independently.[220] 'Thus my mission ended,' he commented in a 1952 retelling for American readers, adding that both of his parents had disapproved of his lack of faith in Germany's ultimate victory – and implied that he had been on some sort of 'mission' for the German resistance.[221]

Louis Ferdinand repeatedly stressed that he would never defy his father's or grandfather's wishes. His father ordered him not to participate in the opposition, just as the ex-Kaiser had forbidden Crown Prince Wilhelm himself from pursuing a candidacy for Reich president in March 1932. But, perhaps more significantly, none of the three royal generations produced a rival to Hitler of sufficient conviction to be of any real use to the coup. Measured against Hohenzollern standards, it was indeed remarkable that Louis Ferdinand engaged in any talks, however general and exploratory, and it seems likely that there was a certain distance – albeit one difficult to determine – between him and the Nazi regime in 1943. However, Louis Ferdinand was not a member of the anti-Hitler resistance. Hohenzollern princes rising up against the regime are figments of the imagination.

Considering how brutally the Nazi regime dealt with any sort of opposition, it is also telling that it never harmed a hair on the head of any Hohenzollern. Agents of the state would have had a relatively easy time disappropriating, exiling, arresting or murdering the entire royal family, had Hitler and his henchmen so desired. The orgies of violence during the Night of the Long Knives and the summer of 1934 had shown how much brutality German elites would tolerate even against individuals from their own ranks. It is an open question whether a comparable campaign against the Hohenzollerns would have provoked resistance from large estate owners, army commanders, diplomats and senior civil servants. In any case, the Nazi leadership didn't seem to have considered any such measures necessary. The regime succeeded with far less force in defusing the potential symbolic influence of the royal family. But that doesn't mean the Nazis underestimated that influence. On the contrary, the regime continued to try to enlist the Hohenzollerns wherever possible, whether by offering the ex-Kaiser the right to return to Germany, by suggesting that he be buried in Potsdam or by sending a gigantic wreath in lieu of an unwanted official delegation to his funeral in Doorn.

Summary: Resistance Resisted

Even totalitarian rule is never total. Just as the regime attacked but could never fully destroy the social codes and values of German Catholics and the German working classes, traditional conservative remnants, niches and alternatives persisted. At least in Protestant Prussia, the Hohenzollerns remained one of the most powerful symbols of a world gone by. The royal family's traditionally strong connections with the military leadership linked the Hohenzollerns with sources of power that could potentially have been turned against the regime – and that in fact were in the summer of 1944.

Gerhard Ritter – an officer in the First World War, an adherent of the DNVP in the Weimar Republic and a supporter of the conservative resistance in the Third Reich – took this line of thinking even further, developing a counterfactual argument that had a lot more to do with reality than any notions of purported 'connections' between the Hohenzollerns and the conservative opposition. 'A Hohenzollern prince who had possessed the enormous courage needed to lead the German resistance', he wrote, 'would have changed the historical situation of the monarchy in Germany in one fell swoop.'[222] Several top international political leaders had seen the situation much the same way. After 1945, none other than Winston Churchill proposed that Hitler would never have come to power had a grandson of the Kaiser occupied the throne.[223] Ten years on from the failed assassination of Hitler, Ritter perfectly summed up the Hohenzollerns' theoretically huge potential. The significance of the German royal family between 1918 and 1945 resided not just in what it did but what it didn't do.

The Hohenzollerns' hostile rejection of the first German democracy is one aspect of their legacy, and their non-participation in the resistance, which was in desperate need of charismatic figures, was another. The royal family could have helped fill that need. Over the past ten years, lawyers for the Hohenzollerns have often questioned whether the family's support had any effect on the Nazi regime. If we pose the same question about the German princes and the anti-Hitler resistance, the only answer is: they had virtually no effect at all. This applies to both Crown Prince Wilhelm and his son Louis Ferdinand. Moreover, not only was Wilhelm *not* a member of the resistance: he did his best to obstruct it, both passively and actively.

There was no way that millions of Germans would simply forget their desires for a king-in-waiting, a role which the crown prince spent so much energy trying to stylize himself for during the Weimar Republic. This mythical figure constantly resonated in the background within the tensions, imagined or not, between the regime and the royal family. Whether individual Hohenzollerns in fact signalled their dissent was less important than the expectations of huge numbers of people that the House of Hohenzollern would represent an alternative to Nazism. Both domestic and international observers continued to believe that the symbolic force of the former German royal family, which the regime was at pains to co-opt at the Day of Potsdam in 1933, could have done something to undermine the new fascist order. Charisma is a source of power that derives its energy less from the sender than the recipients. It is telling that after 20 July 1944 – just as after the Röhm murders, the Blomberg-Fritsch crisis,[224] the attempted Hitler assassination by Georg Elser and the funeral of the crown prince's son – the Nazi surveillance apparatus, the international media and a segment of the German populace initially suspected the crown prince and members of his family of secretly pulling the strings.

Domestic and international observers repeatedly expected that the Hohenzollerns might lead a conservative opposition against the regime, but they were invariably disappointed. The 'vons' weren't generally opposed to Hitler, not one member of the royal family was initiated into Stauffenberg's plot, and the crown prince was never taken away and beheaded, as one French media fantasy had it after the Elser assassination attempt in 1939.[225] The carpenter Elser turned out to have acted alone, but for a time there was no end to speculations about a monarchist coup. Himmler, it was said, was readying a severe blow against a 'gigantic' monarchist plot. Meanwhile the Gestapo were searching the Hohenzollerns' villas, Louis Ferdinand was kept under close surveillance, and monarchist generals in the army leadership were being detained.[226] This shows that the Hohenzollerns' counter-charisma did in fact possess real potential.

The regime quickly denied that anyone in the royal family had been beheaded, arrested or interrogated, and August Wilhelm issued a declaration of loyalty in the name of his family and the German princes in general.[227] The international press and German exile newspapers passed on this statement and others by August Wilhelm's brother, the crown prince.[228] And the allegedly rebellious generals became the architects, eighteen months later, of Germany's attack on the Soviet Union. The expectations of a Hohenzollern-led line of opposition remained a fantasy. The family consistently used what influence it had to further its own interests rather than to counter the Nazi regime. Nonetheless, the myth of the Hohenzollerns' role in the opposition and resistance to the Nazis didn't end within the Third Reich. It continued – and continues to this day.

6.

Tragedy and Farce: The Hohenzollerns and Post-War Germany

The Hohenzollerns did eventually establish close – indeed impressive – contacts with the conservative resistance to Hitler. But this only happened after the Second World War and the Third Reich had ended. In 1946, General Wilhelm von Dommes, who had done so much to advance the family's material interests and to shape their arrangements with National Socialism, stepped down as the family's administrative director. The general, whom one observer described as behaving with 'positively repulsive, insinuating syco-phancy' and as a true 'creature of court'[1] – continued as a consultant for a time but was replaced by a figure of considerable stature. Count Carl-Hans von Hardenberg, the man who took over manag-ing the Hohenzollerns' financial affairs, was a former officer and large estate owner from Brandenburg who had been close to the DNVP and the German Gentlemen's Club before 1933 and had later joined the conservative resistance and survived the Third Reich, despite two suicide attempts while a prisoner in the Sachsenhausen concentration camp. Hardenberg was one of the most impressive resistance figures and among the most important historical and pol-itical heirs to the legacy of 20 July 1944.

The connection between Hardenberg and the Hohenzollerns had nothing to do with the resistance to Hitler. The two sides had contact via traditional institutions such as the elite First Infantry Guard Regiment in Potsdam. Neuhardenberg Castle had been one of the leading meeting points for the conservative aristocrats in the region in the 1920s, and the lord of the manor came from one of most renowned Brandenburg noble families.[2]

Moreover, Hardenberg wasn't the only former member of the

military resistance to enter the Hohenzollerns' service. In 1946, he was joined by lawyer and former officer Fabian von Schlabrendorff. Schlabrendorff was a Doctor of Law who after 1945 went from being part of the innermost circles of the resistance to consulting the Allied secret services and filtering the future officer corps of the Bundeswehr, the democratic post-war German armed forces. He was appointed a judge in the second senate of the Federal Constitutional Court and also served as one of the Hohenzollerns' post-war advisors. Schlabrendorff also represented the former SA Obergruppenführer Landgrave Philipp von Hessen at the latter's de-Nazification hearing.[3] Moreover, Schlabrendorff was also a leading proponent of the myth that conservative elites had opposed Nazism early on and with great vigour and determination. It was down to men like him that this narrative was popularized and firmly anchored during the early days of the Federal Republic.[4]

In Schlabrendorff's idiosyncratic reading of history, even top figures on the extreme Right could appear as pioneers of parliamentary democracy and likeably eccentric opponents of Hitler. Schlabrendorff's bestseller *Offiziere gegen Hitler* (Officers Against Hitler) was a mixture of authentic details from the past and narrative fancy. Few of the surviving military men from the German resistance were able to write as vividly – and with such vivid imagination.[5] The following story is typical. Amidst an interrogation during the Third Reich, a Gestapo commissar told Schlabrendorff, who would be brutally tortured shortly thereafter, why the Nazi state considered him suspicious. He was a Christian, a lawyer, an officer and a 'member of the nobility, i.e., part of a clique that was in some respects a natural enemy of Hitler and Nazism'.[6] This view of the German resistance, lent moral authority because Schlabrendorff had been tortured, was very memorable, if not particularly nuanced.

The recollections of Schlabrendorff, who was also closely connected to the Bismarck family, had a significance far beyond his undeniably meaningful involvement in the plot to assassinate Hitler. Within the community of aristocratic authors and in the flourishing genre of 'noble narratives' after 1945,[7] Schlabrendorff was topped only by the West German cultural icon Countess Marion Dönhoff.[8] In this genre, the high-born passed on oral narratives of aristocratic resistance like latter-day Homeric epics, featuring beautiful countesses, swashbuckling cavalrymen, rustling oak trees, impossibly clever sidekicks and visitors from all over the world travelling to majestic castles, posing in tweed outfits before splendid décor, talking in finely hewn sentences and recognizing the Nazis from the first second on as the greatest source of evil on earth. Such were the heroes and heralds of the didactic conservative literature so popular after 1945.[9] Meanwhile, Schlabrendorff and Hardenberg became the most influential intellectual and strategic organizers of the small circle trying to defend what was left of the Hohenzollerns' family holdings and reputation. The royal family needed to be adapted to fit into the nascent Federal Republic in terms of both its past and its future. That meant a new family narrative of the first half of the twentieth century after the historical caesura of 1945 and a new representative role designed and built atop the ruins of the past. The bonds that gave the family a measure of cohesion during the Weimar Republic and the Third Reich were gone. No one disputed the need to completely remake the Hohenzollerns. In today's advertising terminology, we would call this 'rebranding'.[10]

Hardenberg was an extremely energetic fellow, two metres tall, who had been badly wounded in the First World War and enjoyed an excellent reputation among his fellow officers.[11] In 1951, in conjunction with his activity as a Hohenzollern advisor, he began considering the need for a biography of Wilhelm II, who by then had been dead for a decade. The first attempts to compose such a work by a former guards officer, Joachim von Kürenberg, had appeared in a small Bonn publishing house under the title *Was Everything Wrong?* and didn't pass muster with the Hohenzollerns' advisory staff.[12] In 1946, Dommes had had material collected for potential use by the Pulitzer-Prize-winning author Louis Paul Lochner, presumably with an eye towards influencing American public opinion in favour of the German royal family.[13]

Hardenberg was charged with dealing with the royal family's

historical legacy, and he was under no illusions about the difficulties of presenting Germany's final Kaiser in a positive light. 'Without doubt', he conceded, 'it would be most welcome if a book about His Royal Majesty's person were to be written by a truly good historian.' Hardenberg recognized the importance of Wilhelm II, who was not yet completely defined as a historical figure, for the reputation of the Hohenzollerns and any remaining chances for monarchism in the future. And the former estate owner had a specific historian in mind. Just as three decades previously the royal family had searched for pro-democracy lawyers and historians to depict Crown Prince Wilhelm in a positive light, Hardenberg came up with a surprise solution for polishing the Kaiser's image: Anton Ritthaler, a Bavarian historian who had been a member of the DNVP and frequented Bavarian monarchist circles during the Second World War and who was now living in modest circumstances in Munich. Hardenberg promised Ritthaler access to interviews with suitable individuals from Wilhelm II's closest circles, the chance to travel to do research, a two-year timescale and a budget of 10,000 deutschmarks.[14] But, instead of a comprehensive biography, the project only yielded a slim account of Wilhelm II's life, followed years later by further works composed by the author in his function as Hohenzollern family archivist.[15]

The Hohenzollern family narrative thus remained a work very much in progress after 1945. This chapter will look at some of the main protagonists and examine the leitmotifs and methods of this process, which remains unfinished to this very day.

Resurrected from the Ruins: The Hohenzollerns and the End of the War

On the night of 14 April 1945, some 490 RAF warplanes reduced much of Potsdam to rubble. Twelve days afterwards, advance Soviet battalions crossed the Jungfernsee lake and occupied Cecilienhof, where a short time later a group of Russian officers and soldiers discovered the crown prince's safe. Since the servants at the estate had no idea where the key was, the Russians tried to use sabres from Crown Prince Wilhelm's valuable collection to pry open the door. The sabres were no match, however, for the massive steel door, and the safe would remain closed until a local plumber forced it open with a blowtorch in 1948. The roof of Cecilienhof itself had taken several hits, but the bombs had failed to explode, meaning that the estate survived more or less intact.

The crown prince had left Germany proper for Austria on 3 January 1945, taking with him, among other valuables, 30 of the 280 diamonds in his possession 'for his personal use', although leaving behind in the safe several neckties, some decorated with gemstones. The destruction of Potsdam, the occupation of the crown prince's estate and the threat of the former heir to the throne being disappropriated symbolized both the end of one current in history and the start of new tributaries that still flow today.[16]

With Germany's military defeat in 1945, the Red Army's often pitiless, brutal and sometimes even homicidal treatment of members of the nobility in the east and the communist seizure of property in the Soviet-occupied zone, the Hohenzollerns and many other aristocratic families lost the material basis of the power they had enjoyed for centuries.[17] In the communist interpretation of history, 'the Junkers' had been a main pillar of the Nazi regime. Thus, the Soviet occupiers and later the communist regime of the German Democratic Republic (GDR), or East Germany, made confiscating the property of the landed aristocracy a top priority.

More than 95 per cent of the Hohenzollerns' property in what was now the Soviet occupation zone, Poland and parts of the Soviet Union was confiscated. Amidst all the catastrophic destruction, media interest in the German royal family dwindled to a fraction of what it had been. If we forget for a moment the fate of those groups upon which the Nazi regime had trained its destructive energy, the decline in the House of Hohenzollern's fortunes was indeed dramatic. Compared to the family's situation in 1924 or 1926, its former basis of power lay in a heap of rubble. In 1945, at the request of the crown prince and despite the desolate conditions, Dommes as the 'head of general administration' had tried from Berlin to improvise on the family's behalf and mobilize the help of his friends from the old guard, including radical right-wing agitator Heinrich Class. But in the end Dommes withdrew to his brother's estate in the British-occupied north-west of Germany. In a 1948 letter to Sigurd von Ilsemann, he described his situation in drastic images: 'We come not as humble beggars but as men fighting for their rights against ghouls who are trying to rip away the final scraps of corpses lying on the ground.'[18]

After Germany's defeat, little remained of the pillars, foundations and forms of the House of Hohenzollern. The ex-Kaiser had been interred in a Dutch mausoleum for four years, and his wife, 'Empress' Hermine, lived under Russian military surveillance in a villa in Frankfurt an der Oder, where she died in 1947, surrounded by rumours of pilfered jewels and how she had allegedly been poisoned.[19] Shortly before her death she had given lengthy interviews in which she discussed how she had suffered during the Third Reich, how her family had always opposed Nazism and how terrified Hitler had been of the ex-Kaiser.[20]

On 3 May 1945, Crown Prince Wilhelm was arrested in a small Austrian town after returning from his hunting cabin. An aristocratic French officer recognized him from various international horse-racing events and took him into custody. French newspapers reported that, although the crown prince had been believed dead for a year, he was in fact alive and was now interned in the French occupation zone.[21] In France, he was considered one of the 'premium prisoners', together with those Nazi leaders captured by the First French Army,[22] while Austrian newspapers reported on his arrest as part of the 'ignominious end of the Nazi chieftains'.[23]

Echoing his self-portrayals from 1922, Wilhelm declared in an interview with a French women's magazine that he was nothing more than a simple civilian who wanted to go home. People in Germany were quick to forget, the journalist shot back.[24] By the end of May 1945, the crown prince was already granting interviews and photo

requests for French media from the relative comfort of his confine-
ment in a hotel in the town of Lindau on Lake Constance. French
outlets published page-long pieces on the prince, sporting a white
shirt and holding forth, relaxed and smiling, on world politics. He had
seen the maelstrom coming right from the start, he told journalists.
He had always considered Hitler a 'lunatic blowhard' whom he had
been able to silence with a single resolute thump of his fist on a table.
He had nothing to do with the Third Reich or the Second World War,
he claimed, whereupon journalists composed sarcastic headlines
saying that the Second World War had ended for Wilhelm at the
Battle of Verdun. (The battle of course took place during the *First*
World War.) It was with considerable bewilderment that reporters
registered the crown prince's 'retrospective pacifism'.[25]

Two months following the end of the Second World War, he
posed for photographs as an enviably slim older gentleman, 'with a
beautiful woman, whose name no one knew, constantly at his side'.
The young companion in question was Gerda Puhlmann. The pictorial report also showed his loyal servant Hermann Wölk brushing
Wilhelm's hussar's uniform and focused on a series of bizarre details
such as a hairbrush decorated with a hussar's death's head. The text
referred to the crown prince as a 'daddy's favourite whose life has
been a failure'. The same French media who had pilloried Wilhelm
as the 'butcher of Verdun' thirty years previously now saw him as a
ridiculous old man 'without a penny to his name'. The largest photo
in the report showed the smiling crown prince playing cards with
three French soldiers. It is hard to imagine a better visual representation of the life of a gambler, completely: incapable of self-criticism
and incapable of learning from mistakes, who kept playing even
after he had lost everything.[26]

Bluebloods and the Yellow Press

The French authorities sent the crown prince – by bicycle – from
Lindau on Lake Constance to the Hohenzollerns' hereditary castle

near Hechingen, where he found comfortable quarters.[27] He was called as a witness at the Nuremberg Trials but never faced any charges himself. By 1946, he was again giving interviews – this time mostly to US newspapers – in which he explained the need to establish democracy in Germany and how he had been beseeched to help reconstruct a German monarchy.[28]

Wilhelm moved to the foot of the castle in Hechingen, first to a spacious villa, then a modest, rented, five-room house. By this point, he was separated from Cecilie and spent considerable time with his girlfriend Puhlmann, thirty-six years his junior, whom he had met as an eighteen-year-old in 1937 and who was described in the few existing sources as a 'ticket taker' or a 'number girl' at the Scala. French journalists who visited the May–December couple in the villa in late 1945 mockingly described a good-looking young woman whiling away her days papering the walls with photos of her husband striking various poses.[29] After Puhlmann left the prince for a Swedish officer in 1947, Wilhelm remarked: 'It is hard for me after 10 years of friendship'.[30] He spent the final years of his life in a relationship with another woman more than three decades his junior named Steffi Ritl, who was said to be a divorced hairdresser. It was she who witnessed the former heir to the throne's death. 'Gerda has been succeeded by Steffi,' a family lawyer wrote to Dommes in 1947. 'But she hasn't acclimatized herself and doesn't seem to know what her place is there.'[31]

Dismay at 'the sad physical and mental decline' of the crown prince and princess set the tone for Thomas Mann scholar Klaus W. Jonas's extensive, sympathetic biography in the early 1960s.[32] There were few moral codes any more for Wilhelm to transgress. His correspondence with his old American acquaintance Geraldine Farrar suggests that he lived in financially secure, but no longer opulent, circumstances, although the crown prince and his wife spent considerable amounts of money on trips to Switzerland, where they stayed in luxury accommodation with their respective much younger lovers.

The Hohenzollerns' money managers financed the royal couple's existence primarily by drawing on stocks, art collections and money transferred out of Germany in the months before the end of the Second World War. In late 1943, Wilhelm and Cecilie, together with their two daughters, who lived at Cecilienhof, were paid 409,000 Reichsmarks a year (34,800 Reichsmarks a month) in appanages. Louis Ferdinand received 62,000 Reichsmarks, before taxes, in 1941,[33] and there was money allocated for generous Christmas bonuses as well. In 1943, the latter ranged from 50 Reichsmarks for cleaning ladies to 200 marks for the 'cabinet head' Müldner von Mühlnheim and 300 Reichsmarks for the crown princess.[34] Once handed out, those sums were gone for ever. But the transfers of money abroad directly before Germany's defeat represented a significant nest egg that made it impossible for the royal couple to ever descend into poverty.[35]

Wilhelm's letters to the former opera and Hollywood star Geraldine Farrar combined anti-communist sentiments in line with the new logic of the Cold War and expressions of delight at care packages with requests for more cigarettes, soap, toothpaste, shoes and nylons, size ten, for his 'secretary'.[36] In return, the prince sent photographs of himself and his much younger lover on horseback.[37] One of the leitmotifs in the prince's correspondence was his expectations concerning the Marshall Plan and his hope that the US and Britain would 'remain hard towards the Kremlin'. Wilhelm toed the political line of the early Federal Republic on geopolitics, proposing that Stalin was just like Hitler 'only a little cleverer'.[38] On the whole, his letters were a mixture of the political and the private that meandered from clichés about global political trends and hopes for a US-led international anti-communist alliance to lamentations about greatness lost, especially with regard to his own birthplace, the Marmorpalais in Potsdam's New Garden.

'Dear Geraldine,' he wrote in April 1947,

reading the newspapers I am happy to see that the American public finally recognizes the global danger posed by Bolshevism. General Marshall's appearance in Moscow is also very heartening. Here, spring has arrived. On my birthday, I'll be thinking of our beloved Potsdam, where the Russians are now dwelling. It's said that a Russian officers' mess has been set up in the Marmorpalais. Very tasteful in my opinion. I read a lot of American newspapers that contain extraordinarily interesting articles.[39]

Ferrar confirmed that she had sent 'Miss Gerda' some nylons and agreed with Wilhelm about the global fight against communism: 'We have our troubles with the native Bolshies; horrid breed.'[40]

Roughly a month after securing nylons for his girlfriend, the crown prince testified at Nuremberg in a trial concerning the German Foreign Ministry. He stayed in luxury in a hunting lodge owned by one of the Faber-Castells and was questioned by the American deputy chief prosecutor Robert Kempner, a lawyer from a Jewish family in Freiburg. During his testimony, Wilhelm dismissed the idea that the Foreign Ministry had known nothing about the genocide against Jews as 'absolute nonsense', admitting that he himself had naturally 'been kept in the picture'.[41] When Kempner asked, 'What shocked you most during the past twelve years?' the crown prince answered: 'A lot of things shocked me. The traditions of decency (*die anständigen Traditionen*) in the army were systematically dismantled. The pictures of my father were removed from the officers corps. That hurt.'[42]

Wilhelm's late political communications seem to have stayed basically on that level. Two years before his testimony, shortly after being taken into captivity, the crown prince had occasion to speak with General Jean de Lattre de Tassigny, the commander of the First French Army. In a variation on his pronouncements in Dutch exile, he again proclaimed that all he wanted was to retire to a hunting cabin as a private citizen. His family, he said, had lost all the homes befitting their station. The general, a hero of the Resistance who had fought for sixteen months in the First World War near Verdun and been wounded five times, responded by reminding Wilhelm of the many casualties in that conflict, whom the prince had described as 'long forgotten'. Lattre de Tassigny then terminated the conversation, calling Wilhelm a pathetic wretch, devoid of honour and incapable of thinking about anything but his personal comfort.[43]

The crown prince still cropped up now and again in local newspapers as a lover of sports and a teller of avuncular anecdotes,[44] but as a political figure he had become invisible, losing all influence. There is no evidence that he had any contacts at all with the political class of the early Federal Republic or took stock of the past or developed any ideas for the future. The same was true of his surviving brothers. His correspondence with Farrar showed him as a lonely fellow who had shed his former severe manner and discovered, at least in his letters, his gentler side. That was all the more remarkable considering the pronounced military brusqueness he had previously cultivated. 'All the best for 1948,' he wished Farrar. 'Peace on earth. With love, your old friend Wilhelm.'[45] In his letters to the next generation of German monarchists, he expressed hopes for a revival of 'conservative circles' and sought to build rhetorical bridges with the modern era. 'Without Hohenzollerns, no Prussia, without Prussia no Germany, and without Germany, no Europe,' he declared.[46]

Crown Prince Wilhelm died on 20 July 1951, as a deeply depressed man, largely isolated even among his own relatives. He was buried in the family cemetery in the grounds of Hohenzollern Castle. The West German government sent a wreath of flowers. Playing on the nascent attempts to turn the royal family's ancestral estate in Hechingen into an international tourist attraction, the conservative French newspaper *La Croix* mocked: 'Neither Kaiser nor Reich President. Wilhelm II's son has ended his life as a seller of postcards.' The paper also didn't fail to note that the former crown prince had left behind no political testament.[47]

The testimony of the crown prince and his brother August Wilhelm in Nuremberg in 1947 spoke volumes about the Hohenzollern family's self-image. The prosecutor Kempner was remarkably polite and understanding and made several friendly remarks about the ex-Kaiser. The crown prince's testimony began with a description of his first conversation with Hitler, the exact date of which Wilhelm had forgotten, although he did allege that he had protested against the Nazis' anti-Jewish measures. His account continued in this tenor. In the Bayerisches Viertel neighbourhood of Berlin's Schöneberg district, he claimed, he had once demonstratively sat down on a bench marked as 'Reserved for Jews', drawing disbelieving looks from passers-by.

Reprising his well-rehearsed statements after the First World War, Wilhelm declared that he had known all along that Germany would lose the next global war. So, too, in his son's retelling, had the Kaiser. The crown prince claimed to have taken little note of Germany's post-1933 rearmament, and it never occurred to him that the automotive industry could have been connected with the production of weapons. In his conversations with Hitler, Wilhelm asserted, he had realized that Nazism would lead to a 'Bolshevik system'. Moreover, he was careful to point out, he had many Jewish acquaintances, and his 'best friend' was a non-baptized Jewess married to an officer who served in 'my army'. When asked about concentration camps, Wilhelm cited the fact that his adjutant Louis Müldner von Mülnheim had been detained in such a facility for a short time in 1934. His wife had rejected Nazism just as he had, the crown prince added, and the Nazis had constantly feared his popularity within the armed forces.

The crown prince's brother August Wilhelm's written and oral testimony displayed a degree of stupidity that, if genuine, suggested he was incapable of judgements, opinions or any form of self-reflection. His handwritten declaration and answers to two sessions of live questioning consisted of astonishingly muddled blather lacking both continuity and logic. Along with complaints about how he was being housed and fed, August Wilhelm focused on his early battle against 'Bolshevism', while claiming he had never stood in the 'service' of the brownshirts – despite having been an SA Obergruppenführer. He had known 'slums', poverty and the people from first-hand experience, he added, and had felt, 'for the first time, doubts about the tendencies of the new government' after the

Night of the Long Knives. Conversely, the 'Christian' basis of Nazism had been particularly close to his heart, and he had repeatedly protested against the 'acts of destruction' during the Night of Broken Glass pogroms. In general, he had always believed in peace and protected Jews wherever possible.

It is scarcely credible that the Obergruppenführer, who was capable of reciting with great precision the family trees of half of the high nobility, suffered from a fundamentally faulty memory. Yet, when Kempner sarcastically remarked that many ranking Nazis had testified to being little more than messengers, August Wilhelm merely responded that this was shameful, without uttering a word about his own moral failings.[48] He died on 25 March 1949.

After the Second World War, Crown Princess Cecilie lived from her royal apanage, first in Bad Kissingen, then in a house built especially for her in Stuttgart. She maintained a relationship, considered by Hohenzollern family circles as far too intimate, with her former chauffeur Otto Groha, who was given the absurd title of 'court councillor'. That lead to a variety of conflicts with the clan's administrators, ending only with Cecilie's death in 1954. The crown prince's brothers Eitel Friedrich, Adalbert and Oskar all died between 1942 and 1958.

The final director of the Hohenzollern family administration, Baron Kurt von Plettenberg, who had served as a kind of supreme manager for both the Hohenzollerns and the Schaumburg-Lippes, and thus for two of Germany's agricultural and forestry empires, was arrested in Cecilienhof in March 1945. On behalf of the crown prince, he had spirited away a number of priceless objects, including the crown of the Prussian kings and fifteen snuffboxes that had belonged to Friedrich the Great, from Potsdam to the western German town of Bückeburg, where they were hidden inside the walls of a church.[49] Plettenberg met his end in the terror centre of the Berlin Gestapo and the SS. It is unclear whether he committed suicide to protect various members of the conservative resistance to Hitler, with whom he had contact, or was murdered by the Gestapo.[50]

Müldner von Mülnheim, for decades the crown prince's closest adjutant, committed suicide together with his lover on 26 April 1945 at Cecilienhof after ordering his servant to shoot his hunting dog.[51] Ilsemann, the ex-Kaiser's most trusted advisor, who stayed on in Doorn as an administrator after his master's death, shot himself at his desk on 6 June 1952. Baron Ulrich von Sell, the adjutant, director of finance and one of the most important advisors of the ex-Kaiser, who had opposed the royal family's alliance with Nazism and been close to the conservative resistance, was interned by the Gestapo on 20 July 1944. Released in March 1945, he was arrested in Berlin by Soviet troops a short time later. The following November, he died in a Soviet special internment camp.[52] The crown prince's private secretary Arthur Berg also 'disappeared' after being detained by the Soviets in Potsdam and died in the summer of 1947 in Soviet captivity.[53] By that point, the former Hohenzollern household minister Leopold von Kleist, who unlike Sell, Ilsemann and Plettenberg had encouraged the royal family to align itself with the Nazis, had also died.

The Last Thing Left: The Struggle Over Huis Doorn

In 1946, Dommes, who had been reactivated as general administrator after Plettenberg's death, reported to the Netherlands that Germany was 'a massive pile of rubble – our royal family has been hit especially hard'. The Hohenzollerns' property had been lost and its capital assets seized. The crown prince had separated from his wife, 'Empress' Hermine had fallen into Russian hands, most of the family loyalists had 'passed on', and the younger generation was now 'doing its best to join the economy and perform productive work'. The Dutch government had confiscated Huis Doorn as an 'enemy possession', and, as Dommes put it, the residence was 'pretty much the last thing left undamaged'. Thus, obtaining the release of the ex-Kaiser's home-in-exile was made a major priority.[54]

The crown prince and Ilsemann used much the same language

several weeks later with their contacts in the Netherlands. Russians, Poles and German communists had stolen everything the House of Hohenzollern had possessed, and the crown prince trusted in 'the sense of justice of the Dutch government' so that 'the last' possession of Huis Dorn wouldn't be lost as well. The crown prince hoped that his cause would be helped by the fact that he had intervened directly with the Nazi commissioner for the Netherlands, Arthur Seyss-Inquart, after the arrest of the mayor of Wieringen during the Second World War. Wilhelm seemed not to have considered that his connection to an SS Obergruppenführer who had terrorized the Dutch and was about to be executed in Nuremberg as a war criminal perhaps wasn't the best argument for his case.[55]

In 1947, the Hohenzollerns' application to have the confiscation of Huis Doorn rescinded led to investigations that quickly uncovered unflattering evidence about the German royal family, and what was discovered would return to haunt the clan seventy years later. In several respects, the conflict over Huis Doorn would preview elements also characteristic of the much later German debate. Photo shoots granted by the Hohenzollerns, telegrams to Hitler and Mussolini, articles promoting Nazism, the 1932 election endorsement and various politically symbolic activities became the stuff of scandal.[56] Royal family administrators sought to mitigate the damage by enlisting lawyers, journalists and political contacts in Germany and abroad. For two years, they invested considerable energy in attempts to interpret the telegrams to Hitler and the photos of swastika-sporting Hohenzollerns so that the pictures and documents were no longer seen to depict what they clearly depicted.[57]

The extended correspondence and ultimately the Hohenzollerns' Dutch lawyer used the following arguments.[58] In 1932, there was no predicting how things would develop and, very much in the spirit of democracy, the royal family had remained open to a 'continually growing popular movement'.[59] The Dutch government had offered the ex-Kaiser asylum, and the protection that entailed couldn't be simply withdrawn. As the place where Wilhelm II was buried, Huis Doorn was a kind of 'sacred site' for the Hohenzollerns, who were immensely attached to it. Furthermore, the ex-Kaiser had always clearly positioned himself against National Socialism, and with the lone exception of August Wilhelm, all the members of the family had opposed Nazism. The crown prince had merely been a member of the Nazi Motor Corps, not the Nazi Party, and had remained a 'friend to the Netherlands'. And finally, the Treaty of Versailles and Hitler had been responsible for the Second World War.[60]

For a time, Hohenzollern advocates managed to prevent incriminating photos and documents from being published. But in 1947, when a series of photographs from 1933 and 1934 of German royal family members wearing swastikas ran in the Dutch press, public outrage in the Netherlands reached a level that could not be quelled.[61] Some of these images were the same ones that would play a role in German discussions seventy years later about whether the Hohenzollerns should be compensated for past losses. Several of the ex-Kaiser, Hermine and the crown prince's congratulatory telegrams to Hitler were also made public. The enthusiastic good wishes offered after Germany conquered France, having rolled over Holland along the way, weighed particularly heavily.[62] Attracting particular attention was a 1939 telegram from Wilhelm II to Hitler in which the ex-Kaiser congratulated the Führer on having survived the Elser assassination attempt.[63] Nor was a 1940 telegram from Hermine to Hitler, in which she expressed her hopes that Britain would soon be brought to its knees, especially helpful for advancing the Hohenzollerns' material claims.[64]

In the case of the ex-Kaiser, his supporters could at least stress his religiosity and claim that his motivational telegrams were aimed at 'the troops', not Hitler. With considerable goodwill, Wilhelm II's refusal in his last will and testament to be buried in Germany until the monarchy had been restored was also interpreted as opposition to the Nazi regime. Hohenzollern advocates also claimed that the ex-Kaiser and crown prince hadn't written the telegrams personally.[65] The myth that adjutants to the two leading members of royal family had penned the telegrams without their masters' knowledge would remain in currency for decades within the German royal family and elsewhere.[66] But that was as absurd as it was easy to disprove.[67] And there was no way to repair the damage caused by the crown prince's telegrams, formulated as they were in a tone of submissive admiration for the Führer and in the language of the Third Reich. Immediately after Germany's victory in Poland in 1939, the ex-Kaiser expressed his 'warmly shared enthusiasm' with a 'fervent heart' and proudly pointed out that one of his sons and eight grandchildren were fighting in the Wehrmacht.[68]

For their part, the Netherlands was embroiled at the time in fighting associated with the dissolution of its colonial empire, so a quarrel over an aristocratic estate near Utrecht wasn't near the top of their list of problems. Nonetheless, such a short time after the Second World War and the German occupation of the country, the Dutch public was intensely interested in the conflict. Ilsemann reported receiving more than hundred pieces of correspondence a day referring to the 'unhappy' photos and telegrams. Count Hardenberg tried to stress that the Hohenzollerns had been involved in the Stahlhelm, claiming that the organization had been unrelated to Nazism. He even trotted out the notion that the crown prince had been 'forced' to join the organization.[69] But early in the debate, Crown Prince Wilhelm's 1932 letter to Groener in which he had promoted the SA and the SS was reprinted in its entirety.[70]

Not infrequently, the conflict involved quarrels about minor details such as whether the ex-Kaiser himself had personally provided Wehrmacht soldiers arriving at Huis Doorn in the summer of 1940 with tobacco, lemonade and autographed pictures of himself. Hohenzollern advocates went to great lengths and cited eyewitnesses to refute this,[71] but there was not the slightest doubt about Wilhelm II's enthusiasm for the invasion of the Netherlands and the sight of Wehrmacht soldiers on his doorstep. (We recall here that the ex-Kaiser was described as looking thirty years younger as, decked out in his many medals, he received the troops with great joy and 'fine coffee'.)[72] By contrast, in their correspondence with the Dutch authorities, Hohenzollern advocates now decried the German invasion of the Netherlands as 'ruthless' and 'criminal'.[73]

While the royal family's representatives were trying to rewrite history, they also considered legal and political measures like having the Hohenzollerns' fortune handed over to the crown prince's youngest son, Friedrich, who had married into the British-Irish Guinness family. There was even talk of asking Churchill to personally intervene.[74] Hardenberg tried to enlist the help of a Dutch officer, Willem Frederik Karel Bischoff van Heemskerck, whom he knew as a fellow prisoner at the Sachsenhausen concentration camp and who had become the Dutch queen's stablemaster, to put in a good word with the authorities in the Netherlands.[75] The crown prince insisted upon soliciting the counsel of a Jewish lawyer from New York.[76]

But such efforts were largely in vain. Anecdotes about the crown prince helping opponents of the Nazi regime at considerable risk to himself were largely unfounded and occasionally refuted, for example by the pastor Martin Niemöller, who had in fact been part of the resistance.[77] Meanwhile, investigations were underway as to whether the crown prince or his general administration directors had known that many of the stocks they bought up during the Third Reich had been stripped from their rightful Jewish owners.[78]

A conversation Hardenberg conducted in the Netherlands in July 1948 with the Dutch crown princess's husband, formerly Prince Bernhard zur Lippe-Biesterfeld, proved the high point of these attempts at a conservative management of the past. The prince, who prior to his marriage in 1935 had been a member of the SA, the SS calvary and the Nazi Party, expressed his dismay at the German crown prince's trials and tribulations, arguing that, after all, he himself, the Dutch princess's consort, had been in the SS.[79] But a letter addressed to the Dutch prime minister pleading the Hohenzollerns' case failed to achieve a breakthrough.

To the real and playacted astonishment of the high nobility, among others, it became clear after the Second World War that not all aristocratic families had behaved like the House of Hohenzollern. When Baron Franz von Redwitz, the chief adjutant of Bavaria's Crown Prince Rupprecht, wrote to his Prussian equivalent

Dommes about the sacrifices made in his own family and that of his 'exalted lord', Dommes could only respond that he didn't know anything about that. The two men's brief correspondence magnified the very different positions maintained by the circles around the two crown princes.[80] The contrast between the two royal families is a reminder that it was possible for the high nobility to maintain a distance from Nazism and that some families choose to do this more, and some less. And the greater opposition of the aristocracy in Germany's Catholic south, including the Wittelsbach dynasty, to the Nazis than in the Protestant North is a matter of historical record.[81]

Along with the contention that the crown prince had only learned in 1947 about his own telegrams to Hitler, Hohenzollern advocates rolled out the full arsenal of arguments that had been used by the lawyers for the conservative defendants at the Nuremberg Trials.[82] Hitler had achieved miracles in 'protecting private property' and combatting unemployment, the royal family's lawyers pointed out to justify their clients' lack of opposition to Nazism. Even Churchill and the US ambassador to Germany had greatly admired the Führer – around 1933, the later British prime minister had gone so far as to wish that England had a leader like Hitler capable of eradicating class warfare. This cavalier comparison of the purported good done by Hitler and Churchill was made more than once during the debate. Citing the banker and former Reich economics minister Hjalmar Schacht,[83] who had privately advised the Hohenzollerns and whose lawyers had received an acquittal at the Nuremberg Trials, one conservative advocate wrote:

> Much as some prominent foreigners did, many upstanding, patriotic Germans saw Hitler's early measures as positive for Germany. One of those people was the crown prince who devoted himself to the movement solely for the most noble of reasons. He saw that Germany was in a life-or-death crisis. He saw the immorality reaching out all around and the poisoning of minds through books, plays and films. He saw the massive unemployment and, above all, the peril of

growing Bolshevism. The ideals proclaimed by the Hitler movement addressed the longing of millions of tortured hearts.

In this confoundingly inconsistent interpretation of the past, the
crown prince had both declared his support for Nazism as part
of the battle against 'immorality' and been a dedicated opponent
of the Nazi regime as of 1934, later risking his life by offering to help
the resistance. The photographs of the prince wearing swastikas,
which were so heatedly discussed in the Dutch press, were mere
'camouflage' to conceal his 'true sentiments'.[84]

The Hohenzollerns lost their fight to retain Doorn after failing to
procure the necessary *ontvijandingsverklaring*, or state confirmation
that they were no longer considered official enemies. A Dutch
appeals court was likewise unimpressed by the Hohenzollerns' lawyers' artificially constructed stories. One of the key documents
justifying why the Hohenzollerns' request was originally denied
coolly summarized the judges' reasoning.[85] They could ascertain
neither a pro-Dutch nor an anti-Nazi attitude. The ex-Kaiser had
been given personal asylum and protection until his death, and
there was no such thing as asylum for property. None of the 'hostile
aliens' had been exempted from disappropriation for reasons of
their own emotional attachment to the properties in question. The
telegrams to Hitler, the crown prince's membership in the Nazi
Motor Corps and more than 100 jingoistic nationalist organizations
spoke against him, and existing records listed him as 'a patron
member of the SA and SS storm divisions'.[86] The appeal was thus
dismissed because it could not clear the high hurdles the law
required for a revocation of enemy status, which included proof of
pro-Dutch sentiments and constant residence in the Netherlands. In
any case, exceptions were very rare.[87]

In the years that followed the Hohenzollerns kept trying to negotiate the release of the valuable household effects in Doorn and
have Louis Ferdinand declared their rightful owner, with the family's Jewish lawyers arguing that the crown prince's son had been
part of the resistance.[88] One notable argument made by Louis

Ferdinand himself was that a constitutional monarchy, in which he might be the head of state, would be advantageous for ensuring democracy in Germany. It was thus in the Netherlands' self-interest, he reasoned, to support his claims in Doorn.[89] But such arguments fell flat. By 2014, when the Hohenzollerns made another attempt to regain the ex-Kaiser's home in exile, the idea of monarchy protecting democracy was no longer relevant. Simultaneously with other claims, a law firm in Rotterdam filed a motion on behalf of Prince Georg Friedrich of Prussia to recover ownership of Huis Doorn, its household effects and the attached property. The arguments used were not unlike those that had been advanced before, and the case was dispatched swiftly. In 2015, the Dutch government declared it could see 'no reason' to accede to the Hohenzollerns' demands.[90]

Over the years, Hohenzollern advocates made consistent attempts to affiliate the royal family with the ranks of the victims of the Nazism. There was even an incredible attempt to equate the Hohenzollerns with those whose art the Nazis had looted: Hardenberg considered demanding the return of a painting by Watteau that the family had sold to Hitler for his planned museum in Linz, Austria, for 900,000 Reichsmarks – under the pretext that that the family had surely been forced to part with it. Art was being restored to non-Germans, he argued, so why not to the Hohenzollerns?[91]

Royal Remainders

Along with the 'unhappy' telegrams and photos, the estranged crown prince and princess's propensity for public statements further damaged the Hohenzollerns' reputation. The family's general administrative staff were particularly vexed by the hastily written memoirs both Wilhelm and Cecilie put on the market. The crown prince's recollections initially consisted of a short oral narrative written down by an American journalist and conceived, in line with a familiar pattern, for publication in the United States. The title was to be 'From Bismarck to Hitler', and it was touted to the press as a work that would 'correct numerous misapprehensions by examining the period from the perspective of the time'.[92]

Wilhelm told French journalists that he had always fought against the Nazis and particularly anti-Semitism and called Hitler a blowhard and Goebbels an insidious dwarf with a limp. 'And Now Another Anti-Nazi!' was the sarcastic headline the French newspaper gave to the interview.[93] Meanwhile, in order to prevent publication of this second, poorly done volume of the crown prince's memoirs (the first had appeared in 1922), attempts were made to seize all copies of the manuscript – a difficult undertaking because several were in the possession of a secretary. It was said that even CIA Director Allan W. Dulles took an interest in the case.[94] The idea was to hire a ghost-writer to improve the manuscript, and the search was on for 'a suitable man [to] be hired to process [the crown prince's] thoughts'. Dommes remembered the experienced ghost-writer Karl Rosner from the 1920s. 'He has the right qualities – I just don't know whether he's still energetic enough,' Dommes said.[95] Once contacted, Rosner himself, who was by then over seventy, urgently warned against publishing the memoirs in unfiltered form.[96]

The situation with the crown princess was likewise the source of drama. Shortly after Wilhelm's death in 1951, with the help of an author of kitschy dime-store novels, Cecilie serialized parts of her memoirs and attracted a substantial readership. Originally, the series was to be published under the title 'My Kaiser Without an Empire', but the publishers came up with an even more bathetic title, and in late 1951 this collection of ostensible insights into the crown princess's life appeared as 'Kaiser of My Soul' in *Neue Illustrierte* magazine.[97] A book followed a short time later.[98] Hardenberg, who had begun taking an interest in media law issues with a view towards a potential film about Cecilie's life, called the series 'nice in every sense and also well written'. But the money-hungry publishers also wanted to cash in on the personal recollections of Cecilie's business-minded 'companion' Otto Groha. Publications of this sort were deemed an 'enormous danger', and in 1954 a legal dispute arose over whether private conversations could be exploited for personal gain.[99] Apparently amidst concern that Cecilie could privilege her 'companion' in her will, her mental competence was questioned, and expert evaluators were called in.

Reports about the activity of the chauffeur Groha, who frequently used an invented officer's title, recalled the popular novels of the 1920s about fictional con men. In this instance, the Hohenzollerns' public relations staff needed not just to limit potential damage but to prevent an entire family generation from being dragged through the mud. Germany's leading news magazine *Der Spiegel*, which cynically and precisely dissected the situation in a series of articles between 1952 and 1954, wrote of recollections that had appeared in the tabloids: 'It is understandable that the men who keep the welfare of the House of Hohenzollern close to their hearts don't want to leave these dictated memoirs as the German public's final impression of the crown prince.' Apparently, at the behest of Louis Ferdinand, slightly edited passages from Wilhelm's 1922 memoirs had been given to illustrated magazines, which tried to sell them as sensational revelations. 'Someone needed money,' scoffed *Der Spiegel*. The crown princess was said to have been paid 23,000 marks for her serial, and her son Louis Ferdinand to have demanded 25,000 marks for a 'selection of material' that would show his father as a modern, harmless fellow.[100] By this point, there was an established Hohenzollern tradition of trying to simultaneously manage and monetize the family's history.

When Cecilie died on 6 May 1954, the locks on the doors of her residence were changed, and Groha – in Hardenberg's eyes a mere 'stableboy' who had been given a fake title – was banned from the property. Even parts of the private correspondence between crown prince and princess were a concern.[101] Dommes thought it essential to prevent unauthorized publication of this material and stressed the great responsibility Louis Ferdinand had inherited with the passing of the crown prince. He made his standpoint clear in a private remark that reflected the aged general's dismay at the tawdriness that was overshadowing the royal family's former glory. The 'head of the house' was responsible for defending the family's honour, Dommes told Louis Ferdinand, 'especially when his predecessor has squandered it, as is the case with us'.[102]

Rebranding: Monarchy for Democracy

The generations after the crown prince were responsible for the royal family's transition from the Third Reich to the democratic Federal Republic of Germany, and the changes can be tracked in the relationships concluded by the Hohenzollerns since 1945. The royal clan was and indeed still is, after all, a family where members are expected not to marry 'below their station'. For instance, in 1945, the crown prince's youngest son, Prince Friedrich of Prussia, who spent the Second World War as a POW in Canada and Britain, became a British citizen and, as mentioned earlier, married a daughter of the wealthy Guinness family. This was a union that could be interpreted as a sign of a new era, and it was topped in June 1949, when the crown prince's daughter married an American soldier and interior architect from Amarillo, Texas, at Hohenzollern Castle, with her father in attendance.[103] Photos show a dramatically aged Wilhelm giving the bride away to a former officer of the occupying American forces, whereupon the princess, who renounced her title, prepared to find a new home 'in the endless prairie of Texas'. The German press reported that she wished for nothing else than to be 'a good American housewife' and ran pictures of American cars rolling into the German royal family's ancestral castle – a very symbolic set of images.[104] The marriage and the wedding spectacle can be read as a turning of the tide within the House of Hohenzollern, reflecting the spirit of the early Federal Republic and its new, dominant ideals.

For forty years, one of the main architects and representatives of this realignment was Louis Ferdinand, who became the 'head of the house' upon Wilhelm's death in July 1951. The year before, the news that the son of the crown prince had settled down in Bremen, in the

American occupation zone, as a representative of the Ford Motor Company had made waves as far as the provincial French press.[105] All the way back in June 1946, together with an American army sergeant, who was a film critic in civilian life, Louis Ferdinand had started a German-American club in Bad Kissingen. Its stated mission was to introduce Germans to the democratic culture of debate.[106]

Louis Ferdinand had been living around Bad Kissingen, and in 1950 he and his family permanently settled in 'Wümmehof', a large, restyled turn-of-the-century country manor near Bremen. A newly constructed villa, devoid of all opulence and pomp, in the Grunewald district of the former capital of the Third Reich also gave the 'head of the house' a foothold in Cold War Berlin.[107] Especially compared with the neighbouring villas of West Berlin's richest families, fittingly located on Königsallee (King's Boulevard), Louis Ferdinand's domicile recalled the sober austerity admirers had always lauded in the 'Prussian style'. Symbolic displays of the connection between Prussian tradition and post-war West German democracy were a constant in West Berlin. In 1959, for example, the ex-Kaiser's daughter Viktoria Luise and Prince Louis Ferdinand were the centre of attention at a religious service held in the city's Tiergarten district to commemorate Wilhelm II's 100th birthday.

There is no reason to exaggerate the 'restorative' elements of the early Federal Republic. The dynamics of social and political modernization were just as real and influential in the 1950s, a period of reconstitution, as anti-communism.[108] At the same time, the people who built this new German society didn't just appear out of thin air. Most were elite functionaries who had been active in the Wilhelmine Empire, the Weimar Republic and the Nazi state. Historian Paul Nolte writes: 'Notwithstanding its own ambitions, or at least the expectations of many intellectuals, the Federal Republic didn't create anything radically new. Rather, it reproduced economic, social and political structures from the Wilhelmine Empire and the Weimar Republic.'[109]

When describing 1950s and 1960s German conservativism, it

seems useful to take seriously the restorative aspects of the early Federal Republic's symbolism and emotional energy. Without exception, post-1945 conservative symbols and narratives needed to do two things: to demonstrate distance from 'the Nazis', the Nazi state and its epochal crimes, and to harken back to positively charged traditions from before 1933. The main challenge was not to restore conservative traditions but to adapt them to the 1950s political realities of bourgeois elites constructing the 'Adenauer Republic'. (Konrad Adenauer was the first West German chancellor.) The symbolic centres of the early Federal Republic's restorative elements lay in the west of the country and the bourgeois social milieu depicted in the novels of Heinrich Böll and Wolfgang Koeppen. The shattered remnants of Prussian-German monarchism found neither a functional organizational form nor a symbolic centre, and monarchist political platforms around 1950, however revised they were, sounded like elegies to a lost age: lamentations of aged men whining about their physical frailty and repeating outmoded clichés irrelevant to contemporary reality.[110]

Nonetheless, the uninhabited Hohenzollern Castle became a leading site of monarchist emotions and convictions in the Federal Republic.[111] Of course, places like the castle, Louis Ferdinand and the name of Prussia could not mobilize and embody anything like the powerful feelings that inspired the intense hatred of democracy in the 1920s. But they hadn't, either, in the Third Reich. The relics and holy sites of monarchism didn't completely disappear with the founding of the Federal Republic. The public aggression of Weimar was replaced by a nostalgia practised quietly in symbolically significant locations.

In 1952, for example, the bodies of Friedrich the Great and his father were transferred, 'under cover of night', from Marburg, where they had been temporarily moved after the Russian advance in 1945, to Hohenzollern Castle and reinterred there in a private ceremony.[112] This event was preceded by an extended quarrel about the rightful owners of the coffins and the remains contained therein. Hardenberg had personally registered the family's legal claims with the Elisabeth parish in Marburg, but once again an expert evaluation was commissioned. Schlabrendorff argued, plausibly, that Louis Ferdinand had an 'actionable legal claim' for the coffins to be handed over. Lawyers didn't agree on whether human remains were fundamentally ownable, and in the end, Schlabrendorff justified the reburial on the grounds of German family law, invoking the idea of the 'moral sensibilities of the German people'.[113] The opposing side argued that descendants should not be able to raise claims as 'surviving family members' 200 years after someone's death. The parish council in question declared that 'for Christian, biblical reasons, the church opposed the exhumation of skeletons' and was of 'the opinion that the two coffins were not only family but common property'.

The situation was made more delicate by the Stahlhelm, which had reformed as a secret organization after the war. In a letter in February 1952, the self-appointed militia's 'federal leader', Carl Simon, offered Louis Ferdinand the assistance 'of the entire leader corps of the Stahlhelm, including the federal leader'. Simon signed his letter with the words 'In loyal solidarity and wishes of hail to the front, your Royal Highness's most obedient servant'. Hardenberg was forced to inform him that a parade, with swords drawn, to accompany the relocation of the coffins and the remains was probably not going to be possible – although the count did sign his response with the words 'with comradely greetings'.[114] Before the case went to trial, the issue was resolved politically. Louis Ferdinand was allowed to relocate the coffins, and opposition to the 'privatization' of the Prussian kings came to nought.[115] Representatives of traditional military clubs and monarchist associations were allowed to attend the reburial, but Hardenberg did his best to contain the hyperactive monarchist enthusiasm for the reinterred sarcophagi. Conversely, the monarchists complained about Louis Ferdinand's unmilitary mannerisms.[116]

The fact that the most important artefacts of Prussian conservatism were now kept in a private mausoleum in southern Germany fitted in well with a new modesty that preferred to avoid the public

stage. The crown prince's instructions in his will and Louis Ferdinand's low-key manner accorded well with right-wing intellectuals'
tendency to restrict their appearances to private occasions and 'conversations under the seal of confidentiality'.[117]

Prussia was essential to conservative attempts to obscure right-
wing alliances with Nazism and identify positive legacies from
before 1933. Although the members of the former ruling dynasties
were relegated to the backstage in democratic Germany, they continued to symbolize the positive aspects of Prussia. As long as the
core Prussian territory of Brandenburg remained under communist
control, other places gained importance, and Hohenzollern Castle
was one of the locations where a new German conservative identity
was hammered out, especially during the concerts, lectures and
occasions with Louis Ferdinand in attendance. The royal residence,
the redefined traditions of the Hohenzollern family and its modern,
cosmopolitan head became rallying points for conservatives. Hechingen was by no means a 1950s Doorn, but it was an exclave outside
the mainstream of the times. Tellingly, in 1963, as the first wave of
Beatlemania was conquering the world, the German evening news
reported extensively on the silver anniversary of Prince Louis Ferdinand and the Grand Russian Princess Kira. Viewers were treated to
the spectacle of Porsche convertibles arriving at the castle, European high nobility showing up in extravagant hats and black
limousines, and music professor Karl Münchinger directing a classical concert. The high point was a ball kicked off by torchbearers
dressed in eighteenth-century costumes.[118]

Without doubt, the Hohenzollerns still maintained their own
notions of family traditions and how they were to be preserved.
Favoured historians could count on the active assistance of lawyers
working for the clan. Conversely, when in his 1964 biography of
Wilhelm II the British historian Michael Balfour described in detail
an agreement between the Hohenzollerns and Göring, mentioned
often in scholarly literature, that promised the royal family material
advantages in return for not criticizing the Nazi regime, the crown
prince's nephew Prince Wilhelm Karl von Hohenzollern initiated

legal action. He was represented by the law firm Schlabrendorff and Bismarck, or to be more precise by Fabian von Schlabrendorff, the best-known lawyer of the Hohenzollerns, who two years later would be named to West Germany's Constitutional Court, the highest court in the land. The former officer suggested an alternative wording the author should use. Balfour refused to back down, citing the crown prince's first biographer, Paul Herre, who had known his subject personally and had described the arrangement in question. Balfour succeeded in involving the directorate of the prestigious Institute for Contemporary History in Munich, which commissioned research of its own. The institution considered the existence of such an agreement likely but was never able to document it.

In an astonishingly sharp break with the established tone of apologist literature, Schlabrendorff dismissed the expertise of the institute and declared to the publishers that there had never been any payments by the Nazi state to the Hohenzollern clan. Moreover, he claimed, Göring would never have been able to threaten the royal family with material cutbacks. Balfour's wording that the family had denied the existence of the agreement, thereby removing the most plausible reason for the clan's silence during the Third Reich, was unacceptable to Schlabrendorff, who threatened to sue author and publisher. Having failed to produce documentary evidence, author and publisher later watered down their assertion to say that the arrangement was a possibility, not a fact.[119]

Several years later, when Ilsemann's diaries – one of the most important sources on post-1918 Hohenzollern history – were published, dozens of passages were removed from the page proofs. The world's leading expert on this material, John Röhl, presumed that the changes were made to reflect the wishes of the Hohenzollern family members.[120] The published version of the diaries, for instance, makes no mention of the ex-Kaiser's 1934 demand that 'blood must flow' among the aristocracy and others he felt had abandoned him, and an episode in which the Duke of Braunschweig courted Hitler's favour was also left out.[121] In addition, an entry from March 1934 was deleted. It read: 'The crown prince and his sons have gone fully Nazi, and he has already been seen and photographed in a brown-shirt uniform.'[122] Other omissions included a rhetorical question: 'What judgement would history render if the public were to learn of such interpretations made by the Kaiser? If they saw how ignorant the Kaiser was about the military developments of the World War and how he hardly had a single good word to say about any of its major leaders.'[123]

In contrast to the 1920s, the new political battles over history lacked a militant anti-democratic component. Louis Ferdinand and the culture of Hohenzollern Castle were seen as promoting the acceptance of the Federal Republic on Germany's political Right. One of the most important but sparsely analysed caesurae in post-1945 West Germany was the acceptance of democracy by the aristocracy, which, in extremely sharp contrast to the years after 1918, didn't disrupt the new German republic in any significant way.

In this regard, the new culture in Hechingen and the mission communicated by the new 'head' of the former ruling dynasty to the political Right can be seen as a kind of conservative self-reeducation. Historical fact may have belied the myths of German conservatism – its purported connection to the resistance or the alleged opposition of right-wing elites at the time when Hitler was being handed power. But Germans were able to imagine how the Prussian conservative tradition might be compatible with modern, democratic West Germany. The process was not without parallels to the later attempt by Communist East Germany to encourage a positive attitude towards Prussia and parts of the conservative resistance to Hitler.[124]

The House of Hohenzollern and its new 'head' were less influential players in the great ideological transformations of the early Federal Republic than important symbols of a social caste – no longer enemies of a German republic but rather prominent members of that new republic's conservative camp, who vividly and wholly personified a novel alliance of conservative traditions and democracy. In addition, Hohenzollern family connections and the continuing significant American interest in the German royals also fed into the early Federal Republic's commitment to being part of the West. There was no better symbol of this than the fact that shortly after the Second World War Louis Ferdinand once again started working for Ford in Germany.

In the 1950s, the right-wing elite functionaries who had behaved for a time as *compagnons de route* in the broad 'zones of consensus' between conservatives and Nazis were in desperate need of new narratives and sites of self-reinforcement.[125] Conservative views drew legitimacy during the decade from anti-communism, which was broadly popular, and by narratively burying the conservative–Nazi overlaps that helped create the Third Reich and make it manageable. Collaboration with the Nazis had undermined, hollowed out and compromised many conservative traditions, so there was a great demand for points of orientation that weren't fraught with the horrors of the past.

One of the historians who frequented Hechingen was Hans Rothfels, a Jewish returnee from American exile. As a lieutenant in the First World War, Rothfels had lost a leg, after which he became a charismatic teacher and leader of students and intellectuals of various nationalist, conservative schools of thought in Königsberg (today's Kaliningrad). In 1939, he fled Germany and took up a professorship in Chicago. After the war, he returned to his home country, settling in Tübingen, where he was one of the most important reformers of the discipline of German history. An influential lecture he delivered both there and in Berlin in 1954 began with parallels between 20 July 1944 and the anti-communist uprising in East Germany on 17 June 1953. In keeping with the political winds of the day, this rhetorical gesture was a way of downplaying communist anti-Nazi activity and focusing on resistance among conservatives in the Wehrmacht and the upper civil service.[126] An obituary for Rothfels written in 1976 by a colleague and fellow specialist in the German resistance ended by remarking that his greatest joy in life was the majestic view over the tops of the Schwäbische Alb mountains behind which the outlines of Hohenzollern Castle could be seen in good weather.[127] During the 1960s, Rothfels gave numerous lectures at the castle, including a keynote speech entitled 'Friedrich the Great and the State' that featured a series of concepts central to the myth of Prussia: ethics, devotion, faith in the state, public service and duty. For example, in 'reaching out for Silesia', Rothfels said, Friedrich the Great 'hadn't been interested in power for its own sake, but rather advancing into a space dictated by political reason'.[128]

Delegations from the West Germany military, the Bundeswehr, were among those in attendance at ceremonies marking the '257th birthday of Friedrich the Great' in January 1969. General Hasso Viebig, a former general staff major in the Reichswehr who had been trained militarily in Potsdam, gave a speech at the side of Friedrich's coffin on behalf of the German Defence Ministry, in which he called 'loyalty and service' the leading idea 'every state needed'. Viebig added: 'The demands of our fatherland are largely based on the fact that the community of our people is threatened with destruction . . . In this sense, which I regard as truly Prussian, I bow down before Friedrich the Great, King of Prussia.'[129]

The 'Semper Talis League' – a traditionalist association of the famous Potsdam guards, whose own 'watch battalion', founded in 1957, served as a bridge to the Bundeswehr – also celebrated its anniversary at the castle. During those festivities, Louis Ferdinand repeatedly praised the 'two great kings' and proclaimed his greetings for the 'brothers and sisters in the unfree part of Germany'.[130] Representatives of Germans displaced after the Second World War also frequented the castle, so that the local press began referring to Hechingen as 'the homeland of displaced Germans'.[131]

20 July as a Fountain of Renewal

In 1948, Rothfels had published one of the first and most influential books about the German resistance.[132] This text was the start of a relatively long process in which the protagonists of the military rebellion were transformed in the minds of German conservatives from traitors into heroes. The political orientation of this historian, so significant for the Federal Republic, was later the subject of much heated discussion.[133] As a brilliant German-Jewish intellectual who had felt entirely at home in the anti-democratic culture of East Prussia prior to 1933, Rothfels achieved conceptually what Louis Ferdinand embodied personally. Part of the new right-wing interpretation of the Third Reich as a dictatorship that had subjected its own people to demagoguery and terror and destroyed conservative traditions was the notion that the resistance of conservative elites had come within a hair's breadth of bringing down that dictatorship from within.[134]

Rothfels' contacts with Countess Marion Dönhoff were instrumental in disseminating this interpretation of the past, which lent new legitimacy to conservative tradition, the Prussian nobility and the Hohenzollerns. Born to one of the leading East Prussian aristocratic families, the well-known liberal journalist probably contributed more than anyone to creating a new positive image of the German nobility. The nostalgic image of the aristocracy as a small, rural, traditionally rooted elite, conspicuous in its elegance, which had kept its distance from Nazism and whose legacy was its admirable political resistance to Hitler, was one of the most powerful self-images of the young Federal Republic and still exerts an influence today.

Louis Ferdinand and the young economist Countess Dönhoff, who resided in the majestic Friedrichstein Castle, had similar Prussian roots and enjoyed the same country-estate lifestyles and contacts to the political and military elites of the day. Intellectually, Dönhoff fell somewhere between the prince and the historian Rothfels, but as different as this trio was, all three shared the idea of the nobility and Prussian traditions as antipodes of Nazism. Louis Ferdinand, too, was a promoter of that aristocratic metanarrative in which the nobility recognized Hitler, right from the start, as nothing more than a house painter, a sickly parvenu, a servant, a figure of ridicule and a criminal.

There was no direct line of communication between the

conservative historian's office in the university town of Tübingen and Castle Hohenzollern, which he could see from his window. Nonetheless, the early expert on the German resistance and the highest living representative of the Prussian dynasty stood for the long-term project of redefining both Prussian and conservative traditions for present-day democratic Germany. The interpretations and revisions of intellectuals such as Rothfels needed public representatives, and Louis Ferdinand served as precisely that for the segment of German society still receptive to monarchist signals.

The Hohenzollerns in general were a prominent part of this ultimately successful attempt to reinterpret internal struggles and elitist obscurantism on the German Right as opposition or even resistance to Nazism and to delineate the many levels of collaboration in the creation and leadership of the Nazi dictatorship. This re-interpretive endeavour was equally important to various right-wing intellectual groups and to the self-proclaimed conservative formations, the Prussian nobility and the House of Hohenzollern.[135]

In the early phase of this process, along with managing the Hohenzollerns' affairs, Hardenberg also used his connections with the leading West German circles of elite functionaries to collect sources and material concerning the history of the 20 July assassination attempt. 'Hardenberg is in charge of the whole business,' reported Baron Timo von Wilmowsky, a member of the Krupp board of directors, to the industrialist Paul Reusch in autumn 1947.[136] Hardenberg greatly influenced the later historical treatment of members of the conservative military resistance, whom many on the Right still considered traitors even after the war.[137] He was assisted by an initiative directed by his wife, Countess Renate von Hardenberg, née von der Schulenburg, and the research group 20 July, which continues today to generate important ideas for the depiction and interpretation of the anti-Nazi resistance.[138]

In post-war 1940s Germany, there was a popular – and sadly untranslatable – sarcastic saying about those who tried to whitewash their pasts: 'And when he turned up again, he was part of the resistance.' The same applied, as we will see, to more recent efforts by latter-day Hohenzollerns to rehabilitate Crown Prince Wilhelm in the interests of the family's restitution claims. All the elements of contemporary narratives already existed in the 1940s. As early as 1947, supporters of the royal family had already refined and readied for deployment a narrative, supported by the big names of the German resistance, of the Hohenzollerns as being completely compatible with democracy. Even forty years later, in a lengthy television interview from 1987, Louis Ferdinand repeated this version of the past,[139] and it seems to persist within the family to this very day.

Lots of figures worked in the background to come up with this new self-interpretation, but Louis Ferdinand was its only clear personification, completely overshadowing Crown Prince Wilhelm. Whether he penned them himself or used ghost-writers, his 1952 memoirs put forward an image that read like a caricature of his father's autobiography from the 1920s. Just as the crown prince claimed to have forecast Germany's disaster at the Battle of Marne, Louis Ferdinand was cast as a calm protagonist who had immediately seen through Hitler. Constantly involved in conspiratorial meetings with the elite of the resistance, he remained on call in his West Prussian country estate, ever ready to give the signal to act and horrified at the hesitancy of Germany's generals.[140] The image of the upstanding few who kept a clear overview during a time of 'mass insanity' and stood up to the dictatorship in their inner circles was at the core of conservative self-depictions after 1945.[141] But while that might have been true of a few individuals, where it was applied to collectives it was mere legend.

It didn't take long for critics to analyse and identify this narrative as precisely that – a 'resistance legend'.[142] The word wasn't just a synonym for invention or even lie. It signified a story that developed a special power thanks to omissions, distortions and a reception specific to the times – a story upon which Germans could agree. In terms of the self-depiction of the Hohenzollerns as part of the remaking of German conservativism in the early Federal Republic, we could also speak of a 'myth', understood in the ethically neutral sense of a fundamental programmatic reorientation.[143] The 20 July assassination attempt was indeed one of the most important historical and political myths of the early Federal Republic. It served to accomplish two things: to downplay the communist resistance to Hitler and to appropriate the very idea of resistance on the basis of the tale that conservative elite functionaries had been the most powerful adversaries of, and only realistic alternative to, the Nazi dictatorship.

This interpretation was employed constantly, and more recently it has also been extended back in time to depict those conservative elites as the true opponents of Hitler during 1933 and 1934.[144] From the very beginning, as this narrative would have it, Louis Ferdinand and his circle of advisors were involved in the 'work on the myth', preserving and appropriating the memory of 20 July 1944 – albeit more as personifications and profiteers than major architects.[145] The extensive research on this event has often shown how eyewitness recollections 'can lead down the false path of idealization'.[146] But with the Hohenzollerns, these wrong paths were not mistakes, but rather a conscious attempt to profit from the nascent myth of 20 July and to give it additional legitimacy. This was above all true early on, at a point when the conspirators were considered traitors, not heroes. It was an important signal within German conservatism that the 'head' of the House of Hohenzollerns was present as a guest of honour at the Free University of West Berlin on 20 July 1954, when German President Theodor Heuss paid tribute for the first time in a major public speech to the would-be assassins. Louis Ferdinand never talked much about the Holocaust. He stressed the rescue of Germany's cities and the eventuality that the occupation of a major part of the country by Russian troops might have been prevented had the assassination been successful. By that point, the hypothetical possibility of a monarchy that might have been able to avert the Nazi dictatorship and the Second World War had already been fully developed.[147]

A Warm Hearth

In a 2019 interview with *Der Spiegel*, English author Robert Harris compared his home country with the other nations of Europe. 'For England, the past is like a hearth on which you can warm your hands on a long winter evening,' he told the magazine. 'That's not the case in practically any European nation. That's why we can look on the past with nostalgia.'[148] Harris's words are a precise description of what the German history is *not*, but this sort of nostalgia is by no means unique to Britain and continues to be very powerful among German conservatives to this very day. As unthinkable as the idea of the past as a source of comfort was in 1950s Germany, the parts of Prussia Louis Ferdinand managed to personify did serve as a conservative fireplace.

The prince was an ideal figure to represent the image of the family and conservative desire for positive points of orientation in the past. At least in his own self-depiction, as a global traveller and briefly an assembly line worker at Ford, Louis Ferdinand had nothing to do with the rise of Nazism. Moreover, he had spent the era of the Third Reich on his agricultural estate in Western Prussia and, allegedly, at conspiratorial meetings with members of the conservative opposition. This stylised biography bridged the twelve years of Nazi Germany and symbolically linked the prince with the resistance. People with deep experience of the US early in life were the flavour of the day in the initial years of the Federal Republic, and additionally the prince combined cosmopolitanism and appreciation for the arts while demonstrably distancing himself from the sort of militarism with which Prussia and the Prussian royal family had been associated for centuries around the world.

The same was true for his wife, a cosmopolitan daughter of a grand duke many legitimists had considered the heir to the Russian throne. In the world of the Cold War, where anti-communism was a major source of credit for both conservatives and others, the symbolic value of a Prussian–Romanov union was hard to top. Princess

Kira, some of whose family had been killed by Bolsheviks and whose brother had been arrested by the Gestapo, represented the worldliness of the European high nobility no less effectively than her husband.

His name, biography and self-depiction allowed Louis Ferdinand to personify with elegant ease the combination of anti-communism, connection with the US, reliability and reform, tradition and modernity, and adaptability of the new Germany. Ceremonies at which the prince spoke, always invoking the legacy of the 'great Prussian kings', cast Hohenzollern Castle and Hechingen as a repository of exemplary Prussian virtues far away from the political centres of the Federal Republic.[149] Like few others, Louis Ferdinand personified the German East and the glorious pre-1914 past, which continued to be points of orientation, at least for conservatives, in the 1950s. As a 'refugee' from his home in Western Prussia who maintained residences in Bremen and West Berlin, the prince was a symbol of the new beginnings required of millions of Germans who had to be integrated into the Federal Republic after the Second World War. As a Berliner, he stood for both parts of the divided German capital. Having been born in Potsdam, he embodied connections to the regional state of Brandenburg, which was now in Communist East Germany. As a resident of Bremen, he was able to win over the sympathies of the people of the north and as the lord of the manor in Hechingen also appealed to many parts of the south.

The fact that the uninhabited but frequently used castle remained the possession of both the Brandenburgian-Prussian and Swabian lines of the Hohenzollern family symbolically bridged confessional and regional gaps. In 1952, Kira started a foundation to give socially disadvantaged children – early on above all children from heavily damaged Berlin – the chance to spend their holidays free of charge there.[150] This programme followed in the tradition of charity initiatives by women from the high nobility and underscored the greater German connection to divided Berlin.

Formally standing above political parties and religious confessions, the nominal heir to the throne was ever ready to assume the hereditary royal seat without ever demanding it. As someone who still possessed great wealth, who was not, however, from one of the richest families in Germany and who was known for his modest life-style and unassuming behaviour, Louis Ferdinand seemed to be the epitome of virtuous Prussian austerity. Moreover, the American media continued to take a healthy interest in the prince, which was a major plus in the pro-American post-war West German society. Louis Ferdinand bridged differences of religion, region and political parties while combining tradition and modernity – representing a broad spectrum of people in a way almost none of the other former European ruling families could match.

Louis Ferdinand continued until the 1990s, at least in words, to hold open the possibility of a restoration, although by the 1950s the idea was already far more a statement of attitude than a realistic possibility. Nonetheless, he always stressed in interviews that the ex-Kaiser's abdication in 1918 had been an unfortunate historical exception and that he himself was prepared to become king should the people call for him and a popular monarchy be founded – although all public statements of this ilk were delivered in a playful, self-ironic tone.

The same was true of an episode in which Louis Ferdinand seemed to put himself forward as a candidate for West Germany's largely ceremonial presidency. In the July 1954 parliamentary election of the president, Theodor Heuss received 871 votes to one apiece for the prince and Grand Admiral Karl Dönitz, the final head of state in the dying days of the Third Reich.[151] Far less playful in the 1950s were the prince's occasional remarks about the possibility of shifting Poland back eastwards, negotiating with the Soviet Union over Germany's lost territory in eastern Europe, returning to Germany's 1937 borders and his solidarity with the millions of Germans who had been displaced from their homes. In this context, too, Louis Ferdinand repeated his willingness to become king if the German people wanted him to, connecting this stance to the German resistance to Hitler. 'Precisely because of 20 July 1944, I have this very broad foundation, which back then stretched from [conservative Leipzig mayor Carl] Goerdeler to [social democratic union leader Wilhelm] Leuschner,' he proclaimed. 'This comprehensive community of the German resistance movement is what I have in mind, actually.'[152]

The laconic, relaxed, rakish tone, so typical of Prussia's landed aristocracy, used by the prince in his speeches reflected the decades-long attempt to connect West Germany's present with the country's imperial past while ignoring the Weimar Republic, the Third Reich and communist East Germany. Such speechmaking had little to do with political reality. But in line with the basic laws of the monarchy and its surprising residual appeal in the twentieth century, Louis Ferdinand's words did conjure up the illusion of an alternative Germany that remained very attractive to several segments of society in the Federal Republic. This 'other Germany' was a nation with an intact past that had temporarily fallen victim to Nazism – a democratic Germany as part of the West, standing side by side with the US in opposition to the Eastern bloc, a Germany where the splendour of the Wilhelmine Empire still radiated majestically in the background of the rapidly expanding consumer culture of the Federal Republic's miraculous post-war economic recovery.

As was true for the entire society, the House of Hohenzollern seemed to find a handful of political measures sufficient to wipe out the Nazi past, and Louis Ferdinand typified a country that had transformed itself with remarkable swiftness, much to the world's astonishment, into a pro-American, western democracy.[153] The prince, we should recall, held a doctorate in economics, and in 1947 he granted an interview to the Berlin newspaper *Der Tagesspiegel* on the subject of 'democracy as a natural condition'. In it, he waxed lyrical about an ideal with which he claimed to have become acquainted on the assembly line in an unimaginably prosperous United States, an America where – according to him – working-class families owned four cars, dressed in tuxedoes, played golf, rode horses, never complained, never needed any state support and accepted hierarchies as inevitable. Germans would be happier, he said, as soon as they learned 'to acknowledge democracy as a given in the same way Americans do'.[154]

Louis Ferdinand's reinvented Prussia was as close to the US as it was to Nazism. Hitler – an Austrian and a man without a native land – had always been, in this view, alien to Prussia and the German people. Conversely, Prussia stood for an alternative, better past, whose important symbols included the House of Hohenzollern, which in turn had been part of the resistance.

In 1952, Louis Ferdinand's memoirs were published in Chicago. Tellingly, they were entitled *The Rebel Prince*, and it's safe to assume that the Pulitzer-Prize-winner Louis Lochner had a hand in shaping the text. Lochner had been a friend of Louis Ferdinand since the 1930s and had repeatedly helped him shape his image in the US.[155] The English edition of his recollections self-servingly sought to stress his alleged rebellion against part of German royal tradition. By contrast, the German version, which bore the title *Through the World as the Kaiser's Grandson*, emphasized the prince's cosmopolitanism as the descendant of a family with a glorious past. In that volume, Louis Ferdinand presents himself as a young, dynamic, democratic king – a man globally polished, enlightened by America, eloquent, casual and non-military, who was equally familiar with statesmen and great artists, on the one hand, and assembly lines in Detroit and the steppes of Patagonia, on the other. Written in an entertaining, conversational style and an ironic tone, the memoirs depicted their author as an adventurer whose life consisted both of meeting interesting people in interesting settings and of experiencing at first hand all the great questions of the twentieth century and analysing them from all possible sides.

At the start, the American press lionized Louis Ferdinand as a resistance member, a composer of popular songs and a democratic builder of bridges between Germany and the US. Lochner informed the US public about the prince's plan to preserve world peace in 1938. In 1945, a former US ambassador to Germany suggested that the country should become a constitutional monarchy and that Louis Ferdinand would be 'an excellent choice' to lead it.[156]

Particularly in the US, the prince's book tour for his 1952 memoirs was a PR triumph. The *New York Herald Tribune* published advance excerpts, the other major newspapers were quickly won over, there was no criticism of or doubts about Louis Ferdinand's self-portrayal, and the author was celebrated throughout the country as a charming, pro-American resistance fighter who led a glamorous life in Europe – a man who united past and future.[157]

Yet much as when his father had been reinvented as a modern figure back in 1922, Louis Ferdinand's lightning metamorphosis created friction with the old guard. The widow of a former tutor of the crown prince's children, Hedwig von Ditfurth, wrote an angry letter to protest about Louis Ferdinand's mocking characterization, printed in advance in illustrated German magazines, of her deceased husband Dietrich von Ditfurth's narrow-minded military pretensions. 'I began to hate everything connected with monarchism or conservatism,' the prince had written in one passage.[158] The widow, Hedwig, who had been particularly close to Crown Princess Cecilie, protested that her husband had sacrificed a brilliant military career to serve the House of Hohenzollern between 1917 and 1935 – and that the only thanks he received was now new-fangled derision and mockery of old values. She broke off all contact and requested that the pension she received be discontinued, saying that there was no way she would ever again accept money from the Hohenzollern clan.

A former major in the German armed forces reacted with similar outrage at what he considered the intolerable new style. He complained:

> [The new pretender to throne] doesn't just reject . . . everything traditional and military. By making that seem laughable he also presents himself as an excellent democrat. Wherever possible, he denigrates the past, ignores tradition and feels most at home among the social democrats He proudly calls himself a 'bourgeois' and a 'cosmo-politician' . . . He not only flirts with 'democracy'. He publicly declares his support for it. He disregards all the formalities of court and enjoys behaving in especially coarse fashion.

But the memoirs writer would ultimately founder, the incensed major predicted. He would be seen as a renegade by his loyal followers and learn the painful lesson that 'every democratic king has failed and made himself ridiculous'.

Even the Kaiser's trusted servant Dommes – who had been ennobled relatively late in life in 1913 as a commander of the Guards Hussars Regiment in Potsdam and who was now an old man of eighty-five – directed cautious words of warning to the pretender to the throne about following the trends of the times. In a letter, the general told his 'most gracious prince' and 'lord' that he had received communications from older officers who noted, full of horror, that:

> Your Imperial Majesty is taking a democratic, even social democratic, line and rejecting everything specifically Prussian with such vigour that they simply can no longer follow . . . It isn't the case that we can say these circles belong to us anyway and we can gain others. The right-wing circles are the only ones Your Imperial Majesty can rely upon. Experience from the olden days shows that otherwise one gets caught in the middle between two sides. I can't bring myself to believe that Your Imperial Majesty truly rejects everything that made the Old Prussia great, but I would be a poor servant of His Majesty your grandfather if I didn't openly share with you the above.

Louis Ferdinand responded that he valued everything Prussian but had just returned from Majorca and was preparing for his readings in the US – an answer that probably did little to convince Dommes of any loyalty to tradition.[159]

Louis Ferdinand's liberal, pro-democratic persona, so unpopular among the older generation of monarchists, also had its limits where the Hohenzollern clan itself was concerned. In 1967, when his eldest son, Friedrich Wilhelm, married outside the nobility, violating the 'house rule' of 1938, Louis Ferdinand disinherited him. His second-oldest son, Prince Michael of Prussia, met with the same fate after wedding below his station. Whereas in 1941, in keeping with the prevailing political winds of the times, Crown Prince

Wilhelm had opined that a 'farmer's daughter' made a better wife than a 'degenerate princess', as long as the former was of pure Aryan stock,[160] Louis Ferdinand had little time for notions of either racial or democratic equality. At a time when the Beatles were recording 'All You Need is Love' in London, Jean-Luc Godard was completing *La Chinoise* and the politically radical, free-love Commune I was being founded in Berlin, Louis Ferdinand disowned his sons for wedding women who weren't listed in the first or second volumes of the aristocratic registry.

The mixture of old and new perfectly suited the events at Hohenzollern Castle. Whatever the lowest common denominators may have been between Hans Rothfels, publisher and judge Gerd Bucerius, various American businesspeople and diplomats, conservative writer Ernst Jünger, Fabian von Schlabendorff, a number of repentant former Nazi authors, evangelical resistance members Eugen Gerstenmaier, pedagogical philosopher Eduard Spranger, and German chancellors Kurt Georg Kiesinger and Helmut Kohl, the castle was not only a refuge, but a fortress for representatives of the broken lineage of German conservativism in their search for new homes and combinations. As long as Potsdam remained in communist hands, Sigmaringen was the symbolic political heart of Prussia.

Louis Ferdinand, who found the role of his life in Hechingen, was also the ideal representative of Prussia in early post-war Germany with its mélange of conservative, liberal and pro-American elements. In the summer of 1946, when 'Prince Louis' (a former voter for the Nazis) suggested that young Germans be sent to the US to learn about democracy, a proposal publicized by Lochner (who had helped prepare the English translation of Goebbels' diaries),[161] he was behaving completely in line with the leading ideas of Cold War American cultural diplomacy. It is no exaggeration to say that for the conservative camp the figure of post-1945 Louis Ferdinand was an important example of Germany's 'long path to the West'.[162]

The image of the self-confident, historically informed builder of bridges in divided Germany reached its zenith shortly before the fall of the Berlin Wall, when Louis Ferdinand confidentially negotiated with the communist leader Erich Honecker over questions of Prussian history. The East German leadership was not disinclined to allow the prince a 'stay' in two rooms at Cecilienhof. In June 1989, he laid a wreath in the regional state of Thuringia for his namesake Prince Louis Ferdinand of Prussia, who fell in the Napoleonic Wars. The following month, he sat in the front row at ceremonies marking the restoration of Berlin Cathedral in the east of the divided city. In August, the Eastern German magazine *Neue Zeit* published a full-page private portrayal of Louis Ferdinand in West Berlin that uncritically passed on the self-image promoted by the Hohenzollern 'head of the house'.[163]

In retrospect, it was a short step from there to the 1994 encounter at Hohenzollern Castle at which the state premier of Brandenburg, the social democratic church lawyer Manfred Stolpe, described his 'Imperial Majesty' as a contributor to Brandenburg's post-communist reconstruction and criticized fifty years of the 'demonization' of Germany's loftiest 'aristocratic house'. The Hechingen local newspaper ran a headline reading, 'Stolpe Offers Louis Ferdinand a Villa in Potsdam'.[164]

After the two Germanys were united, the Hohenzollerns' focus shifted from Hechingen and the castle back to Potsdam. The reburial of the remains of the two most famous Prussian kings, which, as we have seen, had undergone a bizarre odyssey between 1943 and 1952,[165] can be interpreted from today's perspective as part of the broader attempt by the family to maintain their connections with Potsdam and their former possessions. In the summer of 1991, the return of Friedrich the Great and Friedrich I to Potsdam was a historical and political spectacle that attracted notice throughout Germany and abroad. A special historic train, which Louis Ferdinand had named the 'Plettenberg' after the Hohenzollerns' general administrator, who had been murdered by the Nazis,[166] transported the remains back to the city near Berlin. The symbolism was unmistakable to initiates: the German resistance of 20 July, represented by a vintage train, was returning the Prussian kings to Potsdam after years in the wilderness.

The spectacle staged between Hechingen and Potsdam, filmed by camera teams from around the world, included the commander of the Bundeswehr Army Command East. Eight staff officers held watch over the coffins, and a funeral march, titled 'Fridericus Rex' and composed by Louis Ferdinand, was played. The music corps of First Armoured Division Hanover greeted the funeral train at the former imperial station of Wildpark. In a symbolic conclusion, around midnight, the Hohenzollerns proceeded through the clan mausoleum with their guests of honour, among them Helmut Kohl, who officially attended as a 'private citizen' and family friend, not as German chancellor.[167] Roughly around this time, Louis Ferdinand also formulated his claims for restitution of Hohenzollern property in Potsdam. These would be rejected by an administrative court in 1999.

In 1994, the German government passed a law, the *Ausgleichsleistungsgesetz*, that enabled the state to compensate those whose property had been disappropriated between 1945 and 1949, if that property could no longer be restored. By the mid-1990s, it appears that compensation claims were filed under this legislation by Louis Ferdinand's general advocate with the regional states of Berlin, Brandenburg and Saxony-Anhalt. After Louis Ferdinand's death in September 1994, Prince Georg Friedrich assumed responsibility as the 'head of the house'. Initial confidential talks took place the following February between the German national government, the regional states of Berlin and Brandenburg and one or more representatives of the Hohenzollerns.

The Development of the 'Hohenzollern Debate'

During the 1980s, Louis Ferdinand once said; 'To put it in good, clear Prussian, I couldn't give a shit about compensation issues. I don't care in the slightest if we don't get a single square metre of our great possessions back.' In 1987, he still considered the 1926 division of wealth 'very generous'.[168] It wasn't until 1991 that Louis

Ferdinand filed for compensation. The end of the Cold War, the fall of the Berlin Wall, German reunification in autumn 1990 and a new set of legislation dealing with the Soviet expropriations between 1945 and 1949 unfroze issues which previously would not have had a chance to even be seriously considered. Like countless other German families who had been expropriated immediately after the war, the Hohenzollerns endeavoured to benefit from the new opportunities. After Louis Ferdinand's death in September, and following years of inheritance disputes within the family, which made it all the way to Germany's highest court, his grand-son Georg Friedrich was declared his main beneficiary and the 'head of the house'. It was now he who would have to interact with the state.

The very first compensation claim led to extremely complex sets of negotiations and a debate that persists until this day. These can be chronologically ordered, divided into legal issues and traced into terms of various levels that were connected with one another and yet followed their own laws. At the centre of these levels were a popular television comedian, professors of German constitutional law and historians of the Third Reich. There is nothing new about historians arguing about how to interpret facts. It's part of the dis-cipline. But the triangular constellation of historical interpretation, political disputes and legal wrangling entailed in the Hohenzollern Debate is quite unusual. Like a spaceship that had travelled back in time and returned, the almost forgotten House of Hohenzollern re-entered the media atmosphere, where it began to glow and then slammed into the surface of democratic Germany. Demands for restitutions and compensations that had been peacefully slumber-ing in the offices of law firms, ministries and government bureaucracies forced their way nearly overnight into a public sphere largely unprepared for the symbolic return of the Prussian king.

At least since 2019, three aspects have become inseparable from one another: the negotiations led by Georg Friedrich with Branden-burg and Berlin, an intense debate in the popular media, and a 1994 law that required an examination of Nazi history in a detail that caused never-ending disputes between historians, lawyers and lay-people. The crux of the issue, as anchored in the law governing compensation, is that the descendants of anyone who 'significantly abetted' (the German legal term is *erhebliche Vorschubleistung*) the Nazi dictatorship are ineligible for restitution of assets.[169] Beginning in 2011, the Hohenzollerns hired multiple respected historians to answer the question of whether the crown prince had done this with regard to the Nazi regime. In a short evaluation, the first of them, Christopher Clark, Regius Professor of History at Cambridge University, arrived at an interpretation favourable to the Hohenzollerns. But citing two other contradictory evaluations, including one written by the present author, the ministry responsible for the case in Potsdam rejected the Hohenzollerns' petition. Georg Friedrich Prinz von Preussen hired another historian, the Weimar Republic and Nazi Germany specialist Wolfram Pyta, to produce a further evaluation and appealed to the administrative court of the regional state of Brandenburg, located in Potsdam. All told, there would be five separate evaluations.[170]

These confidential legal proceedings attracted little attention while they were going on, but they came to develop a mass media dynamic rarely reached by historical issues. The case became public as early as 2014, but for the first time in earnest in November 2019, when the television comedian Jan Böhmermann made the legal battle the subject of his show and posted the four, formerly confidential evaluations on an Internet page with the address hohenzollern.lol. That episode was preceded in July by *Spiegel* magazine and the Berlin daily newspaper *Tagesspiegel* publishing leaked details concerning the confidential negotiations and the claims of the family. Suddenly, the Hohenzollern debate was on the radar screens of Germany's major media outlets. Thus it was that, although the family had not sought out this sort of notoriety, the name Hohenzollern regained some of the attention it had once commanded from millions of Germans. A century-old conflict was back in the news, where it appeared in a new, bizarre light. Depending on one's perspective, one could say that the emotionally charged part of this otherwise specialist debate went back either five or 100 years.[171]

In December 2019, in one of the initial highpoints of the Hohenzollern controversy, a German public television station broadcast a documentary film by Countess Tita von Hardenberg entitled *Who Owns the Kaiser's Treasures?*[172] It allowed both critics and defenders of the royal family to speak their piece. At the end of the film, Prince Michael-Benedikt von Sachsen-Weimar-Eisenach introduced and lauded the example of his own family, who had reached an agreement with the state that involved his renouncing billions in assets. The prince praised the ability of his chief negotiator, who was employed in that same function by the Hohenzollerns, to achieve an amicable settlement. At the same time, he assured viewers that Georg Friedrich von Preussen, whom he knew personally, was 'not a greed head', but a 'responsible man'.

Thereupon, Count Alexander von Schönburg-Glauchau, a member of the editorial board of the tabloid *Bild* newspaper and the author of lifestyle books, wrote of his shock at such public expressions of resentment towards the aristocracy. A theologian and historian declared that in 1926 Wilhelm II had voluntarily 'renounced' some of his family holdings. Historians hired by the Hohenzollerns presented 'new sources' they claimed reopened the question of whether the crown prince had supported the Nazis. One of the family's negotiators, who himself held a doctorate in history, went two steps further and declared that the evaluations indisputably proved there 'could be no talk' of the crown prince ever supporting Nazism.

The underlying message of all these statements was that the best option would be an out-of-court settlement between the royal family and the state. Shortly thereafter, the 'official website of the House of Hohenzollern' promoted Hardenberg's film as 'the most comprehensive documentary about this subject'.[173] Around the same time, the family's legal representatives urged Germany's parliament, the Bundestag, to reach an amicable settlement without a court investigation into the Hohenzollern's relationship to National Socialism.

The conflict took on unusually wide-ranging and intense historical, legal, political and media dimensions, expressed and expanded in the historians' evaluations, articles in Germany's leading daily and weekly newspapers, judgements rendered by civil law, appellate and administrative courts, and in discussions in the Bundestag, two regional parliaments and multiple expert commissions. Among the bodies that brought together the makers of political and academic opinion were the Berlin Institute for Advanced Study, the Leibniz Centre for Advanced Historical Study in Potsdam, the Institute of Contemporary History and the 2021 *Historikertag* conference in Munich. Legal and historical journals discussed the case, high-school students were orally quizzed on it, it was the subject of a dissertation at the University of Cambridge,[174] and it reached an audience of millions via Twitter and Böhmermann's television show. From politicians from the far-right Alternative for Germany (AfD), parliamentary deputies from the Left Party and renowned constitutional law experts and historians to authors of angry letters to the editor, vox pops conducted by television crews and the heads of the culture pages of Germany's newspapers, everyone had an opinion about the Hohenzollerns' restitution claims. German universities used the case as an introduction for first-year history students to the art of interpreting sources. In 2020, three Dutch historians published the first book covering the Hohenzollern Debate,[175] and there have been a host of further studies, of which the present book is one.

Those who follow the debate have often cited Marx's famous dictum that history repeats itself first as tragedy, then as farce. Indeed, in many respects the current conflict seems like a diminutive caricature of the antagonisms of the 1918 German Revolution or the Nuremberg Trials. But there is more to the Hohenzollern Debate than could fit in a popular farce, and it was harder to summarize than the disputes of the 1980s about the proper place of the Holocaust in German history. Even those directly involved in the conflict around the Hohenzollerns are hard pressed to explain why it is so intense.

There can be hardly any question, however, that the debate is about more than the unhappy actions of a potential heir to the throne. The discussions have the form of a Russian Matryoshka doll – the one listed in the *Guinness Book of World Records* as consisting of fifty-one figures. The questions within questions concerning the Hohenzollerns may not be that numerous, but just as the smallest figure in the record-holding doll, which measures only thirty-one millimetres, fits inside the next one, the forgotten figure of the crown prince, who was suddenly remembered in the summer of 2019, may not have been particularly spectacular, but he was part of something much bigger. Prior to 2019, the final crown prince had only been of interest to specialists, but the issue was never just about the man himself. The astonishing energy invested by journalists, historians, lawyers, politicians, comedians, bloggers, authors of letters to editors and millions of people can only be comprehended by remembering that the case involved one of most powerful families in Europe before 1918, the history of the German aristocracy and the elites of the Wilhelmine Empire, and the question of what became of them in the Weimar Republic. If the idea that the Hohenzollerns represented a possible alternative to the Nazi dictatorship was to be taken at all seriously, the question soon arose of who, then, was responsible for destroying the Weimar Republic. The spectre of an authoritarian alternative to Hitler, based upon the Reichswehr and the Stahlhelm and with a monarch at its helm, has haunted German journalism and historical research ever since. Looking at the long-forgotten crown prince allowed people to re-examine the conservative narrative of real and alleged counter-movements to Nazism. Without question, one reason for the intensity of the debate surrounding the royal family's compensation claims is its deep connection to the events of January 1933 and, commensurately, with one of the central questions of German political history: who was responsible for the Nazis attaining power? Historians had provided many solid, plausible answers to questions like this over the previous sixty years. But while the Hohenzollern debate wasn't primarily about uncovering previously unknown facts, it makes observers of history see familiar ones in a new light.

The *Almanach de Gotha*, the genealogical reference work of the European aristocracy, contains three volumes, the first of which is devoted to 'ruling and formerly ruling houses'. This is where the Hohenzollerns can be found. Nazism was by no means dominated by people listed in the *Gotha*, and the listings in the first volume are numerically very small, their cultural codes difficult to read for non-aristocratic historians. That helps explain why, previously, little attention was devoted to the activism of the former ruling German dynasties and why the search in 2019 for experts on the history of the German royal family after 1918 was so difficult.

Among the historical issues affected by the figures sketched out here, the discussion surrounding the creation of the Third Reich in 1933 must be the most significant. But even this question leads to an even bigger Matryoshka doll, at least in popular opinion. After years of confidential judicial negotiations became the subject of public debate, all at once legal categories of ownership became linked in unfamiliar fashion with political, historical and moral issues concerning justice, injustice, victims, damages and compensation. The satirist Jan Böhmermann pilloried the hypocrisy of Germany negotiating a settlement with the Hohenzollerns while the country refused to compensate the Herreros in German colonial Africa. In so doing he took millions of unsuspecting compatriots on an unexpected tour through a largely forgotten bit of history. Böhmermann's free association of the royal family with the genocidal war against the Herreros waged by Germany in 1904 and 1905 may have been rather cavalier, but it could not be dismissed as just a comic routine. There was no shortage of people at the time trying to define criteria for measuring damages caused and compensation deserved. The next largest doll in the series was the larger debate about which groups of twentieth-century victims had been hurt when and by whom and what restitutions had already been made.

Ultimately, all sides of the debate were conditioned by post-war ideas of ownership and inequality. In addition to the complex conceptual universes of legal experts, these took the form of more general questions, posed in angry letters to the editor and tweets: how did the claims raised by the Hohenzollerns compare with the losses suffered by millions of Germans driven from their homes after the Second World War? How could members of a family that, for centuries before 1918, had been among the most powerful German elites present themselves as victims? Why were moneyed aristocratic clans, whose wealth was largely not the product of their own labour, be allowed to negotiate for three decades with the state about art treasures now held in public museums? How did the famous Prussian ideals of frugality, reserve and modesty fit in with the demands the leading Prussian family was now making? There were frequently immense gulfs between the answers provided, on the one hand, by historians, lawyers and negotiators, and, on the other, by those advanced by laypeople and public opinion.

The situation was similar to the emotional debates about property rights that, like all conflicts concerning private property, had both a legal and a non-legal side. In the battle before the courts, one of Georg Friedrich's lawyers asserted that the issue was about 'the claims of a citizen who happens to be an aristocrat'.[176] Of course, the former ruling dynasties of Europe were not 'coincidentally' aristocratic; nor were the origins of their wealth and their attempts to defend it disconnected from their membership of the high nobility. Advocates of the Hohenzollerns continually invoked bourgeois property law and the principles of justice for all in the media, regional parliaments and the Bundestag to portray the entire public debate as a scandal in which the sober standards concerning rights to restitution had regrettably been pushed off the rails. But beyond the legal discussion the issue at stake was also about whether bourgeois property law could or should be applied to wealth whose origins had very little to do with bourgeois concepts of work, performance and acquisitions. That made the case complicated not just legally, but historically and morally as well.

The parliamentary debates featured updated lines of argument from the Weimar Republic. Criticism of the royal family's claims was equated with communism, dictatorship and injustice.[177] Conversely, the conflict also revived discussions of how social injustice originates and is perpetuated. The notion that unearned wealth, passed down through generations, was undeserved wealth was more relevant to the Hohenzollerns' case than practically any other.[178] The debates held in 1921 over the origins and perpetuation of payouts from the Hohenzollern family fortune still interested Germans a century later. No matter whether the case was viewed through a Marxist or liberal-capitalist economic lens, there was no way to square the royal family's enormous wealth with concepts of personal labour and achievement – or normal civil inheritance and property laws.

German laypeople were bewildered by the Hohenzollerns' claims and expressed themselves in far more direct language. 'Where does all that money come from?' one Berlin resident asked, when stopped on the street by Germany's foreign news broadcaster Deutsche Welle. 'You can't tell me that lot ever did any work for it.'[179] In a major article that kicked off the wider public debate, *Spiegel* magazine articulated the views of millions of regular people when it sarcastically labelled the Hohenzollerns a 'Tribe of Takers'.[180]

The comparisons made by the royal family's advocates to the wealth of large corporations and references to the protections of private property anchored in the German constitution may have been legally plausible,[181] but they obscured significant historical differences. The wealth of the European aristocratic dynasties arose in fundamentally different ways from the wealth of master craftsmen, industrialists, large-scale agriculturalists and professorial families. It was difficult to convince Germans that bourgeois ideals of equality before the law applied also to fortunes amassed from centuries of unequal treatment. Even some members of the laissez-faire Free Democratic Party (FDP), whose ranks have included prominent aristocrats, publicly recommend that the Hohenzollerns renounce their demands and accept the principles of meritocracy.[182] A major part of the public outrage at the Hohenzollerns' claims had less to do with historical questions than the issue's implicit and explicit connection to the distribution of wealth and social equity. Such views may not have been legally relevant in any direct sense, but they were politically important.

In his expert testimony to the Brandenburg regional parliament, historian Winfried Süss questioned the legitimacy of claims made by the Kaiser's heirs a century after he abdicated the throne. Süss cited a remark made by the renowned legal historian Michael Stolleis in a related context that it was hard to persuade taxpayers that cultural treasures originally 'acquired with the sweat of [His Majesty's] subjects' should be paid for twice.[183] Indeed, it is hard to see any meritocratic arguments for the royal family as the legitimate owners of the assets in question, even if that fact doesn't suggest any conclusions in the strictly legal sense. The fact remains that today, as was the case a century ago, public debates influence which demands are considered legitimate – and which are not.

Another aspect of the debate is the conflict between the Federal Republic and the formerly German Democratic Republic in the east, where the communists had radically different political, legal and above all historical views from those in the west. Whether the seizure of the Hohenzollerns' assets is seen as an unavoidable consequence of history or a historical injustice in need of remedy won't be decided by laws or judges alone, but in complex negotiations inflected by political articles of faith and ideas of justice. The duration and intensity of the debate is at least partly down to the unusual combination of legal, mass cultural, political and historical issues. As far as history is concerned, the seemingly minor figure of the crown prince takes on increased significance in his connections to other far more weighty historical personages, whose importance also exceeds that of nearly all other personalities in the recent German past.

The Archaeology of Hohenzollern Self-Presentation

For centuries the ruling aristocratic dynasties of Europe, including the House of Hohenzollern, all sought to influence public perception. In the post-monarchist era of the past century, we can approach the Hohenzollerns' efforts like archaeologists carefully uncovering layer after layer: for example, the early years of the Kaiser's exile (1918–23), the period between the end of the Second World War and the establishment of 20 July 1944 as a benchmark for the new Federal Republic (1945–54), or the interval between the commissioning of the first historical evaluation until the present (2011–23). All feature different narratives being adapted to the demands of the day. By brushing the dust from obsolete interpretations, we reveal the self-images of the 'former ruling house' in respective eras and uncover the formal remnants of Hohenzollern self-representation. No matter the period, the royal family always used significant financial resources, published autobiographies and employed lawyers, historians, ghost-writers and PR specialists to influence public opinion.

For the last decade or so, it is worth taking a closer look at the interpretations engendered by the debate over the Hohenzollerns' restitution claims. Whereas the narrative of the royal family's critics has added new facts and research but other otherwise hasn't significantly changed since 2014, Hohenzollern defenders are content with the state of the research in 2015 but have constantly shifted their arguments. They began by depicting the crown prince as a marginal figure, a man stuck in the past who ran around in outdated uniforms, lacking charisma and emotional appeal, so that there was no way he could have mobilized significant support for the Nazi regime, even had he wanted to. That was the essence of Christopher Clark's evaluation in 2011. When closer examination showed the empirical incompleteness in this view, it was replaced by an argument advanced by Wolfram Pyta and Rainer Orth in their 2015 evaluation. Employing new source material, they presented the crown prince as a politically exceptional figure who had actively tried to hinder Hitler. The report, written by a pair of renowned experts and containing 166 pages and 312 footnotes, was originally drawn up to convince governmental authorities but, at least at first glance, it was also intended to win over both experts and laypeople.[184]

Then came Jan Böhmermann. The website Hohenzollern.lol, containing four of the five evaluations, is still up and running,[185] and the corresponding episode of his show *Neo Magazin Royal* has attracted more than four million plays on YouTube alone.[186] Amidst the extraordinary situation of a comedy show plucking historical evaluations from the realm of confidential government documents and putting them at the disposal of millions of ordinary Germans, the shortcomings of the Pyta/Orth evaluation, the most extensive of the four studies, were revealed, and its methodology and conclusions came in for nearly unanimous criticism from other experts.[187] Subsequently, the text and its authors more or less disappeared from the public debate about the Hohenzollerns, and a later academic essay version of this work de-emphasized the role previously given to the crown prince.[188] The original trio of putative 'opponents of Hitler', Schleicher-Strasser-Crown Prince Wilhelm,[189] had essentially become a duo of Schleicher and Strasser, with Wilhelm reduced to a mere supplier of 'top news', whatever that meant.[190]

All variants of the idea of forming a 'broad common front' on the German Right included an alliance with, not opposition to, Nazism. Gregor Strasser, the key figure in such speculations, was one of the Nazi Party's most important leaders and by no means an 'opponent of Hitler', as was also noted in the parliamentary committee that examined the Hohenzollerns' claims.[191] It may be interesting to ponder what a dictatorship might have been like if Hitler had been relegated to a back-up function and Himmler, Heydrich or some other figure had been hoisted into the leadership position. But such thought experiments have little to do with historical analysis.

At the time of writing, no legitimate expert has come forward to defend the idea of the crown prince as a member of the German resistance *avant la lettre*. Despite periodic talk on the margins of the debate about 'new sources' and 'new interpretations',[192] the empirical and methodological objections to the thesis of the crown prince opposing Nazism have never been countered. As it became apparent that experts put even less stock in their second than in their first positive depiction of the crown prince, Hohenzollern apologists again shifted gears. They argued now that there was no consensus among historians and that the Hohenzollern household archives would have to be studied more closely. This reasoning was debuted in an expert hearing of the Bundestag's culture committee in January 2020. There, as in the preceding open debate on the parliamentary floor, members of the CDU, the FDP and the AfD, as well as their chosen experts, defended the Hohenzollerns' claims in sometimes more, sometimes less, contentious fashion. But neither the lengthy Pyta/ Orth evaluation nor the older and much shorter text by Christopher Clark were cited as the most important historical reference points.

The Hohenzollerns' new main contention was that historians had arrived at a 'stalemate'. The expert invited by the conservative CDU to testify, Benjamin Hasselhorn, had never published on the topic but had become the most visible public Hohenzollern defender in previous months. Before the parliamentary session, he avoided staking out a clear position of his own but suggested that he basically agreed with Clark.[193] Hasselhorn's testimony gave the impression, much like the one imparted to a million-strong TV audience by Tita von Hardenberg's documentary, that the questions surrounding the Hohenzollerns were still open,[194] a stance that is only legitimate if four evaluations, commissioned for specific legal purposes, are allowed to completely overshadow sixty years of wide-ranging historical research on the Weimar epoch. Then, and only then, is it possible to speak of a historical stalemate.

The rapid shifts between arguments didn't exactly increase the credibility of the former royal family's advocates. Most historians and most judges in the debate reached conclusions unfavourable to the Hohenzollerns' claims. But while the three existing interpretations – the crown prince as a marginal figure, the same person as an influential Hitler opponent and the purported stalemate over the two interpretations among historians – still flickered sporadically, the pro-Hohenzollern camp again changed its narrative. Commentaries on the wave of lawsuits filed against participants in the debate took on a new, concerned, legalistic timbre. The argument was now that a 'mutual understanding' should be reached regardless of the results of historical investigations. Renowned legal experts stated in prominent public forums that, while the historical debate might have been interesting, its results were by no means definitive since lawyers by nature had to operate with legal instruments beyond the ken of historians. The same historians who had been commissioned by lawyers to interpret a legal issue were now criticized for misusing legal criteria.[195] Whereas the Greens, the SPD and the Left Party urged that the issue be settled in court, members of the CDU, the FDP and the right-wing AfD, together with Prince Georg Friedrich, kept pressing for a compromise political solution. Increasingly Hohenzollern representatives publicly stressed the family's willingness to forgo some of its demands, its desire for an extrajudicial settlement, its appreciation for the historians' work and its regret at the 'misunderstandings' of the past.

A major article in the *New York Times* may have first noted the shift in tone and content,[196] but it soon became apparent to everyone in the media.[197] Assertions about the historical role of the crown prince now sounded very different, as though anticipating the publication of further studies with conclusions disproving the idea of the crown prince as either a completely marginal figure or an opponent of Hitler. In multiple interviews, Georg Friedrich acknowledged that the years from 1930 to 1935 had been a moral 'low point' for the royal family, as he himself could see and assess from his own family archives.

Georg Friedrich claimed to have long supported the most comprehensive, critical, academic study of the crown prince, expressed his regret for the 'misunderstandings' and said his hand remained extended to his detractors in the spirit of dialogue.[198] In light of a decade of effort spent promoting the opposite, the prince's supposed enlightenment is all the more astonishing – not just for the many people, companies and institutions against whom the 'head of the house' has taken legal action. As late as 1993, Louis Ferdinand claimed in an interview with *Spiegel* that Wilhelm II had suffered greatly and been treated unfairly by history. 'I feel I have a duty to protect him from ingratitude and prejudice,' Louis Ferdinand had said. When asked whether his identity as a son and grandson hindered him from engaging in critical reflection, he replied: 'Why should I engage in it? Historians are already doing that. It won't change a thing about the overall situation. As the Americans say, "I don't give a shit."'[199]

The position staked out by Louis Ferdinand's successor as 'head of the house' over the course of 2021 dramatically reversed that position, as previous pro-Hohenzollern narratives became untenable in the face of mounting historical evidence. Together with another announced discovery of 'sensational source material', a new line of argument appeared in the debate over historical interpretation. In the summer of 2021, an author previously uninvolved in the discussion, Lothar Machtan, presented a take on the past that absorbed and empirically expanded upon the existing body of historical evidence between the 1950s and 2014. In fact, Machtan argued, the prince and the Nazis had been close at certain moments and concerning various questions, but that closeness was difficult to interpret. Months in advance, from New York to provincial Brandenburg, the new study of the crown prince was praised as the first to be based on extensive material from the Hohenzollern family archives. In a second television documentary, Tita von Hardenberg offered advance praise for Machtan's work and its allegedly 'new perspective'. In the film, the 'head of the house' claimed that the Hohenzollerns hadn't issued any demands but had merely made an 'offer of a settlement'. In August, the study was finally published – as mentioned at the beginning of this work, the book launch was an opulent affair in the historic setting of Berlin's Kronprinzenpalais (Crown Prince Palace), replete with musical accompaniment and a buffet. There, the acting German economic minister, a historian supported by the Hohenzollerns and Georg Friedrich Prinz von Preussen, introduced Machtan's work, whose scope was limited to 1930–35 and whose subtitle referred rather nebulously to an alleged 'blind spot' on the part of the Hohenzollerns.[200] Surrounded by a spectacle of post-royal symbolism, Machtan secured his spot in the pantheon of writers who worked for the 'head of the house'. Rather astonishingly, he also claimed to have written the first 'academic', impartial, and non-commissioned work on the subject. But the announced 'sensation' never materialized. Despite a variety of new details, no results were presented that deviated from established historical knowledge. Nor did the source material from the family's household archives, touted as the basis for a differentiated portrait of the crown prince, reveal a single new aspect on the topic. In his 'word of welcome', the 'head of the house' stressed his friendship with the author and his readiness for an open attitude that acknowledged the 'dark' sides of Hohenzollern family history and supported critical research. The topic, Georg Friedrich insisted, had been approached 'with the most ruthless honesty'.

Machtan's partial biography paints the crown prince as a playful, politically irrelevant, irresponsible dandy. But its detailed empirical core is embedded in four relativizing assumptions: 1) the influence of the generally insignificant crown prince was brief; 2) without him, nothing in history would have changed; 3) lawyers only should decide the question of whether he had 'abetted' the Nazis – a legal category that would disqualify the royal family from compensation; and 4) the debate had only just begun. But the author never specified what further elements the debate still lacked.[201]

What Can and Cannot Be Said: The Hour of the Lawyers

In the two years before the presentation of Machtan's study, in the context of the debate about Hohenzollern assets, depictions of individual past family members once again gained importance, and as had been the case at various other junctures over the previous 100 years, lawyers took centre stage. When the debate became a *res publica* in 2019, it introduced the additional toolkit of media law to the ongoing political, historical, administrative and financial dimensions of the controversy. Dozens of legal attacks through the field of media law, cease and desist letters and injunctions added an additional battleground that was closely covered by the German media. The result was a series of initially targeted but increasingly scattershot legal actions by Hohenzollern lawyers against people, companies and institutions.

As soon became public, it was clear that a then previously obscure case being heard before an administrative court in Potsdam touched on one of the central questions of German history, and things were about to get nasty. In the autumn of 2014, with the press starting to report on the proceedings and the historians' evaluations, Hohenzollern lawyers sued *Spiegel* magazine over an article entitled 'A Prince with a Screw Loose'.[202] Meanwhile, the newspapers *Die Welt* and the *Märkische Allgemeine Zeitung* reported that a legal complaint had also been filed 'against individuals in the Brandenburg Finance Ministry' for allegedly releasing confidential material.[203] The society magazine *Bunte* ran an article entitled 'The Prince is Fighting for His Inheritance and Honour'.[204] When asked in an interview whether he had filed the complaint, Georg Friedrich replied: 'We have asked the authorities to find out where documents were leaked so as to re-establish a climate of mutual trust.'[205]

Yet lawsuits proved of limited value in re-establishing any such climate, and the Hohenzollerns had a hard time coming by legal victories. In January 2019, one of the journalists most deeply familiar with the case reported that Georg Friedrich had tried, in vain, to muzzle official Brandenburg sources to stop news leaking out. The paper added that the Potsdam administrative court had rejected the request 'to use a gag order to suppress all information given to the press and all public statements about a case concerning millions in compensation for confiscated property'.[206]

In 2015, after I had handed in my own evaluation, a lawyer acting on behalf of Georg Friedrich von Preussen continued the efforts to ensure the confidentiality of the case by using lawsuits and by signalling his readiness to use legal action, if necessary, to promote his own interpretation of the situation.[207] Subsequently, a lawyer contacted the regional office responsible for questions of confiscated assets to protest that the historical evaluator Malinowski 'possessed insufficient knowledge of the material', lacked 'expertise' and had 'political intentions', rendering him 'neither capable nor prepared' to provide the office with expert information. Furthermore, said evaluator had 'misunderstood' his task and was 'out of his depth'. In combination with the previously described lessons on how history was to be correctly interpreted, the lawyer demanded that I be excluded from further proceedings in the matter.

In December of that year, after this initial intervention had failed, I received a letter from the Hamburg Prosecutor's Office informing me that I had become the subject of a criminal investigation for allegedly violating the confidentiality of private matters.[208] Some months before, I had published an article for the news weekly *Die Zeit*, in which I had sketched the historical background of the case and my own historical assessment.[209] When I took up my work as an evaluator in 2014, I hadn't agreed to any particular form of legally binding confidentiality, nor had my article in *Die Zeit* revealed any details about the case that couldn't have been reconstructed from already public sources in the media. As a result, and after the intervention of my lawyer, the baseless investigation and the proceedings themselves were dropped in 2016.[210]

Three years later, the Hohenzollerns stepped up their legal actions in terms of both quantity and intensity. In July 2019, with the press now taking an enhanced interest in the proceedings, journalists started asking many historians for articles and statements. This resulted in my writing two longer articles for the *Frankfurter Allgemeine* and *Süddeutsche Zeitung* newspapers as well as answering an email from a journalist of the German international broadcaster Deutsche Welle, who had asked me for a comment. Between August and October 2019, I received three cease-and-desist demands from one of Georg Friedrich's lawyers. They focused not on the continuing historical debate but on individual sentences. The first letter took issue with a sentence that had demonstrably come from an editor, not from me, and had been added without my knowledge. The second focused on a sentence in which I paraphrased a statement made in an interview by a colleague about the accessibility of private Hohenzollern archives. The third revolved around words in an email to a Deutsche Welle journalist and published without my knowledge and consent in an article on the broadcaster's website. In total, the cease-and-desist letters concerned five statements. My lawyer rejected all of the demands. Only in one case – the statement cut out of an email without my consent – did the Berlin Regional Court follow up on the demands made by the complainants.[211]

Meanwhile, the Hohenzollerns' official website claimed that I was 'inventing my own facts' and their lawyers accused me of cooking up 'fairy tales' and 'lies' and of making 'crude mistakes' and statements with the intent to 'deceive'. In an interview he gave at the start of the series of these legal warnings, Georg Friedrich declared that, while he considered freedom of the press a pillar of democracy, 'lies aren't part of that, and that's the only thing we have tried to straighten out'.[212] In another passage, he dubiously asserted: 'We only go after lies intended to damage me and the House [of Hohenzollern], and we have triumphed in every single instance.'[213]

The word 'lie' was also bandied about in legal documents and on the Hohenzollern family's extensive webpage. No historian wants to be called a liar, a spinner of fairy tales and a fraudster, and in the process of defending myself against accusations of such number that they could be interpreted as a systematic attempt to destroy the credibility of an evaluator and a historian, I countersued. In the end, the opposite side lost the case before the Hanseatic Higher Regional Court in Hamburg (Hanseatisches Oberlandesgericht Hamburg).[214]

As for the case negotiated in Berlin and assessing a sentence cut out off one of my emails, in August 2021, a superior court in Berlin declared upon appeal that the case had been resolved, thus striking down a cease-and-desist order issued by the lower court.[215] On 14 October, that court also ruled that Georg Friedrich would be liable for all costs of the proceedings.

The legal tangle, not always comprehensible to laypeople, of threatening letters, responses and cease-and-desist orders that threatened 'a fine of up to 250,000 euros or six months' imprisonment' – together with letters of application and complaint, justifications for appeals and other correspondence with multiple courts in Berlin and Hamburg – lasted two years, cost me an enormous amount of time and required a five-figure financial outlay. But my own personal experiences were only a very small part of a far more comprehensive and potentially unique campaign of legal actions, interpreted by many as an attempt to influence historical and political interpretations and to intimidate critics of the former royal family. In the months that followed, more and more individuals and institutions received cease-and-desist demands. In February 2020, *Die Welt* newspaper reported Georg Friedrich admitting to '120 such cases'.[216] We only know the number of legal actions filed by the side making the complaints, but with considerable effort we could reconstruct and document at least the outlines of the legal activity. In June 2020, the watchdog website FragdenStaat (AsktheState) started a 'prince fund' for donations to help those who received such demands from Hohenzollern lawyers to pay for their legal defences.[217]

By this point, countless reports in Germany's major media outlets criticized the legal harassment of journalists and others and analysed in depth the 'constrictive effect on the formation of public opinion'.[218] The head of the Leibniz Centre for Contemporary History in Potsdam, Martin Sabrow, publicly went on the offensive about what he called a 'negative culture of intimidation' and a curtailing of academic freedom, and the chairwoman of the Association of German Historians in Germany, Eva Schlotheuber, came out in support of that position.[219] Deputies in the regional parliaments of Berlin and Brandenburg also criticized what was going on, and the parliamentary groups of the Left Party and the Greens held multiple online events about the case. The historical and legal debate made the pages of the *New York Review of Books*[220] and *Le Figaro* and was the subject of a lengthy report by CNN.[221] Richard J. Evans, the renowned Cambridge historian of the Weimar Republic and the Third Reich, wrote a long piece for the *New Statesman* discussing the Hohenzollerns' legal campaign,[222] and Christopher Clark, the historian whose report the royal family's advocates most often cited, explicitly criticized the practice of threatening legal action against journalists and fellow historians.[223]

The press division of the Berlin Regional Court was confronted with no fewer than eighty cease-and-desist demands from Georg Friedrich's media lawyer filed against reporters, bloggers, newspapers, radio stations, politicians and academics,[224] and the actual total was significantly higher, as the 'head of the house' himself publicly confirmed.[225] Among those on the receiving end of the legal actions were the newspapers and magazines *Spiegel*, *Frankfurter Allgemeine Zeitung*, *Welt*, *Zeit*, *Süddeutsche Zeitung* and *Berliner Tagesspiegel*; broadcasters Deutschlandfunk, Deutsche Welle, Norddeutscher Rundfunk and Radio Berlin-Brandenburg; the public employees trade union Verdi; a handful of freelance authors; politicians, particularly from the Left Party; and five historians including Schlotheuber. In June 2021, under the direction of constitutional lawyer Sophie Schönberger and in cooperation with the Association of Historians in Germany, the Heinrich Heine University in Düsseldorf launched an extensive website called 'The Complaints of Hohenzollerns' to permanently document and question the royal family's legal campaign against media outlets and individuals.[226]

At first glance, the issues at stake in these complaints were mostly banal: for instance, whether the family should have a say in exhibitions and museums that contained works loaned from the Hohenzollerns. But, at least subjectively, many of those attacked felt they had no choice but to allow themselves to be called liars and spreaders of false information rather than engage in time-consuming and costly lawsuits. The question needs to be asked: if the only point was to correct supposedly false statements, why didn't the family begin with something other than legal threats? Its representatives could have picked up the phone, sent an email, written letters to the editor, granted interviews or published records on the matters in question. It takes substantial money to make this many legal complaints – just as it does to defend oneself against them. That gives rise to the impression that one of the not unwelcome side-effects of this legal campaign, from the Hohenzollerns' perspective, was to hinder other critics from making unflattering statements about the family and its claims by compelling them to invest immense amounts of time, energy and money.

In the meantime, between the publication of the German and English editions of this book, both the lawsuits against the state at the Administrative Court in Potsdam and the media attacks on individuals and newspapers have ceased. In a major interview with the conservative daily *Die Welt* and at an event organized at great expense, gathering almost the entirety of the German media in Berlin, the 'head of the house' declared in March 2023 that he had 'renounced' those parts of his fortune connected with the historical controversy over the crown prince's closeness to National Socialism. The title of the interview read: 'I want to clear the way for an untroubled debate' – the interview did not specify who or what had previously troubled the debate.[227] The withdrawal of the final lawsuits against a professor of law in Berlin and against two major daily newspapers was announced in March 2023. Only after the news magazine *Der Spiegel* reported on cases that were still before the courts were the last cases withdrawn in July.[228] Many observers found Georg Friedrich's use of the word 'renounce' curious since renunciation implies a legitimate claim. And this was precisely what was increasingly in doubt both in the specialist discussion among historians and in detailed assessments by constitutional lawyers and judges in legal journals.[229] Christopher Clark thoroughly adjusted his original position,[230] and the directors of Germany's two most important contemporary history research institutions stated that there was no historical justification for the Hohenzollerns' compensation claims.[231] Some observers speculated that Georg Friedrich's 'renunciation' was intended to forestall public defeats in court.

In June 2023, the head of the House of Hohenzollern spoke at the 200th anniversary of the Oxford Union Society. As part of a tour through his family history, Georg Friedrich said that the Weimar Republic had compensated his family very generously, and that they had even been allowed to keep many palaces and estates and works of art. He added that, unfortunately, some family members, including Crown Prince Wilhelm, had nevertheless sympathized with National Socialism. He also acknowledged that Wilhelm had openly endorsed Hitler in 1932.[232]

Despite the abandonment of its restitution claims, negotiations between the House of Hohenzollern and the German state on property issues are likely to continue for some time to come. The shift in the family's public position on the past will probably not worsen the Hohenzollerns' negotiating position.

Lawyers have recently described the extensive legal activities of the Hohenzollerns as an example of the 'Streisand effect' – named after the American singer and actress Barbra Streisand, who sued a photographer for fifty million dollars in 2003 for taking a picture of her Californian estate. Much to her dismay, Streisand found that instead of helping to conceal the location of her mansion from the public, the lawsuit led to an endless stream of reports and photos. The Hohenzollerns' cease-and-desist letters have had precisely the same effect.

Summary: The Return of the Twentieth Century

Recent arguments in favour of the Hohenzollerns' restitution demands are fivefold. The first is that focusing on the year 1933 presents a distorted view of the crown prince and an unfairly dark picture of the royal family and Prussia and German history in total. As if history were a commercial ledger, this line of thought seeks to tot up the darkness of the year 1933, on the one hand, and ten centuries of light, on the other. In this logic, the modern German state, the fine arts, the Huguenots, the Jews, the Humboldt brothers, the Enlightenment and the physical beauty of Potsdam owed much, if not everything, to the Hohenzollerns. Historian Michael Wolffsohn, for instance, stressed the 'true achievements of the one-thousand-year Hohenzollern dynasty'.[233] And explicitly reversing the thrust of

Bertolt Brecht's Poem 'Questions of a Literate Worker', the leader of the far right AfD, Alexander Gauland, told the German parliament that Friedrich the Great, not 'the stonemason with his trowel', had built Sanssouci Palace.[234] Moreover, in an article mocking his opponents as 'fumigators' and 'monkish researchers', the chairman of the Prussian Historical Commission, Frank-Lothar Kroll, recalled the Hohenzollerns' 'record of achievements', among which he included 'the cultured [German] state', 'tolerance' and 'socially balanced policies'.[235] The author reached similar conclusion in another article for the aristocratic publication *Deutsches Adelsblatt*.

The hypothetical invocation of an opposition that might have arisen, if conditions had been completely different, is of one historical piece with references to achievements made three centuries ago or things that are promoted today as such. The legally worthless and historically dubious argument about 'achievements' that emanated from the depths of the past and, much as a river does from individual drops of water, enveloped the brief 'dark' period from 1930 to 1935 with '900 years of family history' contributed very little to our understanding of the political situation at the end of the Weimar Republic.[236] Even if we accept that the deeds of eighteenth-century Hohenzollerns were as glorious as some historians of Prussia would like to believe, it would only cast the dynasty's twentieth-century political and moral collapse in an even more unfavourable light.

Secondly, the pro-Hohenzollern position contains a massive number of counterfactual constructions. Since there is no denying the royal family's radical hostility towards Weimar democracy and connections with the Nazi movement, supporters repeatedly invoked traditions, actions, options and princes active in the resistance that never actually existed in reality. At its core, this sort of historical storytelling hypothetically posits a 'restoration' of a monarchy as a conservative alternative – indeed the only one feasible – to the Nazi regime. If post-1918 Germany had become a constitutional monarchy, the logic ran, the country would have developed along the same lines as Britain or Sweden. If the crown prince had been a capable modern leader, if Schleicher and Strasser had been able to mobilize the 'moderate Nazis', and if the Kaiser had not been forced into a position of 'reactive anti-Semitism' and been pushed to the side by radical military officers, and so on, 'the Germans and the world would have been spared a lot [of suffering]'.[237] The extension of this logic is that 'the wrong side' triumphed in 1918. If the Kaiser, who was, of course, in his defenders' eyes a man of peace and by no means an anti-Semite, hadn't become embroiled in war, or if he had won that war, or if Germany had become a constitutional monarchy in 1918, then Hitler and the 'German catastrophe' could 'potentially' have been prevented.[238]

Emphasis has repeatedly been placed on the supposed goal of such a monarchy. In a 2020 interview with CNN, Georg Friedrich claimed that the Stahlhelm had consisted of 'very conservative people' who had advocated the restoration of the monarchy.[239] 'The Hohenzollerns would perhaps have been able to hold on to their crown, if [Wilhelm II] had stepped down in time, around September 1918, and cleared a path for reforms,' the latter-day prince mused.[240] He also claimed that history would have been different if Crown Prince Wilhelm had simply done nothing at all.[241] There was no end to chains of association possible in the realm of hypothesis and with the liberal use of 'could have' and 'would have' constructions. But history is written in the indicative. The value of the subjunctive for historical accounts, however entertaining and charming such speculations may be, is zero.

As a result, counterfactual considerations were pretty much all the crown prince had on his side in the culture sections of newspapers and in the political discussions of the time. Occasionally, these were presented as realistic possibilities even though they radically contradicted actual historical fact. The head of the culture section of *Die Welt* newspaper, Tilman Krause, proposed: 'If a man like Crown Prince Wilhelm had developed a sense of political responsibility, the Germans would have perhaps received a particularly significant push towards civilization.' This line of thought watered down the influence and culpability of the crown prince into the formula: 'Wilhelm's "failure" was the "failure" of his age and his people.'[242]

Such imaginary scenarios serve to obscure historical fact. Reviving a bit of counterfactual speculation from the Pyta/Orth evaluation, another *Welt* author mused about what would have happened 'if Strasser and not Hitler had seized power'. This bit of speculation, which was also promoted in advance as a historical sensation, yielded an impressive chain of hypotheticals, in which Germany would have followed the path of Italy or Hungary, had its 1933 personnel and structure been completely different from what it actually was. Fifty-six subsequent letters to the editor made further propositions about what might have been.[243] When Machtan's 'dossier' was finally published – in March 2023 on the Hohenzollern family's website – it was once again presented as a milestone event, but it didn't contain a single document that altered accepted historical wisdom.[244]

Given the actual course of twentieth-century German history, it's understandable that conservatives look for ways to tell the story of 1933 with imaginary protagonists and configurations. And indeed, versions of an altered past, which Germany was so much in need of after 1945, were successfully marketed, above all to conservative readers.[245] Nevertheless, the real crown prince acted in real circumstances in 1933, not in some imaginary conglomerate universe borrowed from Swedish history, British tradition or Romantic literature.[246]

Moreover, if we were to include counterfactual considerations in evaluations of the crown prince's options, we could turn the tables and ask: what would have happened if the Republic had sought to stabilize itself early on by exiling and expropriating the Hohenzollerns? What effect might a moderate conservatism, supported by the royal family, have had? How might Hindenburg have reacted if the Kaiser, the crown prince and the latter's brothers had issued a public declaration calling for him not to appoint Hitler chancellor? What influence would it have had on conservative elites if the Hohenzollerns had left Germany after the Night of the Long Knives in 1934 or appealed to the Wehrmacht generals on the Eastern Front to rebel in 1943?

These questions are also intriguing, but they are just as fruitless, where historical analysis is concerned, as all the speculations about a Germany with different chancellors, party leaders, monarchs, heirs to the throne or indeed a different native populace. In the rarefied realm of dreams, fantasies about democracy-friendly monarchs may have free rein. But on the *terra firma* of evidence, historians have no choice but to examine the crown princes, Reich chancellors and constellations of power that actually existed, not the ones that may have been more desirable.

Thirdly, Hohenzollern supporters insist that the current state of knowledge is insufficient for forming solid judgements and that historians have reached a stalemate.[247] Even the aforementioned latest public presentation of allegedly new evidence in March 2023 tried to convey the impression that the historical debate was still in its infancy. That view is baffling since no one has come up with any new ground-breaking evidence in the most recent past, and countless legal and historical experts have examined the issue of 'substantial support' over years. Apologists have reacted with not inconsiderable outrage to the assertion that there is no fundamental quarrel or dissent among historians about the crown prince. One small group of respected historians indeed rejected this statement in a public letter, but they didn't cite a single empirical or even theoretical study to support their point. That amounts to simply demanding an academic debate without contributing to one in any concrete form.[248]

No one would dispute that more research is needed on this topic, but where is that *not* the case when history is concerned? A new academic paper in the *Historische Zeitschrift* journal would present new insights, it has been claimed. Georg Friedrich would organize a conference of leading historians at Hohenzollern Castle. Key documents were being kept at the archive in the dynasty's ancestral home in Hechingen, but critics had refused, although invited, to evaluate them. In the Bundestag, the conservative deputy Elisabeth Motschmann – whose remarks might as well have been coordinated with arguments used by Hohenzollern family advisors – subjected historians who testified as experts to a veritable cross-examination. Her core message seemed to be that only those who had inspected the contents of the Hohenzollern family archive in Hechingen should be entitled to offer an opinion on the questions under dispute.[249]

But amidst legal wranglings over the precise conditions for access to the private Hohenzollern archives and Motschmann's rejection of historians' explanations as to what constitutes a source,[250] the parliamentary representatives who vigorously pleaded the Hohenzollerns' case neglected to point out that the contents of those archives have long been a part of the general historical record. For starters, the royal family and their advisors always had access to them. Secondly, as was repeatedly stressed, the evaluators Pyta and Orth had viewed the material. Thirdly, a fifth evaluation, for which two of the most expert individuals within the Hohenzollern family had also examined the house archives, had been around for years. The conclusions of this evaluation, which seems to have been commissioned by the family itself, have never been published but were presented at proceedings at the Brandenburg regional finance ministry, which ended with the rejection of Hohenzollern claims. Given the decades of conflict and the immense effort of lawyers, historians and advisors over more than ten years of proceedings, as well as the fact that the Hohenzollern Castle archives have been examined by various historians commissioned, supported or engaged by the royal family, the likelihood that they contain material exculpating the former ruling German dynasty seems very remote indeed.

The fourth strategy consists of emphasizing the personal and political weakness of the crown prince as proof of his alleged insignificance. In this line of reasoning, neither he nor his father, the Kaiser, possessed any influence worthy of the term after they fled to the Netherlands in 1918. The aura and the symbolic power of the Hohenzollern dynasty, depicted as quite unpopular, had been extinguished – the result being both political and cultural irrelevance.

In a longer newspaper article in April 2021, historians Ulrich Schlie and Thomas Weber promised to resolve both the historical and the legal debate and clear up a 'misapprehension'.[251] But they, too, offered nothing new aside from correcting a false date and contributing a few ancillary details. Essentially, their text merely reprised Clark's arguments. The crown prince, Schlie and Weber proposed, was just 'a ridiculous supporting figure on the margins', and the 'objective category' of having abetted the Nazis could only have been fulfilled, 'if there had been a direct, substantial causal connection between Wilhelm's actions and the establishment and consolidation' of the Nazi system. Whether the two authors are right on this score is one thing,[252] but what's interesting is that they again argued in the subjunctive. If the crown prince had done nothing at all, according to their logic, history would have been just the same. That may be the case. But if the irreplaceability of individuals is the sole criterion, the question becomes: how many Nazi leaders could be deemed to have 'significantly abetted' the Nazi regime? There is no doubt, even hypothetically, that powerful political currents don't simply cease to exist if individual principal figures are removed. The French Revolution would have taken place without Danton, and the Americas would still have been 'discovered' if there had been no Columbus. Likewise, radical anti-Semitism would have affected post-1918 Germany even without the writings of Julius Streicher, the publisher of Germany's most virulently anti-Semitic journal. That does nothing to diminish the historical significance of Danton, Columbus or Streicher.

To support their arguments about the marginality of the crown prince, Schlie and Weber cite a 'Google Ngram analysis' of individual concepts,[253] but this only yields the less-than-surprising insight that media interest in Wilhelm had its downs and ups, with the latter coming in 1918–19, 1923, 1926 and 1933. It is hardly astonishing that the amount of reporting on the crown prince tailed off after

1934. Anyone familiar with the subject matter could have guessed that without the help of Google 'analysis'.[254]

The preceding chapters of this book thoroughly disprove the contention that the crown prince didn't attract any more public interest after 1918. Moreover, the issue can, at least in the general sense, be evaluated quantitively as well. At the beginning of the debate about the Hohenzollerns' relations with Nazism, Clark contended that *The Times* of London had only mentioned the crown prince four times from 1929 to 1945 – a number that would suggest a figure who had completely sunk into obscurity.[255] Ten years later, ignoring the advances in research in the meantime, Schlie and Weber still proposed that quantitative analysis 'revealed' an 'extremely slight' interest in Wilhelm. Regardless of the number games, there can be no doubt that the figure of the crown prince attracted immense attention from the national and international press between 1918 and 1934.[256] If we measure the significance of the crown prince by how often he was mentioned in the foreign press as a whole, he seems to have attracted quite a lot of attention between 1918 and 1945. Although it is by no means a guarantee of statistical validity, anyone carrying out a simple search in English-language data bases will find roughly 23,000 mentions of the 'Hohenzollerns' and some 10,000 for 'Crown Prince Wilhelm'. The numbers in the French press are similar: 19,000 for Hohenzollerns and 22,700 for the crown prince. All these figures are considerably above those various leading conservative politicians in Germany tend to cite, and they reflect the impression made by qualitative analyses.[257]

The attempt to demonstrate the Hohenzollern family's alleged insignificance even cites the prominent differences in the first names Germans gave to their children as of 1917.[258] But the decline in the royal family's aura, as we have seen, was a stop-start, slow and incomplete process. The metaphor of a meandering monarchism after 1918 accurately captures the historical situation. Moreover, the argument that the Hohenzollerns entirely lost their aura and influence after the First World War fails to account for precisely those moments perennially cited in arguments for the royal family as a hypothetical source of opposition to Nazism. The four most important of those moments are Empress Auguste Victoria's funeral in April 1921, that of the crown prince's eldest son in May 1940, the exclusion of Hohenzollern princes from the Wehrmacht and the Nazi rage at the 'blue-blooded swine' after the failed Hitler assassination of 20 July 1944.[259] In the future, the immense attention the family continued to generate at home and abroad and the political battles over the import of the crown prince as a figure may and should be the subject of further examination. But they cannot be sensibly disputed.

Observers both inside and outside Germany described Nazi anxiety about the rival aura possessed by the Hohenzollerns, and examples can be found everywhere. For example, in the wake of Georg Elser's failed assassination of Hitler in November 1939, French newspapers ran reports that the crown prince had been arrested and beheaded.[260] As the authorities searched for the people allegedly behind Elser, it seems that Wilhelm was also briefly considered as one of many suspects. That would be indeed an impressive bit of evidence for the gulf between the Nazi regime and the royal family defenders of the Hohenzollerns, had there been anything at all to those suspicions. But here as well, the distance was purely hypothetical, a potential that was never activated. The fantasy of the crown prince being put to the guillotine for being part of the anti-Hitler opposition was something in which some people may have wanted to believe, but it was never powerful enough to inspire any action. The crown prince was neither arrested nor beheaded, and he never opposed the Nazi regime, either in June 1934 or in July 1944.

By insisting on the weakness of the crown prince and the royal family, many of the Hohenzollerns' advocates returned to the starting point of the debate, Clark's 2011 evaluation, in which he had described Wilhelm as a *Flasche* (nullity), a figure who couldn't have had any significant influence, even if he had wanted to.[261] This initial argument may indeed be the strongest legal and historical one for those seeking to defend the Hohenzollerns' image. But there is no doubting that the royal family retained its aura, emotional appeal and influence for quite some time after the First World War. The only issue under discussion is what individual family members deployed this asset for.

In hindsight it seems surprising that the strongest arguments the defenders of Prussian traditions and the Hohenzollern managed to muster were to invoke the Hohenzollerns' 'achievements' in a remote past, engaging in counter-factual speculations and asserting that the Prussian crown prince was 'a twit', a useless and clueless good-for-nothing.

The fifth and final pro-Hohenzollern line of argument focuses on the personal interests of the family's critics and the ideological fault lines of the twentieth century. One common accusation is that the royal family's detractors are guided by transparently political motives. Now, it certainly is no more plausible to deny that politics were involved in this debate than in any other twentieth-century historical issue. But in this case contrary positions have been accused of departing from the 'foundation of the [German] constitution' – the implication being that Hohenzollern critics side with communism, totalitarianism and, above all, East Germany.[262]

'For you, this is not about the Hohenzollerns,' one far-right AfD representative in the Berlin city-state parliament told a fellow deputy:

> For you, this is about presenting the policies of state confiscation in the Soviet Occupation Zone and East Germany in a more flattering light. That's what you really want, and you should own up to it here and now. Once again, you're trying to whitewash communist policies of confiscating private property, and the Hohenzollerns are easy prey in the public arena.

The AfD deputy also accused his opponent of 'digging out a moth-eaten relic of communist propaganda'.[263] Employing far heavier artillery, the historian Michael Wolffsohn invoked his Jewish family and referred to the 'theft' of aristocratic assets, drawing an equivalence with the disappropriation of Jews in the Third Reich. He also accused Hohenzollern critics of practising 'collective punishment', just as the Nazis had.[264]

The original quarrel about the behaviour of an individual figure revolved around a special issue with which only a few of the combatants engaged empirically. But that was by no means the only reason to broaden the focus and to pose other questions in which the great political metanarratives of the twentieth century collided with one another. In a world in which the simplistic twentieth-century schema of Right versus Left has been succeeded by far more complex conflicts and 'explosive' debates about remembrance,[265] the issue of the Hohenzollerns allowed parties on all sides to journey back to familiar stereotypes of friends and enemies. In this sense it is perhaps precisely the antiquated nature of the debate that accounts for its appeal. Parallel to other, surprisingly lively, discussions about the positive sides of imperial Germany,[266] the Hohenzollern issue seems to revive not only Left–Right divisions in the interpretations of the Third Reich that have been around since the early days of the Federal Republic of Germany, but also the emotions attached to them. The conflict is between a 'leftist' emphasis on the culpability of the Wilhelmine Empire and the old elites and the 'conservative' view that stresses the brighter sides of German history and pins the blame on 'totalitarian' forces and Hitler as an individual. Strikingly, as has been noted in a related context, the accusation of 'political tub-thumping' seems to be reserved solely for the critics of Hohenzollerns.[267]

It is far more plausible to assume that the conflict surrounding the Hohenzollerns, like all of the great historical issues of the twentieth century, is accompanied by predetermined political and ideological opinions on all sides. We can sense a diffuse need, perhaps even demand, for a more friendly, gentle and optimistic version of German history that would help Germans overcome what some perceive as an excessively self-critical examination of their past. A depiction of the past in which the Wilhelmine Empire was an open, highly modern and progressive society, the start of the First World War in the summer 1914 was the result of general European somnambulism, the 1933 transfer of power to the Nazis a mistake made 'on all sides' and the Holocaust as one of many genocides in history would fundamentally alter our estimations of twentieth-century Germany.[268] A Kaiser whose anti-Semitism was merely 'reactive' and a Hohenzollern family who as part of the conservative elite had 'contacts with the resistance' would be major symbolical components of this new view.

Shifts of this sort should not be dismissed as mere revisionism. They arise in various circumstances and develop their own dynamic. Nevertheless, there is every reason to note, along with Andreas Wirsching, the director of the Institute for Contemporary History in Munich, how the longing for a more positive history 'not only guides older Germans of the later war generation, who would love to unburden themselves of what they experienced', but 'revives itself across generations, so that, thirty years on from German reunification, the country is sliding into a debate about its identity'.[269]

Historians can sensibly contribute to the Hohenzollern debate by expanding the corpus of relevant facts with their research and by incorporating new discoveries into the body of historical knowledge according to the rules of the discipline. As soon as the conflict surrounding the royal family focuses more on interpretation than on new empirical facts, it goes down the same path as all the great historical disputes of the Federal Republic: the Fischer controversy of the 1960s over whether Germany was solely responsible for the First World War; the Historians' Dispute of the 1980s about the proper place of the Holocaust in German history; the debate in the 1990s about Daniel Goldhagen's *Hitler's Willing Executioners*; and the scandals around the turn of the millennium about museum exhibits documenting crimes against humanity perpetrated by the Wehrmacht.[270] The difference is that the mounting evidence of the crown prince's public support for the Nazis has never been countered empirically. The historians and journalists who have tried to support the Hohenzollerns' position have never come up with any objective facts beyond those in the Pyta/Orth evaluation.

Indeed, attempts to empirically refute the consensus about the

Hohenzollerns' political behaviour have remained few and far between. It has been more common to accuse the Hohenzollerns' critics of inappropriate ideological motives. For instance, in 2019 the theologist and historian Benjamin Hasselhorn complained about 'deep-seated anti-aristocratic resentment' and dismissed criticism of the royal family as a 'sad continuation' of the largely discredited thesis that German history had taken a fatal detour leading inevitably to Nazism. This line of thought, which had been influential in a part of German post-war historiography for some decades, and which emphasized the strength of anti-democratic traditionalism and the German nobility, was 'basically nothing but First World War anti-German propaganda become history', Hasselhorn fumed.[271]

Meanwhile, the chairman of the Prussian Historical Commission, Frank-Lothar Kroll, identified an 'alarmist campaign'[272] and praised the 'marketing potential' of a 'king' living at Cecilienhof for international tourism. This was the argument Kroll also used to conclude an article in the organ of German aristocrats' organizations, the *Deutsches Adelsblatt*.[273] For his part, Hasselhorn has stressed the Hohenzollerns' support for the arts, the positive aspects of German history and the alleged potential of the monarchy as a counterweight to Nazism.[274] Like Wolffsohn, who concluded one of his articles with the words 'God save the Hohenzollerns', these authors never tire of demanding a more 'differentiated' – i.e. more positive – picture of the Hohenzollerns, the Wilhelmine Empire and German history so that Germans can finally overcome the residual effects of 'Allied war propaganda'.[275]

In the vein of some of the pro-Hohenzollern historians, an AfD parliamentary deputy told the Bundestag that 'overly leftist historians and media' were damaging the image of 'Prussia' and veering dangerously close to the 'Soviet communist ideological view of history'.[276] Almost two years after the start of the public debate, the editor of the culture section of the *Welt* newspaper, Tilman Krause, criticized a general 'mistrust' of the Hohenzollerns, inspired by 'envy, a faulty understanding of history, anti-aristocratic resentment and German self-hatred'. In an op-ed, which the author insisted was

. Adolf Hitler, the ex-Crown Prince and Hermann Göring on 21 March 1933 during the 'Day
f Potsdam'.

The ex-Crown Prince entering the Kroll Opera House in Berlin through a cordon of SA
n at the opening of the Reichstag on 21 March 1933.

17. The ex-Crown Prince in the diplomatic box of the Kroll Opera House at the opening of the Reichstag, 21 March 1933.

18. Meeting of the Queen Luise League in the packed Berlin Sportpalast, May 1933.

. Heinrich Himmler, Ernst Röhm and the ex-Crown Prince at the Stahlhelm's
ichsführertagung, Hanover, September 1933.

SA leader Ernst Röhm greets the ex-Crown Prince at the *Reichsführer*'s Roll-Call.

21. The ex-Crown Prince next to Heinrich Himmler in a propaganda film from 1933.

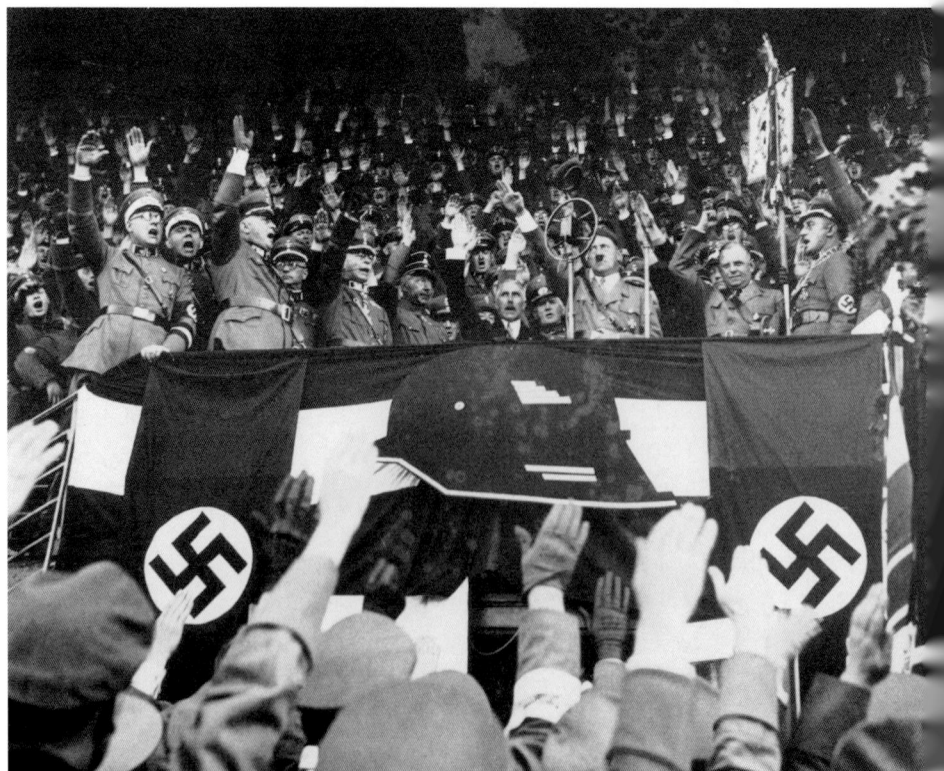

22. Hitler, the ex-Crown Prince, Franz von Papen and Franz Seldte at the Stahlhelm's *Reichsführertagung*.

23. The SA's *Stabschef* Ernst Röhm with the ex-Crown Prince at the *Stahlhelmtag* in Breslau (today Wrocław in Poland), autumn 1933.

4. Louis Ferdinand and his brother Friedrich with US presidential candidate Franklin D. Roosevelt in 1932.

25. The wedding of Kira Kirillovna Romanova and Louis Ferdinand Prince of Prussia, May 1938.

26. Ex-Crown Prince Wilhelm in his *Motor SA* uniform, 1933 or 1934.

Der Marxismus muß sterben

7. The SA officer August Wilhelm Prince of Prussia during a speech at the Sportpalast in 1932
r 1933.

Onrecht in de rechtsstaat Nederland.

RUMOER OM EX-KROONPRINS

. The ex-Crown Prince with his sons Hubertus and Friedrich in 1934, printed in a Dutch
wspaper around 1947.

29. Louis Ferdinand and Kira on board a ship in 1952 on the reading tour for his autobiography, *The Rebel Prince*.

30. Three generations: the former crown prince, the former Kaiser and the former crown prince's oldest son, William Prince of Prussia, at Huis Doorn in the Netherlands, around 1928

not meant satirically, he demanded, 'Mercy for the Hohenzollerns!' Of Georg Friedrich of Prussia, he wrote: 'This likeable, entirely unpretentious man, rather non-glamorous in appearance, is burdened by his inheritance and role. He's a businessman . . . A devoted family man. He enjoys drinking beer.'[277]

Krause didn't spell out what this meant for historical analysis. Although there is no evidence of anyone asserting the contrary, Hohenzollern defenders repeatedly point out that members of the royal family weren't the only ones to support the Nazi regime. AfD parliamentary group leader Alexander Gauland concluded one of his speeches in the Bundestag with the words: 'Let's be forgiving of the Hohenzollerns. They only made the same mistakes which unfortunately many of our grandfathers and grandmothers made millions of times over. In this respect, they were, as Walther Rathenau pointed out about Wilhelm II shortly after the defeat of 1918, an almost perfect example of the confusion of a [whole] people, to which we now should not reduce them.'[278]

The current 'head of the house' and the historians supporting his positions repeatedly stressed that the political blame for the Third Reich was spread across many shoulders. This idea has been around since the 1950s. But as Hannah Arendt put it, where everyone is responsible, no one is.[279] The 'constant task of explaining 1933', as Wirsching has called it, will continue for the foreseeable future. As long as Nazism is not considered an unexplainable 'accident that could have happened anywhere and at any time', Germany will demand that we identify the specific thinking and action of prominent protagonists.[280] One of the leading German historians of the Third Reich, Ulrich Herbert, once tellingly compared the pro-Hohenzollern arguments to the defence of the elite German functionaries used since the Nuremberg Trials for Göring and others. The underlying message, Herbert wrote, was that 'If even they weren't the ones who "aided and abetted", then no one was – so we can all just carry on.'[281]

Conclusion

'Hitler is Reich chancellor. Once again the most fateful alliance, one which Gustav Freytag called the greatest German danger, has come to pass: the alliance between the aristocracy and the mob.'[1]

These are words from the 31 January 1933 diary entry of the theologian and writer Jochen Klepper, who would go on to write an extremely successful novel about King Friedrich Wilhelm I of Prussia that mixed Lutheran faith with a homage to Prussian tradition. In 1931, Klepper had married the Jewish fashion reporter Johanna Stein. In 1942, with Johanna Klepper and their daughter facing the threat of the death camps, the three of them would commit joint suicide. Klepper's diary entry brings together the aristocracy and the mob, two concepts usually considered binary opposites in the twentieth century. Klepper's words unite the crown prince, fallen from grace, and the rapaciously ambitious former painter of postcards Hitler, both of whom set off from very different situations on 9 November 1923 to put an end to the Weimar Republic.

The countless models put forward to explain National Socialism in the past hundred years can often meaningfully be divided into a simplistic dichotomy between Left and Right. The Left stresses the political responsibility of German elites who succeeded during a precarious situation in destroying the labour movement and the protection of workers' interests. The Right conceives of Nazism as a rebellion of the 'mob' against those very elites. From this perspective, the Nazi regime is understood as an 'empire of fascist Jacobinism', the Nazi movement as a bubbling up 'from below' and a form of 'Bolshevism', to use a term employed by Wilhelm II and many aristocrats.

Whereas Klepper's on-the-ground analysis from the time when the Nazis were gaining power encompassed both perspectives, ninety years later most historians have given up on simple models, single causes and assignations of blame to individual groups. Countless works have continued to refine explanations and analysis ever further. Yet as impressive as these attempts at differentiation have been, a model in which 'everyone' is equally responsible would be scarcely credible, little different from the idea that no one bore any responsibility and Nazism was simply Germany's unavoidable fate.

Thus, it remains crucial to continue to describe and distinguish between various groups' scope of alternatives, attitudes and influence. It is well known that the Nazi Party only succeeded in attracting 33.1 per cent of the vote in the last free election of November 1932. The transfer of power to Hitler the following January was thus the result not of an overwhelming electoral triumph, but rather of a decision reached by a small circle of leaders who, acting out of personal interest and because of shared ideology, created a coalition of conservatives and National Socialists. Hitler was, in essence, the unanticipated final stage of the various plans to 'overcome' the Weimar Republic that had been around since 1918. When Hitler was 'levered into power' as Ian Kershaw put it, the Hohenzollerns were either half-hearted supporters or enthusiastic backers of Nazism, but not opponents in any recognizable sense.

The Hohenzollerns and indeed all the former ruling dynasties of Europe are particularly interesting elements of the anti-democratic movement as a whole because, even after 1918, they had immense resources and a special aura at their disposal. Thus, they represent an especially profound example of the erosion of traditional conservatism in this period. This was especially true of the figure who, in the minds of millions of monarchists, would one day inherit an imaginary throne: Crown Prince Wilhelm. The survival of German democracy partly depended on whether the most powerful of the old elites would reach a mutual arrangement with the Weimar Republic. The answer the leading political members of the House of Hohenzollern gave was a clear 'No'.

Opportunists and Collaborators

In his widely read 1946 memoirs, Fabian von Schlabrendorff – lawyer, officer, Hohenzollern legal advisor and member and chronologist of the military resistance to Hitler – presented a simple version of the past. There were three groups in the Third Reich, he wrote: Nazis, non-Nazis and anti-Nazis. 'The non-Nazis were almost worse than the Nazis,' he proposed. 'Their lack of character was more of a burden to us than the Nazis' capriciousness and brutality.' This idea accords well with a central insight of Holocaust research, which holds that a relatively small group of active perpetrators were enabled by far more numerous 'bystanders' and profiteers.[2] One of the leading minds of the German resistance, Count Helmuth James von Moltke, had written about the latter category in 1941:

> In reality, these people, and not the criminals, are the crux and the malady. Criminals are everywhere and always have been. On the other hand, it is the unavoidable duty of all upstanding people to fight against crime, and those who refuse to do this are more guilty than the criminals themselves.[3]

For these reasons, whenever the debate about the crown prince and his family is shoehorned into black-and-white legal concepts, it makes little analytic progress. The hardcore Nazis, among whom none of the Hohenzollerns except August Wilhelm and Hermine can be numbered, could only do what they did with the support of collaborators. In this regard, collaborators were not figures ancillary to the Nazi dictatorship. They were its foundation. At the beginning of the Third Reich, in July 1933, the former state secretary Hans Schäffer wrote from Swedish exile of his hopes that the upstanding members of Germany's elite functionaries would decelerate and constrain the Nazi regime and prevent things from getting 'even worse'. He added, 'Ultimately, much of how things will turn out will depend on the stance of people from the centre of society.'[4]

The cautious hopefulness of this Jewish émigré would prove unfounded. But his words underscore how decisive it was whether German elites in 1933 would go along with the new Nazi order or not. How and why the alliances that created and maintained the Nazi dictatorship arose is a matter of the historical record, but the story can be retold in nuanced fashion from the perspective of the high nobility.

Hitler derived his absolute dominance not just from the fanatical adherents of Nazi Party ideology, but also from the ambivalent collaborators who supported the regime, partially or completely, temporarily or consistently, for selfish or greater motives. Collaborators were able to get behind the Nazi state, as Ulrich Herbert wrote, because they

> didn't see or only recognized too late that the regime was the very essence of evil, regarding it instead as a positive, indeed intoxicating and extremely successful movement that, for all its manifest flaws, was still far preferable to the trauma of defeat and humiliation.[5]

It seems appropriate here to think in terms of opportunists who unscrupulously adapted to every situation – after 1945 Germans also referred to 'fellow travellers' (*Mitläufer*), a category that played a major role in Germany's collective memory of the Second World War.[6] Yet neither of these two images fits the crown prince or most of the royal family and Germany's anti-democratic elites. They were more than just fellow travellers who adapted to their changing political surroundings. After all, they never adapted to the Weimar Republic, pursuing instead a stringently anti-democratic agenda.

Ideologically and politically, and particularly where negative goals were concerned, this agenda had a great deal in common with the Nazi movement. The cooperation between Nazis and traditional movements was often strained but persisted until 1945. Conservative elites went hunting with the Reich forestry minister Hermann Göring, marched alongside Ernst Röhm and discussed how the next war would be waged with military commanders old and new. And the two sides were also united by their mutual hatred of the Weimar Republic, democracy, communists, socialists, pacifists, trade unions and, not least, Jews.

In many cases, it seems more fitting to call conservative elites 'collaborators' who derived considerable personal advantage from their cooperation and who rendered their services in broad, if never total, ideological agreement with the dominant Nazi state. Speculations among elites that cooperation would allow them to ultimately undermine and control the Nazi movement were part and parcel of the sort of voluntary collaboration in which the crown prince and his family engaged.

Depending on their positions within the power structure, millions of individuals and most likely a majority of Germans at the zenith of the Nazi regime's popularity could have been described as fellow travellers, opportunists, bystanders and collaborators. The crown prince stood out from this heterogeneous group because of the enormous attention he and his family commanded. Wilhelm was a figure who, without having to do anything himself, could count on being noticed by millions of people. From a retrospective biographical perspective, he was a lightweight flaneur, an observer, a mediator and a representative of constant new connections and shifts within the German Right. But above all, this seemingly minor figure was the personification and reflection of an entire caste of post-1918 fallen aristocratic and military elites. Aristocrats of his ilk were broken but not fully disempowered, anchored socially and ideologically in a world gone by, restless and fickle in their search for opportunities to collaborate with new, radical right-wing currents, whose dynamism they never completely comprehended. They were too weak, and in many cases of no mind, to lead a conservative alternative to Nazism, even as figureheads. Instead, they supported and helped bring about the conservative coalition without which the Nazis could not have taken power in January 1933.

The Hohenzollerns found their place in an alliance with Germans from all walks of life who worried about their declining social status, a partnership based on the sort of resentment and desperation Hannah Arendt described in her famous study of totalitarianism. Like other Germans, the crown prince, the House of Hohenzollern and the members of Germany's former ruling dynasties had to reinvent themselves as participants in the Weimar Republic and the Third Reich. This is a story largely yet to be written. Nonetheless, the biographies of many of Germany's most prominent nobles vividly reveal the blurring of the lines between conservative and Nazi camps.

The Hohenzollerns' lasting influence is not just a product of manipulation by the family's public relations machinery. In line with Max Weber's famous model of charisma, the abiding connection between the German royal family and parts of the German populace can only be explained by looking at the receivers, not the senders. The Hohenzollerns' influence persisted largely because of the continuing emotional attachments and hopes, as well as the enormous attention, of the German public. The reason that millions of postcards celebrating Crown Prince Wilhelm were printed in 1914 was not that he was a courageous warrior. It was that millions of Germans could project their desires onto him. Before long, this same mechanism would make itself felt with other German leaders.

The Missing Alternative

It is politically understandable why some observers would try to portray the conservative allies of Nazism as an alternative, if not as a group of opponents, to Hitler. But this view contradicts seven decades of empirical historical research about the rise of the Nazi dictatorship. The individuals and groups who actively supported the formation and the solidification of the Third Reich and who played no later role in the resistance began to converge immediately after the First World War. The 1930 statement by the Hugenberg advisor Paul Bang, that there was no way of dismissing a movement as unpatriotic if Prince August Wilhelm marched at its head, speaks to the power the presence of the high nobility in Nazism had for the entire conservative camp.

This was even more true of both the crown prince and princess and the would-be mediators with the Kaiser in Doorn. For millions of Germans, the politically active members of the royal family personified collaboration with the regime. However, their support should by no means be dismissed as 'merely' symbolic. European fascism was most successful where it encountered a weak, diffuse conservativism it could divide and absorb.[7] There were many reasons for the weakness of German conservatives and the porous boundaries to Nazism. The Hohenzollerns, however, specifically contributed to this weakness because the royal family utterly failed to do the one thing the German high nobility would have been capable of doing after 1918: symbolizing and representing a conservative counterweight to Nazism.

Imagined Resistance

The Pyta/Orth evaluation ends with the bold proclamations that the crown prince 'played a thoroughly active part in preventing a Hitler chancellorship' and was 'right from the start close to resistance networks that were forming'.[8] There is no empirical basis for these assertions. Notwithstanding the many nuances and gradations of collaboration in which the Hohenzollerns engaged, the attempt to rewrite history and connect the royal family with the resistance is obscene – particularly when it threatens to obscure the sacrifices of those historical figures who did in fact resist the regime. A good measuring stick for the two groups in question is a list of who became part of Hitler's cabinet in 1933 and who was detained in a concentration camp. This basic measure should continue to inform distinctions between the architects and the opponents of the Third Reich, and it should remain a criterion for assessing the political positions of the most important Hohenzollerns in 1933: a former Kaiser whose attempts at allying himself with the Nazi movement failed and who in his exile sank ever deeper into anti-Semitic fantasies while his spouse continued to court the Nazi elite; a son assisting in a Nazi torture chamber while his brother, the former crown prince, promoted the positive qualities of the Nazi regime and its Führer to an international audience; a grandson who sought to explain to powerful circles in the United States why he had voted for the Nazis and why they should support the regime. Three generations of the royal family promoted the Nazi dictatorship in the key year of 1933. Future discussions of the political orientation within the House of Hohenzollern won't be able to ignore either this historic juncture or the many years leading up to and following it.

'20 July 1944' is one of the most potent cyphers of the alleged gap between conservative Prussian values and the Nazi state. But it by no means reflects the political arc of the House of Hohenzollern or German conservatism in general, nor does it help us evaluate the political biographies of most people at the time. The assassination attempt against Hitler was not typical of the relationship between Nazi elites and their conservative allies. The Hohenzollerns, like most of the German nobility, kept their distance from the resistance.

Those who wish to focus on connections between the influence of conservative groups and '20 July' would be better advised to concentrate not on 1944 but on 1932. On 20 July 1932, Hindenburg disbanded the democratically elected parliament of Prussia, installing Papen as Reich commissar and handed over power to Schleicher. What is known as the 'Prussian coup d'état' (*Preussenschlag*) is widely considered to have paved Hitler's path to power. Unlike the later attempted coup led by Stauffenberg, *this* work of conservative elites was in fact closely interlocked with the plans and wishes of the Hohenzollerns.

Narratives

In 2011, at the beginning of the debate surrounding the political attitudes of the former crown prince, it was said that Wilhelm was one of the least compromised figures in the German high nobility. That assertion, too, would quickly prove untenable. On the contrary, there were few German aristocratic families who opposed the Weimar Republic so unanimously, constantly, radically and influentially as the politically active members of the House of Hohenzollern.

The Nazi dictatorship developed its immense destructive power not only by mobilizing fanatical followers and incorporating millions of people into its apparatuses and organizations. Compromises and alliances with broadly, partially and temporarily collaborating groups were just as important. Collaboration with German elites was especially significant. After 1945, the royal family seems to have had a hard time comprehending this simple truth. The House of Hohenzollern was no different from most of the German populace in refusing to acknowledge its history and engaging in selective memory. Indeed, one could say that the main figures of three generations of Hohenzollerns reflected basic German attitudes from three different epochs. The energy, splendour, dynamism and restlessness of Wilhelm II in the final two decades of the Wilhelmine Empire were typical of a country bursting with strength, energy and a desire to expand, which generated enormous creative energy in all conceivable areas but which was brought down by its own failings. Crown Prince Wilhelm can be seen as a personification of the old elites, who had much in common politically with the Nazi movement and hoped to profit – also in a personal sense – from the Nazi state. Louis Ferdinand reflected the legend, omnipresent in Germany society after 1945, that one's own circles and oneself had allegedly recognized Nazism as a great evil and been 'close to the resistance' right from the start.

After 1945, almost all Germans tried to come up with narratives that would prove their own innocence, claiming that they had known nothing of Nazi atrocities, or hadn't participated in them in any way, or had lots of 'Jewish friends'. The Hohenzollerns and the rest of the German nobility represented a special case, however, in that they had 1,000 years of practice in inventing themselves, and their images and stories had been enthusiastically received by an audience of millions. Their post-1918 attempt to connect with and constrain the Nazi movement reflects the self-overestimation and mistaken calculations of the conservative camp as a whole. Their post-1945 attempt to depict themselves as a part of the centuries-old German resistance was a last flickering of their impressive talent for creating self-serving legends.

Acknowledgements

This book, written under the conditions of the pandemic, has benefited to an unusually large extent from the knowledge and support of others. The responsibility for all remaining errors lies solely with me, and the debt of gratitude I have accumulated is very large regardless of this. I would first and foremost like to thank my friend and lawyer Marcellus Puhlemann, who has defended me against the legal attacks of Georg Friedrich Prinz von Preussen's lawyers since 2015 and has constantly encouraged me to continue working on the subject. I would like to thank my colleague and collaborator Henning Holsten for his excellent research, constant contradiction, criticism and a large number of suggestions, corrections and ideas, many of which have been incorporated into this book. Also Christoph von Wolzogen for intensive discussions about everything that counts, for numerous corrections and organising support. The book owes a great deal to the unrivalled expertise and friendly encouragement of the late John C. G. Röhl, who supported the book from the beginning and made it possible for me to analyse additional sources by giving me access to his extensive estate in the Berlin State Library. His private collections also gave me access to some parts of the 'house archives' of the former royal family, which I was unfortunately unable to access while working on this book. John Röhl's expertise, helpfulness and friendliness were everything and more one could expect from an 'Old Master'. Among the colleagues who have helped me with criticism and knowledge exceeding my own by dimensions, I would like to thank Jürgen Luh, one of Germany's finest and most complete scholars of Prussian history, first and foremost. His expert advice in the field of Prussian history and his criticism on individual issues were of immense value. In Ulrich Wank I had an editor from whose knowledge, experience, care and commitment both text and author have benefited more than can be said here. In a very comprehensive sense, I would like to thank my brother Andreas Malinowski for his support in terms of content and organisation and for his reliable advice in all situations. My thanks also go to Karina Urbach, who persuaded me to take the subject seriously and supported me with countless tips and her expertise. This book would not exist without Kristin Rotter, who convinced me to put the topic into a book and discussed all the questions with me. She made sure that the text actually became a book and organised support for the author that was ideal in every respect. I would like to thank Ullstein Verlag, headed by Karsten Kredel and Urban van Melis, for their dedicated support of my work. Jack Gartmann, Miriam Gries, Oswald Immel and Peter Palmer also contributed significantly to the improvement of the text and the design of the book. Juliane Junghans did an excellent job with the press work, and I would like to thank Barbara Wenner for establishing the most important contacts and for her support during the writing process. Thomas Kemper, Sophie Schönberger, Daniel Schönpflug and Tristan Straub gave me important advice on art historical, legal and historical questions. Among the student assistants, I am particularly grateful to Lydia Bucher and Freddy Ykema, who made important discoveries, suggestions, contributions and research that were not possible in Scotland, and to Leonie von Wangenheim and Katja Binder for further research in German archives. Ernst-Alexander von Gersdorff, Philipp von Sell and Karl-Wilhelm von Plettenberg provided me with documents from private collections and discussed individual sources with me. I would like to thank them for their openness, which is anything but a matter of course. I would also like to thank Sabine Mangold-Will, who gave me access to extracts from the edition of Alfred Haehner's diaries being prepared at the University of Cologne and provided important suggestions. I am grateful to Kees van der Sluijs, Peter Trotier and Hans-Jörg Volkmann for their important corrections of remaining mistakes.

The present English version of the book owes its existence first and foremost to the interest and masterful overview of Simon Winder. I would like to thank Annemarie Blumenhagen for her great commitment in clearing formal hurdles. In Jefferson Chase I had a translator whose immense experience was as impressive as his masterful resolution of countless questions. I thank David Watson for countless improvements to the English manuscript and his precise work on the final version.

The original book has benefited in various ways from the advice and criticism of a large number of additional colleagues and other people involved in the Hohenzollern debate. These include Volker R. Berghahn, Sabine Bichler, Thomas Biskup, Gisela Bock, Frank Bösch, Christian Bommarius, Magnus Brechtken, Ewen Cameron, Bruce Campbell, Eckart Conze, Enda Delaney, Norman Domeier, Jan Eckel, Jacques Ehrenfreund, Richard J. Evans, Detlef Felken, Detlev Flachs, Birte Förster, Marcus Funck, Manfred Gailus, Robert Gerwarth, Constantin Goschler, Beatrice de Graaf, Erhard Grundl, Matthias Grünzig, Chris Harding, Susanne Heim, Fabian Hilfrich, Hans Günter Hockerts, Alexander vom Hofe, Phillip Hofmann, Larry E. Jones, Otmar Jung, Helmut Kappelhoff, Linda von Keyserlingk-Rehbein, Georg H. Kleine, Martin Kohlrausch, Stefan J. Link, Sabine Mangold-Will, Stefanie Middendorf, David Milne, Reiner Möckelmann, David Motadel, Frank Lorenz Müller, Armin Nolzen, Frederik Orlowski, Jacco Pekelder, Kim Priemel, Till van Rahden, Cornelia Rauh, Heinz Reif, James Retallack, Julius Ruiz, Martin Sabrow, Konstantin Sakkas, Eva Schlotheuber, Christoph Schönberger, Arne Semsrott, Daniel Siemens, Peter Steinbach, Alexa Stiller, Winfried Süß, Rüdiger von Treskow, Johannes Tuchel, Tereza Valny, Peer Oliver Volkmann, Daniel Wesener, Thomas Werneke, Thomas Wernicke, Leonie Wolters and Andreas Zielcke.

Bibliography

Archives

Akten der Reichskanzlei, Weimarer Republik Online, published by the
   Historische Kommission of the Bayerische Akademie der Wissen-
   schaften and the Bundesarchiv
Archiv der Freiherren von Aretin
   Correspondence Erwein Freiherr von Aretin
   Correspondence Rupprecht von Bayern
Badische Landesbibliothek Karlsruhe
   Correspondence between Cecilie Prinzessin von Preussen and Rein-
   hold Schneider
Benson Ford Research Center – The Henry Ford – Dearborn, Michigan
   Acc. 23 (Correspondence Louis Ferdinand Prinz von Preussen)
Bundesarchiv Berlin (BAB)
   Louis Müldner von Mülnheim estate
   Franz Sontag (Junius Alter) estate
   SS personnel file Friedrich Graf von der Schulenburg
Bundesarchiv Militärarchiv Freiburg (BAMA)
   Kurt von Schleicher estate
   Eberhard von Selasen-Selasinsky estate
   Karl von Einem estate
   Max Bauer estate
Center for Jewish History / Leo Back Institute
   Hans Schäffer Papers (AR 7177/MF 512), Series I: Correspondence,
   1933–1994; Series II: Diaries, 1924–1933
Deutsches Adelsarchiv, Marburg
   Holdings of the Deutsche Adelsgenossenschaft
Geheimes Staatsarchiv Preussischer Kulturbesitz, Berlin (GStA PK)
   Brandenburgisch-Preussisches Hausarchiv Rep 100 A

Bibliography

Brandenburgisch-Preussisches Hausarchiv Rep 53 (Wilhelm II.) and 54 (Kronprinz Wilhelm)

Arthur Berg estate

Wilhelm von Dommes estate

Ulrich Freiherr von Sell estate

Hilde Wagner estate

Eugen Zimmermann estate

Alfred Haehner Diaries, Best 1193a. Quoted from the DFG edition project developed at the University of Cologne: The Last German Imperial Couple and His Personal Physician: Wilhelm II and Auguste Victoria in Dutch Exile (1919–1924) as Reflected in the Diaries of Dr. med. Alfred Haehner (1880–1949)

Harvard University Archives, Cambridge, MA

Brüning Papers

Hechingen local press cuttings (partly undated newspaper articles, local/regional press, 1950s–1970s, private collection of Stephan Malinowski)

Het Utrechts Archief

Archival estate of Wilhelm II for the period 1918–1941

Historical Papers Research Archive, University of the Witwatersrand Johannesburg, WITS, South Africa

Adolf Victor von Koerber Papers

Correspondence with Wilhelm Prince of Prussia, A807/Ab

Historisches Archiv der Stadt Köln (Cologne)

Institut für Zeitgeschichte (Munich)

General Max Rudolf Viebahn interviewed by Otto John (ZS/A 33/5)

Landeskirchliches Archiv Kassel

KS C 3.3.1., Nr. 170 (Akten zur Überführung der Hohenzollern-Särge)

Library of Congress, Washington, DC

Geraldine Farrar Papers, ML31.F4, Box 11, Folder 34 and Folder 35

Maurice Frankenhuis Memoirs of the Frankenhuis Collection, New York, Courtesy of Aaron Oppenheim

Militärhistorisches Museum der Bundeswehr, Dresden (MHMB, Dresden)

Ludwig Beck estate

Friedrich Wilhelm Heinz estate

Nachlass John C. G. Röhl, Handschriftenabteilung der Staatsbibliothek zu Berlin. Röhl's collection contains unprinted and printed sources from 185 estates.

Nationaal Archief, Den Haag
C27036, Collectie J. B. Kan
Privatarchiv Christoph Freiherr von Wolzogen
Privatarchiv Ernst-Alexander von Gersdorff
Privatarchiv Karl-Wilhelm Freiherr von Plettenberg
Privatarchiv Philipp von Sell
Stiftung Preussische Schlösser und Gärten, print collection (Potsdam)
Sichert, Heinz, Cecilienhof. Geschichte eines Schlosses. 2 vols. Manuscript, 1982
The National Archives / Public Record Office (PRO), London
Foreign Office: Political Departments: General Correspondence 1906–1966
United States Holocaust Memorial Museum (USHMM), Washington, DC
Kempner Papers, Box 313, Folder 19
Universität Augsburg, Universitätsbibliothek
Klaus W. Jonas estate
Wisconsin Historical Society Archives, Madison, Wisconsin
Sigrid Schultz Papers

Newspapers and Journals

Alaska Daily – Albuquerque Morning Journal – Allgemeiner Tiroler Anzeiger – Algemeen handelsblad voor Nederlandsch-Indië – Ambiance – Americus Times-Recorder – Arbeiterwille – Arbeiter Zeitung – Arizona Republican – Aufbau – Aux écoutes – Basler Nachrichten – Berlingske illustreret Tidende – Berliner Börsenzeitung – Berliner Lokal-Anzeiger – Berliner Tageblatt – Birmingham Daily Gazette – Bismarck Tribune – Bonsoir – Boston Daily Globe – Brownsville Herald – Ce Soir – Chattanooga News – Chicago Daily Tribune – China Weekly Review (Shanghai) – Chinese Newspaper Collection – Christlichsoziale Arbeiterzeitung – Cicero – Cincinnati Enquirer – Courrier de la Saône-et-Loire – Current History (New York) – Current Opinion – Daedalus – Dagblad van Noord-Brabant – Daily

Bibliography

Mail – Daily Monitor – Daily Union – Das Historisch 1 Politische Buch – Das illustrierte Blatt – Das Interessante Blatt – Das Reich – Das Tage-Buch – Der Abend – Der Angriff – Der Aufrechte – Der Kuckuck – Der Morgen – Der neue Tag – Der Reichswart – Der Ring – Der Spiegel – Der Stahlhelm – Der Tag (Vienna) – Der Tagesspiegel – Der Türmer – Detroit Tribune – Deutsche Allgemeine Zeitung – Deutsche Juristen-Zeitung – Deutsche Kavallerie-Zeitung – Deutsches Adelsblatt – Die Stunde – Die Welt – Die Weltbühne – Die Welt am Montag – Die Welt am Sonntag – Die Zeit – Die Zukunft – El Paso Herald – Engadiner Post – European Journal of Marketing – Evening Journal (Washington, DC) – Evening Star (Washington, DC) – Excelsior (Paris) – Frankfurter Allgemeine Zeitung (FAZ) – Flensburger Tagesblatt – France-Soir – Freiburger Nachrichten – Freiburger Zeitung – Freie Presse/La Presse Libre (Strasbourg) – Freie Stimmen – Freiheit – Generalanzeiger Dortmund – Germania – Geschichte in der Gegenwart – Geschichte und Gesellschaft – Grazer Tageblatt – Gubener Zeitung – Haagsche Post – Hamburgischer Correspondent – Hamburger Echo – Hamburger Nachrichten – Hebdo-madaire illustré – Henderson Daily Dispatch – Historical Research – Hohenzollernsche Zeitung – Illustrierte Kronen Zeitung – Indi-anapolis Times – Innsbrucker Nachrichten – Interpress (Hamburg) – Irish Times – Jahrbuch der Juridischen Zeitgeschichte – Je suis partout – Journal du Cher – Journal des débats politiques et littéraires – Journal of Contemporary History – Kleine Volkszeitung – Kölner Lokal-Anzeiger – Kölnische Zeitung – Kreuzzeitung (= Neue Preussische Zeitung) – L'Action Française – L'Africain – L'Ami du peuple – L'Aube – L'Avenir Normand – L'Écho d'Alger – L'Écho de Paris – L'Ère nouvelle – L'Europe nouvelle – L'Événement – L'Express de Mulhouse – L'Humanité – L'Indépendance Belge – L'Intransigeant – L'Œuvre – L'Ouest-Éclair (Rennes) – La Charente – La Croix – La Dépêche – La Dépêche du Berry – La France de Bordeaux et du Sud-Ouest – La Gazette provençale – La Lanterne – La Liberté – La Petite Gironde – La Presse – La Revue des jeunes – La Tribune de l'Aube – La Volonté – Lake Country Times – Le Figaro – Le Jour – Le Journal – Le Nouvelliste de Bretagne – Le Matin – Le Midi socialiste – Le Petit bleu de Paris – Le Petit Courrier – Le Petit Journal – Le Petit Marseillais – Le Petit Parisien – Le Petit Provençal – Le Phare de la

Bibliography

Loire – *Le Progrès de la Côte-d'Or* – *Le Quotidien* – *Le Radical* – *Le Rappel* – *Les Annales politiques et littéraires* – *Leuchtrakete* – *Leviathan* – *Linzer Tages-Post* – *Linzer Volksblatt* – *Los Angeles Times* – *Lyon républicain* – *Märkische Allgemeine Zeitung* – *Mercure de France* – *Midland Journal* – *Montag Morgen* – *Morgenpost* – *Nachrichten für Stadt und Land* – *Nationalsozialistische Landpost* – *Neptune (Antwerpen)* – *Neue Freie Presse* – *Neue Preussische Kreuzzeitung* – *Neue Zeit* – *Neues Deutschland* – *Neues Wiener Journal* – *Neues Wiener Tageblatt* – *Neue Züricher Nachrichten* – *Neue Züricher Zeitung (NZZ)* – *New Britain Herald* – *New York American* – *New York Herald Tribune* – *New York Review of Books* – *New York Times* – *New York Tribune* – *Nuit et Jour* – *Oberländer Opinion* – *Oberländer Tagesblatt* – *Omaha Daily Bee* – *Paris-Presse* – *Paris-Soir* – *Pariser Tageszeitung* – *Perth Amboy Evening News* – *Pester Lloyd* – *Pforzheimer Anzeiger* – *Potsdamer Neueste Nachrichten* – *Prager Tageblatt* – *Prescott Daily News* – *Preussische Jahrbücher* – *Preussischer Pressedienst* – *Public History Weekly* – *Reichspost* – *Revue d'Allemagne et des pays de langue allemande* – *Revue du Rhin et de la Moselle* – *Richmond Palladium* – *Rock Island Argus* – *Rote Fahne* – *Salzburger Chronik* – *Salzburger Volksblatt* – *Salzburger Wacht* – *San Francisco Chronicle* – *Schlesische Zeitung* – *Simplicissimus* – *South Bend News Times* – *South China Morning Post* – *Spandauer Zeitung* – *Sport im Bild* – *Süddeutsche Zeitung* – *Sun Telegram* – *Sunday Star* (Washington) – *Telegraph* – *De Telegraaf* (Amsterdam) – *Teltower Kreisblatt* – *The Atlanta Constitution* – *The Austin American* – *The Austin Statesman* – *The China Press* (Shanghai) – *The Christian Science Monitor* (Boston) – *The Daily Ardmoreite* – *The Economist* – *The Evening Bulletin (Philadephia)* – *The Illustrated London News* – *The Globe* (Toronto) – *The Hartford Courant* – *The Manchester Guardian* – *The Minneapolis Star* – *The New Statesman* – *The North China Herald and Supreme Court & Consular Gazette* – *The Observer* – *The Philadelphia Inquirer Public Ledger* – *The Scotsman* – *The Star* (Christchurch, NZ) – *The Sun* (Baltimore) – *The Sun* (New York) – *The Times* – *The Washington Post* – *Tidens* (Norway) – *Topeka State Journal* – *Union nationale des femmes: revue des électrices (UNF)* – *Unsere Partei* – *Voilà* – *Völkischer Beobachter* – *Volkspost* – *Volksstimme* – *Vorarlberger Landes-Zeitung* – *Vorwärts* – *Vossische Zeitung* – *Weltbühne* – *Welt am Abend – Welt am Sonntag – Welt-Spiegel – Westfälischer Beobachter – Wiener Illustrierte Zeitung – Wiener Salonblatt – Wiener Sonn- und Montagszeitung*

Published Sources

Akten der Partei-Kanzlei der NSDAP, *Rekonstruktion eines verlorengegangenen Bestandes* (published by Institut für Zeitgeschichte), part 1: *Regesten*, vol. 1, edited by Helmut Heiber, Vienna, Munich 1984.

Alter, Junius [Franz Sontag], *Nationalisten. Deutschlands nationales Führertum der Nachkriegszeit*, Leipzig 1930.

An Empress in Exile. My Days in Doorn. By Empress Hermine, London 1927.

Anker, Kurt, *Kronprinz Wilhelm*, revised and completed on the basis of documents and memoranda, Berlin 1922.

Anker, Kurt, *Unsere Stunde kommt! Erinnerungen und Betrachtungen über das nach-revolutionäre Deutschland*, Leipzig 1923.

Appens, Wilhelm, *Charleville. Dunkle Punkte aus dem Etappenleben*, Dortmund 1919.

Behind the Gates at Doorn; Prinzessin Hermine Reuss, Mijn leven en hoe ik den Keizer trouwde, Amsterdam 1927.

The Berlin Diaries. The Private Journals of a General in the German War Ministry Revealing the Secret Intrigue and Political Barratry of 1932–33, edited by Dr Helmuth Klotz, London 1934.

Binder, Heinrich, *Die Schuld des Kaisers*, Munich 1918.

Channon, Henry 'Chips', *The Diaries. 1918–1938*, edited by Simon Heffer, London 2021.

Das Reichsbanner, *Weimar und Potsdam*, edited by Ortsgruppe Potsdam des Reichsbanners Schwarz Rot Gold, Berlin n.d.

Deutscher Bundestag, Ausschuss für Kultur und Medien, Wortprotokoll der 42. Sitzung. Öffentliche Anhörung. 29. 1. 2020, Protokoll 19/42.

Die Erzeugungsschlacht im Kriege, edited by Reichsministerium für Ernährung und Landwirtschaft, Munich 1940.

Dietrich, Otto, *Zwölf Jahre mit Hitler*, Cologne 1955.

Documents on British Foreign Policy 1919–1939, First Series, vol. XII, European, including Russian, Questions, January 1920–April 1921, edited by Rohan Butler and J. P. T. Bury with the collaboration of M. E. Lambert. London: HMSO 1962.

Domela, Harry, *Der falsche Prinz. Leben und Abenteuer. Im Gefängnis zu Köln von ihm selbst geschrieben, Januar bis Juni 1927* (1927), Berlin 1983.

Dumur, Louis, *Le Boucher de Verdun*, Paris 1921.

Einem, Karl von, *Ein Armeeführer erlebt den Weltkrieg*, Leipzig 1938.

Eppstein, Georg Freiherr von, *Der Deutsche Kronprinz. Der Mensch, der Staatsmann, der Geschichtsschreiber*, Leipzig 1926.

Fraenkel, Ernst, *The Dual State. A Contribution to the Theory of Dictatorship*, New York/London/Toronto 1941.

François-Poncet, André, *Souvenirs d'une Ambassade à Berlin 1931–1938*, with Preface and notes by Jean-Paul Bled, Paris.

Friedrich, Julius (i.e. Joachim von Ostau), *Wer spielte falsch? Hitler, Hindenburg, der Kronprinz, Hugenberg, Schleicher. Ein Tatsachenbericht aus Deutschlands jüngster Vergangenheit nach authentischem Material*, Hamburg 1949.

Frymann, Daniel (i.e. Heinrich Class), *Wenn ich der Kaiser wär'*, Leipzig 1912.

Goebbels, Joseph, *Tagebücher = Die Tagebücher von Joseph Goebbels*, part 1: *Aufzeichnungen 1923–1941*, edited by Elke Fröhlich, 14 vols., Munich 1998–2005.

Goethes Werke, Sophien-Ausgabe, vol. 5, part 1: *Gedichte*, Weimar 1893.

Grosser Generalstab, Kriegsgeschichtliche Abteilung (ed.), *Kriegsbrauch im Landkriege*, Berlin 1902.

Guevara, Ernesto, *Guerrilla Warfare* (1961), Introduction by Marc Becker, Lincoln 1961.

Gumbel, Emil Julius, *Vier Jahre politischer Mord*, Berlin 1922.

Günther, Hans F. K., *Adel und Rasse*, Munich 1926

Günther, Hans F. K., *Rassenkunde des deutschen Volkes*, Munich 1930.

Günther, Hans F. K., *Rassenkunde des Europas*, Munich 1929.

Harden, Maximilian, *Köpfe. Porträts, Briefe und Dokumente*, edited by Hans-Jürgen Fröhlich, Hamburg 1963.

Hassell, Ulrich von, *Vom anderen Deutschland. Aus den nachgelassenen Tagebüchern 1938–1944*, Zürich and Freiburg im Breisgau, 3rd edn, 1946.

Heilmann, Ernst (anon.), *Verdienste der Hohenzollern*, Berlin 1921.

Heinig, Kurt, *Fürstenabfindung? Ein Lesebuch zum Volksentscheid*, Berlin 1926.

Heinig, Kurt, *Hohenzollern. Wilhelm II. und sein Haus. Der Kampf um den Kronbesitz*, Berlin 1921.

Hermelin, Baron, *Der Prinz auf Wiereland, Erlebtes und Erlauschtes*, Berlin 1926.

Heuss, Theodor, *Hitlers Weg. Eine Schrift aus dem Jahre 1932*, edited by Eberhard Jäckel, Tübingen 1968.

Hitler, Adolf, *Mein Kampf. Eine kritische Edition*, edited on behalf of the Institut für Zeitgeschichte München-Berlin by Christian Hartmann, Thomas Vordermayer, Othmar Plöckinger, Roman Töppel, with the collaboration of Pascal Trees, Angelika Reizle, Martina Seewald-Mooser, Munich/Berlin 2015.

Hugo, Victor, *L'homme qui rit*, Paris 1869.

Hünefeld, Ehrenfried Günther von, *Der Kronprinz im Exil. Stimmungsbilder aus Holland*, Berlin 1922.

Hünefeld, Ehrenfried Günther von, *Insel der Verbannung. Hohenzollern im Exil. Stimmungsbilder aus Holland*, Berlin 1920.

Hupfeld, Hans (ed.), *Reichstags-Eröffnungsfeier in Potsdam. Das Erlebnis des 21. März in Wort und Bild*, Potsdam 1933.

Illard, Gustav (i.e. Gustav Steinbömer), *Herren und Narren der Welt*, Munich 1954.

Ilsemann, Sigurd von, *Der Kaiser in Holland. Aufzeichnungen des letzten Flügeladjutanten Kaiser Wilhelms II.*, Munich 1968.

Jünger, Ernst, *Der Arbeiter. Herrschaft und Gestalt*, Hamburg 1932.

Jünger, Ernst, *Der Kampf als inneres Erlebnis*, Berlin 1922.

Jünger, Ernst, *In Stahlgewittern*, Leipzig 1920.

'Kaiser, Kronprinz & Cie. Caricatures et images de guerre', frontispiece of Robida, *184 caricatures françaises et étrangères*, Paris 1916.

Kleist-Schmenzin, Ewald von, *Die letzte Möglichkeit. Zur Ernennung Hitlers zum Reichskanzler am 30. Januar 1933*, posthumously published in *Politische Studien* 10 (1959), 89–92.

Klemperer, Victor, *I Shall Bear Witness: The Diaries of Victor Klemperer 1933–41*, trans. Martin Chalmers, London 1998

Klepper, Jochen, *Unter dem Schatten deiner Flügel. Aus den Tagebüchern der Jahre 1932–1942*, Giessen 1997.

Kreutzer, Guido, *Der deutsche Kronprinz und die Frauen in seinem Leben. Nach authentischen Aufzeichnungen, Belegen und Untersuchungen*, Leipzig 1923.

Bibliography

Kronprinz Wilhelm, *Erinnerungen*, Stuttgart/Berlin 1922.

Kronprinz Wilhelm, *Ich suche die Wahrheit! Ein Buch zur Kriegsschuldfrage*, Stuttgart/ Berlin 1925.

Kronprinz Wilhelm, *Meine Erinnerungen aus Deutschlands Heldenkampf*, Berlin 1923.

Lange, Carl, *Der Kronprinz und sein wahres Gesicht*, Leipzig 1921.

Lange, Carl, *Der Kronprinz*, Berlin 1934 (= *Schlieffen-Bücherei: Geist von Potsdam*, vol. 3).

Lehndorff, Hans Graf von, *Ostpreussisches Tagebuch. Aufzeichnungen eines Arztes aus den Jahren 1945–1947*, Munich 1961.

Liman, Paul, *Der Kronprinz. Gedanken über Deutschlands Zukunft*, Minden 1914.

Maistre, Joseph de, *Lettres d'un Royaliste Savoisien à ses compatriotes*, 2nd corrected edition, n.p. 1793.

Mann, Thomas, *Ein Appell an die Vernunft, Essays*, vol. 3, Frankfurt am Main 1994.

Mao Zedong, *On Guerrilla Warfare* (1937), US Marine Corps, Department of the Navy, Washington, DC, 1989.

Meinecke, Friedrich, *Politische Schriften und Reden*, edited by Georg Kotowski, Darmstadt 1958.

The Memoirs of the Crown Prince of Germany, London 1922.

Moeller van den Bruck, *Arthur: Das Dritte Reich*, 3rd edn, Hamburg 1931.

Moltke, Helmuth von, *Gesammelte Schriften und Denkwürdigkeiten*, vol. 5, Berlin 1892.

Mowrer, Edgar Ansel, *Germany Puts the Clock Back* (1933), rev. edn, New York.

Müller, Ernst, *Wilhelm II. Eine historische und psychiatrische Studie*, n.p. 1927.

Musil, Robert, *Der Mann ohne Eigenschaften*, vol. 1, Berlin 1930.

Niemoeller-von Sell, Sibylle, *'Furchtbar einfach, wird gemacht'. Erinnerungen*, Berlin/Frankfurt am Main 1992.

Nowak, Karl Friedrich, *Das Dritte Deutsche Kaiserreich*, vol. 1: *Die übersprungene Generation*, Leipzig/Berlin 1929.

Nowak, Karl Friedrich, *Das Dritte Deutsche Kaiserreich*, vol. 2: *Deutschlands Weg in die Einkreisung*, Leipzig/Berlin 1931.

Preussen, Cecilie von, *Erinnerungen*, Leipzig 1930.

Preussen, Cecilie von, *Erinnerungen an den Deutschen Kronprinzen*, Biberach an der Riss 1952.

495

Preussen, Louis Ferdinand Prinz von, *Als Kaiserenkel durch die Welt*, Berlin 1952.

Preussen, Louis Ferdinand Prinz von, *Die Geschichte meines Lebens*, Göttingen 1968.

Preussen, Louis Ferdinand Prinz von, *Im Strom der Geschichte*, Munich / Vienna 1983.

Preussen, Wilhelm Prinz von, *Der Marne-Feldzug 1914*, Berlin 1926.

Preussen, Wilhelm Prinz von, *Der Sieg war zum Greifen nahe!*, Berlin 1922.

Preussen, Wilhelm von, *Die letzte Nacht in Doorn. Am Sarge Ihrer Majestät der Kaiserin und Königin Auguste Victoria*, Berlin 1928.

Preussen, Wilhelm von, *Erinnerungen des Kronprinzen Wilhelm. Aus den Aufzeichnungen, Dokumenten, Tagebüchern und Gesprächen*, edited by Karl Rosner, Stuttgart 1922.

Preussen, Wilhelm von, *Ich suche die Wahrheit! Ein Buch zur Kriegsschuldfrage*, Stuttgart / Berlin 1925.

Preussen, Wilhelm von, *Meine Erinnerungen aus Deutschlands Heldenkampf*, Berlin 1923.

Prince Louis Ferdinand of Prussia, *The Rebel Prince*, Chicago 1952.

Reibnitz, Kurt Freiherr von, *Im Dreieck Schleicher, Hitler, Hindenburg. Männer des deutschen Schicksals*, Dresden 1933.

Reibnitz, Kurt Freiherr von, *Wilhelm II. und Hermine. Geschichte und Kritik von Doorn*, Dresden 1929.

Reinowski, Hans, *Terror in Braunschweig. Aus dem ersten Quartal der Hitlerherrschaft*, report edited by Kommission zur Untersuchung der Lage der politischen Gefangenen, Verlag Sozialistische Arbeiter-Internationale, Zürich 1933.

Reisen ins Reich 1933 bis 1945. Ausländische Autoren berichten aus Deutschland, compiled and with an Introduction by Oliver Lubrich, Frankfurt am Main 2004.

Reuss, Prinzessin Hermine, *Days in Doorn*, London 1928.

Reuss, Prinzessin Hermine, *Der Kaiser und ich. Mein Leben mit Kaiser Wilhelm II. Im Exil*, Göttingen 2008.

Reuss, Prinzessin Hermine, *Mijn leven en hoe ik den Keizer trouwde*, Amsterdam 1927.

Reventlow, Ernst zu, *Kaiser Wilhelm II. und die Byzantiner*, Munich 1906.

Reventlow, Ernst zu, *Monarchie?*, Leipzig 1926.

Reventlow, Ernst zu, *Von Potsdam nach Doorn*, Berlin 1940.

Rosner, Karl, *Der König. Weg und Wende*, Stuttgart 1921.

Sartre, Jean-Paul, *Kean*, Paris 1954.

Schlabrendorff, Fabian von, *Begegnungen in fünf Jahrzehnten*, Tübingen 1979.

Schlabrendorff, Fabian von, *Offiziere gegen Hitler*, Zürich 1946.

Schleich, Carl Ludwig, *Besonnte Vergangenheit. Lebenserinnerungen eines Arztes*, Berlin 1920.

Schneider, Reinhold, *Verhüllter Tag*, Cologne 1956.

Schotte, Walter, *Der Neue Staat*, Berlin 1932.

Schultz, Edmund, *Das Gesicht der Demokratie: Ein Bilderwerk zur Geschichte der deutschen Nachkriegszeit*, with an Introduction by Friedrich Georg Jünger, Leipzig 1931.

Semi-Imperator. 1888–1918. Eine genealogisch-rassengeschichtliche Aufklärung zur Warnung für die Zukunft – ein packender Kommentar zu den Semi-Alliancen im besonderen und semi-gothaischen Erkenntnissen im allgemeinen, Munich 1919.

Severing, Carl, *Mein Lebensweg*, 2 vols., Cologne 1950.

Sichert, Heinz, 'Cecilienhof. Geschichte eines Schlosses', 2 vols., manuscript, 1982, print collection, SPSG, Potsdam 1982.

Steinhauer, Gustav, *Der Meisterspion des Kaisers. Was der Detektiv Wilhelms II. In seiner Praxis erlebte. Erinnerungen*, Berlin 1930.

Stresemann, Gustav, 'Väter und Söhne' (1926), in Gustav Stresemann, *Reden und Schriften. Politik – Geschichte – Literatur 1897–1926*, edited by Hartmuth Becker, Berlin 2008, 459–64.

Stresemann, Wolfgang, *Mein Vater Gustav Stresemann*, Berlin 1979.

Studnitz, Hans-Georg von, *Seitensprünge. Erlebnisse und Begegnungen 1907–1970*, Stuttgart 1975.

Sturm 33 – Hans Maikowski, Berlin-Schöneberg 1933.

Szende, Stefan, *Zwischen Gewalt und Toleranz: Zeugnisse und Reflexionen eines Sozialisten*, Frankfurt 1975.

Thaer, Albrecht von, *Generalstabsdienst an der Front und in der Obersten Heeresleitung. Aus Briefen und Tagebuchaufzeichnungen 1915–1919*, Göttingen 1958.

Trebitsch-Lincoln, Ignatius Timothy, *Der grösste Abenteurer des 20. Jahrhunderts! Die Wahrheit über mein Leben*, Leipzig / Zürich / Vienna 1931.

Tschirschky, Fritz Günther von, *Erinnerungen eines Hochverräters*, Stuttgart 1972.

Verhandlungen des Preussischen Landtags / Sitzungsberichte des Preussischen Landtags (various years).

Verhandlungen des Reichstags, IX. Wahlperiode 1933, vol. 458, Berlin 1936.

Viereck, George Sylvester, 'Crown Prince Wilhelm Bares His Heart', in idem, *Glimpses of the Great*, London 1930, 134–45.

Viereck, George Sylvester, *The Kaiser on Trial*, New York 1937.

Viscount d'Abernon, *Ein Botschafter der Zeitwende: Memoiren*, vol. 2, Leipzig 1929.

Voegelin, Eric, *Die politischen Religionen* (1938), edited and with an Afterword by Peter J. Opitz, Munich 1993.

Wandt, Heinrich, *Der Gefangene von Potsdam*, vol. 2, Vienna / Berlin 1927.

Wandt, Heinrich, *Erotik und Spionage in der Etappe Gent*, Vienna / Berlin 1929.

Wandt, Heinrich, *Etappe Gent. Streiflichter zum Zusammenbruch*, Vienna / Berlin 1926.

Westarp, Kuno Graf von, *Das Ende der Monarchie am 9. November 1918*, with an Afterword by Werner Conze, Berlin 1952.

Wiegand, Karl H. von, *Current Misconceptions about the War*, New York 1915.

Wilamowitz-Moellendorff, Fanny Gräfin von, *Carin Göring*, with an Afterword by Martin H. Sommerfeldt, Berlin 1934.

Wilhelm II, *Aus meinem Leben. 1859–1888*, Leipzig 1926.

Wilhelm II, *Ereignisse und Gestalten aus den Jahren 1878–1918*, Leipzig / Berlin 1922.

Zoller, Albert, *Hitler privat. Erlebnisbericht seiner Geheimsekretärin*, Düsseldorf 1949.

Zoubkoff, Alexander, *Mein Leben und Lieben. Memoiren* (1928), Bonn 2005.

Secondary Literature

Afflerbach, Holger, *Auf Messers Schneide. Wie das Deutsche Reich den Ersten Weltkrieg verlor*, Munich 2018.

Bibliography

Ahlheim, Hannah, '*Deutsche, kauft nicht bei Juden!*' *Antisemitismus und politischer Boykott in Deutschland 1924 bis 1935*, Göttingen 2011.

Albertz, Anuschka, *Exemplarisches Heldentum. Die Rezeptionsgeschichte der Schlacht an den Thermoplylen von der Antike bis zur Gegenwart*, Munich 2006.

Almeida, Fabrice d', *Hakenkreuz und Kaviar. Das mondäne Leben im Nationalsozialismus*, Düsseldorf 2007.

Almeida, Fabrice d', *La vie mondaine sous le nazisme*, Paris 2006.

Aly, Götz, *Hitler's Beneficiaries: Plunder, Racial War, and the Nazi Welfare State*, New York 2007.

Aly, Götz, *Hitlers Volksstaat. Raub, Rassenkrieg und nationaler Sozialismus*, Frankfurt am Main 2005.

Aly, Götz / Heim, Susanne, *Architects of Annihilation: Auschwitz and the Logic of Destruction*, London 2003.

Angeloch, Jürgen, 'Ein ambivalenter Fanatiker. Sigmund Freuds Briefwechsel mit dem Poeten, Publizisten und Propagandisten George Sylvester Viereck (1919–1936)', in *Psyche. Zeitschrift für Psychoanalyse und ihre Anwendungen* 68 (2014), 633–65.

Arendt, Hannah, *Eichmann in Jerusalem. Ein Bericht von der Banalität des Bösen*, with an introductory essay by Hans Mommsen, Munich/ Zürich 1986.

Arendt, Hannah, *Elemente und Ursprünge totaler Herrschaft*, Frankfurt am Main 1955. New edition, edited by Thomas Meyer, Munich 2023.

Aretin, Karl Otmar Freiherr von, 'Der bayerische Adel. Von der Monarchie zum Dritten Reich', in Martin Broszat, Elke Fröhlich and Anton Grossmann (eds.), *Bayern in der NS-Zeit*, vol. 3, Munich 1981, 513–67.

Aron, Raymond, 'Hannah Arendt, *The Origins of Totalitarianism*', in *L'Essence du totalitarisme*, New York 1951, 195–213 (first published in *Critique* 80).

Balfour, Michael, *Der Kaiser. Wilhelm II, und seine Zeit*, Berlin 1979.

Banerjee, Milinda et al. (eds.), *Transnational Histories of the 'Royal Nation'*, Basingstoke 2017.

Baur, Johannes, *Die russische Kolonie in München 1900–1945. Deutsch-russische Beziehungen im 20. Jahrhundert*, Wiesbaden 1998.

Beck, Hermann, *The Fateful Alliance: German Conservatives and Nazis in 1933. The Machtergreifung in a New Light*, New York 2008.

Bibliography

Becker, Manuel / Studt, Christoph (eds.), *Der Umgang des Dritten Reiches mit den Feinden des Regimes*, Münster 2010.

Beckert, Jens, *Unverdientes Vermögen. Soziologie des Erbrechts*, Frankfurt am Main / New York 2004.

Beigel, Thorsten / Mangold-Will, Sabine (eds.), *Wilhelm II. Archäologie und Politik um 1900*, Stuttgart 2017.

Bein, Reinhard, *Zeitzeichen. Stadt und Land Braunschweig 1930–1945*, Braunschweig 2006.

Bender, Philipp / Hillgruber, Christian, 'Hat der ehemalige Kronprinz Wilhelm von Preussen dem nationalsozialistischen System erheblichen Vorschub geleistet? Zur Auslegung und Anwendung von § 1 Abs. 4 Ausgleichsleistungsgesetz', in *Deutsches Verwaltungsblatt* 136 (2021), 427–34.

Benjamin, Walter, *Das Kunstwerk im Zeitalter seiner technischen Reproduzierbarkeit*, Frankfurt 1980.

Berghahn, Volker R., *America and the Intellectual Cold Wars in Europe*, Princeton / Oxford 2001.

Berghahn, Volker R., 'Das Ende des "Stahlhelm"', in *Vierteljahrshefte für Zeitgeschichte* 13 / 4 (1965), 446–51.

Berghahn, Volker R., *Der Stahlhelm. Bund der Frontsoldaten 1918–1935*, Düsseldorf 1966.

Besier, Gerhard, *Die Kirchen und das Dritte Reich*, vol. 3: *Spaltungen und Abwehrkämpfe 1934–1937*, Berlin 2001.

Besier, Gerhard, *Spaltungen und Abwehrkämpfe 1934–1937*, Berlin 2001.

Bessel, Richard, 'The Potempa Murder', in *Central European History* 10 / 3 (1977), 241–54.

Biskup, Thomas / Kohlrausch, Martin (eds.), *Das Erbe der Monarchie. Nachwirkungen einer deutschen Institution seit 1918*, Frankfurt am Main 2008.

Biskup, Thomas / Vu Minh, Truc / Luh, Jürgen (eds.), *Preussendämmerung. Die Abdankung der Hohenzollern und das Ende Preussens*, Heidelberg 2019.

Blasius, Dirk, *Weimars Ende. Bürgerkrieg und Politik 1930–1933*, Göttingen 2006.

Bloch, Max, *Albert Südekum (1871–1944). Ein deutscher Sozialdemokrat zwischen Kaiserreich und Diktatur. Eine politische Biographie*, Düsseldorf 2009.

Bloks, Moniek, *Hermine. An Empress in Exile, The Untold Story of the Kaiser's Second Wife*, Winchester, 2020.

Bibliography

Bluche, Frédéric, *Manuel d'histoire politique de la France contemporaine*, Paris 2008.

Bock, Gisela / Schönpflug, Daniel (eds.), *Friedrich Meinecke in seiner Zeit: Studien zu Leben und Werk*, Stuttgart 2006.

Böhler, Jochen, *Auftakt zum Vernichtungskrieg. Die Wehrmacht in Polen 1939*, Bonn 2006.

Bommarius, Christian, *Im Rausch des Aufruhrs. Deutschland 1923*, Munich 2022.

Borchmeyer, Dieter, 'Der aufgeklärte Herrscher im Spiegel von Goethes Schauspiel', in *Aufklärung 2* (1987), 49–74.

Bouverie, Tim, *Appeasing Hitler: Chamberlain, Churchill and the Road to War*, London 2019.

Bracher, Karl Dietrich, *Die Auflösung der Weimarer Republik*, Düsseldorf 1984.

Bracher, Karl Dietrich / Sauer, Wolfgang / Schulz, Gerhard, *Die national-sozialistische Machtergreifung*, Cologne / Opladen 1961.

Brelot, Claude-Isabelle, *La Noblesse réinventée. Nobles de Franche-Comté de 1814 à 1870*, vol. 1: *Restaurations et reconversions*, vol. 2: *De la tradition à l'innovation*, Paris 1992.

Breuer, Stefan, *Ordnungen der Ungleichheit*, Darmstadt 2001.

Brosman, Catharine Savage, 'Sartre's Kean and Self-Portrait', in *The French Review* 55/7 (1982), 109–22.

Buchstein, Hubertus / Göhler, Gerhard, *Vom Sozialismus zum Pluralismus*, Baden-Baden 2000.

Budrass, Lutz, *Adler und Kranich. Die Lufthansa und ihre Geschichte 1926–1955*, Munich 2016.

Büschel, Hubertus, *Hitlers adeliger Diplomat. Der Herzog von Coburg und das Dritte Reich*, Frankfurt am Main 2016.

Cannadine, David, *Winston Churchill. Abenteurer, Monarchist, Staatsmann*, Berlin 2005.

Carter Hett, Benjamin / Wala, Michael, *Otto John. Patriot oder Verräter: Eine deutsche Biographie*, Hamburg 2019.

Chapoutot, Johann, *Le Meurtre de Weimar*, Paris 2015.

Chickering, Roger, *We Men Who Feel Most German. A Cultural Story of the Pan-German League, 1886–1914*, New York 1984.

501

Clark, Christopher, *Iron Kingdom: The Rise and Downfall of Prussia, 1600–1947*, London 2007.

Clark, Christopher, *Wilhelm II. Die Herrschaft des letzten deutschen Kaisers*, Munich 2008.

Confino, Alon / Fritzsche, Peter (ed.), *Memory Work in Germany*, Urbana / Chicago 2002.

Conrad, Sebastian, 'Erinnerung im globalen Zeitalter: Warum die Vergangenheitsdebatte gerade explodiert', in *Merkur* 867 (August 2021), 5–17.

Conze, Eckart, *Adel und Adeligkeit im Widerstand des 20. Juli 1944*, Berlin 1991.

Conze, Eckart (ed.), *Kleines Lexikon des Adels. Titel, Throne, Traditionen*, Munich 2005, 220–21.

Conze, Eckart, *Schatten des Kaiserreichs. Die Reichsgründung von 1871 und ihr schwieriges Erbe*, Munich 2020.

Conze, Eckart, *Von deutschem Adel. Die Grafen v. Bernstorff im 20. Jahrhundert*, Stuttgart / Munich 2000.

Conze, Eckart / Meteling, Wencke / Schuster, Jörg (eds.), *Aristokratismus und Moderne. Adel als politisches und kulturelles Konzept 1890–1945*, Cologne 2013.

Conze, Eckart / Wienfort, Monika (ed.), *Adel und Moderne. Deutschland im europäischen Vergleich im 19. und 20. Jahrhundert*, Cologne 2004.

Corni, Gustavo / Gies, Horst, *Blut und Boden. Rassenideologie und Agrarpolitik im Staat Hitlers*, Idstein 1994.

Corni, Gustavo / Gies, Horst, *Brot – Butter – Kanonen. Die Ernährungswirtschaft in Deutschland unter der Diktatur Hitlers*, Berlin 1997

Darré, Richard Walther, *Neuadel aus Blut und Boden*, Munich 1930.

Dehé, John / Wolzogen Kühr, Paul von, *Wilhelm, een omstreden eilandgast*, Bussum 2020.

Del Boca, Angelo, *La guerra d'Etiopia. L'ultima guerra del colonialismo*, Mailand 2010.

Der Reichskanzler Dr Heinrich Brüning, *Das Brüning-Bild in der zeitgeschichtlichen Forschung. Gedenkveranstaltung zum 100. Geburtstag*, edited by Franz Matuszcyk, Münster 1986.

Dettmar, Klaus / Breunig, Werner (ed.), *Berlin in Geschichte und Gegenwart. Jahrbuch des Landesarchivs Berlin 2006*, Berlin 2007.

Bibliography

Dipper, Christof, 'Der deutsche Widerstand und die Juden', in *Geschichte und Gesellschaft* 9 (1983), 343–80.

Domeier, Norman, *Weltöffentlichkeit und Diktatur. Die amerikanischen Auslandskorrespondenten im 'Dritten Reich'*, Göttingen 2021.

Dominioni, Matteo, *Lo sfascio dell'Impero. Gli italiani in Etiopia 1936–1941*, with a Preface by Angelo Del Boca, Bari 2008.

Donig, Simon, *Adel ohne Land – Land ohne Adel? Lebenswelt, Gedächtnis und materielle Kultur des schlesischen Adels nach 1945*, Berlin / Boston 2020.

Dornheim, Andreas, 'Die Thüringer Fürstenhäuser zwischen Erbhof-Realität und Reichsstatthalter-Träumen', in Detlev Heiden and Gunther Mai (eds.), *Nationalsozialismus in Thüringen*, Weimar / Cologne / Vienna 1995, 269–92.

Dornheim, Andreas, *Rasse, Raum und Autarkie. Sachverständigengutachten zur Rolle des Reichsministeriums für Ernährung und Landwirtschaft in der NS-Zeit*, prepared for the Bundesministerium für Ernährung, Landwirtschaft und Verbraucherschutz, Bamberg 2006.

Ebbinghausen, Rolf / Neckel, Sighard (eds.), *Anatomie des politischen Skandals*, Frankfurt am Main 1989.

Eckel, Jan, *Hans Rothfels. Eine intellektuelle Biographie im 20. Jahrhundert*, Göttingen 2005.

Eckel, Julia / Ruchatz, Jens / Wirth, Sabine (eds.), *Exploring the Selfie. Historical, Theoretical, and Analytical Approaches to Digital Self-Photography*, London 2018.

Entgrenzte Gewalt. Täterinnen und Täter im Nationalsozialismus, Bremen 2002 (= vol. 7 of *Beiträge zur Geschichte der nationalsozialistischen Verfolgung in Norddeutschland*).

Epkenhans, Michael / Winkel, Carmen (eds.), *Die Garnisonkirche Potsdam. Zwischen Mythos und Erinnerung. Im Auftrag des Zentrums für Militärgeschichte und Sozialwissenschaften der Bundeswehr*, Freiburg im Breisgau 2013.

Esser, Hartmut (ed.), *Der Wandel nach der Wende*, Wiesbaden 2000.

Evaluation Brandt (Peter Brandt, Gutachten zur politischen Einstellung und zum politischen Verhalten des ehemaligen preussischen und reichsdeutschen Kronprinzen Wilhelm, August 2014, http://www.hohenzollern.lol/#gutachten).

Evaluation Clark (Christopher Clark, Hat Kronprinz Wilhelm dem nation-alsozialistischen System *erheblichen Vorschub* geleistet?, Cambridge 2011, http: // www.hohenzollern.lol / #gutachten).

Evaluation Malinowski (Stephan Malinowski, Gutachten zum politischen Verhalten des ehemaligen Kronprinzen (Wilhelm Prinz von Preussen, 1882–1951), Edinburgh, June 2014, http: // www.hohenzollern.lol / #gutachten).

Evaluation Pyta / Orth (Pyta, Wolfram / Orth, Rainer, Gutachten über die politische Haltung und das politische Verhalten von Wilhelm Prinz von Preussen (1882–1951), letzter Kronprinz des Deutschen Reiches und von Preussen, in den Jahren 1923 bis 1945, (2015 or 2016), http: // www.hohen-zollern.lol / #gutachten).

Evans, Richard J., *Altered Pasts. Counterfactuals in History*, London 2014.

Evans, Richard J., *The Coming of the Third Reich*, London 2003.

Evans, Richard J., *Das Dritte Reich*, vol. 1: *Aufstieg*, Munich 2004.

Ewen, Stuart, *PR! A Social History of Spin*, New York 1996.

Farmer, Walter I., *Die Bewahrer des Erbes. Das Schicksal deutscher Kulturgüter am Ende des Zweiten Weltkrieges*, Berlin 2002.

Ferguson, Niall, *Der falsche Krieg. Der Erste Weltkrieg und das 20. Jahrhundert*, Stuttgart 1999.

Förster, Birte, Der Königin Luise-Mythos. *Mediengeschichte des 'Idealbilds Deutscher Weiblichkeit'*, Göttingen 2011.

Förster, Stig, *Der doppelte Militarismus*, Darmstadt 1985.

Franck, Georg, *Ökonomie der Aufmerksamkeit. Ein Entwurf*, Munich 1998.

Fraschka, Mark A., *Franz Pfeffer von Salomon. Hitlers vergessener Oberster SA-Führer*, Göttingen 2016.

Frei, Norbert, *Der Führerstaat. Nationalsozialistische Herrschaft 1933 bis 1945*, Munich 2013.

Frei, Norbert (ed.), *Hitlers Eliten nach 1945*, Frankfurt am Main 2001.

Frei, Norbert, *Vergangenheitspolitik. Die Anfänge der Bundesrepublik und die NS-Vergangenheit*, Munich 2012.

Frevert, Ute, 'Gefühlspolitik und Herrschaftskommunikation im 19. Jahr-hundert', in idem, *Gefühle in der Geschichte*, Göttingen 2021, 285–305.

Frevert, Ute, *Mächtige Gefühle. Von A wie Angst bis Z wie Zuneigung. Deutsche Geschichte seit 1900*, Frankfurt am Main 2020.

Fricke, Dieter (ed.), *Lexikon zur Parteiengeschichte. Die bürgerlichen und klein-bürgerlichen Parteien und Verbände in Deutschland (1789–1945)*, vol. 2, Leipzig 1984.

Friedländer, Saul, *Das Dritte Reich und die Juden*, Munich 2007.

Friedländer, Saul, *Les Années d'Extermination. L'Allemagne nazie et les Juifs 1939–1945*, Paris 2007.

Friedländer, Saul, *Nazi Germany and the Jews. The Years of Persecution 1933–39*, London 1997.

From Weimar to Hitler. Studies in the Dissolution of the Weimar Republic and the Establishment of the Third Reich, 1932–1934, edited by Hermann Beck and Larry Eugene Jones, Oxford 2020.

Funck, Marcus, 'The Meaning of Dying. East Elbian Noble Families as Warrior-Tribes in the 19th and 20th Centuries', in Greg Eghigian and Matt Berg (eds.), *Sacrifice and National Belonging in 20th-Century Germany*, Arlington 2002, 26–63.

Funck, Marcus, 'Schock und Chance. Der preussische Militäradel in der Weimarer Republik zwischen Stand und Profession', in Heinz Reif (ed.), *Adel und Bürgertum in Deutschland*, vol. 2, Berlin 2001, 127–71.

Galbraith, John Kenneth, 'Hereditary Land in the Third Reich', *The Quarterly Journal of Economics* 53, 3 (May 1939), 465–76.

Gallus, Alexander, 'Eine kontinuitätsgebremste Revolution. Deutschland an der Wegscheide zwischen Monarchie und Demokratie', in Biskup, Luh and Vu Minh (eds.), *Preussendämmerung*, 23–38.

Gärditz, Klaus, 'Die Rolle der Verwaltungsgerichtsbarkeit in geschichtspolitischen Auseinandersetzungen. Der Fall "Hohenzollern"', in *Das öffentliche Recht der Gegenwart. Jahrbuch des öffentlichen Rechts der Gegenwart*, new series, vol. 69, edited by Oliver Lepsius, Angelika Nussberger, Christoph Schönberger, Christian Waldhoff and Christian Walter, Tübingen 2021, 269–310.

Gassert, Philipp, *Amerika im Dritten Reich: Ideologie, Propaganda und Volksmeinung 1933–1945*, Stuttgart 1997.

Gasteiger, Daniela, *Kuno von Westarp (1864–1945). Parlamentarismus, Monarchismus und Herrschaftsutopien im deutschen Konservatismus*, Berlin 2018.

Geheimdienst und Propaganda im Ersten Weltkrieg. Die Aufzeichnungen von Oberst Walter Nicolai 1914 bis 1918. Im Auftrag des Zentrums für

Militärgeschichte und Sozialwissenschaften der Bundeswehr, edited by Michael Epkenhans, Gerhard P. Gross, Markus Pöhlmann and Christian Stachelbeck, Berlin/Boston 2019.

Gerbet, Klaus, *Carl-Hans Graf von Hardenberg 1891–1958. Ein preussischer Konservativer in Deutschland*, Berlin 1993.

Gerstner, Alexandra, *Neuer Adel. Aristokratische Elitekonzeptionen zwischen Jahrhundertwende und Nationalsozialismus*, Darmstadt 2008.

Gerwarth, Robert, *Der Bismarck-Mythos. Die Deutschen und der Eiserne Kanzler*, Munich 2007.

Geyer, Martin H., *Kapitalismus und politische Moral in der Zwischenkriegszeit oder: Wer war Julius Barmat?*, Hamburg 2018.

Geyer, Martin H., *Verkehrte Welt. Revolution, Inflation und Moderne, Munich 1914–1924*, Göttingen 1998.

Gies, Horst, *Richard Walther Darré*, Cologne 2019.

Giloi, Eva, *Monarchy, Myth and Material Culture in Germany 1750–1950*, Cambridge 2012.

Görlitz, Walter, *Die Junker. Adel und Bauer im deutschen Osten*, Limburg 1981.

Goschler, Constantin, Prinzen, 'Bürger und Preussen. Die Eigentumsfrage in Ostdeutschland und die Entschädigungsforderungen der Hohenzollern', in *Zeitschrift für Geschichtswissenschaft* 69 (2020), 322–36.

Granier, Gerhard, *Magnus von Levetzow. Seeoffizier, Monarchist und Wegbereiter Hitlers. Lebensweg und ausgewählte Dokumente*, Boppard am Rhein 1982.

Grass, Karl Martin, *Jung, Papenkreis und Röhmkrise 1933/1934*, Heidelberg 1966.

Grawe, Lukas (ed.), *Die militärische Elite des Kaiserreichs. 24 Lebensläufe*, Darmstadt 2020.

Groh, Thomas et al. (eds.), *Verfassungsrecht, Völkerrecht, Menschenrechte – Vom Recht im Zentrum der Internationalen Beziehungen*, Heidelberg 2019.

Gross, Raphael, *November 1938. Die Katastrophe vor der Katastrophe*, Munich 2013.

Grünzig, Matthias, *Für Deutschtum und Vaterland. Die Potsdamer Garnisonkirche im 20. Jahrhundert*, Berlin 2017.

Gusy, Christoph, *Weimar – die wehrlose Republik? Verfassungsschutzrecht und Verfassungsschutz in der Weimarer Republik*, Tübingen 1991.

Gutsche, Willibald, *Ein Kaiser im Exil. Der letzte deutsche Kaiser Wilhelm II. in Holland*, Marburg 1991.

Bibliography

Hadeln, Charlotte von, *In Sonne und Sturm*, Rudolstadt 1935.

Hamann, Brigitte, *Hitlers Wien*, Munich 2012.

Hamann, Brigitte, *Winifred Wagner oder Hitlers Bayreuth*, Munich / Zürich 2002.

Hamerow, Theodore S., *Die Attentäter. Der 20. Juli – von der Kollaboration zum Widerstand*, Munich 1999.

Hardenberg, Reinhild Gräfin von, *Auf immer neuen Wegen. Erinnerungen an Neuhardenberg und den Widerstand gegen den Nationalsozialismus*, Berlin 2003.

Hardtwig, Wolfgang, *Geschichtskultur und Wissenschaft*, Munich 1990.

Harpprecht, Klaus, *Die Gräfin: Marion Dönhoff*, Reinbek 2008.

Harpprecht, Klaus, *Thomas Mann, eine Biographie*, Frankfurt am Main 1995.

Hartley, L. P., *The Go-Between*, London 1953.

Haslam, Jonathan, *The Spectre of War: International Communism and the Origins of World War II*, Princeton 2021.

Hasselhorn, Benjamin, *Königstod: 1918 und das Ende der Monarchie in Deutschland*, Leipzig 2018.

Haupt, Heinz-Gerhard, 'Der Adel in einer entadelten Gesellschaft. Frankreich seit 1830', in *Geschichte und Gesellschaft*, special edn, vol. 13: *Europäischer Adel 1750–1950* (1990), 286–305.

Hausherr, Rainer (ed.), *Die Zeit der Staufer. Geschichte – Kunst – Kultur*, vol. 3, Stuttgart 1977.

Heiden, Detlev / Mai, Gunther (eds.), *Nationalsozialismus in Thüringen*, Weimar / Cologne / Vienna 1995.

Heinen, Ernst / Schoeps, Hans Julius (eds.), *Geschichte in der Gegenwart. Festschrift für Kurt Kluxen*, Paderborn 1972, 199–210.

Heinrich, Gerd, *Geschichte Preussens. Staat und Dynastie*, Frankfurt am Main / Berlin 1984.

Herbert, Ulrich, *Geschichte Deutschlands im 20. Jahrhundert*, Munich 2014.

Herbert, Ulrich, *Wer waren die Nationalsozialisten?*, Munich 2021.

Herbst, Ludolf, *Hitlers Charisma. Die Erfindung eines deutschen Messias*, Frankfurt am Main 2010.

Herre, Paul, *Kronprinz Wilhelm. Seine Rolle in der deutschen Politik*, Munich 1954.

Herzogin Viktoria Luise, *Die Kronprinzessin*, Göttingen 1977.

Heynickx, Rajesh, 'Bridging the Abyss: Victor Basch's Political and Aesthetic Mindset', in *Modern Intellectual History* 10 (2013), 87–107.

Higham, Nicholas J., *King Arthur: Myth-Making and History*, London/New York 2002.

Hiller von Gaertringen, Friedrich Freiherr, 'Zur Beurteilung des Monarchismus in der Weimarer Republik', in Gotthard Jasper (ed.), *Tradition und Reform in der deutschen Politik. Gedenkschrift für Waldemar Besson*, Frankfurt am Main 1976.

Hitler aus nächster Nähe. Aufzeichnungen eines Vertrauten 1929–1932, edited by Henry Ashby Turner, Frankfurt am Main 1978.

Hochstetter, Dorothee, *Motorisierung und 'Volksgemeinschaft': Das Nationalsozialistische Kraftfahrkorps (NSKK) 1931–1945*, Munich 2005.

Hoepke, Klaus Peter, *Die deutsche Rechte und der italienische Faschismus*, Düsseldorf 1968.

Hofe, Alexander vom, *Vier Prinzen zu Schaumburg-Lippe und das parallele Unrechtssystem*, n.p. 2006.

Hofe, Alexander vom, *Vier Prinzen zu Schaumburg-Lippe, Kammler und von Behr*, n.p. 2013.

Hofmann, Arne, '*Wir sind das alte Deutschland, Das Deutschland, wie es war . . .' Der 'Bund der Aufrechten' und der Monarchismus in der Weimarer Republik*, Frankfurt am Main 1998.

Hoffmann, Dieter, *Der Skandal. Hindenburgs Entscheidung für Hitler*, Bremen 2020.

Hoffmann, Peter, *Claus Schenk Graf von Stauffenberg und seine Brüder*, Stuttgart 1992.

Hofmann, Arne, 'Obsoleter Monarchismus als Erbe der Monarchie. Das Nachleben der Monarchie im Monarchismus nach 1918', in Biskup and Kohlrausch (eds.), *Das Erbe der Monarchie*, 241–60.

Hofmann, Arne, '*Wir sind das alte Deutschland, das Deutschland, wie es war . . .' Der 'Bund der Aufrechten' und der Monarchismus in der Weimarer Republik*, Frankfurt am Main 1998.

Hofmann, Gunter, *Marion Dönhoff. Die Gräfin, ihre Freunde und das andere Deutschland*, Munich 2019.

Hohenlohe, Franz zu, *Stephanie. Das Leben meiner Mutter*, Munich 1991.

Höhne, Heinz, *Mordsache Röhm. Hitlers Durchbruch zur Alleinherrschaft 1933–1934*, Reinbek bei Hamburg 1991.

Holzhauer, Heinz, 'Die Vermögensauseinandersetzung der Republik Preussen mit ihrem vormals regierenden Königshaus', in *Juristen Zeitung (JZ)* 76 (2021), 87–94.

Honneth, Axel, *Kampf um Anerkennung. Zur moralischen Grammatik sozialer Konflikte*, Frankfurt am Main 2008.

Horne, John / Gerwarth, Robert (eds.), *Krieg im Frieden: Paramilitärische Gewalt nach dem Ersten Weltkrieg*, Göttingen 2013.

Huber, Ernst Rudolf, *Deutsche Verfassungsgeschichte seit 1789*, vol. 5, Stuttgart / Berlin 1978.

Hull, Isabell, *The Entourage of Wilhelm II, 1888–1918*, Cambridge 1982.

The IAF Handbook of Group Facilitation. Best Practices from the Leading Organization in Facilitation. Edited by Sandy Schuman, San Francisco 2005.

Ilsemann, Sigurd von, *Der Kaiser in Holland. Aufzeichnungen des letzten Flügeladjutanten Kaiser Wilhelms II.*, edited by Harald von Koenigswald, vol. 1: *Amerongen und Doorn, 1918–1923*, Munich 1967.

Ilsemann, Sigurd von, *Der Kaiser in Holland. Aufzeichnungen des letzten Flügeladjutanten Kaiser Wilhelms II.*, edited by Harald von Koenigswald, vol. 2: *Monarchie und Nationalsozialismus, 1924–1941*, Munich 1968.

Ilsemann, Sigurd von, *Wilhelm II in Nederland 1918–1941. Dagboekfragmenten bezorgd door Jacco Pekelder en Wendy Landewé*, Soesterberg 2014.

Jacobsen, Wolfgang / Kaes, Anton / Prinzler, Hans Helmut (eds.), *Geschichte des deutschen Films. 2., aktualisierte und erweiterte Auflage*. Stuttgart 2004.

Jasper, Gotthard, *Die gescheiterte Zähmung. Wege zur Machtergreifung Hitlers 1930–1934*, Frankfurt am Main 1986.

Jasper, Gotthard (ed.), *Tradition und Reform in der deutschen Politik. Gedenkschrift für Waldemar Besson*, Frankfurt am Main 1976.

Johnson, Neil M., *George Sylvester Viereck. German-American Propagandist*, Chicago 1972.

Jonas, Klaus W., *Der Kronprinz Wilhelm*, Frankfurt am Main 1962.

Jonas, Klaus W., *The Life of Crown Prince William*, London 1961.

Jones, Larry E., ' "The Greatest Stupidity of my Life". Alfred Hugenberg and the Formation of the Hitler Cabinet, January 1933', in *Journal of Contemporary History* 27 (1992), 63–87.

Jones, Larry E., 'Taming the Nazi Beast: Kurt von Schleicher and the End of the Weimar Republic', in Hermann Beck and Larry Eugene Jones (eds.), *From Weimar to Hitler. Studies in the Dissolution of the Weimar Republic and the Establishment of the Third Reich, 1932–1934*, New York 2018.

Jones, Larry E., 'The Limits of Collaboration. Edgar Jung, Herbert von Bose, and the Origins of the Conservative Resistance to Hitler, 1933–34', in Larry Eugene Jones and James Retallack (eds.), *Between Reform, Reaction, and Resistance. Studies in the History of German Conservatism from 1789 to 1945*, Providence 1993, 465–501.

Jones, Larry E. / Beck, Hermann (ed.), *From Weimar to Hitler: Studies in the Dissolution of the Weimar Republic and the Establishment of the Third Reich, 1932–1934*, New York 2019.

Jones, Larry Eugene, *Hitler versus Hindenburg. The 1932 Presidential Elections and the End of the Weimar Republic*, Cambridge 2016.

Jones, Larry Eugene, *The German Right 1918–1930. Political Parties, Organized Interests, and Patriotic Associations in the Struggle against Weimar Democracy*, Cambridge 2020.

Jones, Larry Eugene / Pyta, Wolfram (eds.), *'Ich bin der letzte Preusse.' Der politische Lebensweg des konservativen Politikers Kuno Graf von Westarp (1864–1945)*, Cologne / Weimar / Vienna 2006.

Jones, Mark, *Am Anfang war Gewalt. Die deutsche Revolution 1918/1919 und der Beginn der Weimarer Republik*, Berlin 2017.

Jung, Otmar, *Senatspräsident Freymuth. Richter, Sozialdemokrat und Pazifist in der Weimarer Republik. Eine politische Biographie*, Frankfurt am Main 1989.

Jung, Otmar, *Volksgesetzgebung. Die 'Weimarer Erfahrungen' aus dem Fall der Vermögensauseinandersetzungen zwischen Freistaaten und ehemaligen Fürsten*, 2 vols., Hamburg 1996.

Kaehler, Siegfried, 'Vier quellenkritische Untersuchungen zum Kriegsende 1918', in *Studien zur deutschen Geschichte des 19. und 20. Jahrhunderts. Aufsätze und Vorträge*, Göttingen 1961.

Bibliography

The Kaiser's Daughter. Memoirs of H. R. H. Viktoria Luise Duchess of Brunswick and Lüneburg, Princess of Prussia, London 1977.

Kampwirth, Karen, *Women and Guerilla Movements. Nicaragua, El Salvador, Chiapas, Cuba*, Penn State University 2002.

Kantorowicz, Ernst H., *Kaiser Friedrich der Zweite*, Berlin 1927.

Kantorowicz, Ernst H., *The King's Two Bodies. A Study in Medieval Political Theology*, Princeton / Oxford 1957.

Karlauf, Thomas, *Stauffenberg. Porträt eines Attentäters*, Munich 2019.

Karlauf, Thomas, *Stefan George. Die Entdeckung des Charisma. Biografie*, Munich 2007.

Kaufmann, Walter H., *Monarchism in the Weimar Republic*, New York 1953.

Keitz, Ursula von, *Filme vor Gericht. Theorie und Praxis der Filmprüfung in Deutschland 1920 bis 1938*, Frankfurt am Main 1999.

Kellerhoff, Sven Felix, *Geschichte in Geschichten. Ortstermin Mitte. Auf Spurensuche in Berlin Innenstadt*, Berlin 2007.

Kellogg, Michael, *The Russian Roots of Nazism: White Émigrés and the Making of National Socialism, 1917–1945*, Cambridge 2005.

Kershaw, Ian, *Der Hitler-Mythos: Führerkult und Volksmeinung*, Munich 2018.

Kershaw, Ian, *Hitler*, Munich 2009.

Kershaw, Ian, *Popular Opinion and Political Dissent in the Third Reich. Bavaria 1933–1945*, Oxford 1983.

Kessler, Harry Graf, *Das Tagebuch*, vol. 9: *1926–1937*, edited by Sabine Gruber und Ulrich Ott, Stuttgart 2010.

Keyserlingk-Rehbein, Linda von, *Nur eine 'ganz kleine Clique'? Die NS-Ermittlungen über das Netzwerk vom 20. Juli 1944*, Berlin 2018.

Kiesel, Helmuth, *Ernst Jünger. Die Biographie*, Munich 2007.

Kirschstein, Jörg, *Auguste Victoria. Porträt einer Kaiserin*, Berlin 2021.

Kirschstein, Jörg, *Cecilie (1886–1954). Deutschlands letzte Kronprinzessin zwischen Monarchie und Republik*, edited by the Stiftung Preussische Schlösser and Gärten Berlin-Brandenburg, Potsdam 2004.

Kirschstein, Jörg, *Kronprinzessin Cecilie. Eine Bildbiographie*, Berlin 2004.

Kirsten, Jens, *Nennen Sie mich einfach Prinz. Das Lebensabenteuer des Harry Domela*, Weimar 2010.

Kissenkoetter, Udo, *Gregor Strasser und die NSDAP*, Munich 1978.

Klausa, Ekkehard, 'Sie kamen aus dem "Stahlhelm". Frühe Kampf-
genossen Hitlers, die früh in den Widerstand gingen', in *BIOS* 28
(2015), 218–30.

Klee, Ernst, *Das Personenlexikon zum Dritten Reich. Wer war was vor und nach
1945*, Frankfurt am Main 2007.

Kleine, Georg H., 'Adelsgenossenschaft und Nationalsozialismus', in *Vierteljahrshefte für Zeitgeschichte* 26 (1978), 100–143.

Klemperer, Victor, *LTI. Notizbuch eines Philologen*, Leipzig 1996.

Klemperer, Victor, *The Language of the Third Reich*, translated by Martin
Brady, London/New York 2002.

Klingler, Anita, 'Negotiating Violence. Defining the Legitimacy of Political Violence in Interwar Britain and Germany 1918–1938', PhD,
University of Edinburgh 2020.

Kluck, Thomas, *Protestantismus und Protest in der Weimarer Republik*,
Bern 1996.

Kluge, Ulrich, *Agrarwirtschaft und ländliche Gesellschaft im 20. Jahrhundert*,
Munich 2005.

Koch, Lars (ed.), *Modernisierung als Amerikanisierung. Entwicklungslinien
der westdeutschen Kultur 1945–1960*, Bielefeld 2007.

Kohlrausch, Martin, *Der Monarch im Skandal: Die Logik der Massenmedien
und die Transformation der wilhelminischen Elite*, Berlin 2005.

Kohlrausch, Martin, 'Die Flucht des Kaisers. Doppeltes Scheitern adlig-
bürgerlicher Monarchiekonzepte', in Reif (ed.), *Adel und Bürgertum in
Deutschland*, vol. 2, 65–102.

Kohlrausch, Martin, 'Meer dan eenden voederen. Nieuwe literatuur over
keizer Wilhelm II en Nederland', in *Tijdschrift voor Geschiedenis* 130/4
(2017), 625–42.

Kohlrausch, Martin (ed.), *Samt und Stahl. Kaiser Wilhelm II. im Urteil seiner
Zeitgenossen*, Berlin 2006.

Kopke, Christoph / Tress, Werner (ed.), *Der Tag von Potsdam. Der 21.
März 1933 und die Errichtung der nationalsozialistischen Diktatur*, Boston,
Mass. 2013.

Kopper, Christopher, *Hjalmar Schacht: Aufstieg und Fall von Hitlers mächtig-
stem Bankier*, Munich 2006.

Bibliography

Korschanowski, Jessica, 'Rot dominiert – Funktion und Ausstattung des Weissen Salons im Schloss Cecilienhof während der Potsdamer Konferenz 1945. Betrachtungen anlässlich der Sonderausstellung 2020 – Teil 1', in Texte des RECS #36, 26/02/2020, https://recs.hypotheses.org/5790.

Kronprinzessin Cecilie, *Erinnerungen an den deutschen Kronprinzen*, Biberach an der Riss 1952.

Krüger-Bulcke, Ingrid, *Der Hohenzollern-Hindenburg-Zwischenfall in Marburg 1947. Wiederaufleben nationalistischer Strömungen der Sturm im Wasserglas?*, Marburg 1989.

Kühnl, Reinhard, *Die nationalsozialistische Linke 1925–1930*, Meisenheim am Glan 1966.

Kürenberg, Joachim von, *War alles falsch? Das Leben Kaiser Wilhelms II.*, Bonn 1951.

Kurtz, Michael, *America and the Return of Nazi Contraband*, Cambridge 2004.

Laak, Dirk van, *Gespräche in der Sicherheit des Schweigens: Carl Schmitt in der politischen Geistesgeschichte der frühen Bundesrepublik*, Berlin 2002.

Laak, Dirk van, 'Symbolische Politik in Praxis und Kritik. Neue Perspektiven auf die Weimarer Republik', in Ute Daniel (ed.), *Politische Kultur und Medienwirklichkeiten in den 1920er Jahren*, Munich 2010, 25–46.

Landau, Peter, *Juristen jüdischer Herkunft im Kaiserreich und in der Weimarer Republik. Mit einem Nachwort von Michael Stolleis*, Munich 2020.

Landtag Brandenburg, 'Ausschuss für Wissenschaft', in *Forschung und Kultur*, 20 January 2021, P-AWFK 7/13.

Lehmann, Hartmut (ed.), *Historikerkontroversen*, Göttingen 2000.

Lerner, Robert E., *Ernst Kantorowicz. Eine Biografie*, Stuttgart 2020.

Ley, Michael / Schoeps, Julius H. (eds.), *Der Nationalsozialismus als politische Religion*, Bodenheim bei Mainz 1997.

Lier, Barbara, *Das 'Hilfswerk 20. Juli 1944'. Die Geschichte der Hinterbliebenen der Hitler-Attentäter von 1944 bis 1974*, Augsburg 2020.

Lindenberger, Thomas, *Strassenpolitik. Zur Sozialgeschichte der öffentlichen Ordnung in Berlin 1900 bis 1914*, Bonn 1995.

Link, Stefan J., *Forging Global Fordism. Nazi Germany, Soviet Russia and the Contest over the Industrial Order*, Princeton/Oxford 2020.

Link, Stefan J., 'Rethinking the Ford–Nazi Connection', in *Bulletin of the GHI Washington*, 49 (2011), 135–50.

Linse, Ulrich, *Barfüssige Propheten*, Berlin 1983.

Lipp, Carola (ed.), *Medien populärer Kultur. Erzählung, Bild und Objekt in der volkskundlichen Forschung*, Frankfurt am Main / New York 1995, 60–70.

Longerich, Peter, *Die braunen Bataillone. Geschichte der SA*, Munich 1989.

Longerich, Peter, *Goebbels: A Biography*, New York 2015.

Lubrich, Oliver (ed.), *Reisen ins Reich 1933–1945. Ausländische Autoren berichten aus Deutschland*, Frankfurt am Main 2004.

Ludwig, Bernhard, 'Victor Basch et l'Allemagne. Esquisse d'une relation particulière', in *Revue d'Allemagne et des pays de langue allemande* 36 (2004), 341–58.

Luh, Jürgen, 'Carl Lange und "Der Kronprinz"', in Texte des RECS #42, 11/05/2021, https://recs.hypotheses.org/6381.

Luh, Jürgen, *Der Kronprinz und das Dritte Reich. Wilhelm von Preussen und der Aufstieg des Nationalsozialismus*, Munich 2023.

Luh, Jürgen, 'Die "Langemarck-Denkmalweihe" in Naumburg 1933, Franz Seldte und der Kronprinz', in Texte des RECS #44, 18/10/2021, https://recs.hypotheses.org/6630.

Luh, Jürgen, 'Düsseldorf 1933. Der 3. Waffentag der deutschen Kavallerie oder Wie die alten Soldaten in den "neuen Staat" überführt wurden', in Texte des RECS #40, 18/03/2021, https://recs.hypotheses.org/6279.

Luh, Jürgen, 'Fiat Lux? Lothar Machtans "Quellen zur politischen Biografie des letzten deutschen Kronprinzen unter besonderer Berücksichtigung der 1930er Jahre"', Berlin 2023, in RECS-Buchbesprechungen, 13/11/2023, https://recs.hypotheses.org/11826.

Luh, Jürgen (ed.), *Potsdamer Konferenz 1945. Die Neuordnung der Welt*, Potsdam 2020.

Luh, Jürgen / Bauer, Alexandra Nina, 'Cecilie und die Dynastie während der Weimarer Republik und dem Dritten Reich', in *Cecilie. Deutschlands letzte Kronprinzessin zwischen Monarchie und Republik*, Potsdam 2004, 47–59.

Lundestad, Geir, 'Empire by Invitation? The United States and Western Europe, 1945–1952', in *Journal of Peace Research* 23 (1986), 263–77.

Machtan, Lothar, *Der Kaisersohn bei Hitler*, Hamburg 2006.

Machtan, Lothar, *Der Kronprinz und die Nazis. Hohenzollerns blinder Fleck*, Berlin 2021.

Machtan, Lothar, *Die Abdankung. Wie Deutschlands gekrönte Häupter aus der Geschichte fielen*, Munich 2008.

Machtan, Lothar (ed.), *Quellen zur politischen Biografie des letzten deutschen Kronprinzen unter besonderer Berücksichtigung der 1930er Jahre*, Berlin 2023, https://www.preussen.de/forum-preussen/epaper-Machtan_Dossier_V3/index.html#0.

Maier, Hans, ' "Totalitarismus" und "Politische Religionen". Konzepte des Diktaturvergleichs', in Eckard Jesse (ed.), *Totalitarismus im 20. Jahrhundert. Eine Bilanz der internationalen Forschung*, Baden-Baden 1996, 118–34.

Malinowski, Stephan, ' "Führertum" und "Neuer Adel". Die Deutsche Adelsgenossenschaft und der Deutsche Herrenklub in der Weimarer Republik', in Reif (ed.), *Adel und Bürgertum*, vol. 2, Berlin 2001, 173–211.

Malinowski, Stephan, *Nazis and Nobles. The History of a Misalliance*, Oxford 2020.

Malinowski, Stephan, 'Politische Skandale als Zerrspiegel der Demokratie. Die Fälle Barmat und Sklarek im Kalkül der Weimarer Rechten', in *Jahrbuch für Antisemitismusforschung* 5, 1996, 46–64.

Malinowski, Stephan, *Vom König zum Führer. Sozialer Niedergang und politische Radikalisierung im deutschen Adel zwischen Kaiserreich und NS-Staat*, Berlin 2003.

Malinowski, Stephan / Funck, Marcus, 'Masters of Memory. The Strategic Use of Memory in Autobiographies of the German Nobility', in Alan Confino and Peter Fritzsche (eds.), *Memory Work in Germany*, Urbana, 2002.

Mansel, Philip / Riotte, Torsten (eds.), *Monarchy and Exile. The Politics of Legitimacy from Marie de Médicis to Wilhelm II.*, Basingstoke 2011.

Mattioli, Aram, *Experimentierfeld der Gewalt. Der Abessinienkrieg und seine internationale Bedeutung 1935–1941*, Zürich 2005.

Meinl, Susanne, *Nationalsozialisten gegen Hitler. Die nationalrevolutionäre Opposition um Friedrich Wilhelm Heinz*, Berlin 2000.

Merkenich, Stephanie, *Grüne Front gegen Weimar. Reichs-Landbund und agrarischer Lobbyismus 1918–1933*, Düsseldorf 1998.

Bibliography

Merz, Kai-Uwe, *Das Schreckbild. Deutschland und der Bolschewismus 1917 bis 1921*, Berlin 1995.

Merziger, Patrick / Stöber, Rudolf / Körber, Esther-Beate / Schulz, Jürgen Michael (eds.), *Geschichte, Öffentlichkeit, Kommunikation. Festschrift für Bernd Sösemann zum 65. Geburtstag*, Stuttgart 2010.

Middendorf, Stefanie, 'Ausserwirtschaftlicher Wille? Antiliberale Haltungen zu Kapitalismus und Demokratie bei Johannes Popitz und Carl Schmitt', in Detlef Lehnert (ed.), *Soziale Demokratie und Kapitalismus. Die Weimarer Republik im Vergleich*, Berlin 2019, 173–208.

Minia, Hans-Georg, *Die Fridericus-Gedenkfeiern auf der Burg Hohenzollern 1976– 1991. Mit den Reden seiner Kaiserlichen und Königlichen Hoheit Prinz Louis Ferdinand von Preussen und des Prinzen Hohenzollern-Emden*, Ulm 2007.

Moeyes, Paul, *Het kleine keizersdrama in Amerongen. Keizer Wilhelm II op kasteel Amerongen*, Stichting Kasteel Amerongen 2018.

Möllers, Heiner, *Reichswehrminister Otto Gessler. Eine Studie zu 'unpolitischer' Militärpolitik in der Weimarer Republik*, Frankfurt am Main 1998.

Mommsen, Hans, *Alternative zu Hitler. Studien zur Geschichte des deutschen Widerstandes*, Munich 2000.

Mommsen, Hans, *Der Nationalsozialismus und die deutsche Gesellschaft. Ausgewählte Aufsätze. Zum 60. Geburtstag herausgegeben von Lutz Niethammer und Bernd Weisbrod*, Reinbek bei Hamburg 1991.

Mommsen, Hans, *Die verspielte Freiheit. Aufstieg und Untergang der Weimarer Republik. Durchgesehen und mit einem Nachwort versehen von Detlef Lehnert*, Berlin 2018.

Mommsen, Hans, 'Gesellschaftsbild und Verfassungspläne des deutschen Widerstands', in Walter Schmitthenner and Hans Buchheim (eds.), *Der deutsche Widerstand gegen Hitler. Vier historisch-kritische Studien*, Cologne 1966, 73–16.

Morat, Daniel, *Von der Tat zur Gelassenheit. Konservatives Denken bei Martin Heidegger, Ernst Jünger und Friedrich Georg Jünger 1920–1960*, Göttingen 2007.

Morsey, Rudolf, *Der Untergang des politischen Katholizismus. Die Zentrumspartei zwischen christlichem Selbstverständnis und 'Nationaler Erhebung' 1932/33*, Stuttgart 1977.

Morsey, Rudolf, *Fritz Gerlich. Ein früher Gegner Hitlers und des Nationalsozialismus*, Paderborn 2016.

Morsey, Rudolf, *Zur Entstehung, Authentizität und Kritik von Brünings Memoiren 1918–1934*, Opladen 1975.

Moses, A. Dirk, 'Der Katechismus der Deutschen', in *Geschichte der Gegenwart*, 23 May 2021, https://geschichtedergegenwart.ch/der-katechismus-der-deutschen/.

Moses, A. Dirk, *The Problems of Genocide: Permanent Security and the Language of Transgression*, Cambridge 2021.

Müller, Frank Lorenz, *Die Thronfolger. Macht und Zukunft der Monarchie im 19. Jahrhundert*, Munich 2019.

Müller, Klaus-Jürgen, *Generaloberst Ludwig Beck. Eine Biographie*, Paderborn 2008.

Müller, Mario H., *Fabian von Schlabrendorff. Ein Leben im Widerstand gegen Hitler und für Gerechtigkeit in Deutschland*, Berlin 2023.

Müller, Yves / Zilkenat, Reiner (eds.), *Bürgerkriegsarmee. Forschungen zur nationalsozialistischen Sturmabteilung (SA)*, Frankfurt am Main 2013.

Münkler, Herfried, *Der Partisan. Theorie, Strategie, Gestalt*, Opladen 1990.

Nagel, I., *Fememorde und Fememordprozesse in der Weimarer Republik*, Cologne 1991.

Nerdinger, Winfried / Hockerts, Hans Günter / Krauss, Marita (eds.), *München und der Nationalsozialismus*, Munich 2015.

Neumann, Franz, *Behemoth. Struktur und Praxis des Nationalsozialismus 1933–1944* (1942/1944), edited by Alfons Söllner and Michael Wildt, Hamburg.

Niemoeller-von Sell, Sibylle, '*Furchtbar einfach, wird gemacht*', Berlin 1994.

Nivet, Philippe, *La France occupée 1914–1918*, 2nd edn, Paris 2014.

Noakes, Jeremy, 'German Conservatives and the Third Reich. An Ambiguous Relationship', in Martin Blinkhorn (ed.), *Fascists and Conservatives. The Radical Right and the Establishment in Twentieth-Century Europe*, London 1990, 71–97.

Oexle, Otto Gerhard, *Geschichtswissenschaften im Zeichen des Historismus*, Göttingen 1996.

Orth, Rainer, '*Der Amtssitz der Opposition?' Politik und Staatsumbaupläne im Büro des Stellvertreters des Reichskanzlers in den Jahren 1933–1934*, Cologne / Weimar / Vienna 2016.

Bibliography

Otto, Frank / Schulz, Thilo (eds.), *Grossbritannien und Deutschland. Gesellschaftliche, kulturelle und politische Beziehungen im 19. und 20. Jahrhundert. Festschrift für Bernd-Jürgen Wendt zu seinem 65. Geburtstag*, Rheinfelden 1999.

Parssinen, Terry, *Die vergessene Verschwörung. Hans Oster und der militärische Widerstand gegen Hitler*, Berlin 2008.

Paul, Gerhard, *Aufstand der Bilder. Die NS-Propaganda vor 1933*, Bonn 1990.

Paul, Gerhard / Mallmann, Klaus-Michael (eds.), *Die Gestapo. Mythos und Realität*, Darmstadt 1995.

Payne, Stanley G., *A History of Fascism*, London 1996.

Pekelder, Jacco, 'Leven in een luchtkasteel. De dagboeken van Sigurd von Ilsemann als historisch document over Wilhelm II', in Sigurd von Ilsemann (ed.), *Wilhelm II in Nederland 1918–1941. Dagboekfragmenten bezorgd door Jacco Pekelder en Wendy Landewé*, Soesterberg 2014.

Pekelder, Jacco / Schenk, Joep / van der Bas, Cornelis, *De keizer en het Derde Rijk – De familie Hohenzollern en het nationaalsocialisme*, Soesterberg 2020.

Pekelder, Jacco / Schenk, Joep / van der Bas, Cornelis, *Der Kaiser und das 'Dritte Reich'. Die Hohenzollern zwischen Restauration und Nationalsozialismus*, Göttingen 2021.

Petropoulos, Jonathan, *Royals and the Reich. The Princes von Hessen in Nazi Germany*, Oxford 2006.

Petzinna, Berthold, *Erziehung zum deutschen Lebensstil. Ursprung und Entwicklung des jungkonservativen 'Ring'-Kreises 1918–1933*, Berlin 2000.

Pohl, Karl Heinrich, *Gustav Stresemann. Biographie eines Grenzgängers*, Göttingen 2015.

Pomp, Rainer, *Bauern und Grossgrundbesitzer auf ihrem Weg ins Dritte Reich: Der Brandenburgische Landbund 1919–1933*, Berlin 2010.

Pomp, Rainer, *Brandenburgischer Landadel und die Weimarer Republik. Konflikte um Oppositionsstrategien und Elitenkonzepte*, Berlin 1996.

Preussen, Friedrich Wilhelm Prinz von, 'Die Hohenzollern in Potsdam', in *Schloss Cecilienhof und die Potsdamer Konferenz 1945. Von der Hohenzollernwohnung zur Gedenkstätte*, Berlin / Kleinmachnow / Potsdam 1995.

Preussen, Friedrich Wilhelm Prinz von, *'Gott helfe unserem Vaterland'. Das Haus Hohenzollern 1918–1945*. With 61 pages of documents. Second revised and expanded new edition, Munich 2003.

Bibliography

Preussen, Louis Ferdinand Prinz von, 'Kaiser auf Abruf', TV interview, *Zeugen des Jahrhunderts*, 1987. Prinz Louis Ferdinand von Preussen in conversation with Friedrich Müller, https://www.youtube.com/watch?v=y5eveUVrO9M.

Preussen, Louis Ferdinand Prinz von, *The Rebel Prince*, Chicago 1952.

Puschner, Uwe, *Die völkische Bewegung im wilhelminischen Kaiserreich. Sprache – Rasse – Religion*, Darmstadt 2001.

Pyta, Wolfram, 'Die Kunst des rechtzeitigen Thronverzichts. Neue Einsichten zur Überlebenschance der parlamentarischen Monarchie in Deutschland im Herbst 1918', in Patrick Merziger et al., *Geschichte, Öffentlichkeit. Kommunikation. Festschrift für Bernd Sösemann*, Stuttgart 2010.

Pyta, Wolfram, *Hindenburg. Herrschaft zwischen Hohenzollern und Hitler*, Munich 2007.

Pyta, Wolfram, 'Konstitutionelle Demokratie statt monarchischer Restauration. Die verfassungspolitische Konzeption Schleichers in der Weimarer Staatskrise', in *Vierteljahrshefte für Zeitgeschichte* 47 (1999), 417–41.

Pyta, Wolfram, 'Verfassungsumbau, Staatsnotstand und Querfront: Schleichers Versuche zur Fernhaltung Hitlers von der Reichskanzlerschaft August 1932 bis Januar 1933', in Wolfram Pyta and Ludwig Richter (eds.), *Gestaltungskraft des Politischen. Festschrift für Eberhard Kolb*, Berlin 1998, 173–97.

Pyta, Wolfram, 'Vorbereitungen für den militärischen Ausnahmezustand unter den Regierungen Papen/Schleicher', in *Militärgeschichtliche Mitteilungen* 51 (1992), 385–428.

Pyta, Wolfram / Orth, Rainer, *Nicht alternativlos. Wie ein Reichskanzler Hitler hätte verhindert werden können*, in HZ 312 (2021), 400–444.

Raulff, Ulrich, *Kreis ohne Meister. Stefan Georges Nachleben*, Munich 2009.

Reichardt, Sven, *Faschistische Kampfbünde. Gewalt und Gemeinschaft im italienischen Squadrismus und in der deutschen SA*, Cologne/Weimar/Vienna 2002.

Reif, Heinz (ed.), *Adel und Bürgertum in Deutschland*, vol. 2, Berlin 2001.

Reventlow, Eugen Graf zu, in 'Die Sprache der Monarchie', edited by the project 'Anpassungsstrategien der späten mitteleuropäischen Monarchie am preussischen Beispiel (1786–1918)', Berlin-Brandenburgische

Bibliography

Akademie der Wissenschaften, Berlin. Version 3, 3 December 2020, https://actaborussica.bbaw.de/v3/P0001898.

Riotte, Torsten, *Der Monarch im Exil. Eine andere Geschichte von Staatswerdung und Legitimismus im 19. Jahrhundert*, Göttingen 2018.

Rissmann, Michael, *Hitlers Gott. Vorsehungsglaube und Sendungsbewusstsein des deutschen Diktators*, Zürich/Munich 2001.

Ritter, Gerhard, *Carl Goerdeler und die deutsche Widerstandsbewegung*, Stuttgart 1954.

Ritthaler, Anton, *Die Hohenzollern. Ein Bildwerk*, Frankfurt am Main 1961.

Ritthaler, Anton, *Wilhelm II. Herrscher in einer Zeitwende. Tradition und Leben*, Cologne 1958.

Rödder, Andreas, 'Dichtung und Wahrheit. Der Quellenwert von Heinrich Brünings Memoiren und seine Kanzlerschaft', in *Historische Zeitschrift* 265 (1997), 77–116.

Röhl, John C. G., 'Hof und Hofgesellschaft unter Wilhelm II.', in Karl Ferdinand Werner (ed.), *Hof, Kultur und Politik im 19. Jahrhundert. Akten des 18. Deutsch-Französischen Historikerkolloquiums, Darmstadt vom 27.–30. September 1982*, Bonn (Röhrscheid) 1985, 237–89.

Röhl, John C. G., *Kaiser, Hof und Staat. Wilhelm II. und die deutsche Politik*, Munich 2002.

Röhl, John C. G., 'Kaiser Wilhelm II. und der deutsche Antisemitismus', in idem, *Kaiser, Hof und Staat*, Munich 1987, 203–22.

Röhl, John C. G., 'The Emperor's New Clothes: A Character Sketch of Kaiser Wilhelm II', in John C. G. Röhl and Nicolaus Sombart (eds.), *Kaiser Wilhelm II. New Interpretations. The Corfu Papers*, Cambridge 1982.

Röhl, John C. G., *Wilhelm II.*, vol. 1: *Die Jugend des Kaisers, 1859–1888*, Munich 1993.

Röhl, John C. G., *Wilhelm II.*, vol. 2: *Der Aufbau der persönlichen Monarchie*, Munich 2001.

Röhl, John C. G., *Wilhelm II.*, vol. 3: *Der Weg in den Abgrund 1900–1941*, Munich 2008.

Roloff, Ernst-August, *Bürgertum und Nationalsozialismus 1930–1933. Braunschweigs Weg ins Dritte Reich*, Hanover 1961.

Rothfels, Hans, 'Das politische Vermächtnis des deutschen Widerstands', in *Vierteljahrshefte für Zeitgeschichte* 2 (1954), 329–43.

Rothfels, Hans, *Die deutsche Opposition gegen Hitler. Eine Würdigung*, Krefeld 1949.

Rouette, Hans-Peter, 'Die Widerstandslegende. Produktion und Funktion der Legende vom Widerstand im Kontext der gesellschaftlichen Auseinandersetzungen in Deutschland nach dem Zweiten Weltkrieg', doctoral dissertation, FU Berlin 1983.

Ryback, Timothy W., *Hitler's First Victims and One Man's Race for Justice*, London 2015.

Sabrow, Martin, 'Das Bild der Hohenzollern', unpublished lecture, Potsdam 15 September 2020.

Sabrow, Martin, *Der Rathenau-Mord und die deutsche Gegenrevolution*, Frankfurt 1999.

Sabrow, Martin (ed.), *Die Macht der Bilder*, Leipzig 2013.

Sabrow, Martin, 'Die vergessene Republik. Zum Ort der Weimarer Demokratie in der deutschen Zeitgeschichte', in Hanno Hochmuth et al. (eds.), *Weimars Wirkung. Das Nachleben der ersten deutschen Republik*, Göttingen 2020, 9–27.

Sabrow, Martin / Jessen, Ralph / Grosse Kracht, Klaus (eds.), *Zeitgeschichte als Streitgeschichte. Grosse Kontroversen nach 1945*, Munich 2003.

Sartre, Jean-Paul, *Kean*, Reinbek bei Hamburg 1993.

Sartre, Jean-Paul, *The War Diaries of Jean-Paul Sartre: November 1939/March 1940*, trans. by Quintin Hoare, New York 1984.

Schabas, William A., *The Trial of the Kaiser*, Oxford 2018.

Scheel, Klaus, *1933. Der Tag von Potsdam*, Berlin 1996.

Schieder, Wolfgang, 'Das italienische Experiment. Der Faschismus als Vorbild in der Krise der Weimarer Republik', in *HZ* 262 (1996), 73–125.

Schilde, Kurt, 'Opfer des NS-Terrors 1933 in Berlin. Biographische Skizzen', in Kopke and Tress (eds.), *Tag von Potsdam*, 178–211.

Schildt, Axel, *Militärdiktatur mit Massenbasis? Die Querfrontkonzeption der Reichswehrführung um General von Schleicher am Ende der Weimarer Republik*, Frankfurt am Main 1981.

Schildt, Axel / Sywottek, Arnold, *Modernisierung im Wiederaufbau. Die westdeutsche Gesellschaft der 50er Jahre*, Bonn 1998.

Schleusener, Jan, *Eigentumspolitik im NS-Staat: Der staatliche Umgang mit Handlungs- und Verfügungsrechten über privates Eigentum 1933–1939*, Frankfurt am Main 2009.

Schlögel, Karl, *Der grosse Exodus: Die Russische Emigration und ihre Zentren 1917 bis 1941*, Munich 1994.

Schloss Cecilienhof und die Potsdamer Konferenz 1945. Von der Hohenzollernwohnung zur Gedenkstätte, Berlin / Kleinmachnow / Potsdam 1995.

Schmädeke, Jürgen / Steinbachm, Peter (eds.), *Der Widerstand gegen den Nationalsozialismus: Die deutsche Gesellschaft und der Widerstand gegen Hitler*, Munich 1985.

Schmeling, Anke, *Josias Erbprinz zu Waldeck und Pyrmont: Der politische Weg eines hohen SS-Führers*, Kassel 1993.

Schmidt, Eberhard, *Kurt von Plettenberg. Im Kreis der Verschwörer um Stauffenberg. Ein Lebensweg*, Munich 2014.

Schöck-Quinteros, Eva, 'Der Bund Königin Luise. "Unser Kampfplatz ist die Familie . . ."', in Eva Schöck-Quinteros and Christiane Streubel (eds.), *Ihrem Volk verantwortlich. Frauen der politischen Rechten (1890–1933). Organisationen – Agitationen – Ideologien*, Berlin 2007, 231–70.

Schöllgen, Gregor, *Ulrich von Hassell. 1881–1944. Ein Konservativer in der Opposition. Aktualisierte Neuausgabe*, Munich 2004.

Schönberger, Paul, *The History Management of the East-Elbian Nobility after 1945*, PhD dissertation, University of Cambridge, 2017.

Schönberger, Sophie, *Was soll zurück? Die Restitution von Kulturgütern im Zeitalter der Nostalgie*, Munich 2021.

Schönberger, Sophie, 'Wiedergänger. Die Entschädigungsforderungen der Hohenzollern zwischen Geschichte, Recht und politischer Gestaltung', in *Zeitschrift für Geschichtswissenschaft*, 68 (2020), 337–47.

Schönpflug, Daniel, *Luise von Preussen. Königin der Herzen. Eine Biographie*, Munich 2010.

Schreiner, Klaus, 'Die Staufer in Sage, Legende und Prophetie', in *Die Zeit der Staufer. Geschichte – Kunst – Kultur*, Stuttgart 1977.

Schröder, Wilhelm Heinz / Hachtmann, Rüdiger, 'Die Reichstagsabgeordneten der Weimarer Republik als Opfer des Nationalsozialismus:

vorläufige Bestandsaufnahme und biographische Dokumentation', in *Historical Social Research* 10/4 (1985), 55–98.

Schumacher, Martin (ed.), M. d. R. *Die Reichstagsabgeordneten der Weimarer Republik in der Zeit des Nationalsozialismus. Politische Verfolgung, Emigration und Ausbürgerung, 1933–1945. Eine biographische Dokumentation.* 3rd, considerably expanded and revised, edn, Düsseldorf 1994.

Schumann, Dirk, *Politische Gewalt in der Weimarer Republik. Kampf um die Strasse und Furcht vor dem Bürgerkrieg*, Essen 2001.

Schüren, Ulrich, *Der Volksentscheid zur Fürstenenteignung 1926*, Düsseldorf 1979.

Schuster, Martin, 'Die SA in der nationalsozialistischen Machtergreifung in Berlin und Brandenburg 1926–1934', dissertation, Berlin 2004.

Schwab, Sebastian, 'Historische Ambiguität und Recht. Zur Frage der Ausgleichsleistungen für die "Hohenzollern" und der Stellung historischen Wissens im Prozessrecht', in *Juristen Zeitung* 76 (2021), 500–508.

Schwan, Gesine, 'Der Mitläufer', in Étienne François and Hagen Schulze (eds.), *Deutsche Erinnerungsorte*, vol. 1, Munich 2001, 654–72.

Schwerin, Detlef Graf von, ' "Dann sind's die besten Köpfe, die man henkt." Die junge Generation im deutschen Widerstand', Munich 1994.

Schwerin von Krosigk, Lutz Graf, *Es geschah in Deutschland*, Tübingen 1951.

Self, Robert, *Neville Chamberlain: A Biography*, London/Burlington 2006.

Seliger, Hubert, *Politische Anwälte? Die Verteidiger der Nürnberger Prozesse*, Baden-Baden 2016.

Siemens, Daniel, *Stormtroopers. A New History of Hitler's Brownshirts*, New Haven 2017.

Siemens, Daniel, *Sturmabteilung. Die Geschichte der SA*, Munich 2019.

SKH Prinz Louis Ferdinand von Preussen zum 75. Geburtstag am 9. November 1982. Eine Festschrift, Moers 1983.

Smith, Gary (ed.), *'Eichmann in Jerusalem' und die Folgen*, Frankfurt am Main 2000.

Smith, Gary (ed.), *Hannah Arendt Revisited: 'Eichmann in Jerusalem' und die Folgen*, Frankfurt am Main 2009.

Sombart, Nicolaus, *Wilhelm II. Sündenbock und Herr der Mitte*, Berlin 1996.

Spreti, Heinrich Graf von, *Imlau. Ein Herrenhaus und seine Bewohner*, Munich 1998.

Stachura, Peter D., *Gregor Strasser and the Rise of Nazism*, London 1983.

Stark, Gary D., *Banned in Berlin. Literary Censorship in Imperial Germany, 1871–1918*, New York/London 2009.

Steinbach, Peter / Tuchel, Johannes (eds.), *Widerstand gegen die nationalsozialistische Diktatur 1933–1945*, Berlin 2004.

Stiftung Preussische Schlösser und Gärten Berlin-Brandenburg (ed.), *Cecilie. Deutschlands letzte Kronprinzessin zwischen Monarchie und Republik*, Potsdam 2004, 47–62.

Strenge, Irene, *Kurt von Schleicher, Politik im Reichswehrministerium am Ende der Weimarer Republik*, Berlin 2006.

Strenge, Irene, *Ferdinand von Bredow. Notizen vom 20. 2. 1933 bis 31. 12. 1933. Tägliche Aufzeichnungen vom 1. 1. 1934 bis 28. 6. 1934*, Berlin 2009.

Stresemann, Gustav, *Reden und Schriften. Politik – Geschichte – Literatur 1897–1926*, 2nd edn, edited by Hartmuth Becker, Berlin 2008.

Stribrny, Wolfgang, 'Der Versuch einer Kandidatur des Kronprinzen Wilhelm bei der Reichspräsidentenwahl 1932', in Ernst Heinen and Hans Julius Schoeps (eds.), *Geschichte und Gegenwart. Festschrift für Kurt Kluxen zu seinem 60. Geburtstag*, Paderborn 1972, 199–210.

Studnitz, Hans-Georg von, *Seitensprünge. Erlebnisse und Begegnungen 1907–1970*, Stuttgart 1975.

Süchting-Hänger, Andrea, *Das 'Gewissen der Nation'. Nationales Engagement und politisches Handeln konservativer Frauenorganisationen 1900 bis 1937*, Düsseldorf 2002.

Sweetman, Jack, *The Unforgotten Crowns: The German Monarchist Movements, 1918–1945*, Ann Arbor 1988.

Thamer, Hans-Ulrich, *Verführung und Gewalt. Deutschland 1933–1945*, Munich 1994.

Theweleit, Klaus, *Männerphantasien*, vol. 1: *Frauen, Fluten, Körper, Geschichte* (1977), Munich 1995.

Thimme, Anneliese (ed.), *Friedrich Thimme, 1868–1938. Ein politischer Historiker, Publizist und Schriftsteller in seinen Briefen*, Boppard am Rhein 1994.

Thimme, Anneliese, *Gustav Stresemann. Eine politische Biographie zur Geschichte der Weimarer Republik*, Hanover/Frankfurt am Main 1957.

Thompson, John B., *Political Scandal. Power and Visibility in the Media Age*, Cambridge 2000.

Toyka-Seid, Christiane, 'Gralshüter, Notgemeinschaft oder gesellschaftliche "Pressure-group"? Die Stiftung "Hilfswerk 20. Juli 1944" im ersten Nachkriegsjahrzehnt', in Gerd R. Ueberschär (ed.), *Der 20. Juli 1944. Bewertung und Rezeption des deutschen Widerstands gegen das NS-Regime*, Cologne, 1998, 159–78.

Totalitarismus im 20. Jahrhundert. Eine Bilanz der internationalen Forschung, edited by Eckard Jesse, Bonn 1996.

Turner, Henry Ashby, *Die Grossunternehmer und der Aufstieg Hitlers*, Berlin 1985.

Turner, Henry Ashby, 'The Myth of Chancellor von Schleicher's Querfront Strategy', in *Central European History* 41 (2008), 673–81.

Tye, Larry, *The Father of Spin. Edward L. Bernays and the Birth of Public Relations*, New York 1998.

Ueberschär, Gerd R. (ed.), *Der 20. Juli 1944. Bewertung und Rezeption des deutschen Widerstandes gegen das NS-Regime*, Cologne 1994.

Ueberschär, Gerd R. (ed.), *Hitlers militärische Elite. Vom Kriegsbeginn bis zum Weltkriegsende*, vol. 2, Darmstadt 1998.

Ueberschär, Gerd R. / Vogel, Winfried, *Dienen und Verdienen. Hitlers Geschenke an seine Eliten*, Frankfurt am Main 2000.

Urbach, Karina, *Go-Betweens for Hitler*, Oxford 2015.

Urbach, Karina, *Hitlers heimliche Helfer. Der Adel im Dienst der Macht*, Stuttgart 2016.

Urbach, Karina, ' "Nützliche Idioten". Die Hohenzollern und Hitler', in Biskup, Vu Minh and Luh (eds.), *Preussendämmerung. Die Abdankung der Hohenzollern und das Ende Preussens*, Heidelberg 2019, 65–93.

Urbach, Karina, 'Useful Idiots: The Hohenzollerns and Hitler', in *Historical Research* 93/261 (August 2020), 526–50.

Urbach, Karina, 'Zwischen Aktion und Reaktion. Die süddeutschen Standesherren 1914–1919', in Conze and Wienfort (eds.), *Adel und Moderne*, 323–54.

Vince, Natalya, *Our Fighting Sisters. Nation, Memory and Gender in Algeria, 1954– 2012*, Manchester 2015.

Vogelsang, Thilo, *Reichswehr, Staat und NSDAP*, Stuttgart 1962.

Volkmann, Peer Oliver, *Heinrich Brüning (1885–1970), Nationalist ohne Heimat. Eine Teilbiographie*, Düsseldorf 2007.

Wachsmann, Nikolaus, *KL. Die Geschichte der nationalsozialistischen Konzentrationslager*, Munich 2015.

Wachsmann, Nikolaus / Steinbacher, Sibylle (eds.), *Die Linke im Visier: Zur Errichtung der Konzentrationslager 1933*, Göttingen 2014.

Walter, Dirk, *Antisemitische Gewalt und Kriminalität. Judenfeindschaft in der Weimarer Republik*, Bonn 1999.

Wasserstein, Bernard, *The Secret Lives of Trebitsch Lincoln*, New Haven / London 1988.

Weber, Thomas, *Hitler's First War. Adolf Hitler, the Men of the List Regiment, and the First World War*, Oxford 2010.

Wehler, Hans-Ulrich, *Der Nationalsozialismus. Bewegung, Führerherrschaft, Verbrechen. 1919–1945*, Munich 2009.

Wehler, Hans-Ulrich, *Deutsche Gesellschaftsgeschichte*, vol. 3: *Von der 'Deutschen Doppelrevolution' bis zum Beginn des Ersten Weltkrieges 1849–1914*, Munich 2007.

Wehler, Hans-Ulrich, *Deutsche Gesellschaftsgeschichte*, vol. 4: *Vom Beginn des Ersten Weltkriegs bis zur Gründung der beiden deutschen Staaten 1914–1949*, Munich 2003.

Wehler, Hans-Ulrich, *Krisenherde des Kaiserreichs 1871–1918*, Göttingen 1979.

Weisbrod, Bernd, 'Gewalt in der Politik. Zur politischen Kultur in Deutschland zwischen den beiden Weltkriegen', in *GWU* 43 (1992), 391–404.

Weiss, Dieter J., *Kronprinz Rupprecht von Bayern (1869–1955). Eine politische Biografie*, Regensburg 2007.

Weiss, Hermann / Hoser, Paul (eds.), *Die Deutschnationalen und die Zerstörung der Weimarer Republik. Aus dem Tagebuch von Reinhold Quaatz 1928–1933*, Munich 1989.

Weiss, Volker, *Moderne Antimoderne. Arthur Moeller van den Bruck und der Wandel des Konservatismus*, Paderborn 2013.

Welzer, Harald / Moller, Sabine / Tschuggnall, Karoline, *'Opa war kein Nazi'. Nationalsozialismus und Holocaust im Familiengedächtnis*, Frankfurt am Main 2002.

Wernicke, Thomas, *Der Handschlag am 'Tag von Potsdam'. Der Tag von Potsdam: Der 21. März 1933 und die Errichtung der nationalsozialistischen*

Diktatur, edited by Christoph Kopke and Werner Tress, Berlin, Boston 2013.

Wheeler-Bennett, John W., *Die Nemesis der Macht. Die deutsche Armee in der Politik 1918–1945*, Düsseldorf 1954.

Whittle, Tyler, *Kaiser Wilhelm II. Eine Biographie*, Berlin 1981.

Wichmann, Manfred, *Waldemar Pabst und die Gesellschaft zum Studium des Faschismus (1931–1934)*, Berlin 2013.

Wienfort, Monika, *Monarchie in der bürgerlichen Gesellschaft. Deutschland und England 1640 bis 1848*, Göttingen 1993.

Wilderotter, Hans, 'Haus Doorn. Die verkleinert Kopie eines Hofstaats', in Hans von Wilderotter and Klaus-D. Pohl (eds.), *Der letzte Kaiser. Wilhelm II. im Exil*, Gütersloh / Munich 1991, 113–22.

Wilderotter, Hans / Pohl, Klaus-D., *Der letzte Kaiser. Wilhelm II. im Exil*, Gütersloh 1991.

Winkler, Heinrich August, *Der lange Weg nach Westen*. 2 vols., Munich 2000.

Winkler, Heinrich August, *Die deutsche Staatskrise 1930–1933*, Munich 1992.

Winkler, Heinrich August, *Weimar 1918–1933*, Munich 2018.

Wirsching, Andreas, 'Review of Hermann Beck, *The Fateful Alliance: German Conservatives and Nazis in 1933*; The Machtergreifung in a New Light', in *The Journal of Modern History* 82/3 (2010), 754–6.

Wirtz, Verena, 'Flaggenstreit. Zur politischen Sinnlichkeit der Weimarer Demokratie', in Andreas Braune and Michael Dreyer (eds.), *Republikanischer Alltag. Die Weimarer Demokratie und die Suche nach Normalität*, Stuttgart 2017, 51–66.

Wolzogen, Christoph von, *Drei Schwestern – Innenansichten eines Jahrhunderts in Briefen und Tagebuch*, Frankfurt 2020.

Wolzogen, Christoph von, 'Nach dem Tee in die Mördergrube. Essays zu Helmuth James von Moltke', manuscript, appeared 2022.

Wolzogen, Christoph von, 'Parva Aristocratia. Essays zu einer Philosophie des Adels', unpublished manuscript, 2020.

Wright, Jonathan, *Gustav Stresemann. Weimar's Greatest Statesman*, Oxford 2002.

Zajonz, Michael, *Das kronprinzliche Landhaus Cecilienhof in Potsdam*, 2 vols., Berlin, 1998.

Bibliography

Zboralski, Dietrich, 'Quellenfunde zur neuesten Geschichte des Hohen-
zollernhauses [Berichte und Bemerkungen]', in *ZfG* 3 (1955), 772–4.

Zelinsky, Hartmut, 'Verfall, Vernichtung, Weltentrückung. Richard Wag-
ners antisemitische Werk-Idee als Kunstreligion und Zivilisationskritik
und ihre Verbreitung bis 1933', in Saul Friedländer and Jörn Rüsen (eds.),
Richard Wagner im Dritten Reich, Munich 2000, 309–41.

Ziblatt, Daniel, *Conservative Parties and the Birth of Democracy*, Cambridge,
MA 2017.

Zorgbibe, Charles, *Guillaume II. Le dernier empereur allemand*, Paris 2013.

Zwehl, Konrad, 'Die Deutschlandpolitik Englands von 1922 bis 1924 unter
besonderer Berücksichtigung der Reparationen und Sanktionen', doctoral dissertation, Munich 1974.

Notes

Introduction

1 Following the conventions of history, this book will refer to Hohenzollerns and largely omit the suffix 'of Prussia'. The 'House of
Hohenzollern' refers exclusive to the Brandenburgian-Prussian and
not the Swabian branch of the family. Statements concerning 'the
Hohenzollerns' and the 'Hohenzollern family' never refer to all
family members, but rather only to those whose actions are part of
the historical record and who took clear political positions. The use
of terms such as 'Kaiser', 'crown prince', 'princess' and 'prince' have
been retained to reflect the historic language of the aristocratic
milieu, which is the subject of this book. For readability and clarity's
sake, this book will refer simply to Crown Prince Wilhelm and not
former Crown Prince Wilhelm.

2 See Haupt, 'Adel in einer entadelten Gesellschaft'; Brelot, *La noblesse
réinventée*.

3 'Aus der Reichshauptstadt', *Der Tag*, 10 Nov. 1917; 'Die Taufe der Kron-
prinzentochter', *Kreuzzeitung*, 10 Nov. 1917; 'Aus der Gesellschaft',
Sport im Bild, 23 Nov. 1917, 642.

4 Such works include Herre, *Kronprinz Wilhelm*; Jonas, *Der Kronprinz*;
Preussen, *Gott helfe*; Granier, *Magnus von Levetzow*; Gutsche, *Ein
Kaiser im Exil*.

5 Such works include Röhl, *Wilhelm II. Der Weg in den Abgrund*; Malinow-
ski, *Vom König zum Führer*; Malinowski, *Nazis and Nobles*; Machtan, *Der
Kaisersohn*; Petropoulos, *Royals and the Reich*; Urbach, *Go-Betweens*;
Urbach, *Useful Idiots*; Pekelder/Schenk/van der Bas, *Der Kaiser*;
Machtan, *Der Kronprinz und die Nazis*; Luh, *Der Kronprinz*.

6 Wehler, *Deutsche Gesellschaftsgeschichte*, vol. 3, 805.

7 This oft-cited mocking phrase, most frequently attributed to Kurt

Tucholsky, referred to the mediating role played by the German president Paul von Hindenburg's son Prince Oskar in negotiations over the naming of Hitler as German chancellor. But it can be applied just as well to the majority of post-1918 aristocratic communications, which ran contrary to the spirit of the Weimar Constitution.

1. The Hohenzollerns in Exile: Outposts in the Counter-Revolution (1918–23)

1 'Des Kaisers Heldentod. Ein neudeutsches Lesestück', *Vorwärts*, 9 Nov. 1932.

2 Thaer, *Generalstabsdienst an der Front*, 251–3.

3 Huber, *Verfassungsgeschichte*, 658–70. See also Pyta, 'Die Kunst'; and Gallus, 'Eine kontinuitätsgebremste Revolution'.

4 'Hohenzollernbriefe aus den Novembertagen', *Vorwärts*, 26 March 1919; 'Die Briefe der Hohenzollern', *Neue Freie Presse*, 27 March 1919; 'Die letzte Audienz Hindenburgs', *Neues Wiener Tagblatt*, 6 April 1919; 'Wie Kaiser Wilhelm abgedankt hat', *Neues Wiener Journal*, 5 April 1919. See also Wilhelm Heye, 'Im Hauptquartier am 9. November 1918', *Deutsche Allgemeine Zeitung*, 22 Jan. 1922.

5 'Die Flucht Wilhelms Hohenzollern', *Freiheit*, 5 April 1919; 'Graf Westarps Protokoll', *Kreuzzeitung*, 27 July 1919.

6 Machtan, *Die Abdankung*, 271.

7 Herre, *Kronprinz Wilhelm*, 152–73.

8 Ibid., 166–7.

9 Einem, *Ein Armeeführer*, 466; Herre, *Kronprinz Wilhelm*, 167–8.

10 Jonas, *Der Kronprinz*, 160–68.

11 'Wilhelm Prinz von Preussen an Fürst Solms, März 1919,' GStA PK, Rep. 45, No. 17a.

12 Malinowski, *Vom König zum Führer*, 104–18, 228–58, 488–500; Kohlrausch, *Der Monarch im Skandal*, 427–43.

13 Schlabrendorff, *Begegnungen in fünf Jahrzehnten*, 26.

14 'Rosy Fürstin zu Salm-Horstmar an Marie Prinzessin zur Lippe, 17. 11. 1918', private collection, Christoph Freiherr von Wolzogen.

15 Ibid.

16 Herre, *Kronprinz Wilhelm*, 168.

17 Wilhelm II., 'Zusatz zum Testament, 25. 5. 1937', GStA PK, BPH, Rep. 192, Nachlass Dommes, No. 19.

18 'Der deutsche Kronprinz und seine Schwiegermutter', *Neue Freie Presse*, 19 Feb. 1919; 'Won't Get Me Alive Says Crown Prince', *Boston Daily Globe*, 12 Jan. 1919; 'Crown Prince's Defiance', *The Observer*, 6 July 1919; 'Only Dead Body to Foes', *New York Times*, 7 July 1919.

19 Ilsemann, *Der Kaiser in Holland* vol. 1 (hereafter Ilsemann I) 38–9 (9 Nov. 1918).

20 Ibid., 44–5 (10 Nov. 1918).

21 Martin Kohlrausch, 'Der Kampf als inneres Erlebnis', *FAZ*, 19 Nov. 2018. See also Kohlrausch, 'Der Monarch im Skandal', 362–86.

22 Jünger, *Kampf als inneres Erlebnis*, 52.

23 Albertz, *Exemplarisches Heldentum*, 250–93.

24 See Funck, *The Meaning of Dying*; Hull, *The Entourage of Wilhelm II* ; Wehler, *Deutsch Gesellschaftsgeschichte*, vol. 3, 873–85.

25 'Gefälschtes Reisedokument auf den Namen Johannes Hoogenstein, datiert auf den 28. 9. 1918', in Algemeen, Rijksarchief, Depot, Collectie 151 (Mr H. P. Marchant), No. 162. Thanks to Freddy Ykema for alerting me to this source.

26 Machtan, *Die Abdankung*, 278–82, Kirschstein, *Auguste Victoria*, 146–66.

27 Machtan, *Die Abdankung*, 277–8.

28 Schönpflug, *Luise von Preussen*, 199–256; Kohlrausch, *Der Monarch im Skandal*, 405; Wienfort, *Monarchie*, 173–5.

29 'Rosy Fürstin zu Salm-Horstmar, 10. 12. 1918', private collection, Christoph Freiherr von Wolzogen.

30 Cecilie von Preussen, *Erinnerungen*, 249.

31 Estimates from Jones, *Am Anfang war Gewalt*, 12.

32 See Klingler, *Negotiating Violence*.

33 'Immer wieder konterrevolutionäre Aktionen', *Freiheit*, 12 Dec. 1918; 'Schlimme Zustände in Potsdam', *Freiheit*, 14 Dec. 1918.

34 'Sie bleiben Monarchisten', *Vorwärts*, 16 Dec. 1918.

35 'Konservative Kriegserklärung', *Vorwärts*, 5 July 1919; 'Monarchists in Germany Grow. May Try a Coup', *The Sun* (New York), 6 July 1919.

36 'Neue Ludendorff-Demonstration', *Vorwärts*, 26 Nov. 1919; 'An die

falsche Adresse', *Vorwärts*, 1 Dec. 1919; 'Der Monarchistenkrach in Potsdam', *Freiheit*, 27 Nov. 1919; 'Die monarchistischen Kundgebungen in Potsdam', *Neues Wiener Abendblatt*, 26 Nov. 1919.

37 'Philipp Zorn, Das Verlangen nach Auslieferung Wilhelms II.', *Neue Freie Presse*, 26 Jan. 1919.

38 Holzhauer, *Die Vermögensauseinandersetzung*, 91–3.

39 Ilsemann I, 275 (7 May 1923).

40 Ibid.

41 Louis Ferdinand of Prussia, *The Rebel Prince*, 105–6, 112, 125.

42 Machtan, *Die Abdankung*, 283–4.

43 Ilsemann I, 115 (27 Sept. 1919); ibid., 236–7 (4 Aug. 1922).

44 Ibid., 99 (22 May 1928).

45 See, for example, Kohlrausch, 'Meer dan eenden voederen'.

46 Harald von Königswald, 'Vorwort', Ilsemann I, 8.

47 'Bei der "gefährlichen" Hermine', *Neues Wiener Journal*, 24 April 1927.

48 'Sic 'em!' (cartoon), *Rock Island Argus*, 5 Dec. 1918.

49 'Prussian Militarism' (cartoon), *Rock Island Argus*, 17 March 1919; 'Crazy Old German Eagle' (cartoon), *Rock Island Argus*, 7 July 1919; 'Hen Still Has Hopes' (cartoon), *Rock Island Argus*, 13 March 1919.

50 Reibnitz, *Wilhelm II. und Hermine*, 208.

51 Klaus Büstrin, 'Schriftsteller Harald von Koenigswald. Preusse, Kein Nazi', *Potsdamer Neueste Nachrichten*, 15 May 2015.

52 The originals are kept in the city of Cologne's historical archive. See the edition being published by the University of Cologne: *Das letzte deutsche Kaiserpaar und sein Leibarzt: Wilhelm II. und Auguste Victoria im niederländischen Exil (1919–1924) im Spiegel der Tagebücher des Dr. med. Alfred Haehner (1880–1949)*. Thanks to Sabine Mangold-Will for allowing me to view the diaries and giving me a number of important hints.

53 Kohlrausch, 'Meer dan eenden voederen', 629.

54 Wilhelm-Viktor von Ilsemann in interview with Boudewijn Buch (Dutch) in 1998, https://www.youtube.com/watch?v= kAcLUe3Fo7E, 7:26–9:00 min. See 'Stichting Vriendenkring Kasteel Amerongen', bulletin, September 2015, 6, http://vrienden.kasteel-amerongen.nl/

content/5-bulletins/91-bulletin-september-2015.pdf. See also Röhl, 'The Emperor's New Clothes', 25, 32.

55 See the information in chapter 6 of this book, which is based John Röhl's precise critique of the sources.

56 Hellmuth Killer, 'Säge-Leistung' (letter to the editor), *FAZ*, 8 Nov. 1967, 10.

57 Heinz Bindokat, 'Drei Arbeiter sägten mit' (letter to the editor), *FAZ*, 22 Nov. 1967, 12. Those around the Kaiser worried that the dramatic reduction in the number of trees would expose him to the peering eyes of curiosity seekers and the paparazzi cameras. See Ilsemann I, 138, 151, 166, 172, 204, 207–8.

58 Werner Freiherr von Rheinbaben, 'Die Schönfärberei in Doorn' (letter to the editor), *FAZ*, 2 Nov. 1968, 14.

59 Michael Salewski, 'Rezension', *Das Historisch Politische Buch*, 16 (1968), 117.

60 Wilhelm Karl Prinz von Preussen, 'Kaiser Wilhelm II. – Kind seiner Zeit' (letter to the editor), *FAZ*, 8 Dec. 1967, 9.

61 Carl Gero von Ilsemann, *FAZ*, 20 Jan. 1968, 6.

62 Haehner, 'Tagebuch, Eintrag vom 20. 4. 1923, 24. 8. 1923', Cologne Historical Archive.

63 Haehner, 'Tagebuch, Eintrag vom 8. 3. 1921', Cologne Historical Archive.

64 'Wilhelm II. an Hofprediger Vogel, 10. 3. 1923' (emphasis in original), Nachlass John Röhl, Berlin, vol. 86, no. 23. See also 'Wilhelm II., Anmerkungen zu Chamberlains Mensch und Gott', in ibid., no. 33–41.

65 George Sylvester Viereck, 'Wilhelm on the Bible, Miracles, and Reasons for Human Faith', *New York American*, 26 July 1925; 'Wilhelm II. an Viereck, 30. 12. 1925', Nachlass John Röhl, Berlin, vol. 86, no. 349–54.

66 Well documented in both volumes of Ilsemann's journals, especially Ilsemann, *Der Kaiser in Holland*, vol. 2 (hereafter Ilsemann II), 11–13 (February/August 1924), 36 (1 May 1926), 77 (13 Dec. 1927), 89 (5 March 1928); and in Röhl, *Wilhelm II. Der Weg in den Abgrund*, 1247–329, especially 1277–81.

67 Ilsemann II, 36 (1 May 1926).

68 B. Graf Finck von Finckenstein, 'Doorn', *Deutscher Jägerbund*, special printing, 1924; see Nachlass John Röhl, Berlin, vol. 86, no. 53.

69 Wilhelm II himself was quite sceptical about Mackesen's preparedness to do battle. See Ilsemann II, 13 (25 July 1924).

70 See Röhl, *Wilhelm II. Der Weg in den Abgrund*, 1272.

71 Röhl, *Kaiser, Hof und Staat*, 23. Thanks to John Röhl for alerting me to this source. Some of the printing proofs for Ilsemann's journals are contained in the Nachlass John Röhl in Berlin's Staatsbibliothek library.

72 Kessler, *Das Tagebuch* (3 April 1923); Röhl, *Wilhelm II. Der Weg in den Abgrund*, 1279–80; Haehner, 'Tagebuch, Eintrag vom 30. 8. 1921'.

73 'Berlin Assassins Severely Wound Maximillian Harden' and 'Asks Why Kaiser Is Silent', *New York Times*, 4 July 1922.

74 'Wilhelm II. an Bigelow, 18. 2. 1926, Wilhelm II. an Viereck, 2. 3. 1923', Vorlass John Röhl, Berlin, vol. 87.

75 Maximilian Harden, 'Plot Kaiser's Return, With Murder Toll 317', *Evening Star* (Washington, DC), 2 July 1922. The article was a revised version of Harden's final piece for *Die Zukunft*, 'In der Mördergrube', 1 July 1922. See also 'Young Wilhelm Chided by Harden', *Evening Star* (Washington, DC), 14 May 1922; 'Attack Maximilian Harden; Kaiser's Foe Badly Injured', *New York Herald*, 4 July 1922.

76 Harden, *Köpfe. Porträts, Briefe und Dokumente*, 244–6; Kurt Tucholsky, 'Prozess Harden', *Die Weltbühne*, 21 Dec. 1922, 638–45, quote on 643.

77 Malinowski, *Vom König zum Führer*, 200–228; Urbach, *Zwischen Aktion und Reaktion*, 323–54.

78 'Ein Putsch in München. Ein preussischer Prinz als Führer', *Vorwärts*, 20 Feb. 1919; 'Missglückter Putsch', *Freiheit*, 20 Feb. 1919; 'Komplott in München', *Freiheit*, 25 Feb. 1919; Frederick Moore, 'Eisner, a Great Loss', *New York Tribune*, 25 Feb. 1919; 'A Lesson for Us', *New York Tribune*, 2 March 1919.

79 Ilsemann, printer's proofs, 28 Feb. 1925, Nachlass John Röhl, Berlin, vol. 115, no. 1 and 4.

80 'Hohenzollern-Debatte im Reichstag', *Vossische Zeitung*, 23 Nov. 1920; see also Heinig, *Hohenzollern. Wilhelm II. und sein Haus*, Berlin 1921.

81 Bloch, *Albert Südekum*, 250–55.

82 Röhl, *Wilhelm II.*, III, 1248; Wilderotter, 113–14.

83 Reibnitz, *Wilhelm II. und Hermine*, 210; 'Former Kaiser Was Richest Person in Germany in 1914', *New York Tribune*, 8 Dec. 1918.

84 'Ex-Kaiser Land Poor Says Berlin Manager: He Denies Wilhelm Hohenzollern is Richest Individual of the German Nation', *New York Times*, 7 July 1929, 45.

85 Pekelder, 'Leven in een luchtkasteel', 38.

86 Marc Schalenberg, 'Schlösser zu Museen: Umnutzungen von Residenzbauten in Berlin und München während der Weimarer Republik', in Biskup/Kohlrausch (ed.), *Das Erbe der Monarchie*, 189; Martin Sabrow, 'Das Bild der Hohenzollern', lecture 15, Sept. 2020.

87 'Die Kaiserkomödie. Falsche Sensation – Unmögliche Rückkehr Wilhelms II', *Vorwärts*, 26 Oct. 1926.

88 Röhl, *Wilhelm II. Der Weg in den Abgrund*, 1250.

89 'Lloyd George zum Friedensvertrag', *Vorwärts*, 4 July 1919.

90 'Zur Auslieferungsfrage', *Vorwärts*, 10 Jan. 1920 (evening); 'Zur Auslieferung W. Hohenzollerns', *Freiheit*, 11 Jan. 1920.

91 Ilsemann I, 75, 112. On the alleged attempts to flee, see *Freiheit*, 27 June 1919, *Vorwärts*, 28 June 1919, *The Sun* (New York), 3 July 1919.

92 See Schabas, *The Trial of the Kaiser*; Röhl, *Wilhelm II. Der Weg in den Abgrund*, 1250–57; 'Acht amerikanische Soldaten wollten Wilhelm II. Entführen', *Pariser Tagesszeitung*, 3 Jan. 1938; Moeyes, *Het kleine keizersdrama*, 81.

93 For example, *New York Tribune*, 1 Dec. 1918; *Evening Star* (Washington), 29 June 1919, *De Courant*, 11 Oct. 1919, *Punch*, 21 Jan. 1920.

94 Ilsemann I, 236–7 (4 Aug. 1922).

95 'French Mother Plots Revenge on Ex-Kaiser', *New York Times*, 22 Dec. 1922; 'Doch ein Attentat gegen Wilhelm', *Der Tag* (Vienna), 21 Dec. 1932; no title, *Die Stunde*, 17 Dec. 1932; 'Der "Attentäter" von Doorn', *Illustrierte Kronen-Zeitung*, 17 Dec. 1932; 'Morden oder Politisieren?': *Illustrierte Kronen-Zeitung*, 20 April 1933; 'Anschlag in Haus Doorn vereitelt', *Hamburger Nachrichten*, 13 Dec. 1932.

96 See Beigel/Mangold-Will (eds.), *Wilhelm II. Archäologie und Politik*.

97 Ilsemann I, 287 (7 Oct. 1923).

Notes

98 See Linse, *Barfüssige Propheten*; Puschner, *Die völkische Bewegung*; Breuer, *Ordnungen der Ungleichheit*.

99 Röhl, *Wilhelm II. Der Weg in den Abgrund*, 1272.

100 David Freis, 'Diagnosing the Kaiser: Psychiatry, Wilhelm II and the Question of German War Guilt', *Modern History* 62 (2018), 273–94.

101 Röhl, *Wilhelm II. Der Weg in den Abgrund*, 1289.

102 'Wilhelm Has Chosen Second Bride With Temperament Like His Own', *Evening Star* (Washington), 5 Nov. 1922.

103 J. B., 'Ein Kaiser-Interview', *Tage-Buch*, 18 Dec. 1926, 1938–9.

104 Viktoria Luise Duchess of Brunswick and Lüneburg, Princess of Prussia, *The Kaiser's Daughter*, 159–62.

105 Ilsemann I, 218–58 (June–December 1922); 'Ex-Kaiser's Daughter Meets Stepmother. Reconciliation Ascribed to Monarchist Party Wishes for Hohenzollern Family Unity', *New York Times*, 6 Aug. 1923, 5. See also Bloks, *Hermine. An Empress in Exile*, 46–66.

106 Ilsemann I, 269 (9 April 1923).

107 'Ex-Kaiser Wilhelm to Wed in November. Old Nobility Is Peeved', *New York Times*, 20 Sept. 1922.

108 Fritz Löwe, 'Die Kaiserbraut. Aus der Heimat der Prinzessin Hermine' [September 1922], Utrechts Archief, NL-UtHUA, A17235.

109 Ilsemann I, 258, 283 (27 Dec. 1922, 1 Sept. 1923).

110 Empress Hermine, *An Empress in Exile* and 'Behind the Gates at Doorn; An Intimate Portrait of the Former Kaiser by His Wife', *New York Times*, 14 Oct. 1928.

111 'Kletterhermine' (cartoon), *Simplicissimus* 32 (1927), vol. 3 (18 April 1927), 27. Reprinted in Reibnitz, *Wilhelm II. und Hermine*, 208.

112 'Die Pfiffigen und der deutsche Staat', *Salzburger Wacht*, 23 August 1923.

113 Reibnitz, *Wilhelm II. und Hermine*, 140–43. One son from her first marriage died young, in 1927.

114 'Der Reporterskandal in Doorn. Intimes von den Hochzeitstagen', *Neues Wiener Journal*, 10 Nov. 1922; Reibnitz, *Wilhelm II. und Hermine*, 128–34.

115 'Mrs. William Hohenzollern', *Albuquerque Morning Journal*, 24 Dec. 1922; pictorial series, *New York Tribune*, 19 Nov. 1922; pictures of arrival and limousine, *Das illustrierte Blatt* (Frankfurt), 15 Dec. 1918; 'Wilhelm Sells Photo', *New York Times*, 24 Dec. 1922.

116 'Im Glashaus zu Doorn. Exkaiser Wilhelm dementiert "gewisse Ger-
    üchte" ', *Der Tag* (Vienna), 28 Aug. 1923. See also Martin Kohlrausch,
    'Wilhelm II. als Medienkaiser', in Sabrow (ed.), *Die Macht der Bilder*,
    51–70.

117 'Ex-Kaiser to Wed a Young Widow', *New York Times*, 19 Sept. 1922; 'Ex-
    Kaiser Denies Knowing of Plots', *New York Times*, 31 July 1923; 'Stone
    Hits Kaiser's Wife', *New York Times*, 21 October 1923; 'Wilhelm Eager
    to Return', *New York Times*, 14 Nov. 1923; 'The Ex-Kaiser Speaks His
    Mind. Intimate Letters to an American Woman', *New York Times*, 13
    July 1925; 'First Kaiser Barred Bathtub from Palace. Hermine Has
    Installed One', *New York Times*, 30 March 1927; 'Ex-Kaiser's Wife Gets
    His Former Palace in Berlin for Her Vacation', *New York Times*, 5 July
    1927; 'Behind the Gates at Doorn. An Intimate Portrait of the Former
    Kaiser by His Wife', *New York Times*, 14 Aug. 1928; 'Reunion for Kaiser
    Largest Since 1914', *New York Times*, 27 Jan. 1929; 'Princess Hermine Is
    Dead in Germany', *New York Times*, 13 Aug. 1947.

118 'Film Prince at Wieringen. Movie Agents Take Pictures', *The Globe*, 7
    Jan. 1919.

119 'Honeymoon Walks Have Ceased and William Appears Much Older
    and Thinner', *New York Times*, 25 Feb. 1923; 'First Exclusive Picture
    of Ex-Kaiser and His Bride!', *Boston Daily Globe*, 21 Dec. 1922. On the
    constant siege of photographers and journalists, see Ilsemann I, 70,
    110, 130, 207–8 (6 Dec. 1918; 26 June 1919; 22 Dec. 1919; 21/27 April 1922);
    'Maurice Frankenhuis, Interview with Prince Louis Ferdinand von
    Preussen, 21 Jan. 1965', in the Frankenhuis collection. Thanks to
    Aaron Oppenheim for providing access to the interview.

120 See Moeyes, *Het kleine keizersdrama*.

121 Clifford Geertz, 'Deep Play: Notes on the Balinese Cockfight', *Daeda-
    lus* 101/1 (1972), 1–37.

122 Reibnitz, *Wilhelm II. und Hermine*, 87; Röhl, *Kaiser, Hof und Staat*, 90.

123 Ilsemann I, 124–5.

124 Studnitz, *Seitensprünge*, 24; Moeyes, *Het kleine keizersdrama*, 115; Haeh-
    ner, 'Tagebuch, Eintrag vom 4. 5. 1923'.

125 Ilsemann II, 78 (13 Dec. 1927).

126 Ibid., 203 (2 Sept. 1932).

127 Ibid., 259 (25 May 1934).

128 'Burchard Prinz von Preussen' (a son of Prince Oskar), 25 Jan. 1935, Utrechts Archief, NL-UtHUA, A16662, fol. 71.

129 Ilsemann II, 16 (2 Oct. 1924); ibid., 186 (5 March 1932).

130 Haehner, 'Tagebuch, Eintrag vom 23. 2. 1924'.

131 Ilsemann I, 120 (27 Oct. 1919).

132 Ibid., 132 (30 Dec. 1919).

133 Ibid., 128 (4 Dec. 1919).

134 Stefan Grossmann, 'Der Kronprinz. Zu seinem 50. Geburtstag', *Neue Freie Presse*, 18 May 1932.

135 'Friedrich Solms Baruth an Wilhelm II., Klitschdorf, 9. November 1934', Utrechts Archief, NL-UtHUA, A16666_000262.

136 Percy Ernst Schramm, 'Notizen über einen Besuch in Doorn', in Kohlrausch (ed.), *Samt und Stahl*, 401–2.

137 Ilsemann II, 234 (3 Oct. 1933).

138 See 'Briefwechsel mit Ludwig Beck', MHMB, Dresden, BBAV5790, 5788, 5789, 5781, and Ilsemann II, 96 (12 May 1928).

139 'Der deutsche Exkronprinz', *Neues Wiener Journal*, 1 May 1919.

140 See Geraldine Farrar holdings, Library of Congress, Washington, DC, Box 11, Folder 34–5, and 'Koerber Papers', WITS, Johannesburg, A807/Ab (Crown Prince).

141 Eckel/Ruchatz/Wirth (eds.), *Exploring the Selfie*.

142 'Koerber an Kronprinz, 27. 8. 1936', Adolf Victor Koerber Papers, WITS, Johannesburg, A807/Ab (Folder 1936–1939).

143 'Fürstenberg an Wilhelm II., 28. 10. 1939', Nachlass John Röhl, Berlin, vol. 91, no. 117.

144 Ilsemann II, 46 (30 Jan. 1927).

145 Ilsemann I, 113 (25 Sept. 1919).

146 Johann Wolfgang Goethe, *Sämtliche Werke*, vol. 5, part 1, *Gedichte: 5. Theil Erste Abteilung*, Weimar,1893, 153. See Borchmeyer, *Der aufgeklärte Herrscher*, 49–74.

147 Moeller van den Bruck, *Das dritte Reich*, 233.

148 'Tagebuch Alfred Haehner, 17. 4. 1921', 31–6; Ilsemann I, 177–8 (17 April 1921); Kirchstein, *Auguste Victoria*, 160–66.

149 *Vossische Zeitung* in Sabrow, *Das Bild der Hohenzollern*, 5.

150 Schönpflug, *Luise von Preussen*, 7–26, 250–56.

151 Thomas Wehrlin, 'Der Prinzenbrief', *Das Tage-Buch*, 26 Feb. 1921.

152 See Sabrow, 'Die Hohenzollern und die Demokratie'.

153 'Die Überführung der Kaiserin', *Nachrichten für Stadt und Land*, 19 April 1921.

154 'Die Wallfahrt nach Potsdam', *Freiheit*, 19 April 1921; 'Der grosse Tag der Monarchisten', *Freiheit*, 20 April 1921.

155 Hans Siemsen, 'Das Begräbnis', *Freiheit*, 22 April 1921 (evening).

156 Kirchstein, *Auguste Victoria*, 166–73.

157 See Ute Frevert, *Gefühlspolitik und Herrschaftskommunikation*.

158 Röhl, *Wilhelm II. Der Weg in den Abgrund*, 1264; film footage: https://www.filmportal.de/video/das-begraebnis-der-ehemaligen-kaiserin-auguste-viktoria.

159 'Hohenzollern-Pläne. Die Wahrheit über Kaiser Wilhelm II. und den Kronprinzen', *Neues Wiener Journal*, 30 Oct. 1919.

160 Photos in *The Sun* (New York), 22 Dec. 1918; 'En Route to Oblivion', *Chicago Daily Tribune*, 29 Dec. 1918; 'Die Ankunft des Exkronprinzen in Wieringen', *Welt-Spiegel*, 8 Dec. 1918; 'Der flüchtige Kronprinz', *Freiheit*, 23 Nov. 1918, 'Die Fahrt des ehemaligen Kronprinzen', *Neues Wiener Tagblatt*, 23 Nov. 1918.

161 See the photo of the village in the Frankenhuis collection. See also Dehé/von Wolzogen Kühr, *Wilhelm, een omstreden eilandgast*; 'Wieringen, Where Former Crown Prince Lives', *Prescott Daily News*, 22 Jan. 1920.

162 https://www.akpool.ode/ansichtskarten/26798794kuenstler-ansichtskarte-postkarte-kronprinz-wilhelm-von-preussen-ringen-bis-zum-ende-im-exil-in-wieringen.

163 'Für Wilhelm II. (Aufruf von Friedrich Wilhelm Prinz zur Lippe)', *Vorarlberger Landes-Zeitung*, 11 July 1919; 'Offener Brief S. K. H. des Prinzen Heinrich von Preussen an Seine Majestät König Georg V. von England', *Hamburger Nachrichten*, 3 Aug. 1919; 'Der Kronprinz will sich für die anderen opfern', *Neue Züricher Nachrichten*, 11 Feb. 1920.

164 'Wilhelm von Preussen an King George V, 9. 2. 1920', *Documents on British Foreign Policy 1919–1939*, ser. 1, vol. 7 (9 Feb. 1920); Ilsemann I, 111 (12 July 1919).

165 'Ex-Crown Prince Plots to Be King', *New York Times*, 25 Oct. 1919.

166 T. Walter Williams, 'The Crownless Crown Prince and His Island', *New York Times*, 21 Sept. 1919.

167 'No Ground for Scandals around Ex-Crown Prince', *Chicago Daily Tribune*, 19 July 1920.

168 Haehner, 'Tagebuch, Eintrag vom 20./21. 5. 1921'.

169 Typed calendar of the most important dates on Wieringen November 1918–Summer 1921, GStA PK, BPH, Rep. 192, Nachlass Arthur Berg, No. 19.

170 'Friedrich Wilhelm von Preussen, Kronprinz, an eine unbekannte Empfängerin, Wieringen/Holland, 8. Mai 1920', Antiquariat Huesken, Kat.-No. 509, Provenienz Slg. B. Döring, Heidelberg.

171 'Kronprinz an Ludwig Beck, 14. 2. 1919', MHMB, Dresden, Nachlass Beck, BBAV, 5771.

172 'Kronprinz an Ludwig Beck, 2. 8. 1921', MHMB, Dresden, Nachlass Beck, BBAV 5795. See also Sabrow, *Der Rathenau-Mord*, 149–51; Haehner, 'Tagebuch, Eintrag vom 22. 10. 1921'.

173 'Kronprinz an Ludwig Beck, 23. 5. 1921', MHMB, Dresden, Nachlass Beck, BBAV 5790.

174 T. Walter Williams, 'Ex-Crown Prince Predicts Another War in Ten Years', *New York Times*, 11 June 1919; 'The Jonkheer Hohenzollern', *New York Tribune*, 12 June 1919.

175 'An Adventurer in Many Lands. Trebitsch Lincoln's Life Story', *South China Post*, 18 Sept. 1931; 'Trebitsch-Lincoln', *Times Literary Supplement*, 8 Oct. 1931, 770; Ignatius Lincoln, 'International Spy', *New York Tribune*, 16 May 1920. See also generally Trebitsch-Lincoln's autobiography *Der grösste Abenteurer des 20. Jahrhunderts*.

176 'Kaiser Still Silent. Ex-Spy Lincoln Fails to Get Statement to Public', *Washington Post* and *Boston Daily Globe*, 22 Sept. 1919; 'Trebitsch Lincoln. A Mysterious Visit to Amerongen', *The Manchester Guardian*, 23 Sept. 1919.

177 'German Plot Frustrated. Central European Monarchist Had Great Plans', *Los Angeles Times*, 2 May 1921.

178 Wasserstein, *The Secret Lives of Trebitsch Lincoln*, 124–47.

179 Heiko Suhr, 'Oberst Max Bauer', in Grawe (ed.), *Die militärische Elite des Kaiserreichs*, 17–28.

180 Karl H. von Wiegand, 'Restoration of German Monarchy', *Omaha Daily Bee*, 9 Dec. 1919.

181 'Former Kaiser Is Reported Insane', *The Sun* (New York), 10 Jan. 1920; 'Exile Raves Like Maniac', *Washington Times*, 10 Jan. 1920.

182 Wasserstein, *The Secret Lives*, 136–7.

183 'Kronprinz an Bauer, 12. 7. 1919', and 'Bauer an Kronprinz, 1. 2. 1920', Bundesarchiv Freiburg, N1022, (Nachlass Max Bauer), No. 21, 21–3, 93–6.

184 'Crown Prince Plots Rising, Berlin Hears', *Boston Daily Globe*, 10 Aug. 1919; 'Denkschrift an den Kronprinzen, vermutlich von Fürst Otto II. zu Salm-Horstmar', 1924, BAMA, Nachlass Selasen-Selasinsky, No. 432/3.

185 Haehner, 'Tagebuch, Eintrag 13. 3. 1920 (fol. 111)'.

186 'Sir R. Graham to Earl Curzon, 16. 3. 1920', *Documents on British Foreign Policy 1919–1939*, ser. 1, vol. 9, Reference: 185744/9019/39.

187 Bernard Wasserstein, 'On the Trail of Trebitsch Lincoln, Triple Agent', *New York Times*, 8 May 1988.

188 'Ignaz Trebitsch-Lincoln, Bluff, Dummheit und hohe Politik. Die Macher des Kapp-Putsches in ihrer wahren Gestalt', *Der Abend* (Vienna), 4 March 1931.

189 'Eine Komödie der Weltkorruption. "Konjunktur" von Leo Lania im Lessingtheater', *Vorwärts*, 11 April 1928.

190 Manfred Weissbecker, 'Deutschvölkische Freiheitspartei 1922–1933', in Fricke (ed.), *Lexikon zur Parteiengeschichte*, 558; Schumacher (ed.), *M. d. R. Die Reichstagsabgeordneten*, 1556.

191 'Obituary: Colonel Bauer', *The Manchester Guardian*, 7 May 1929.

192 Kershaw, *Hitler*, 239; Hans Günther Hockerts, 'Warum München? Wie Bayerns Metropolie die "Hauptstadt der Bewegung" wurde', in Nerdinger/Hockerts/Krauss (eds.), *München und der Nationalsozialismus*, 387–97.

193 'Schriftwechsel Müldner von Mülnheim-Friedrich Graf von der Schulenburg', undated, pre-1923, Bundesarchiv Berlin (formerly: Bundesarchiv Potsdam, 90 Mu 1, Bd. 1. fol. 163).

194 Hans Wilderotter, 'Haus Doorn. Die verkleinerte Kopie eines Hofstaats', in Wilderotter/Pohl (eds.), *Der letzte Kaiser*, 116.

195 'Probably It Would Run Backward Easier', *Perth Amboy Evening News*, 17 Oct. 1919.

196 'Ex-Crown Prince Plots to Be King', *New York Times*, 25 Oct. 1919; 'Hohenzollern Intrigues', *The Observer*, 19 Oct. 1919.

197 *Vorwärts*, 16 and 19 July 1914.

198 Malinowski, *Vom König zum Führer*, 73–89.

199 Haehner, 'Tagebuch, Eintrag vom 30. 12. 1919 (fol. 75)' and 'November 1920, (fol. 181)'.

200 Paul Liman, 'Der Kronprinz, Ausschnitt', *Hamburger Nachrichten*, 20 April 1914. See also *Vorwärts*, 11 May 1914. For more context, see Röhl, *Wilhelm II. Der Weg in den Abgrund*, 1025–37.

201 See Frymann (i.e. Heinrich Class), *Wenn ich der Kaiser wär'*; Malinowski, *Vom König zum Führer*, 170–97; Kohlrausch, *Monarch im Skandal*, 414–26.

202 Maximilian Harden, 'Der deutsche Kronprinz. Ein Porträt', *Neues Wiener Journal*, 14 Feb. 1922, 3.

203 Gustav Stresemann, 'Väter und Söhne', *Deutsche Stimmen*, 26 Feb. 1922; Stresemann, *Reden und Schriften*, 462.

204 Karl von Wiegand, 'Crown Prince Writing Book', *Los Angeles Times*, 2 April 1919; Karl von Wiegand, 'Ex-Crown Prince Is Willing to Be Tried by U.S.', *The Sun* (New York), 20 July 1919.

205 Haehner, 'Tagebücher, Nachträgliche Aufzeichnungen aus den Monaten Mai-Oktober 1920, fol. 138–140'.

206 Röhl, *Wilhelm II. Der Weg in den Abgrund*, 1257.

207 Ilsemann I, 171 (16 Jan. 1921).

208 Kronprinz Wilhelm, *Erinnerungen*; *Meine Erinnerungen aus Deutschlands Heldenkampf*; *Ich suche die Wahrheit! Ein Buch zur Kriegsschuldfrage*.

209 'Schulenburg an Müldner 6. 12. 1921', Bundesarchiv Berlin, Nachlass Müldner von Mülnheim (formerly Bundesarchiv Potsdam 90 Mu1, Bd. 3, Bl. 54). 'Briefe Müldners an Beck, 27. 5. 1921, 21. 6. 1921, 3. 7. 1921', MHMB Dresden, Nachlass Beck, BBAV 5792-5794; 'Kronprinz an Ludwig Beck, 22. 7. 1922 und undatiert (1922)', ibid., BBAV 5844 and BBAV 5800. See also *Vorwärts*, 3 June 1922 (evening); 'Les Palais du Kaiser', *Mercure de France*, 15 September 1925, 857.

210 'Allerlei vom Tage. Ein Brief des Kronprinzen', *Hamburgischer Corres-pondent*, 6 Aug. 1919.

211 'Mémoires du Kronprinz', *Les Annales politiques et littéraires*, 20 Aug. 1922.

212 'Exkaiser und Exkronprinz', *Vorwärts* (evening), 1 Feb. 1922.

213 'Die Alldeutschen gegen den deutschen Kronprinzen', *Pester Lloyd*, 22 June 1922; *Prager Tageblatt*, 24 June 1922; *Vorwärts*, 30 May, 3, 6 and 10 June 1922; *Völkischer Beobachter*, 7 May 1922. Rosner had no Jewish heritage and won a lawsuit for significant compensation in 1943, see 'General Max Rudolf Viebahn im Verhör durch Otto John', IfZ, ZS / A 33 / 5, 28 Jan. 1948, fol. 369–86.

214 *Semi-Imperator. 1888–1918. Eine genealogisch-rassengeschichtliche Aufklärung zur Warnung für die Zukunft – ein packender Kommentar zu den Semi-Alliancen im besonderen und semi-gothaischen Erkenntnissen im allgemeinen*, Munich, 1919; 'Wilhelm II. – ein Halbjude! Eine groteske alldeutsch-antisemitische Entdeckung', *Neues Wiener Journal*, 22 Oct. 1920.

215 Henry Bidou, 'Karl Rosner, Der König', *Les Annales politiques et litté-raires*, 9 Dec. 1923; Rosner, *Der König. Weg und Wende.*

216 [Wilhelm II.], *Ereignisse und Gestalten aus den Jahren 1878–1918; Aus meinem Leben. 1859–1888*; Röhl, *Wilhelm II., Der Weg in den Abgrund*, 1273; Haehner, 'Tagebuch, Eintrag vom 1. 11. 1922'. See also the sarcas-tic commentaries in *Vorwärts*, 9 May, 19 Aug., 19 Sept. and 17 Oct. 1922.

217 'Wilhelm II. an Ulrich Freiherr von Sell, 24. 3. 1932', GStA PK, Nachlass Sell, No. 1; 'Wilhelm II an George Sylvester Viereck, 21. 3. 1926', Nachlass John Röhl, Berlin, vol. 87.

218 Nowak, *Das Dritte Deutsche Kaiserreich*, vol. 1, *Die übersprungene Gener-ation*; idem., *Das Dritte Deutsche Kaiserreich*, vol. 2, *Deutschlands Weg in die Einkreisung*; Röhl, *Wilhelm II. Der Weg in den Abgrund*, 1275; Pekelder / Schenk / van der Bas, *Der Kaiser*, 27.

219 'Sigmund Freud an George Sylvester Viereck, 30. 10. 1927', Angeloch, *Ein ambivalenter Fanatiker*, 646; Viereck, *Crown Prince Wilhelm Bares His Heart*, 134–45.

220 See Karl Rosner's letter of 12 May 1947 and the correspondence and documents in: GStA PK, Rep. 192, Nachlass Dommes, No. 6. See also 'Monsieur Hohenzollern' schreibt ein Buch', *Aufbau*, 20 Aug. 1948.

Notes

221 Hans Reimann, 'Das Buch eines wirklichen Scharfrichters', *Das Tage-Buch*, 1 Sept. 1923, 1237. According to Reimann, the Kaiser earned $250,000 from the book.

222 See Lange, *Der Kronprinz und sein wahres Gesicht*; Anker, *Kronprinz Wilhelm*; von Hünefeld, *Insel der Verbannung*; von Hünefeld, *Der Kronprinz im Exil*.

223 Eppstein, *Der Deutsche Kronprinz*; Anker, *Kronprinz Wilhelm*; Anker, *Unsere Stunde kommt!*.

224 Ilsemann I, 212, 215, 265.

225 Ibid., 215, (19 May 1922); ibid., 202 (3 March 1922). See also Reibnitz, *Wilhelm II. und Hermine*. I, 215 (19 May 1922) and 202 (3 March 1922).

226 'Sir R. Graham to Earl Curzon, 17. 12. 1919', *Documents on British Foreign Policy 1919–1939*, ser. 1, vol. 5, Reference: 164126/9019/39.

227 Ilsemann I, 284 (12 Sept. 1923), 295 (31 Oct. 1923).

228 Ibid., 212 (6 Nov. 1919).

229 Ibid., 121, 147, Binder, *Schuld des Kaisers*, 43–6.

230 Röhl, *Wilhelm II. Der Weg in den Abgrund*, 1259–61.

231 Hans-Ulrich Wehler, 'Der Fall Zabern von 1913/14 als Verfassungskrise des Wilhelminischen Kaiserreichs', in *Krisenherde des Kaiserreichs*, 70–88, 449–58; Röhl, *Wilhelm II. Der Weg in den Abgrund*, 1025–37.

232 Müller, *Die Thronfolger*, 343–4.

233 See Dumur, *Le Boucher de Verdun*.

234 Jonas, *Der Kronprinz*, 153.

235 Hugo, *L'homme qui rit*. In 1928, the novel was adapted into a silent film called *The Man Who Laughs* by German expressionist director Paul Leni. It is considered one of the models for the Joker character in the Batman comics.

236 Stresemann, 'Väter und Söhne', 462.

237 'Der Kronprinz als Soldat', *Kreuzzeitung*, 14 Dec. 1933, 13; Carl Lange, *Der Kronprinz*, Berlin 1933; 'Ein Buch über Kronprinz Wilhelm', *Berliner Börsenzeitung*, 15 Dec. 1933.

238 Ilsemann I, 175 (14 April 1921); Graf Adalbert Sternberg, 'Als der deutsche Kronprinz in Wien weilte', *Neues Wiener Journal*, 7 Aug. 1934.

239 Malinowski, *Vom König zum Führer*, 90–104.

240 See Anker, *Kronprinz Wilhelm*; and Kronprinz Wilhelm, *Erinnerungen*.

544

He repeated his statements in 1934. 'Erinnerungen an ein abendliches Gespräch, das der deutsche Kronprinz allein mit uns am Kaminfeuer in der grossen Halle in Cecilienhof führte. Dez. 1934', GStA PK, VI HA Nachlass Hilde Wagner, No. 4.

241 Kronprinzessin Cecilie, *Erinnerungen*, 250.
242 Eppstein, *Der Deutsche Kronprinz*.
243 'Vom Tage', *Simplicissimus*, 16 Feb. 1921, 636; photo of the crown prince in the village smithy: *Evening Star* (Washington), 14 Nov. 1920; 'Der deutsche Ex-Kronprinz als Schmied', *Wiener Illustrierte Zeitung*, 21 Nov. 1920; 'Das Hufeisen "von Gottes Gnaden"', *Vorwärts*, 25 Nov. 1920 (evening); 'Der ehemalige deutsche Kronprinz als Schmied', *Freiburger Nachrichten*, 5 Aug. 1921.
244 'Der Schmied von Wieringen', *Simplicissimus*, 2 Nov. 1923, 439; See also the satirical poems in *Simplicissimus*, 24 May 1922, 116; 1 June 1924, 182; 8 March 1926, 698; 14 June 1926, 146; 12 March 1928, 683.
245 Jonas, *Der Kronprinz*, 181–97. Kurt von Schleicher also played a central role in the complicated arrangements for the crown prince's return, see Herre, *Kronprinz Wilhelm*, 181–6.
246 Eppstein, *Der Deutsche Kronprinz*, 403.
247 'Am Prinzen gescheitert', *Vossische Zeitung*, 27 July 1920.
248 'Müldner von Mülnheim an Ludwig Beck, 20. 4. 1927', MHMB, Dresden, Nachlass Beck, BBAV; 'Friedrich von Berg an Selasen-Selasinsky, 22. 11. 1932', BAMA, Nachlass Selasen-Selansinsky, 432/4; Kurt Anker, 'Die letzten Stunden des Kaiserreichs', *Berliner Tageblatt*, 29 Dec. 1926.
249 'Kurt Anker an den Kronprinzen, 29. 8. 1920', Bundesarchiv Berlin, Nachlass Müldner von Mülnheim (previously Bundesarchiv Potsdam 90 Mu1, Bd. 3, 140–41).
250 Jonas, *Der Kronprinz*, 181, Gasteiger, *Kuno von Westarp*, 217. On the period during the war, see Müller, *Die Thronfolger*, 340–53.
251 'Das Kronprinzliche Dirnenhauptquartier', *Freiheit*, 26 Jan. 1922; 'Das Kronprinzliche Harem', *Vorwärts*, 25 Jan. 1922 (evening); 'Das Harem des Kronprinzen', *Engadiner Post*, 2 Feb. 1922.
252 'Mob Prince for Visiting Modiste. Police Take a Hand', *Washington Post*, Dec. 1918; 'Wie Kronprinz Friedrich Wilhelm im Exil lebt', *Neues Wiener Journal*, 24 Jan. 1919; *Linzer Tages-Post*, 23 Nov. 1918.

253 'Peereboom an J. B. Kan, 20. 12. 1918', Nationaal Archief, Den Haag, C27036, Collectie J. B. Kan, No. 14; Haehner, 'Tagebuch, Einträge vom 12. 10. 1922, 21. 10. 1923, 2. 11. 1922, 10. 11. 1922, 10. 1. 1924'.

254 'Blanche und der Kronprinz', *Prager Tageblatt*, 5 June 1921; 'Die Geliebte des Kronprinzen', *Salzburger Volksblatt*, 24 June 1921; 'Pariser Brief', *Neues Wiener Tageblatt*, 26 June 1921; 'Aus der "guten Gesellschaft"', *Rote Fahne* (Vienna), 21 May 1921; 'Die Hölle von Verdun', *Illustrierte Kronenzeitung*, 17 May 1921.

255 Wandt, *Der Gefangene von Potsdam*, 129–64.

256 See Wandt, *Etappe Gent*; idem., *Erotik und Spionage in der Etappe Gent*.

257 Wandt, *Etappe Gent*, 3.

258 Wandt, *Erotik und Spionage in der Etappe Gent*, 199.

259 Ibid., 92.

260 Ibid., 205.

261 'Crown Prince More Taken with Gay Adventures Than the Problems of Strategy', *South Bend New Times*, 31 Dec. 1918; 'Don Juan from Beyond the Rhine', *Chattanooga News*, 31 Dec. 1918.

262 'Die Heldenfamilie', *Vorwärts*, 27 Oct. 1932 (evening). Emphasis in original.

263 Haehner, 'Tagebuch, 12. 10. 1922'; Ilsemann I, 191–5 (October–December 1921). Thanks to Kees van der Sluijs for his corrections on this score.

264 Sichert, *Cecilienhof*, 65; Wolfram Pyta, 'Kurt von Schleicher, Gregor Strasser und Kronprinz Wilhelm gegen Hitler', lecture, Katholische Akademie in Bayern, 5 March 2018, https://www.youtube.com/watch?v= EOnoPFomPtA.

265 http://cafe-deutschland.blogspot.com/2013/10/hommage-cecilie-2-wilhelm-auf-wieringen.html.

266 https://picclick.de/Wilhelm-II-junior-Postkarte-alt-ungelaufen-Insel-Wieringen-233106720909.html.

267 'Bericht an Oberst Bauer' (undated), BAMA, Nachlass Bauer, N1022, No. 21, fol. 1–3.

268 *Geheimdienst und Propaganda im Ersten Weltkrieg*, 386, 392–3, 534–7, 555.

269 Ibid., 555.

270 'Was ist mit Oskar? Wo ist das militärische Heldentum? Oskars Heldentaten', *Vorwärts*, 23 Feb. 1932. On the ideal of the heroic death in the Prussian nobility, see Funck, *The Meaning of Dying*.

271 'Crown Prince Would Go Back "As a Laborer" ', *Chicago Daily Tribune*, 4 Dec. 1918.

272 Prince Alexander Hohenlohe, 'A Hohenlohe Scores Crown Prince's Memoirs', *New York Herald*, 23 July 1922.

273 'Kaiserdebatte im Reichstag', *Vorwärts*, 10 Nov. 1926.

274 Karl H. von Wiegand, 'Crown Prince of Germany Interviewed', in *Current Misconceptions About the War*, 3–11.

275 'No Ground for Scandals Around Ex-Crown Prince', *Chicago Daily Tribune*, 19 July 1920.

276 'Latest Picture of Crown Prince and Family', *Rock Island Argus and Daily Union*, 22 April 1922; 'At Ex-Kaiser's Home', *Arizona Republican* (Phoenix), 9 Dec. 1921; *Evening Star* (Washington, DC), 19 Oct. 1919; 'Ex-Princess Visits Husband at Wieringen', *The Daily Ardmoreite*, 17 Oct. 1919.

277 'Der Salonwagen der Exkronprinzessin', *Neues Wiener Journal*, 10 Sept. 1919.

278 See photos 'Die Ankunft der deutschen Exkronprinzessin', *Das interessante Blatt*, 2 Oct. 1919; 'Mit der Familie vereint', *Wiener Bilder*, 26 Oct. 1919; 'At Ex-Kaiser's Home', *Evening Journal* (Washington, DC), 21 Dec. 1921; photo with Cecilie, *The Sun* (New York), 30 Nov. 1919; 'Ex-Kaiser's Family Holds a Reunion', *Americus Times-Recorder*, 19 July 1922; 'Latest Picture of Crown Prince and Family', *Rock Island Argus and Daily Union*, 22 April 1922; 'Former Crown Prince Rejoins His Family', *Omaha Morning Bee*, 18 Nov. 1923.

279 Kurt Mühsam, 'Der deutsche Exkronprinz und die Frauen', *Neues Wiener Journal*, 8 Aug. 1926.

280 See Kreutzer, *Der deutsche Kronprinz und die Frauen in seinem Leben*; and Nivet, *La France occupée 1914–1918*, 138.

281 'Farrar-Prince Romance Told. Son of Ex Kaiser Madly Loved Opera Star', *Chicago Daily Tribune*, 22 June 1923.

282 *Geheimdienst und Propaganda im Ersten Weltkrieg*, 537.

283 'Die Ehen der Hohenzollern', *Das Tage-Buch*, 25 Sept. 1926, 1420.

284 Kreutzer, *Der deutsche Kronprinz und die Frauen*, 82–3, 185–9.

285 Ibid., 204.

286 Sichert, *Cecilienhof*, vol. 1, 98–101. See also 'Erinnerungen an ein abendliches Gespräch, das der deutsche Kronprinz allein mit uns am Kaminfeuer in der grossen Halle in Cecilienhof führte. Dez. 1934', GStA PK, Nachlass Wagner, No. 4 ('Hohenzollernhumor').

287 Hardenberg, *Auf immer neuen Wegen*, 135–6.

288 'General Max Rudolf Viebahn im Verhör durch Otto John', IfZ, ZS/A 33/5, 28 Jan. 1948, fol. 369–86. For a different version of this anecdote, see Jonas, *Der Kronprinz*, 195, and Sichert, *Cecilienhof*, vol. 1, 65–6.

289 'Brief des Kronprinzen vom 2. 4. 1919', in GStA PK Rep. 192, Nachlass Eugen Zimmermann, No. 80. See also Binder, *Schuld des Kaisers*, 45; 'Müldner von Mülnheim an Ludwig Beck, 7. 5. 1929', MHMB Dresden, Nachlass Beck, BBAV5821. On jokes within circles including Hindenburg, Groener, Schulenburg, Stülpnagel; Viscount d'Abernon, *Ein Botschafter der Zeitwende: Memoiren*, vol. 2, Leipzig 1929, 311.

290 Förster, *Königin Luise-Mythos*, 334–5.

291 'Rosy Salm-Horstmar an Marie Fürstin zu Ysenburg und Büdingen, 5. 11. 1925', in Wolzogen, *Drei Schwestern*, 261.

292 Reibnitz, *Wilhelm II. und Hermine*, 189.

293 Kessler, *Tagebücher*, vol. 9, 384 (10 October 1930). See also Reibnitz, *Wilhelm II. und Hermine*, 190.

294 For examples, see Wilderotter/Pohl, *Der letzte Kaiser*; Pekelder/Schenk/van der Bas, *Der Kaiser*.

295 'Eugen Zimmermann an Hermine, 12. 8. 1918', GStA PK, Nachlass Eugen Zimmermann, No. 88.

296 www. alamy.de, Bild-ID: TA3BXX.

297 *Lake Country Times*, 17 March 1922.

298 Wilhelm Prinz von Preussen, *Der Sieg war zum Greifen nahe!*; Wilhelm Prinz von Preussen, *Der Marne-Feldzug 1914*.

299 'Crown Prince Would Go Back "As a Laborer"', *Chicago Daily Tribune*, 4 Dec. 1918; *Wiener Zeitung*, 6 Dec. 1918; 'Der doppelzüngige Kronprinz', *Arbeiterwille*, 8 Dec. 1918; 'Erklärungen des Ex-Kronprinzen', *Freiheit*, 6 Dec. 1918.

300 'Eitel Friedrich Wants to Be Just "a Simple Citizen"', *Chicago Daily Tribune*, 29 Dec. 1918.

301 *The Memoirs of the Crown Prince of Germany*, 104, 168, 200, 224, 276, 280, 292.

302 Sartre, *War Diaries*, 304. See also Wolzogen, *Parva Aristocratia*, 48–55.

303 Musil, *The Man Without Qualities*, https://uberty.org/wp-content/uploads/2015/12/musil-1.pdf, 109–10.

304 Sartre, *War Diaries*, 537.

305 Hitler, *Mein Kampf*, vol. 1, 557. See also Weber, *Hitler's First War*, 129–226.

Chapter 2: Guerrillas: The Hohenzollerns Versus the Weimar Republic (1923–31)

1 'Brückenbauer Stresemann' (cartoon), *Vorwärts*, 7 Oct. 1924.

2 'Zirkusspiel', *Vorwärts*, 7 Feb. 1925.

3 *Lachen Links. Das republikanische Witzblatt* (Kaiser's birthday edition), 25 Jan. 1924.

4 'Le Kronprinz est revenue en Silésie. Ludendorf a été mis en liberté "sur parole"', *Le Petit Journal*, 11 Nov. 1923; 'Le kronprinz est rentré en Allemagne', *Le Rappel*, 11 Nov. 1923.

5 'Une nouvelle menace. Le Kronprinz', *La Presse*, 13 Nov. 1923; 'Le Reich ne s'est pas opposé à la rentrée du kronprinz', *Le Rappel*, 13 Nov. 1923; 'Le Retour du Kronprinz est une menace pour la paix', *Journal du Cher*, 15 Nov. 1923; 'L'Allemagne a laissé rentrer l'Ex-kronprinz', *Le Figaro*, 11 Nov. 1923; 'Le kronprinz arrive à son château d'Oels en Silésie', *Le Matin*, 12 Nov. 1923; 'L'ex-kronprinz quitte la Hollande et rentre en Allemagne', *L'Ouest-Éclair*, 11 Nov. 1923; 'Le kronprinz est rentré en Allemagne', *Le Quotidien*, 11 Nov. 1923; 'Le kronprinz est rentré en Allemagne', *La Lanterne*, 11 Nov. 1923; 'Le kronprinz est rentré en Allemagne', *L'Action Française*, 11 Nov. 1923.

6 Curzon, 29 Oct. 1923 and 22 Nov. 1923, cited in Zwehl, *Die Deutschlandpolitik Englands*, 618–19.

7 See Bommarius, *Im Rausch des Aufruhrs*.

8 Pohl, *Gustav Stresemann*, 113–218.

9 Ibid., 270–84; Wright, *Gustav Stresemann*, 231–60; Thimme, *Gustav Stresemann*; Stresemann, *Mein Vater Gustav Stresemann*, 146–8.

10 Gustav Stresemann, 'Väter und Söhne', *Deutsche Stimmen*, 26 Feb. 1922, cited in Stresemann, *Reden und Schriften*, 459–64.

11 Afflerbach, *Auf Messers Schneide*, 324–6.

12 Stresemann, 'Väter und Söhne', 463–4.

13 Stefan Grossmann, 'Der Kronprinz. Zu seinem 50. Geburtstag', *Neue Freie Presse*, 18 May 1932.

14 Jung, *Volksgesetzgebung*, 490, 495–6.

15 Holzhauer, *Die Vermögensauseinandersetzung*, 89–91.

16 Farmer, *Die Bewahrer des Erbes*, 135; Kurtz, *America and the Return of Nazi Contraband*, 24.

17 'The Ex-Kaiser and War Loot', *The Washington Post*, 20 Oct. 1924. See also 'Der Raub des Genter Altars', *Vossische Zeitung*, 2 July 1920 (evening).

18 'Le kronprinz aime les pendules; la kronprinzessin leur préfère les vases de Sèvres', *Le Petit bleu de Paris*, 15 May 1926.

19 Stresemann, 'Väter und Söhne', 463.

20 'The Hohenzollern Problem', *South China Morning Post*, 28 Nov. 1923.

21 'Dr. Stresemann's Explanation', *The Times*, 15 Nov. 1923.

22 'Eine geistige Potenz', *Vorwärts*, 1 March 1922; *Rosenheimer Anzeiger*, 16 Nov. 1923; 'Der deutsche Exkronprinz. Wie Stresemann ihn sieht', *Neues Wiener Journal*, 1 March 1922; 'Stresemann, der Exkronprinz und die "Hamburger Nachrichten"', *Hamburger Echo*, 4 March 1922; 'Gerechtigkeit für den Kronprinzen', *Hamburger Nachrichten*, 3 March 1922.

23 'Stresemann an Kronprinz, 24. 10. 1923', Nationaal Archief, Den Haag, C27036, Collectie J. B. Kan, No. 14.

24 Annelise Thimme, 'Einmal um die Uhr. Die Stresemannkontroverse von 1927 bis 1929', in Lehmann (ed.), *Historikerkontroversen*, 31–85.

25 'Das Ehrenwort des Kronprinzen. Aufruf für Hitler', *Vossische Zeitung*, 3 April 1932 (evening).

26 Jürgen Luh, 'Eine Erbschaft der Monarchie: Das Hohenzollern-Museum', in Biskup/Kohlrausch (ed.), *Das Erbe der Monarchie*, 200–216; Jürgen Luh, 'Die Historiographie über die Hohenzollern nach der Abdankung Wilhelms II. 1918 bis zur Auflösung Preussens 1947', in Biskup/Luh/Vu Minh (eds.) *Preussendämmerung*, 95–106;

Wolfgang Hardtwig, 'Von Preussens Aufgabe in Deutschland zu Deutschlands Aufgabe in der Welt. Liberalismus und borussianisches Geschichtsbild zwischen Revolution und Imperialismus', in Hardtwig, *Geschichtskultur und Wissenschaft*, 103–60.

27 Ewen, *PR! A Social History of Spin*; Tye, *The Father of Spin. Edward L. Bernays and the Birth of Public Relations*.

28 See Wolzogen, *Parva Aristocratia*, 15–28.

29 De Maistre, *Lettres d'un Royaliste Savoisien à ses compatriotes*, 5 (Préface).

30 See Franck, *Ökonomie der Aufmerksamkeit*; Honneth, *Kampf um Anerkennung*.

31 'Der deutsche Kronprinz besucht seine Eltern', *Der neue Tag* (Vienna), 14 Oct. 1919; 'Der Aufenthalt des deutschen Exkronprinzen', *Neues Wiener Journal*, 4 Oct. 1919; 'Kronprinz bleibt in Wieringen', *Arbeiter-Zeitung*, 4 Oct. 1919; 'Former Crown Prince Ends Visit to Ex-Kaiser', *The Sun* (Baltimore), 4 Feb. 1926.

32 'Der ehemalige deutsche Kronprinz in Wien?', *Allgemeiner Tiroler Anzeiger*, 25 April 1924; 'Anwesenheit eines früheren deutschen Prinzen in Wien', *Neues Wiener Tageblatt*, 25 April 1924; 'Keine Anwesenheit eines früheren deutschen Prinzen in Wien', *Kleine Volkszeitung*, 26 April 1924; 'Der deutsche Exkronprinz nicht in Wien', *Neues Wiener Journal*, 26 April 1924; 'Der Wiener Besuch des deutschen Kronprinzen. Er reist heute nach München ab', 29 August 1927; 'Der deutsche Exkronprinz in Wien', *Die Stunde*, 30 August 1927.

33 'Le kronprinz et le chancelier von Papen ont assisté à la projection d'un film dans un cinéma de Berlin sur la parade des casques d'acier qu'ils présidèrent', *Excelsior*, 12 Oct. 1932. See such vacuous reports as 'L'ex-kronprinz à Doorn', *L'ami du peuple*, 26 Nov. 1933; and 'Wilhelm n'ira pas à Londres', *Aux écoutes*, 18 March 1933.

34 'Fausse Nouvelle. L'ex-kronprinz n'a pas séjourné dans le Var', *La Liberté*, 12 July 1934.

35 'Queen "Won't Watch the Harry and Meghan Circus"', *The Times*, 7 March 2021. This was the top story in the newspaper's online edition.

36 'Der frühere Kronprinz als Demokrat. Ein Brief an Professor Zorn', *Berliner Tageblatt*, 1 Feb. 1922 (evening); 'Der Kronprinz und die Republik', *Der Reichswart*, 11 Feb. 1922, 1–2; Gasteiger, *Kuno von Westarp*, 218.

37 'Der frühere Kronprinz als Demokrat. Ein Brief an Professor Zorn', *Berliner Tageblatt*, 1 Feb. 1922 (evening).

38 'Was will der Kronprinz?; Antwort Reventlow an Hünefeld', *Der Reichswart*, 4 March 1922, 10, 12.

39 Ernst Graf zu Reventlow, 'Der Kronprinz und die Republik', *Der Reichswart*, 11 Feb. 1922, 4, 6.

40 Ernst Graf zu Reventlow, 'Monarchie?', *Der Reichswart*, 15 Oct. 1920. Count Kuno von Westarp felt exactly the same. See Gasteiger, *Kuno von Westarp*, 208.

41 Ernst Graf zu Reventlow, 'Rückkehr des Kronprinzen?' and 'Der Kronprinz und die Republik', *Der Reichswart*, 10 Nov. 1923 and 11 Feb. 1922; 'Replik auf Hünefeld', *Der Reichswart*, 25 March 1922.

42 'Vaterländische in Not', *Vorwärts*, 21 Dec. 1927. On the conflict within the Stahlhelm in 1926, see the correspondence in DAAM, Nachlass Lüninck, No. 768; *Der Stahlhelm*, 12 Dec. 1926; 'Cramon an Mackensen, 4. 12. 1926 und 16. 12. 1926', and 'Kapitän Ehrhardt und die Fürstenabdankung', Nachlass John Röhl, Berlin, vol. 87.

43 Hünefeld, *Insel der Verbannung*.

44 'So sieht er aus!', *Vorwärts*, 10 July 1928 (evening); 'Der Lachmann. Baron v. Hünefeld jüdischer Herkunft', *Vorwärts*, 26 July 1928.

45 'Grösse der Zeit. Der Amerikaflug', *Vorwärts*, 15 April 1928; 'Tod des Ozeanfliegers Hünefeld', *Neues Wiener Journal*, 27 Feb. 1929; 'Der Monarchist Hünefeld', *Grazer Tagblatt*, 27 April 1928; 'Helden für 10,000 Mark', *Vorwärts*, 11 July 1928 (evening).

46 Freiherr von Hünefeld, 'Kronprinz und Monarchie', *Der Reichswart*, 12 (25 March 1922), 10.

47 Hermelin, *Der Prinz auf Wiereland*, 416, 427. See also 'Der Prinz auf Wiereland', *Vorwärts*, 28 Nov. 1926.

48 See Gumbel, *Vier Jahre politischer Mord*; Sabrow, *Der Rathenau-mord*; Nagel, *Fememorde*; Horne/Gerwarth (eds.), *Krieg im Frieden*; Jones, *Am Anfang war Gewalt*; Weisbrod, *Gewalt in der Politik*; Schumann, *Politische Gewalt*.

49 *Verhandlungen des Reichstags. Stenographische Berichte, I. Wahlperiode 1920*, vol. 356, session of 25 Feb. 1922, Berlin 1922, 8054–8.

50 Gusy, *Weimar – die wehrlose Republik?*, 139–70.

Notes

51 *Verhandlungen des Deutschen Reichstags*, 244th session, 5 July 1922, and 249th session, 12 July 1922.

52 *Akten der Reichskanzlei, Kabinett Cuno*, vol. 1, document 207, 'Aufzeichnung von Mackensen, 3.7.1923'; ibid., *Kabinette Stresemann I/II*, vol. 2, document 167, 'Kabinettssitzung 23.10.1923'; ibid., vol. 2, supplement 1, 'Materialsammlung des Generalleutnants z. V. Lieber vom 10. 11. 1923'.

53 See 'Die Rückkehr des Kronprinzen', *Vorwärts*, 14 Nov. 1923 (morning).

54 'Hohenzollernfimmel', *Vorwärts*, 11 April 1924 (evening).

55 'Der Schlossherr von Oels', *Berliner Tageblatt*, 18 Aug. 1924.

56 'Der ehemalige Kronprinz deutschnationaler Reichstagskandidat?', *Berliner Tageblatt*, 24 Oct. 1924; Erhard Ocke, 'Der Kronprinz M.d.R.', *Weltbühne*, 4 Nov. 1924, 710.

57 'Die Kaiserkomödie. Falsche Sensation. Unmögliche Rückkehr Wilhelm II.', *Vorwärts*, 26 Nov. 1926.

58 'Die Kronprinzen-Erklärung. Stresemann-Brief in geänderter Fassung', *Vossische Zeitung*, 24 May 1932 (evening).

59 Gustav Stresemann, 'Vermächtnis. Die Rückkehr des Exkronprinzen aus Holland', *Vossische Zeitung*, 2 March 1932 (evening); 'Eine Kontroverse um Stresemanns "Vermächtnis"', *Vossische Zeitung*, 20 May 1932 (evening); 'Stresemann und Kronprinzen-Versprechen', *Vorwärts*, 21 May 1932; Sollmann, 'Hohenzollern-Ehrenwort. Was hat der Exkronprinz Stresemann versprochen?', *Vorwärts*, 20 May 1932; 'Das Hohenzollernwort. Der Exkronprinz will von nichts wissen', *Vorwärts*, 24 May 1932.

60 Wilhelm Sollmann, 'Legende oder Wahrheit. Die Verpflichtung des Exkronprinzen', *Vorwärts*, 25 May 1932.

61 Thimme (ed.), *Friedrich Thimme*.

62 Friedrich Thimme, 'Der ehemalige Kronprinz als Politiker', *Preussische Jahrbücher*, 181 (December 1920), 361–80, here 363.

63 Friedrich Thimme, 'Die Kronprinzenfrage', *Kölnische Zeitung*, 28 Nov. 1923; Friedrich Thimme, 'Kaiser Wilhelm II. Erinnerungen und Gespräche', *Kölnische Zeitung*, 6 Jan. 1923.

64 *Deutsche Allgemeine Zeitung*, no. 237 (1932).

65 'Die Erklärung des Kronprinzen', *Kreuzzeitung*, 26 May 1932.

66 'L'Activité politique de l'ex-kronprinz', *L'Ouest-Éclair*, 11 March 1932.

67 'Der Berg kann gehen', *Vorwärts*, 7 Dec. 1926; 'Der Schrecken der Monarchisten', *Vorwärts* (evening), 25 Nov. 1926.

68 ' "Ehrenwörter" des "Dritten Reichs" ', *Christlichsoziale Arbeiterzeitung*, 16 April 1932.

69 *Das Tage-Buch*, 8 May 1932, 816–17.

70 *New York Herald*, 1 April 1924.

71 'Das Wort des Exkronprinzen', *Vorwärts*, 24 May 1932. See also the chapter 'Der Wille zum Aufstieg', in Pohl, *Gustav Stresemann*, 71–112.

72 Stresemann, *Mein Vater Gustav Stresemann*, 146–8.

73 See the detailed description in Röhl, *Hof und Hofgesellschaft unter Wilhelm II.*, 81–7.

74 Jung, *Volksgesetzgebung*, 446–50.

75 Ibid., 431–4, here 433.

76 Gerhard Anschütz (Heidelberg), Max Fleischmann (Königsberg), Otto von Gierke (Berlin), Heinrich Triepel (Berlin) and Walther Schücking (Marburg).

77 Jung, *Volksgesetzgebung*, 459.

78 Heinz Holzhauer, 'Kaisertreue Gutachter', *FAZ*, 9 Aug. 2019, Holzhauer, *Die Vermögensauseinandersetzung*, 91–3.

79 'The Fortune of the Hohenzollern Family. Letters to the Editor' (letter to the editor written by the lawyer Rechtsanwalt Karl Siebert), *The Christian Science Monitor* (Boston), 3 March 1925.

80 *Freiheit*, 18 Aug. 1922; *Vorwärts*, 18 Aug. 1922.

81 'Hoch die Fürsten!', *Vorwärts*, 6 Dec. 1924.

82 'Fürstenkompromiss und Rechtsausschuss', *Vorwärts*, 3 Feb. 1926.

83 'Ex-Kaiser Appeals for African Property', *New York Times*, 14 June 1926.

84 'Schreiben des Kronprinzen vom 9.12.1941', GStA PK, I.HA, Rep. 100A, No. 212; 'The Hohenzollern Estates', *The Irish Times*, 20 Sept. 1932.

85 Urbach, *Go-Betweens for Hitler*, 153–216.

86 'An Unusual Referendum', *Boston Daily Globe*, 19 May 1926.

87 'Berg an Wilhelm II, 8. 2. 1926, 29. 3. 1926 und 20. 5. 1926', Nachlass John Röhl, Berlin, vol. 87.

88 'Wilhelm II., Order vom 26. 7. 1926', ibid.

89 Kühnl, *Die nationalsozialistische Linke*, 43–55; Kershaw, *Hitler*, 353–5; Longerich, *Goebbels*, 66.

90 Mommsen, *Verspielte Freiheit*, 331–6.

91 'Was soll werden?', *Vorwärts*, 19 June 1926; See also the cartoon 'Reaktionäre Moral', *Vorwärts*, 18 June 1926.

92 Ernst Seeger, the head of German film oversight, would continue his career under Goebbels until his death in 1937. See Keitz, *Filme vor Gericht*; Martin Loiperdinger, 'Filmzensur und Selbstkontrolle', in Jacobsen / Kaes / Prinzler (eds.), *Geschichte des deutschen Films*, 534–7.

93 'Eine nötige Korrektur', *Vorwärts*, 14 June 1926; 'Ein Film gegen die Fürsten', *Arbeiter-Zeitung*, 15 June 1926; 'Freigabe des Propagandafilms', *Vorwärts*, 17 June 1926.

94 Heinig, *Fürstenabfindung?*, 32–43.

95 Schüren, *Volksentscheid*, 28.

96 Kluck, *Protestantismus und Protest in der Weimarer Republik*, 54.

97 Karl Freiherr von Plettenberg, 'Erinnerungen, Eintrag von 1933 oder 1934', Karl-Wilhelm Freiherr von Plettenberg private archive.

98 'The Hohenzollern Claims. Public Hostility', *The Observer*, 21 March 1926.

99 Jung, *Volksgesetzgebung*, 439.

100 'Berg an Wilhelm II., Januar 1926', Nachlass John Röhl, Berlin, vol. 87.

101 This and the quote above: Morus [Richard Lewinsohn], 'Hohenzollern-Beute', *Weltbühne*, 12 Oct. 1926, 577–81.

102 Carl von Ossietzky, 'Vanity Fair', *Weltbühne*, 14 Sept. 1926.

103 'Der Hohenzollernvergleich im Landtag', *Vorwärts*, 12 Oct. 1926; 'Annahme des Hohenzollernvergleichs', *Vorwärts*, 16 Oct. 1926; 'Riot Marks Debate in Prussian Diet', *The Sun* (New York), 13 Oct. 1926.

104 'Hohenzollern Claims Squeezing the Republic', *Irish Times* 29 Jan. 1926; 'The Hohenzollern Claims. Public Hostility', *The Observer*, 21 March 1926.

105 Carl von Ossietzky, 'Die Mittelmänner', *Die Weltbühne*, 19 Oct. 1926.

106 'Liebesgaben an die Hohenzollern', *Vorwärts*, 6 Nov. 1925.

107 'Der Hohenzollernvergleich. Aussprache der Berliner Parteifunktionäre', *Vorwärts*, 27 Oct. 1926.

108 Henri Guilbeaux, 'L'Indemnisation des Hohenzollern et l'étrange attitude des social-démocrates', *L'Humanité*, 19 Oct. 1926.

109 'Le kronprinz réclame son argenterie', *Le Matin*, 20 Feb. 1925.

110 'La grande misère des Hohenzollern', *Revue du Rhin et de la Moselle*, 5 Feb. 1925, 79–83; 'Le peuple allemand contre les exigences financières de ses princes déchus', *La Revue des jeunes*, 25 May 1926; 'On les connait les affaires de la famille des Hohenzollern', *Le Petit Bleu de Paris*, 28 Nov. 1926.

111 'Der Minister gegen das Monokel', *Wiener Morgenzeitung*, 19 Jan. 1921; Stefan Grossmann, 'Assessor Wehrhahns Ende', *Neue Freie Presse*, 3 Feb. 1921.

112 Jung, *Volksgesetzgebung*, 439–40, 466, 471–3, 482, 490, 513.

113 Ibid., 502, 507.

114 Merz, *Das Schreckbild*.

115 Mommsen, *Die verspielte Freiheit*, 9–129, here 129; Winkler, *Weimar*, 13–98.

116 'Der Berg kann gehen', *Vorwärts*, 7 Dec. 1926.

117 Geyer, *Verkehrte Welt*.

118 'Verhaftung eines Berliner Bankiers', *Neue Freie Presse*, 10 June 1925, 'Verhaftung des Geheimen Kommerzienrats Grusser', *Neues Wiener Journal*, 9 June 1925; 'Barmat vs. Grusser', *Vorwärts*, 22 March 1925; 'Der Schieber der Hohenzollern', *Vorwärts*, 13 May 1922 (evening); 'Der Schwarze und der Weisse', *Vorwärts*, 20 May 1921 (evening); 'Hohenzollerns Involved in Big Smuggling Plot', *New York Tribune*, 24 Nov. 1920; 'Ex-Royalty in 250 000 000 Marks Smuggling Plot', *Evening Star* (Washington, DC), 23 Nov. 1920; 'Royal Germans Smuggle Millions', 24 Nov. 1920.

119 See the figures given in 'Das Vermögen Wilhelm II.', *Neues Wiener Journal*, 26 Dec. 1920; and 'Ein Dementi des deutschen Kronprinzen', *Innsbrucker Nachrichten*, 2 Dec. 1920; 'Kalender der wichtigsten Wieringer Daten', January 1920, GStA PK, BPH, Rep. 192, Nachlass Arthur Berg, No. 19.

120 'Die Millionenschiebungen der Hohenzollern. Weitere Einzelheiten', *Neues Wiener Journal*, 20 Nov. 1920.

121 'Der verurteilte Hohenzollern. Eitel Friedrich wegen Kapitalverschiebung bestraft', *Prager Tagblatt*, 19 May 1921; 'Eitel Friedrich Is Convicted of Smuggling Cash to Holland', *New York Tribune*, 16 May 1921; 'Ein Hohenzollern-Prinz auf der Anklagebank', *Neues Wiener Journal*, 19 May 1921.

122 'Die unverdächtigen Hohenzollern. Schutz dem Milliarden-Diadem', *Vorwärts*, 4 Nov. 1922.

123 'Unsere Hohenzollern', *Weltbühne*, 4 Nov. 1924, 703; *Vorwärts*, 17 June 1931 (evening) and 15 Aug. 1931.

124 'Verhandlungen des Deutschen Reichstags 32. Sitzung, 22. 11. 1920', 1189.

125 Ibid., 1175.

126 Ibid., 1193.

127 'Monarchistisches aus der Schweiz', *Vorwärts*, 14 Oct. 1919 (evening); 'Die Aufklärung der Zwanzig-Millionen-Schiebung', *Vorwärts*, 28 Aug. 1919.

128 Heilmann, *Verdienste der Hohenzollern*, 26.

129 'Verhandlungen des Deutschen Reichstags 32. Sitzung, 22. 11. 1920', 1198.

130 'Smuggling Princes Hit in Reichstag', *New York Times*, 24 Nov. 1920.

131 'Kaiser's Family Charged with Stealing', *Boston Daily Globe*, 16 Jan. 1921.

132 Landau, *Juristen jüdischer Herkunft im Kaiserreich und in der Weimarer Republik*; Otmar Jung, 'Arnold Freymuth – eine Nachlese', *Jahrbuch der Juristischen Zeitgeschichte*, 10 (2008/9), 209–45.

133 See Heilmann, *Verdienste der Hohenzollern*. The title plays upon the dual meaning of the German word *Verdienste* as 'services' and 'earnings'.

134 'Die Habgier der Hohenzollern. Die Debatte im deutschen Reichstag', *Arbeiterwille*, 2 Dec. 1920; 'Ums Hohenzollerngeld. Zur gestrigen Sitzung der Landesversammlung', *Vorwärts*, 1 Dec. 1920; 'Was Wilhelm will', *Vorwärts*, 30 Nov. 1920 (evening).

135 'Schieber', *Die Gleichheit*, 4 Dec. 1920; 'Neue Hohenzollern-Ballade', *Vorwärts*, 1 Dec. 1920 (evening).

136 Bloch, *Albert Südekum*, 230–31, 250–55.

137 Tobias Schlot, 'Der Vater der Fürstenabfindung', *Prager Tageblatt*, 22 June 1926; 'Südekum auf Schloss Sacrow', *Prager Tageblatt*, 13 July 1926; 'Wie der Genosse Finanzminister Schlossherr wurde', *Salzburger Chronik*, 31 July 1926; 'Maximilian Harden gegen den Reichskanzler Ebert', *Neues Wiener Journal*, 2 Feb. 1921; Bloch, *Albert Südekum*, 270–71.

138 Jung, *Volksgesetzgebung*, 455–75, 489–507.

139 KPD election slogan, cited by Jung, *Volksgesetzgebung*, 483.

140 Heilmann, *Verdienste der Hohenzollern*, 7–10.

141 Jung, *Volksgesetzgebung*, 480; 'Return of Royal Dynasties Seen as Possible in France', *The Christian Science Monitor*, 4 Oct. 1923.

142 The reference was to a speech Bismarck made to the lower chamber of the Prussian regional parliament on 13 February 1869.

143 Heilmann, *Verdienste der Hohenzollern*, 13, 18–20.

144 'Ein schwarzer Tag für die Monarchisten', *Freiheit*, 23 Nov. 1920.

145 Heilmann, *Verdienste der Hohenzollern*, 30.

146 'Bill and His Boys Are on Their Uppers – Looking for Jobs. Don't Want to Work, Don't Know How; It's a Tough Life', *Topeka State Journal*, 28 Dec. 1918.

147 'Ex-Kings Swelling the Ranks of the Unemployed Forces', *Alaska Daily*, 3 April 1919; 'Ex-Kaiser Fights for Large Estates', *The Hartford Courant*, 27 Nov. 1925.

148 Afflerbach, *Auf Messers Schneide*, 326–8.

149 'Der deutsche Blut-Tag von Halle', *Vorwärts*, 19 May 1924.

150 'Die Heldenfamilie. Zurückhaltung im Krieg – aber grosses Portemonnaie', *Vorwärts*, 27 Oct. 1932.

151 'Kriegsheld Auwi. Wie ein Kaisersohn verwundet wurde', *Arbeiter-Zeitung*, 29 July 1932; Machtan, *Der Kaisersohn*, 53–7.

152 'Fight to Deprive W. Hohenzollern of Goods Begins', *The Atlanta Constitution*, 4 March 1920.

153 'Monarchie. Die elendste aller Staatsformen', *Volksstimme* (Magdeburg), 1 Nov. 1932.

154 Ernst Jünger, *In Stahlgewittern*; Jünger, *Der Arbeiter*; Kiesel, *Ernst Jünger*, 394–7.

155 See the section entitled 'The Drones' in the pacifist pamphlet by Wilhelm Appens, *Charleville. Dunkle Punkte aus dem Etappenleben*, 15–18.

156 Reibnitz, *Wilhelm II. und Hermine*, 193.

157 'Parade der Prinzenbegehrler', *Vorwärts*, 31 May 1931.

158 'A Quiet Life at Potsdam', *The Observer*, 18 Nov. 1923; 'Royalty Living Simply', *The Sun* (New York), 1 Aug. 1926; 'Kaiser's Son Farms', *Washington Times*, 2 April 1922.

159 'A Hohenzollern Goes into Banking', *The Manchester Guardian*, 9 March 1929.

160 'Ex-Kaiser Land Poor Says Berlin Manager. He Denies Wilhelm Hohenzollern Is Richest Individual of the German Nation', *New York Times*, 7 July 1929, 45.

161 'Pourquoi les Hohenzollern ne sont-ils pas encore restauré?', *Je suis partout*, 29 Oct. 1932.

162 Walter von Molo, 'Drei Schriftstücke an eine falsche Adresse', *Berliner Tageblatt*, 10 June 1926.

163 See Gerstner, *Neuer Adel*; Malinowski, *Nazis and Nobles*, 129–207; and Conze/Meteling/Schuster (eds.), *Aristokratismus*.

164 Alois Fürst zu Löwenstein, 'Aufgaben des Adels in der Gegenwart', in 'Adel', *Staatslexikon* (Görres Society), Freiburg 1926, vol. 1, 44.

165 Studnitz, *Seitensprünge*, 27.

166 Musil, *Der Mann ohne Eigenschaften*, book 1, part 2, chapter 24.

167 'Ein Hohenzollernprinz als Egalité', *Salzburger Volksblatt*, 22 Jan. 1919; 'Ein prinzlicher Umlerner', *Tägliche Rundschau*, 25 Nov. 1918; 'Immer wieder konter-revolutonäre Aktionen von Offizieren', *Freiheit*, 12 Dec. 1918; *New York Times*, 11 Dec. 1918; Nicholas M. Railton, 'The "Red Prince" and Freemansonry. Scenes from the German Revolution 1918', *JGMO* 2012, 67–92; 76–9; Heinig, *Hohenzollern*, 150–56.

168 'A Lucky Hohenzollern. Prince Leopold's Rapid Promotion Causes Envy', *New York Tribune*, 9 July 1893.

169 See Heinrich Graf von Spreti, *Imlau. Ein Herrenhaus und seine Bewohner*, Munich, 1998.

170 *Wiener Salonblatt*, 24 July 1927.

171 'Prinz Heinrich an die Familienmitglieder des ehemals königlich preussischen Hauses', *Berliner Tageblatt*, 4. Dec. 1918.

172 'Die Entmündigung des Prinzen Friedrich Leopold', *Frankfurter Zeitung*, 2 Oct. 1917; Karl Friedrichs, 'Der Entmündigungsstreit im Königlichen Hause', *Deutsche Juristen-Zeitung* 23/24 (1917), 988–91; 'Das Verfahren gegen den Prinzen Friedrich Leopold', *Deutsche Allgemeine Zeitung*, 12 April 1921; 'Entmündigungsprozess Prinz Friedrich Leopold', *Tägliche Rundschau*, 19 June 1918; 'Die Beschlagnahme der Juwelen des Prinzen Leopold', *Deutsche Allgemeine Zeitung*, 19 July 1921; Steinhauer, *Der Meisterspion des Kaisers*. See also Jung, *Volksgesetzgebung*, 484–9.

173 Hellmut von Gerlach, 'Friedrich Leopold', *Die Weltbühne*, 22 Sept. 1931, 456–7; Studnitz, *Seitensprünge*, 20–21; Railton, 'The "Red Prince"', 67–92; 'Kaiser's Relative a Spender', *Arizona Republican*, 6 April 1919.

174 Jung, *Volksgesetzgebung*, 484–9.

175 'Die Forderungen der Hohenzollern', *Weltbühne*, 25 Sept. 1924, 475.

176 'Die fürstlichen Millionenschieber. Die Debatte im Reichstag', *Arbeiterwille*, 24 Nov. 1920; 'Sturm im Reichstag. Eine Hohenzollern-Debatte', *Neues Wiener Journal*, 23 Nov. 1920.

177 'Kaiser's Son Is Lucky Gambler, Says Paper', *Hartford Republican*, 29 Aug. 1919; 'King as Good as a Socialist Here', *Washington Times*, 6 Aug. 1919; 'Ex-Kaiser's Son Buys Villa in Switzerland', *The Globe* (Toronto), 20 June 1919; 'Prince Joachim Gambles', *El Paso Herald*, 21 July 1919; 'Joachim Plays Roulette. Ex-Kaiser's Son Known as Greatest Gambler at Campione', *Washington Post*, 11 May 1919; 'Kaiser's Son in Italy', *Washington Post*, 27 April 1919. See also Jonas, *Der Kronprinz*, 178.

178 'Preussenprinz verjuxt ganzes Vermögen', *New Ulm Post*, 12 Aug. 1921.

179 Malinowski, *Politische Skandale*, 46–64; Geyer, *Kapitalismus und politische Moral*.

180 Schultz, *Das Gesicht der Demokratie*, 96.

181 'Old Time Prussian Pomp Precedes Uprising by Reds', *Bismarck Tribune*, 31 March 1920; 'German Pomp at Funeral for Ex-Empress', *Perth Amboy Evening News*, 4 May 1920; 'Revival of Old Kaiserlich Guard Causes Stir in Germany', *Lake County Times*, 21 June 1921; 'Prince Eitel Friedrich, Ludendorff View Reunion of German Front Troops', *Albuquerque Morning Times*, 24 Sept. 1921.

182 Grünzig, *Für Deutschtum*, 80–104.

183 Studnitz, *Seitensprünge*, 23, 27.

184 Prince Louis Ferdinand of Prussia, *The Rebel Prince*, 50–66.

185 Grünzig, *Für Deutschtum*, 113–14; Severing, *Mein Lebensweg*, vol. 2, 24–6.

186 Bernard Ludwig, 'Victor Basch et l'Allemagne. Esquisse d'une relation particulière', *Revue d'Allemagne et des pays de langue allemande*, 36 (2004), 341–58 ; Rajesh Heynickx, 'Bridging the Abyss: Victor Basch's Political and Aesthetic Mindset', *Modern Intellectual History*, 10 (2013), 87–107.

187 See Sabrow, *Die vergessene Republik*.

188 'Die "Baschisten"', *Stahlhelm*, 12 Oct. 1924; 'Nachklänge zum Potsdamer

Baschistenabend', *Stahlhelm*, 19 Oct. 1924; 'Die Taktlosigkeiten des Monsieur Basch', *Grazer Tageblatt*, 14 Oct. 1924.

189 'Weimar und Potsdam' and 'Das Reichsbanner in Potsdam', in *Das Reichsbanner. Weimar und Potsdam*, published by the Potsdam chapter of the Reichsbanners Schwarz Rot Gold, Berlin, no year, 13–18.

190 Thomas Wernicke, 'Der Handschlag am "Tag von Potsdam"', 11–12.

191 'Stahlhelm-Blamage in Potsdam', *Vorwärts*, 7 Oct. 1924; 'Stresemann und Reichsbanner', *Vorwärts*, 6 Dec. 1924; 'Weltfriedenskongress in Berlin', *Vorwärts*, 6 Oct. 1924; 'Victor Basch in Berlin', *Vorwärts*, 2 Oct. 1924; 'Die deutsche Politik am Scheidewege', *Vorwärts*, 30 Sept. 1924 (evening).

192 Lindenberger, *Strassenpolitik*.

193 'Junker Plots Rumored in Berlin', *New York Times*, 26 Feb. 1921.

194 Mao Zedong, *On Guerrilla Warfare*; Guevara, *Guerrilla Warfare*; Münkler, *Der Partisan*.

195 Laak, *Symbolische Politik in Praxis und Kritik*, 46.

196 See Lindenberger, *Strassenpolitik*; Chickering, *We Men Who Feel Most German*.

197 'Die Parade der Gestrigen', *Vorwärts*, 3 June 1931.

198 Ernst Jünger, in 'Die Standarte. Beiträge zur geistigen Vertiefung des Frontgedankens, 8/1925', 151–2, quoted by Morat, *Von der Tat zur Gelassenheit*, 58.

199 Frevert, *Mächtige Gefühle*, 167–83.

200 'Der Hass des Stahlhelms', *Vorwärts*, 18 Sept. 1928; Berghahn, *Stahlhelm*, 113–14.

201 'Ex-Kaiser's Son, Who May Be in Plot', *Richmond Palladium* and *Sun Telegram*, 17 March 1920.

202 'Intensify Attack on Hohenzollerns', *New York Times*, 18 Oct. 1926.

203 'Die Zigaretten des Prinzen Oskar', *Frankfurter Zeitung*, 3 Nov. 1926; 'Die Zigaretten des Prinzen. Ein sonderbarer Sympathiebeweis', *Hamburgischer Correspondent*, 3 Nov. 1926; 'Eine merkwürdige Erklärung', *Berliner Tageblatt*, 4 Nov. 1926; 'Der harmlose Prinz', *Frankfurter Zeitung*, 4 Nov. 1926; 'Der unschuldige Oskar', *Vorwärts*, 4 Nov. 1926; 'Oskar und Stresemann-Attentäter', *Vorwärts*, 31 Oct. 1926; 'Auwi, der Seelentröster' (cartoon) *Vorwärts*, 30 Dec. 1931.

204 Klingler, *Negotiating Violence*, 35–83, 192–215.

205 Schleich, *Besonnte Vergangenheit*. See also Frevert, *Mächtige Gefühle*, 274–7.

206 Tobias Becker, 'Eine kleine Geschichte der Nostalgie', *Merkur*, 72 (2018), 66–73.

207 'Kommando für besondere Verwendung', *Berliner Tageblatt*, 25 March 1927; 'Die Zeugen in Giessen, *Vossische Zeitung*, 25 March 1927; 'Eine Aussage über die Ermordung Rathenaus', *Neue Freie Presse*, 25 March 1927; *Der Tag*, 26 March 1927.

208 'Stahlhelmtag in Berlin', *Wiener Sonn- und Montagszeitung*, 9 May 1927; 'Stahlhelmtag in Berlin', *Freie Stimmen*, 10 May 1927.

209 'Parade der Prinzenbegehrler', *Vorwärts*, 31 May 1931.

210 'Die Pläne der Kaiserin Hermine. Besorgnisse der preussischen Staatsregierung', *Neues Wiener Journal*, 25 March 1927.

211 'Ein Berliner Beispiel: Ein Kriegerdenkmal in Berlin' *Vorwärts*, 24 June 1924; 'Hohenzollernparade', *Arbeiterzeitung*, 15 June 1924.

212 'Der deutsche Blut-Tag von Halle', *Vorwärts*, 19 May 1924.

213 'Blutiger Tag in Halle', *Vorwärts*, 12 May 1924; 'Der Putschistenaufmarsch', *Vorwärts*, 21 May 1924; 'Severing über den Skandal von Halle', *Vorwärts*, 22 May 1924; 'Die blutige Moltke-Feier in Halle', *Linzer Volksblatt*, 14 May 1924.

214 'Ex-Crown Prince – Reappearance in the Social World. New Monarchist Tactics', *The Observer*, 13 July 1924.

215 'Geburtstagsfeier in Potsdam', *Prager Tageblatt*, 29 January 1924.

216 'A Hohenzollern Whose Sword Sleeps in Its Scabbard', *Current Opinion*, January–June 1924, 26.

217 'Der ausgepfiffene Kronprinz', *Oberländer Tagblatt*, 23 Nov. 1926; Reibnitz, *Wilhelm II. und Hermine*, 87, 185; 'Kronprinz Wilhelm, der Sportsmann', *Pforzheimer Anzeiger*, 17 March 1950.

218 'Heil Dir im Bürgerblock. Der Kronprinz demonstriert', *Vorwärts*, 2 Feb. 1925 (evening), 1; 'Die Zollforderungen des Schlesischen Landbundes', *Vossische Zeitung*, 2 Feb. 1925 (evening), 3.

219 'Der frühere Kronprinz beim Landbund. Teilnahme an einer politischen Tagung', *Berliner Tageblatt*, 2 Feb. 1925 (evening), 4.

220 'Zirkusspiel', *Vorwärts*, 7 Feb. 1925, 11.

Notes

221 'À Berlin l'ex-kronprinz paraît en public et se fait acclamer par la foule', *L'Ouest-Éclair* (Rennes), 19 Feb. 1925; 'Le kronprinz et sa femme sont acclamés à Berlin', *Le Quotidien*, 19 Feb.1925; 'Le kronprinz ne se gène plus', *La Dépêche*, 19 Feb. 1925.

222 Ch. Le Gendre, 'Le kronprinz sera-t-il président de la République allemande?', *L'Événement*, 2 March 1925; 'Londres craint un coup d'État de l'ex-kronprinz', *Le Rappel*, 2 March 1925; 'Un républicain ou un des kronprinz allemands', *Le Nouvelliste de Bretagne*, 1 March 1925; 'L'ex-kronprinz acclamé par les hobereaux allemands', *Le Radical*, 19 Feb. 1925.

223 'Kronprinz an J. B. Kan, 8. 5. 1925', Nationaal Archief, Den Haag, C27036, Collectie J. B. Kan, No. 10.

224 'Sons of Ex-Kaiser at War Monument. Parade on Street Barred', *New York Times*, 25 May 1924.

225 'Wieder eine Hohenzollernparade', *Freiheit*, 25 June 1921.

226 'Republikanische Reichswehr?', *Vorwärts*, 11 Feb. 1925.

227 See Gasteiger, *Kuno von Westarp*, 203.

228 Wirtz, *Flaggenstreit*, 51–66.

229 Grünzig, *Für Deutschtum*, 106–11.

230 Petzinna, *Erziehung zum deutschen Lebensstil*, 190–240; Malinowski, *'Führertum' und 'Neuer Adel'*.

231 'Seeckt zurückgetreten', *Vorwärts*, 7 Oct. 1926; 'Keine Einstellung eines Kronprinzensohnes in die Reichswehr', *Berliner Tageblatt*, 28 Sept. 1926 (evening), 3.

232 'Zeitfreiwilliger Hohenzollern. Der "Prinz" und die Reichswehr', *Vorwärts*, 30 Sept. 1926 (morning), 2; 'Kronprinzensohn und Reichswehr. Antwort auf das Dementi des Reichswehrministers', *Vorwärts*, 3 Oct. 1926 (morning), 2; 'Der Zeitfreiwillige Hohenzollern. Disziplinierung des Schuldigen?', *Vorwärts*, 5 Oct. 1926 (evening), 2.

233 'Die Folge von Seeckts Missgriff', *Vorwärts*, 9 Oct. 1926 (evening), 2.

234 'Seeckt zurückgetreten. Konflikt mit Gessler um den Prinzen in der Reichswehr. Vor der Entscheidung des Reichspräsidenten', *Vorwärts*, 7 Oct. 1926 (morning), 1; 'Die Manövertage des Kronprinzensohnes. Gessler beim Reichspräsidenten', *Berliner Tageblatt*, 6 Oct. 1926 (evening), 1.

235 'Gessler fängt an. Es geht schon, wenn man nur will!', *Vorwärts*, 9 Oct. 1926 (morning), 1–2.

236 'Friedrich Graf von der Schulenburg an Generalleutnant Max von Viebahn, 25. 3. 1938', SS-Personalakte Schulenburg, BAB, R436-III / 555316.

237 'Der Prinzleutnant. Hat er den Eid auf die Republik geschworen?', *Vorwärts*, 8 Oct. 1926 (evening), 1. See also Stresemann, *Mein Vater*, 452.

238 'Erbprinz, Wiking, Reichswehraspirant. Der Fall Sachsen-Koburg-Gotha', *Vorwärts*, 9 Oct. 1926 (morning), 2.

239 'Die Entlassung des Generals Seeckt. Heute Nachmittag Entschluss des Reichspräsidenten', *Vorwärts*, 7 Oct. 1926 (evening), 1; 'Der Fall Seeckt. Noch keine Entscheidung des Reichspräsidenten', *Vorwärts*, 8 Oct. 1926 (morning), 1; 'Fall Seeckt und Frankreich. Urteile der Pariser Presse', *Vorwärts*, 8 Oct. 1926 (morning), 3.

240 Möllers, *Reichswehrminister Otto Gessler*, 318–24.

241 Theodor Wolff, 'Abschiedsgesuch des Generaloberst v. Seeckt', *Berliner Tageblatt*, 7 Oct. 1926 (morning), 1–2.

242 Carl von Ossietzky, 'Von Germersheim bis Münsingen', *Die Weltbühne*, 5 Oct. 1926.

243 'Von Seeckt Victim of Plot by Cecilie', *New York Times*, 8 Oct. 1926.

244 'Amerika und Seeckts Rücktritt. Funktelegramm unseres Korrespondenten', *Berliner Tageblatt*, 9 Oct. 1926 (morning), 1; 'End of Seeckt Gives New Impetus to European Peace', *The Globe*, 8 Oct. 1926.

245 'The Hohenzollern Nuisance', *The Economist*, 16 Oct. 1926.

246 *Germania*, 6 Oct. 1926.

247 Zoubkoff, *Mein Leben und Lieben*; Röhl, *Wilhelm II.*, vol. 2, 718–19.

248 'A Hohenzollern', *Irish Times*, 14 Nov. 1929; 'The Zubkov Sale', *The Observer*, 20 Oct. 1929.

249 'Princess Divorces Hohenzollern Scion', *The Washington Post*, 23 Oct. 1926; 'Two Hohenzollern Princes Confirmed', *The Washington Post*, 3 July 1927; 'Hohenzollern Princess Now Learning to Cook', *The Hartford Courant*, 18 March 1928; 'Hohenzollern Lawsuit. Custody of Joachim's Son', *South China Morning Post*, 16 Sept. 1921; ' "Am Prinzen gescheitert" ', *Vossische Zeitung*, 27 July 1920; 'Der Kampf um das Kind der Prinzessin Joachim', *Deutsche Allgemeine Zeitung*, 10

Nov. 1920; 'Scheidung von Eitel Friedrich', *Hamburger Nachrichten*, 16 Nov. 1926.

250 'Die Tragödie eines Hohenzollernsohnes', *Prager Tageblatt*, 26 Oct. 1922; 'Der Freund der Prinzessin Joachim. Ein geheimer Betrugsprozess', *Neues Wiener Journal*, 28 Oct. 1922.

251 'Prince Joachim Victim of Hohenzollern Taint', *The Sun* (New York), 20 July 1920; Machtan, *Der Kaisersohn*, 103; Kirschstein, *Auguste Victoria*, 157–9.

252 'Say Eitel Seeks Divorce', *New York Times*, 17 March 1919; 'Ex-Kaiser's Second Son Seeks Divorce', *Boston Daily Globe*, 17 March 1919.

253 'Hohenzollern von heute. Die Ehescheidung Eitel Friedrichs', *Prager Tageblatt*, 29 Sept. 1926.

254 'Prince Eitel to Sue in Wife's Defense', *New York Times*, 6 May 1922; 'Princess Admits Divorce Suit Guilt', *New York Times*, 11 March 1922.

255 'Princess Eitel Friedrich Gets Divorce For "Mental Suffering"', *Boston Daily Globe*, 22 Oct 1926; 'Ex-Kaiser's Daughter-in-Law to Wed Policeman', *The Sun* (Baltimore), 17 Oct. 1926; 'Eitel Friedrich, Second Son of Ex-Kaiser, Dies', *New York Herald Tribune*, 28 Dec. 1942.

256 'Prince Eitel, Ex-Kaiser's Son, Asks Divorce, Charging Film-Struck Wife Is Humiliating', *New York Times*, 21 Sept. 1926.

257 'Aus dem Mittelalter. Eitel-Schieberich und sein Orden', *Vorwärts*, 16 Nov. 1926.

258 Haehner, 'Tagebuch, 20.12.1919, fol. 68'; Machtan, *Der Kaisersohn*, 105–20.

259 'Die Prinzessin im Wohnwagen', *Flensburger Tageblatt*, 20 June 2015.

260 'Separation Reported Won by German Crown Princess', *New York Tribune*, 20 Nov. 1919; 'Divorce Case May Reveal More Sensational Chapters in Hohenzollern Family History', *Richmond Palladium*, 20 March 1920; 'Ex-Kaiser's Sons Seek Divorces', *South Bend News Times*, 14 Jan. 1920; 'Decree Granted Outcome of Cecilie's Divorce Suit', *New York Tribune*, 20 Nov. 1919; 'Ex-Kaiser's Son Facing Divorce', *San Francisco Chronicle*, 18 April 1919; 'Angebliche Scheidungsabsichten der ehemaligen deutschen Kronprinzessin', *Neue Freie Presse*, 13 April 1919; *Wiener Zeitung*, 17 April 1919.

261 'Exkronprinzens Sehnsucht', *Freiheit*, 16 July 1921; Haehner, 'Tagebuch, 9. 12. 1919, fol. 52'.

262 'Ex-Crown Princess of Germany to Wed an American?', *The Washington Post*, 15 July 1919.

263 Domela, *Der falsche Prinz*.

264 Kirsten, *Nennen Sie mich einfach Prinz*.

265 Sartre, *Kean*, 81, 165–6. See Brosman, *Sartre's Kean*, 109–22.

266 'Der Zollernprinz vor Gericht, *Vorwärts*, 16 April 1920; 'Hohenzollern Prince Fined for Assault', *New York Times*, 17 April 1920; 'Das "gerichtliche" Nachspiel zum Adlon Skandal', *Freiheit*, 17 April 1920; 'Ein Hohenzoller auf der Anklagebank', *Neues Wiener Journal*, 17 April 1920.

267 'Won to Jazz', *New Britain Herald*, 21 March 1928; Joachim de Hohenzollern, 'Chef d'orchestre dans un cabaret berlinois nous parle du Kaiser, son oncle', *Le Quotidien*, 6 June 1932.

268 Heinrich Petermeyer, 'Bei entthronten Fürstlichkeiten', *Neues Wiener Tageblatt*, 10 April 1921; *Neues Wiener Journal*, 10 Sept. 1932.

269 Jonas, *Der Kronprinz*, 206, 211–13.

270 'Une tournée de propagande de l'ex-Kronprinz en Prusse Orientale', *Excelsior*, 16 Oct. 1925.

271 See Jonas, *Der Kronprinz* , 213.

272 Gasteiger, *Kuno von Westarp*, 215–16, 224–5, 470.

273 'Protokoll einer Unterredung Ausfeld/Müldner am 11. 5. 1928', Bundesarchiv Berlin, R 72, No. 10, 68–70.

274 Gutsche, *Ein Kaiser im Exil*, 90.

275 Stahlhelm, 'Internes Schreiben an Wilhelm Prinz von Preussen, 27. 11. 1931', Bundesarchiv Berlin, R 72, No. 42, 182–3.

276 Ilsemann II, 169–71 (26 May and 11 June 1931).

277 'Rumbold to Henderson', 3 June 1931, Documents on British Foreign Policy 1919–1939, ser. 2, vol. 2, Reference: C 3847 / 11 / 18.

278 'Protokoll einer Unterredung Ausfeld/Müldner am 11. 5. 1928', BAB, R 42, No. 10, 68–70; 'Bericht an Müldner, 21. 7. 1929', BAB, R 42, No. 39, 255–6.

279 Gasteiger, *Kuno von Westarp*, 218.

280 Ilsemann II, 173–4 (13 Oct. 1931).

281 Ilsemann I, 250 (6 Nov. 1922).

282 'Kaiser Wilhelm über das Italien Mussolinis (Bericht über ein

Interview Wilhelms II. mit Pietro Solari in der Gazzetta del Popolo)',
Berliner Börsenzeitung, 6 May 1932.

283 Ilsemann II, 95–6 (12 May 1928).

284 'Brief des Kronprinzen an seinen Vater, 7. 5. 1928', in Ilsemann II, 95.

285 'Kronprinz Wilhelm an von Dryander 14.5.1924', GStA PK, Rep. 54, No. 21.

286 Malinowski/Funck, 'Masters of Memory'; Malinowski, *Vom König zum Führer*, 47–117.

287 Friedrich Wilhelm von Preussen, *Gott helfe*, 45–55.

288 Louis Ferdinand, *The Rebel Prince*, 239–40; Louis Ferdinand, Prinz von Preussen, *Im Strom der Geschichte*, 262; Urbach, *Useful Idiots*, 526–50.

289 Jonas, *Der Kronprinz*, 286.

290 Wichmann, *Waldemar Pabst*.

291 See evaluation Pyta/Orth, 147–9. The evaluators complete ignored the topic of Mussolini and Italian fascism, although Pyta did write of it on another occasion. See Pyta, *Hindenburg*, 675; Stribrny, *Der Versuch*, 208; Herre, *Kronprinz Wilhelm*, 212; and for additional information Hoepke, *Die deutsche Rechte*, 295–303; Petropoulos, *Royals*; and Schieder, *Das italienische Experiment*, 73–125.

292 See Urbach, *Zwischen Aktion und Reaktion*; Malinowski, *Vom König zum Führer*, 290–92, 413–21.

293 'Nationalsozialistische Huldigung für den Faschismus', *Freie Stimmen*, 20 Nov. 1932.

294 'The Revived Bayreuth Festival', *New York Herald*, 17 Aug. 1924; 'Wagner a Political Storm Center', *New York Times*, 24 Aug. 1924; Hamann, *Winifred Wagner*, 117–56.

295 'Politisches aus Bayreuth', *Neues Wiener Journal*, 6 Aug. 1925; 'In Bayreuth muss man "hoffähig" sein', *Die Stunde*, 5 Sept. 1925.

296 The Hohenzollerns were also conspicuously present at Chamberlain's funeral. See 'Chamberlains Begräbnis', *Der Wiener Tag*, 13 Jan. 1927; 'Die Einäscherung Houston Stewart Chamberlains', *Neues Wiener Journal*, 13 Jan. 1927; Hamann, *Winifred Wagner*, 157–8.

297 Hamann, *Winifred Wagner*, 73–100; Zelinsky, *Verfall, Vernichtung, Weltentrückung*.

298 'Stahlhelmer Friedrich Wilhelm', *Vorwärts*, 7 Oct. 1930 (morning).

299 Wilamowitz-Moellendorff, *Carin Göring*, 119–20.

300 *München und der Nationalsozialismus. Katalog des NS-Dokumentationszentrums München*, ed. Winfried Nerdinger, Munich 2015, 15–397.

301 Sichert, *Cecilienhof*, 28, 59.

302 Zajonz, *Das kronprinzliche Landhaus*, vol. 1, 61, 63.

303 'To Build Modern Home. Crown Prince William and Wife Break Away from Hohenzollern Tradition', *Boston Daily Globe*, 13 April 1913.

304 Zajonz, *Das kronprinzliche Landhaus*, vol. 1, 7.

305 Grünzig, *Für Deutschtum*, 311–16.

306 Friedrich Wilhelm Prinz von Preussen, 'Die Hohenzollern in Potsdam', *Schloss Cecilienhof und die Potsdamer Konferenz 1945*, 54.

307 Grünzig, *Für Deutschtum*, 311.

308 Sichert, *Cecilienhof*, 40.

309 Ibid., 136.

310 'Meine Kindheit in Oels / Schloss Oels, diverse Entwurfsschreiben, Alexandra oder Cecilie v. Preussen, zum Teil undatiert, um 1936', GSta PK, Nachlass Hilde Wagner, No. 82.

311 Ilsemann II, 257 (9 March 1934).

312 Reibnitz, *Wilhelm II. Und Hermine*, 122, 174 f.

313 Reibnitz, *Im Dreieck*, 201; Jonas, *Der Kronprinz*, 171; Mowrer, *Germany Puts the Clock Back*, 144; '4200 Parteibuchbeamte', *Vorwärts*, 30 April 1932.

314 Petzinna, *Erziehung zum deutschen Lebensstil*, 190–240.

315 Almeida, *Hakenkreuz und Kaviar*; Urbach, *Hitlers heimliche Helfer*.

316 On the political influence of the eastern aristocracy, see Hoffmann, *Der Skandal*.

317 Sichert, *Cecilienhof*, 105–7, on Prince Louis Ferdinand's 1938 wedding.

318 Ilsemann II, 259–63, 269–70 (May–August 1934).

319 'Wilhelm II. an Frhr. v. Sell', in Ilsemann II, 150 (20 Oct. 1930).

320 'Heinrich Prinz von Preussen an seinen Bruder Wilhelm II., 12. 3. 1924', Nachlass John Röhl, Berlin, vol. 86, fol. 93.

321 'Koerber an Kronprinz, 25. 6. 1932 (mit Bezug auf frühere Jahre)', in Koerber Papers, A807 / Ab, Folder 1931–1936.

322 That was the attitude of Ilsemann and Prince Friedrich Wilhelm von Preussen in *Gott helfe*, 52–157.

323 'The Ex-Kaiser at Doorn', *New York Herald Tribune*, 27 May 1928; Urbach, *Useful Idiots*, 20; Viereck, *The Kaiser on Trial*.

324 Dominic Angeloch, 'Ein ambivalenter Fanatiker. Sigmund Freuds Briefwechsel mit dem Poeten, Publizisten und Propagandisten George Sylvester Viereck (1919–1936)', *Psyche. Zeitschrift für Psychoanalyse*, 68 (2014), 633–65, here 659.

325 Fritz Solmitz, 'Die Pfiffigen und der deutsche Staat', *Salzburger Wacht*, 23 Aug. 1927; abridged as 'Republik und Spiesserliebe', *Linzer Tagblatt*, 23 Aug. 1927.

326 'Rund um Doorn', *Linzer Tagblatt*, 30 July 1931.

327 Röhl, *Wilhelm II.*, vol. 3, 1295.

328 'Abteilung IA, Bericht vom 18.10.1930', Landeshauptarchiv Brandenburg, Rep. 2 A I Pol No. 1100, 272–302, here 290.

329 Machtan, *Der Kaisersohn*, 177, 417.

330 'Vernehmung August Wilhelm Prinz von Preussens in Nürnberg, 14. 5. 1947', USHMM, Kempner Papers, Box 313, Folder 19, 4.

331 'Politisierende Prinzen', *Der Kuckuck*, 14 June 1931.

332 'Die Stiege zum Hohenzollern-Thron', *Leuchtrakete* 11 (March 1933).

Chapter 3: Almost a King

1 Schneider, *Verhüllter Tag*, 102.

2 Prince Louis Ferdinand, *The Rebel Prince*, 317.

3 Friedrich Wilhelm von Preussen, *Gott helfe*, 88.

4 *Fridericus*, 20 March 1933, in GStA PK, BPH, Rep. 192, Nachlass Dommes, vol. 14.

5 Granier, *Magnus von Levetzow*, 174; Stribrny, *Der Versuch*, 203.

6 'Der Kandidat des Kronprinzen', *Vossische Zeitung*, 5 March 1932.

7 Ilsemann II, 157 (27 Jan. 1931).

8 Machtan, *Der Kaisersohn*, 230.

9 Dietrich, *Zwölf Jahre mit Hitler*, 244.

10 'Kronprinzen im Wahlfeldzug', *Die Stunde*, 10 March 1932; 'Hohenzollernprinzen im Wahlkampf', *Altonaer Nachrichten*, 10 March 1932.

Notes

11 'L'ex-kronprinz déploie la plus grande activité', *Paris-Soir*, 11 March 1932.

12 This was the plausible reading of the situation in an otherwise mistaken letter from Heinrich Brüning to Joachim von Ostau on 19 Feb. 1951. See Brüning Papers, Harvard University Archives, Cambridge, MA, HUG (FP) Acc. 13634, Box 1, Folder 5.

13 'Bericht Günther von Einems, 1. 4. 1932', BAMA, Nachlass Einem, vol. 29, 123–31.

14 Ostau, 'Offener Brief an Hitler', *Fridericus*, 3 Oct. 1932. Ostau was barred from the Nazi Party that month.

15 Herre, *Kronprinz Wilhelm*, 206.

16 Jonas, *Der Kronprinz*, 225–30.

17 Granier, *Magnus von Levetzow*, 174. See also Friedrich, *Wer spielte falsch?*, 14–16.

18 See Wolfgang Stribrny, 'Der Versuch einer Kandidatur des Kronprinzen Wilhelm bei der Reichspräsidentenwahl 1932', in Heinen/Schoeps (eds.), *Geschichte in der Gegenwart*, 199–210; Pyta, *Hindenburg*, 673–8; Machtan, *Der Kaisersohn*, 238–43; Jonas, *Der Kronprinz*, 224–31; Granier, *Magnus von Levetzow*, 173–5; Ilsemann II, 188, 190–92, 199; Herre, *Kronprinz Wilhelm*, 203–10; Jonas, *Der Kronprinz*, 224–31, Sweetman, *Unforgotten Crowns*, 310–17; Vogelsang, *Reichswehr*, 155–6; Bracher, *Auflösung*, 420.

19 Ilsemann II, 243 (2 Dec. 1933).

20 Wilhelm II., 'Allerhöchste Ordre (April 1932) sowie ein Schreiben Wilhelms II. an Hausminister und Söhne (15. 4. 1932)', GStA PK, BPH, Rep. 192, Nachlass Dommes, No. 14.

21 'Wilhelm II. an Kronprinz und an Oskar Prinz von Preussen, 5.4.1932', GStA PK, BPH, Rep. 192, Nachlass Dommes, No. 14.

22 'Kronprinz an Selasen-Selasinsky, 1. 4. 1932', BAMA, N432/10. Wilhelm stressed the services of Joachim von Ostau as a mediator.

23 'Kronprinz an Günther von Einem, 1. 4. 1932', BAMA, Nachlass Einem, vol. 29, 108.

24 'Eugen Zimmermann an Hermine, 14. 6. 1932', in GStA PK, Rep. 192, Nachlass Eugen Zimmermann, No. 88.

25 'Hitler wollte den Exkronprinzen zum Reichspräsidenten machen', in *Arbeiter Zeitung*, 8. 4. 1932; 'Crown Princes Candidacy Vetoed',

Chicago Daily Tribune, 8 April 1932, 5; Hans Schäffer, 'Tagebucheintrag, 15. 4. 1932', in Hans Schäffer-Papers, Series II: Diaries,
1924–1933.

26 *Vossische Zeitung*, 6 and 9 June 1932; 'Papen bereitet Monarchie vor',
Volkspost, 21 Oct. 1932; 'Der Ex-Kronprinz will Kaiser werden', *Volkspost*, 14 Oct. 1932.

27 The article went so far as to claim that the crown prince wished to
become Reich administrator. *Der Wahre Jakob*, 19 Nov. 1932.

28 'Hitler verspricht Exkaiser den Thron. Hohenzollern sollen wieder
herrschen – Gegenleistung für den Naziführer', *Welt am Abend*, 21 April
1932; 'Anweisungen aus Doorn. Wilhelm II. Hitlers Hauptaktionär',
MM, *Montag Morgen*, 4 April 1932; 'Wer ist für Hitler? Die Aris-
tokraten!', *Arbeiter-Zeitung*, 24 Sept. 1932.

29 'Soll der Ex-Kronprinz Reichsverweser werden?', *Welt am Abend*, 3
June 1932; 'Deutsche Monarchisten sondieren in London', *Vossische
Zeitung*, 22 June 1932 (evening); 'Sphinx auf Oels', *Vossische Zeitung*
(evening), 9 June 1932.

30 *Der Gerade Weg*, 10 July 1932. See also Rudolf Morsey, *Fritz Gerlich. Ein
früher Gegner Hitlers und des Nationalsozialismus*, Paderborn 2016,
185–248.

31 Hans Schäffer, 'Tagebucheintrag, 7. 6. 1932, 17. 6. 1932, 15. 8. 1932',
Hans Schäffer-Papers, Series II: Diaries, 1924–1933, 568, 590, 747–8.

32 'Vers une proche restauration des Hohenzollern outre-Rhin?', *Le
Phare de la Loire*, 18 Oct. 1932; 'Le Reich à la veille d'une restauration?',
L'Ami du peuple, 17 Oct. 1932.

33 'La propagande pour le retour des Hohenzollern prend en Allemagne
un charactère presque officiel', *L'Ami du peuple*, 18 Oct. 1932;
'Réflexions', *Aux écoutes*, 13 Aug. 1932; 'L'ex-kronprinz proposerait la
restauration des Hohenzollern', *Le Quotidien*, 12 Oct. 1932.

34 '20 000 Cheer Five Ex-Princes in Berlin', *New York Tribune*, 3 Sept. 1932.

35 Georges Simenon, 'La génération du désordre', *Voilà*, 22 April 1933,
abridged as Georges Simenon, 'Hitler im Fahrstuhl', in Lubrich (ed.),
Reisen ins Reich 1933 bis 1945, 45–8.

36 *La Charente*, 31 Aug. 1932.

37 'Ex-Kaiser Wilhelm Will Soon Be Back, Is Son's Assertion', *The Globe*,

30 Aug. 1932; 'Ex-Kaiser Sees Hohenzollerns Reigning Again', *New York Herald Tribune*, 25 Sept. 1932; 'Hohenzollern's Return Seen by Prince Wilhelm', *The Washington Post*, 25 July 1932.

38 William Shirer, 'German Crown Prince in Vienna Plot Suspected', *Chicago Daily Tribune*, 23 July 1932; 'German Prince Accused of Plot to Seize Rule', *Chicago Daily Tribune*, 12 Oct. 1932.

39 Sweetman, *Unforgotten Crowns*, 354. Ronald Graham to John Simon, 14 Nov. 1932, Woodward and Butler, *Documents on British Foreign Policy*, Series 2, VI, 83n.

40 'Hitler Playing Leading Role in Monarchy Plan', *The Minneapolis Star*, 10 June 1932. See also 'Son and Ex-Kaiser Talk on Restoring Hohenzollern', *The Austin Statesman*, 24 June 1932; 'Germany Deeply Stirred by Rumored Plan to Restore Monarchy', Chinese Newspaper collection, 6 June 1932; 'Hohenzollern Restoration Looms Large in Germany', *The China Press* (Shanghai), 19 Oct. 1932; 'Hohenzollern Stock Rises Under New Regime', *New York Times*, 14 July 1932; 'Hohenzollern Move Seen', *New York Times*, 22 Nov. 1932; 'No Hohenzollern Restoration: Chancellor Denies Reports', *Irish Times*, 25 Oct. 1932; 'Hindenburg May Quit Presidency', *Daily Boston Globe*, 1 Dec. 1932. See also the astonishingly detailed and precise report by the American socialist Ludwig Lore, 'Will the Hohenzollern Return?', *Current History* (New York), 1 Dec. 1932.

41 Kaufmann, *Monarchism in the Weimar Republic*, 210–13. See also the hard-to-distinguish mix of fantasy and reality in *The Berlin Diaries*.

42 Thomas Theodor Heine, 'Das neue Märchen vom Froschkönig', *Simplicissimus*, 13 Nov. 1932.

43 'Gerüchte um den früheren Kronprinzen', *Vossische Zeitung*, 12 Oct. 1932; 'Umtriebe des Ex-Kronprinzen', *Vorwärts*, 11 Oct. 1932; 'Papens Hilfstruppen', *Vorwärts*, 16 Oct. 1932.

44 *N. S. – Der Nationale Sozialist*, 6 Sept. 1930.

45 'Tagebucheintrag Hans Schäffer, 15. 4. 1932', Hans Schäffer Papers, Series II: Diaries, 1924–1933, 461; Edgar Ansel Mowrer, *Germany Puts the Clock Back*, revised edition New York 1939, 140–45 (originally 1933).

46 'Parteigenossen', *Der Kuckuck*, 22 May 1932; 'Die Hitlerei im Golde des Exkaisers', *Salzburger Wacht*, 5 April 1932; 'Wer finanziert Hitler?', *Prager*

Tageblatt, 1 July 1932; 'Hitlers Geldgeber', *Linzer Volksblatt*, 9 April 1932; Hans Petersen, 'Wer finanziert Hitler?', *Der rote Aufbau*, June 1932.

47 'Max Weber, Hitler und das Haus Hohenzollern, Bericht vom 21. 4. 1934', Bayerisches HStA V, Abteilung Nachlässe und Sammlungen, Nachlass Gerlich 49, Dokument 32/Z/49/1842. Thanks to Paul Hoser for alerting me to this source.

48 Quietus [Walther Karsch], 'Hitlers Finanzen', *Weltbühne*, 19 April 1932, 584.

49 'Der Hakenkreuzkaiser', *Arbeiter Zeitung*, 24 May 1932.

50 'Die SA wird finanziert. Ein feudaler Bettelsack', *Vorwärts*, 30 April 1932.

51 Karina Urbach, 'Militarismus und echte Führerliebe', *Taz*, 31 Jan. 2021; Machtan, *Der Kaisersohn*, 223.

52 Paul, *Aufstand der Bilder*, Bild No. 22; Parteigenossen, *Der Kuckuck*, 22 May 1932; Petropoulos, *Royals and the Reich*, 120.

53 'Le Kronprinz électeur d'Adolf Hitler', *La Liberté*, 6 April 1932.

54 Herre, *Kronprinz Wilhelm*, 210–11.

55 Goebbels, *Tagebücher*, 294–5 (1 and 3 June 1932).

56 '195,000 German vets pledged to Junkers', *Daily Boston Globe*, 5 Sept. 1932; 'The First Official German Recognition of the Stahlhelm: A Great Rally in Berlin – The March-Past before the Chancellor and Other Ministers on the Tempelhoferfeld', *The Illustrated London News*, 10 Sept. 1932.

57 'En Allemagne républicaine: 180000 Casques d'Acier en uniforme ont defilé durant trois heures sur le terrain de Tempelhof', *Le Quotidien*, 5 Sept. 1932. See also the front pages of *L'Ouest-Éclair*, 5 Sept.1932, *L'Excelsior*, 5 Sept. 1932, *L'Écho de Paris*, 5 Sept. 1932, and 'La grande parade: L'armée verte défile au pas de l'oie devant l'ex-kronprinz et vingt princes déchus', *L'Écho d'Alger*, 5 Sept. 1932.

58 '180000 Casques d'Acier ont défilé aujourd'hui sur le terrain de Tempelhof', *Paris-Soir*, 5 Sept. 1932.

59 'L'armée du fascisme et de la dictature des trusts. Devant von Papen et l'ex-Kronprinz, 160 000 Casques d'acier défilent à Berlin', *L'Humanité*, 5 Sept. 1932.

60 'Après la parade de Tempelhof. Les princes allemands relèvent la tête', *La Dépêche du Berry*, 7 Sept. 1932.

Notes

61 'Le kronprinz et le chancelier von Papen ont assisté à la projection d'un film dans un cinéma de Berlin sur la parade des Casques d'Acier qu'ils présidèrent', *Excelsior*, 12 Oct. 1932.

62 *Schlesische Zeitung*, 3 April 1932.

63 'Der Standpunkt des Stahlhelms: Über den Parteien!', *Neue Preussische Kreuzzeitung*, 1 April 1932, supplement.

64 *Schlesische Zeitung*, 3 April 1932; 'Erklärung des Kronprinzen', *Der Tag*, 3 April 1932; 'Das Ehrenwort des Kronprinzen. Aufruf für Hitler', *Vossische Zeitung*, 3 April 1932; 'Der Kronprinz für Hitler', *Berliner Lokal-Anzeiger*, 3 April 1932; 'Der richtige Mann für Hitler. Der Exkronprinz als führende Person des deutschen Geisteslebens', *Vorwärts*, 3 April 1932; 'Väter und Söhne', *Frankfurter Zeitung*, 3 April 1932; 'Eine Kundgebung aus Oels', *Germania*, 3 April 1932; 'Gebrochenes Ehrenwort. Der frühere Kronprinz wirbt für Hitler', *Berliner Tageblatt*, 3 April 1932; 'Der gewesene deutsche Kronprinz wählt Hitler', *Reichspost*, 3 April 1932; 'Der Kronprinz als Wahlhelfer. Ein Geheimabkommen mit dem Hause Hohenzollern', *Die Welt am Sonntag*, 4 April 1932. See also the crown prince's rejection of a call to vote for Hindenburg, BLHA, Rep. 37 Lübbenau, No. 6643; Bracher, *Auflösung*, 477; Gutsche, *Ein Kaiser im Exil*, 140; Herre, *Kronprinz Wilhelm*, 209–10; Jonas, *Der Kronprinz*, 230–31; Pomp, *Landadel*, 213–16; Berghahn, *Stahlhelm*, 195–219.

65 'Gewaltige Agitation', *Prager Tageblatt*, 3 April 1932; 'Der deutsche Kronprinz für Hitler. Sensationelle Erklärung', *Neues Wiener Journal*, 3 April 1932; 'Der Kronprinz wählt Hitler', *Das Kleine Blatt* (Vienna), 3 April 1932; 'Der neue Wahlkampf in Deutschland. Der frühere Kronprinz für Hitler', *Arbeiter-Zeitung*, 3 April 1932; 'Das Eintreten des Exkronprinzen für Hitler', *Neue Freie Presse*, 4 April 1932; 'Exkaiser Wilhelm finanziert die Nazi [sic]', *Der Morgen* (Vienna), 4 April 1932; 'Exkaiser Wilhelm für Hitler. Die Gründe des Aufrufs des Ex-Kronprinzen', *Der Tag* (Vienna), 4 April 1932; 'Sensation im deutschen Wahlkampf. Eine Erklärung des früheren Kronprinzen für Hitler', *Salzburger Volksblatt*, 4 April 1932; 'Nach dem Burgfrieden', *Salzburger Chronik*, 4 April 1932; 'Das Eintreten des Exkronprinzen für Hitler', *Neue Freie Presse*, 4 April 1932; 'Hohenzollernprinzen gegen Hindenburg und für Hitler', *Grazer Tageblatt*, 4

Notes

April 1932; 'Exkaiser Wilhelm und der Kronprinz für Hitler', *Rote Fahne* (Vienna), 5 April 1932; 'Wilhelm II. als "Hauptaktionär" Hitlers', *Die Stunde*, 5 April 1932.

66 '"Je voterai pour Hitler" fait placarder le Kronprinz', *L'Action Française*, 3 April 1932; '"Je voterai pour Hitler!" déclare l'ex-kronprinz', *L'Écho de Paris*, 3 April 1932; 'L'ex-kronprinz Wilhelm se rallie à Hitler', *Le Figaro*, 3 April 1932; 'Le manifeste de l'ex-kronprinz', *L'Ouest-Éclair* (Rennes), 5 April 1932; 'Hitler et le Kronprinz', *L'Ère nouvelle*, 5 April 1932; 'Qui inspira le manifeste du kronprinz?', *L'Intransigeant*, 5 April 1932; 'Le Kronprinz électeur d'Adolf Hitler', *La Liberté*, 6 April 1932; 'Nazis Prepare for Attack. Hitler Forces Plan Strenuous Drive – Former Crown Prince Supports It', *New York Times*, 3 April 1932; 'Former Crown Heir to Vote for Hitler', *The Washington Post*, 3 April 1932; 'Hitler Wins Vote of Ex-Kaiser's Heir for "Nazis": Former Crown Prince to Act in Support of Policy of Closed Nationalist Front', *New York Herald Tribune*, 3 April 1932; 'Ex-Crown Prince of Germany for Hitler Candidacy', *The Austin American*, 3 April 1932; 'Former Crown Prince Comes Out for Hitler', *The Sun* (Baltimore), 3 April 1932; 'Ex-Kaiser's Heir Declares for Hitler', *Daily Boston Globe*, 3 April 1932; 'Presidency of Germany. Ex-Crown Prince and the Nazis', *The Times*, 4 April 1932; ' "No Gentleman". Ex-Crown Prince Criticized Asking Votes for Hitler', *The Scotsman*, 4 April 1932; 'Crown Prince and Hitler', *Irish Times*, 4 April 1932; 'Political Sensation in Germany. Prince's Manifesto', *Times of India* (Mumbai), 4 April 1932; 'Hitler's Whirlwind Tour of Cities Week's Campaign Supported by Ex-Crown Prince', *The Manchester Guardian*, 4 April 1932; 'Manifesto Issued. Ex-Crown Prince Creates a Sensation', *South China Morning Post*, 4 April 1932; 'Hitler's Crown Prince', *The Star* (Christchurch, NZ), 4 April 1932; 'Hitler Can Have Him. Crown Prince as Voter', *Ashburton Guardian* (NZ), 4 April 1932.

67 *Das Kleine Blatt*, 6 April 1932.

68 *Chicago Daily Tribune*, 3 April 1932.

69 Stribrny, *Der Versuch*, 208. Historian Wolfgang Stribrny (1935–2011), a professor at the University of Flensburg, was the spokesman of the 'Zollern Circle', which was founded in 1969 at Hohenzollern Castle,

575

a Knight of Justice of the Order of St John and the president of the Prussian Institute, whose stated goals included the 'reconstitution of Prussia wherever it is desired'.

70 Jonas, *Der Kronprinz*, 230.

71 Herre, *Kronprinz Wilhelm*, 209.

72 See *Der Tag, Germania* and *Berliner Tageblatt*, 3 and 4 April 1932; *MM der Montag Morgen*, 4 April 1932; *Eisleber Tageblatt*, 5 April 1932; *Berliner Tageblatt*, 8 April 1932.

73 *Welt am Montag*, 4 April 1932.

74 'L'Ordre de Doorn', *L'Africain. Hebdomadaire Illustré*, 22 April 1932.

75 For conservative voices endorsing Hindenburg, see *Der Ring*, 15 April 1932, and on the broader context and the fissures within German aristocratic society, see Malinowski, *König*, 355–7.

76 'Die Selbstvernichtung des Monarchismus', *Tägliche Rundschau*, 5 April 1932.

77 Granier, *Magnus von Levetzow*, 173.

78 *Völkischer Beobachter*, 13, 27 and 29 March and 3, 4 April 1932; letters from Levetzow to Göring (25 March 1932) and Class (3 March 1932), in Granier, *Magnus von Levetzow*, 333–5. On the regional parliamentary election, see *Salzburger Wacht*, 5 April 1932.

79 Crown Prince to Lord Rothermere, 20 June 1934, The Hoover Institution Archives, Stanford, Collection Number 77020. See also Machtan, *Der Kaisersohn*, 244; Hohenlohe, *Stephanie*, 100 f. Although born a bourgeois in Vienna, Hohenlohe's mother Princess Stéphanie zu Hohenlohe-Waldenburg-Schillingsfürst's rise up the social ladder epitomized in some respects the connection between the high nobility and the Nazi leadership. See Urbach, *Go-Betweens*, 217–78.

80 Salomon Grumbach, 'Zwischen zwei Wahlen in Deutschland', *Freie Presse (La Presse Libre)*, 19 April 1932.

81 Evaluation Malinowski, 66–7; evaluation Pyta/Orth, 49–61 evaluation Clark, 8–9; evaluation Brandt, 47–50; and Bender/Hillgruber, *Hat der ehemalige Kronprinz*, 430–31.

82 Friedrich Wilhelm von Preussen, *Gott helfe*, 89.

83 Weiss/ Hoser (eds.), *Die Deutschnationalen und die Zerstörung der Weimarer Republik*, (25 March 1932), 185.

Notes

84 Friedrich Wilhelm von Preussen, *Gott helfe*, 91; Ilsemann II, 192 (20 May 1932).

85 Blasius, *Weimars Ende*, 41–54; Bernd Ulrich, 'Letzter Abwehrversuch', radio report Deutschlandfunk, 13 April 2007.

86 Funck, *Schock und Chance*; Schwarzmüller, 'Generalfeldmarschall August von Mackensen', in Grawe, *Die militärische Elite*, 215–26.

87 'Görings Reichstagsrede gegen Brüning-Groener / Groener antwortet stockend und aufgeregt', *Grazer Tageblatt*, 11 May 1932; Winkler, *Weimar*, 464–74.

88 'Kronprinz an Groener, 14. 4. 1932', GStA PK, BPH Rep. 192, Nachlass Dommes, No. 7. See also Jonas, *Der Kronprinz*, 232–3; Friedrich Wilhelm von Preussen, *Gott helfe*, 213–14.

89 'Brief des Kronprinzen, Ende Juni 1932, unter anderem an Hindenburg, in Kopien an Berg, Schleicher, Hindenburg, Papen und Neurath, Juni 1932', BAMA, N 42, No. 27, 43–9.

90 Friedrich Wilhelm von Preussen, *Gott helfe*, 214.

91 'Groener an Kronprinz, April 1932 (Entwurf)', BAMA, Nachlass Groener, No. 152, 69–70.

92 'Immer feste druff! Der gewesene Kronprinz für die Nazis', *Arbeiter-Zeitung* (Vienna), 16 Oct. 1932; 'Der Nazi-Kronprinz', *Linzer Tageblatt*, 17 Oct. 1932; 'Ex-Crown Prince Tried to Control War Office', *Chicago Daily Tribune*, 16 Oct. 1932.

93 Carl von Ossietzky, 'Das Verbot der SA', *Die Weltbühne*, 19 April 1932, 580.

94 'Aus der Gesellschaft', *Sport im Bild* 9, 1932.

95 'Much under discussion in German Political Circles – The Former Crown Prince', *The Illustrated London News*, 11 June 1932.

96 Jonas, *Der Kronprinz*, 234.

97 *Chicago Daily Tribune*, 7 May 1932. See also Kellerhoff, *Geschichte in Geschichten*, 180–81.

98 *Hitler aus nächster Nähe*, 86–91.

99 Dietrich, *Zwölf Jahre mit Hitler*, 245; Machtan, *Der Kaisersohn*, 231–4.

100 'Das Programm der NSDAP. NSDAP und monarchische Frage', *Unsere Partei*, 15 April 1932.

101 Cartoon, 'Intermezzo im Kaiserhof', *Unsere Partei*, 24 Oct. 1932.

102 'Feine Leute in der NSDAP', *Unsere Partei*, 1 Oct. 1932.

103 'Unsere Partei', 13 April 1932, 2nd special edition, 100. See also *Vorwärts*, 19 April 1932 (morning).

104 'Der Stahlhelm marschiert' and 'Splitter', *Unsere Partei*, 15 Sept. 1932; Longerich, *Goebbels: A Biography*, 28–153.

105 Pomp, *Bauern und Grossgrundbesitzer*, 304–88.

106 'Nationalsozialistisches Untermenschentum', *Unsere Partei*, 15 Oct. 1932.

107 'Deutschnationale Riesenkundgebung in der Hasenheide. Bolschewistische Methoden der NSDAP', *Unsere Partei*, 8 Oct. 1932.

108 'Eine deutsche Rechtsfront? Bemühungen des Exkronprinzen', *Grazer Tageblatt*, 24 Oct. 1932; 'Der deutsche Exkronprinz für Steigerung des Wehrwillens', *Neue Freie Presse*, 15 Oct. 1932; 'Der Nazi-Kronprinz', *Linzer Tageblatt*, 17 Oct. 1932.

109 'Nazi-Stahlhelm Clashes', *The Times*, 17 Oct. 1932.

110 'Kronprinz an Hitler, 25. 9. 1932', 'Kronprinz an seinen Vater, 1. 10. 1932', 'Hitler an Kronprinz, 28. 9. 1932', GStA PK, BPH Rep. 53 and Rep. 54, also cited in Friedrich Wilhelm von Preussen, *Gott helfe*, 99–106.

111 Hans Schäffer, 'Tagebucheintrag, 7. 6. 1932', Hans Schäffer-Papers, Series II: Diaries, 1924–1933, 568.

112 Herre, *Kronprinz Wilhelm*, 214.

113 Goebbels, *Tagebücher*, 1 June 1932.

114 Machtan, *Der Kaisersohn*, 246.

115 Selasen-Selasinsky to the Crown Prince, 13 Dec. 1932, N 432/2, 40–44.

116 'Berg an Sela, 22. 11. 1932, und Berg an Sela, 17. 1. 1933', BAMA, N 432/4; 'Selasen-Selasinsky an Kronprinz, 13. 12. 1932', BAMA N 432/2. See also 'Nationalsozialisten gegen Kronprinz Wilhelm', *Salzburger Chronik*, 19 Nov. 1932; 'Kube gegen Kronprinz', *Vossische Zeitung*, 19 Nov. 1932 (morning).

117 'Hitlers Kampfjahr', *Vossische Zeitung*, 19 April 1933 (morning).

118 Wilhelm Kube, 'Moskau, Monarchie oder Nationalsozialismus', *Preussischer Pressedienst*, 18 Nov. 1932. See also the conservative-nationalist response in *Unsere Partei*, 2 Dec. 1932.

119 'Julius Friedrich Lehmann an Selasen-Selasinsky, 6. 7. 1921', BAMA, N

432/3; 'Krückmann an Selasen-Selasinsky', 21 Nov. 1924, BAMA, N432/7.

120 Goebbels, *Tagebücher*, vol. 2/III, 118 (29 January 1933); Hitler, *Mein Kampf. Eine kritische Edition*, vol. I, 250–53, vol. II, 42. For more context, see Malinowski, *Vom König zum Führer*, 157–97, 482–8, 520–31.

121 'Müldner an Selasen-Selasinsky', 14. Aug. 1924, BAMA, N 432/3.

122 See the article by Wilhelm Kube and Reich Administrator Wilhelm Friedrich Loeper, 'An die Monarchisten', *Gubener Zeitung*, 26 Jan. 1934.

123 'Nationalsozialistisches Bekenntnis zu Hohenzollern', *Reichspost*, 3 June 1932; 'Nationalsozialisten und Hohenzollern', *Grazer Tag*, 4 June 1932.

124 See Günther, *Rassenkunde Europas*; Günther, *Rassenkunde des deutschen Volkes*. For more detail, see Malinowski, *Vom König zum Führer*, 516–31.

125 Günther, *Adel und Rasse*, 82–6.

126 Müller, *Wilhelm II.*, 12 and 77–80.

127 See Darré, *Neuadel aus Blut*.

128 Ibid., 11, 163.

129 'Richard Walter Darré', *Nationalsozialistische Landpost*, 27 Nov. 1932.

130 'Wie lange noch, Darré?', *Die Partei*, 2 Dec. 1932; 'Der Jude Saalfeld in der NSDAP', *Die Partei*, 15 Oct. 1932.

131 See Corni/Gies, *Blut und Boden*; Gies, *Richard Walter Darré*.

132 Jasper, *Gescheiterte Zähmung*, 123; Thamer, *Verführung und Gewalt*, 220–21.

133 'Wilhelm II. an Sell 22. 10. 1932', GStA PK, Rep. 192, Nachlass Sell, No. 2.

134 See Urbach, *Go Betweens*, Malinowski, *Nazis and Nobles*; Petropoulos, *Royals and the Reich*; Schmeling, *Josias Erbprinz zu Waldeck*.

135 'Carl Landeskroener an Holtz [Fridericus], 15. 4. 1932', BAMA, 432/2.

136 Müller, *Die Thronfolger*, 104–6.

137 Bredow, *Notizen*, 191–4.

138 See the papers of Crown Prince Wilhelm's friend Princess Stephanie zu Hohenlohe-Waldenburg-Schillingsfürst, The Hoover Institution Archives, Stanford, Collection Number 77020.

139 Evaluation Pyta/Orth, 28–31.

140 'Arthur Berg an Selasen-Selasinsky, 22. 1. 1933', 'Kronprinz an Wilhelm II., 13. 11. 1932', Nachlass John Röhl, Berlin, vol. 90.

142 'Kronprinz an Selasen-Selasinsky, 14. 12. 1932'; 'Selasen-Selasinsky an Heinrichsbauer, 22. 12. 1932'; 'Chef des Stahlhelm-Nachrichtendienstes an Bundesführer des Stahlhelms, 15. 11. 1932', BAMA, N 432/8.

143 'Märchen über Prinz August Wilhelm', Völkischer Beobachter, 13 Jan. 1933.

144 'Hans Schäffer, Tagebucheintrag, 17. 6. 1932', Hans Schäffer-Papers, Series II: Diaries, 1924–1933, 590.

145 'Kronprinz an Selasen-Selasinsky, 14. 12. 1932', BAMA, N 432/2.

146 'Kronprinz an Schleicher, 3. 12. 1932', BAMA, N 24/88.

147 'Hörauf an Kronprinz, 12. 1. 1933', BAMA, N 42/23, 58-58 A.

148 'Müldner an Selasen-Selasinsky, 8. 11. 1932', in BAMA, 432/3.

149 'Hörauf an Kronprinz zur Weitergabe an Schleicher, 21. 12. 1932', BAMA, N 42/23, 47–48 A. The Pyta/Orth evaluation (42) refers to this letter but doesn't cite the passage in question.

150 'Selasen-Selasinsky an Kronprinz, 16. 12. 1932', in BAMA, Nachlass Schleicher, No. 13, 10–11.

151 At a large DNVP meeting in September 1932, the landowner Elard von Oldenburg-Januschau spoke of his impression 'that Hitler is still the only sensible person among them', in Unsere Partei, 1 October 1932; see also Deutsche Allgemeine Zeitung, 28 September 1932.

152 Kershaw, Der Hitler-Mythos, 107–63; Michael Wildt, 'Wenn das der Führer wüsste', Die Zeit, 30 March 2000.

153 Mommsen, Verspielte Freiheit, 674–86; Winkler, Weimar, 560–70; Stachura, Gregor Strasser; Bracher, Die Auflösung, 662–85; Kershaw, Hitler, 492–501; Evans, The Coming of the Third Reich, 302–3. See also the differing interpretations of the latter-day evaluations in Pyta/Orth, Nicht alternativlos, 423–38.

154 Kissenkoetter, Strasser, 175.

155 Turner, Die Grossunternehmer, 234–7, 316–17, 348–9.

156 Peter Hayes, '"A Question Mark with Epaulettes?" Kurt von Schleicher and Weimar Politic', The Journal of Modern History, 52, 1

Notes

(1980), 35–65; Turner, 'The Myth of Chancellor Von Schleicher's Querfront Strategy', 673–81; Jones, 'Taming the Nazi Beast'.

157 Turner, *The Myth*, 681. Strangely, the Pyta/Orth evaluation ignores Turner's work.

158 Sven Felix Kellerhoff, 'Es gab 1933 eine Alternative zu Hitler', *Die Welt*, 20 March 2021.

159 *Daily Mail*, 6 June 1932. See also 'Rothermere Predicts Hohenzollern Return', *New York Times*, 6 June 1932; and *New York Times*, 7 and 10 June 1932; 'Rothermere Predicts Hohenzollerns Will Be Restored in Germany', *The Hartford Courant*, 6 June 1932.

160 'Mémoires van Wilhelm II', *Dagblad van Noord-Brabant*, 21 Nov. 1932.

161 'Hindenburg-Krise. Ex-Kronprinz soll Reichsverweser werden', *Die Stunde*, 31 Jan. 1933.

162 'Hinein ins Dritte Reich!' (cartoon), *Der Abend* (Vienna), 31 Jan. 1933; 'Restaurationspläne', *MM der Montag Morgen*, 13 Feb. 1933.

163 Friedrich Freiherr Hiller von Gaertringen, 'Zur Beurteilung des Monarchismus in der Weimarer Republik', in Jasper (ed.), *Tradition und Reform*, 138–85.

164 Winston Churchill on 8 April 1945, cited in 'The Royal Legacy', *The Washington Post*, 30 Dec. 1995.

165 Winston Churchill, telegram of 26 April 1945 to Hughe Knatchbull-Hugessen, British Ambassador to Turkey, quoted in Gilbert, *Road to Victory*, 1314.

166 See evaluation Pyta/Orth; Pyta/Orth, *Nicht alternativlos*.

167 This is particularly drastic in the case of Hasselhorn, *Königstod, der Fall*.

168 See Riotte, *Der Monarch im Exil*; Mansel/Riotte (eds.), *Monarchy and Exile*; Müller, *Die Thronfolger*.

169 Kantorowicz, *The King's Two Bodies*, 3.

170 It's no accident that the third volume of Tolkien's *Lord of the Rings* is entitled the *Return of the King*.

171 Higham, *King Arthur*.

172 Heine, *Reisebilder*, in *Sämtliche Werke*, 181.

173 See Kershaw, *Hitler Mythos*; Herbst, *Hitlers Charisma*.

174 François-Poncet, *Memoiren*, cited in Sichert, *Cecilienhof*, 86 f.

581

175 *Deutschlandbericht der Sopade*, November 1935, A28.

176 Ilsemann I, 116 (18 Oct. 1919).

177 Ibid., 144–5 (8–12 Feb. 1920).

178 Ibid., 157–63 (September–November 1920).

179 Ibid., 190 (6 Sept. 1921).

180 Ibid., 263, 269 (4 Jan. 1923, 9 April 1923).

181 Ibid., 267–8 (9 April 1923).

182 Ibid., 272 (9 April 1923).

183 See Jones/Pyta (eds.), *Ich bin der letzte Preusse*; Gasteiger, *Kuno von Westarp*.

184 Ilsemann I, 274 (9 April 1923); 'Ex-Kaiser Denies Knowing of Plots', *New York Times*, 31 July 1923.

185 'Ronald Graham to Earl Curzon', *Documents on British Foreign Policy 1919–1939*, ser. 1, vol. 5, Reference: 164126/9019/39 (17 Dec. 1919).

186 'Die Qual der Wahl. Unstimmigkeiten im Lager der Monarchisten', *Vorwärts*, 10 June 1922.

187 Ilsemann I, 278–9 (24/25 May 1923).

188 Ilsemann II, 62, 73, 78, (7 July 1927, 24 Nov. 1927).

189 Ibid., 87, 88 (27/28 Feb. 1928).

190 Ibid., 23 (6 April 1925), 84, 88, 92, 96, 100, 108, 181 (January 1928–January 1932).

191 Ibid., 104–15 (5 Aug. 1928).

192 Ibid., 156 (26 Jan. 1931).

193 Ibid., 166 (9 April 1931).

194 Ibid., 187 (8 March 1932).

195 Pyta, *Hindenburg*, 413–31, 621–7, 673–8, 749–50, 855–71; Horst Mühleisen, 'Das Testament Hindenburgs vom 11. Mai 1934', *VfZ* 44 (1996), 355–71.

196 'Kronprinz an Ludwig Beck, 21. 9. 1925', BBAV 5814.

197 See Schotte, *Der Neue Staat*; Bracher, *Die Auflösung der Weimarer Republik*, 471–9; Petzinna, *Erziehung zum deutschen Lebensstil*, 257–86.

198 'Breitscheid über die Pläne des Exkronprinzen', *Berliner Tageblatt*, 13 Oct. 1932; 'Monarchie ohne Monarchen', *Die Welt am Montag*, 12 Sept. 1932; 'Monarchistische Pläne des Exkronprinzen', *Generalanzeiger Dortmund*, 12 Oct. 1932; 'Dunkle Pläne', *Berliner Tageblatt*, 12 Oct. 1932.

199 'Can Hohenzollern Return to Power?', *The Globe* (Toronto), 26 Oct. 1932; 'Monarchists of Germany: Active Preparations Said to Be Going On to Restore the Hohenzollerns', *The North China Herald and Supreme Court & Consular Gazette*, 26 Oct. 1932; 'Hindenburg Retires on Oct. 2, Is Report', *The Washington Post*, 5 June 1932.

200 'Sphinx auf Oels', *Vossische Zeitung*, 9 June 1932 (evening); 'Er will sich nicht festlegen. Der Herr von Oels und die Restaurationsfrage', *Vorwärts*, 9 June 1932.

201 See Sombart, *Herr der Mitte*.

202 See Machtan, *Der Kaisersohn*, 157–8.

203 See the letter of 17 Sept. 1932 quoted in its entirety in Friedrich Wilhelm von Preussen, *Gott helfe*, 97–8. A copy is contained in Nachlass John Röhl, Berlin, vol. 90.

204 Friedrich Wilhelm von Preussen, *Gott helfe*, 97–106; Ilsemann II, 204–6, 208 (3 Oct. and 15 Nov. 1932); Sweetman, *Unforgotten Crowns*, 351–4; Sichert, *Cecilienhof*, 250.

205 See the page proofs of Ilsemann, *Tagebücher*, 17 Sept. 1931, 140, Nachlass John Röhl, Berlin, vol. 115, entry. The passage was stricken from the published version of Ilsemann's memoirs.

206 'Entwurf eines Schreibens Wilhelms II. an Levetzow, 11.1.1933', GStA PK, BPH, Rep. 192, Nachlass Dommes; 'Levetzow an Hermine, 12. 12. 1932', 'Levetzow an Wilhelm II. 22. 12. 1932', Granier, *Magnus von Levetzow*, 184–9, 347–53.

207 'Aufzeichnungen Sells vom 3.2.1933', 'Kleist an Schwerin, 4.1.1933', 'Wilhelm II. an Kleist, 31.12.1932', 'Kronprinz an Wilhelm II., 13.12.1932', 'Sell an Schwerin, 20. 10. 1932', 'Dommes an Dirksen, 27. 1. 1937 und 4. 12. 1937', 'Aufzeichnung Dommes vom 25. 4. 1940', Nachlass John Röhl, Berlin, vol. 90.

208 'Schulenburg an Arnim, 10. 12. 1919', Sammlung Eliten-Projekt, TU Berlin.

209 'Schulenburg an Müldner, November 1920', BAP, 90 Mu 1, vol. 3, entry. 75 f. See also Lukas Grawe, 'General der Kavallerie Friedrich Graf von der Schulenburg', in Grawe (ed.), *Die militärische Elite*.

210 'Die Rückkehr des Kronprinzen', *Vorwärts*, 14 Nov. 1923 (morning).

211 'Joachim von Stülpnagel an Müldner, August 1924', Bundesarchiv

Berlin, Nachlass Müldner, previously Bundesarchiv Potsdam 90 Mu 1, vol. 3, 169.

212 Ilsemann II, 14–15 (4 Sept. 1924).

213 'Wilhelm II. an seinen Sohn Oskar, 26. 4. 1932', Ilsemann II, 190.

214 Ilsemann II, 220 (29 April 1933); 244 (8 Dec. 1933).

215 '"Ohne mich könnt ihr nichts tun!" Ansprache Wilhelms II. in Doorn, 18. 5. 1930', BAMA, N 239/49, 70–76. Emphasis in the original. Wilhelm II's 'court marshal' transmitted this speech back to Germany.

216 'Erinnerungen an ein abendliches Gespräch, das der deutsche Kronprinz allein mit uns am Kaminfeuer in der grossen Halle in Cecilienhof führte. Dez. 1934', GStA PK, Nachlass Hilde Wagner, No. 4.

217 Granier, *Magnus von Levetzow*, 160; Ilsemann II, 155 (19 Jan. 1931).

218 Ilsemann II, 91 (18 March 1928).

219 Kessler, *Tagebücher*, vol. 9, 518 (16 Oct. 1932), see also 514. In addition, see Reibnitz, *Im Dreieck*, 209.

220 'The Other Hohenzollern Princes', *The Observer*, 18 Nov. 1923.

221 Ilsemann II, 155 (19 Jan. 1931), 164 (19 March 1931).

222 Hellmut von Gerlach, 'Renaissance der Monarchie', *Weltbühne*, 18 Oct. 1932, 591; Hans Schäffer, 'Tagebucheintrag über Wilhelm Groener, 17. 6. 1932', Hans Schäffer Papers, Series II: Diaries, 1924–1933.

223 Zum Nationalen Deutschen Damen-Automobilclub siehe den Exkurs: Frauen am Steuer: Die Deutschen Damen-Automobilclubs, in Hochstetter, *Motorisierung*, 217 ff.

224 Wolzogen, *Drei Schwestern*, 309, 310, 326.

225 Ilsemann II, 219 (22 April 1933).

226 Haehner, 'Tagebücher, Einträge vom 13. 5. 1921, 18. 10. 1923', Historisches Archiv der Stadt Köln.

227 Ilsemann II, 132 (7 Nov. 1929).

228 'Selasen-Selasinsky an Kronprinz, 23. 12. 1932', BAMA, 432/2.

229 See Gerwarth, *Der Bismarck-Mythos*.

230 Goebbels, *Tagebücher*, 294 (1 June 1932).

231 See Tschirschky, *Erinnerungen eines Hochverräters*. See also Orth,

Notes

'Amtssitz der Opposition', 73–9, 206–23, and Ilsemann II, 307, 319 (2 Aug. 1938 and 13 March 1939).

232 Friedrich [Joachim v. Ostau], *Wer spielte falsch*, 74.

233 Sweetman, *Unforgotten Crowns*, 124–71, 365–402, 570–604; Kaufmann, *Monarchism*, 215–20; Arne Hoffmann, 'Bund der Aufrechten', 27–8, 81–5.

234 Reibnitz, *Wilhelm II*, 212–13; Reibnitz, *Im Dreieck*, 209.

235 Ilsemann II, 17 April 1932, 188; Hans Schäffer, 'Tagebucheintrag, 7. 6. 1932', Hans Schäffer-Papers, Series II: Diaries, 1924–1933, 568; Weiss/Hoser, *Die Deutschnationalen*, 179; 'Prince Oscar to Run for Presidency', *South China Morning Post*, 20 Feb. 1932; 'Le rétablissement éventuel de la monarchie en Allemagne', *Excelsior*, 11 Feb. 1933.

236 Junius Alter [Franz Sontag], 'Die Stahlhelmprinzen', *Nationalisten. Deutschlands nationales Führertum der Nachkriegszeit*, Leipzig 1930, 190–204.

237 'Der Kaiser von Deutschland. Oskar, der Rückschlag auf den Urgrossvater', *Vorwärts*, 23 Nov. 1930; 'Hohenzollern gegen Hindenburg. Kandidat der Harzburger: Prinz Oskar von Preussen?', *Vorwärts*, 18 Feb. 1932.

238 Sweetman, *Unforgotten Crowns*, 354.

239 Reibnitz, *Wilhelm II.*, 213.

240 See Mansel/Riotte (eds.), *Monarchy and Exile*.

241 See Reventlow, *Monarchie?*, 86, 100, 104, 119. Also cited in Reibnitz, *Im Dreieck*, 207.

242 Frederick T. Birchall, 'Germany's Junkers Await a New Dawn', *New York Times*, 9 Oct. 1932.

243 Kessler, *Tagebuch*, vol. 9, 20. July 1935, 650.

244 Reventlow, *Monarchie?*, 115.

245 Hans Schäffer, 'Tagebucheintrag, 28. 10. 1932', Hans Schäffer-Papers, Series II: Diaries, 1924–1933, 945.

246 Morsey, *Zur Entstehung*.

247 Andreas Rödder, 'Dichtung und Wahrheit. Der Quellenwert von Heinrich Brünings Memoiren und seine Kanzlerschaft', *Historische Zeitschrift*, 265 (1997), 77–116. See also Volkmann, *Heinrich Brüning (1885–1970)*.

248 Gasteiger, *Kuno von Westarp*, 202, 218–19, 470.

249 'Vernehmung vom 17. 6. 1947', USHMM, Kempner Papers, Box 310, Folder 19, 2.

250 See Hoffmann, 'Obsoleter Monarchismus' 243–7.

251 Reibnitz, *Wilhelm II. und Hermine*, 110.

252 Ilsemann II, 112 (11 Jan. 1929).

253 See Kohlrausch, *Der Monarch im Skandal*; Malinowski, *Vom König zum Führer*; evaluation Pyta/Orth; Hasselhorn, *Königstod*.

254 'Tagebucheintrag Hans Schäffer, 28. 10. 1932', Hans Schäffer-Papers, Series II: Diaries, 1924–1933, 945.

255 Ilsemann II, 233 (1 Oct. 1933).

256 GStA PK, BPH, Rep. 53, No. 167/2; Sichert, *Cecilienhof*, 180–86; Ilsemann II, 258 (8 May 1934) and 290 (14. Aug. 1936).

257 Pyta, *Hindenburg*, 748–51. In their evaluation (29–31), Pyta and Orth also cite Hindenburg's refusal to support the main arguments of monarchism. See also Ilsemann II, 232 (1 Oct. 1933).

258 *New York Times*, 10 June 1932; Sweetman, *Unforgotten Crowns*, 332–3.

259 Hellmut von Gerlach, 'Renaissance der Monarchie', *Weltbühne*, 18 Oct. 1932, 591.

260 Similar arguments are made in Hoffmann, *Obsoleter Monarchismus*, 258–60.

261 Pyta, *Hindenburg*, 747. See also Sweetman, *Unforgotten Crowns*; Malinowski, *Vom König zum Führer*.

262 Evaluation Pyta/Orth, 28.

263 Ludwig Marcuse, 'Die Hohenzollern warten aufs Schlüsselwort', *Aufbau*, 19 April 1946.

264 Rödder, *Dichtung und Wahrheit*, 91–2, 116; Volkmann, *Heinrich Brüning (1885–1970)*, 175–86; Frank Müller, 'Zum "englischen Vorbild" in den Verfassungsplänen Heinrich Brünings', in Otto/Schulz (eds.), *Grossbritannien und Deutschland*, 57–76.

265 Ilsemann I, 250 (6 Nov. 1920).

266 Wilhelm II, 'Vatikan und Völkerbund (Exposé, Juni 1926)', Nachlass John Röhl, Berlin, vol. 87.

267 'Prinz August Wilhelm huldigt dem Faschismus', *Salzburger Chronik*, 21 Nov. 1932; Kessler, *Tagebuch*, vol. 9, 483–4 (5 Aug. 1932).

268 Ilsemann II, 222 (2 June 1933).

269 Meinecke coined the phrase in 1918. See Meinecke, 'Verfassung und Verwaltung der deutschen Republik', in *Politische Schriften und Reden*, 281; Nikolai Wehrs, 'Demokratie durch Diktatur? Friedrich Meinecke als Vernunftsrepublikaner in der Weimarer Republik', in Bock/Schönpflug (eds.), *Friedrich Meinecke in seiner Zeit*, 95–118; Mann, *Ein Appell an die Vernunft*, vol. 3: *Essays*, 259–79; Harpprecht, *Thomas Mann, eine Biographie*, 664–8.

270 See Riotte, *Der Monarch im Exil*.

271 Camilla G. Kaul, 'Erfindung eines Mythos – Die Rezeption von Friedrich Barbarossa im Kyffhäuser im frühen 19. Jahrhundert und ihre national-politische Implikation', *Zeitschrift für Literaturwissenschaft und Linguistik*, 38 (2008), 107–47.

272 Friedrich Rückert, 'Der alte Barbarossa' (1817).

273 See Förster, *Der doppelte Militarismus*; Grünzig, *Für Deutschtum*, 68–71.

274 Gerstner, *Neuer Adel*; Malinowski, *Vom König zum Führer*, 293–320; Malinowski, *Nazis and Nobles*, 129–60; Conze/Meteling (eds.), *Aristokratismus und Moderne*.

275 Granier, *Levetzow*, 351.

276 Kantorowicz, *Kaiser Friedrich der Zweite*.

277 Karlauf, *Stefan George*, 547–62; Lerner, *Ernst Kantorowicz*, 101–16; Hoffmann, *Claus Schenk Graf von Stauffenberg*, 61–72; Otto Gerhard Oexle, 'Das Mittelalter als Waffe', in Oexle, *Geschichtswissenschaften im Zeichen des Historismus*, 163–215; Schreiner, 'Die Staufer in Sage, Legende und Prophetie', vol. 3, 249–62.

278 Lerner, *Kantorowicz*, 114–15.

279 Ibid., 115; Klaus Harpprecht, *Die Gräfin*, 188.

280 Voegelin, *Die politischen Religionen*; Philippe Burrin, 'Die politischen Religionen: Das Mythologisch-Symbolische in einer säkularisierten Welt', in Ley and Schoeps (eds.), *Der Nationalsozialismus als politische Religion*, 168–85; Arendt, *Elemente und Ursprünge*, chapters 10 and 11.

281 Raulff, *Kreis ohne Meister*, 168.

282 Ibid., 169.

283 Reibnitz, *Wilhelm II. und Hermine*, 201–3; *An Empress in Exile. My Days in Doorn. By Empress Hermine*, London 1927.

284 Wehler, *Deutsche Gesellschaftsgeschichte*, vol. 4, 485; Kohlrausch, *Der*

Monarch im Skandal, 439–41, 469–74; Kohlrausch, *Die Flucht des Kaisers*, 98; Hofmann, *Obsoleter Monarchismus*, 260.

285 See Biskup/Kohlrausch (eds.), *Das Erbe der Monarchie*; Hofmann, *'Wir sind das alte Deutschland, das Deutschland wie es war . . .'*.

286 See Eric Voegelin, *Die politischen Religionen*; Aron, 'Hannah Arendt, The Origins of Totalitarianism'; Maier, ' "Totalitarismus" und "Politische Religionen" '; Rissmann, *Hitlers Gott*.

287 Sichert, *Cecilienhof* 163.

288 'Schulenburg an Arnim, 15. 4. 1928', Briefwechsel Arnim/Schulenburg.

289 'Schulenburg an Arnim, 25. 11. 1928', Briefwechsel Arnim/Schulenburg. An almost identical wording is used in a letter one year later. 'Friedrich Graf von der Schulenburg an Heinrich Prinz von Schönburg-Waldenburg, 28. 12. 1929', Christoph von Wolzogen, private collection.

290 'Kronprinz Wilhelm an von Dryander, 14.5.1924', GStA PK, Rep. 54, No. 21.

291 'Oskar Prinz von Preussen an Sontag, 30. 12. 1924', BAK, Nachlass Alter, No. 17. See also Friedrich Wilhelm von Preussen, *Gott helfe*, 245.

292 Maximilian Harden, 'Monarchen-Erziehung', *Die Zukunft* 1 (1892), 625–32, 630. See also Martin Kohlrausch, 'Loss of Control: Kaiser Wilhelm II., Mass Media, and the National Identity of the Second German Reich', in M. Banerjee et al. (eds.), *Transnational Histories*, 93–4. For more background, see Kohlrausch, *Der Monarch im Skandal*.

293 Friedrich Wilhelm von Preussen, *Gott helfe*, 229.

294 'Wilhelm II. an Louis Ferdinand, 23. 2. 1932', Nachlass John Röhl, Berlin, vol. 90. See also Urbach, *Useful Idiots*, 553.

295 *The IAF Handbook of Group Facilitation*.

Chapter 4: Collapsing Constraints: The Hohenzollerns in 1933

1 Erich Kästner, 'Gerda und der Kronprinz. Neues von einer alten Burg', *Aufbau*, 14 Dec. 1945 – which reproduces the interview with the crown prince in *Weltwoche*.

2 'Monsieur Wilhelm, ex-kronprinz nous apprend qu'il a des idées sur tout', *France-Soir*, 15 Sept. 1946.

3 Machtan, *Der Kaisersohn*, 306.

4 Schneider, *Verhüllter Tag*, 100; Sichert, *Cecilienhof*, 203–5.

5 Sichert, *Cecilienhof*, 195–6.

6 Ilsemann II, 257 (9 March 1934).

7 'Kronprinz an Ludwig Beck, 21. 9. 1925', MHMB, Dresden, Nachlass Beck, BBAV5814.

8 Jonas, *Der Kronprinz*, 242; evaluation Pyta/Orth, 114–17, 124–37.

9 Jonas, *Der Kronprinz*, 224–5.

10 See Jasper, *Die gescheiterte Zähmung*.

11 Friedrich Wilhelm von Preussen, *Gott helfe*, 219–21; evaluation Pyta/Orth, especially 126–38.

12 See Sturm 33, 'Hans Maikowski', Berlin 1933; Bernhard Sauer, 'Goebbels' "Rabauken". Zur Geschichte der SA in Berlin-Brandenburg', in Dettmar/Breunig (eds.), *Berlin in Geschichte und Gegenwart*. 107–64.

13 'Neue Zusammenstösse in mehreren Städten', *Die Stunde*, 4 Feb. 1933.

14 'Fürstenwalder Zeitung', 7 Feb. 1933; 'Das Staatsbegräbnis', *Vorwärts*, 7 Feb. 1933.

15 Alamy/Süddeutsche Zeitung Photo/Alamy Stock Photo, Image ID: DYYT4C; 'Das Staatsbegräbnis', *Vorwärts*, 7 Feb. 1933.

16 Süddeutsche Zeitung Photo/Alamy Stock Photo, Image ID: DYYT4B.

17 August von Mackensen, 'Wie ich zu Adolf Hitler gekommen bin, 1. 2. 1942', Nachlass John Röhl, Berlin, vol. 92 (dated 16 Dec. 1939 / 1 Feb. 1942).

18 Bundesarchiv Bildarchiv, Bild 102–14283, cf. another view of the scene in *Spandauer Zeitung*, 6 February 1933.

19 'Brauner Rundfunk – Goebbels und der Kronprinz', *Vorwärts*, 7 Feb. 1933.

20 Goebbels, *Tagebücher*, vol. 2/III, 124–6 (6 and 10 Feb. 1933). See also the photo of the crowd and the SA men in front of the Berlin Cathedral on 5 Feb. 1933, Ullstein Bild, 00962847.

21 *Fürstenwalder Zeitung*, 7 Feb. 1933,1f.

22 'Beisetzung der Charlottenburger Opfer. Die Trauerfeier im Dom', *Vossische Zeitung*, 6 Feb. 1933.

23 Frederick T. Birchall, 'Watchfully, the Hohenzollerns Wait', *New York Times*, 19 March 1933, 5.

24 'Rundfunkreportage zum Staatsakt am 5.2.1933', Deutsches Rund-
funkarchiv Wiesbaden.

25 Martin Schuster, *Die SA*, 111–19.

26 'Kaiser Sends His Baggage into Germany. Restored Monarchy Is Suspected', *Chicago Daily Tribune*, 7 Feb. 1933.

27 'Hitler and the Crown Prince', *Chicago Daily Tribune*, 8 Feb. 1933;
Sigrid Schultz, 'Ex-Kaiser's Son Joins Hitler at Nazi Funeral. Thousands at Burial of Slain Fascists', *Chicago Daily Tribune*, 6 Feb. 1933.

28 'Un cortège immense où figurait l'ex-kronprinz', *Le Journal*, 6 Feb.
1933; 'Grande parade raciste à Berlin. Le kronprinz y assiste aux côtés
du chancelier', *Le Petit Journal*, 6 Feb. 1933; 'Obsèques à Berlin', *Le
Matin*, 6 Feb. 1933.

29 Fraenkel, *The Dual State*. See also Alexander von Brünneck, 'Ernst
Fraenkels Urdoppelstaat von 1938 und der Doppelstaat von 1941/1974',
in Buchstein/Göhler, *Vom Sozialismus zum Pluralismus*, 29–42; Michael
Wildt, 'Die politische Ordnung der Volksgemeinschaft. Ernst Fraenkels "Doppelstaat" neu betrachtet', *Mittelweg*, 36, 12 (2003), issue 2,
45–61.

30 Neumann, *Behemoth*.

31 See Bernhard Sauer, 'Goebbels' "Rabauken". Zur Geschichte der SA
in Berlin-Brandenburg', in Dettmar/Breunig (eds.), *Berlin in Geschichte
und Gegenwart* , 107–64.

32 *Der Gerade Weg*, 25 Jan. 1933; *Senftenberger Anzeiger*, 23 Jan. 1933. See
also evaluation Pyta/Orth, 63–70.

33 Luh, *Der Kronprinz*, 128, 184.

34 Evaluation Pyta/Orth, 72–85, here 77.

35 Bracher/Sauer/Schulz, *Die nationalsozialistische Machtergreifung*, 54–
8, 72–4, 82–8.

36 Heuss, *Hitlers Weg*, 48.

37 See Grünzig, *Für Deutschtum*; Clark, *Iron Kingdom*, 655–61; Scheel,
1933. Der Tag von Potsdam; Kopke/Tress, *Der Tag von Potsdam*, John
Zimmermann, 'Der Tag von Potsdam', in Epkenhans/Winkel (eds.),
Die Garnisonkirche Potsdam, 69–90.

38 Grünzig, *Für Deutschtum*, 144–61.

39 Martin Sabrow, 'Der "Tag von Potsdam". Zur doppelten Karriere

eines politischen Mythos', in Kopke/Tress, *Der Tag von Potsdam*, 47–86, here 47.

40 See evaluation Pyta/Orth, 96–7; and Morsey, *Der Untergang des politischen Katholizismus*.

41 Ilsemann II, 215 (21 March 1933).

42 Goebbels, *Tagebücher*, 17 March 1933.

43 'Der Staatsakt in Potsdam. Die Platzverteilung in der Garnisonkirche', *Kölner Lokal-Anzeiger* (morning), 21 March 1933, 2. See also evaluation Pyta/Orth, 85–96.

44 François-Poncet, *Souvenirs d'une Ambassade à Berlin*, 163.

45 *Kölner Lokal-Anzeiger*, 21 March 1933 (evening).

46 'An den Gräbern der Preussischen Könige', *Tägliche Rundschau*, 22 March 1933; 'Der Feierliche Staatsakt', *Kreuzzeitung*, 22 March 1933; Hupfeld (ed.), *Reichstags-Eröffnungsfeier in Potsdam*, 54; Scheel, *Der Tag von Potsdam*, 43–44; Herre, *Kronprinz Wilhelm*, 214–15; Grünzig, *Für Deutschtum*, 161–8; François-Poncet, *Souvenirs d'une Ambassade à Berlin*, 163.

47 André Waltz, 'La rentrée solennelle du nouveau Reichstag à Potsdam', *Le Petit Journal*, 22 March 1933.

48 'Avant la séance solennelle du nouveau Reichstag hier à Potsdam', *Paris-Soir*, 23 March 1933; 'La rentrée du Reichstag', *Le Petit Courrier*, 22 March 1933.

49 Scheel, *Tag von Potsdam*, 44–5.

50 'Der Feierliche Staatsakt', *Kreuzzeitung*, 22 March 1933.

51 François-Poncet, *Souvenirs d'une Ambassade à Berlin*, 165.

52 'An Outburst of Militarism in Germany: 125,000 "Steelhelmets" on Parade', *The Illustrated London News*, 11 Oct. 1930.

53 *Kölner Lokal-Anzeiger*, 21 March 1933 (evening), 2.

54 'Erinnerungen des späteren Heeresgruppenoberbefehlshabers Maximilian Frhr. von Weichs (1881–1954) an den Tag von Potsdam', BAMA, N19/5, fol. 4, cited in Scheel, *Tag von Potsdam*, 123. See also Friedrich-Christian Stahl, 'Generalfeldmarschall Maximilian Freiherr von und zu Weichs an der Glonn', in Gerd R. Ueberschär (ed.), *Hitlers militärische Elite. Vom Kriegsbeginn bis zum Weltkriegsende*, vol. 2, Darmstadt 1998, 276–82.

55 Bundesarchiv, Bildarchiv, No. 102–02315 and No. 102–14437.

56 'Kronprinz, hinter Hindenburg und Macksensen stehend, 21. 3. 1933', Ullstein Bild, No. 00070492.

57 Martin Sabrow, Der '"Tag von Potsdam". Zur doppelten Karriere eines politischen Mythos', in Kopke/Tress, *Der 'Tag von Potsdam'*, 47–86, here 75.

58 For a different interpretation, see evaluation Pyta/Orth, 84–114.

59 See Philippe Barrès, 'L'hitlérisme au pouvoir organise l'unité du Reich', *Le Matin*, 22 March 1933; Ambroise Got, 'La monarchie, peut-elle être restaurée en Allemagne', *Le Phare de la Loire*, 24 March 1933; 'Le discours de Hitler aux députés du Reichstag', *La Volonté*, 19 May 1933.

60 'Zweierlei Reklameprinzen', *Rumpelstilzchen*, 22 Nov. 1928; Alter [Franz Sontag], 'Die Stahlhelmprinzen', 196.

61 For a somewhat divergent interpretation see Sabrow, 'Der Tag von Potsdam' and *Das Bild der Hohenzollern*, 16.

62 See Richard J. Evans, 'The German History Wars', *The New Statesman*, 12 May 2021.

63 Photo in 'Avant la séance solennelle du nouveau Reichstag hier à Potsdam', *Paris-Soir*, 23 March 1933.

64 https://www.bundestag.de/parlament/geschichte/schauplaetze/kroll_oper/kroll_oper-199642 (accessed on 4 July 2021).

65 Schröder/Hachtmann, *Die Reichstagsabgeordneten*, 55–98, here 59.

66 'Bunter Bilderbogen aus dem Dritten Reich', *Der Kuckuck*, 2 April 1933.

67 *Westfälischer Beobachter*, 21 March 1933.

68 See 'Die erste Reichstagssitzung', *Vossische Zeitung*, 22 March 1933; *Kölner Lokal-Anzeiger*, 22 March 1933 (morning). See also 'Kronprinz Wilhelm am Eingang der Berliner Kroll-Oper, 21. 3. 1933', Ullstein Bild, No. 00070548; 'Kronprinz Wilhelm und Blomberg in der Kroll-Oper, 21. 3. 1933', Ullstein Bild, No. 00070554.

69 Scheel, *Der Tag von Potsdam*, 50; Hubert Schonger, 'Hakenkreuz am Stahlhelm (1933)', Bundesarchiv, Filmarchiv, Signatur: K 23686–1.

70 *Berliner Illustrierte Zeitung*, special edition, 21 March 1933. 'Die Staatsfeierlichkeiten bei der Reichstagseröffnung', 21–2.

71 André Waltz, 'La séance de pure forme au Reichstag', *Le Petit Journal*, 22 March 1933; 'M. Goering, réélu président', *L'Ouest-Éclair* (Rennes), 22 March 1933.

72 Jonas, *Der Kronprinz*, 236, and Preussen, *Gott helfe*, 205. See also 'Bunter Bilderbogen aus dem Dritten Reich / Der Kronprinz vor dem Reichstag', *Der Kuckuck*, 2 April 1933.

73 Wehler, *Gesellschaftsgeschichte*, vol. 4, 606.

74 Evaluation Clark, 4, 10; evaluation Pyta / Orth, 90–94.

75 Scheel, *Tag von Potsdam*, 48; Sabrow, *Tag von Potsdam*, 74–9, here 75.

76 'Der feierliche Staatsakt in der Garnisonkirche', *Völkischer Beobachter*, 22 March 1933, first supplement.

77 'Der Preussische Landtag', in *Walliser Volksfreund*, 24 March 1933.

78 Ullstein Bild, No. 00205806.

79 'Die Parade von Potsdam. Das graue und braune Heer Schulter an Schulter', *Völkischer Beobachter*, 22 March 1933, first supplement.

80 Scheel, *Tag von Potsdam*, 29.

81 *Kölner Lokal-Anzeiger*, 21 March 1933 (evening).

82 Gutsche, *Ein Kaiser im Exil*, 213–16.

83 'Parade vor Hindenburg', *Kreuzzeitung*, 22 March 1933.

84 Pomp, *Bauern und Grossgrundbesitzer*, 250–64; Malinowski, *Vom König zum Führer*, 531–52.

85 Ernst Graf zu Reventlow, 'Führer wollen wir – keine Herren', *Reichswart*, 5 March 1933.

86 See Pomp, *Bauern und Grossgrundbesitzer*; Horst Gies, 'NSDAP und landwirtschaftliche Organisationen in der Endphase der Weimarer Republik', *VfZG* 15 / 1967, 341–76; and Merkenich, *Grüne Front gegen Weimar*.

87 See Malinowski, *Vom König zum Führer*, and the analysis of the form and funtion of 'high society' in the Third Reich in Fabrice d'Almeida, *La vie mondaine sous le nazisme*, Paris 2006.

88 Napoleon's famous declaration on 11 November 1799 proclaiming the post-coup alliance of the revolution and the *ancien régime* was: 'Citoyens, la Révolution est fixée aux principes qui l'ont commencée, elle est finie.' Cited in Bluche, *Manuel d'histoire politique de la France contemporaine*, 90.

89 'Kronprinz an Lord Rothermere, 20.6.1934', The Hoover Institution Archives, Stanford, Collection Number 77020; Jonas, *Der Kronprinz*, 286.

90 'Hitler bleibt dem katholischen Gottesdienst fern. Eine amtliche Aufklärung', *Kölner Lokal-Anzeiger*, 21 March 1933 (evening), 2.

91 Ernst Graf zu Reventlow, 'Kanzler und Kirche', *Reichswart*, 25 March 1933.

92 Ernst Graf zu Reventlow, 'Das Ereignis des 21. März', *Reichswart*, 25 March 1933.

93 See the photo in Röhl, *Wilhelm II.*, vol. 3, 1251.

94 *Kreuzzeitung*, 22 March 1933, first supplement, 1.

95 Albert Esderts, 'Erwachendes Deutschland', *Der Aufrechte*, 5 April 1933.

96 'Wie die Presse Potsdam sieht', *Vossische Zeitung*, 21 March 1933.

97 Scheel, *Der Tag von Potsdam*, 52–3.

98 Bredow, *Notizen*, 234.

99 *Lokal-Anzeiger für Stadt und Land*, 29 May 1933 (morning).

100 For details on the course of events and the significance of the 'Weapons Day', see Luh, *Der Kronprinz*, 17–34.

101 Luh, *Düsseldorf 1933*, 10.

102 Ibid., 15.

103 '"Ich bin von Düsseldorf begeistert." Der Kronprinz plaudert über seine Eindrücke und Erinnerungen', *Deutsche Kavallerie-Zeitung*, 1 Aug. 1933, 123–4.

104 Arendt was quoting Otto Kirchheimer's *Political Justice* (1961) here. *Eichmann in Jerusalem*, 1963/1965 edition, 127.

105 Wilhelm II stated his position on his sons' political activities in a letter to his grandson Prince Louis-Ferdinand of 23 Feb. 1932. See Jonas, *Der Kronprinz*, 223.

106 Ilsemann II, 215 (21 March 1933).

107 Ibid., 215–16 (21 and 25 March 1933).

108 Studnitz, *Seitensprünge*, 22.

109 'Nicht im Traum wollte er Kaiser sein, Interview mit Georg Friedrich Prinz von Preussen', *Stuttgarter Nachrichten*, 19 June 2017.

110 Hellmut von Gerlach, 'Renaissance der Monarchie', *Weltbühne*, 18 Oct. 1932, 591.

111 'Kronprinz an Joseph Goebbels, 11.4.1933', in GStA PK, Rep. 100A, No. 388/2.

112 'Kronprinz an Lord Lothian, 17.6.1933', GStA PK, Rep. 100 A, No. 388/2.

113 Crown Prince Wilhelm of Prussia, 'Ewiges Preussentum', GStA PK, Rep. 100 A, No. 388/2. This article was published in the cultural magazine *Der Türmer*, 4 Jan. 1934, 289–90, and elsewhere.

114 Süchting-Hänger, *Das 'Gewissen' der Nation*, 202; Förster, *Königin Luise-Mythos*, 333; Schöck-Quinteros, *Der Bund Königin Luise*, 231–70; Hadeln, *In Sonne und Sturm*, 248.

115 'Die einen und die anderen', *Der Kuckuck*, 2 Oct. 1932.

116 Luh/Bauer, *Cecilie*, 52–3; Förster, *Königin Luise-Mythos*, 331.

117 'Potsdam im Zeichen der Kornblume', *Nachrichten aus Potsdam*, 19 Sept. 1932. Bundesarchiv-Bildarchiv, Bild 183-2003-1014-500.

118 Förster, *Königin Luise-Mythos*, 333.

119 Ibid., 334.

120 'Stahlhelm und Königin-Luise-Bund für Begnadigung', *Kreuzzeitung*, 26 Aug. 1932. See also Bessel, *The Potempa Murder*, 241–54; Chapoutot, *Le Meurtre de Weimar*; Klingler, *Negotiating Violence*, 192–212.

121 Förster, *Königin Luise Mythos*, 341.

122 Hadeln, *In Sonne und Sturm*, 1935.

123 'Zehn Jahre Freiheitskampf des Bundes Königin Luise. Rede der deutschen Kronprinzessin auf der Fest-Veranstaltung', *Der Tag*, 16 May 1933, 3.

124 The speech was printed in *Die deutsche Frau*, 27 (1933), 215. See also Förster, *Königin Luise Mythos*, 432–3; Luh/Bauer, *Cecilie*, 53–4; Süchting-Hänger, *'Gewissen der Nation'*, 387.

125 Luh/Bauer, *Cecilie*, 53–4. Cecilie als Rednerin: Bundesarchiv, Bildarchiv, Bild 102–14605 and Bild 102–14604.

126 Klaus Theweleit, *Männerphantasien*, vol. 1.

127 *Freiburger Zeitung*, 15 March 1933 (evening).

128 *Kölner Lokal-Anzeiger für Stadt und Land*, 15 May 1933 (morning).

129 'Zehn Jahre Freiheitskampf des Bundes Königin Luise. Rede der deutschen Kronprinzessin auf der Fest-Veranstaltung', *Der Tag*, 16 May 1933, 3; Franz Seldte, 'Ein Appell an die Hausfrauen', *Morgenpost*, 17 May 1933; '8. Tagung des Bundes Königin Luise', *Teltower Kreisblatt*, 15 May 1933.

130 Image in Bundesarchiv-Bildarchiv, 183-2003-1014-500; Luh/Bauer, *Cecilie*, 53.

131 'La propagande de l'ex-kronprinzessin', *Le Matin*, 15 May 1933; 'l'ex-kronprinzessin fait l'éloge de Hitler', *L'Œuvre*, 15 May 1933; 'L'ex-kronprinzessin préside le Congrès des femmes nationalistes allemandes', *Le Petit Journal*, 15 May 1933; 'La femme de l'ex-kronprinz fait acclamer le nom d'Hitler', *L'Ami du peuple*, 15 May 1933; '40000 Allemandes réunies sous la présidence de la kronprinzessin celèbrent l'esprit de Potsdam', *L'Action Française*, 15 May 1933.

132 'Der Kronprinz als Soldat', *Kreuzzeitung*, 14 Dec. 1933, 13. The letter to Pückler was written on 24 June 1933. See also 'Der frühere Kronprinz an den Stahlhelm', *Salzburger Volksblatt*, 26 June 1933.

133 'Wilhelm II. an die NSDAP-Ortsgruppe Bockenheim, 11. 3. 1933, und an Eitel Friedrich, 4. 7. 1933', Reichsarchiv Utrecht, Nachlass Wilhelm II., No. 18. See also Gutsche, *Ein Kaiser im Exil*, 160–61.

134 'Der Kronprinz mahnt zur Einheit', *Kreuzzeitung*, 16 Oct. 1932; 'Der Kronprinz gegen den nationalen Bruderkampf', *Linzer Tages-Post*, 17 Oct. 1932; 'Zusammenschluss der deutschen Rechtsfront? Bemühungen des Exkronprinzen', *Innsbrucker Nachrichten*, 24 Oct. 1932.

135 'Freie Presse', *La Presse Libre. Sozialistisches Organ für das Departement des Nieder-Rheins*, 16 May 1933.

136 'Die Rechte ist erledigt. Das Ende einer Illusion'; 'Die Auflösung der bürgerlichen Parteien'; 'SA frisst den Stahlhelm auf', *Arbeiter-Zeitung*, 14 April 1933.

137 'Aufmarsch in Hannover, 24. 9. 1933', Bundesarchiv Bildarchiv, Bild 102–03043. See also the photo in *Der Kuckuck*, 8 Oct. 1933.

138 'A Hohenzollern Wears the Nazi Emblem', *Evening Star* (Washington, DC), 15 Oct. 1933; 'L'Ex-Kronprinz à la réunion des casques d'acier à Hanovre', *Paris-Soir*, 27 Sept. 1933; *L'Ouest-Éclair*, 28 Sept. 1932.

139 Hubert Schonger, 'Hakenkreuz am Stahlhelm Soldaten gehören zusammen. Ein Bildbericht von der Erhebung und Einung des deutschen Soldatentums, 1933', Bundesarchiv, Filmarchiv, Signatur: K 23686–1. See also 'Kronprinz beim Treueschwur', *Der Wiener Tag*, 27 Sept. 1933, 12.

140 Collectie Huis Doorn HuDF-1246; Röhl, *Wilhelm II.*, vol. 3, 1311; Jacco Pekelder, 'Dromen van de monarchie. Wilhelm II en de nazi's',

Geschiedenis Magazine, 4, May/June 2020, 26, https://www.huisdoorn.
nl/files/25-27-gsm20-tds-nr-4-2.pdf.

141 'L'Ex-Kronprinz chez les "Nazis"', *Paris-Soir*, 13 Oct. 1933; *L'Ouest-Éclair*, 17 Oct. 1933.

142 Crown Prince Wilhelm, 'Novembertage', 9 Nov. 1933, in GStA PK, Rep. 100A, No. 388/2. It was published in the *Kreuzzeitung* and the *Bayerischen Staatszeitung*. The national election, dominated by Nazi coercion, was held on 12 Nov. 1933.

143 Evaluation Pyta/Orth, 124–42.

144 Ilsemann II, 241–4 (November/December 1934).

145 Malinowski, *Vom König zum Führer*, 357.

146 'Ein erlauchter Nazi', *Der Abend*, 16 Dec. 1933.

147 See Luh, *Düsseldorf 1933*.

148 *Die Leuchtrakete*, February 1933.

149 'Le Clown-Prince', *Neptune* (Antwerp), 7 March 1934.

150 See evaluation Pytha/Orth, 126–38.

151 Ibid., 133.

152 *De Beiaard*, 22 November 1947. This series of photographs was used as evidence in the legal conflicts over Huis Doorn between the Dutch government and the Hohenzollerns after 1945. See F. A. J. van der Ven, 'De onteigening van Huis Doorn: een hoofdstuk uit de Nederlandse geschiedenis', *Rechtsgeleerd Magazijn Themis*, 2001, 67–81.

153 'Hos den kejserlige S.A.-Mand i Potsdam', *Berlingske illustreret Tidende*, 22 April 1934.

154 *The Illustrated London News*, 7 April 1934; *Soerabaijasch Handelsblad*, 21 April 1934; *Algemeen handelsblad voor Nederlandsch-Indie*, 11 May 1934.

155 'Der Kronprinz, die Idioten und die schöne Frau', *Die Zeitung*, 25 May 1945.

156 'Prussian Junker, in Letter to Bouton, Praises Hitler as Leader Country Needs', *The Sun* (New York), 17 June 1934; 'Hitler's Reign of Terror', 55 min. film by Michael Mindlin and Cornelius Vanderbilt, premiered 30 April 1934.

157 'The Former Crown Prince in Nazi Uniform', *Chicago Tribune*, 8 April 1934.

158 'The Emperor of Doorn House: The Most Intimate Photographs Yet

Taken of the Exiled Kaiser at His Home in Holland', *The Illustrated London News*, 24 Dec. 1933.

159 'Kronprinz an Selasen-Selasinsky, 13. 3. 1933', BAMA Freiburg, Nachlass Selasen-Selasinsky, No. 432/2.

160 Ibid., 21–3.

161 Gutsche, *Ein Kaiser im Exil*, 164; Sichert, *Cecilienhof*, 165–7. For reasons unknown his letter is missing from GStA PK, I. HA Rep. 100 A, No. 388/2.

162 'Leopold von Kleist, 27. 3. 1931, an Wilhelm II. und an Cecilie'; 'Wilhelm II. an seinen Enkel Wilhelm von Preussen, 31. 3. 1931', Nachlass John Röhl, Berlin, vol. 90 (emphasis in original).

163 Ilsemann II, 165–7 (9–11 April 1931).

164 'Ex-Kaiser Wilhelm at 75 Becomes a Great-Grandfather', *Chicago Tribune*, 7 Sept. 1934.

165 'Verzeichnis der für die Prinzen des Königlichen Hauses eventuell in Frage kommenden heiratsfähigen Prinzessinnen aus den evangelischen Fürstenhäusern der Abt. III des Gotha (Fürstliche Familien des niederen Adels), Stand: 1940', GSta PK, BPH, Rep. 192, Nachlass Dommes, No. 13.

166 'Verzeichnis der für die Prinzen des Königlichen Hauses eventuell in Frage kommenden, z. Zt. heiratsfähigen Töchter der evangelischen deutschen standesherrlichen Fürstlichen und Gräflichen Häuser, mit dem Recht der Ebenbürtigkeit mit den regierenden und ehemals regierenden Fürstenhäusern; Stand: August 1933', and 'Wilhelm von Dommes an Cecilie Prinzessin von Preussen, 22. 6. 1934', GStA PK, I. HA Rep. 100 A, No. 349.

167 'Ergebnisse des Ausschusses zur Prüfung der Ebenbürtigkeits-Regeln, genehmigt durch Wilhelm II., 12. 9. 1940', GStA PK, I. HA Rep. 100 A, No. 349. See also Malinowski, *Vom König zum Führer*, 336–58, 482–8.

168 'Oskar Prinz von Preussen, Zukunftsgedanken, 30. 10. 1934', GStA PK, I. HA Rep. 100 A, No. 349.

169 'Kronprinz Wilhelm, Meine Gedanken zur Frage der Erweiterung bzw. Abänderung der Bestimmungen über ebenbürtige Heiraten der Familienmitglieder unseres Hauses, 14. 3. 1941', in GStA PK, I. HA Rep. 100 A, No. 349.

170 'Notiz des Kronprinzen an den Familienrat, 13. 8. 1940', in GStA PK, I. HA Rep. 100 A, No. 349.

171 Louis Ferdinand of Prussia, *The Rebel Prince*, 235–7.

172 'Le kronprinz au concours hippique de Rome', *Paris-Soir*, 6 May 1933.

173 'Die Deutschen gewinnen endgültig die Coppa Mussolini', *Wiener Salonblatt*, 21 May 1933; Louis Ferdinand of Prussia, *The Rebel Prince*, 239–40.

174 'Wilhelm II. an Sell, 29. 4. 1933', GStA PK, Nachlass Sell, No. 4.

175 'Der deutsche Kronprinz amüsiert sich', *Das Kleine Blatt*, 29 Sept. 1932; 'Kennst du das Land, wo . . . ?', *Der Kuckuck*, 2 Oct. 1932.

176 On Hitler in Essen, see footage from the British Pathé: https://youtube/oWL5vFRBS9M.

177 'Distanz' (cartoon), *Die Leuchtrakete*, September 1932.

178 Herbst, *Hitlers Charisma*, 59–176; Kershaw, *Hitler*, vol. 1: *1889–1936*, 149–399; Hamann, *Hitlers Wien*; Weber, *Hitler's First War*.

179 Peter Driessen, 'Die deutschen Kaisersöhne, wie sie heute leben', *Neues Wiener Journal*, 10 Sept. 1932.

180 https://www.youtube.com/watch?v=dM8PMIa8PIA (accessed 1 June 2021).

181 '"Trump ist der Aufbruch einer Eiterbeule, die sich vorher gebildet hatte". Interview mit Wolfgang Schivelbusch', *Spiegel Online*, 2 Dec. 2020.

182 'Der Exkronprinz preist Hitlers "magnetische Kraft". Interview mit dem Exkronprinzen', *Basler Nachrichten*, 15 Aug. 1934.

183 Benjamin, *Das Kunstwerk*, 506.

184 George Sylvester Viereck (1884–1962) was a German-American writer known for his 'services' as a Nazi propagandist. Goebbels privately loathed him but stressed his usefulness. See Goebbels, *Tagebücher*, 19 Sept. 1933; Urbach, *Useful Idiots*, 20; Röhl, *Wilhelm II.*, vol. 3, 1274–5, 1294; Johnson, *George Sylvester Viereck*.

185 'Eine Mahnung des Kronprinzen', *Der Tag*, 29 March 1933; 'Der Kronprinz gegen Greuelpropaganda', *Senftenberger Anzeiger*, 29 March 1933; 'Der deutsche Kronprinz', *Völkischer Beobachter*, 29 March 1933 (first supplement); 'Einsicht im Auslande. Erfolg der deutschen Aktion gegen die Greuel-Propaganda. / Der Kronprinz gegen Greuel-Propaganda', *Berliner Lokal-Anzeiger*, 28 March 1933.

186 Angeloch, *Ein ambivalenter Fanatiker*, 655–6; 'L'ex-kronprinz croit devoir démentir les atrocités commises', *Lyon républicain*, 29 March 1933.

187 Geraldine Farrar (1882–1967) was a friend of the crown prince's family and had a relationship with him. After training in Boston from 1901 to 1906, she was a member of the Berlin Court Opera and later a superstar at the Metropolitan Opera in New York and in Hollywood during the silent film era, where she appeared alongside Enrico Caruso and Wallace Reid and was honoured with two stars on the Hollywood Walk of Fame. Farrar's estate in the Library of Congress (Washington, DC) documents an exchange that lasted until the death of the crown prince.

188 'Kronprinz an Geraldine Farrar', GStA PK, I. HA Rep. 100 A, No. 388/2, reprinted in Machtan, *Der Kaisersohn*, 291–2. Prince Friedrich Wilhelm inexplicably failed to include this letter in *Gott helfe*.

189 Goebbels, *Tagebücher*, 10 Feb. 1933.

190 Ibid., 16 March 1933.

191 https://www.lottissimo.com/de-de/auction-catalogues/hermann-historica-ohg/catalogue-id-srher10023/lot-decedaf7-4f8c-42ea-8bd6-a5e901584fc1 (accessed on 4 July 2021). See also Sichert, *Cecilienhof*, vol. 1, 255; and Goebbels, *Tagebücher*, 31 March 1933 and 5 Aug. 1933; 'Du message Roosevelt au discours d'Hitler', *L'Ouest-Éclair*, 19 May 1933.

192 See, for instance, Goebbels, *Tagebücher*, 19 Sept. 1933.

193 'Grosskampf gegen Greuel-Lügen. Nationale Bewegung Hand in Hand', *Kreuzzeitung*, 27 March 1933; 'Hitler stellt Greuelmeldungen richtig', *Berliner Lokal-Anzeiger* (evening), 24 March 1933.

194 'Einsicht im Auslande / Der Kronprinz gegen Greuel-Propaganda', *Berliner Lokal-Anzeiger*, 28 March 1933.

195 'Abflauende Hetze in England', *Kreuzzeitung*, 4 April 1933.

196 On the first wave of disenfranchisement, harassment and terrorizing of Jewish Germans, see Friedländer, *Nazi Germany and the Jews*, 14–40.

197 Wachsmann, *KL*, 33–98; Evans, *The Coming of the Third Reich*, 309–90; Wachsmann/Steinbacher (eds.), *Die Linke im Visier*.

198 Bernhard Sauer, 'Goebbels' "Rabauken". Zur Geschichte der SA in Berlin-Brandenburg', in Dettmar/Breunig (eds.), *Berlin in Geschichte*

und Gegenwart; and Kurt Schilde, 'Opfer des NS-Terrors 1933 in Berlin. Biographische Skizzen', in Kopke/Tress (eds.), *Der Tag von Potsdam*, 178–211.

199 See Friedländer, *Das Dritte Reich und die Juden*, 30–38; Ahlheim, '*Deutsche, kauft nicht bei Juden!*'.

200 Klemperer, *The Language of the Third Reich*, 36 (27 March 1933).

201 'Was bleibt? Es bleibt die Muttersprache. Günter Gaus im Gespräch mit Hannah Arendt', TV interview, 28 Oct. 1964.

202 'Bunter Bilderbogen aus dem Dritten Reich', *Der Kuckuck*, 2 April 1933.

203 'Grosskampf gegen Greuel-Lügen', *Kreuzzeitung*, 27 March 1933.

204 Timothy W. Ryback, *Hitler's First Victims and One Man's Race for Justice*, London 2015.

205 'Abwehr der Greuelpropaganda. Aufruf der NSDAP', *Gubener Zeitung*, 29 March 1933; 'Wir sind gerüstet – Boykott organisiert', *Der Angriff*, 30/31 March 1933.

206 Goebbels, *Tagebücher* (25 March 1933).

207 *Völkischer Beobachter*, 29 March 1933 (first supplement).

208 Scheel, *Tag von Potsdam*, 146; Wachsmann, *KL*, 42.

209 'Menace d'emprisonnement à l'égard des journalistes étrangers en Allemagne', *Le Matin*, 22 March 1933.

210 Schuster, *Die SA*, 230–52, here 239. Szende, *Zwischen Gewalt und Toleranz*, 15–20; Machtan, *Der Kaisersohn*, 305–6.

211 Stephan Szende, 'Prinz Auwi verhört', *Sozialistische Warte*, 15 Feb. 1937, 81–4. Szende was arrested on 26 Nov. 1933.

212 'Hassfeldzug gegen Deutschland. Systematische Greuellügen gegen Deutschland', *Berliner Lokal-Anzeiger* (evening), 23 March 1933.

213 Report by Horace Rumbold to British Foreign Secretary John Simon on 21 March 1933, *Documents on British Foreign Policy 1919–1939*, Second Series, vol. IV, London 1950, 401–2.

214 Klemperer, *Diaries*, 35–6 (21–2 March 1933, emphasis in original).

215 'Der Kronprinz über die Greuelpropaganda', *Vossische Zeitung* (evening), 28 March 1933.

216 'Ex-Crown Prince Denies Atrocities', *New York Times*, 28 March 1933, 14; 'Hohenzollern Prince Denies Atrocity Tales', *New York Herald Tribune*, 28 March 1933, 3; 'Ex-Crown Prince Deplores "Propaganda of

Lies"', *Boston Globe*, 28 March 1933, 2; 'Crown Prince Denies Germany Is Abusing Jews', *Chicago Tribune*, 28 March 1933, 4; 'Former Crown Prince Protests Cruelty Reports', *Los Angeles Times*, 28 March 1933, 4.

217 'Brief an Lord Lothian, 17. 6. 1933', GStA PK, Rep. 100 A, No. 388/2.

218 'Nazi-Kronprinz Wilhelm gegen den Antisemitismus', *Der Morgen*, 21 Aug. 1933.

219 Otto König, 'Gespräch mit Kronprinz Wilhelm', *Neues Wiener Journal*, 1 Sept. 1931, 8.

220 'Une interview de l'ex-kronprinz', *L'Express de Mulhouse*, 25 Feb. 1932. The interview also appeared in the Norwegian newspaper *Tidens*.

221 Pekelder/Schenk/van der Bas, *Der Kaiser*, 37–44.

222 Kershaw, *Popular Opinion and Political Dissent in the Third Reich*, 277.

223 Rivka Weinberg, 'The Road to Auschwitz Wasn't Paved With Indifference', *New York Times*, 21 Jan. 2020.

224 See the evaluation Pyta/Orth, 23, which is as far as the authors' analysis of anti-Semitism goes.

225 See Walter, *Antisemitische Gewalt*.

226 On the crown prince's reception on 5 July 1933, see BAB, R43/4063.

227 'Der Kronprinz über die deutsche Revolution', *Vossische Zeitung*, 5 Aug. 1933.

228 Schilde, *Opfer des NS-Terrors*, 178–211.

229 Wilhelm Prinz von Preussen, 'Why Is the World Against Us?', *New York Herald Tribune*, 27 Aug. 1933; '"Warum ist die Welt gegen uns?" Der Kronprinz über die Lage in Deutschland', *Berliner Börsenzeitung*, 12 Sept. 1933.

230 Machtan, *Der Kaisersohn*, 279–97.

231 Johannes Sivers, 'Aus meinem Leben', Berlin 1966, typed manuscript, Graphische Sammlung, SPSG, Potsdam, 374. Sivers was a lecturing counsel and a professor in the culture division of the German Foreign Ministry.

232 'Politisches aus Bayreuth', *Neues Wiener Journal*, 6 Aug. 1925; photo with the singer Friedrich Schorr, *Die Stunde*, 5 Sept. 1925.

233 'Heinrich Arnhold an August Wilhelm Prinz von Preussen, 15. 5. 1930',

Leo Baeck Institute Center for Jewish History, AR2920, Arnhold Family Collection 1830–1987. See also Machtan, *Der Kaisersohn*, 145.

234 'Ex-Crown Prince Joins Nazis', *Birmingham Daily Gazette*, 7 March 1934, 5; 'L'ex-kronprinz adhère au parti hitlérien', *La Tribune de l'Aube*, 24 May 1933.

235 Ilsemann II, 238 (16 Nov. 1933).

236 Ibid., 239–44 (26 Nov.–8 Dec. 1933).

237 Ibid., 253 (21 Feb. 1934).

238 Evaluation Pyta/Orth, 133–4.

239 Ilsemann II, 253–5 (21 and 25 Feb. 1934).

240 See the lists in the evaluations Brandt, Malinowski, Pyta/Orth; Ilsemann II, 283 (24 Aug. 1935); Jonas, *Der Kronprinz*, 237–43.

241 See Luh, *Düsseldorf 1933*.

242 See Luh, 'Die "Langemarck-Denkmalweihe"'; and Luh, *Der Kronprinz*, 51–72. See also http://www.naumburg1933.de/geschichte/langemarck.htm (accessed 4 July 2021).

243 *Leuchtrakete*, July 1933, 8.

244 Ilsemann II, 254–7 (February/March 1934), here 254 (21 Feb. 1934).

245 See evaluation Pyta/Orth, 120.

246 Moltke, *Gesammelte Schriften und Denkwürdigkeiten*, vol. 5, Berlin 1892, 194.

247 Grosser Generalstab, Kriegsgeschichtliche Abteilung (ed.), *Kriegsbrauch im Landkriege*, 1902, cited in Daniel-Erasmus Khan, 'Der ewige Friede ist ein Traum, und nicht einmal ein schöner . . . Anmerkungen zu einem Briefwechsel zwischen Johann Caspar Bluntschli und Helmuth Graf von Moltke', in Groh et al. (eds.), *Verfassungsrecht*, 159–74, here 171.

248 'Diverse Briefe, Bauer-Kronprinz, 1919–1920', BAMA, Nachlass Bauer, N 1022, No. 21.

249 See *Der Kuckuck*, 2 Oct. 1932.

250 'Erwein Freiherr von Aretin an Kronprinz Rupprecht, 1. 8. 1926', AFA. In late 1930, Count Karl August von Drechsel rejected the Stahl-helms for similar reasons, specifically voicing his disappointment in the northern German aristocracy's enthusiasm for Nazis. 'Drechsel an Friedrich von Berg, 17. 12. 1930', DAAM, LAB, vol. 1, H. 30/31. See also Malinowski, *Vom König zum Führer*, 367–85.

251 'Erwein Freiherr von Aretin an Kronprinz Rupprecht, 27. 12. 1929', AFA.

252 'Erwein Freiherr von Aretin an Kronprinz Rupprecht, 17. 5. 1928', ibid.

253 'Kronprinz Rupprecht an Erwein Aretin, 18. 5. 1927', ibid.

254 'Erwein Frhr. v. Aretin an Kronprinz Rupprecht, 23. 12. 1927', ibid.

255 'Erwein Freiherr von Aretin an Kronprinz Rupprecht, 23. 12. 1930', ibid.

256 https://www.youtube.com/watch?v=y5eveUVrO9M.

257 See *Der Abend*, 6 Sept. 1932, 12; *Kleine Volkszeitung*, 4 Sept. 1932; *Linzer Tagespost*, 6 Sept. 1932; *Salzburger Chronik*, 10 Sept. 1932; 'Neues, Interessantes, Merkwürdiges', and 'Wo steht die Reichswehr', *Der Kuckuck*, 11 Sept. 1932; 'Aus einer sonderbaren Republik', *Der Abend*, 22 June 1932, 12.

258 'The past is a foreign country. They do things differently there', L. P. Hartley, *The Go-Between*, London 1953.

259 See Gasteiger, *Kuno von Westarp*, 205–6; Malinowski, *Vom König zum Führer*, 208; Funck, *The Meaning of Dying*.

260 'Oskar Prinz von Preussen an seinen Vater, 23. 3. 1930', Utrechts Archief, NL-Ut-HUA, A16662, fol. 102–3.

261 'Bericht über meine Reise auf Allerhöchsten Befehl zur Beisetzung Seiner Kaiserlichen und Königlichen Hoheit des Erzherzogs Friedrich nach Magyarovar 4. bis 6. 1. 1937 (Oskar Prinz von Preussen an seinen Vater), 11. 1. 1937', Utrechts Archief, NL-UtHUA_A16662, fol. 104–7.

262 'Eitel Friedrich Prinz zu Preussen, Brieflicher Bericht ("Lieber Papa!") über den Regimentstag des Ersten Garde-Regiments zu Fuss in Potsdam und Berlin, 28. 5. 1934', Utrechts Archief, NL-UtHUA A16662, fol. 93–5.

263 See the correspondence in GStA PK, BPH, Rep. 192, Nachlass Dommes, No. 7., here a letter dated 1 May 1947; see also the evaluation Pyta/Orth, 135–6.

264 Beck, *The Fateful Alliance*, 219–52. See also Wirsching's criticism of Beck's account, 'Review of Hermann Beck', 754–6.

265 Anke Hoffstadt, 'Eine Frage der Ehre – Zur "Beziehungsgeschichte" von "Stahlhelm. Bund der Frontsoldaten" und SA', in Müller/Zileknat (eds), *Bürgerkriegsarmee*, 267–96; Berghahn, *Stahlhelm*, 187–275.

266 Roloff, *Bürgertum und Nationalsozialismus 1930–1933*, 148; Bein, *Zeitzeichen*, 53–4; Reinowski, *Terror in Braunschweig*; Berghahn, *Stahlhelm*, 263–6.

267 'Alfred Hugenberg an Hitler, 12 April 1933', BAB, Akten der Reichskanzlei, NSDAP, R34 II, No. 1195, 211–35.

268 Beck, *A Fateful Alliance*, 236–52.

269 'Nazis and the Stahlhelm. Quarrel Goes On', *The Manchester Guardian*, 28 May 1934.

270 'Berg an Selasen-Selasinsky, 23. 6. 1933', BAMA Freiburg, Nachlass Selasen-Selasinsky, No. 432/4.

271 'Protokoll der Unterredung Hitlers mit Reichsminister und Bundesführer Franz Seldte, 12. 8. 1935', in Berghahn, *Stahlhelm*, 446–51, here 450.

272 Klausa, *Sie kamen aus dem 'Stahlhelm'*, 218–30; Beck, *The Fateful Alliance*, 83–113.

273 'Der deutsche Adel hat es schwer', *Linzer Tageblatt*, 12 Oct. 1932, See also Noakes, 'German Conservatives and the Third Reich', in Blinkhorn (ed.) *Fascists and Conservatives*, 71–98; Beck, *The Fateful Alliance*; Jones, *Hitler versus Hindenburg*; Kleine, *Adelsgenossenschaft*; Malinowski, *Vom König zum Führer*, 556–60.

274 'Das Trümmerfeld der Harzburger Front', *Reichspost*, 12 Oct. 1932, 3.

275 Evaluation Pyta/Orth, 25, 84–97, 114–17, 154.

276 See *Die Kirchen und das Dritte Reich*, vol. 3: Gerhard Besier, *Spaltungen und Abwehrkämpfe 1934–1937*, Berlin 2001.

277 *DAZ*, 22 June 1933.

278 Berghahn, *Stahlhelm*, 263–74; evaluation Pyta/Orth, 124–36.

279 Longerich, *Die braunen Bataillone*, 159, 184; Siemens, *Stormtroopers*, 142.

280 Ilsemann II, 212 (1 Feb. 1933); Friedrich Wilhelm von Preussen, *Gott helfe*, 204. The Pyta/Orth evaluation doesn't mention the Hohenzollerns' reaction to the appointment of the Hitler cabinet as documented by Ilsemann. Ilsemann is only mentioned once (106) in a reference to the Marburg Speech.

281 Ilsemann II, 212 (1 Feb. 1933).

282 'Telegramm Hitlers an den Kronprinzen, 4. 2. 1933', BAK, R51/2205. See also Sweetman, *Unforgotten Crowns*, 412.

283 Prince Louis Ferdinand of Prussia, *The Rebel Prince*, 223–4.
284 Evaluation Pyta / Orth, 60–97.
285 Ewald von Kleist-Schmenzin, 'Die letzte Möglichkeit. Zur Ernennung Hitlers zum Reichskanzler am 30. Januar 1933', *Politische Studien* 10 (1959), 89–92; Schwerin von Krosigk, *Es geschah in Deutschland*, 147.
286 Berghahn, *Stahlhelm*, 278.
287 Cited in Malinowski, *Vom König zum Führer*, 480.
288 Strenge, *Ferdinand von Bredow*, 69.
289 Hoover Institution Archives, Stanford, Collection Number 77020.
290 'Kronprinz an Hitler, 29. 12. 1934', BAB, R43 / 4063. See also Machtan, *Der Kaisersohn*, 363.
291 'Der Exkronprinz preist Hitlers 'magnetische Kraft'. Interview mit dem Exkronprinzen', *Basler Nachrichten*, 15 Aug. 1934. The French original was 'Il n'y aura plus de guerre franco-allemande. Telle est l'opinion que le kronprinz exprime', *Le Petit Journal*, 15 Aug. 1934.

Chapter 5 Abysses: The Hohenzollerns in the Third Reich (1934–45)

1 Ilsemann II, 346 (25 June 1940).
2 Karl Richard Ganzer, 'Zwischen Leistung und Traum', *Das Reich*, 25 June 1941; Friedrich Wilhelm von Preussen, *Gott helfe*, 267–71.
3 Ilsemann II, 347 (1941, without exact date).
4 Wilhelm II, 'Zusatz zum Testament, 25. 12. 1933', GStA PK, BPH, Rep. 192, Nachlass Dommes, No. 19.
5 Evans, *Das Dritte Reich*, 417–512; Herbert, *Geschichte Deutschlands*, 305–68; Kershaw, *Hitler*, 627–62; Orth, *'Der Amtssitz der Opposition?'*, 291–310.
6 See Jones, 'The Greatest Stupidity'.
7 See Malinowski, *Vom König zum Führer*; Malinowski, *Nazis and Nobles*.
8 See Schmeling, *Josias Erbprinz zu Waldeck und Pyrmont*; Urbach, *Go-Betweens for Hitler*; Büschel, *Hitlers adliger Diplomat*; Petropoulos, *Royals and the Reich*.
9 Petropoulos, *Royals and the Reich*, 380–89; Malinowski, *Vom König zum Führer*, 569–78.
10 Machtan, *Der Kaisersohn*, 309–87.

11 Stiftung Preussische Schlösser und Gärten, Archiv, Akte 2/4062.

12 GStA PK, BPH, Rep. 100 A, No. 360, 361. Cf. Machtan, *Der Kaisersohn*, 375–6.

13 Ilsemann II, 211–13 (February/March 1933).

14 Ibid., 268–9 (28 July 1934) and 270 (4 Aug. 1934).

15 Ibid, 274–5 (22 Aug., 23 Aug., 15 Sept. 1934).

16 Wilhelm II himself doubted that he would ever be ready to 'whistle.' Ibid., 13 (25 July 1924).

17 'Protokolle der drei Begegnungen mit Hitler (9. 5. 1933, 24. 10. 1933, 2. 2. 1934) und zu einer Begegnung mit Hitlers Staatssekretär Hans Heinrich Lammers (26. 9. 1933)', GStA PK, BPH, Rep. 53, No. 167, 1–6; Nachlass John Röhl, Berlin, vol. 91, 68–85. Partially reprinted in Gutsche/Petzold, *Verhältnis*, 934–9; Gutsche, *Kaiser*, 169–79, und Friedrich Wilhelm von Preussen, *Gott helfe*, 182–222.

18 'Cramon an Mackensen, 19. 1. 1934', Nachlass John Röhl, Berlin, vol. 91, 174.

19 'Argumente für eine Rückkehr Seiner Majestät des Kaisers und Königs in Seine Rechte anlässlich des 75. Geburtstages', BAMA, N 266, No. 46, fol. 1–4, and Hindenburg's answer, ibid., No. 83, fol. 17 f.

20 Gasteiger, *Kuno von Westarp*, 467–86, Biskup/Kohlrausch (eds.), *Erbe der Monarchie*, 11–34; Kohlrausch, *Der Monarch im Skandal*, 386–444, 469–75.

21 'Wilhelm II. an Poultney Bigelow, 4. 7. 1933', Nachlass John Röhl, Berlin, vol. 91, 88–9.

22 'Wilhelm II. an seine Schwester Margarete (Mossy), Abschrift, 13. 10. 1933', Nachlass John Röhl, Berlin, vol. 91, 105 (emphasis in original).

23 Ilsemann II, 247–50, here 248.

24 'Ex-Kaiser Plots for Monarchy, Nazi Chief Avers', *Chicago Tribune*, 19 Jan. 1934; 'Deutliche Worte gegen die Reaktion', *Morgenpost*, 19 Jan. 1934. See also the press clippings in Nachlass John Röhl, Berlin, vol. 91, 162–8.

25 Hans Graf von Reischach, 'Aufgang nur für Herrschaften', *Nationalsozialistische Schlesische Tageszeitung*, 24 Jan. 1934.

26 Membership record, Rüdiger Graf von der Goltz, born 8 Dec. 1865, at BAB (BDC).

27 'Generalmajor a. D. Rüdiger Graf von der Goltz an Johann von Leers, 27. 1. 1934', BAMA, N 266, No. 42, fol. 1–12.

28 Fromm, *Hitler*, 175–6; 'Johann von Leers an Cramon, 31. 1. 1934', BAMA, N 266, No. 42, fol. 14–16.

29 Achim von Arnim, 'Der Adel am Scheidewege!', *DAB*, 12 Aug. 1933.

30 'Wilhelm von Dommes an Hitler, 2. 2. 1934', GStA PK, BPH, Rep. 192, Nachlass Dommes, No. 13; 'Briefentwurf Dommes, 30. 1. 1934', GStA PK, BPH, Rep. 53, No. 167/5.

31 'Nazis Against Monarchists', *The Manchester Guardian*, 29 Jan. 1934.

32 'Nazis End Hope of Monarchists by Wide Rebuff', *New York Herald Tribune*, 4 Feb. 1934.

33 'Überwinden und zermalmen!', *Salzburger Chronik*, 27 Jan. 1934.

34 Ilsemann II, 256 (28 Feb. 1934).

35 Hitler, 'Rede im Reichstag am 30.1.1934', *Verhandlungen des Reichstags, IX. Wahlperiode 1933*, vol. 458, 5, 11, 12. See also 'Hitlers Rede im Reichstag', *Neue Freie Presse*, 31 Jan. 1934.

36 'Göring an Frick, 30. 1. 1934', *Vossische Zeitung* 31 Jan. 1934; Sichert, *Cecilienhof*, 239–41.

37 Ilsemann II, 241, 250–52 (27 Nov. 1933, 1, 2, and 7 Feb. 1934).

38 Goebbels, *Tagebücher*, vol. 2/III, 241 (7 Aug. 1933).

39 'Hitler et la kronprinzessin', *Aux écoutes*, 8 April 1933.

40 'Einem an Mackensen, 25. 1. 1934', Nachlass John Röhl, Berlin, vol. 91, 178.

41 Karl von Einem, 'Aufruf!', *Der Aufrechte*, 12/1933 (June 1933), 89.

42 'Hermine an August von Cramon, 19. 5. 1933', Nachlass John Röhl, Berlin, vol. 91, 64.

43 See Grass/Jung, *Papenkreis und Röhmkrise*; Höhne, *Mordsache Röhm*; Kershaw, *Hitler*, 627–62; Orth, 'Amtssitz der Opposition?', 451–518; Siemens, *Sturmabteilung*, 225–54; Jones, *The Limits of Collaboration*.

44 Siemens, *Sturmabteilung*, 108–20; Reichardt, *Faschistische Kampfbünde*, 254–345.

45 Orth, 'Amtssitz der Opposition?', 451–72.

46 Frei, *Führerstaat*, 28.

47 'Der Schlag gegen rechts', *Neue Züricher Zeitung*, 3 July 1934; Ilsemann II, 265 (2 July 1934); Orth, 'Amtssitz der Opposition?', 473.

Notes

48 'Der Führer schützt das Recht. Zur Reichstagsrede Adolf Hitlers vom 13. Juli 1934', *Deutsche Juristen-Zeitung*, 1 Aug. 1934; 'Der Exkronprinz preist Hitlers "magnetische Kraft". Interview mit dem Exkronprinzen', *Basler Nachrichten*, 15 Aug. 1934; Machtan, *Der Kaisersohn*, 333–50.

49 Frei, *Der Führerstaat*, 37.

50 Wolzogen, *Drei Schwestern*, 365.

51 Röhl, *Wilhelm II.*, vol. 3, 1314.

52 Ilsemann II, 264–5 (2 July 1934). See also 266–7 (4, 6, 23 and 28 July 1934).

53 Evaluation Pyta/Orth, 103–10; Ilsemann II, 267 (28 July 1934).

54 Wolzogen, *Drei Schwestern*, 364.

55 'Les exécutions en Allemagne ont été beaucoup plus nombreuses', *L'Écho de Paris*, 2 July 1934; 'Répression sanglante d'Hitler', *Le Petit Provençal*, 2 July 1934; 'Le kronprinz est-il au Danemark?', *Le Progrès de la Côte-d'Or*, 3 July 1934; 'L'ex-kronprinz a été expulsé', *Le Petit Provençal*, 4 July 1934; 'Nouvelles contradictoires au sujet du kronprinz', *Le Quotidien*, 3 July 1934; 'Hohenzollerns Who Are Found Guiltless of Plot', *New York Herald Tribune*, 3 July 1934; 'Family Is Unanimous', *Cincinnati Enquirer*, 2 July 1934; 'Hohenzollern Immune', *The Philadelphia Inquirer Public Ledger*, 2 July 1934; 'Ex-Crown Prince & August Wilhelm', *The Manchester Guardian*, 3 July 1934.

56 Prince Louis Ferdinand of Prussia, *The Rebel Prince*, 24042.

57 Link, *Forging Global Fordism*, 150–57; Pekelder/Schenk/van der Bas, *Der Kaiser*, 96–100; Urbach, *Useful Idiots*, 534–9.

58 'Keppler to Louis Ferdinand, 9 Aug. 1934' and 'Louis Ferdinand to Charles Sorensen, 26 June 1934', Benson Ford Research Center, Dearborn, Michigan, Acc. 572, Box 16, FMC 11.14; 'Louis Ferdinand to Ford, 29 Jan. 1935 and 3 Jan. 1935', Benson Ford Research Center, Dearborn, Michigan, Acc. 6, Box 227. See also the photo in Link, *Rethinking the Ford–Nazi Connection*, 147.

59 'Heinrich F. Albert to Charles Sorensen, 6 Dec. 1935', Benson Ford Research Center, Dearborn, Michigan, Acc. 38, Box 28.

60 'Louis Ferdinand to Henry Ford, 29 Jan. 1935', Benson Ford Research Center, Dearborn, Michigan, Acc. 6, Box 227.

61 'Royal Salesman', *Indianapolis Times*, 28 July 1928.

62 See Gassert, *Amerika im Dritten Reich*.

63 Link, *Forging Global Fordism*, 131–71.

64 'Royalty Calls at White House', *Henderson Daily Dispatch*, 11 June 1938; 'Prince Greets American "Pal" ', *Henderson Daily Dispatch*, 15 June 1938.

65 Budrass, *Adler und Kranich*, 141–372.

66 'Fascism to Monarchy?', *Sunday Star* (Washington), 13 Dec. 1936. 'Kaiser's Kind Hyde Park Guests', *Henderson Daily Dispatch*, 30 May 1938.

67 'Charles Lindbergh rencontre le Kronprinz', *Paris-soir*, 29 July 1936; 'En quelques lignes', *L'Express de Mulhouse*, 29 July 1936.

68 'Fête aérienne à Berlin', *Paris-soir*, 4 April 1934; 'Hitler, Goering, Goebbels, Guillaume de Hohenzollern vus de près', *La Petite Gironde*, 29 Feb. 1936; 'Allemagne 1934', *L'Écho d'Alger*, 6 April 1934. See Link, *Forging Global Fordism*, 154.

69 The term was coined by Charles Wright Mills in 1956 and came to lasting fame through its use in Dwight D. Eisenhower's farewell speech on 17 January 1961.

70 Channon, *The Diaries*, 323, 328, 558–9, 561–4, 730–35, here 556. See also Karina Urbach, 'Blick in den Abgrund', *Taz*, 11 April 2021. Thanks to Urbach for alerting me to Channon. On the function of Nazi high society, see D'Almeida, *Hakenkreuz und Kaviar*, 210–88; Petropoulos, *Royals and the Reich*, 176–269.

71 Channon, *The Diaries*, 563.

72 'Ein Buch über Kronprinz Wilhelm', *Berliner Börsen-Zeitung*, 15 Dec. 1933.

73 Lange, *Der Kronprinz und sein wahres Gesicht*.

74 Ibid.

75 See Jürgen Luh, 'Carl Lange und "Der Kronprinz" ', *Texte des RECS* #42, 11 May 2021, https://recs.hypotheses.org/6381; and Luh, *Der Kronprinz*, 35–50.

76 'Die Winterfahrt-Sieger. Deutsche Erzeugnisse in allen Klassen überlegen', *Kreuzzeitung*, 6 March 1934.

77 'Rundschreiben Nr.101/35 des Stellvertreters des Führers (Hess), 23.5.1935', BAB, NS 6, No. 219.

78 Pekelder/Schenk/van der Bas, *Der Kaiser*, 100.

79 'Grossfürst Kyrill von Russland. Der Prätendent auf den Thron der Romanows', *Deutsche Allgemeine Zeitung*, 14 Oct. 1938.

Notes

80 'Le grand-duc Wladimir se verra-t-il offrir la couronne d'Ukraine?', *La Dépêche*, 17 Dec. 1938; 'Le Prétendant au trône impérial de Russie recontrera-t-il le dirigeant du Reich?', *L'Indépendance Belge*, 18 Dec. 1938; 'Grand Duke Vladimir's Visit to Germany', *The Times*, 19 Dec. 1938.

81 *Evening Star* (Washington), 28 June 1941; 'Russian Throne?', *Midland Journal*, 18 July 1941; Talbot Lake, 'Proposed Soviet Puppet Former Ford Employee', *Daily Monitor*, 23 July. Report by R. A. Butler, 16 June 1941, PRO, FO 371/29467; 'Soviet Troops Hold Up German Drive. Monarchist Restoration', *China Weekly Review* (Shanghai), 12 June 1941; 'Berlin Speculates on Russian Regime', *New York Times*, 26 June 1941; 'Red Army Deemed Set to Spring Surprises', *The Washington Post*, 29 June 1941; 'One Touch of Royalty Makes Some Heads Spin', *The Washington Post*, 8 June 1941.

82 See Schlögel, *Der grosse Exodus*; Kellogg, *The Russian Roots of Nazism*; Baur, *Die russische Kolonie*, 253–314.

83 'Czarist Pretender Arouses German Ire', *New York Times*, 26 April 1942; 'Nazis Seize Staff of Pretender to Russian Throne', *New York Herald Tribune*, 26 April 1942.

84 Sigrid Schultz Papers, Box 40, Folder 11. Thanks to David Milne for pointing out this source.

85 'Une princesse allemande à Londres', *Paris-soir*, 18 Dec. 1936.

86 'Hermine to General W. H. H. Waters, 15. 3. 1936', Nachlass John Röhl, Berlin, vol. 91, fol. 425.

87 Prince Friedrich Wilhelm (*Gott helfe*, 231–2) would later write of a 'document of his intrepidness'.

88 See Haslam, *The Spectre of War*, 258–325; Self, *Neville Chamberlain*, 235–350; Bouverie, *Appeasing Hitler*.

89 See Urbach, *Go-Betweens for Hitler*.

90 Müller, *Generaloberst Ludwig Beck*, 307–64.

91 See the paper of Ludwig Beck in Dresden's Militärhistorisches Museum.

92 Müller, *Generaloberst Ludwig Beck*, 63–132.

93 Meinl, *Nationalsozialisten gegen Hitler*, 268–98; Parssinen, *Die vergessene Verschwörung*, 179–83. See also the apparently coded letter from Prince Wilhelm of Prussia to Friedrich Wilhelm Heinz on 14 Sept. 1938, MHMB, Dresden, Nachlass Heinz, BBAT 2549.

94 'Hitler Seeking Unity, Avers Kin of Kaiser Here', *Chicago Tribune*, 4 August 1934.

95 Jonas, *Der Kronprinz*, 249.

96 Prince Louis Ferdinand of Prussia, *The Rebel Prince*, 224–6.

97 'Louis Ferdinand to Ernest Liebold, 21 March 1933', Benson Ford Research Center, Dearborn, Michigan, Acc. 23, Box 6. See also Link, *Forging Global Fordism*, 150. Thanks to Stefan J. Link for alerting me to this source and the archive as a whole.

98 Röhl, *Wilhelm II.*, vols. 1, and 2.

99 'Wilhelm II. an Gräfin von der Goltz, 7. 8. 1940', NL-UtHUA A16712, 000027.

100 Haehner, 'Tagebuch, Eintrag vom 11. 11. 1919'. Wilhelm II's praise was directed at Dinter's anti-Semitic popular novel *Sünde wider das Blut* (Sin Against Blood).

101 'L'ex-kronprinz salue la dépouille du grand soldat', *Paris-soir*, 4 Aug. 1934; 'L'Allemagne fête ses morts', *L'Ère nouvelle*, 18 March 1935; 'En présence du kronprinz et du führer', *L'Ami du Peuple*, 9 May 1936; 'Le kronprinz est reçu par le Führer', *Le Petit Journal*, 6 Feb. 1935; 'La récente visite à Hitler', *Le Petit Parisien*, 9 Feb. 1935; 'En causant, à Berlin avec l'ex-kronprinz', *Le Petit Journal*, 23 May 1935; 'Devant le Kronprinz en uniforme de feld-maréchal Hitler a passé une revue des troupes', *L'Ouest-Éclair* (Rennes), 18 March 1935.

102 '"L'Europe devrait remercier Hitler," déclare l'ex-kronprinz', *L'Express de Mulhouse*, 29 May 1935.

103 'La popularité du kronprinz', *La Liberté*, 16 Feb. 1937.

104 Sichert, *Cecilienhof*, 195–7.

105 'Ex-Crown Prince "Bawled Out" for Slouching in Nazi Ranks', *New York Herald Tribune*, 22 April 1934, 1; '"The former 'highness' is a private in the Brown Shirt motor corps; in other words a truck driver": 'Ex-Crown Prince Is "Just in Army Now"', *The Hartford Courant*, 18 April 1934. See also Sichert, *Cecilienhof*, 195–7.

106 'Ex-Kaiser's Son Will Beg for Coins', *Chicago Tribune*, 24 Feb. 1934; 'Former Kaiser's Son Proves His Success as a Beggar Prince', *Chicago Tribune*, 25 Feb. 1934.

107 See Del Boca, *La guerra d'Etiopia*; Dominioni, *Lo sfascio dell'Impero*; Mattioli, *Experimentierfeld der Gewalt*.

108 'Telegramm aus Oels', *Das Schwarze Korps*, 14 May 1936, 2.

109 'Un télégramme du kronprinz à M. Mussolini', *Le Progrès de la Côte-d'Or*, 10 May 1936; 'La presse nazi critique l'ex-kronprinz', *La Liberté*, 18 May 1936; 'Le kronprinz étroitement surveillé', *L'Ami du peuple*, 21 May 1936; 'L'Hitlerisme contre les Hohenzollern', *L'Intransigeant*, 1 June 1936.

110 'Schreiben des SA-Standarten- und Stabsführers Kwalo, 1. 11. 1937, über den freiwilligen Austritt des Kronprinzen im Juli 1936 nebst anderen Dokumenten über den Austritt in den SA-Personalakten im Bundesarchiv', copies in Sammlung LARoV, vol. 24, hier fol. 232.

111 Preussen, *Gott helfe*, 219 f., 375 f.

112 See Gross, *November 1938*.

113 Ilsemann II, 313–14 (14 and 24 November 1938); Röhl, *Wilhelm II.*, vol. 3, 1321; Friedrich Wilhelm von Preussen, *Gott helfe*, 195–6.

114 Clark, *Wilhelm II.*, 330, passes this assertion from Balfour (*Der Kaiser*, 456) and Gutsche (*Kaiser im Exil* 208), who in turn cite Jonas's *The Life of Crown Prince William* (175, 190 – where there is no mention of any such interview) and Whittle (*Kaiser Wilhelm II*, 387), who refers back to Balfour (456). The legend has also been passed on by Zorgbibe (*Guillaume II*, 374) and the historian Pauline Piettre in a major documentary film by Maud Guillaumin, *Les Monarchies face à Hitler* (2021). The French newspaper interview shown there ('Une entrevue sensationelle: Guillaume II déclare à l'envoyé spécial de Voilà ce qu'il pense d'Hitler et des événements actuels', in *Voilà*, 30 Sept. 1938) was probably a fake and was published in any case five weeks before the Night of Broken Glass pogrom and thus could not have commented on it. Versions of this text later turned up in the American and British press: 'Hitler Made Germany Nation of Fanatics', *The Minneapolis Star*, 8 Dec. 1938; 'Germany Has Been Turned into a Country of Fanatics, Says Kaiser, Accusing Hitler', *The Enquirer* (Cincinnati), 8. Dec. 1938; 'The Kaiser Attacks Hitler', *The Scotsman*, 8 Dec. 1938.

115 'Een gefingeerd interview. De ex-keizer en Hitler', *Het Vaderland*, 8

Dec. 1938; 'Het gefingeerde interview te Doorn', *Het Vaderland*, 9 Dec. 1938; 'Kaiser Disapproves Outrages', *New York Times*, 18 Nov. 1938; 'Ex-Kaiser's Denial of Reported Interview', *The Manchester Guardian*, 9 Dec. 1938; 'Story Denied', *South China Morning Post*, 9 Dec. 1938; 'Denial by Kaiser', *South China Morning Post*, 16 Dec. 1938.

116 'Wilhelm II. an General Waters, 29. 12. 1938', in Nachlass John Röhl, Stabi Berlin, Bd. 91, Bl. 685.

117 Wilhelm II., 'Losungen, Eintrag vom 10. 11. 1938', Nachlass John Röhl, Stabi Berlin.

118 Machtan, *Der Kaisersohn*, 364–5.

119 Galbraith, 'Hereditary Land in the Third Reich'.

120 *Die Erzeugungsschlacht im Kriege*, published by Reichsministerium für Ernährung und Landwirtschaft, Munich 1940; Corni / Gies, *Brot-Butter-Kanonen*, 261–318; Kluge, *Agrarwirtschaft und ländliche Gesellschaft*, 88–98.

121 See Hofe, *Vier Prinzen*.

122 See, for example, Ilsemann II, 250, 306, 313 (1 Feb. 1934, 28 July and 14 Nov. 1938).

123 Dommes, 'Notizen für eine Besprechung mit Lammers', September 1933, in Nachlass John Röhl, Berlin, vol. 91, 70–71.

124 'Hitler et les Hohenzollern', *L'Express de Mulhouse*, 29 June 1936.

125 Ilsemann II, 255 (23 Feb. 1934).

126 See ibid., 255–6 (23 and 26 Feb. 1934); Sichert, *Cecilienhof*, 340–42.

127 'Les Hohenzollern aux ordres', *Le Figaro*, 4 Feb. 1934.

128 *Pariser Tageszeitung*, 19 May 1937.

129 Ilsemann II, 306–8, (28 July, 12 and 13 August 1938).

130 'Aktenvermerk Reichskanzlei, 16. 8. 1938', BAB, R43 II / 287, fol. 259. See also Dornheim, *Die Thüringer Fürstenhäuser*.

131 Gutsche, *Ein Kaiser im Exil*, 211.

132 See Schleusener, *Eigentumspolitik im NS-Staat*.

133 Letter to the editor by Racheli Edelman, *New York Review of Books*, 26 March 2020; 'Israelische Verlegerin wirft Hohenzollern Arisierung vor', *Der Spiegel*, 27 March 2020; Klaus Wiegrefe, 'Kumpanei mit den Nazis könnte für die Hohenzollern teuer werden', *Der Spiegel*, 24 Jan. 2020; 'Helping Hitler: An Exchange', *New York Review*

of Books, 9 April 2020. See also the corrrespondence in GStA PK, BPH, Rep. 192 Dommes, No. 3 und No. 4; 'Schreiben betr. der Rohtex AG, zur Kenntnisnahme an Plettenberg und Berg, 18. 9. 1943', GStA PK, Rep. 100 A, 220.

134 Zboralski, *Quellenfunde*, 772–4; Gutsche, *Ein Kaiser*, 193–224.

135 Aly und Heim, *Architects of Annihilation*, 260–61.

136 'Nikolaus Erbgrossherzog von Oldenburg an Himmler, 2. 6. 1941': BAB (BDC), Nikolaus Erbgrossherzog von Oldenburg, 10. 8. 1897. Further examples include 'Erasmus Freiherr von Malsen-Ponickau, 16. 6. 1941, an Reichstatthalter in Posen, Adolf Fürst zu Bentheim-Tecklenburg-Rheda, Schreiben von 1939', BAB (BDC); 'Schreiben der Ehefrau Heinrich von Bismarcks für ihren "im Felde" stehenden Ehemann vom 18. 11. 1939', BAB (BDC), PA: Heinrich von Bismarck, 22. 10. 1905; and 'Bismarcks Schreiben vom 10. 2. 1943'. See also Malinowski, *Nazis and Nobles*, 288–302.

137 'Schriftwechsel zwischen den Brüdern Wolrad und Heinrich Schaumburg-Lippe, April 1943', Hofe, *Vier Prinzen*, 154.

138 Dornheim, *Rasse, Raum und Autarkie*, 88–96.

139 Hofe, *Vier Prinzen*, 92–3.

140 https://www.vierprinzen.com/2019/12/praktikum-in-ausschliessungsgrunde-teil.html?m=1; Hofe, *Vier Prinzen*, 80–82.

141 'Siebert an Lammers, 29. 7. 1938', BAB, R43, No. 4063, fol. 41–6.

142 See 'Erbhof-Antrag von Erbprinz Reuss vom 31. 10. 1938': Dornheim, *Die Thüringer Fürstenhäuser*, 282–90; Malinowski, *Vom König zum Führer*, 524–5.

143 'Kronprinz an Hermann Göring, 29. 6. 1939', BAB, R43, 4063, 3, 99–101.

144 See evaluation Clark, 11–12.

145 Petropoulos, *Royals and the Reich*, 264; Schmeling, *Waldeck*, 71–2; Malinowski, *Vom König zum Führer*, 564–9.

146 Ilsemann II, 308, 312–15 (13 Aug., 29 Oct., 24 and 27 Nov. 1938); Machtan, *Der Kaisersohn*, 364–5.

147 Zboralski, *Quellenfunde*, 774; Hoffmann, *Der Skandal*, 188.

148 'Der Osthilfesumpf', *Vorwärts*, 25 Feb. 1933; 'Noch nicht genug?', *Berliner Tageblatt*, 25 Jan. 1933; ibid., 2 and 7 Feb. 1933; 'Osthilfe im Rampenlicht', *Frankfurter Zeitung*, 20 Jan. 1933.

149 See Hoffmann, *Der Skandal.*

150 Kessler, *Das Tagebuch*, vol. 9, 535 (28 Jan. 1933).

151 Theodor Wolff, 'Die hungrigen Raben', *Berliner Tageblatt*, 29 Jan. 1933.

152 See Aly, *Hitler's Beneficiaries.* See also the forum for reviews organized by Winfried Süss in *Sehepunkte*, 5, 7 / 8 (2005); Michael Wildt, 'Vertrautes Ressentiment', *Die Zeit*, 4 May 2005; Hans-Ulrich Wehler, 'Engstirniger Materialismus', *Der Spiegel*, 3 April 2005; Mark Spoerer, 'Rezension zu Aly, Hitlers Volksstaat', *H-Soz-Kult*, 26 May 2005; Adam Tooze, 'A New Look at Nazi Plunder', *Telegraph*, 9 Aug. 2007.

153 Hitler cited in Sichert, *Cecilienhof*, 350–51.

154 'Crown Prince's Son to Enlist in German Army', *Chicago Tribune*, 30 Oct. 1934.

155 'Kaiser's Grandson Is Killed in Action', *New York Times*, 17 Sept. 1939; Friedrich Wilhelm von Preussen, *Gott helfe*, 272–3.

156 'Toujours des bruits relatifs à un mouvement monarchiste', *Le Journal*, 15 Nov. 1939.

157 See Böhler, *Auftakt zum Vernichtungskrieg.*

158 'Wilhelm Prinz von Preussen an Friedrich Wilhelm Heinz, 16. 10. 1939', MHMB, Dresden, Nachlass Heinz, BBAT 25575.

159 See Funck, *The Meaning of Dying.*

160 'Gedenkblatt des Corps Saxo Borussia für SKH Wilhelm Prinz von Preussen, 26. 9. 1940', Utrechts Archief, NL-UtHUA, A16712000133:

161 Friedrich Wilhelm von Preussen, *Gott helfe*, 272–7; Jonas, *Der Kronprinz*, 262–4. Cf. other records in Petropoulos, *Royals and the Reich*, 282–3.

162 Heinrich, *Geschichte Preussens*, 515–16.

163 Friedrich Wilhelm von Preussen, *Gott helfe*, 275; Klee, *Personenlexikon*, 385; Ueberschär / Vogel, *Dienen und Verdienen*; 'Mackensen an Wilhelm II., 25. 03. 1935', Nachlass John Röhl, Berlin, vol. 91, fol. 374–5.

164 August von Mackensen, 'Wie ich zu Adolf Hitler gekommen bin, 1. 2. 1942', Nachlass John Röhl, Berlin, vol. 92 (dated 16 Dec. 1939 / 1 Feb. 1942).

165 'Marie Fürstin zu Ysenburg an Olga Prinzessin zur Lippe, 29. 1. 1944', Privatarchiv Christoph Freiherr von Wolzogen. This letter is preserved together with the announcement of the death of decorated Major Prince Heinrich zu Sayn-Wittgenstein-Sayn, who had fallen in 'aerial battle after his 83rd nighttime sortie true to the tradition of his

house in battle for the fatherland he so passionately loved'. See also *Akten der Partei-Kanzlei der NSDAP*, 887; 'Brief Hermines, 23. 1. 1942', GStA PK, BPH, Rep. 53, 372.

166 'Eidesstattliche Erklärung August Wilhelm Prinz von Preussen vor dem Verhör mit Robert Kempner, 16. 5. 1947', USHMM, Kempner Papers, Box 313, Folder 19.

167 Wolzogen, *Drei Schwestern*, 405.

168 'Kordt an Dommes, 11. 9. 1940', and 'Briefe vom 19. 9. 1940, 28. 6. 1941, 30. 10. 1941', GStA PK, BPH Rep. 192, Nachlass Berg, No. 6. See also 'Friedrich Prinz von Preussen an Bigelow, Januar 1941', Utrechts Archief, NL-UtHUA, A16712000232.

169 'Kronprinz an Farrar, 10. 1. 1941', Library of Congress, Farrar Papers, Correspondence, Box 11, Folder 34.

170 'Friedrich Graf von der Schulenburg an Heinrich Prinz von Schönburg-Waldenburg, 28. 12. 1929', Privatbesitz Christoph von Wolzogen.

171 'Friedrich Graf von der Schulenburg an Generalleutnant Max von Viebahn, 25. 3. 1938', SS-Personalakte, BAB, R436-III/555316.

172 'Oberkommando der Wehrmacht (gezeichnet von Wilhelm Keitel), Verbot der Beteiligung von Wehrmachtsangehörigen an Feierlichkeiten aus Anlass des 80. Geburtstags Wilhelm II, 21. 12. 1938', GStA PK, BPH, Rep. 192, Nachlass Dommes, No. 13.

173 Halifax, correspondence and telegrams 10 and 11 May 1940, National Archives, London, Foreign Office, Political Department, FO 371 24422.

174 Ilsemann II, 259–63, 269–70 (May–August 1934).

175 Gutsche, *Ein Kaiser im Exil*, 198–200; Röhl, *Wilhelm II.*, vol. 3, 1319.

176 'Bericht des Leibarztes Wilhelms II., Dr. von Ortenberg, (Abschrift, Mai 1940)', Utrechts Archief, NL-UtHUA, A 16712, 000143, copy in Nachlass John Röhl, Berlin, vol. 92.

177 Gutsche, *Ein Kaiser im Exil*, 205–6.

178 'Hermine an Margarete Landgräfin von Hessen-Kassel, die Schwester Wilhelms II., 28. 6. 1940', Nachlass John Röhl, Berlin, vol. 92.

179 'Hermine an Prinzessin Solms-Braunfels, 6. 6. 1940', ibid.

180 See the various telegrams to Hitler and Lammers and the responses in BAB, R 43/40–3.

181 'Telegramm an Hitler ('Mein Führer!')', BAB, R 43/40–3.

182 'Telegramme Kaiser-Hitler, 25. 9. 1939, 17. 6. 1940 und 25. 6. 1940', GStA PK, BPH, Rep. 192 Nachlass Dommes, No. 17.

183 'Meerwald an Cecilie, 20.4.1939', Bundesarchiv Berlin-Lichterfelde, R 43-II/287, fol. 265–6.

184 https://www.alexautographs.com/auction-lot/hermann-goering_822409F847/#0 (accessed 21 May 2021).

185 Zoller, *Hitler privat*, 186.

186 'Die Todesstunde der Reaktion', *Völkischer Beobachter*, 10 Aug. 1944.

187 Conze, *Adel und Adeligkeit*, 269–70.

188 SS-Personalakte Friedrich Graf von der Schulenburg, BAB, R436-III/555316.

189 See the comments made by a Hohenzollern family lawyer on 'Gerichte und Geschichte. Die Forderungen der Hohenzollern', HR2 radio programme *Der Tag*, 29 July 2021.

190 'Exclusif. Notre entretien sans tabou avec Georg Friedrich de Prusse', *Point de Vue*, 30 July 2021.

191 'Nicht im Traum wollte er Kaiser sein, Interview mit Georg Friedrich Prinz von Preussen', *Stuttgarter Nachrichten*, 19 June 2017.

192 Friedrich Wilhelm von Preussen, *Gott helfe*, 280–302, quote on 301.

193 See Benjamin Hasselhorn's commentary, 'Streit um Entschädigung. Wem gehörte der Hohenzollernschatz?', SWR2 radio programme *Forum*, 7 Aug. 2019.

194 See Schlabrendorff, *Begegnungen*, 271, 311. Over the course of 400 pages, the author only mentions Crown Prince Wilhelm twice, both times in the context of Ludwig Beck's aversion to him.

195 See Schlabrendorff, *Offiziere gegen Hitler*. See also Müller, *Fabian von Schlabrendorff*.

196 Keyserlingk-Rehbein, *Nur eine 'ganz kleine Clique'*, 326–7, 466–7. By way of comparison, the author mentioned the House of Hohenzollern four times and never in conjunction with any activity that could be described as resistance. See ibid., 128, 144, 539, 663.

197 This assertion is based on a viewing of the catalogue and information provided by the memorial's director Peter Steinbach and Johannes

Tuchel on 6 August 2019. See Steinbach/Tuchel (eds.), *Widerstand gegen die nationalsozialistische Diktatur.*

198 See Machtan, *Der Kronprinz und die Nazis*; Machtan, *Quellen.* On Lothar Machtan's idiosyncratically composed selection of sources, see the meticulous review by Luh, 'Fiat Lux?'.

199 'Franz von Papen an Klaus W. Jonas, 26. 3. 1958'; Wernher von Braun an Jonas, 31. 10. 1961'; 'Magnus Freiherr von Braun an Jonas, 8. 10. 1961', Universität Augsburg, Nachlass Klaus W. Jonas.

200 Jonas, *Der Kronprinz*, 269.

201 See Paul/Mallmann (eds.), *Die Gestapo.*

202 Prince Louis Ferdinand of Prussia, *The Rebel Prince*, 321–34; Prinz Louis Ferdinand von Preussen, *Die Geschichte meines Lebens*, 288–308.

203 See Becker/Studt, *Der Umgang des Dritten Reichs.*

204 Schmidt, *Plettenberg*, 221, 243.

205 Maurice Frankenhuis, 'Interview mit Louis Ferdinand Prinz von Preussen in New York, 21. 1. 1965', Maurice Frankenhuis Collection, used with the kind permission of Aaron Oppenheim.

206 See Middendorf, *Ausserwirtschaftlicher Wille?*; Dipper, *Der deutsche Widerstand*; Friedländer, *Les années d'extermination*, 632, 775–8.

207 Carter Hett/Wala, *Otto John*, 15–36.

208 Ibid., 289–331. See also the evidence from John and other memoirs in Friedrich Wilhelm von Preussen, *Gott helfe*, 322–5.

209 McCannon, 'Generalfeldmarschall Georg von Küchler', in Ueberschär (ed.), *Hitlers militärische Elite*, vol. 1, 138–45; Klee, *Personenlexikon*, 347; Prinz Louis Ferdinand, *Die Geschichte meines Lebens*, 290–91.

210 See Schwerin, *'Dann sind's die besten Köpfe, die man henkt'*; Karlauf, *Stauffenberg. Porträt eines Attentäters*; Hoffmann, *Stauffenberg und seine Brüder.*

211 Wheeler-Bennett, *Nemesis der Macht*, 529; Sichert, *Cecilienhof*, 371–3.

212 Wolfgang Schieder, 'Zwei Generationen im militärischen Widerstand gegen Hitler', in Schmädeke/Steinbach, *Der Widerstand gegen den Nationalsozialismus*, 436–59. On the attitudes of major members of the resistance, see Hoffmann, *Claus Schenk Graf von Stauffenberg und seine Brüder*, 61–78; Hans Mommsen, 'Fritz-Dietlof Graf von

der Schulenburg und die preussische Tradition', *VfZ* 1977, 213–39; Mommsen, *Alternative zu Hitler*.

213 See Mommsen, 'Gesellschaftsbild'.

214 Ritter, *Carl Goerdeler*, 567–8; Jonas, *Der Kronprinz*, 273–5.

215 The spectrum of interpretations runs from Hamerow, *Die Attentäter*, to Schöllgen, *Ulrich von Hassell*. See also Hassel, *Vom anderen Deutschland*, 240–41.

216 Roderick Stackelberg, 'Theodore S. Hamerow, On the Road to the Wolf's Lair: German Resistance to Hitler', *Central European History*, 33, 1 (2000), 150–51, here 151.

217 Ritter, *Goerdeler*; cf. also the earlier standard text by Hans Rothfels, *Die deutsche Opposition gegen Hitler*.

218 See the prince's own account in Louis Ferdinand von Preussen, *Als Kaiserenkel durch die Welt*, 358–368; Jonas, *Der Kronprinz*, 275–7.

219 Ritter, *Goerdeler*, 290–94, 504 f., 567 f., quote on 292. See also Hassell, *Vom anderen Deutschland*, 94, 174, 213, 224, 240–42. In light of these two sources, it is astonishing that Prince Friedrich Wilhelm (*Hohenzollern*, 274 f.) would claim that the crown prince decided not to get involved 'after many years of fruitless back and forth within the resistance movement'. See also the partially unsubstantiated account in Herre, *Kronprinz Wilhelm*, 229–39.

220 Prince Louis Ferdinand of Prussia, *The Rebel Prince*, 317–18; Louis Ferdinand von Preussen 'Kaiser auf Abruf', TV Interview, 1987; Ritter, *Carl Goerdeler*, 290–93, 504–5.

221 Prince Louis Ferdinand of Prussia, *The Rebel Prince*, 317–18.

222 Ritter, *Goerdeler*, 293.

223 Cannadine, *Winston Churchill*, 89–91, 113.

224 See, for instance, *Courrier de Saône-et-Loire*, 7 Feb. 1938.

225 'Qu'est devenu le kronprinz', *Le Jour*, 14 Nov. 1939; 'Le kronprinz décapité', *Le Midi socialiste*, 14 Nov. 1939; 'L'ex-kronpriz n'a pas été décapité par les nazis', *Le Petit Marseillais*, 14 Nov. 1939; 'L'ex-kronprinz est gardé à vue', *Le Petit Courrier*, 10 Nov. 1939; 'Le " Complot" monarchiste', *L'Ouest-Éclair* (Rennes), 17 Nov. 1939; 'Le régime hitlérien sévit contre les Hohenzollern', *Le Matin*, 17 Nov. 1939; 'Toujours des bruits relatifs à un mouvement monarchiste', *Le Journal*, 15 Nov. 1939.

226 'Pour briser l'opposition monarchiste la Gestapo a arrêté plusieurs offi-
ciers supérieurs', *La France de Bordeaux et du Sud-Ouest*, 17 Nov. 1939; 'La
Gestapo fouille les maison des Hohenzollern', *Paris-soir*, 15 Nov. 1939.

227 'Une déclaration écrite de l'ex-kronprinz', *Excelsior*, 23 Nov. 1939; 'La
répression. Himmler et les Hohenzollern', *L'Europe nouvelle*, 2 Dec.
1939; 'Journal des débats politiques et littéraires', 22 Nov. 1939.

228 *Pariser Tageszeitung*, 15, 22 and 23 Nov. 1939.

Chapter 6: Tragedy and Farce: The Hohenzollerns and Post-War Germany

1 Haehner, 'Tagebuch, Eintrag vom 28. 2. 1920', Historisches Archiv
der Stadt Köln, 108.

2 Hardenberg, *Auf immer neuen Wegen*, 30–96, esp. 62–3; Gerbet, *Carl-
Hans Graf von Hardenberg*, 12–96.

3 Petropoulos, *Royals and the Reich*, 281.

4 See Schlabrendorff, *Offiziere gegen Hitler*. The English translation is
titled *The Secret War against Hitler*.

5 See Schlabrendorff's depictions of Heinrich Class and Elard von
Oldenburg-Januschau, in *Begegnungen in fünf Jahrzehnten*, 51–58, 149–67.

6 Schlabrendorff, *Offiziere gegen Hitler*, 168–9.

7 Albrecht Lehmann, ' "Grafenerzählungen". Gehobene Heimat- und
Erinnerungsprosa für Bürger von heute', in Lipp (ed.), *Medien populärer Kultur*, 60–70.

8 See Hofmann, *Marion Dönhoff*; Malinowski, *Nazis and Nobles*, 261–6,
321–6; Malinowski, 'Hüter des Grals. Wie der Adel seit 1945 vom Widerstand erzählt', *Die Zeit*, 17 July 2019.

9 See Malinowski, 'Die Hüter des Grals'.

10 Laurent Muzellec/Mary Lambkin, 'Corporate Rebranding: Destroying, Transferring or Creating Brand Equity?', *European Journal of
Marketing* 40 (2006), 803–24.

11 Schlabrendorff, *Begegnungen in fünf Jahrzehnten*, 239–53.

12 Kürenberg, *War alles falsch?*.

13 'Material für Mr. Louis P. Lochner, September 1946', GStA PK, BPH,
Rep. 192, Nachlass Dommes, No. 15.

14 'Schreiben Hardenbergs vom 28. 5. 1952', GStA PK, Rep. 192, Nachlass Dommes, No. 3.

15 Ritthaler, *Wilhelm II* ; Ritthaler, *Die Hohenzollern*.

16 Sichert, *Cecilienhof*, 129–32, 159, 171.

17 See Lehndorff, *Ostpreussisches Tagebuch*; Görlitz, *Die Junker*, 410–31. On aristocratic lives and the post-1945 aristocratic cult of memory, see also Donig, *Adel ohne Land*.

18 'Dommes an Ilsemann, 29. 6. 1948', GStA PK, BPH, Rep. 192 Dommes, No. 8; Klaus Schlegel, 'Wilhelm von Dommes. Zur 100. Wiederkehr seines Geburtstages am 15. 9. 1967', GStA PK, BPH, Rep. 192 Dommes, No. 23.

19 *New York Times*, 11 and 12 Aug. 1947. See also 'Farrar an Kronprinz, 13. 8. 1947'; 'Kronprinz an Farrar, 22. 8. 1947 und 5. 9. 1947', Library of Congress, Farrar Papers, Correspondence, Box 11, Folder 35.

20 'Kaiser's Widow Says Ex-Ruler Detested Hitler', *New York Herald Tribune*, 20 April 1947. See also the material in GStA PK, BPH, Rep. 192 Dommes, No. 10.

21 'Le monde hippique est parfois mêlé', *Combat*, 6 May 1945; 'Le kronprinz est vivant', *L'Aube*, 6 May 1945.

22 'Les prisonniers de marque', *La Croix*, 8 May 1945.

23 'Ruhmloses Ende der Nazihäuptlinge', *Österreichische Zeitung*, 9 May 1945.

24 Henriette Chandet, 'En Allemagne', *UNF – Union nationale des femmes. Revue des électrices*, 1 June 1945.

25 'Pour le Kronprinz la guerre s'est arrêtée à Verdun', *Nuit et Jour. Le grand journal illustré*, 31 May 1945; Paul Bringuier, 'Visite à Lindau', *France Soir*, 31 July 1945.

26 'Et le Kronprinz joue à la belote', *Ambiance*, 18 July 1945; Louis Parrot, 'Le Kronprinz pleure misère . . . Et les Hohenzollern mènent la vie de château un peu à l'étroit', *Ce Soir*, 23 Feb. 1946; 'Revue de Presse', *L'Avenir Normand*, 22 Aug. 1946.

27 Martin Sabrow, 'Die Hohenzollern und die Demokratie nach 1918 Teil II', *Deutschland Archiv*, 18. 12. 2020, www.bpb.de / 324802.

28 'Allies Are Not Practicing Democracy in Germany, Crown Prince

Says', *The Evening Bulletin* (Philadelphia), 8 Nov. 1946, Library of Congress, Farrar Papers, Correspondence, Box 11, Folder 35.

29 Jacques Forestier, 'Le Kronprinz trouve Hitler bavard, Goebbels infâme et voudrait voyager', *Paris-Presse*, 8 Nov. 1945.

30 'Kronprinz an Farrar, 5. 9. 1947', Library of Congress, Farrar Papers, Correspondence, Box 11, Folder 35.

31 'Kupsch an Dommes, 25. 9. 1947', GStA PK, BPH, Rep. 192 Dommes, No. 1.

32 Jonas, *Der Kronprinz*, 295–304, here 298; Sichert, *Cecilienhof*, vol. 1, 66–70.

33 'Aufstellung vom 30. 6. 1941', GStA PK, I. HA Rep. 100 A, No. 363.

34 'Aufstellungen vom 2. 4. 1943 und vom 6. 12. 1943', GStA PK, I. HA Rep. 100 A, No. 247.

35 Sichert, *Cecilienhof*, vol. 1, 118–32.

36 See 'Kronprinz an Farrar, 18. 1. 1947', and the rest of their extensive correspondence in Farrar Papers, Library of Congress.

37 Library of Congress, Farrar Papers, Correspondence, Box 11, Folder 34.

38 'Kronprinz an Farrar, 24. 1. 1948', Library of Congress, Farrar Papers, Correspondence, Box 11, Folder 35.

39 'Crown Prince to Farrar, 16 April 1947', Library of Congress, Farrar Papers, Correspondence, Box 11, Folder 35.

40 'Farrar an Kronprinz, 21. 5. 1947', Library of Congress, Farrar Papers, Correspondence, Box 11, Folder 35.

41 'Ex-Kronprinz Wilhelm sagte in Nürnberg aus', *Weltpresse*, 21 June 1947.

42 'Vernehmung vom 17. 6. 1947', USHMM, Kempner Papers, Box 310, Folder 19, 10. See also Jonas, *Der Kronprinz*, 294.

43 Conversation on 17 May 1945, described in Jonas, *Der Kronprinz*, 283–4.

44 'Kronprinz Wilhelm, der Sportsmann', *Pforzheimer Anzeiger*, 17 March 1950.

45 Kronprinz an Farrar, 2. 12. 1947, Library of Congress, Farrar Papers, Correspondence, Box 11, Folder 35.

46 'Kronprinz an Franz Sontag, 17. 8. 1948', BAB, N 1064, No. 17.

47 'La mort du kronprinz. Ni empereur ni président de la République le fils de Guillaume II a fini sa vie comme marchand de cartes postales',

La Croix, 27 July 1951; 'Le kronprinz n'a pas laissé de testament politique', *La Croix*, 3 Aug. 1951.

48 'August Wilhelm von Preussen, Eidesstattliche Erklärung, 16. 5. 1947, sowie seine Vernehmung durch Robert Kempner, 14. 5. und 19. 5. 1947', USHMM, Kempner Papers, Box 313, Folder 19. See also Machtan, *Der Kaisersohn*, 380–87.

49 Schmidt, *Plettenberg*, 203.

50 Ibid., 207–38, Sichert, *Cecilienhof*, vol. 1, 147–54; 'Brief des Hofrats Arthur Berg an den Kronprinzen, 26. 3. 1945', GStA PK, I. HA Rep. 100 A, No. 67/1.

51 Sichert, *Cecilienhof*, vol. 1, 160–69.

52 'Zwischen Kaisertum und Widerstand: Die politischen Umbrüche in Deutschland gespiegelt an der Vita Ulrich von Sells' (biographical sketch, private holding of Philipp von Sell); Sibylle Niemoeller von Sell, '*Furchtbar einfach, wird gemacht*', 334–49.

53 'Kronprinz an Farrar, 3. 3. 1947', Farrar Papers, Library of Congress, Box 11, Folder 35.

54 'Dommes an Kan, 30.5.1946', Nationaal Archief, Den Haag, Collectie J. B. Kan 2.21.375,15, 47–8.

55 'Ilsemann an Kan, 21. 10. 1946, mit direkten Zitaten aus einem Brief des Kronprinzen', Nationaal Archief, Den Haag, Collectie J. B. Kan 2.21.375,15, 45–56.

56 See the material in GStA PK, BPH, Rep. 192 Dommes, No. 9.

57 See Dommes's lists of photos and other material in his letter to Hardenberg, 16 Jan. 1949, GStA PK, BPH, Rep. 192 Dommes, No. 9.

58 'Schreiben des Anwalts vom 21. 6. 1948', GStA PK, BPH, Rep. 192 Dommes, No. 8.

59 'Entwurf für einen Artikel in einer Niederländischen Zeitung, 27. 3. 1948', GStA PK, BPH, Rep. 192 Dommes, No. 8.

60 'Schreiben von Dommes, 20. 8. 1948', GStA PK, BPH, Rep. 192 Dommes, No. 8.

61 'De Duitsche Kroonprins en zijn Non-Enemy Verklaring', *Haagsche Post*, 5 July 1947.

62 'Haus Doorn enteignet', *Telegraf*, 30 Dec. 1948.

63 'Dommes 1. 1. 1949', GStA PK, BPH, Rep. 192 Dommes, No. 2.

64 'Trouw 24. 12. 1948'; 'Haus Doorn enteignet', *Telegraf*, 30 Dec. 1948, both in ibid.

65 'Telefonprotokoll eines Gespräches zwischen Ilsemann mit einem Anwalt, 27. 9. 1948', GStA PK, BPH, Rep. 192 Dommes, No. 8.

66 Friedrich Wilhelm von Preussen , *Gott helfe*, 233–4; Jonas, *Der Kronprinz*, 264–5, 300.

67 'Schreiben vom 7. 1. 1941 und vom 14. 10. 1939', GStA PK, I. HA Rep. 100 A, No. 363. See also 'Schreiben von 1975', GStA PK, BPH, Rep. 192, Nachlass Berg, No. 16.

68 'Schreiben vom 14. 10. 1939, im Auftrag des Kaisers an Kronprinzessin', GStA PK, I. HA Rep. 100 A, No. 363. In fact, twelve and not eight of the ex-Kaiser's grandsons were deployed 'directly at the front'. See Friedrich Wilhelm von Preussen , *Gott helfe*, 272–3.

69 'Entwurf eines Schreibens an die niederländische Regierung, 11. 4. 1946'; 'Schreiben vom 1. 5. 1947, Hardenberg, 8. 7. 1947'; 'Ilsemann an Dommes, 31. 7. 1947'; 'Dommes 7. 8. 1947', GStA PK, BPH, Rep. 192 Dommes, No. 7.

70 Paul Hertz, 'Exkronprinz Wilhelm ein Nazi!', *Telegraf*, 20 Dec. 1947.

71 'Widerspruch des niederländischen Rechtsanwalts der Familie, 21. 6. 1948' and the article placed in *Der Spiegel*, 14 June 1947, both in GStA PK, BPH, Rep. 192 Dommes, No. 8.

72 Ilsemann, II, 342–3; Gutsche, *Ein Kaiser*, 201, 205–6; 'Bericht des Leibarztes Wilhelms II., (Abschrift, Mai 1940)', Utrechts Archief, NL-UtHUA, A 16712, 000143.

73 Dommes, 'Erwiderung an Gericht, 20. 8. 1948', GStA PK, BPH, Rep. 192 Dommes, No. 8; 'Dommes, 1. 1. 1949', GStA PK, BPH, Rep. 192 Dommes, No. 9.

74 Friedrich Prinz von Preussen an Kronprinz, 14. 11. 1947', GStA PK, BPH, Rep. 192 Dommes, No. 7.

75 'Reisebericht Hardenbergs, 13.–25. 7. 1948', GStA PK, BPH, Rep. 192 Dommes, No. 1.

76 'Schreiben an Hardenberg 12. 8. 1948'; 'Telegramm des Kronprinzen vom 30. 9. 1948' and other correspondence, GStA PK, BPH, Rep. 192 Dommes, No. 8. See also 'Reisebericht Hardenbergs Januar 1951, über Gespräche mit Louis Ferdinand und Prof. Dr. Cohn in Hamburg', GStA PK, BPH, Rep. 192 Dommes, No. 3.

77 Jonas, *Der Kronprinz*, 301.

78 'Schlabrendorff an Dommes, 12. 12. 1951', GStA PK, BPH, Rep. 192 Dommes, No. 3. See also 'Israelische Verlegerin wirft Hohenzollern Arisierung vor', *Der Spiegel*, 27 March 2020; Klaus Wiegrefe, 'Kumpanei mit den Nazis könnte für die Hohenzollern teuer werden', *Der Spiegel*, 24 Jan. 2020.

79 'Reisebericht Hardenbergs 13.–25. 7. 1948', GStA PK, BPH, Rep. 192 Dommes, No. 1.

80 'Redwitz an Dommes, 12. 9. 1947', and other correspondence, GStA PK, BPH, Rep. 192 Dommes, No. 6.

81 See Aretin, *Der bayerische Adel*; Sweetman, *Unforgotten Crowns*, 570–604; Malinowski, *Vom König zum Führer*, 367–85, 504–16; Weiss, *Kronprinz Rupprecht*.

82 See Seliger, *Politische Anwälte?*.

83 Hjalmar Schacht, 'Abrechnung mit Hitler', *Die Zeit*, 16, 23 and 30 Sept. 1948. See also generally Kopper, *Hjalmar Schacht*.

84 'Nicht signiertes sechsseitiges Schreiben zur Verteidigung der Berufung, wahrscheinlich von Dommes, Anfang 1949', GStA PK, BPH, Rep. 192 Dommes, No. 9.

85 'Zurückweisung des Einspruchs, Ablehnungschreiben 26. 7. 1948' GStA PK, BPH, Rep. 192 Dommes, No. 8.

86 See the telegram and membership documentation in GStA PK, BPH, Rep. 192 Dommes, No. 8. See also Pekelder/Schenk/van der Bas, *Der Kaiser*, 103–6.

87 'Ilsemann an Dommes, 27. 5. 1949'; 'Niederländische Urteilsbegründung vom 21.6.1949', 'Ilsemann an Kronprinz, 22. 6. 1947', GStA PK, BPH, Rep. 192 Dommes, No. 9. See also Pekelder/Schenk/van der Bas, *Der Kaiser*, 105–6.

88 'Reisebericht Hardenbergs, 26.–27. 12. 1952', GStAPK, BPH, Rep. 192 Dommes, No. 4.

89 Foskea van der Ven, 'De onteigening van Huis Doorn: een hoofdstuk uit de Nederlandse geschiedenis', *Rechtsgeleerd Magazijn Themis*, 2001, 67–81; Pekelder/Schenk/van der Bas, *Der Kaiser*, 106–7.

90 'Besluit op Wobverzoek over mogelijke restitutieclaims over (de collectie van) Huis Doorn vom 26. 9. 2014 und 26. 5. 2015', https://www.

rijksoverheid.nl/documenten/wob-verzoeken/2020/10/15/besluit-op-wob-verzoek-over-huis-doorn. See also Schönberger, *Was soll zurück?*, 29; Pekelder/Schenk/van der Bas, *Der Kaiser* 108–10; Rob Savelberg, 'De Nederlands-Duitse slag om Huis Doorn. Student vond correspondentie van nazaten keizer Wilhelm II', *De Telegraaf*, 24 Nov. 2020; Klaus Wiegrefe, 'Scharf aufs Silber', *Der Spiegel*, 21 Nov. 2020.

91 'Reisebericht Hardenberg, 26. 3. 1949'; 'Schreiben vom 19. 2. 1949', GStA PK, BPH, Rep. 192 Dommes, No. 2.

92 'Wer? Was? Wo?', *Welt am Abend*, 25 Sept. 1947.

93 'Et voici un antinazi de plus!: Jacques Forestier, Le Kronprinz trouve Hitler bavard, Goebbels infâme et voudrait voyager', *Paris-Presse*, 8 Nov. 1945.

94 'Kupsch für Hardenberg an Dommes, 24. 10. 1949'; 'Rosner an Müller 12.6.1947', GStA PK, BPH, Rep. 192 Dommes, No. 6. See also Jonas, *Der Kronprinz*, 286.

95 'Dommes, 11. 11. 1949', 'Bericht Hardenbergs, 24.–31. 10. 1949', GStA PK, BPH, Rep. 192 Dommes, No. 2.

96 'Rosner, 12. 6. 1947', GStA PK, BPH, Rep. 192 Dommes, No. 6.

97 Kronprinzessin Cecilie, 'Kaiser meiner Seele', *Neue Illustrierte*, 19. Dec. 1951.

98 Cecilie von Preussen, *Erinnerungen an den deutschen Kronprinzen*.

99 'Die Bänder der Cecilie', *Der Spiegel*, 4 May 1955, 15–21; 'Schriftwechsel 1954 um Prozess gegen Otto Groha', GStA PK, BPH, Rep. 192 Dommes, vol. 5.

100 'Hohenzollern-Geschichten. Des Hofrats Verdienste', *Der Spiegel*, 6 April 1954, 10–16, here 12, 15–16.

101 'Hohenzollern. Neue Schlösser', *Der Spiegel*, 19 May 1954, 8–10; Kirchstein, *Kronprinzessin Cecilie*, 112–21.

102 'Reisebericht Hardenbergs 15.–18.12.1951' and 'Dommes an Hardenberg, 27. 2. 1952', GStA PK, BPH, Rep. 192 Dommes, No. 3.

103 *New York Times*, 22 June 1949.

104 See articles such as 'Hochzeit auf Burg Hohenzollern' and 'Prinzen ohne Romantik. Das Haus Hohenzollern – heute' in the Hechingen local press.

105 'Le fils du kronprinz deviendrait agent des automobiles Ford en Alle-magne', *La Gazette provençale*, 17 April 1948.

106 'German-American Club Formed in U.S. Zone', *New York Times*, 20 June 1946.

107 Sichert, *Cecilienhof*, vol. 1, 191–3, further mentions a villa in Switzerland.

108 Schildt/Sywottek, *Modernisierung im Wiederaufbau*, 649–97.

109 Paul Nolte, 'Einführung: Die Bundesrepublik in der deutschen Geschichte des 20. Jahrhunderts', *Geschichte und Gesellschaft*, 28 (2002), 175–82, here 176.

110 'Programmatisches Schreiben von Franz Sontag, 18. 12. 1951', BAB, N 1064, No. 16, and the correspondence between Louis Ferdinand and Hardenberg, among others, ibid., Nos. 15, 16 und 17.

111 Giloi, *Monarchy*; Jürgen Luh, 'Eine Erbschaft der Monarchie: Das Hohenzollern-Museum', in Biskup/Kohlrausch, *Das Erbe*, 184–99.

112 See Sabrow, *Die Hohenzollern und die Demokratie*, part II.

113 'Rechtsgutachten Fabian von Schlabrendorff, 11. 1. 1952', Landeskirch-liches Archiv KS C 3.3.1., No. 170.

114 'Stahlhelm-Bundesführer Simon, 19.2.1952', and 'Hardenberg, 28. 2. 1952', BAB, N 1064, No. 15.

115 'Epd-Landesdienst Hessen-Kassel, No. 7, 22. 3. 1952', Landeskirchliches Archiv KS C 3.3.1., No. 170; Krüger-Bulcke, *Der Hohenzollern-Hindenburg-Zwischenfall*, 345–7.

116 'Franz Sontag an Hardenberg, 26. 8. 1952', and 'Hardenberg, 29. 8. und 1. 9. 1952', BAB, N 1064, No. 15.

117 Laak, *Gespräche in der Sicherheit des Schweigens*; Morat, *Von der Tat zur Gelassenheit*.

118 'Silberhochzeit auf Burg Hohenzollern', SWR Retro – *Abendschau* TV programme, 2 July 1963; 'Beisetzung von Fürst Friedrich Viktor von Hohenzollern', SWR Retro – *Abendschau* TV programme, 12 Feb. 1965.

119 See the extensive correspondence between Schlabrendorff and Balfour's publisher The Crescent Press and others in Nachlass John Röhl, Berlin, vol. 91, fol. 1–24. See also Jonas, *Der Kronprinz*, 239; Jung, *Volksgesetzgebung*, 544–5.

120 It is impossible to ascertain all the deviations between the manuscript and the page proofs, but John Röhl did offer an assessment of the differences. See Nachlass John Röhl, Berlin, vol. 115; Röhl, *The Emperor's New Clothes*, 25, 32; Röhl, *Kaiser, Hof und Staat*, 23. In two emails with the present author, Röhl confirmed that it is unclear who ordered the changes made.

121 Ilsemann, 'Druckfahnen, Eintrag vom 22. 8. 1934', Nachlass John Röhl, Berlin, vol. 115, fol. 35 (223 of the page proofs).

122 Ilsemann, 'Druckfahnen, Eintrag vom 8. 3. 1934 und 2. 8. 1934', Nachlass John Röhl, Berlin, vol. 115, fol. 31, 38 (208, 251 of the page proofs).

123 Ilsemann, 'Druckfahnen, Eintrag vom 23. 7. 1927', Nachlass John Röhl, Berlin, vol. 115, fol. 14.

124 Marcus Colla, 'Constructing the Prussia-Myth in East Germany, 1945–61', *Journal of Contemporary History*, 54 (2019), 527–50.

125 Hans-Ulrich Wehler's phrase, cited in Jochen Kirchhoff, 'Tagungsbericht: Hans Rothfels und die deutsche Zeitgeschichte, 16. 07. 2003– 17. 07. 2003 München', *H-Soz-Kult*, 13 Aug. 2003.

126 Hans Rothfels, 'Das politische Vermächtnis des deutschen Widerstands', *Vierteljahrshefte für Zeitgeschichte*, 2 (1954), 329–43, here 329.

127 Klemens von Klemperer, 'Hans Rothfels, 1891–1976', *Central European History*, 9 (1976), 381–3, here 383.

128 See 'Friedrich der Grosse und der Staat. Professor Dr. Rothfels hielt die geschichtlich souveräne Festrede', in the Hechingen local press.

129 See 'Auch für uns gültig: Treue und Dienen', in the Hechingen local press.

130 See 'Das Jubliäum des Semper-talis-Bundes. Eindrucksvolle Morgenfeier auf der Burg Hohenzollern', article in Hechingen local press.

131 'Hechingen als Heimat der Vertriebenen. Treffen der Danziger Vertriebenen in Hechingen – Louis Ferdinand ausgezeichnet', article in Hechingen local press.

132 See Rothfels, *Die deutsche Opposition gegen Hitler*; Jan Eckel, 'An Intellectual Biography in the Age of Extremes', *Journal of Contemporary History*, 42 (2007), 421–46.

133 'Tagungsbericht: Hans Rothfels und die deutsche Zeitgeschichte, 16. 07. 2003–17. 07. 2003 München', *H-Soz-Kult*, 13 Aug. 2003.

134 Eckel, *Hans Rothfels*, 237–68, 351–7.

135 Weiss, *Moderne Antimoderne*, 313–21.

136 Wilmowsky an Reusch, 20. 10. 1947, quoted by Gerbet, *Carl-Hans Graf von Hardenberg*, 197.

137 Ueberschär (ed.), *Der 20. Juli 1944*, Cologne, 1994.

138 See Lier, *Das 'Hilfswerk 20. Juli 1944'*; Tokya-Seid, *Gralshüter*.

139 Louis Ferdinand von Preussen, 'Kaiser auf Abruf'.

140 Prince Louis Ferdinand of Prussia, *The Rebel Prince*, 314.

141 See the speech given by resistance member Axel von dem Bussche, 'Zur Erinnerung an Kurt Plettenberg, 28.4.1985', Privatarchiv Karl-Wilhelm Freiherr von Plettenberg.

142 See Rouette, *Die Widerstandslegende*.

143 Herfried Münkler, 'Wirtschaftswunder oder antifaschistischer Widerstand – politische Gründungsmythen der Bundesrepublik Deutschland und der DDR', in Esser (ed.), *Der Wandel nach der Wende*, Wiesbaden 2000, 41–65.

144 See Pyta / Orth, *Nicht alternativlos*.

145 Ulrich Heinemann, 'Arbeit am Mythos. Neuere Literatur zum bürgerlich-aristokratischen Widerstand gegen Hitler und zum 20. Juli 1944 (Teil I)', *Geschichte und Gesellschaft*, 21 (1995), 111–39; Ulrich Heinemann / Michael Krüger-Charlé, 'Arbeit am Mythos. Der 20. Juli 1944 in Publizistik und wissenschaftlicher Literatur des Jubiläumsjahres 1994 (Teil II)', *Geschichte und Gesellschaft*, 23 (1997), 475–501.

146 Heinemann / Charlé, *Arbeit am Mythos*, 484 (referring here to Countess Marion Dönhoff).

147 'Heuss Hails Dead in Plot on Hitler', *New York Times*, 20 July 1954; 'Berlin as a capital of Germany', *The Manchester Guardian*, 21 July 1954.

148 ' "Diese Leute in der Regierung sind Lügner", Interview mit Robert Harris', *Der Spiegel*, 16 Oct. 2019.

149 Minia, *Die Fridericus-Gedenkfeiern; SKH Prinz Louis Ferdinand von Preussen zum 75. Geburtstag am 9. November 1982. Eine Festschrift*.

150 https://kira-stiftung.de.

151 'Unverzichtbare Kaiserkrone', *Der Spiegel*, 17 Nov. 1968; 'Prinz weint dem Thron nach', *Berliner Zeitung*, 29 April 1993.

152 ' "Wenn ich Kaiser wär". Interview mit Louis Ferdinand Prinz von

Preussen', *Der Spiegel*, 9 April 1957; 'Der Preussenprinz und der 20. Juli', *Hamburger Freie Presse*, 3 May 1947.

153 See Frei, *Hitlers Eliten nach 1945*; Frei, *Vergangenheitspolitik*; Koch (ed.), *Modernisierung als Amerikanisierung?*.

154 Dr Louis Ferdinand Prinz von Preussen, 'Demokratie als Naturzustand', *Der Tagesspiegel*, 29 June 1947.

155 'Louis Ferdinand an Edsel Ford, 21. 2. 1935', Benson Ford Research Center, Acc 6, Box 230, 1936, FMC Subsidary. See Urbach, *Useful Idiots*, 533, 548, 550; Norman Domeier, 'Der US-Journalist, der heimlich mit den Nazis paktierte', *Der Spiegel*, 12 March 2021. At the start of the Second World War, as the chief Berlin correspondent of the Associated Press, Lochner had close contact with Joseph Goebbels and later edited the English translation of his diaries. On the cooperation between foreign journalists and Nazi leaders, see Domeier, *Weltöffentlichkeit und Diktatur*.

156 Louis P. Lochner, 'Kaiser's Grandson Says He Aided Peace Move by Roosevelt', *Evening Star* (Washington), 17 June 1945; 'Ex-Envoy to Germany Would Return Country to Hohenzollern Rule', *Evening Star* (Washington), 5 June 1945; 'Kaiser's Grandson Arrives in Baltimore on Freightner', *Evening Star* (Washington), 8 Dec. 1948; 'The Prince of Prussia Writes Popular Tunes' *Evening Star* (Washington), 12 Oct. 1956; 'Prussian Prince Visits Capital', *Detroit Tribune*, 31 Oct. 1959; 'Ex-Secretaries Skeptical', *New York Times*, 17 June 1945.

157 'The Rebel Prince', *New York Herald Tribune*, 21 Dec. 1952; 'Books', *New York Times*, 3 Oct. 1952; 'German Prince in for 17-day lecture tour', *New York Herald Tribune*, 14 Oct. 1952; Felix E. Hirsch, 'After Pomp and Glory', *New York Herald Tribune*, 26 Oct. 1952; William L. Shirer, 'The Prince and His "Ifs"', *New York Times*, 26 Oct. 1952.

158 Prince Louis Ferdinand of Prussia, *The Rebel Prince*, 29–31, 53–4, 58–63, 75–9, here 59.

159 'Hedwig von Ditfurth an Hardenberg, 5. 7. 1952', 'Dommes an Louis Ferdinand, 28. 8. 1952', 'Louis Ferdinand an Dommes, 7. 9. 1952', and other correspondence GStA PK, BPH, Rep. 192, Nachlass Dommes, No. 3.

160 Kronprinz Wilhelm, 'Meine Gedanken zur Frage der Erweiterung

bzw. Abänderung der Bestimmungen über ebenbürtige Heiraten der Familienmitglieder unseres Hauses, 14. 3. 1941', GStA PK, Rep. 100 A, No. 349.

161 Louis P. Lochner, 'Prince Louis Proposes Democratic Training for Germans in U.S.', *Evening Star* (Washington), 30 Aug. 1946.

162 See Winkler, *Der lange Weg nach Westen*. See also Lundestad, 'Empire by Invitation', and Berghahn, *America and the Intellectual Cold Wars*.

163 'Chef des Hauses Hohenzollern ehrte gefallenen Prinzen', *Neues Deutschland*, 3 June. 1989; 'Prinz Louis Ferdinand im Gespräch mit "Neue Zeit"', *Neue Zeit*, 1 July 1989; 'Zwiesprache mit der Geschichte im Haus "Monbijou". Eine nicht alltägliche Begegnung bei den Hohenzollern', *Neue Zeit*, 26 Aug. 1989; Martin Sabrow, 'Geheimverhandlungen schon mit der DDR', *FAZ*, 18 Dec. 2019.

164 'Stolpe bietet Louis Ferdinand eine Villa in Potsdam an', *Hohenzollernsche Zeitung*, 18 Feb. 1994.

165 Martin Sabrow, 'Die Hohenzollern und die Demokratie nach 1918. Teil II', *Deutschland Archiv*, 18 Dec. 2020, www.bpb.de/324802.

166 *Die Museums-Eisenbahn. Zeitschrift für Freunde der Dampf-Eisenbahn* 3/1991, Privatarchiv Karl-Wilhelm Freiherr von Plettenberg.

167 'Aktion Sarg und Asche', *Der Spiegel*, 11 Aug. 1991; Martin Sabrow, 'Die Hohenzollern und die Demokratie nach 1918, Teil II', *Deutschland Archiv*, 18 Dec. 2020, www.bpb.de/324802; *Friedrichs Heimfahrt*, Spiegel TV, 18 Aug. 1991: https://www.spiegel.de/video/friedrichs-heimfahrt-video-99009916.html.

168 Interview with Louis Ferdinand Prinz von Preussen: 'Der Verzicht auf die Krone 1918 war ein historischer Betriebsunfall', in *Der Spiegel*, special edition: *1000 Jahre Preussenstadt Potsdam*, April 1993; Louis Ferdinand von Preussen, 'Kaiser auf Abruf', TV interview 1987.

169 The main law in question is the 'Gesetz über die Entschädigung nach dem Gesetz zur Regelung offener Vermögensfragen und über staatliche Ausgleichsleistungen für Enteignungen auf besatzungsrechtlicher oder besatzungshoheitlicher Grundlage (Entschädigungs- und Ausgleichsleistungsgesetz)', 27 Sept. 1994. See Goschler, *Prinzen, Bürger und Preussen*, 322–36; Schönberger, *Wiedergänger*, 337–47; ' "Die

Forderungen aus dem Adel waren teilweise unverschämt". Interview mit Johannes Gerster', *Der Spiegel*, 21 Feb. 2020.

170 'Kein Geld für die Hohenzollern', *Der Tagesspiegel*, 14 Jan. 2016; Pekelder/Schenk/van der Bas, *Der Kaiser*, 118. It remains unknown whether the claim preceded the evaluation or vice versa.

171 Klaus Wiegrefe, 'Vom Stamme Nimm', *Der Spiegel*, 12 July 2019; Thorsten Metzner, 'Hohenzollern erheben Ansprüche auf tausende bedeutende Kunstwerke', *Der Tagesspiegel*, 13 July 2019; Thorsten Metzner, 'Wie der Streit zwischen Kaiser-Ururenkel und Bund eskalieren konnte', *Der Tagesspiegel*, 13 July 2019.

172 'Wem gehören die Schätze des Kaisers?', first broadcast on 21 Dec. 2019, 3Sat/ZDF.

173 https://www.preussen.de/wem-gehoeren-die-schaetze-des-kaisers/.

174 Schönberger, *The History Management of the East-Elbian Nobility after 1945*, 271–328.

175 Pekelder/Schenk/van der Bas, *De keizer en het Derde Rijk*.

176 Markus Hennig in the television show *Titel, Thesen, Temperamente*, ARD, 4 Aug. 2019. The same sentiments were advanced by the conservative parliamentarian Elisabeth Motschmann (CDU) in the Bundestag, 16 Jan. 2020, Plenarprotokoll 19/140, 17492.

177 Parliamentary debate (Bundestag) 16 January 2020, discussion of the motion by Jan Korte, Friedrich Straetmanns, Simone Barrientos, other MPs and Die Linke parliamentary group (printed matter 19/14729), 'Keine Entschädigungen an Nachkommen der Monarchie' (No compensation to descendants of the monarchy), 16 January 2020. See here the contributions to the debate by Arnim-Paul Hampel (AfD), Elisabeth Motschmann (CDU), Alexander Gauland (AfD), Hartmut Ebbing (FDP).

178 Beckert, *Unverdientes Vermögen*.

179 *Der Tag*, daily news programme, Deutsche Welle, 23 July 2019.

180 Wiegrefe, 'Vom Stamme Nimm', *Der Spiegel*, 12 July 2019.

181 Klaus Ferdinand Gärditz, speech in the Landtag Brandenburg (regional parliament), 7. Wahlperiode, Ausschuss für Wissenschaft, Forschung und Kultur, Protokoll der Sitzung vom 20. 1. 2021, 25.

182 Stefan Förster (FDP), speech in the Berlin city-state parliament, 25 March 2021; Plenarprotokoll 18/76, 8941.

183 Winfried Süss, speech in the Landtag Brandenburg, 7.Wahlperiode, Ausschuss für Wissenschaft, Forschung und Kultur, Protokoll der Sitzung vom 20. 1. 2021, 21. See also Michael Stolleis, 'Wer weitere Schwabenstreiche verhindern will, lese dieses Buch!', *FAZ*, 30 March 2007.

184 The orientation of this evaluation is reflected by the frequency with which the authors mentioned the names of the other historians who contributed to the debate: Volker Berghahn 2x, Axel Schildt 2x, Larry E. Jones 4x, Heinrich-August Winkler 17x, Peter Brandt 17x and Stephan Malinowski 99x. These figures do not mirror the significance for Weimar history of the scholars named. Instead, they express the text's stated intent of countering the 'accusations' made by 'hostile detractors' of the crown prince (evaluation Pyta/Orth, 12).

185 http://hohenzollern.lol/#gutachten.

186 'Neo Magazin Royal', 14 Nov. 2019, https://www.youtube.com/watch?v=kFZKaXi7HyM (accessed 5 April 2023).

187 Chronologically: Stephan Malinowski/Peter Brandt, 'Ein Prinz im Widerstand?', *Die Zeit*, 13 Nov. 2019; Ulrich Herbert, 'Vier Gutachter, ein Kronprinz und die nationale Diktatur', *FAZ*, 1 Dec. 2019; Richard J. Evans, 'Das Gewissen eines Gutachters', *FAZ*, 10 Dec. 2019; 'Der Kronprinz war ein reaktionärer Opportunist. Interview mit Heinrich-August Winkler', *Die Zeit*, 11 Dec. 2019; Jörn Leonhard, 'Sperrige Widergänger', *FAZ*, 21 Dec. 2019; Martin Sabrow, 'Die Hohenzollern und die Demokratie nach 1918, Teil I', *Deutschland Archiv*, 18 Dec. 2020, www.bpb.de/324774.

188 Sven Felix Kellerhoff, 'So wollte Preussens Kronprinz Hitler verhindern', *Die Welt*, 11 Feb. 2016; Sven Felix Kellerhoff, 'Wenn Strasser statt Hitler die Macht ergriffen hätte', *Die Welt*, 22 March 2021.

189 Wolfram Pyta, 'Kurt von Schleicher, Gregor Strasser und Kronprinz Wilhelm gegen Hitler', lecture, Katholische Akademie in Bayern, 5 March 2018, https://www.youtube.com/watch?v=EOnoPFomPtA.

190 See Pyta/Orth, *Nicht alternativlos*.

191 See Stefanie Middendorf, speech to the Deutscher Bundestag,

Ausschuss für Kultur und Medien, 29. 1. 2020, Protokoll 19/42, 24, 28–9, 13.

192 For example: Frank-Lothar Kroll, 'Das Recht der Hohenzollern', *Deutsches Adelsblatt*, April 2020, 6–11, here 8; Hans-Christof Kraus, 'In der Begriffsnacht bequem gemacht (Leserbrief)', *FAZ*, 4 Dec. 2019; commentary by Benjamin Hasselhorn, 'Streit um Entschädigung. Wem gehörte der Hohenzollernschatz?', *SWR2, Forum*, 7 Aug. 2019.

193 Speech by Benjamin Hasselhorn, in Deutscher Bundestag, Ausschuss für Kultur und Medien, 29. 1. 2020, Protokoll 19/42, 37–38.

194 'Pars pro toto: Gutachter uneinig im Konflikt um Hohenzollern', *Die Welt*, 29 Jan. 2020.

195 Klaus F. Gärditz, 'Geschichte vor Gericht', *FAZ*, 23 Sept. 2020; Klaus F. Gärditz, speech, Ausschuss für Wissenschaft, Forschung und Kultur, Landtag Brandenburg, 20. 1. 2021, P-AWFK 7/13, 17, 24–5; Gärditz, 'Die Rolle der Verwaltungsgerichtsbarkeit', 306–9.

196 Catherine Hickley, 'His Ancestors Were German Kings. He Wants Their Treasures Back', *New York Times*, 12 March 2021.

197 Thorsten Metzner, 'Hohenzollern-Streit: Prinz Georg Friedrich übt Selbstkritik', *Der Tagesspiegel*, 16 March 2021.

198 'Prinz Georg Friedrich von Preussen äussert sich erstmals im Streit um Entschädigung und gibt Fehler zu', *Märkische Oderzeitung*, 19 March 2021.

199 Interview with Louis Ferdinand Prinz von Preussen: 'Der Verzicht auf die Krone 1918 war ein historischer Betriebsunfall'.

200 See Machtan, *Der Kronprinz und die Nazis*.

201 Andreas Kilb, 'Die braune Blume der Monarchie', *FAZ*, 11 Aug. 2021; Kilb, 'Zwei gute Freunde und ein böser Prinz', *FAZ*, 20 Aug. 2021; Klaus Wiegrefe, 'Der Kronprinz und der liebe "Don Adolfo"', *Der Spiegel*, 6 Aug. 2021; Jörg Häntzschel, 'Der etwas peinliche Onkel der Familie', *Süddeutsche Zeitung*, 19 Aug. 2021.

202 Klaus Wiegrefe, 'Prinz mit Schuss', *Der Spiegel*, 7 Sept. 2014.

203 'Haus Hohenzollern erstattet Strafanzeige', *Die Welt*, 9 Sept. 2014; 'Hohenzollern zeigen Finanzministerium an', *Märkische Allgemeine Zeitung*, 9 Sept. 2014.

204 'Der Prinz kämpft um Erbe und Ehre!', www.bunte.de, 23 March 2015.

205 Johannes Boie/Rainer Haubrich, ' "Da heisst es in den Medien, der Prinz will plötzlich Schlösser zurückhaben" ', *Die Welt*, 28 July 2019.

206 Thorsten Metzner, 'Keine Steuermillion für Hohenzollern', *Potsdamer Neueste Nachrichten*, 15 Jan. 2016.

207 Marcellus Puhlemann, ' "Wenn er Versöhnung will, soll er die Klagen fallen lassen" ', *Der Tagesspiegel*, 24 March 2021.

208 Hamburg Prosecutor's Office letter to Malinowski, 21 Dec. 2015.

209 Stephan Malinowski, 'Der braune Kronprinz', *Die Zeit*, 13 Aug. 2015.

210 Hamburg Prosecutor's Office letter to Malinowski's lawyer Marcellus Puhlemann, 26 Sept. 2016.

211 Stephan Malinowski, 'Die Selbstversenkung', *FAZ*, 22 July 2019; Stephan Malinowski, 'Wir Stauffenbergs', *Süddeutsche Zeitung*, 7 Aug. 2019.

212 'Georg Friedrich von Preussen über die Nazi-Vergangenheit seines Vorfahren: "Ein schrecklicher Irrglaube" ', www bunte.de, 9 Aug. 2020.

213 Susanne Gaschke, 'Familie mit Licht und Schatten', *Welt am Sonntag*, 2 Feb. 2020.

214 See the verdict rendered by the Hanseatisches Oberlandesgericht Hamburg, Urteil, 23. 3. 2021, Az: 7 U 42/20–324 O 52/20. See Thorsten Metzner, 'Hohenzollern verlieren in Hamburg. Gericht verbietet Vorwurf der Desinformation gegen NS-Forscher', *Der Tagesspiegel*, 24 March 2019.

215 See the press release Pressemitteilung des Kammergerichts, 19. 8. 2021 for Verfahren 10 U 1009/20 (PM No. 30/2021).

216 Susanne Gaschke, 'Familie mit Licht und Schatten', *Welt am Sonntag*, 2 Feb. 2020.

217 https://fragdenstaat.de/aktionen/prinzenfonds/ (28. 4. 2021). See also Johanna Christner, 'Ein "Prinzenfonds" gegen den Prinzen, *FAZ*, 19 June 2020; Christian Orth, 'Prinzenfonds hilft Journalisten', radio report, Deutschlandfunk, 28 July 2020; Danny Kringiel, 'Mit dem "Prinzenfonds" gegen Kaiser Wilhelms Nachfahren', *Der Spiegel*, 18 June 2020.

218 Anne Haeming, 'Es droht eine systematische Beeinflussung der öffentlichen Meinung', *UeberMedien*, 2 July 2020.

219 Martin Sabrow, ' "Ihr Vorgehen greift die Freiheit der Wissenschaft an" ', *Der Tagesspiegel*, 21 Dec. 2019; Eva Schlotheuber and Eckart

Conze, 'Die Ehre Der Familie', *FAZ*, 9 Sept. 2020; Eva Schotheu-ber, ' "Das ist schon eine ziemliche Drohkulisse" ', radio report, Deutschlandfunk Kultur, 9 Sept. 2020.

220 David Motadel, 'What Do the Hohenzollern Deserve?', *New York Review of Books*, 26 March 2020.

221 Pierre Avril, 'Les Hohenzollern veulent récupérer les châteaux du temps de leur splendeur', *Le Figaro*, 2 Oct. 2019; Scott McLean, 'Germany's Ex-Royals Want Their Riches Back, but Past Ties to Hitler Stand in the Way', CNN, 30 Dec. 2020, https://edition.cnn.com/style/article/hohenzollern-prince-georg-prussia/index. html (accessed 28 April 2021).

222 Richard J. Evans, 'The German History Wars', *The New Statesman*, 13 May 2021.

223 ' "Der Mann war eine Flasche". Interview mit Christopher Clark', *Der Spiegel*, 25 Oct. 2019. See also Christopher Clark's contributions to the online discussion 'Brandenburg und der Streit mit den Hohen-zollern', Die Linke, Fraktion im Landtag Brandenburg, 19. 1. 2021; and 'Wilhelm wollte Hitler nicht zähmen. Interview mit Christopher Clark', *FAZ*, 4 Nov. 2020.

224 ' "Herr Prinz von Preussen lehnt sich sehr weit aus dem Fenster". Interview mit Sophie Schönberger', *Der Spiegel*, 14 June 2021.

225 'The prince himself admits to 120 cases', Susanne Gaschke, 'Familie mit Licht und Schatten', *Welt am Sonntag*, 2 Feb. 2020.

226 www.die-klagen-der-hohenzollern.de. See also 'Die Klagen der Hohenzollern – eine Dokumentation, Podiumsdiskussion zum Launch der Website am 15. 6. 2021', https://lisa.gerda-henkel-stiftung. de/wiki_hohenzollern; Christian Staas, 'Die Klagen des Prinzen', *Die Zeit*, 15 June 2021.

227 'Ich will den Weg freimachen für eine unbelastete Debatte', inter-view in *Die Welt*, 9 March 2023; 'Warum die Hohenzollern klein beigeben', *Der Spiegel*, 8 March 2023.

228 Klaus Wiegrefe, 'Die Prozesshanselei des Georg Friedrich Prinz von Preussen', *Der Spiegel*, 9 June 2023; Thorsten Metzner, 'Verfahren gegen Medien und Wissenschaftler', *Der Tagesspiegel*, 4 July 2023.

229 Sophie Schönberger, 'Geschichte vor dem Verwaltungsgericht',

NVwZ, 2022; Georg Herbert, 'Hochmut und Fehlurteil. Eine kurze Geschichte der Vorschubleistung des Hohenzollern', *NVwZ Extra*, July 2022, 1–8.

230 Christopher Clark, 'Die zwei Körper des Kronprinzen', *Die Zeit*, 11 October 2021.

231 Andreas Wirsching: 'Doppelbesprechung zu den Neuerscheinungen von Lothar Machtan und Stephan Malinowski', *sehepunkte*, 21, 11 (2021), http://www.sehepunkte.de/2021/11/36179.html (accessed on 23 Jan. 2023); Martin Sabrow, 'Erkenntnis und Evidenz. Zur zeithistorischen Bedeutung der Hohenzollerndebatte', *Der Tagesspiegel*, 23 Dec. 2022.

232 'Address by Georg Friedrich Prinz von Preussen, Oxford Union Society – June 13, 2023', https://www.preussen.de/wp-content/uploads/2023/06/20230613_Oxford-Union-Address-GF-final-delivered.pdf.

233 Michael Wolffsohn, 'Geist und Geister: (fast) tausend Jahre Hohenzollern – eine kleine Chronologie der historischen Ereignisse wider die Hohenzollern-Dämonologie', *Neue Züricher Zeitung*, 1 March 2020.

234 Alexander Gauland (AfD), speech in the Deutscher Bundestag, 16 Jan. 2020, Plenarprotokoll 19/140, 17494.

235 Frank-Lothar Kroll, 'Das Recht der Hohenzollern', *FAZ*, 21 Oct. 2020.

236 See, in response to Kroll, Andreas Pečar, 'Zur Aufrechnung historischer "Leistungen" der Hohenzollern in der politischen Debatte', *Debatte*, 25. Nov. 2020, https://recs.hypotheses.org/6131.

237 Michael Wolffsohn, 'Geist und Geister: (fast) tausend Jahre Hohenzollern', *NZZ*, 1 March 2020.

238 Hasselhorn, *Königstod*, 106–19, who significantly alters an argument by Niall Ferguson.

239 Scott McLean, 'Germany's Ex-Royals Want Their Riches Back', CNN, 23 Sept. 2020.

240 Lothar Machtan, ' "Die Monarchie hätte überleben können". Interview', *Märkische Allgemeine Zeitung*, 1 Nov. 2018.

241 Ulrich Schlie/Thomas Weber, 'Historiker entlasten den Hohenzollern-Kronprinzen', *Die Welt*, 15. 4. 2021.

242 Tilman Krause, 'Auch die Hohenzollern gehören zu Deutschland', *Die Welt*, 16 April 2021.

243 Sven Felix Kellerhoff, 'Wenn Strasser statt Hitler die Macht ergriffen hätte', *Die Welt*, 22 March 2021. See also the reader comments on the newspaper's website.

244 Machtan (ed.), *Quellen*. On this collection: Stephan Malinowski, 'Die PR-Kampagne der Hohenzollern', *FAZ*, 15, March 2023; and Luh, 'Fiat lux?'. https://www.preussen.de/forum-preussen/epaper-Machtan_Dossier_V3/index.html#2. On this collection: Stephan Malinowski, 'Die PR-Kampagne der Hohenzollern', *FAZ*, 15 March 2023.

245 See Evans, *Altered Pasts*.

246 Hasselhorn, *Königstod*, 147–56.

247 See Elisabeth Motschmann (CDU), speech in Deutscher Bundestag, 16 Jan. 2020; Robbin Juhnke (CDU), speech in Berliner Abgeordnetenhaus, 25 March 2021; Plenarprotokoll 18/76, 8935; Marc Jongen (AfD), speech in Deutscher Bundestag, 16 Jan. 2020, Plenarprotokoll 19/140, 17500; Hartmut Ebbing (FDP), speech in Deutscher Bundestag, 16 Jan. 2020, Plenarprotokoll 19/140, 17496.

248 Reinhard Müller, 'Wer will hier eine Debatte unterbinden?', *FAZ*, 15 Sept. 2020.

249 Deutscher Bundestag, Ausschuss für Kultur und Medien, 29 Jan. 2020, Protokoll 19/42, 24, 20–24.

250 Testimony by Stefanie Middendorf and Stephan Malinowski, Deutscher Bundestag, Ausschuss für Kultur und Medien, 29 Jan. 2020, Protokoll 19/42, 24, 28–9.

251 Ulrich Schlie/Thomas Weber, 'Historikerstreit: Die Hohenzollern und Hitler – eine Fehleinschätzung', *Die Welt*, 15 April 2021.

252 See the judgement in the case of Hugenberg by the Federal Administrative Court, which concluded that 'abetting' in the sense of the law in question (§1 Abs.4 AusglLeistG) meant nothing other than 'promotion' in the sense of the corresponding compensation law for civil servants (§ 8 Abs. 1 BWGöD), i.e. 'support' and 'improvement' of conditions for the system in question. See also the verdict in the case involving Bismarck, BVerwG, Urteil, 18. 09. 2009; Az; – 5 C 1 /09.

253 Ulrich Schlie/Thomas Weber, 'Historikerstreit: Die Hohenzollern und Hitler – eine Fehleinschätzung', *Die Welt*, 15. April 21.

254 A comparison of the Vorwärts, ANNO, ProQuest, Chronicling

America, The Times and RetroNews databases confirms this as a general trend. Thanks to Henning Holsten and Thomas Werneke for giving me an overview of the databases.

255 Evaluation Clark, 18.

256 Depending on how Crown Prince Wilhelm is referred to, the Times Digital Archive turns up 2,000 mentions between 1918 and 1945, and 200–300 mentions for the period after 1930.

257 As of 12 Sept. 2021, searches for the period 9 Nov. 1918–8 May 1945 in RetroNews turned up 22,700 hits for 'crown prince', 33,200 for 'Papen', 11,500 for 'Schleicher', 14,000 for 'Hugenberg' and 6,300 for 'Westarp'. A superficial search of the Austrian press turns up 8,300 mentions of 'Hohenzollerns' and some 2,500 of the crown prince in his various designations.

258 Michael Wolffsohn, 'Hohenzollern-Streit: Deutschlands Verweigerungshaltung ist ein Skandal', *Neue Zürcher Zeitung*, 8 March 2021; 'Christopher Clark in der Anhörung', online discussion Brandenburg und der Streit mit den Hohenzollern, 19 Jan. 2021; Benjamin Hasselhorn, speech to Deutscher Bundestag, Ausschuss für Kultur und Medien, 29. 1. 2020, Protokoll 19/42, 9; Ulrich Schlie/Thomas Weber, 'Historikerstreit: Die Hohenzollern und Hitler – eine Fehleinschätzung', *Die Welt*, 15 April 21; Tilman Krause, 'Auch die Hohenzollern gehören zu Deutschland', *Die Welt*, 16 April 2021; Jürgen Aretz, commentary in the TV documentary, *Wem gehören die Schätze des Kaisers?*, first broadcast 21 Dec. 2019, 3Sat/ZDF.

259 Eckart Conze, 'Adel und Adeligkeit im Widerstand des 20. Juli 1944', in Reif, *Adel und Bürgertum in Deutschland* II, 269–96, here 269.

260 'Qu'est devenu le kronprinz', *Le Jour*, 14 Nov. 1939; 'Le kronprinz décapité', *Le Midi socialiste*, 14 Nov. 1939; 'L'ex-kronpriz n'a pas été décapité par les nazis', *Le Petit Marseillais*, 14 Nov. 1939; 'L'ex-kronprinz est gardé à vue', *Le Petit Courrier*, 10 Nov. 1939; 'Une déclaration écrite de l'ex-kronprinz', *Excelsior*, 23 Nov. 1939.

261 '"Der Mann war eine Flasche". Interview mit Christopher Clark', *Der Spiegel*, 25 Oct. 2019.

262 Elisabeth Motschmann (CDU), speech in the Deutscher Bundestag, 16. 1. 2020, Plenarprotokoll 19/140, 17493.

263 Martin Trefzer (AfD), speech to the Berliner Abgeordnetenhaus, 25. 3. 2021; Plenarprotokoll 18/76, 8937.

264 Michael Wolffsohn, 'Hohenzollern-Streit: Deutschlands Verweigerungshaltung ist ein Skandal', *NZZ*, 8 March 2021.

265 See Conrad, *Erinnerung im globalen Zeitalter.*

266 Oliver F. R. Haardt, 'Im Zweifel für den Zweifel', *Süddeutsche Zeitung*, 4 Feb. 2021; Heinrich August Winkler, 'Gab es ihn doch, den deutschen Sonderweg? Anmerkungen zu einer Kontroverse', *Merkur*, 75 (2021), 17–28.

267 Sonja Dolinsek / Claudia Gatzka, 'Konfliktlinien deutscher Demokratiegeschichtsschreibung', *Public History Weekly*, 29 April 2021.

268 See Moses, *The Problems of Genocide*; Moses, *Der Katechismus der Deutschen.*

269 'Stammt die Ideologie Hitlers aus dem Kaiserreich? Interview mit Andreas Wirsching', *Der Spiegel*, 7 June 2021.

270 See Lehmann (ed.), *Historikerkontroversen*; Sabrow / Jessen / Kracht (eds.), *Zeitgeschichte als Streitgeschichte.*

271 Benjamin Hasselhorn, 'Und ewig grüsst der Sonderweg', *Cicero*, 30 July 2019.

272 Frank-Lothar Kroll, 'Das Recht der Hohenzollern', *FAZ*, 21 Oct. 2020.

273 Frank-Lothar Kroll, 'Das Recht der Hohenzollern – Bilanz und Perspektive', *Deutsches Adelsblatt*, April 2020, 6–11.

274 Benjamin Hasselhorn, commentary in *Streit um Entschädigung – Wem gehört der Hohenzollern-Schatz?*, radio broadcast SWR II Forum, 9 Aug. 2019.

275 Benjamin Hasselhorn, 'Wenn es um den Adel geht, scheint es in Deutschland keine Hemmungen zu geben', *NZZ*, 11 Dec. 2019; Michael Wolffsohn, 'Geist und Geister: (fast) tausend Jahre Hohenzollern', *NZZ*, 1 March 2020.

276 Marc Jongen (AfD), speech to the Deutscher Bundestag, 16. 1. 2020, Plenarprotokoll 19/140, 17500.

277 Tilman Krause, 'Auch die Hohenzollern gehören zu Deutschland', *Die Welt*, 16 April 2021, https://www.welt.de/kultur/plus230384853/NS-Verstrickung-Auch-die-Hohenzollern-gehoeren-zu-Deutschland.html;

Alexander Gauland (AfD), speech to the Deutscher Bundestag, 16. I. 2020, Plenarprotokoll 19/140, 17494.

278 Alexander Gauland (AfD), speech to the Deutscher Bundestag, 16. I. 2020, Plenarprotokoll 19/140, 17494.

279 Arendt, *Eichmann in Jerusalem*, 348–404; Smith (ed.), *Hannah Arendt*, 163–76, 231–90.

280 'Stammt die Ideologie Hitlers aus dem Kaiserreich? Interview mit Andreas Wirsching', *Der Spiegel*, 7 June 2021.

281 Ulrich Herbert, 'Vier Gutachter, ein Kronprinz und die nationale Diktatur', *FAZ*, 1 Dec. 2019.

Conclusion

1 *Unter dem Schatten Deiner Flügel. Aus den Tagebüchern der Jahre 1932–1942 von Jochen Klepper. Mit einem Geleitwort von Reinhold Schneider*, ed. by Hildegard Klepper, Stuttgart 1955 (31 Jan. 1933).

2 See, for instance, Friedländer, *Das Dritte Reich und die Juden*.

3 Moltke on 6 Nov. 1941, cited in Wolzogen, *Nach dem Tee in die Mördergrube*, section XXVIII.

4 'Hans Schäffer an Heimann, 21. 7. 1933', Hans Schäffer Papers Series I: Correspondence, 1933–1994.

5 Herbert, *Wer waren die Nationalsozialisten?*, 38.

6 See, for instance, Schwan, *Der Mitläufer*.

7 See Jones, *The German Right 1918–1930*, 2, 14–15, 589–97; Gasteiger, *Kuno von Westarp*, 477–84; Ziblatt, *Conservative Parties*, 297–333, 363–8; Noakes, *German Conservatives*; Payne, *A History of Fascism*.

8 Evaluation Pyta/Orth, 154.

Index

Adalbert, Prince (Kaiser's son), 43, 164, 230, 403
Adalheid von Sachsen-Meiningen, Princess, 164
Adenauer, Konrad, 416
agrarian associations, 120, 204, 212, 215, 217, 274, 319, 323, 329
Aldenburg-Bentinck, Count Godard van, 28
Alexander, Prince (August Wilhelm's son), 203–4, 230, 238, 272
Alexandra zu Schleswig-Holstein-Sonderburg-Glücksburg, Princess, 160–61
Alter, Junius, 239
Alternative for Germany (AfD), 440, 448, 449, 458–9, 467, 470, 471
Aly, Götz, 366
Anker, Kurt, 65, 74, 82
anti-Semitism: attacks on royal family/nobility from radical right, 61, 66, 105, 208–9, 210–11; of August Wilhelm, 308–9; and 'Barmat scandal' (1924–5), 143–4; Basch visit to Potsdam, 145–6; in British elites, 346–7; and the crown prince, 13, 108, 300–302, 305–7, 402, 412; defaming of Jewish financiers/merchants, 128; and disappropriation initiative (1925–6), 120, 122; of German Aristocratic Society (DAG), 294; global conspiracy theories, 55;

'Jewification' of the aristocracy, 66, 210–11; of Kaiser, 12, 13, 30–31, 181, 245, 293, 307, 355, 358, 460, 469, 478–9; in legal system, 133; Nazi state persecution of Jews, 290, 301–4, 305–7, 357, 358, 402, 403, 412, 467–8; of Queen Luise Association, 281; and Stresemann's support for crown prince, 99, 104–5; and Trebitsch-Lincoln, 56; in USA, 22, 31, 180, 300, 345, 346; writings of Streicher, 464 *see also* Holocaust, Jewish
Arendt, Hannah, 58, 249, 278, 303, 471, 477
Aretin, Baron Erwein von, 314–15
aristocracy/nobility: and 20 July 1944 plot, 43, 377–9, 380, 381–5, 389, 391, 392, 422–3, 424, 426, 429–30; acquiring of formerly Jewish-owned property, 361, 363, 408; anti-Semitic attacks on from radical Right, 66, 208–9, 210–11, 306; aristocrat-of-the-people image, 88–92; Bavarian, 196, 227, 238, 251, 314–16, 394, 408–9; behaviour behind Western Front, 74–80, 81, 82–3, 136–7, 140–41; central disciplines/pursuits of, 8, 61–3, 165, 175; collaboration with Nazi state, 258, 274, 275, 287–93, 330–40, 341–3, 351–2, 358–67, 474–8,

643

communism: anti-Bolshevik Russians in exile, 348–50, 418, 427–8; Cold War sentiments against, 399–400, 415, 421, 427–8, 430; communist press in France, 126, 196; conservative downplaying of resistance to Hitler from, 421, 426; conservative labelling of Nazis as 'Bolshevists', 179, 205–6, 212, 218, 357, 360, 402, 472; defeat of (end of Cold War), 434–5; Italian fascist responses to, 168; and Kaiser's 'strategic plan', 178, 374; KPD (German communist party), 118–19, 125, 134, 188, 202, 270; Nazi state's suppression of, 209, 270, 301, 305–6, 335, 343, 345; right-wing exploitation of fear of, 18, 21, 122, 127, 308, 351–2, 353, 409–10, 443–4, 467–8; and the SPD, 125–7, 134; street battles with right-wing forces, 151, 171; victory of in east (1945), 394–5, 418, 421, 428, 430, 434, 445; in Weimar Republic, 110, 116–17, 118–19, 125–7, 130, 134, 151, 188, 202

conservatism/right-wing politics: and 20 July 1944 plot, 43, 320, 321, 377–9, 380, 381–5, 389, 391, 392, 422–3, 424, 426, 429–30; and Augusta Viktoria's memorial ceremonies, 48, 49–50; and 'Barmat scandal' (1924–5), 143–4; Christian resistance to Hitler, 257, 322; and Cold War anti-communism, 399–400, 415, 421, 427–8, 430; collaboration between segments of, 1–2, 55–6, 58–9; counterfactual constructions of

pro-Hohenzollern position, 220–21, 459–62, 464–5, 467; counter-revolutionary tradition after French Revolution, 246; coup d'état' (*Preussenschlag*) (20 July 1932), 210, 214, 479; creation of alliances with Third Reich (1933), 265–9, 271–85, 291–3; crown prince as pre-1914 ally of, 61–3, 97–8; crown prince's Nazi mediator role, 206–7, 211–12, 253, 255, 279–80, 284–5, 324–6, 476; development of alliance with Nazis, 174, 183–92, 193–201, 202–8, 213–20, 324–6; elite embrace of violence, 21, 32–3, 108–10, 149–50, 151, 168; fantasies over Kaiser's self sacrifice, 10–11, 14–16; 'Finsterwalde Declaration of Hate' (1928), 148; forums/circles outside institutions of Republic, 155; guerrilla warfare against Weimar Republic, 144–58, 163–71; Hohenzollerns' role in (before 1932), 21–2, 24–5, 27–8, 46–51, 54–8, 92, 95–6, 144–58, 163–71, 174–82; hotspots/hubs of counter-revolution, 171–9; ideals of womanhood, 19, 81, 173; impact of Day of Potsdam, 275, 276, 331–2, 353; Kaiser as too 'liberal' for radical right, 61, 105; longing for a more positive history, 427–8, 468–9; myth of early opposition to Nazism, 392; Nazi state decouples from allies, 329–43, 344–54, 355–8; Nazis as victors within, 7, 163, 184; negotiation phase with Hitler (July 1932–January 1933), 214–20,

East Germany, 395, 420, 422, 428, 430,
434–5, 445, 467; anti-communist
uprising (17 June 1953), 421
Ebert, Friedrich, 153–4
Ehrhardt, Hermann, 54, 106
Einem, Günther von, 188, 190, 340
Einem, Karl von, 339–40
Eisner, Kurt, 33
Eitel Friedrich, Prince (Kaiser's son),
14, 88, 106, 117, 122, 138, 189, 229;
at Augusta Vikoria's funeral, 50;
death of, 403; divorce of (1926),
160; fined for covert bank
account, 129–30, 142–3; lives in
Villa Ingenheim, 19, 160; mooted
as possible successor, 149; and
Nazi movement, 150, 186–7, 274,
309; and Night of the Long
Knives, 343; obesity of, 62, 303;
and Prussian military culture, 21,
144, 318–19; as Stahlhelm
member, 196, 273, 274, 309, 321
Elser, Georg, 368, 389, 406, 466
Epp, Ritter von, 181
Eppstein, Georg Freiherr von, 72, 73–4
Ernst, Karl, 257, 304
Erzberger, Matthias, 32, 33, 108–9,
149–50
Ethiopia, 356
Eulenburg, Count, 21
Evans, Richard J., 455–6
Everling, Friedrich, 117

Farrar, Geraldine, 300, 371, 398,
399–400, 401
fascist movements: Arendt's analysis
of, 58, 249, 278, 303, 471, 477;
Walter Benjamin on, 300; and
cross-class alliances, 58–9, 244–5,
472, 476–7; crown prince's

enthusiasm for Italian model, 167,
168–70, 215, 244–5, 252–3, 281, 289,
295, 356; Kaiser's enthusiasm for,
168, 244–5; monarch-dictator
combination in Italy, 244–5; and
'popular Kaiserdom' idea, 167–70;
and Queen Luise Association,
281–4; Society for the Study of
Fascism, 169, 244–5; and staged/
symbolic spectacle, 259–74, 277–8,
280, 282–3, 285–6, 290, 311; and
weak conservatism, 478 *see also*
Nazism/National Socialism;
Third Reich
Finckenstein, Count Finck von, 31, 337
First World War: Allied 'Hundred
Days Offensive', 9; ceasefire in
Compiegne (November 1918), 33,
108–9; construction of
Cecilienhof during, 3–4, 172–3;
corruption and profiteering
during, 128, 132, 143–4; crown
prince's claimed prescience, 65,
88, 97–8, 105, 402; crown prince's
sexual behaviour during, 74–80,
81, 82–3, 86; German refusal to
accept outcome, 22, 23, 55;
Germany military victory on
Eastern Front, 4, 317; idea of
German culpability for, 22, 31,
148, 154, 267, 468–9; and ideal of
heroic death, 17, 18; impact on
Weimar Republic, 128, 312, 313;
and Lattre de Tassigny, 400–401;
royal family's service during, 4,
18, 65, 74–83, 86, 97–8, 135–8, 158,
263, 313; 'stab in the back' myth,
13, 22, 33, 57, 76, 108–9, 300, 313,
355; USA enters, 172
Fischer, Fritz, 469

resistance / opposition – *cont'd.*
447–8, 478–9; crown prince's
obstruction of, 386, 388; *Die
deutsche Opposition gegen Hitler*
(Rothfels), 422–3; former
members in post-war royal
service, 13, 391–3; Hohenzollerns
as not involved, 323, 325–6, 343,
352, 379, 380–82, 385, 388, 389, 466,
473, 478–9; Hohenzollerns'
post-1945 claims, 220–21, 222, 320,
353–4, 357–8, 367, 379–90, 397, 402,
406–12, 420, 423–6; idea of an
'elite monarchy', 238; and
Königswald, 28; myth of crown
prince's connection with, 325–6,
379–84, 386, 388, 389–90, 397, 402,
408, 410, 412, 425, 447–8, 478–9,
480–81; myth of early
conservative opposition, 392, 393;
myth of Louis Ferdinand's
connection with, 379–80, 381–4,
386–7, 388, 389, 410–11, 425–7,
429–33, 480; post-1945 genre of
'noble narratives', 392–3;
post-war conservative
reinterpretations, 421–6, 429–33,
447–8, 478–9; potential rival
camps to Nazis, 319–23; research
group 20 July, 424; view of
'bystanders' and profiteers, 474
see also 20 July 1944 plot against
Hitler
Reusch, Paul, 424
Reventlow, Count Ernst von, 104–8,
240, 241
Ribbentrop, Joachim von, 346, 353
Richthofen, Baron Prätorius von, 153
Ritl, Steffi, 398
Ritter, Gerhard, 385–6, 388

Ritthaler, Anton, 394
Röhl, John, 37, 354
Röhm, Ernst, 184–5, 215, 216–17, 219,
220, 285, 286, 326, 340, 389
Romanov family, 348–50, 418, 427–8
Rominten, East Prussia, 361
Roosevelt, Franklin D., 301–2, 384
Rosner, Karl, 65–6, 343, 412
Rothermore, Lord, 199–200, 215,
221, 326
Rothfels, Hans, 421–2, 423–4, 434; *Die
deutsche Opposition gegen Hitler*,
422–3
Rückert, Friedrich, 246–7
Rupprecht, Crown Prince of Bavaria,
227, 315, 408–9

SA: August Wilhelm in, 170, 205, 255,
257, 263, 273, 308, 341–2, 402–3; ban
on (April 1932), 201–3; and crown
prince, 202–3, 215, 216–17, 257–9,
288–9, 310–12, 356, 410; death cult
within, 262; and dual structure of
Nazi rule, 263, 264; fraternal ideal,
316; Horst Wessel cult, 263; and
Nazi state ceremonial, 260–64,
268, 269, 270, 271–2, 273, 274,
277–8; Night of the Long Knives
(30 June 1934), 214, 219, 220, 326,
340–43, 387, 389, 402–3; 'planned
acts of terror' on conservative
events, 206; proposed alliance
with SS / Stahlhelm, 206–7, 284–5,
287, 321, 407; reign of terror in
early Nazi era, 263–4, 302, 304–5;
and the Stahlhelm, 203, 204–7, 217,
314, 316, 320–22, 407; Stahlhelm's
incorporation into, 287, 310, 311,
322; storms monarchist
celebration (27 January 1934), 335,

Index